Assessment of At-Risk and Special Needs Children

Assessment of At-Risk and Special Needs Children

SECOND EDITION

JOSEPH C. WITT
Louisiana State University

STEPHEN N. ELLIOTT
University of Wisconsin–Madison

EDWARD J. DALY III
University of Cincinnati

FRANK M. GRESHAM
University of California, Riverside

JACK J. KRAMER
University of Nebraska, Lincoln

Boston, Massachusetts Burr Ridge, Illinois Dubuque, Iowa
Madison, Wisconsin New York, New York San Francisco, California St. Louis, Missouri

McGraw-Hill

A Division of The ***McGraw-Hill*** *Companies*

ASSESSMENT OF AT-RISK AND SPECIAL NEEDS CHILDREN

 This book is printed on recycled paper containing 10% postconsumer waste.

4 5 6 7 8 9 0 HAM HAM 0 9 8 7 6 5 4 3

ISBN 0–697–24447–4

Sponsoring editor: *Beth Kaufman*
Marketing manager: *Dan Loch*
Project manager: *Terry Routley*
Production supervisor: *Laura Fuller*
Cover designer: *ZGraphics, Ltd.*
Interior designer: *Kathleen F. Theis*
Photo research coordinator: *Carrie Burger*
Compositor: *Shepherd, Inc.*
Typeface: *10/12 Garamond Light*
Printer: *Hamco/NetPub Corporation*

Photographs: **Section Openers: 1:** © Digital Stock/Babies and Children; **2:** © David Frazier Photo Library; **3:** © David Frazier Photo Library. **Chapter Openers: 1, 2, 4, 7, 9, 10, 12, 13, 14, 15:** © James L. Shaffer; **3, 11:** © Elizabeth Crews/The Image Works; **5, 6:** © Michael Siluk; **8:** © Bob Kalman/The Image Works; **Chapter 12: figure 12.3:** Reproduced with permission of The Riverside Publishing Company, Chicago, IL.

Library of Congress Cataloging-in-Publication Data

Assessment of at-risk and special needs children / Joseph C. Witt . . . [et al.]. -- 2nd ed.
p. cm.
Rev. ed. of: Assessment of children. c1994.
Includes bibliographical references and index.
ISBN 0–697–24447–4
1. Handicapped children--Education--United States. 2. Handicapped children--United States--Ability testing. 3. Educational tests and measurements--United States. I. Witt, Joseph C. II. Assessment of children.
LC4031.A69 1997
372.91'0973--dc21 97-8561
CIP

http://www.mhhe.com

To my mother, Wilma Anne Witt.
J.C.W.

For my favorite companions,
Anita, Dustin, Drew, and Scooter.
S.N.E.

To my parents, Mary and Ed Daly;
to my wife, Anne, and our
children, Chloé, Madeline,
Alexandre, and Bérénice.
E.J.D.

To my son Matt Gresham, someone
who tops out the distribution on
courage and will.
F.M.G.

To Ron Edwards who taught me
that most of psychoeducational
assessment is irrelevent.
J.J.K.

Contents

Expanded Table of Contents 

Preface

Purpose of the Text

This book is intended for professionals who wish to improve student academic performance. In that sense it is not merely about assessing children and finding out whether anything is "wrong" with them. Instead, the approach to assessment presented here is one that is more concerned with learning how to help children improve than in applying a label or diagnosis.

As authors we also wanted to write an interesting and readable text. We were concerned that an encyclopedic listing of tests and an overemphasis on the technology (e.g., statistics) of assessment might overshadow the more important and interesting features of the field. We wanted to present stories of children like Rhonda K., who, because of cerebral palsy, had very poor control of her arms and legs and was thought to be mentally disabled. However, skillful testing with nontraditional methods indicated she was a bright young girl who could benefit from a much higher level of instruction than traditional tests had suggested. This practical focus, based on our experience, is interwoven with a clear, accurate, and readable description of all the essential information one would expect to find in an introductory text on assessment in special education.

We have stressed the application of assessment in two ways. First, there is a strong emphasis on the linking of assessment with intervention and instruction through a problem-solving process. In fact, this book evolved out of a perception that specialists wanted a source of information that would link assessment to intervention and the solution of important educational problems. The goals, therefore, are to describe how assessment data can be obtained and used by individuals engaged in the problem-solving process within educational settings and to integrate the assessment process typically used in schools with test instruments. Application also has been stressed through the frequent discussion of actual case studies, examples, and special sections entitled "Focus on Practice" that show real people dealing with real problems. To describe a field as broad and diverse as assessment and still convey that it is an organized and coherent body of knowledge, it was necessary to maintain uniformity from chapter to chapter by emphasizing the following common themes: (a) linking assessment and intervention, and (b) using and interpreting tests.

Linking Assessment and Intervention

This book is based on the assumption that when a child is referred for assessment, the goal is to solve the child's problem by developing appropriate academic or social interventions. Thus, the focus is on using tests within a problem-solving process. For too long, giving tests has been equated with problem solving, but the link between assessment and intervention must be explicitly planned and practiced. The text first details the assessment process and then examines several areas of concern, such as reading, math, language, and preschool readiness, to illustrate how to understand a child experiencing problems in each of these domains.

Using and Interpreting Tests

The text also helps test users master assessment fundamentals so that instruments can be administered and interpreted correctly. Because assessment data play a major role in determining how children will be educated, they can be harmful as well as helpful, depending on their use. Irrevocable damage can be done by individuals misinformed about the limitations of tests; thus, every test user is responsible for knowing what tests can and cannot do.

New to the Second Edition

This edition represents a wholly revised approach to the book and a radical, but logical extension of the concepts presented in the first edition. The practice of school-based assessment is undergoing tremendous change. There have been marked changes over the last five years from traditional norm-referenced assessment to a more functional assessment process and philosophy. What does this mean? It means that assessment specialists are learning that the environment matters. That assessment is much more than labeling. That it is at least as important to know how to teach the child as to know what the child *has*.

In this edition, you will find both the content and an orientation which is steeped in the new functional assessment practices. Hence, we have added a systematic model for determining how children learn best. This model includes a series of "tests" but the tests are really short-term interventions to determine *what works* best with the child. For example, some children, when tested with the usual methods (e.g., a norm-referenced reading test), do not score very well. Some of these children, however, can read relatively well. They simply do not want to read. Hence, one of the "tests" described is a process to determine if a child "Can't" or "Won't" read. We have also included new chapters on a functional approach to problem solving, performance assessment and portfolio assessment.

This edition has integrated some of the literature on inclusion, rights without labels, and the regular education initiative into the assessment process. Special education is changing. Hence, assessment practices connected with special education must also change.

We have also updated information relevant to curriculum-based assessment. Curriculum-based assessment is becoming standard practice, yet the research behind it is still emerging. This edition integrates research into practice in a way which can be consumed by front line assessment specialists.

Finally, many of the changes are reflected in a new title, which reflects our intent to more sharply focus the test on children who are being assessed for special education and those at risk for placement and/or other interventions.

Audience for This Book

Special education professionals taking their first course in assessment are the audience for this book. We have assumed no previous knowledge of or work in educational measurement or statistics. The book is designed for individuals who will be working with special needs children and who must be able to use and interpret both standardized and informal tests. This text will also benefit counselors, school psychologists, educational administrators, speech and language pathologists, social workers, and others directly or indirectly involved in the education of preschool children, children with behavior problems, and those with mild or severe disabilities.

Learning Aids Accompanying the Book

The instructor using this book will have access to a comprehensive Instructor's Manual. This manual includes detailed summaries of each of the chapters in the text, lists of key terms used in each chapter, ideas for lectures on critical or controversial issues in assessment, and a variety of test questions (i.e., multiple-choice, true or false, and short answer essay) that can be used to facilitate studying or to evaluate learning. The Instructor's Manual also includes blackline masters for nearly 50 of the key tables or figures from the text.

Assessment of At-Risk and Special Needs Children

Part One

Foundations of Assessment

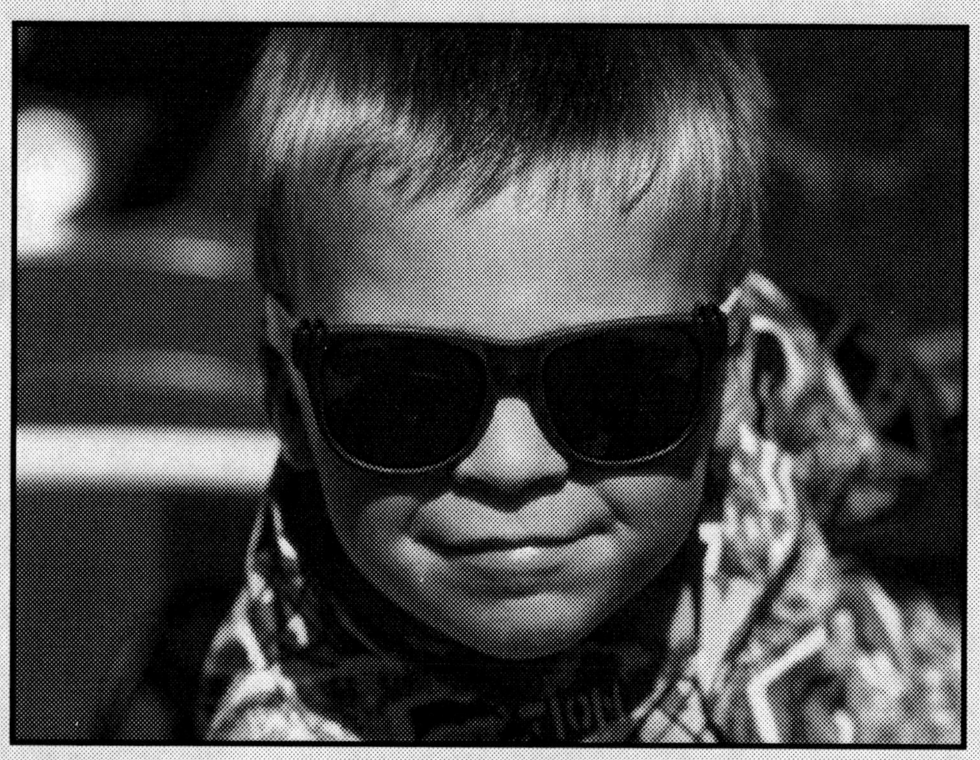

Whether one is building a house or teaching fifth-grade math, it is both necessary and important to set a proper foundation. A good foundation is also important to school-based assessment of children for special education, and this first part of the book introduces basic assumptions and terminology upon which the remainder of the book is based. This part also provides a context within which assessment can be placed.

This book is mostly about children—children who are experiencing problems of one type or another. Individuals working directly with these children both want and demand solutions to the problems. In chapter 1, assessment is presented as a vital source of the information needed to address these problems. More specifically, assessment should yield information that helps identify the nature of the problems, the factors that may be contributing to them, and, most important, possible remedies.

Chapter 2 is about being a critical consumer of tests and test information. Tests are not perfect, and the wise consumer knows the strengths and weaknesses of all assessment practices and uses this information to assist and advocate for children.

In chapter 3, problem solving is placed within the context of the laws and regulations that govern the education of children with handicaps. These laws govern not only the day-to-day functioning of the special education assessment process but also its very existence. The application of the various laws and regulations is described to explain how the assessment process works. By the time you complete this section, you should have a richer understanding of why we assess, the legal foundation of the assessment process, and the context within which that process exists.

Chapters 4 and 5 provide a technical foundation for all that is to follow. In chapter 4, basic statistics needed to understand and interpret tests are presented. Chapter 5 discusses reliability, validity, and other essential characteristics of tests.

CHAPTER 1

Assessment and the Problem-Solving Model

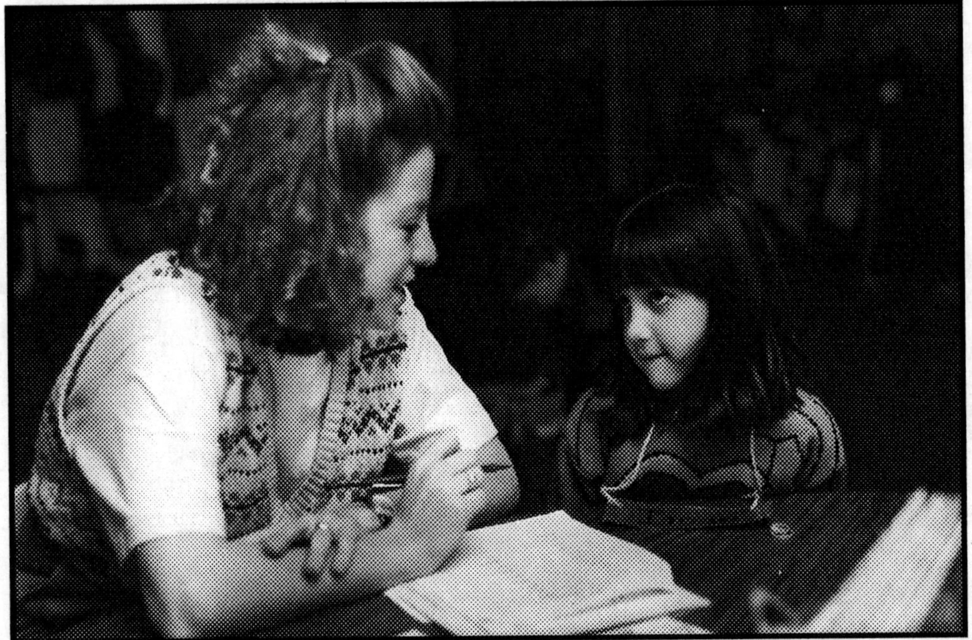

Imagine, or perhaps recall, being confronted with statements such as the following:

- "Shawn has a significant discrepancy between his verbal and performance scores on the IQ test. Further testing indicated that he has auditory processing deficits relative to his strong visual-motor processing skills."
- "I gave Kathy two reading tests. She has a grade equivalent score of approximately 2.3 on the standardized achievement test for Word Recognition. She didn't do as well on the Comprehension section. When I assessed her processing strengths, I found that she was a kinesthetic learner."
- "We know that Jaquan has difficulty learning to read. That's why he is classified as learning disabled. However, we want to know exactly what skills he has and what kinds of expectations you have for his performance."

Each statement involves assessment in some way. In the first and second scenario, you are being asked to be a consumer of assessment information. In the last scenario, you are being asked to produce assessment information. We expect that there will be a wide variety of reactions to these statements regarding assessment. Some of you may not be able to interpret the information at this point. We also expect, however, that all readers of this text have at least one thing in common: seeking to be better prepared to respond to reasonable professional demands in a manner that ultimately helps the student, be it participating in a decision, choosing an action, or providing information to others.

Building a Professional Model of Assessment

A reflective educator thinks critically about the myriad circumstances confronting him or her in meeting the responsibilities of the job. Thinking critically involves, among other things, having high standards for the quality of evaluation information used as a basis for decision making, being an active participant in the full range of educational decisions for students, and systematically problem solving to confront the demands of effectiveness and accountability. Having high standards for the quality of evaluation information means that teachers are knowledgeable about which assessment practices yield the best information for the kinds of educational decisions that they need to make. Critical educators are knowledgeable about these practices so that when they are called on to make instructional planning decisions, classification decisions, and decisions about the effectiveness of programs for children, they do so in an informed manner. Finally, critical educators must be systematic in problem solving in order to understand the effects that instruction and the school environment are having on the student. The image of the educator that is emerging from this description is one of a professional who has a strong professional model of practice, a model that is robust in that it allows the educator to problem-solve effectively across a wide variety of circumstances (Good & Kaminski, 1996). Our intention is to help you build a model of assessment practice that lives up to these standards.

An effective teacher does more than just present curricular activities to the students. An effective teacher plans instruction, chooses instructional materials, arranges the environment and teaching sequence to promote student learning, instructs, evaluates student learning, and plans future instruction accordingly. Obviously, decision making plays a key role in being a good teacher. Teachers follow a pattern to make instructional decisions. Figure 1.1 presents a model of how teachers affect student achievement. Teachers make observations about what students know and how well they are responding to instruction. Based on those observations, they make decisions about where to place students in the curriculum, what instructional procedures to use, how to group students, what materials are appropriate for instruction, how to motivate students, and how much time students need to spend on instructional activities. Those decisions dictate whether teachers will maintain or modify their instructional practices for individual students. These actions will

Figure 1.1 Qualities and Potential Outcomes of a Good Instructional Decision-Making Model

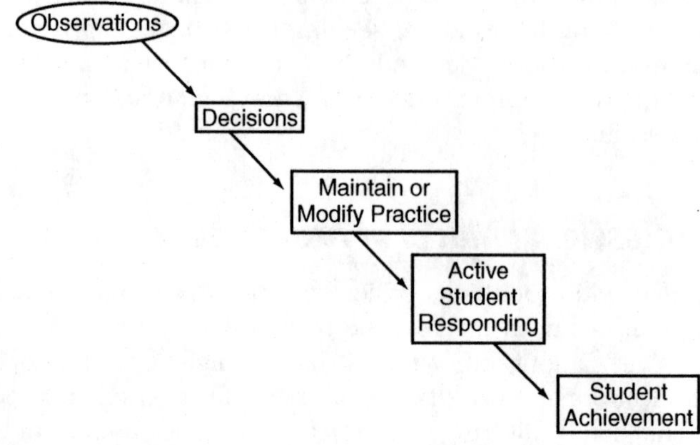

affect how well students respond to instruction. The more students engage in active responding that is directly related to curricular objectives, the more likely it is that students will achieve (Greenwood, Terry, Marquis, & Walker, 1994). Whether you are a teacher or a professional who helps teachers, it is important to understand how children learn and perform. Through this knowledge, it is then possible to determine wherein the problem lies when a child does not learn.

Effective teachers instruct well because they make good decisions that lead to actions that promote student responding and achievement. Good decision making involves (a) knowing which instructional procedures are effective under which conditions and (b) having good information about student performance. This is where assessment comes in. The primary purpose of assessment is to gather information about student performance to make decisions about how and where students should be instructed. Assessment is the process of making structured observations about students. Increasing the quality of observations is likely to increase the quality of decisions about student performance. Therefore, to the degree that teachers are knowledgeable about assessment, they increase the likelihood of making good decisions about the students in their classrooms. In essence, effective teaching boils down to good instruction, good evaluation (which informs instruction), and using each to do the other better.

The purpose of this book is to help teachers and other professionals to be knowledgeable about conceptual and technical issues related to assessment and various assessment practices. Although the issues may appear initially to be very complex, we believe that the foundations for good assessment practice are intuitive once you've grappled with understanding their application. We have had the good fortune of seeing professionals grasp the importance of these issues and relate them to their own personal, professional experiences. The ultimate test is how well you are able to integrate your understanding of these issues in your decision making for students. Like anything we learn, it will take practice. If you persist, however, in developing, practicing, and refining an assessment model, we believe that you will improve the quality of decisions that you make about the students that you teach. Our goal is to give you the tools for building your professional model of assessment.

Assessment must be integrated in all educational activities. Assessment as we just described it is a feedback mechanism. Teachers who routinely gather assessment information and make instructional modifications according to student performance increase student achievement (Fuchs & Fuchs, 1986). It stands to reason that better assessment information will lead to better decision making. Integrating assessment into practice also serves the purpose of providing professional accountability. Student performance is affected by a host of factors, only a small portion of which the teacher directly controls. However, teachers can make significant contributions to children's lives by being aware of those factors over which they have control, taking responsibility for them, and examining the outcomes of their efforts. Given the emerging climate of increasing accountability in the eyes of the broader society, we believe that it behooves us to have a good model of professional accountability for our practices. Indeed, if we as educators fail to develop assessment practices that demonstrate accountability, we run the risk of having business leaders, legislators, and others do it for us.

General Assumptions About Assessment

Assessment is the process of gathering information about student performance. Many conceptual and technical issues compose the rules by which we can judge whether the assessment information is accurate, reliable, and valid. Some of the confusion surrounding assessment can be directly attributed to the fact that various individuals approach assessment with differing assumptions concerning how and when tests can be utilized. This problem is complicated further by the lack of any one universally accepted theory guiding the development, use, and interpretation of tests. Hence, we feel that it is important to be explicit about the assumptions that we use in the model of assessment practice that we are promoting. We invite you to reflect critically on these assumptions. They are the foundation for our assessment model.

Assumption 1: Individual Differences Among Children Derive Their Meaning from the Situation in Which They Occur

In assessing the many attributes and behaviors of a particular child, it is very likely that the child will differ, perhaps markedly, from his or her peers on at least one dimension. It must be determined if we should be concerned about such differences. That determination depends on the child's situation, acculturation, and the expectations placed on the child in that situation. Behaviors considered normal in one setting may be considered abnormal in another, and skills considered adequate in one school may cause problems in another school. The point is that tests can determine whether a child is different from the norm but not whether this difference is a problem.

Children differ on innumerable attributes, some of which are important while others are not. For example, a child's hearing is measured frequently during the school years, and those with a hearing loss are identified because this is a problem that may interfere with learning. However, some children have a quite different hearing abnormality: They are able to perceive extremely high-pitched sounds (i.e., those in excess of 20,000 cycles per second). At present, this capability has no practical importance in our society (except perhaps to people who test dog whistles). Children who cannot hear sounds in this range are not considered hearing impaired because there is no expectation that they should be able to hear sounds at such high frequencies. Suppose, however, that it suddenly became important for children to be able to hear sounds of 20,000 cycles per second. Children who could hear at such frequencies would be valued highly by our culture, whereas those who could not probably would be viewed as less capable and possibly marked for placement in classrooms for the hearing impaired.

Consider the more realistic example of a child who moves from south-central Los Angeles (an inner-city environment) to Scarsdale, a suburb of New York City (an upper-class, professional community). According to a nationally standardized reading test, the child's reading ability would be approximately a half year below grade level, yet when he was in the Los Angeles neighborhood his reading ability was not considered a problem. In fact, there he was a good student. However, in Scarsdale he is immediately referred for specialized programming because the average child in that community scores more than one year above grade level on the national test. The obvious conclusion is that a test score becomes most meaningful when the conditions and expectations under which the child must operate are known. With the growing number of children from different cultures—different environments, different expectations for behavior, and different values—the task of meaningful and unbiased assessment will be an ongoing challenge for professionals.

Assessment data must also be interpreted in terms of developmental norms, which evaluate a child's performance relative to what other children that age are doing. For example, an interview with a mother indicates that she is concerned about her 5-year-old son who is frequently disobedient at home. Reference to developmental norms suggests that such behavior is relatively normal for children that age. In fact, 56 percent of normal boys are considered disobedient at one time or another. Similarly, kindergarten and first-grade children are referred frequently to speech clinicians because of problems articulating the letters *s* and *r*. Generally, however, speech therapy is not initiated with such young children because the problems often disappear with another year or two of experience in the natural environment. It is important to assume that test data derive their meaning from the social context, because viewing test scores as meaningful by themselves can lead to their misuse.

It is important to state this explicitly because all too often tests that are interpreted naively and mechanically do more harm than good. Simply because a child may score in the impaired range on a particular test should not be sufficient evidence to label the child as handicapped. Most importantly, a test score in the impaired range does not always correspond to impaired performance in other situations.

Assumption 2: Tests Are Samples of Behavior That Assist in Decision Making

Tests do not make and should not make decisions. People make decisions based on a full consideration of all the issues. The assumption that test data will be only a portion of the information used to make a decision about a child is related to the first assumption and pertains to how test data are used. Unfortunately, in practice, test data are frequently the only information considered. Children are placed in programs based on very specific criteria often operationalized by exact scores on tests. For example, a score of 130 or above on an intelligence test may be needed for placement in a program for gifted youngsters, and a score of 129 simply will not suffice. Perhaps if other criteria were examined, a child with a 129 IQ may be more suited to the program than a child with an IQ in the 140 range. Tests are simply not accurate enough, nor do they measure a wide enough range of variables, to be used as the sole criterion for most decisions. They are only samples of behavior, and common sense must be used in judging their contribution to decisions.

A simple decision, such as placement in the proper reading group, may be fraught with difficulty if a test score is the major determiner. Two children with scores indicating they read at the third-grade level may have quite different reading abilities, especially if they were given different tests or were tested in different aspects of reading. One child may have approached the task with a cavalier attitude and, because of carelessness, responded incorrectly in some relatively minor areas. Another child may have approached the test very anxiously and struggled all the way through, as evidenced by grimacing, stammering, and statements suggesting self-doubt. A test score may suggest that the two children should be in the same reading group, yet it may be very difficult to teach them in the same manner and at the same rate. In addition to knowing a test score and the manner in which it was achieved, it may be helpful to have information that is not in any test (e.g., whether the child learns best in a group or one-to-one situation, whether the child responds best in written form or orally, and whether the child could be taught more effectively by a teacher or a peer). Good educational programming is seldom based on test scores alone but instead considers the complex array of variables that influence student learning.

The problem of misusing test scores as a basis for placement decisions can be partially overcome by making sure an adequate sample of behavior is included in assessment. For example, the assessment of intelligence should measure a wide range of behaviors that have been associated with the construct of intelligence. In addition, it is important that the child is properly motivated and puts forth an optimal or nearly optimal effort. By doing this, it is possible to predict more accurately what the child can do given proper motivation in the classroom.

Assumption 3: A Primary Reason to Conduct an Assessment Is to Improve Instructional or Intervention Activities

What are the goals of assessment? To find out how to eliminate a problem? To find out why a child performs as he or she does? To determine the appropriate placement for a child? Some may argue that determining etiology and finding the cause of a problem are primary reasons for conducting an assessment. In ordinary educational practice, this is true, however, only to the extent that assessment also points to an effective intervention for the child's problem. Identifying an educational classification may be necessary in many states to provide special education services, but such classifications do not provide information for planning daily lessons. For example, knowing a child has a learning disability does not lead to the same level of treatment specificity as does knowing the child has a medical problem, such as phenylketonuria (PKU). On this topic, Howell, Kaplan, and O'Connell (1979) noted:

> When the problem is academic deficiency, the variables for classification are less specific. . . . Yet educators have tended to treat students who fail academically as if they have enzyme deficiencies. That is, they have sought to label students and then make treatment statements from the label. . . . Of course, our educational levels are far from precise. (p. 16)

Consider a teacher or a psychologist who knows only that a child completes assignments in a sloppy fashion because he or she is "impulse-ridden" or a youngster frequently displays aggressive and inappropriate behavior because he or she is "socially maladjusted." Labels are useful only to the extent that they lead to a successful intervention. If a prescribed treatment exists for the "impulse-ridden" child, then using that label is advantageous; however, if no such prescription is available, such a label may actually interfere with treatment by clouding the variables that influence the problem.

All too often educational specialists have considered their job to be completed when they have labeled the child to determine the classification and made some general recommendations. This attitude may be partially attributable to the categorical system of special education established in most states and the heavy demands on specialists to conduct large numbers of assessments. By law a child must be classified as eligible to receive special education services. Thus, some specialists may communicate only the appropriate categorical label and leave teachers and therapists, who do most of the direct, daily work with the child, to develop the individualized educational programming.

Assumption 4: The Assessor Is Properly Trained

Since many potential sources of error exist in administering and interpreting tests and other assessment devices, it is extremely important that they be administered by individuals who are knowledgeable about both assessment and human behavior. For example, an acquaintance of the authors told of a college student who was gaining experience administering tests to children in a small rural school. In discussing the results of the testing with the college student, our friend learned that two Native American students would not respond to any test questions. Our friend then readministered the test but allowed more time than usual for answering each question. Although perhaps 30 seconds were required for the students to respond to each question, they did eventually respond, and very accurately. They simply needed more time to respond than white middle-class children. A person less familiar with the response times of individuals from some Native American tribes may have assumed a lack of knowledge on their part. Thus, skill in administering an assessment device encompasses more than the simple mechanics of test giving and requires knowledge and training in many aspects of human behavior.

The lack of highly skilled assessors has been a major problem in special education because of the sudden and dramatic demand for individuals in this field after the passing of P.L. 94–142. As a result, states allowed people to become "provisionally" or temporarily certified. Master's degree programs in speech pathology, school psychology, and special education sprang up to meet the demand for practitioners. Some of these programs have provided adequate training, but others have not.

Ample evidence exists that many in the field of special education are inadequately trained in assessment practices. Bennett and Shepard (1982), for example, reported that on the average, a sample of learning disability specialists missed 50 percent of the items on a test reflecting their knowledge of basic measurement (such as reliability, validity, and use of norms). This lack of skill often translates into the misuse of tests and misinterpretation of assessment information.

The assumption that a person doing an assessment is properly trained implies that people can be trained at different levels. At one level, regular classroom teachers are well trained to administer a number of assessment instruments. In fact, in many cases they are the persons of choice to conduct an assessment, for they are familiar with the classroom materials and the demands that will be placed on the child, have access to almost unlimited samples of the child's behavior, and have more contacts with the child than almost any other individual (Moran, 1978; Wiggins, 1989). At a more complex level, more specialized tests, such as individually administered intelligence tests, require supervised training to learn to administer. Most professional codes of ethics admonish individuals to administer only those tests for which they have the training and skills.

Assumption 5: All Forms of Assessment Contain Error

Information provided by lie detectors is inadmissible as evidence in court because of an error rate of between 10 percent and 25 percent (Bersoff, 1983a). Unfortunately, many of the tests administered to schoolchildren contain even greater error. Measuring such variables as anxiety, motivation, intelligence, and self-concept without error is simply not possible.

Error is introduced into the assessment of children by several factors. First, tests themselves often have low reliability and validity. A common and frustrating example is that different reading and math achievement tests provide different grade equivalent scores. Second, the same test may indicate different results when administered to the same child on different occasions. Test scores should be expected to fluctuate slightly because the child will remember some of the items and may feel more at ease when the test is repeated. Marked variations in scores can result because of other factors as well. For example, a child may feel more motivated on one occasion than another or the conditions under which the test is given may change from one testing to another.

The assumption that error is present in all forms of evaluation influences practice in two primary ways. First, it mandates that we be aware of and try to minimize factors that might contribute to inaccurate test scores. Every effort should be made to see that an assessment reflects the attribute being measured to the fullest possible extent. Second, the presence of error makes it all the more necessary to use and interpret test data in a cautious and professional manner. Fortunately, with standardized tests we can statistically estimate error. This point provides a convenient springboard to chapters 2, 4, and 5, in which technical procedures used in determining the worth of a test will be introduced.

Assumption 6: Good Assessment Involves Gathering Information *Directly* Related to the Problem

Let's say that Chad, a fourth-grade student, is having more difficulty learning to read than the other children in his reading group. You could assess the problem in different ways. Using one approach, you could test Chad with a common achievement test. Based on the results of this test, you could then infer why Chad is having difficulty learning to read in the fourth-grade curriculum. Using another approach, you could have Chad read from the curriculum the teacher is using, noting the kinds of errors that he makes. You might have him read different passages of differing difficulty levels. Based on your observations of his reading performance in the curriculum, you could also infer why Chad is having difficulty learning to read. In both situations, you made observations and collected information that led you to infer something about the nature of the problem. In the first scenario, the test helped you to evaluate how well Chad is doing relative to what a national sample of fourth graders can do. In the second scenario, the information collected was focused on Chad's reading in the actual curriculum.

Which type of information is better? It depends. If your goal is to compare Chad with other fourth-grade students in general, then the first technique is better. If your goal is to examine Chad's reading proficiency in the curriculum and identify the kinds of mistakes he makes, then the second process is better. The problem comes if you try to use a test for the wrong purpose. If, for example, you wish to know what Chad's problems in his curriculum are and use a nationally standardized test, then it will require a great leap of faith on your part to believe that the fourth-grade material sampled by the national test is the same material Chad's teacher used for instruction. Maybe Chad can read a lot of sight words but can't sound out words. His teacher is perhaps using a reading book with lots of proper names like Zimbabwe and Sulawes. Chad's problem may not be reading in general but reading proper names. The national test may not tell you this!

The point is that there are numerous ways to assess problems. All assessment strategies cause you to make inferences. Some inferences will be better than others. That is, they will help us to solve the problem efficiently and effectively. We suspect that you would have chosen the latter assessment strategy rather than the former, believing it to be a more efficient and effective method. We also suspect that the basis for your belief is that you are more willing to consider the information that is more directly related to the problem than the information that is further removed from the actual circumstances of the problem.

The importance of gathering information that is directly related to the problem seems clear. Yet, this is often not how assessment practices are conducted. In a survey of teachers and school psychologists about which measures they felt were most useful for instructional planning, Thurlow and Ysseldyke (1982) found that, although both teachers and school psychologists reported that standardized tests were most useful, school psychologists reported them most useful much more so than teachers and teachers relied more on other sources of information. The teachers and school psychologists in this sample reported that information related to intelligence, perceptual skills, and normative comparisons of achievement skills are the most useful assessment tools for planning for instruction. We view this situation as problematic because none of these assessment practices actually involve assessing student performance in the curriculum, the very criterion for performance itself and the most direct sample of the kinds of information that teachers need to plan instruction.

Assumption 7: Good Assessment Involves Gathering Information About the Environment in Which the Student Is Functioning

Once again, when we gather assessment information, we make inferences about the nature of the problem. The kind of assessment information that we gather dictates the kinds of inferences that we will make. If we only gather information about the student, we are more likely to make inferences that suggest that the student is the problem. This is the situation that classifying students with disabilities creates. The standard of practice is to compare the referred child with other children his or her age on measures of aptitude and achievement. Little to no information is gathered about the environment in which the child is expected to function (i.e., the classroom). Therefore, we make inferences about factors within the child, using labels such as learning disabilities, attention deficit disorder, and so on—labels believed to describe conditions affecting his or her performance. If you don't believe that the environment is important for learning, think about how much you study for a university class. Will you study more or less than usual the week before a test? If you never had a test, would you study at all? Some would. But if you were in fourth grade and the teacher never checked your work, would you do it accurately? Some would, but some would not.

Let's return to Chad for a moment. Suppose you gathered information not only about how well Chad reads under different conditions with different textbooks, but about how much time Chad actually spent reading in your classroom. Suppose you discovered that Chad was only reading about 4 minutes a day in your classroom. He was not getting enough practice. What would you do? Chances are that you would look for strategies to increase the amount of time that Chad was reading in your classroom on a daily basis. When we are assessing a problem, we have to gather information about the environment in which the child is functioning. We are looking for factors over which we have control that are related to the problem. Chapter 9 describes in detail a range of factors over which teachers have control and provides a model for how to consider these factors when problem solving.

Assumption 8: Good Assessment Is Grounded in Detecting Naturally Occurring Observable Patterns of Behavior

Assessment must be based on observable student learning patterns in the natural classroom environment under typical curricular demands. By focusing on naturally occurring observable patterns of behavior, we can develop hypotheses about what is influencing student learning and test out our hypotheses with strategies that are known to influence student learning. For instance, simple observable patterns of behavior can have profound consequences for children's academic achievement. When we are assessing students, we are trying to provide an account of student learning. All assessment practices are tied to models of how students learn.

Different models yield different assessment practices. In the model that we present in this book, our primary concern is with describing assessment practices that allow for reliable inferences about student learning as a basis for developing effective instructional practices. These practices will direct our observations to attend more carefully to certain factors (e.g., student performance in the curriculum, the amount of time the student has to practice skills, etc.) over other factors. For instance, one assessment model, broadly labeled Aptitude by Treatment Interaction (ATI), attempts to predict student achievement based on assessments of student "aptitudes," inferred mental constructs that are believed to account for an individual's learning performance (using such terms as visual-motor processing, simultaneous processing versus sequential processing, verbal versus perceptual organization profiles, etc.). According to this approach, the task of assessment is to diagnose "processing styles" so that teachers can match instruction to the child's processing style. Unfortunately, the research on ATI indicates that this assessment model doesn't work (Arter & Jenkins, 1979; Kavale, 1990; Snider, 1992). In fact, in several studies that examined how well assessed learning styles predicted which instructional approach was most effective, the investigators found the exact opposite of what the model predicted (Ayres & Cooley, 1986; Ayres, Cooley, & Severson, 1988; Good, Vollmer, Creek, Katz, & Chowdri, 1993)!

The ATI approach has not worked for a number of reasons (see Howell, Fox, and Morehead (1993) for a concise, informative discussion of this issue). We would like to highlight one fundamental reason for ATI's failure that has been neglected in these discussions. The ATI approach doesn't work because the things that are assessed with diagnostic tests (inferred mental constructs) differ from the things that are assessed as outcomes of adapting instruction (e.g., reading). In other words, when Emily is referred for a reading problem, what we assess in our diagnostic assessments (e.g., Emily's visual-motor integration, hemispheric dominance, auditory processing, etc.) is different from the kinds of assessments that we make to determine whether the problem is solved (e.g., listening to Emily read and having her answer comprehension questions). There is no clear link between the things that we assess and how we evaluate outcomes for intervention because the patterns of behavior that are assessed using the ATI model cannot be reliably related to the observable patterns of behavior that students display as they acquire skills in classrooms.

In contrast to this approach, a group of researchers at Juniper Gardens Children's Project undertook a series of investigations to examine the amount of time students spent actively responding to classroom instruction (e.g., reading aloud, writing responses, responding to teacher questions, etc.) across students of low and high socioeconomic levels (SES). They found that high-SES students spent 364 more cumulative hours actively engaged in responding to curricular materials by the end of elementary school than their low-SES counterparts. By the end of middle school, the cumulative difference between high-SES students and low-SES students was 475 hours on average (Greenwood, 1991a). Greenwood (1991a) concluded that low-SES students would need to attend school an extra 1.6 years to attain the same educational experience. When researchers examined instructional practices, they found that instructional practices that "decelerate" student learning (e.g., frequent use of overhead projectors and lectures during prime-time instruction) were used more frequently with low-SES students. In the face of these overwhelming statistics reflecting simple patterns of observable student behavior, Greenwood and his colleagues developed "classwide peer tutoring" to increase the amount of time that students are actively responding to classroom instruction. Few academic interventions have been as successful or powerful as classwide peer tutoring (Greenwood, 1991b; Greenwood, Delquadri, & Hall, 1984). By focusing on naturally occurring observable patterns of behavior that were reliably assessed, Greenwood and his colleagues were able to develop an effective solution to a chronic problem.

Assumption 9: Good Assessment Practices Seek to Link Assessment Information Explicitly to Interventions

First let us clarify what we mean by "intervention." Intervention can be incorrectly interpreted to mean that the teacher has not done anything to help the student having a problem. Clearly, in most instances, teachers are trying a variety of strategies for helping students who are having difficulty. What we mean by **intervention** is a planned modification of a student's (or students') educational programming in response to evidence that the student (or students) is (are) not progressing academically or socially. Sometimes interventions are effective and sometimes they are ineffective. In seeking to link assessment information to interventions, we endeavor to assess student and environmental variables that are known through empirical research to be related to each other (Nelson & Hayes, 1986). For example, in an assessment of disruptive classroom behavior, Broussard and Northup (1995) found that students who displayed high rates of off-task behavior responded differently to available teacher attention, peer attention, and classroom demands. They demonstrated that in some instances students were seeking adult attention; in other instances they were seeking the attention of their peers; and in yet other instances students were trying to get out of their assigned work (escaping the tasks). In each instance, Broussard and Northup (1995) designed effective interventions to promote students' on-task behavior based on their knowledge of *why* the particular student was misbehaving.

In an investigation on the relationship between student behavior and classroom demands, Kern, Childs, Dunlap, Clarke, and Falk (1994) found that factors such as the length of tasks, the kinds of problems given, and where the student was placed in the classroom were related to levels of student on-task behavior. To demonstrate these relationships between student behavior and the classroom environment, the investigators had to systematically assess both student behavior, how the classroom was arranged, how instruction was delivered, and the extent to which teacher and peer attention were available for misbehavior. By gathering information about how student behavior was related to events in the classroom such as available attention and instructional demands, they developed intervention strategies that were effective.

The Process of Assessment and Decision Making

Assessment requires the collection and interpretation of many pieces of information. A primary goal of any assessment is to determine what a student can and cannot do and how that student learns best in order that successful interventions can be designed. To accomplish this goal efficiently and effectively, a systematic plan is needed for the collection and interpretation of data. Such a plan functions like a road map, since it can provide direction and landmarks for moving from the problem state to the intervention state in the delivery of psychoeducational services.

The activities and decisions that occur during assessment can be thought of as *process* components, and the information collected represents *content* components. For example, the decision to use interview and direct observation techniques instead of a test to assess a disruptive student represents a process component, whereas the information derived from the interview and observation would represent a content component. This chapter focuses on the process components of assessment. We will explore the steps involved in an individual assessment and how to use the assessment information to make decisions about students. Later chapters focus on the content components of assessment relating to intelligence, reading, math, and adaptive behavior. Knowledge of the process of assessment may be used or generalized across all types of assessment situations. Thus, knowledge of the assessment process, from our perspective, is prerequisite to knowledge of the various content domains because it serves as the framework to organize assessment activities.

Purposes of Assessment

The overriding purpose of all assessments is to gather information to facilitate effective decision making. Within education, assessment is used to help people (i.e., teachers, administrators, psychologists, parents, and students) make at least five kinds of decisions: screening, classification and placement, student progress, programming or instruction, and program effectiveness decisions (Hawkins, 1979; Salvia & Ysseldyke, 1991; Ysseldyke, 1979). Each type of decision requires the collection of a variety of data on students' backgrounds, interests, and abilities as well as the environmental conditions and expectations of their families and school. The type of data collected to make any of these decisions can be very similar. In other words, academic achievement data (such as scores on standardized achievement tests, grades, or classwork samples) or behavior rating data can be used to help make any of the five kinds of decisions. It is the criteria and standards used to interpret the data that vary across the five kinds of decisions. In addition, as highlighted in figure 1.2, different consumers of assessment information use it for a wide array of purposes, all of which are subsumed under the five basic decisions facilitated by assessment. We examine each of these next.

Figure 1.2 The Many Purposes of Assessment from the Viewpoints of Parents, Students, Teachers, Administrators, and Policymakers

Policymakers need assessments to:	• Set standards • Focus on goals • Monitor the quality of education • Reward/sanction various practices • Formulate policies • Direct resources including personnel and money
Administrators need assessments to:	• Monitor program effectiveness • Identify program strengths and weaknesses • Designate program priorities • Assess alternatives • Plan and improve programs
Teachers and administrators use assessment for:	• Grouping decisions • Individual diagnosis and prescription • Monitoring student progress • Curriculum evaluation and refinement • Fostering mastery/promotion/grading and other feedback • Motivating students • Grading
Parents and student can use assessments to:	• Gauge student progress • Assess student strengths and weaknesses • Evaluate school accountability

Screening Decisions

Screening is a procedure in which an entire population of students, such as those entering kindergarten, are evaluated to determine whether they may need additional assessment from educational, psychological, or medical specialists. Abilities and skills assessed during a screening process are often believed to be basic or prerequisite to success in regular education settings. Therefore, individuals who cannot or do not perform at least at a specified level of competency on screening tasks are labeled "at risk" and are usually targeted for a more detailed, individualized examination of their abilities.

Assessment for educational screening purposes is generally carried out by teachers and involves brief tests, skill inventories, and behavioral checklists. These instruments are characterized by ease of administration, brevity, and only moderate levels of reliability. In addition to teachers, speech, vision, and hearing specialists are routinely involved in screening. Many school systems also require regular health screenings of students.

Classification and Placement Decisions

Students whose abilities or behaviors seem to differ significantly from those of "normal" peers are often targeted by teachers or parents for consideration for placement in special instructional programs. Some of these students have persistent learning difficulties, others have behavioral or emotional disorders, and still others are intellectually gifted or talented. Of course, assessment will indicate that some of the students referred have no serious difficulties and do not require special services. Regardless of the reason for the referral, if an appropriate referral is made, it becomes the collective responsibility of educators, parents, and specialists to gather data on which to base informed decisions.

A classification decision technically is separate from a placement decision and in fact must precede it with regard to special education actions. Historically, psychologists have been responsible for the classification of individuals' learning and behavior problems, whereas educators have decided where to teach such individuals. However, with the passage of the Individuals with Disabilities Education Act (IDEA; originally referred to as the Education for All Handicapped Children Act of 1975, Public Law 94–142), eligibility, classification, and placement decisions must now be made by teams of knowledgeable professionals and parents. Such a legal requirement provides a strong rationale for the development of assessment knowledge and skills in all teachers.

Although a classification decision is a very serious action intended to help students obtain needed services, it can have adverse effects if improperly used (Edelbrock, 1988; Hobbs, 1975). Therefore, for intelligent classification and placement decisions to be made, specific and accurate data must be gathered concerning a student's ability and present educational setting (e.g., materials, seating arrangement, and teacher's methods and learning expectations). Assessment information typically used to make such decisions includes direct behavior observations, results from individually administered intelligence and achievement tests, behavior rating scales, and class performance indicators such as work samples. Unfortunately, as we will see in the next chapter, making accurate and consistent classification decisions based on these assessment data is often next to impossible.

Student Progress Decisions

The educational development of a student or a group of students generally is of much interest to parents, teachers, and students themselves. An effective teacher continuously monitors and evaluates student progress in numerous areas. On a daily basis, students' work samples and classroom performances provide information for progress decisions. However, since the learning of many concepts and skills requires considerable time, most progress decisions can be made only after significant time has elapsed. Data concerning student progress are likely to consist of standardized group achievement tests, curriculum-based checklists of objectives accomplished, and teachers' subjective reports of growth. Students receiving special or remedial services often are given the same test at the beginning and end of each school year to enable educators to document their progress more accurately.

Programming or Instructional Decisions

Teachers need information about a student's abilities, curriculum content, and teaching methods to make intelligent programming or instructional decisions, for such decisions are complex and cannot be made automatically because students with similar abilities do not always learn in the same way (Cronbach & Snow, 1977; Elliott, Kratochwill, Littlefield & Travers 1996; Ysseldyke, 1977). Therefore, a student's progress within a particular curriculum, and under given instructional methods, must be assessed regularly if effective programming decisions are to be reached. Standardized intelligence and achievement tests often have been used to develop instructional programs for exceptional students, but unless these tests correspond well with the content of a given curriculum, such use must be questioned. Instead, direct assessment of a student's performance on classroom materials and teacher-prepared tests can provide detailed, reliable information for specific programming decisions.

Program Effectiveness Decisions

Assessing the effectiveness of an educational program is difficult, because generally more than one student or educator is involved and the criteria for determining effectiveness are often undefined. Nevertheless, educators must be accountable for their programs. Hence, program evaluation has become a major activity of educational administrators and psychologists. Assessment data such as those used to make decisions about students' progress are particularly helpful in making decisions about a given program's effectiveness. Of course, data from individual students must be integrated to obtain an overall picture of the educational impact of a program. Published investigations of the effectiveness of various special education programs have appeared recently in several major educational and psychological journals and provide interesting reading (see e.g., Kavale, 1990).

Approaches to Assessment

A theory determines the types of variables that will be measured during the assessment process. The assessment of different types of variables in turn leads to the use of different approaches to assessment. Major traditional approaches to assessment include **norm-referenced** assessment, **criterion-**

referenced assessment, **functional** assessment, and **ecological** assessment. They differ not only with respect to what is measured but also with respect to how it is measured. This section provides a critical analysis of the various approaches to assessment, including a discussion of the strengths and weaknesses of each.

Norm-Referenced Assessment

Perhaps the most common approach to testing is norm-referenced assessment. It derives its name from the method in which test scores get their meaning by comparison to a representative group of scores. For example, a test score of 86 is considered good if it is higher than 95 percent of the scores with which it is compared, but it is not so good if it is lower than 70 percent of the other scores. In other words, norm-referenced assessments compare one child's behavior or performance with other children's behavior or performances. Thus, other children play a major role in providing a standard for interpreting the target child's performance.

Typically, in the development of norm-referenced tests, a large, collectively representative sample of the general population is tested. These people are referred to as the **norm group.** On one of the most common children's intelligence tests, such as the Wechsler Intelligence Scale for Children-Revised (WISC-R and more recently the WISC-III), the norm group has an average score of 100 (this is the result of a rather complex transformation process whereby raw scores are transferred to a scale with a mean of 100). The properties of this test have been extensively studied, and the test manual suggests, for example, that less than 5 percent of the population score above 130. Because it is norm-referenced, any WISC-R score can be meaningfully interpreted by comparing it with the norm group. Norm-referenced assessment can be used to answer the following types of questions: How does Sarah compare in reading comprehension with a nationally normed sample of same-age peers? Are Julie's SAT scores high enough to qualify her for admission to the university of her choice?

Advantages of Norm-Referenced Assessment

Norm-referenced tests are widely used in special and remedial education for several reasons. First, many decisions involve categorizing children as "exceptional" or "special." These are essentially norm-referenced decisions because information is needed (and sometimes is required by law) on who is legally eligible for special services and who will probably be in greatest need of such services. Second, norm-referenced assessment provides information that is easily communicated to parents and others unfamiliar with tests. Telling parents that their child is in the lower 5 percent of the population with respect to hearing ability is usually more meaningful than providing data about their child's decibel (loudness) levels. Third, norm-referenced tests have received a lot of attention in terms of technical data and research.

Disadvantages of Norm-Referenced Assessment

A major difficulty with norm-referenced assessment is that it typically provides information that may be too general to be useful in everyday classroom teaching activities. Many educators disregard the prognostic and interpretative types of data provided by standardized tests because the information is often not directly applicable to developing daily instructional activities or interventions. What does knowing a child's WISC-III score or grade equivalent in reading specifically tell a teacher about what and how to teach? Does the child need to learn initial consonants or is he or she having difficulty with comprehension?

Another problem is that because most norm-referenced tests are designed for a broad national use, often a discrepancy exists between what is taught in an individual classroom and what is tested. For example, the spelling subtest of the Peabody Individual Achievement Test-Revised (PIAT-R) requires the respondent to choose the one word out of a list of four that is spelled incorrectly. The problem with this test is that most classroom spelling tests require the respondent to write words from memory as they are dictated by a teacher. Thus, the PIAT-R would provide information that not only lacks the specificity to guide remediation but also would probably be inaccurate unless a child's ability to recognize a correctly spelled word corresponded perfectly to his or her ability to recall and write spelling words from memory.

Another form of the problem concerning the discrepancy between what is taught and what is tested reveals itself in the form of content differences that frequently exist between published tests and the curriculum content taught in any given classroom. For example, the numerous norm-referenced achievement tests on the market today differentially sample the many curricula used in schools (Jenkins & Pany, 1978; Marston, 1989). Without careful attention to the potential testing-teaching overlap, or lack thereof, test scores do not truly index students' skill levels, since they do not adequately sample what the students have learned.

A fourth problem with norm-referenced tests is that, because their primary purpose is to compare one student with another, they tend to promote and reinforce the belief that the locus of the problem is within the child. However, although a child may differ from the norm, the real problem may not be within the child but in the teaching, placement, or curriculum. Educational specialists must begin to assess teacher's behaviors, curriculum content and sequencing, and other variables not measured by norm-referenced tests.

Criterion-Referenced Assessment

Whether a child can perform a particular skill is the question that criterion-referenced assessment seeks to answer. In contrast to norm-referenced assessment, which compares, or references, one person's performance with others', criterion-referenced assessment seeks to determine which individuals have reached some preestablished level or standard of performance. Typically, skills within a subject are hierarchically arranged so that those that must be learned first are tested first. In math, for example, addition skills would be evaluated (and taught) before multiplication skills. These tests usually are criterion-referenced because a student must achieve competence at one level before being taught at a higher level; criterion-referenced tests help to determine if a person is ready to move on to the next level. No effort is made to determine how much better or worse than the criterion a student performs but merely to assess, in a pass-fail manner, if a student possesses a certain skill.

Criterion-referenced assessment can be further illustrated by referring to differences in the methods used by some graduate and professional schools to evaluate students. A medical school, for example, may be concerned that everyone achieve surgery skills at some established criterion level (e.g., the patient must recover in a minimal amount of time with no complications). However, some professional schools may use a norm-referenced approach in which they admit more students than they expect to graduate and then "weed out" the weaker ones by administering difficult tests and passing only those with the highest scores.

Conceptually, much of what is occurring in the recent authentic assessment and outcome-based education movements is consistent with criterion-referenced assessment (Elliott, 1991; Gresham, 1991a). That is, educators are reacting against the use of norm-referenced tests and arguing for the use of assessment methods that compare a student's performance or products with some agreed-upon standard. This approach to assessment is discussed later in this chapter, but it clearly is consistent with the notion that standards or criteria for performing can be identified in advance of the performance and can be used to judge a performance in an objective manner.

Advantages of Criterion-Referenced Assessment

The primary usefulness of criterion-referenced assessment is in identifying a child's specific skills. Since most skills have been extensively studied and broken down into a series of steps or hierarchies, the test results could be used to determine the next most logical skill to teach. Thus, the implications for teaching are more direct with criterion-referenced tests than with norm-referenced tests.

A related advantage is the ability to use criterion-referenced tests in formative evaluation, which means assessing a child regularly, usually daily, when skills are being learned. This makes it possible to note student progress, determine if instruction is effective, and help plan the next skill to be taught. Since the focus is on skills instead of comparison with others, knowing what to teach and how to measure it becomes simplified.

Disadvantages of Criterion-Referenced Assessment

The primary problem with this form of assessment is establishing a suitable criterion. If a test were needed to determine whether students had mastered high school mathematics, for example, there is the challenge of determining exactly which skills should be included in the test. Some may feel that geometry must be included, but others may disagree. After the decision to measure a particular skill is made, the level at which the skill must be performed for the student to pass must be determined. Should a student pass the test if 90 percent of the questions are answered correctly or only if 100 percent are correct? These decisions must be carefully considered, because setting inappropriate criteria may cause a student to struggle unnecessarily with a concept. Currently, many more educators are demonstrating an interest in determining the essential learning outcomes of schooling, so it is likely that there will be increased use of criterion-referenced assessments in the schools of the 1990s (e.g., Spady & Kit, 1991).

Advocates of criterion-referenced testing assume that a child who fails to master a concept does so because of lack of exposure to the material. It is further assumed that additional instruction related to the concept will enable a child to pass the test. However, these assumptions may be inaccurate for some youngsters in special education, because additional instruction of the wrong type may not benefit some children and may result in repeated failures.

A potentially troublesome aspect of this form of test, for some educators, is that the skills assessed may become the goals of instruction rather than selected samples exemplifying what the child should know (Ebel, 1975). Teachers may then narrow the focus of their instruction and simply teach in accordance with what is measured on the test, which can result in a loss of the richness and variety that characterize good instruction.

Functional Assessment

Watching grandparents interact with their grandchildren is a good opportunity to see a wide range of assessment activities. For example, a 3-year-old might be asked to count to 10, to follow simple directions, to color with crayons, or to name the animals in a book. Such tasks may or may not be present at that age, but grandparents derive a great deal of satisfaction whatever the outcome. This type of assessment is ongoing and occurs in a very flexible and open social atmosphere. The tasks are obviously not standardized.

Similarly, teachers who analyze a child's writing for error patterns, special education teachers who observe a child in the regular classroom, speech therapists who just listen to a child talk, and psychologists who look at a child's mannerisms during oral reading may all be using informal assessment. Such techniques tell how a child learns and what a child knows.

Since the late 1980s terms such as **authentic** or **performance** assessment (Airasian, 1991) have been introduced into the literature. The process is really basic functional assessment and represents a structured and systematized problem-solving approach (see, e.g., the systems suggested by Eaves & McLaughlin, 1977; Elliott, 1991, 1994; Elliott & Piersel, 1982). Specifically, the intent is to emphasize the use of curriculum-based tests, behavioral observations, and trial teaching in the assessment of children.

Individuals who utilize informal assessment seem to view themselves as detectives. If a child is experiencing failure, assessment consists of collecting clues and facts about what contributes to the problem. Is it a problem with the child, such as a lack of ability or low motivation, or with the task being too difficult, insufficiently explained, or not worth learning? Or is it a problem with the setting, such as poor teaching or the lack of a quiet place to study? A good detective attempts to evaluate every area that might possibly contribute to the problem. A major assumption of this approach is that the closer the evaluation is to the actual situation in which the child is experiencing difficulty, the more accurate the identification processes and remedial interventions.

Advantages of Functional Assessment

The primary benefit of functional assessment over either norm-referenced or criterion-referenced assessment is its relevance to developing instructional or intervention activities. In general, norm-referenced tests can be used to select those who need instruction, and criterion-referenced tests help to determine what needs to be taught. Functional assessment practices also provide information about what a child needs to learn, but they do so using the actual materials and stimuli that the child encounters daily. Additionally, functional assessment is unique in providing information about *how* instruction should be given. By experimenting and playing detective, one can determine whether a child should be seated at the front or back of the room, what reinforces him or her, and when performance is best and worst.

Another reason that functional assessment is so applicable to instruction is that only very small inferences are needed to use the test data for instruction. Compare, for example, the degree of inference required to apply data from a nationally standardized norm-referenced test of reading ability versus information from a child's reading in a book used in the classroom with different amounts of help (see chapter 9). Since functional assessment typically occurs in the child's natural environment, assessors do not have the problem of generalizing the results from one situation to another. For example, consider a child who is being evaluated for a behavior problem. One evaluator may take the child into a quiet place for interviewing and formal testing. Another person may choose to observe the child in the classroom and on the playground under a variety of conditions. It is easy to question the degree to which the formal testing generalizes, since it was conducted in a small, quiet room on a one-to-one basis. Even the informal aspects of this situation are suspect because whether the child behaves normally during the individual session may have little relevance to how he or she may behave in a classroom with 25 other children who may encourage and reinforce the child's behavior. The observations in the classroom, on the other hand, can be structured to examine how the child responds to things like teacher attention, different activities, and so on, and may be more easily generalized because they took place in the child's actual environment.

Another major advantage of functional assessment is its flexibility. It can be utilized nearly any time, any place, and with any problem. Virtually the only limits are the users' knowledge of specific subjects and possible modifications and the means of gathering reliable data about important behavior. Little problems occur very frequently when working with children. It is usually best to check out such difficulties before they become big problems. The flexibility of functional assessment enhances its use over other types of assessment because users can take whatever materials are available and obtain a quick and simple check in a problem area. In general, fast and economical assessment procedures are preferred to those that are equally effective but require more personnel and material resources. The acceptability of functional assessment methods is attested to by the plethora of articles published in major education journals and presentations given at national conventions during the past several years.

Disadvantages of Functional Assessment

One drawback to functional assessment is that it places a great deal of burden on a teacher or an examiner to select appropriate tasks, be a good detective, and to correctly interpret the results in the absence of a test manual or formal guidelines. Functional assessment also requires good training in the content area in which assessment occurs and good problem-solving skills. For example, if a teacher notices that a kindergarten child consistently is reversing the letters *b* and *d,* does this mean that the child might have a learning disability? In this case, a little knowledge (that *b* and *d* reversals are bad) might cause problems, because *b* and *d* reversals are relatively common among kindergarten and first-grade children and may reflect a developmental immaturity rather than a learning disability.

A related problem with functional assessment is that the values and biases of the assessor can influence testing. For example, most people believe that boys are more aggressive and create more problems in school than girls. The difficulty with this and other biases is that judgment does not always correspond to reality. Observations of primary-grade children, for example, indicate that girls display as many deviant behaviors as boys but that teachers are more likely to respond to boys' misbehavior in a negative way (Patterson, 1982). Similar biases affect how functional assessment methods are chosen, implemented, and interpreted. Systematically approaching functional assessment and being aware of personal biases may help reduce bias.

Finally, functional assessment does not have the long history of supportive research and theory enjoyed by criterion-referenced and norm-referenced assessment. Consequently, functional assessment has seldom been included in teacher or psychologist training programs. Although many practitioners use it on an ongoing basis, few have received any formal training in functional assessment. Its outward simplicity compared with the grand statistical underpinnings of formal testing causes some individuals to question its adequacy. Although researchers suggest that educational programming can be accomplished just as effectively with functional assessment as with standardized testing (Lovitt & Fantasia, 1980; Wiggins, 1990), some practitioners are still reluctant to adopt functional assessment procedures.

Ecological Assessment

Anyone who has ever worked with children is aware of some of the complex interrelationships that exist between student and teacher, student and student, student and environment, teacher and community, and the like. Children are affected by other children, approaching holidays, the subject matter they are learning, the social mores of their community, their family situations, and even world economic conditions, especially if their parents are unemployed. It may be impossible to assess every factor that can influence student learning and behavior, but it is possible to move beyond an almost exclusive focus on the child. Ecological assessment must include an analysis of the teacher as well as the child (e.g., does the teacher use appropriate feedback and instructional techniques?), the teacher's expectations (e.g., does the teacher expect the child to be perfectly still and docile?), the environment (e.g., is the temperature at the proper level and are the desks arranged in a manner consistent with what the teacher wants to accomplish?), and the task (e.g., was the material worth learning and related to the content?).

Consider a teacher who is concerned about the number of students who have begun to turn in incomplete assignments during the last month. Previously, the rate of assignment completion had been excellent for the entire class. An analysis of the situation suggests the problem really began when construction was initiated on a new wing of the school. The building activities were clearly visible to the students through an open window, and many enjoyed watching the progress. An easy solution would be to close the curtains or turn the students' desks away from the window. However, a less complete, child-centered analysis may have resulted in the time-consuming and possibly less successful remedy of modifying student behavior in spite of an environment that encouraged off-task behavior.

Ecological assessment is not a category of tests or even a theory of assessment. Instead, it is more of a viewpoint of assessment. Virtually any type of criterion-referenced, norm-referenced, or informal test could be used in an ecological approach, for it offers the freedom to use assessment devices in unique and creative ways. A wide range of variables can influence student learning and behavior, many of which can be measured using a variety of assessment approaches.

Recently, Ysseldyke and Christenson (1987, 1993) developed a formal systematic procedure that can be used to gather data on the nature of an instructional environment for an individual student. After reviewing the research and conceptual literature on effective instruction, models of schooling, and instructional psychology, Ysseldyke and Christenson developed The Instructional Environment Scale, revised as The Instructional Environment

System-II or TIES-II. TIES-II provides an excellent illustration of the components in a comprehensive education-focused ecological assessment. Specifically, TIES-II is a qualitative observation scale that provides information on 17 descriptive indicators of a student's learning environment. These include information on instructional planning (i.e., instructional match and teacher expectations), instructional management (i.e., classroom environment), instructional delivery (i.e., instructional presentation, cognitive emphasis, motivational strategies, and informed feedback), instructional monitoring and evaluation (i.e., academic engaged time, adaptive instruction, progress evaluation, and student understanding), and home support for learning components (i.e., expectations and attributions, discipline orientation, home affective environment, parent participation, and structure for learning).

Advantages of Ecological Assessment

The ecological model has four major advantages over other forms of assessment. First, because it is a process of assessment, it is more than a collection of tests: It is a way of viewing all forms of assessment. Second, it has helped to expand the focus of assessment. Rather than simply focusing on the child, an intensive study of the student is made in relationship to his or her environment. Third, ecological assessment increases our awareness of the complexity of human behavior. Finally, this model causes us to question the validity of simplistic and mechanical assessment practices that diagnose a child's problem on the basis of only one or two standardized tests.

Disadvantages of Ecological Assessment

The most obvious problem in using ecological assessment is its complexity. Instead of administering a test or observing one or two behaviors, an evaluator is faced with the additional possibilities of interviewing other adults, observing the child in multiple situations, and collecting and synthesizing a large amount of information. This process may be too time-consuming or impractical for many situations. Professionals using the ecological approach must be careful to collect enough information so that the problem can be understood, yet not so much that it cannot be used or comprehended.

A second problem with this form of assessment is the lack of adequate instruments. To a large extent, assessors are left on their own to determine what and how to assess, although tools like TIES certainly provide some useful structure to one's ecological assessment. A related problem is the lack of research into factors, such as the seating arrangement or the type of instruction, that significantly affect learning.

An Integration of Assessment Models and Approaches

Each of the various approaches to the assessment of children has some advantages and disadvantages for professionals entrusted to assess children experiencing difficulties in school. There is no perfect or foolproof assessment approach; however, when confronted with the task of assessing a child who is experiencing academic or behavior difficulties, we have found it helpful to focus assessment activities on six general variables: the target child, his/her teacher(s), his/her parent(s), the school materials, the task(s), and his/her peers. We have found that for most cases, we need to collect information about each of these six variables (child, teacher, parent, materials, tasks, and peers) to discern how they relate to the target child's problems. The collection of information often involves the use of direct observations, standardized and informal tests, interviews, and examination of products produced by the student. Thus, these six variables organize most of our assessment efforts. In addition, we have found that by changing aspects of one or more of these six variables, we are likely to improve the target child's functioning.

In summary, by using the best features of the various assessment models and approaches and by focusing one's activities on six practical variables, one generally can conduct a meaningful assessment—one that leads to changes in instructional tactics and outcomes. Let's now examine how a structured problem-solving sequence can guide assessment activities and the conclusions one draws from assessment results.

Problem Solving and the Role of Assessment

Assessment is never an end in itself. Rather, as part of the problem-solving process, assessment is used in screening, classifying and placing, progress monitoring, programming, and determining program effectiveness. Numerous psychologists and educators have written about problem-solving strategies; however, less has been written about how such strategies or schemes apply to assessment.

Before examining a general model of problem solving, we must define the term "problem." Most people think of a problem as something negative, subaverage, or at least bothersome. Although this is often true, numerous situations occur in which individuals are functioning well above average but still have problems or concerns. For example, a student may be functioning several grades above average in math yet experience significant difficulties when placed in an accelerated math program. In addition, the student's self-concept may be influenced negatively because of the failures in the accelerated program. *Problem* is thus a relative concept and can be said to exist when an individual (child, teacher, or parent) reports a significant discrepancy between a target person's current level of performance and a desired level of performance.

A number of aspects of this definition require elaboration. First, although the person reporting the problem may or may not be the target person, the reporter in most cases would be considered a component of the problem. Second, the determination of whether a problem involves a "significant discrepancy" is initially not questioned; however, once the current and desired levels of performance are defined operationally, this significant discrepancy becomes the focal point of assessment. This approach to problem definition is based on the belief that such problems grow out of the unsuccessful or discrepant interactions between persons (e.g., child and peers, child and teacher, child and parent, and parent and teacher). Thus, the person targeted as having a problem and his or her interactions with the environment must be examined first to understand and then to change the problem behavior. Several models have been developed for problem solving by professionals in educational settings.

A General Model of Problem Solving

The problem-solving model that we will describe here is a four-step process that outlines objectives for each step of the process (Kratochwill & Bergan, 1990). The steps are as follows:

1. Identifying a problem
2. Analyzing a problem
3. Implementing an intervention
4. Evaluating the intervention

Within this process the first step is to achieve a clear, objective definition of the problem. Once a problem has been identified and defined, we are ready to analyze factors that may be influencing the targeted problem. After a comprehensive assessment of the problem and the factors influencing it, some intervention designed to treat the problem must be developed and implemented. Finally, after a suitable time period, the intervention plan is evaluated to determine its effectiveness. Each step of the model requires gathering information to proceed to the next step. Some of the information is gathered by interviewing teachers, parents, or even the students themselves. Some of the information requires observational assessment. Assessment of the individual will provide some information as well. The overall goal is to integrate different sources of information to resolve the problem.

This model will serve as a template for helping us to decide what assessment activities are necessary as we try to resolve problems. The objectives of each step of the problem-solving model are described in figure 1.3. The objectives that require assessment are in boldface. In many instances of this type, teachers refer the child to a multidisciplinary team. It is the responsibility of the entire team (including the teacher) to work cooperatively with the parents to develop an intervention plan. Some teams will do a "diagnostic assessment" to see if the child qualifies for a handicapping condition. In the case below, however, the multidisciplinary team will first work to try to solve the problem in the classroom. The process will require meetings, coordinating responsibilities, and assessment.

Identifying a Problem

The first priority in problem solving is ensuring that we get a comprehensive description of all of the concerns about the student. Let's say that Mrs. Lowery

Figure 1.3 Problem-Solving Model Steps and Objectives

Identifying a Problem

- Articulate all concerns.
- Prioritize and identify a target problem area.
- Define the behavior in observable, measurable terms.
- Describe planned methods of assessment.
- Describe typical events preceding the target behavior.
- Describe typical events following the problem behavior.
- Describe the discrepancy between actual and expected performance.
- Set goals.

Analyzing a Problem

- Make reasonable hypotheses about factors affecting the problem.
- Focus on factors over which we have control.
- Generate a solution based on the presumed function of the target behavior.

Implementing a Solution

- Define responsibilities.
- Ensure that it gets done.
- Assess whether it gets done.
- Assess student outcomes.
- Assess whether the outcomes are viewed as positive by all the relevant stakeholders (i.e., the child, the teacher(s), the parents, etc.).

Evaluating the Solution

- Evaluate whether the solution was implemented.
- Evaluate whether the solution was effective.
- Evaluate whether the solution led to valued outcomes.

---

has referred Derrick, a repeating fourth-grade student, because of concerns about Derrick's poor reading skills. In our interview, she explained that he has been retained once and is being instructed in reading in her lowest reading group. Mrs. Lowery uses the lower-level third-grade book of the district basal reading series. She said that when Derrick reads, his reading is halting and that he has poor decoding skills, a lot of difficulty reading the passages in the reading group, and difficulty answering the comprehension questions. To make sure that Mrs. Lowery had described all of her concerns, we asked her directly if there were any other problems. She responded that Derrick is fine otherwise. Mrs. Lowery said that she discussed the problem with the parents, who are aware of Derrick's difficulties and are willing to help. The next objective is to prioritize concerns and identify a target problem area. In Derrick's case, Mrs. Lowery was concerned primarily about Derrick's poor oral reading skills. She felt that if he read more fluently, his comprehension would probably improve.

Given that the general concern was reading, the team wanted to get more specific and to define the reading problem in observable, measurable terms. The team decided that the school psychologist, Ms. Wright, would observe Derrick during reading instruction. She also had Derrick read passages from the basal readers as well as lists of phonetically regular words (e.g., words with common vowel combinations, words with vowel-r combinations, and words with two short vowels). During reading group, Ms. Wright observed that Derrick displayed high rates of on-task behavior. He read orally with poor accuracy and fluency, but he gave generally accurate responses to the comprehension questions. During independent seat work, Derrick displayed lower rates of on-task behavior; he was distracted but not disruptive. Derrick completed his worksheets with 60 percent accuracy. Derrick and a group of his classroom peers read aloud three passages randomly chosen for one minute from the fourth- and third-grade basal readers. Ms. Wright found that in the fourth-grade texts, whereas Derrick read at an average rate of 75 correctly read words per minute with 7 errors, the average peer read at an average rate of 137 correctly read words per minute with 3 errors. In the third-grade text, Derrick read at an average rate of 93 correctly read words per minute with 4 errors; the average third-grade peer read at an average rate of 118 correctly read words per minute with 3 errors. When Derrick read lists of words that were phonetically regular, he read words with common vowel combinations (e.g., may, teach, soak), a second-grade curricular objective with only 72 percent accuracy, words with vowel-r combinations (e.g., star, dirt, cord), a third-grade objective, with 52 percent accuracy, and words with two short vowels (e.g., kitten, hopping), also a third-grade objective, with 40 percent accuracy.

These assessment activities allowed the team to describe the problem in the following manner: Derrick is reading at a rate of 75 correctly read words per minute with 7 errors (a high error rate) in the fourth-grade curriculum while the average student is reading at a rate of 137 correctly read words per minute with 3 errors under the same conditions. Also, Derrick has poor phonic decoding skills, as evidenced by his low accuracy in reading phonetically regular words in isolation.

The team agreed that the goal would be for Derrick to improve his oral reading fluency in the fourth-grade basal reader, as this was the instructional goal for Derrick. As such, they assessed Derrick's oral reading fluency in the fourth-grade reader two more times to make sure that the assessment information was stable (and that the previous estimate of 75 correctly read words per minute was not a fluke). They plotted this data on a graph to display it visually, calling this the "baseline data," which implies data gathered prior to intervention (displayed in figure 1.4). They decided that their goal statement would read as follows: "When given a randomly selected passage from the fourth-grade reader of the Silver, Burdett, and Ginn reading series, Derrick will read at least 105 words correctly per minute with 3 or fewer errors by April 12." A precise goal statement was possible because of the assessment data that they had collected. Oral reading fluency is a good measure of reading skills, and it is quite sensitive to student growth (Shinn, 1989). The team members also decided to assess Derrick's oral reading fluency at least once a week to see how it would progress over the next eight weeks following any instructional modifications that would be made. Because they had a precise goal, they were able

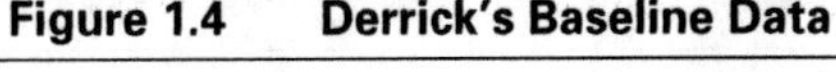

Figure 1.4 Derrick's Baseline Data

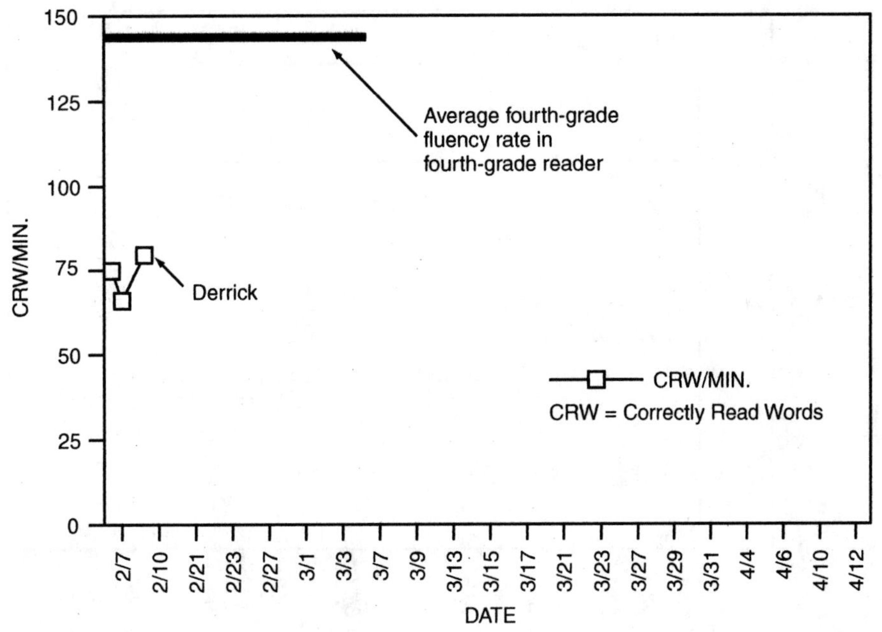

to draw a line—referred to as an "aim line"—from where Derrick was reading (75 correctly read words per minute) to where he was expected to be reading in eight weeks time (105 correctly read words per minute) (see figure 1.5).

Analyzing a Problem

Given the information that they had collected, the team members had to consider reasonable hypotheses about what would make Derrick a better reader. We will use the term *reasonable hypotheses* throughout this text. It is simply an inference or an educated guess limited to factors over which we have control based on the information we have collected. In examining the information that they had gathered so far, Derrick's team noted and concluded the following:

- Derrick was displaying low rates of oral reading accuracy and fluency (i.e., speed) in curricular reading materials.
- He had poor mastery of phonics.
- Therefore, during reading instruction, Derrick makes many errors and does not read fluently at the level at which he is being instructed.

Figure 1.5 Derrick's Projected Aim Line

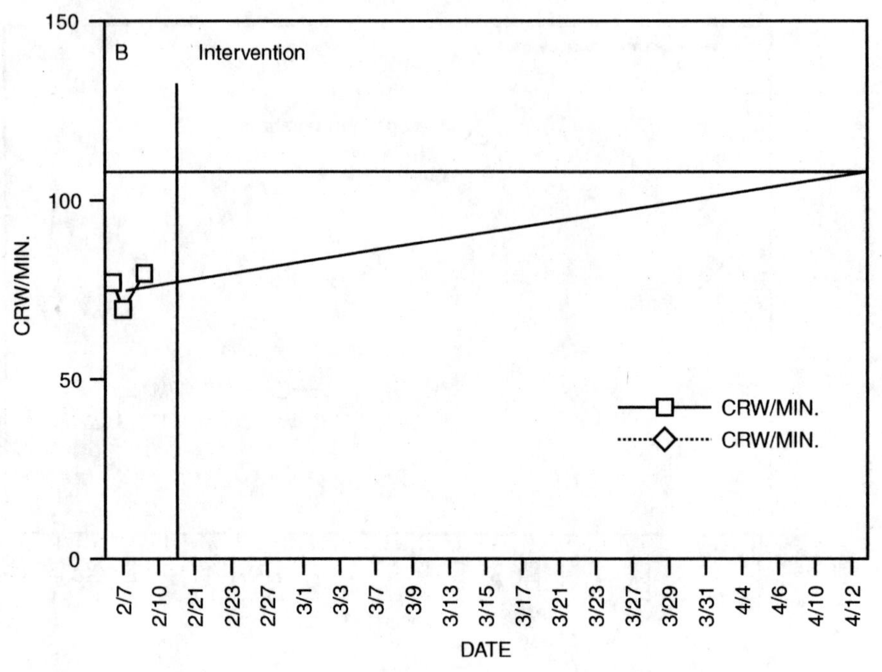

The team hypothesized that Derrick's oral reading accuracy and fluency would improve through modifications designed to (a) supplement current instruction with instruction in materials at a lower instructional level, (b) increase modeling of accurate and fluent reading, and (c) increase reading practice. Team members, including the vice principal (the chair of the multidisciplinary team), the teacher, and the school psychologist, met with Derrick's parents to share the results of the assessments, how they interpreted the assessment results, and the factors that they felt were affecting Derrick's performance. They also wanted to see if Derrick's parents were able to be a part of the intervention that they would develop.

Implementing a Solution

The purpose of this step is to generate an intervention, decide who will be responsible for implementing it, and how long it will be tried before a decision is made about how effective it is. Based on the team's hypotheses concerning factors affecting Derrick's performance, the teacher agreed to implement several modifications to Derrick's reading program, and his parents agreed to spend time reading with him in the evening. Mrs. Lowery would continue to instruct Derrick in the third-grade basal reader in the reading group but would supplement instruction for the group three times a week with another reading series with carefully controlled (i.e., phonetically regular) vocabulary words by reducing the amount of independent seat work, reading the passage to the students (modeling accurate and fluent reading), and having students practice reading the passage with a partner. Furthermore, a peer tutor was to work with Derrick three times a week to (a) read passages to him from phonetically regular texts that contained high percentages of the kinds of phonics words that Derrick had not yet mastered and (b) have Derrick read the passages orally (a form of drill or practice) while correcting Derrick's mistakes (error correction). Finally, Derrick would read aloud to his parents three or four times a week from the basal reader in which he was being instructed to practice reading the passages before reading group.

To help everyone remember their responsibilities, checklists were developed for each part of the intervention. The checklists described each step in detail. In this way, if one of the key players was having difficulty doing the intervention, the team could try to come up with alternative solutions. The team then trained everyone to use the checklists. Assessment data were gathered continuously throughout this period on Derrick's oral reading fluency and the frequency with which he was receiving the instructional modifications in the classroom (e.g., peer tutoring and parent tutoring).

Evaluating the Solution

The purpose of this step is to decide whether the intervention was effective or not. If it was effective, it is then necessary to decide whether the intervention should be continued or terminated. If it was not effective, the team must consider what factors were responsible for poor outcomes and decide how to modify the intervention to increase the chances that it will be effective in the future. At the end of the eight-week period, the team members examined the data to see if there was an increasing trend in Derrick's oral reading fluency. The aim line allowed them to determine whether Derrick was progressing at the expected rate of improvement. Indeed, in this instance, the instructional modifications were successful at increasing Derrick's oral reading fluency (see figure 1.6). Mrs. Lowery reported that Derrick was more confident in reading group, that he answered the comprehension questions accurately during reading group, and that he had developed a special relationship with his peer tutor. Mrs. Lowery was very pleased with the outcomes as were Derrick's parents, who said that he was enjoying the one-on-one time that he was receiving in the evening.

In Derrick's case, the initial modifications were quite successful at improving his performance in the targeted area. Any teacher knows, however, that it doesn't always work like this. You try something and see if it works. The problem-solving process has several features, however, that make it a

Figure 1.6 Derrick's Outcome Data

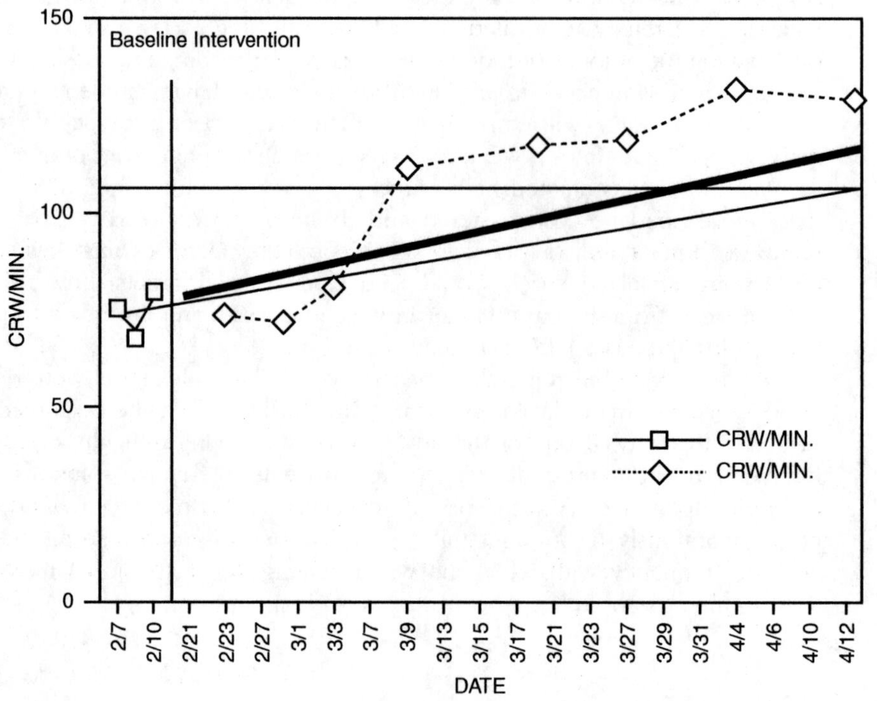

particularly useful model. First, the process can be repeated if you're not successful initially. Information from the first attempt can be used to improve the process during later attempts. Second, the problem-solving process encourages us to look at the environment in which children are functioning for factors over which we have control. This feature is particularly useful because we will start with simple solutions before considering complex solutions. Simple solutions, when effective, are more likely to be carried out more consistently than complex solutions that may also be effective because they are also a more efficient use of resources (Noell & Gresham, 1993).

The problem-solving model has been described as "robust," because it can be very effective and applicable to a lot of different problem situations. It will not, however, tell us what kind of assessment information we need to gather. It merely creates an outline for the kind of information that we should be seeking at each step of the process. Nonetheless, when we are using the problem-solving process, we know what the objective of each step is as well as the ultimate outcome. In Derrick's case, the team gathered assessment data about Derrick's functioning in the curriculum as well as data about the classroom environment and linked the two in a series of hypotheses about what would make Derrick a better reader. For these reasons, we will use the problem-solving process throughout the remainder of the text in our discussions of assessment techniques to help you to see the value of different techniques in answering different questions.

Chapter Summary

In this chapter, we have emphasized the need for developing a model of assessment. Each educator has an individual responsibility to develop his or her own professional model of assessment. As we have seen, your model of assessment will dictate the kinds of things you assess and the kinds of decisions you make about students. We are encouraging you to be a critical, reflective educator who understands the limitations of assessment information and the effects that assessment data will have on the decisions that you make. A solid professional model of assessment is grounded in standards that can be shown to increase students' academic and social competence. These recommendations are in line with the *Standards for Educational and Psychological Testing* developed jointly by the American Educational Research Association, the American Psychological Association, and the National Council on Measurement in Education (1985). They state:

> The *Standards* emphasizes that test users should have a sound technical and professional basis for their actions, much of which can be derived from research done by test developers and publishers. In selecting a test, a potential user should depend heavily upon the developer's research documentation that is clearly related to the intended application. Although the test developer should supply the needed information, the ultimate responsibility for appropriate test use lies with the user. (p. 3)

We have explicitly described nine assumptions and principles of the assessment model that we embrace. The remaining chapters of this first section will describe many of the conceptual issues in assessment that you must face in being a good educator. They will also describe the technical issues related to evaluating the accuracy, reliability, and validity of assessment data. The next section will describe assessment strategies that examine student functioning in the curriculum and in the classroom. In the final section, we will review the technical adequacy of some common norm-referenced measures used in psychoeducational assessments.

CHAPTER 2

A Practical Look at Current Assessment Practices with Some Suggestions for Avoiding Trouble[1]

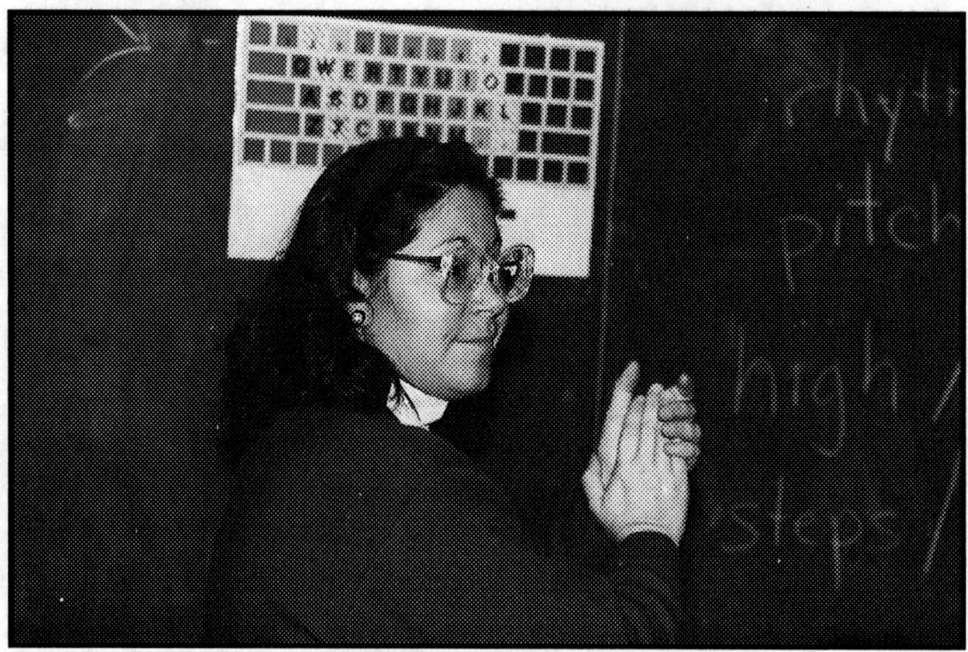

You may be faced with a struggle between the way that you think practices should be and the way that they are. In the previous chapter, we described the assumptions, objectives, and practices associated with the problem-solving model used in this text. This problem-solving approach differs from a traditional "testing" approach but is quite compatible with current demands on practitioners to be active in resolving problems rather than simply labeling children or their problems (Reschly & Ysseldyke, 1995). Teachers and others who work directly with children want to know *how to* improve a child's reading or decrease a problem behavior, not merely that the child has a learning disability or a behavior disorder. Hence, the most important reason to utilize a problem-solving approach is that it is useful. Traditional "testing" is not only

[1]David W. Barnett, University of Cincinnati, was coauthor for this chapter.

less useful, it can be harmful. What is it like to experience decision making using traditional assessment methods? This chapter starts with an example of a typical scenario of a teacher referring a child because of academic problems and describes traditional testing from the perspective of a teacher. Next, problems with the testing approach are discussed. Finally, we describe some assessment practices that try to correct for those mistakes that have had detrimental consequences for children and youth.

The Case of Tony and Mrs. Grier

Imagine the following situation confronted by Mrs. Grier, a third-grade regular education classroom teacher, and ask yourself, "Did Mrs. Grier receive the help she needed?"

Mrs. Grier has a student, Tony, who is having difficulty learning to read in her classroom. After talking to Tony's parents on several occasions and trying different strategies for improving his reading, Mrs. Grier referred Tony to the school's multidisciplinary team (MDT). Tony's parents were in agreement that it would be a good idea to get more professionals involved. Mrs. Grier has never been to the MDT before but hopes that the team will be able to do something that will get Tony back on track.

Mrs. Grier walks into a room of six people, including the vice principal, who serves as the chair of the MDT, a special education teacher, an educational diagnostician, a school psychologist, a speech pathologist, and a social worker. Tony has not been referred before so none of the team members are familiar with him. The social worker has worked with the family, since Tony has an older sibling who is medically fragile and the social worker had to coordinate contacts between the family, the school, and community medical services two years ago.

Team members ask Mrs. Grier various questions about what grade level he is at instructionally, how extreme of a problem she feels it is, whether he has any communication difficulties, and a few questions about the strategies that she has used to try to improve his reading skills. Finally, the vice principal proposes that the educational diagnostician, the speech pathologist, and the school psychologist conduct screenings (i.e., use brief tests to begin to discover the problem) to gather more information. The team will return in three weeks[2] to discuss the results of the screenings and decide how to proceed. Mrs. Grier asked what the screenings would entail. Team members responded that they would determine where Tony's skill levels are and whether they should do a full evaluation to determine if he qualifies for services as a student with a learning disability. Note that the team will have two sets of estimates of Tony's skills following the screening—one based on classroom performance according to Mrs. Grier, the teacher, and a second

---

[2]Note that this preliminary testing will require three weeks. In most states, MDTs have 30 to 60 working days by law to evaluate the child. Meanwhile there is often nothing done to help the child during this time period.

from standardized test scores from professionals who are not familiar with Tony. Mrs. Grier wonders to herself why they want to assess his reading level because she has just told them his reading level.

Before the next meeting, each of the professionals at various times removed Tony from the classroom and worked with him individually in an isolated testing room. When the team reconvened, the vice principal asked team members to review their test results. The educational diagnostician said that she had checked Tony's records and found that he scored at the 25th percentile in reading and at the 77th percentile in math on the standardized group-administered tests at the end of second grade, a bit lower in reading than what would be expected. However, she gave him the Woodcock Johnson-Revised and found that he obtained grade equivalency scores of 3.2 in reading and 3.6 in math. She concluded that he seemed to be doing fine academically. Mrs. Grier sits silently and says to herself, "No way he reads at the third-grade level!"

The school psychologist gave some parts of an IQ test to try to predict what Tony's IQ score would be if he were given the full battery. The school psychologist reports that Tony's IQ seems to be in the average range. The school psychologist also gave Tony the Bender Gestalt, a test that involves copying complex geometric forms to see if there might be a visual processing deficit, a supposed diagnostic indicator of a learning disability. He reported that Tony committed several "scorable" errors but he believed that the errors reflected an emotional basis rather than a processing deficit, explaining that the task was laborious for Tony, "his line quality was tremulous," and that he made several self-deprecating statements while he was doing the drawings. Mrs. Grier says to the team in a serious manner that Tony is one of the most emotionally normal kids she has but that there are four or five other children who do seem to have some emotional problems.

The speech pathologist said that she examined Tony's vocabulary skills, comprehension skills, and articulation skills (which overlaps with what the school psychologist may have done). She reported that he seemed to be fine in all areas.

The ensuing discussion led the team members to the conclusion that Tony would probably not qualify for services as a learning disabled student if a full evaluation was done but that he might have some emotional difficulties that could be explored with the parents. Therefore, the team decided to not do an evaluation for services but recommended that the teacher talk to the parents about Tony's self-esteem.

How do you think that Mrs. Grier might respond to this process and this outcome given the discrepancy between what she is observing in the classroom (the first source of information) and the testing results (the second source of information)? How would you respond? How would you express *your* point of view?

Mrs. Grier has several options. She can acquiesce and decide that these professionals should know what they are doing given all the testing that they performed and the confidence they appear to have in their conclusions. In this case, Mrs. Grier will continue to instruct Tony as best she can and may take the team's recommendation to discuss his self-esteem with the parents. Mrs. Grier, however, may decide, based on confidence in her own observations, that she doesn't agree with the testing results and that Tony truly does have a problem with reading. Stated differently, the testing process did not match the perceptions which Mrs. Grier has of Tony. Furthermore, emotional problems, if they do exist, may be Tony's *reactions* to his struggles in school or maybe the school psychologist simply made Tony nervous. On what grounds can Mrs. Grier make such assertions?

We stated in chapter 1 that to be an active participant in the full range of educational decisions affecting Tony, Mrs. Grier needs to be a critical educator. In this case, knowledge *is* power. Mrs. Grier must be able to articulate why she thinks that the screening process was not helpful to Tony's educational programming and be able to request more helpful assistance. We have met many teachers who have encountered situations like the one just described. The critical educator understands the assumptions and limitations of assessment practices and works from a model that has been shown to increase student achievement through improved educational decisions. We will return to Mrs. Grier at various points throughout the remainder of the chapter as we describe some of the problems with tests and why Mrs. Grier can place more confidence in her own information about Tony, which has been acquired through working with him five to six hours per day for several months. In the following sections, we will discuss some of the more important problems associated with traditional assessment practices. A summary of the major problems is presented in table 2.1.

Sources of Error in Assessment

Barnett and Macmann (1992a) suggested that two questions be asked about assessment: (a) What can be said with confidence? and (b) What can be said that might be helpful? How confident can we be about what we say about the assessment results? Each facet of assessment may potentially contribute information *and* error. The worst part of assessment and decision making is that it contains error with potential harmful and expensive consequences. Although *any time* we measure something, *there will be error* in our measurement, tests were designed to *improve* decision making and for this reason many types of errors are insidious. We will examine the statistical implications of error in chapter 5. Here we will show how error from traditional tests can affect decision making.

First let's distinguish between two kinds of error: systematic error and random error. *Systematic error* is due to a flaw in the measurement device. It's like having a short ruler. The error is always there. Unfortunately, it's not always possible for the average professional to know whether a test has systematic error. If there is systematic error, you need to dismiss the results of

Table 2.1 Four Problems Associated with Traditional Psychoeducational Assessment Practices

1. Tests contain surprising amounts and kinds of error. Screening and classification practices with norm-referenced academic and other developmental tests lead to high error rates in identifying students when they are subjected to proper analysis of the accuracy and consistency of decision outcomes.
2. Traditional tests do not assess what is being taught or expected in the classroom, nor do they yield useful information directly relevant to the setting in which students are supposed to be learning.
3. MDTs do not use assessment information in their decision making according to federal and authoritative guidelines for classification decisions.
4. Traditional tests are useless for developing interventions. Tests have little to no utility in identifying problems targeted for intervention, assessing factors related to the problem(s), and monitoring effects of interventions.

the measurement procedures. *Random error,* on the other hand, affects all assessment practices. Random error is due to events affecting student performance that were not considered in the interpretation of the results. For example, if a child guesses correctly or likes the person doing the testing, he or she may perform better. If the child is sick, performance may suffer.

Measurement error is everywhere, but error emerges in different forms in the traditional versus problem-solving models as a result of different assumptions and tactics of each approach. Therefore, it is critical to understand potential sources of error in both assessment approaches in order to know what we can say confidently about test results. The remainder of this section describes sources of error in the traditional testing approach. We will examine sources of error in the problem-solving approach later in the chapter after looking at some problem-solving assessment techniques.

Assessment involves gathering samples of behavior under structured conditions to describe the student's performance. In education, assessment is traditionally conducted for screening of problems and for classifying students (as having a disability). The test instructions, the kinds of test items, the way in which the student is expected to respond (e.g., in written form versus saying the answer verbally), time limits, and scoring rules for responses are some of the conditions that are defined prior to assessment. All of these conditions will affect how we interpret student responses and, ultimately, the decision that we will make. For example, an interpretation of a typical norm-referenced test of reading might be something like, "When asked to read a list of words orally, Lashawnda scored as well as or better than 67 percent of her same-age peers in the standardization sample." This finding, however, may not correspond to typical classroom performance or the results of reading assessments using different methods, because the rules imposed by the test are different from the rules in the classroom. For example, one test of spelling ability requires students to identify the correctly spelled word from a list of four words. Most teachers, however, dictate words and the child must *recall* them, not *recognize* them.

To meaningfully interpret, understand, and convey assessment results, a set of rules for planning assessments and organizing the results was needed. Standard procedures for how to assess are developed based on these rules. By standardizing the conditions, it is possible to compare Lashawnda's performance with other third graders under the same conditions. But this leads to many questions. To which third graders should Lashawnda be compared? Those in her classroom or national samples? Those of the same age, gender, culture, and other experiences? What is a correct response to questions on the test? Are there multiple correct responses? Are some responses more correct than others? In general, numbers are assigned to student responses in order to produce a score that will allow us to make some statement about student performance.

Obviously, the conditions in which someone is tested and the scoring rules are important to the interpretations of the assessment data. You also can see the importance of having assessment conditions that reflect real-life demands when we are making decisions about what to do in real-life circumstances (e.g., what instructional materials to use, where to place a child, etc). So, for instance, when measuring a student's mastery of grammar, will we design a test that requires students to write grammar rules verbatim or will we design a test that allows us to analyze the grammatical content of student writing samples? The answer depends on what you wish to infer. If you want to infer whether students have memorized grammar rules, the former is probably a better approach. If you want to infer whether students write papers using correct grammar, the latter is probably a better approach.

In a traditional model, it is important for the assessment data to be consistent across other items of the same type, across time, across settings, and across examiners (Cronbach, Gleser, Nanda, & Rajaratnam, 1972). These tests are designed to produce consistent results. Thus, the goal is for the test to give the same result regardless of who is doing the testing, where the test is administered, and so on.

Numerous factors, however, can adversely affect the consistency of assessment results in a traditional assessment approach. For example, test items may not adequately sample the domain that we are assessing. If we are trying to measure students' multiplication performance but the test contains only two multiplication problems, then our sample of "multiplication knowledge" was too small.

Another form of inconsistency occurs when examiners or observers don't agree. This kind of error suggests that the rules for scoring performance are not clear enough to ensure that student performance is scored in a consistent manner. For example, a test item may ask a child to tell what the word *teacher* means. A child might respond, "A teacher is a person." If the scoring rules for the test are poor, then one examiner may score this response correct and another may not.

A third source of inconsistency is the normal daily fluctuations in student performance that occur from one day to the next. The fluctuations may be the result of (a) how the student is feeling physically on one day or another, (b) competition for the student's attention across different days, or (c) changes in skills. Fluctuations of student performance also may occur across settings. The presence of one teacher or the physical arrangement of a room may affect student performance. These daily fluctuations have a significant impact on student performance, reducing our confidence in conclusions about students' mastery of, for example, multiplication. The traditional approach regards these differences as random fluctuations that decrease the reliability of the results but that must be tolerated. A problem-solving approach, on the other hand, regards these differences as potentially important clues about environmental factors that may be affecting student behavior.

Another factor that may interfere with truly understanding the test results is the testing method. In our multiplication test, we could have students circle the correct response (from a list of four alternatives) or write the correct response to the query, "4 × 4 = ?" Having students write the response is probably a more accurate indicator of the actual skill than having them select among alternatives because this is what will be expected by the curriculum and actual life demands.

Why is it important to know that tests contain error? When we interpret tests using a traditional approach, we must be cognizant of the fact that student performance may differ from one time to the next, from one setting to the next, or from one method of assessing to the next. All of these factors decrease our confidence in interpretation and may introduce error in our decision making if they are not accounted for. Therefore, it is critical to understand the various sources of error present in testing results. From a problem-solving approach, these differences across time, settings, and methods are the very information that we are seeking to make inferences about what is affecting student performance.

How Error Affects Traditional Screening and Testing Practices

Two common reasons for assessment are screening and classification. We would like to examine in more depth how error affects decisions made about students like Tony, students who are of concern for teachers. The problems associated with screening and classification affect decision making to a much greater degree than commonly thought.

Screening

Educators use many formal assessment procedures (e.g., standardized tests) to conduct screening where information is gathered using brief tests to help educators decide whether to pursue further testing. Because the outcomes for screening don't appear to be as hazardous as evaluation for classification, many professionals adopt a "crude initial screening" frame of reference (Meehl & Rosen, 1955) and promote the use of lower standards and questionable techniques for screening decisions. For instance, there is a longstanding tradition of examining developmental functioning based on human figure drawings where professionals assess aptitude and emotional functioning using children's drawings of humans. Many scoring systems have been developed for inferring aspects of development, such as a child's IQ, based on his or her drawing of a person. Drawing a person, like other screening techniques, is quick, requiring only a few minutes. These quick (and sometimes dirty) procedures that do not seem to be at first glance costly to administer and can be given quickly are justified because decisions made on the basis of screening tests supposedly do not have the same consequences as other, more weighty decisions. However, screening decisions are often as important as classification decisions because they dictate whether a child will be considered for classification. It is difficult to measure emotional adjustment or learning ability, let alone to do so quickly. Screening can be a waste of professional time and give misleading information. This is merely one of the problems with screening measures.

A second problem with screening is the *base rate* problem. To understand base rates, consider two early childhood programs. One program is in an affluent community and another is in an economically depressed urban setting. You may find enormous differences in the presence of language problems and preacademic skills between these two groups of children. The frequency of a condition is referred to as the base rate. In one setting, the base rate for deficits in preacademic skills (e.g., phoneme segmentation, letter naming, number naming, letter copying, etc.) may be 70 percent. That is, 70 percent of the students may display deficits in important preacademic skills that will make it difficult for them to benefit later from instruction in basic academic skills like reading and math. In the other setting, the base rate may be much smaller (e.g., 5% of the children), meaning that only a few children have such problems. In the setting where there are a lot of children with poor preacademic skills, rather than spending considerable professional time and money on screening practices, it may be wiser to teach preacademic skills to all students, assuming that *everyone* will benefit. In the setting with a low base rate for preacademic skills problems, traditional screening of all children will be expensive and will have a low yield, not identifying many children because only 5 percent have problems. Other methods, such as teacher consultation, may be explored.

Most screening measures suffer from problems so severe that their primary advantage, efficiency, is very small relative to the negative consequences of using them. As a starter, across screening instruments designed to identify children who are at risk for academic failure, for every *one* case where the screening results agree with a second screening test, there are about *three to five* cases of disagreement for each case of agreement (Barnett & Macmann, 1992a). This should not be surprising given that the situation isn't any better with more esteemed intelligence and achievement measures (Macmann, Barnett, Lombard, Belton-Kocher, & Sharpe, 1989).

Finally, we must consider the *utility* of screening instruments. The utility of a measure refers to how helpful it is in improving accuracy of decisions when costs also are considered. In Mrs. Grier's case, the screening instruments had no utility in further clarifying the description of the problem, factors contributing to the problem, or the design of an intervention. Traditional screening procedures are generally created based on inferred traits (e.g., developmental functioning, achievement, language, etc.) that have limited utility for identifying specific targets for intervention, the first step in problem solving. Consequently, the screening results are generally not useful for identifying areas where intervention is needed. Therefore, screening practices with norm-referenced tests are likely to lead to high error rates in identifying individual students with educational problems when all factors have been considered (see problem 1 in table 2.1).

Assessment for Classification

Classification practices in schools burgeoned with the advent of federal legislation creating special education funds based on categorical identification of students as being disabled. Often referred to as psychoeducational assessment, the original intent was to provide a nonbiased, comprehensive evaluation of students across broad domains, such as cognitive development, physical development, communication skills, social/emotional development, and adaptive behavior. In practice, the law was translated into giving a battery of tests to compare student performance with other same-age or same-grade students in different areas of functioning.

In the case of Tony, had the MDT done a complete evaluation, team members would have administered norm-referenced achievement and cognitive abilities tests and may have included a test of visual-motor skills or ratings of social behaviors. Inferences might be drawn about the degree to which Tony's IQ is affecting his learning, conclusions that have a high degree of inference. The IQ test that we would give to Tony would require him to put together blocks in geometric designs, define some vocabulary words, put together several puzzles, and some other such activities. The inference that would be drawn from the IQ test is that Tony learns well or does not learn well based on a comparison with same-age peers on the same tasks. Imagine all of the different learning situations about which we are generalizing given these novel samples of behaviors (e.g., asking vocabulary and comprehension questions, etc.) that have little to do with any of the relevant learning environments to which we are predicting Tony's performance in the first place! As shown in figure 2.1, this is clearly a high-inference assessment practice that may have high stakes for Tony's educational future. Even achievement tests don't necessarily measure what Tony has been taught *in his classroom* (see figure 2.2) or what should be taught, nor do they yield information directly

Figure 2.1 Problems with the Traditional Model: The Levels of Inference Problem

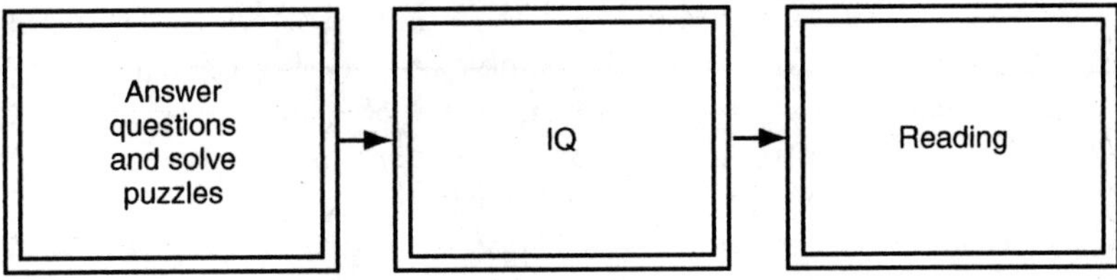

If you want to know about reading, test reading. Don't test puzzle solving!

Figure 2.2 The Levels of Inference Problem: Reading Assessment

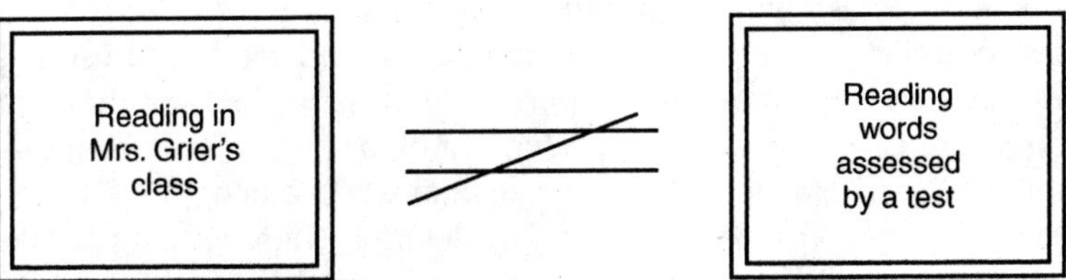

The words used on the test may not match the words used in the reading book in Mrs. Grier's class. Test using the actual curriculum (i.e., words) from Mrs. Grier's class.

relevant to the setting in which students are supposed to be learning. (These issues are directly relevant to problem 2 in table 2.1.) Tony's standing on these tests would then be compared to federal, state, and local guidelines to determine if he qualified for services as a student with a disability (e.g., learning disability). In addition, Tony's test scores would be analyzed to determine strengths and weaknesses (as in the ATI approach described in chapter 1) in order to make recommendations for curricular modifications.

Several unforeseen and unfortunate consequences have occurred with the emergence of these assessment practices as the standard for evaluating students. First, there has been an overreliance on standard test batteries without differentiating assessment according to the type of problem the student is displaying (Thurlow & Ysseldyke, 1979). In other words, MDTs are prone to give the same battery of tests to all students regardless of the reason that the student was referred. Other problems include a child-centered view of student problems that neglects the contributing role of the family, social, and academic environments. As a result, designing interventions has involved primarily labeling and placing children in special classes (Barnett & Macmann, 1992b).

Another set of problems with many tests has to do with the numbers they produce. A reading test, for example, may say that a child has a score of 110 in reading, meaning the child is slightly above average. These numbers seem very *exact.* When you count the number of points for example, in a ball game, you get a number that is the exact number of points scored. There is no question about this. However, one would be wrong to conclude that the 110 on the reading test was an exact score. In fact, it is possible to harm a child by assuming the scores are exact. One way this is apparent is if you give two tests of reading. Depending on the tests that we give, we may arrive at very different conclusions about the same child. We may decide to classify a child based on one test and decide to not classify a child if we give another test.

If we administer different tests to determine strengths and weaknesses across different areas of functioning (e.g., motor functioning versus language functioning), chances are that this profile, or overall impression of strengths and weaknesses, will be unreliable. Indeed, Macmann et al. (1989) found a maximum *upper limit* of about 80 percent agreement across tests used to classify individual students as learning disabled based on presumed strengths and weaknesses. Although 80 percent may seem high, authoritative sources suggest reliabilities of .90 or preferably higher for important individual decisions. Also, in practice, decision reliabilities are much worse (Barnett & Macmann, 1992b). So if we are trying to determine strengths or weaknesses and find that a child's motor skills are stronger than her language skills, we could get very different results, depending on the motor and language tests that we give. We are even likely to get different results if we give the same tests at different times! Experienced MDTs know these problems, and *some* may even exploit them by continuing to administer different tests until a child qualifies for special education or does not qualify, depending on how the team wants the results to turn out, rather than communicating to parents the uncertainty and error in decisions.

These problems occur for several reasons. Tests that are supposed to be measuring the same thing (e.g., academic functioning) are usually only somewhat related to each other (although not well), meaning that they don't really all measure one aspect of development specifically. Tests that are supposed to be measuring different things are also somewhat related to each other, meaning that they may really measure similar things. The same problem is greatest when we are trying to analyze student strengths and weaknesses within the same test (Barnett & Macmann, 1992b). If your head is spinning, you're understanding that testing is not as straightforward as some would have us believe. Describing children's performance by using a profile of strengths and weaknesses should be a red flag to indicate error. However, it is done every day with unpredictable results for children. The bottom line is that we lack good measures for classifying students and for classifying strengths and weaknesses based on tests. Existing achievement and development measures are all somewhat related to each other, creating unreliable results when we want to compare one score to another. Therefore, beware of test score comparisons. At best, we don't know what they mean with confidence for individual children! We return once again to problem 1 in table 2.1.

If the situation appears bleak, brace yourself. . . . It gets even worse. A number of studies have shown that MDTs don't even use the information from these assessments for classification purposes. O'Reilly, Northcraft, and Sabers (1989) found that different school psychologists recommended different classifications even when they were interpreting the same evaluation data. Their classification recommendations were more consistent on average with the type of referral, "learning disabled" or "gifted." Ysseldyke, Algozzine, Richey, and Graden (1982) asked, "Why bother with the data?" after examining actual team placement meetings. They found only the quantity of data affected team decisions: The more data presented at the meeting, the more likely the team was to reach a decision of classifying the child. They also found that 83 percent of the statements made at the meeting were irrelevant to the classification decisions made! There were no significant relationships between the team placement decisions and statements about criteria for classification (ability/achievement discrepancies, verbal/performance discrepancies, or federal definition criteria). In short, teams are not considering the assessment data in their placement decisions except where they collect enough data to justify a classification decision.

In a more recent series of investigations, investigators have found that only a small percentage of actual classification decisions for mental disabilities are consistent with administrative (e.g., state education guidelines, local district policies) and authoritative (e.g., American Association on Mental Retardation) guidelines for classifying students (MacMillan, Gresham, & Bocian, 1996; MacMillan, Gresham, Siperstein, & Bocian, in press; MacMillan, Siperstein, Gresham, & Bocian, in press). In summarizing these results, Gresham and Witt (in press) commented, "Schools frequently do not follow authoritative definitions of mild disability groups and appear to make classification decisions irrespective of IQ test results." They concluded that "the entire enterprise of intelligence testing is time consuming, expensive, and largely irrelevant in treatment planning, differential diagnosis, and classification/placement decisions." These issues are directly relevant to problems 3 and 4 in table 2.1.

Some Alternatives to Traditional Assessment Practices

Given the problems mentioned above with traditional assessment approaches, it is important to consider alternatives. We refer you back to assumptions 6 and 8 in chapter 1. Assumption 6 states, "Good assessment involves gathering information that is directly related to the problem." Assumption 8 states, "Good assessment is grounded in detecting naturally occurring observable patterns of behavior." Once again, we want to be reasonably confident about how we use assessment data to make inferences that are helpful in educating students. Adhering carefully to practices that are consistent with assumptions 6 and 8 will help you to do so. The question is, what are the guidelines for choosing assessment strategies that are consistent with these assumptions?

An evaluator needs to consider two features. First, the professional should seek assessment practices that measure behavior in the natural setting under natural conditions. To this end, we will next describe several assessment techniques that are designed to gather information about student functioning in the natural environment (e.g., interviews, observations, and curriculum-based measurement). Second, the professional should take steps to reduce error. One important way to reduce the likely effects of error is to start by making decisions that have less grave consequences than those associated with screening and classification. We will elaborate on ways that this can be done, describing one approach to low-inference decision making that has been shown to positively affect student achievement—formative evaluation.

Interviews

Interviews serve the dual functions of allowing us to identify problems and to analyze problem situations with key individuals who know the child (parents, teachers, etc.). An "ecobehavioral" interview involves "mapping" the child's and family's place in the community, allowing us to examine social networks or relationships among and between settings. Through the use of an ecobehavioral interview, we can develop detailed descriptions of behaviors across settings (Hartman, 1978; Kanfer & Grimm, 1977; Peterson, 1968; Wahler & Cormier, 1970). Parents describe daily events, focusing on routines and behavior from the time the child wakes up in the morning to the time that the child goes to bed. Teachers describe events such as transportation to and from school, entering school, class activities, transitions, lunch, and other activities. The interview often reveals behaviors and settings of greatest concern to parents and teachers, as well as key persons, time periods, settings, and circumstances related to child behavior and caregiver concerns. Ecobehavioral interviews also have the objective of clarifying concerns of parents and teachers and examining the extent to which teachers and parents will be able to participate in creating modifications intended to correct the problem. The interested reader is referred to Barnett and Carey's (1992) text for examples of actual ecobehavioral interviews. The primary advantage of interviews of this type as a source of assessment information is that they provide information about how the child functions in the natural settings of home and school, information that norm-referenced tests neglect.

Observation

Reliable and valid observations of the child allow us to understand how the child functions in his or her environment. Preliminary observations help to clarify important situations and behaviors that will require further problem solving. Additional observations are made to assist in analyzing environmental events that may be linked to the problem behavior. We have devoted an entire chapter (see chapter 8) to observation methods in the third section.

Curriculum-Based Measurement

Curriculum-based measurement (CBM) is a set of standardized assessment techniques for evaluating student performance in basic academic skills using the student's own curricular materials (Shinn, 1989). Curriculum-based measures are well validated for making individual instructional decisions (Marston, 1989), easy to use (i.e., requiring only a few minutes to administer), use materials from the actual curriculum, provide estimates of student accuracy and fluency, and are sensitive to change, allowing educators to monitor student performance across time. We also have devoted an entire chapter to describing curriculum-based assessment techniques in the third section.

CBM is a very direct form of assessment because if we want to know how Tony is reading, we assess his reading using his own textbook. Other assessment practices are less direct and require that we make an inference (i.e., an educated guess) about how Tony might be expected to do. Using CBM, we might make inferences about how well he is doing in the curriculum and how well the classroom environment is designed to meet Tony's needs.

Formative Evaluation

Consistent with the problem-solving approach that was described in the first chapter, another approach would be to use formative evaluation. Formative evaluation is not an assessment technique per se. It is a process of gathering assessment data on important skills from curricular materials to make instructional decisions based on student trends in performance (Deno, 1986). Formative evaluation has two core characteristics. First, we have to acknowledge that we don't know what interventions will work for students until we try something. We saw in chapter 1 that trying to predict which interventions will work well for individual students has not been a fruitful endeavor. Therefore, we must test curricular modifications empirically. Second, formative evaluation involves analyzing student performance across time. The purpose is to make individual or group decisions about the effectiveness of curricular modifications based on gathering frequent and routine data on basic academic skills. Formative evaluation generally incorporates curriculum-based measurement strategies.

Fuchs and Fuchs (1986) quantitatively analyzed all of the studies conducted on formative evaluation up until 1986. The results were quite compelling. They found that in instances where formative evaluation was integrated with instruction, and teachers used systematic rules about modifying instruction, there were large gains in achievement relative to students whose teachers did not use formative evaluation.

Formative evaluation is a process that directly corresponds to the problem-solving process: defining problem situations through descriptions of student behavior in terms of valid indicators of basic academic skills, developing goals for student progress, testing modifications empirically, and evaluating outcomes on an individual basis by looking at the trend across time. In Mrs. Grier and Tony's case, we would be making decisions about the effectiveness of instruction for improving Tony's reading skills. This is very different than high-inference decisions about how likely he is to learn across different environments based on knowledge of his IQ score.

Problem Solving May Contain Error Too

In contrast to traditional assessment practices, problem-solving assessment is conducted for improving planning for instruction, planning for interventions, monitoring student progress, and evaluating instruction or other interventions. Errors may be present in this type of assessment in other ways. In this case, error may influence our professional decisions by affecting (a) how we define a problem situation or measure key variables, (b) steps that we follow in problem solving, (c) whether we develop useful hypotheses concerning children's problem behaviors and needs, (d) the kinds of strategies that we choose for teaching targeted skills, and (e) whether outcomes are reliably and validly measured. Problem-solving assessment relies on techniques that describe how the student is functioning in the natural environment and factors that may be affecting student performance. Decision making is adversely affected when interview, observational, or direct assessment results (e.g., CBM) lead to errors in items "a" through "e" above.

Chapter Summary

We have attempted to describe in this chapter some key assessment issues that affect educational decision making. We have seen that there are four key reasons (table 2.1) that a teacher such as Mrs. Grier would be justified in criticizing the evaluation procedures used to assess Tony's "problem" (which is still yet undefined). Mrs. Grier will be more helpful to Tony if she is able to contribute to effective team problem solving. Mrs. Grier will have to work within the current organizational structure of her building to promote awareness of these issues and, whenever possible, adoption of functional, intervention-based service delivery models that will be more effective at meeting her students' needs.

We are not saying that one educator can do all of the things outlined above. Child assessment should be a multidisciplinary process involving *all* individuals responsible for promoting a child's growth. Assessment needs to be a core element of the organization of schools, involving teachers, parents, administrators, support personnel, and relevant community agencies. In Mrs. Grier's case, she would support the process through her own careful obser-

Figure 2.3 A List of Questions Mrs. Grier Might Ask

- How well do the test items overlap with what Mrs. Grier taught in the classroom? In other words, were they testing what Tony was being taught?
- How relevant were the assessment tasks (e.g., reading words in isolation, drawing complex geometric forms, etc.) to the instructional objectives that Mrs. Grier has for Tony?
- How well do the tests provide an indication of Tony's rate of learning in school?
- How likely is it that Tony's behavior in the 1:1 assessment situation reflects Tony's behavior in the classroom?
- How well are the assessment techniques adapted to the referral problem?
- How sure of the inferences can we be?
- What can Mrs. Grier observe that may be useful?
- What could Mrs. Grier hypothesize and try out?

vations leading to formative evaluation, being concerned primarily with how to better instruct Tony, and clarification of support that Tony could have, or that she should have. You may participate in this process by conducting functional assessments (like those described in chapter 1), helping the school or the school district to set up guidelines for assessment practices, or being a part of a team that makes educational decisions about students, and ultimately helping carry out plans.

We hope that the professional model for assessment that you are developing permeates all facets of your service to students and makes you a useful contributor to improving decision making for the students you serve. Given what you now know, what kinds of questions would you ask if you were in Mrs. Grier's shoes? We made up our own list of questions (see figure 2.3) that Mrs. Grier might ask. Check yours to see if they are in agreement with ours. These questions, however, apply to *all* assessment practices, not just screening and classification. They are critical indicators, if you will, of how much confidence we can have in the assessment results and how useful the assessment results might be for educating Tony. If we continuously ask them, we may actually learn from past mistakes.

Chapter 3

Assessment and the Law

Most school districts currently provide a relatively wide array of special education services for children with mild to severe disabilities. We do not have to go back much more than 10 years, however, to discover that this level of service to children with disabilities did not always exist. At one time most children with disabilities were denied any type of education. Parents were encouraged to find an institutional setting for the child or do what they could at home. Now, schools have elaborate procedures not only to admit and educate all children with disabilities but also to search for such children whose parents may not be aware that services are available.

What has brought about this marked change in school attitudes in such a short period? Could it be that benevolent school districts have suddenly become aware of the learning potential of children with even the most severe disabilities? Have school districts proactively taken steps to ensure that all children receive the education to which they are entitled? Unfortunately most school systems have been neither benevolent nor proactive in responding to the needs of children with disabilities. Instead, parents of children with disabilities have argued successfully in one lawsuit after another that it is illegal to deny children with disabilities their basic right to an education. Thus, school systems have been required to provide an education to all children. In this chapter we describe how the law has influenced how we conduct assessment, classification, and intervention activities with potentially disabled children.

Legal Influences on Assessment and Special Education

Court Decisions Establishing a Free and Appropriate Public Education

The issue at the heart of all the litigation between parents of children with disabilities and school systems has been that all children have a basic right to an education. The legal basis used by parents to establish this right is the Fourteenth Amendment to the United States Constitution, which forbids any state from denying "to any person within its jurisdiction the equal protection of the laws." This is frequently referred to as the equal protection clause and has been interpreted by the courts as directing schools to provide equal educational opportunities to all students.

The first and most significant court decision invoking the equal protection clause was *Brown v. Board of Education* (1954). Although *Brown* was filed in behalf of black students without disabilities, the logic behind the case has been subsequently used in defending the rights of children with disabilities. *Brown* was filed because it was believed that black children were not receiving an education equivalent to that given to white children. In its ruling, the U.S. Supreme Court agreed with this argument and stipulated that black students must receive an equivalent education using equivalent resources. This decision is relevant to children with disabilities because in this case the Court considered students to be a class of persons in society. According to the Constitution, all members of a class must be treated equally. In cases involving children with disabilities, *Brown* has been used as a precedent to argue that both students with and without disabilities should be defined as a class and must therefore be treated equally. Just as the Court indicated in *Brown* that black children had been denied equal protection because of an unalterable and unchosen trait, their race, in subsequent cases involving children with disabilities the Court has stipulated that such children have been denied an equal education because of an unalterable and uncontrollable trait, their disability.

Among the major post-*Brown* cases that helped gain equal education for children with disabilities, the most important were *Pennsylvania Association for Retarded Children (PARC) v. Commonwealth of Pennsylvania* (1972) and *Mills v. Board of Education of the District of Columbia* (1972). In *PARC* the suit was filed because Pennsylvania state law relieved a board of education "from any obligation to educate a child whom a public school psychologist certified as uneducable or untrainable" and permitted "an indefinite postponement of admission to public school of any child who has not obtained a mental age of 5 years" (*PARC,* 1972, p. 282). The U.S. Supreme Court struck down this state law, stipulating that all children with mental disabilities are capable of benefiting from an education and the state has the responsibility to provide all such children between the ages of 6 and 21 years access to a free education.

After the *PARC* decision, the Court heard the *Mills* case, in which the school system did not deny that all children had the right to a free education but rather argued that the system lacked the financial resources to fulfill its obligation to handicapped children. Although the Court acknowledged that the education of children with severe disabilities can be very expensive, it did not accept this as an excuse for failing to provide an education to children with disabilities, ruling that if sufficient funds are not available to finance all of the services and programs needed and desirable in the system, then the available funds must be expended equitably in such manner that no child is entirely excluded from a publicly supported education that is consistent with the child's needs and ability to benefit from it. The inadequacies of the District of Columbia public school system, whether occasioned by insufficient funding or administrative inefficiency, certainly could not be permitted to bear more heavily on the child who is "exceptional" or disabled than on the normal child (*Mills,* 1972).

In both the *PARC* and *Mills* cases, the Court went beyond establishing that children with disabilities had a right to a free and appropriate public education, for it imposed many procedural and due process requirements on school systems. Due process is a means of ensuring that schools perform as the law mandates. For example, in the *PARC* decision, the court declared that the state must locate all children with mental disabilities in the state, that those children should be placed in as normal an environment as possible, and that their progress should be reviewed yearly or at the parents' request. In both *PARC* and *Mills,* the Court recognized that the advances granted to parents by the law would be meaningless if due process procedures were not also specified. These procedures make it clear to school systems that parents are to be involved and may challenge decisions about their children made by the system.

The Education of All Handicapped Children Act of 1975

The *PARC* and *Mills* cases as well as many subsequent decisions have had a profound effect on who is educated, how they are educated, and which due process procedures are available to safeguard the children and their parents. The most obvious result was the recognition by Congress that federal legislation and funding would be necessary to guarantee a free and appropriate public education for all children. Congress accordingly enacted the Education of All Handicapped Children Act of 1975, Public Law 94–142, which goes far beyond simply establishing each child's right to an education by specifying the process through which education must occur (e.g., describing the steps in the assessment process and declaring that children must be educated in the least restrictive environment).

Table 3.1 Summary of Major Changes from P.L. 94–142 to IDEA

- New programs for transition
- New programs for children with serious emotional disturbance
- New research and information dissemination program on Attention Deficit Disorder
- Added transition and assistive technology services
- Included rehabilitation counseling and social work as related services
- Services expanded to more fully include children with autism and traumatic brain injury

P.L. 94–142 was amended by P.L. 101–476 in 1990 and is now called the Individuals with Disabilities Education Act (IDEA). Although P.L. 94–142 and IDEA are similar, Congress did revise and extend the law in some important ways (see table 3.1 for a summary). Seven major provisions of this law are summarized in table 3.2. Its importance for individuals concerned with the assessment and placement of children with disabilities cannot be overstated, because it literally directs practitioners' daily activities.

The law has been a two-edged sword in the field of special education. On one hand, it has created a vast network of services for children with disabilities who were often denied any publicly supported education prior to the 1970s. On the other hand, it has made the assessment of children more complex. Generally, this increased complexity is not unnecessarily constricting. In fact, in most cases what was once simply good educational practice is now the law.

From time to time, concern is focused on the expense of educating children with disabilities, and there are calls within U.S. Congress to repeal IDEA. This often causes fear among those whose employment in special education depends on the existence of the law. However, such fear is probably unfounded for three reasons. First, IDEA is based directly on case law, which in turn is influenced by the U.S. Constitution. Thus, as long as a free education is offered to children without disabilities, a free and appropriate public education must also be granted to children with disabilities. Congress cannot alter this right unless it amends the Constitution. Second, many states have adopted laws that are highly similar to IDEA. Many are even more procedurally specific than the federal law and would remain in effect if the latter were changed. Finally, there is still considerable support in Congress for IDEA. Originally, the bill passed by a margin of 87 to 7 in the Senate and 404 to 7 in the House. Evidence of the continued support for the law in Congress is provided by the passage in October 1986 of the Education of the Handicapped Amendments, Public Law 99–457, which serves to amend IDEA by requiring states to provide special education services to not only school-aged children but also preschoolers as young as three years. Thus, it

Table 3.2 Major Provisions of IDEA

Free and Appropriate Public Education

All children are entitled to a free and appropriate public education, regardless of the nature or severity of their disability.

Nondiscriminatory Assessment

Requires the establishment of procedures to ensure that testing and evaluation materials and procedures utilized for evaluation and placement of children with disabilities will be selected and administered so as not to be culturally or racially discriminatory.

Development of an Individual Education Plan (IEP)

Requires the development of a written IEP for each child with a disability that will include a statement of current levels of educational achievement, annual and short-term goals, specific educational services to be provided, dates of initiation and duration of services, and criteria for evaluating the degree to which the objectives are achieved.

Due Process

Requires an opportunity to present complaints with respect to any matter relating to the identification, evaluation, or educational placement of a child. Specific due process procedures include: (a) written notification to parents before evaluation, (b) written notification when initiating or refusing to initiate a change in educational placement, (c) opportunity to obtain an independent evaluation of the child, and (d) an opportunity for an impartial due process hearing.

Privacy and Records

Requires that educational and psychological records pertaining to a child remain confidential except to those individuals who are directly involved in a child's education and who have a specific reason for reviewing the records. Further, the law provides an opportunity for the parents or guardian of a child with a disability to examine all relevant records with respect to the identification, evaluation, and educational placement of the child.

Least Restrictive Environment

Requires to the maximum extent appropriate that children with disabilities be educated with children who are not disabled in as normal an environment as possible.

Related Services

Requires support services (e.g., psychological, audiology, occupational therapy, music therapy) are required to assist the child with a disability to benefit from special education.

Source: Adapted from Individuals with Disabilities Education Act, P.L. 101–476.

seems likely that the fundamental philosophy of IDEA will influence the profession of special education and the delivery of psychoeducational services for years to come.

P.L. 99–457, Handicapped Infants and Toddlers

P.L. 99–457 extended the Education of the Handicapped Act (i.e., IDEA, Part H), which targeted primarily school-age children, to include infants and toddlers. The law provides governmental support for early intervention and was viewed by Congress as cost effective because problems that are targeted and perhaps resolved early minimize the need for more intensive and costly services later. Infants and toddlers who are eligible for services include those who (a) experience a measured developmental delay in areas such as cognitive, physical, psychosocial, or language functioning, (b) have a diagnosed physical or mental condition such as Down's syndrome, or (c) are "at risk" for having developmental delays if early intervention services are not provided. Factors that may place an infant at risk include poverty, teenage parentage, low birth weight, physical abuse or neglect, malnutrition, and environmental poisoning (Garwood and Sheehan, 1989).

Parent involvement is a major factor incorporated into P.L. 99–457. Specifically, there is a requirement that an Individualized Family Services Plan (IFSP) be developed for each child and family. The emphasis on family needs, in name and intent, comes from a recognition that children with disabilities are better served when parents are actively involved and served as well. Hence, P.L. 99–457 moved away from the more or less exclusive focus on the child found in IDEA and provided a mechanism where parents could receive mental health services, parent training, and other services to help them be more effective caretakers of their infant or toddler with a disability.

An IFSP is to be based on a multidisciplinary evaluation that includes an assessment of the child's current developmental levels as well as the family's strengths and weaknesses. The content of the IFSP should include the following:

1. Statement of assessment results relative to six major areas of functioning
2. Statement of the family's strengths and weaknesses relating to enhancing the development of the family's infant or toddler with a disability
3. A statement of major outcomes expected
4. A statement of specific early intervention services necessary to meet the unique needs of the child or the family
5. The projected dates of services and the name of the case manager, from the profession most immediately relevant to the specified needs, who will coordinate services

P.L. 99–457 appears to come from a theoretical and research base that is on the cutting edge. Unfortunately, for those involved in the assessment process, what the law requires is ahead of the available technology. That is, the quality and availability of tests and other assessment procedures for infants and toddlers leaves a lot to be desired. In addition to problems with the reliability and validity of tests, there are problems inherent in obtaining a stable assessment of young children. Also, the idea of assessing the family is a relatively new one and quality assessment instruments need to be developed and refined.

Section 504 of the Rehabilitation Act of 1973

Typically, children in school settings are classified as disabled under IDEA because it pertains directly to educational settings. Increasingly, however, schools are being required to provide special services to children classified as "disordered" or "disabled" by other professions (e.g., physicians, private psychologists) using classification systems such as the *Diagnostic and Statistical Manual of the American Psychiatric Association, Fourth Edition* (*DSM-IV*). The basis in law for obtaining services for children who do not qualify for services under IDEA but who have a disorder according to some other diagnostic scheme has typically been Section 504 of the Rehabilitation Act of 1973. Section 504 is an antidiscrimination law that grants equal access for all. The law is far-ranging and does everything from requiring wheelchair ramps in buildings to ensuring that individuals are not discriminated against on the basis of race.

Section 504 has been used increasingly in schools to get services for children classified as having a disorder under DSM-IV. For example, a child diagnosed as depressed by a psychiatrist may not qualify for services under IDEA but may be eligible under Section 504. The U.S. Office of Civil Rights (OCR) has been relatively vigorous in enforcing this new interpretation of Section 504. Like IDEA, schools have a duty to inform parents that their child classified, for example, as Attention Deficit-Hyperactivity Disorder, may be eligible for special education services. Unlike IDEA, school districts can be found liable for civil damages for not serving children with disabilities in a timely and appropriate manner.

The potential influence of Section 504 is great because educational institutions, guided by each state's department of education, have been relatively self-contained in deciding who is disabled, and under IDEA it was possible to legally tell parents their child did not fit one of the IDEA "pigeonholes." Under Section 504 all public institutions must provide equal access to all and as Hackola (1992) has indicated: "OCR has found that students with conditions such as sleep disorders, allergies/asthma, AIDS/HIV, dyslexia, mental illness, arthritis, and obesity that do not fit with an IDEA category may be entitled under Section 504 to special education services and procedural safeguards."

Schools who expel or suspend students without due process are particularly vulnerable under Section 504 because, unlike IDEA, a formal evaluation must be conducted prior to any change in placement, including exclusion from school (Hackola, 1992). Hence, a child who has been diagnosed as being conduct disordered, depressed, alcoholic, and so on would appear to need a formal evaluation by the school to determine if the problem for which he or she was being suspended was due to the disorder. Section 504 appears to require this even though the school has not diagnosed the problem or even made any formal recognition of it.

Historically, many schools have only done as much for children with disabilities as they have been forced to do. Because of the "teeth" in Section 504 they will probably adhere to the procedures closely and quickly. In addition to the potential loss of federal funds for noncompliance, Hackola has indicated there is increasing support for the award of monetary damages that is "more than a special education dispute about the adequacy of services; it may allege violations of federal constitutional and civil rights laws, laws which have historically served as a basis for money damages to compensate for the individual's injuries" (Hackola, 1992).

Legal Influences in the Assessment Phase

Parental Consent

Legal regulation of the education of children with disabilities starts even before assessment begins. The law requires that parental approval is necessary before the evaluation of any child for potential placement in special education. Under ordinary circumstances, a regular classroom teacher who is administering tests to the entire class for the purpose of improving educational programming within the classroom does not need to obtain parental permission to give the tests. Likewise, permission is not usually required for a school district to administer routine educational tests to all children. In general, parental permission is usually not required if a test is administered to all children, if it does not reveal information that is educationally irrelevant (e.g., questions about drug use), and if the test is not used to change a child's educational placement.

According to IDEA, parental permission is required when an educational agency proposes to initiate (or refuses to initiate) or change the classification, evaluation, or educational placement of a child or the provisions of a free and appropriate public education for the child. Thus, parental permission is a legal necessity when a child is singled out and removed from the classroom to be tested by a psychologist, speech clinician, or special education teacher, regardless of whether the child eventually is placed in special education. Parents have a right to know when a potential change is being considered. It is not enough simply to tell parents that an evaluation of their child is planned. The notice must also meet the legal requirements of informed consent, which means that parents must be informed about—in writing, in their primary language—the purpose of the evaluation, the specific tests that will be administered, what they measure, how the information will be used, and the likely outcomes of such an assessment.

Focus on Practice

How Does the Prudent School-Based Specialist Steer Clear of Problems with Section 504?

The following recommendations were offered by Stuart Hackola (1992), an attorney, with respect to Attention Deficit Disorder (ADD). Although this model policy is most relevant to ADD, the general process to comply with Section 504 is applicable to other disorders.

Identification Procedures

1. Ensure that the identification mechanism includes referral for evaluation of suspected ADD and other disorders and that children receive the formal multidisciplinary evaluations mandated by the IDEA, with consent to evaluate and full notice of parental rights. Conducting "prescreening" for eligibility without parental consent and involvement is legally questionable.
2. Have the evaluation team first consider the student's eligibility under the IDEA and address eligibility under Section 504 only if the student does not meet IDEA criteria. Note, however, that students found eligible under the IDEA criteria still have Section 504 rights, including the right to an evaluation prior to long-term suspension/expulsion or any other significant change in placement.
3. Convene an IEP Committee within the required timelines. If the IEP Committee finds the student ineligible under the IDEA, the same group of persons should immediately reconstitute itself as a "Section 504 Committee" to consider eligibility under the broader criteria. If the Section 504 Committee finds the student eligible under Section 504, a written plan of service is required. Again, using the existing IEP form will assure compliance.
4. Provide parents and guardians with full notice of rights under both IDEA and Section 504; for example, if a student is found eligible under the IDEA to challenge the IDEA eligibility denial via independent educational evaluations and/or impartial due process hearings.

Provision of Services

5. Ensure that the decision-making team, whether constituted as an IEP Committee or as a "Section 504 Committee," considers the entire range of special education and related services needed to meet the student's unique needs. For students with ADD, such may include medical evaluations (including ongoing monitoring and medication), counseling/psychotherapy, and behavioral management plans. Consideration should also be given to securing parental consent to any behavior management plan and/or to the administration of medication by school personnel.

6. Provide guidance to the IEP Committee/Section 504 Committee in implementing the legal mandate that children be placed in the most normal or least restrictive environment possible. For children with ADD, the team should consider support services and modification of the regular education classroom environment and/or curriculum.

Behavioral Control

7. Ensure that the IEP Committees or Section 504 Committees proactively address the behavioral needs of students with ADD by establishing adequate behavior plans and services.
8. Ensure that the school's code of conduct provides for the detailed procedures required for disciplining handicapped students and that these special procedures extend to students protected by Section 504.
9. Ensure proper evaluation prior to long-term suspension/expulsion. This evaluation should precede IEPC consideration of whether the misconduct is a manifestation of disability. The evaluation and the IEP Committee should be completed within 10 days of the initial exclusion. There should also be provisions for disciplining students who have not yet been evaluated for special education but who are suspected of having a disability. Such students may be entitled to remain in school pending full and immediate evaluation of their eligibility under the IDEA and Section 504.
10. Ensure adequate compliance with the special protections of special education laws and with the constitutional right of due process.

Nondiscriminatory Assessment

By far the most intense involvement in assessment by courts and legislatures has been to establish procedures to ensure that assessment materials and procedures utilized for the evaluation and placement of children with disabilities will be selected and administered so as not to be culturally or racially discriminatory. The impetus for the development of law in this area has its roots in the civil rights struggles of the 1950s, when minorities fought for and won the right for their children to have the same education as white children, as in *Brown*. Many schools, however, sought to circumvent the rights of minority children by placing them in "special" classrooms on the basis of their performance on standardized tests. The courts (see, e.g., *Larry P. v. Wilson Riles et al.*, 1979) have often concluded that the intelligence and achievement tests used to place these children are biased or discriminatory and result in a disproportionate number of minority children in special education classrooms. Many tests have been considered discriminatory because of the lack of minority group children in the sample on which they were standardized and because children from minority cultures tend to achieve lower scores than middle-class white children (cf. Reynolds, 1982).

The issue of discriminatory assessment has not always received a fair appraisal in the courts because many of the individuals responsible for making decisions have appeared to ignore the scientific evidence concerning assessment instruments and have instead relied on intuition and inference. The problem of deciding intuitively whether a test is biased has been examined by Reschly and Sabers (1979), who argued that evaluating a test without reference to research can lead to inaccurate conclusions. They pointed out, for example, that the widely criticized item from the Wechsler Intelligence Scale for Children-Revised, "What is the thing to do if a boy (girl) much smaller than yourself starts to fight with you?" may actually be easier for black children to answer than for white children. Without consulting the research on this particular question, it would be easy to conclude that it was biased against poor children because turning your back on anyone who hits you in the ghetto would not be an intelligent thing to do. Determining whether a test is biased is a complex social and psychometric issue that has challenged researchers from many scientific disciplines.

Larry P. concerned the overrepresentation of minority students in special education classrooms. The plaintiffs portrayed the "culturally biased" intelligence test as the primary reason that black children were placed in "isolating," "inferior," "deadened," and "stigmatizing" classes for those with mild mental disabilities. The logic of this statement has been questioned, and the court has been faulted for not inquiring as to why so many black children are even brought into the referral process (MacMillan & Meyers, 1980).

The question of why so many minority children are referred in the first place played a central role in *Marshall et al. v. Georgia* (1984) (Reschly, Kicklighter, & McKee, 1988). In *Larry P.* the court pointed an accusing finger at IQ tests, blaming these instruments for many of the problems surrounding minority children, including and especially their overrepresentation in special education. However, in *Marshall,* it was argued that referral occurs not because children come from a minority culture but because children often are not able to learn from standard curricula and teaching practices and because schools may lack sufficient educational options for remedying children's deficits. Although defendant school districts in the *Marshall* case did have an overrepresentation of minority children in special education, they argued that this was simply because more minority children exhibit severe achievement problems and need help.

Marshall is an important case for school-based professionals because it provides specific recommendations for providing quality services to children. According to Reschly and colleagues (1988), a critical difference between *Marshall* and previous cases, such as *Larry P.,* where schools had been criticized for placing disproportionate numbers of minority children in special education, was the ability of the schools in *Marshall* to show positive outcomes for minority students. In *Larry P.* and cases before it, schools appeared to be using IQ tests as a rationale for first segregating minority children and then educating them in an inferior fashion. However, in *Marshall,* school districts were able to prove that placement of children was related to low achievement and that placement resulted in positive outcomes.

IDEA contains a good summary of the legalities influencing assessment. This law emphasizes the use of a wide range of assessment information that is collected by a variety of professionals so as to be as culturally fair as possible. Table 3.3 provides an overview of portions of the law relevant to testing and assessment.

Access to Records

IDEA, as well as another federal law, the Family Educational Rights and Privacy Act (FERPA) of 1977 (often referred to as the Buckley Amendment), govern the handling of records in educational settings. These laws require that all public educational institutions

1. allow parents access to all official educational records related to their child and provide an interpretation of the records if necessary;
2. allow parents to challenge records that may be inaccurate or misleading; and
3. obtain the written consent of parents before releasing a child's records to a third party.

Basic to understanding the regulations contained within these laws is the legal definition of "educational records." Simply stated, educational records are any records directly related to a student that are maintained by an educational institution. Stated even more simply by Trachtman (1972), a record is "anything put in writing for others to see" (p. 45). Obviously all reports and other official documentation of evaluation, classification, and placement should be open for parental inspection. Frequently school districts appoint an individual to review the records with parents so that explanations and interpretations can be offered if needed.

To follow the law is not always a straightforward matter, and the issue of access to records provides an excellent example of the problems that may be encountered. The fact that FERPA allows parents to see the educational records of their child runs counter to the rights of some test publishers, who argue that test forms and test protocol must not be shown to anyone except qualified professionals because to do so would jeopardize test security. Since many of these test protocols contain actual test items, publishers are concerned that parents might tell others about test content, thus jeopardizing the validity of the test. Individuals who provide interpretations of test results to parents can usually avoid problems by telling parents the general type of items on the test and giving examples that are similar but not identical to the ones actually on the test.

Although FERPA allows parents wide latitude in having access to records, it is quite specific in denying access to all other persons except those who have a "legitimate educational interest" in the child. For example, if a child moves from one school system to another, the new system may

Table 3.3 Major Requirements Concerning Testing and Assessment in IDEA

1. Each state educational agency shall ensure that each public agency establishes and implements procedures that meet the requirements of this law.
2. Testing and evaluation materials and procedures used for the purposes of evaluation and placement of children with disabilities must be selected and administered so as not to be racially or culturally discriminatory.
3. Before any action is taken with respect to the initial placement of a child with a disability in a special education program, a full and individual evaluation of the child's educational needs must be conducted in accordance with the requirements of this law.
4. State and local educational agencies shall ensure, at a minimum, that tests and other evaluation materials:
   a. Are provided and administered in the child's native language or other mode of communication, unless it is clearly not feasible to do so;
   b. Have been validated for the specific purpose for which they are used; and
   c. Are administered by trained personnel in conformance with the instructions provided by their producer.
5. Tests and other evaluation materials include those tailored to assess specific areas of educational need and not merely those designed to provide a single general intelligence quotient.
6. Tests are selected and administered so as best to ensure that when a test is administered to a child with impaired sensory, manual, or speaking skills, the test results accurately reflect the child's aptitude or achievement level or whatever other factors the test purports to measure, rather than reflecting the child's impaired sensory, manual, or speaking skills (except when those skills are the factors that the test purports to measure).
7. No single procedure is used as the sole criterion for determining an appropriate educational program for a child.
8. The evaluation is made by a multidisciplinary team or group of persons, including at least one teacher or other specialist with knowledge in the area of suspected disability.
9. The child is assessed in all areas related to the suspected disability, including, where appropriate, health, vision, hearing, social and emotional status, general intelligence, academic performance, communicative status, and motor abilities.
10. In interpreting evaluation data and in making placement decisions, each public agency shall:
    a. Draw upon information from a variety of sources, including aptitude and achievement tests, teacher recommendations, physical condition, social or cultural background, and adaptive behavior.
    b. Ensure that information obtained from all of these sources is documented and carefully considered.
    c. Ensure that the placement decision is made by a group of persons, including persons knowledgeable about the child, the meaning of the evaluation data, and the placement options.
    d. Ensure that the placement decision is made in conformity with the least restrictive environment rules.
11. If a determination is made that a child is disabled and needs special education and related services, an Individualized Education Program must be developed for the child.

Source: Adapted from IDEA.

want to know the results of special education evaluations conducted by the former district. However, no records can be released unless the parents give written permission. Parents have the right to know what records are being disclosed and to whom and the purposes of the disclosure. In addition, parents have the right to a copy of all records being disclosed.

An issue that arises with some frequency involves telephone requests for information about a child with whom an educational specialist has had some contact. The caller may or may not have permission to see the records and could be an individual from another school district or the private sector (such as a speech pathologist or psychologist) or even a relative of the child. According to FERPA, it is clearly not prudent to provide information over the telephone. First, it is difficult to be completely certain to whom you are talking. Second, although the caller may have the child's best interests in mind, the law requires parental permission be obtained before information is released. Third, the specialist must exercise reasonable care in ensuring that information is disclosed to parties who have obtained such permission.

Legal Influences in the Classification and Placement Phase

Multidisciplinary Decision Making

After the assessment phase has been completed, the classification phase typically begins with a group of professionals meeting to make decisions about classification and placement. IDEA requires that the evaluation be made by a multidisciplinary team or group of persons, including at least one teacher or other specialist with knowledge in the area of suspected disability. The law further requires each school to ensure that the placement decision is made by a group of persons, including persons knowledgeable about the child, the meaning of the evaluation data, and the placement options. Thus, educational decision-making teams composed of teachers, parents, and support personnel (e.g., psychologists, counselors, nurses, physical and occupational therapists, speech pathologists, and social workers) have been required to ensure such a mandate is carried out. Children can also be a part of this team, although they are rarely present during formal team meetings. According to Fenton, Yoshida, Maxwell, and Kaufman (1979), teams should try to accomplish 11 goals for every student with special needs:

1. Determine the student's eligibility for special education.
2. Determine whether sufficient information about the student exists before the placement team makes decisions affecting the student's instructional program.
3. Evaluate the educational significance of such data.
4. Determine the student's placement.
5. Formulate appropriate yearlong educational goals and objectives for the student.

6. Develop specific short-term instructional objectives for the student.
7. Communicate with the parents about changes in the student's educational program.
8. Decide which information is needed for the future review of the student's program and progress.
9. Establish the date for the placement team's review.
10. Review the continued appropriateness of the student's educational program.
11. Review the student's educational progress.

The implicit rationale for a team approach to special education decision making is the belief that a group decision provides safeguards against individual errors in judgment while enhancing adherence to due process requirements (Pfeiffer, 1980). According to Pfeiffer (1981), "the key elements of a multidisciplinary team are a common purpose, cooperative problem-solving by different professionals who possess unique skills and orientation, and a coordination of activities" (p. 330). Thus, multidisciplinary teams provide a number of benefits beyond those provided by a single individual, including:

1. greater accuracy in assessment, classification, and placement decisions;
2. a forum for sharing differing views;
3. provisions for specialized consultative services to school personnel, parents, and community groups; and
4. the resources for developing and evaluating Individualized Educational Programs for exceptional students.

Classification and Diagnosis

A major goal of the multidisciplinary decision-making process is to determine if a child qualifies for placement in special education. Although the terms *classification* and *diagnosis* are often used interchangeably, they refer to different processes. Within an educational setting, classification involves the ordering or grouping of the attributes, characteristics, or behaviors of children into distinct categories. Effective classification systems use objective criteria or rules to decide whether a particular child belongs in a specific category. For example, to be classified as mentally disabled a child must have a score that is less than 70 (or two standard deviations below the mean) on a comprehensive intelligence test and significantly subaverage adaptive behavior. In this case, test scores provide relatively objective criteria upon which to base a decision to classify a child as mentally disabled. Classification is thus the system used to categorize the characteristics and behaviors of children.

Diagnosis follows from classification and is the process of assigning a child to a particular category within the classification system. In education, the development of the classification system has involved the establishment of a series of categories such as mentally disabled, learning disabled, and behavior disordered. The diagnostic process that evolves from this classification scheme requires that the attributes of a particular child be compared with the criteria that define each category. Diagnosis is thus simply the process of assigning a child to one of the classification categories (such as mentally disabled).

Classification in Educational Settings

Although a number of educational classification systems are available, one derived from the federal guidelines (i.e., IDEA) is used almost without exception throughout the United States. This system, which is typically interpreted in a slightly different manner by each state's department of education, is widely used because funding from the federal government to state governments and from state governments to local school districts is based on the system. Thus, local school districts are reimbursed by state governments for each child classified as disabled. Typically, children with the more severe disabilities entitle their school district to more funding than do children with mild disabilities. As mentioned previously, schools are increasingly being required to serve children diagnosed as "disabled" under classification systems other than those derived from IDEA. Diagnoses derived from DSM-IV, in particular, are being used more frequently in connection with Section 504.

Evaluation of the Educational Classification System

Ysseldyke and Thurlow (1984) collected considerable data on how well the educational classification system works. They found that approximately 5 percent of the elementary school population is referred for evaluation during any given year. Once a student is referred, 92 percent are evaluated, and 73 percent of the students who are evaluated are actually placed in special education. Thus, teachers who refer a student for evaluation appear to have an astoundingly high prediction rate; that is, most students who are referred for testing are diagnosed as disabled and placed in special education. Ysseldyke and Thurlow (1984) attribute this phenomenon not to the keen eye of teachers but instead to negative features of the diagnostic process itself. They characterize the multidisciplinary decision-making process as a "search for pathology" during which it is "assumed that *if* a teacher refers a student, then the student must have a problem; it is assumed that the task of the decision-making team is to find the problem" (Ysseldyke & Thurlow, 1984, p. 125). This perspective, although probably true in many cases, fails to acknowledge the ability that teachers develop for identifying children experiencing problems (Hoge, 1983).

Children diagnosed as disabled are most frequently placed in situations involving part-day services in a resource room with the remainder of their time in school being spent in the regular classroom. According to Ysseldyke and Algozzine (1982), the overall outcome of the educational classification process, which often involves the use of psychometrically inadequate tests, is the overinclusion of children on a one-way street into special education programs.

Needless to say, the educational classification system has been a matter of intense debate. We have already examined some of the serious shortcomings of classifying children in chapter 2. Although proponents of the system recognize that it could be improved, they also argue that it offers a number of advantages, including several administrative necessities, not the least of which are record keeping and a means for funding. Readers interested in an extensive discussion of issues surrounding the classification of children should consult other sources, including the Project on the Classification of Exceptional Children, a comprehensive and systematic analysis of the educational classification system. This project, coordinated by Nicholas Hobbs and funded by the federal government, was eventually published as *Issues in the Classification of Children* (Hobbs, 1975), and, although somewhat dated, should be required reading for anyone involved with children with disabilities.

Legal Influences in the Intervention Phase

Individualized Education Plan

After a child has been assessed and classified, IDEA requires that a team of individuals, including the child's parents, develop an **Individualized Education Plan,** or **IEP,** which is a written document describing the goals, objectives, and procedures that will be used to provide an appropriate education for the child with a disability. The plan must contain at least the following types of information:

1. A statement of the child's present levels of educational performance
2. A statement of annual goals, including short-term instructional objectives
3. A statement of the specific special education and related services to be provided and the extent to which the child will be able to participate in regular education programs
4. The projected dates of the initiation of services and the anticipated duration
5. Objective criteria and evaluation procedures for determining, at least annually, whether the short-term instructional objectives are being achieved
6. A statement of the needed transition services for students beginning no later than age 16 including, when appropriate, a statement of the interagency responsibilities or linkages (or both), before the student leaves the school setting.

After the IEP is developed, the special education and related service personnel who will implement the objectives are given copies of the final document to guide their interventions. There are at least two major problems with a follow-up evaluation of an IEP. First, the review of an IEP is required only annually. Although it is possible to review goals more frequently, the process of meeting with a number of different professionals can be time-consuming and expensive. The problem with only a yearly review, however, is that the needs of and goals for a child can change several times during that period.

IDEA calls for the specification of short-term objectives, but it provides no formal mechanism for monitoring the realization of these objectives or changing them as they are determined to be ineffective or inappropriate. Therefore, a high probability exists that problems with an IEP will not be discovered until an entire year has passed and it is time for the annual review of the IEP. Of course, active parental involvement in their child's education enhances the accountability of educators and increases the probability the objectives are accomplished or adjusted when needed.

A second major problem with the review of the IEP is that school personnel are often concerned that their professional credibility will be damaged if a child's educational objectives are *not* achieved. They have this concern despite explicit statements in the regulations governing special education that educational personnel will not be held accountable if educational objectives are not met. This fear among school personnel can lead to the establishment of only minimal annual goals that can be easily attained.

Least Restrictive Environment

In making placement and intervention decisions, multidisciplinary teams must take care to ensure that education occurs in the **least restrictive environment,** which is best defined within the context of a continuum of educational services for children with disabilities. One such continuum is illustrated in figure 3.1. The figure is organized from top to bottom, with services at the top (i.e., those provided in the regular classroom) being less restrictive than those at the bottom (i.e., those provided in a residential school). The idea behind the principle of least restrictive environment is that children must be educated in as normal an environment as their disability allows. Thus, children with minor disabilities, such as a minor reading problem, can be educated in their home school where they socialize with their neighborhood friends. Children with very severe disabilities, such as autism, may require placement in a school that specializes in that disability.

Education in the least restrictive environment is sometimes referred to as **inclusion, mainstreaming,** because many children with mild disabilities are pulled out of their regular education classes for part of the day and placed in a resource room where they receive specialized services for impairments such as learning disabilities or mild mental disabilities. The remainder of the day they are "mainstreamed," or included, with children without disabilities for socialization and instruction in subjects in which their deficits do not interfere with their ability to benefit from the teaching.

Appropriate Education

The major purpose of the entire special education referral, assessment, and placement process is to ensure that children with disabilities receive an *appropriate* education. Typically, this is a straightforward process (see, e.g., figure 3.2)

Figure 3.1 Continuum of Special Education Services Along Three Dimensions

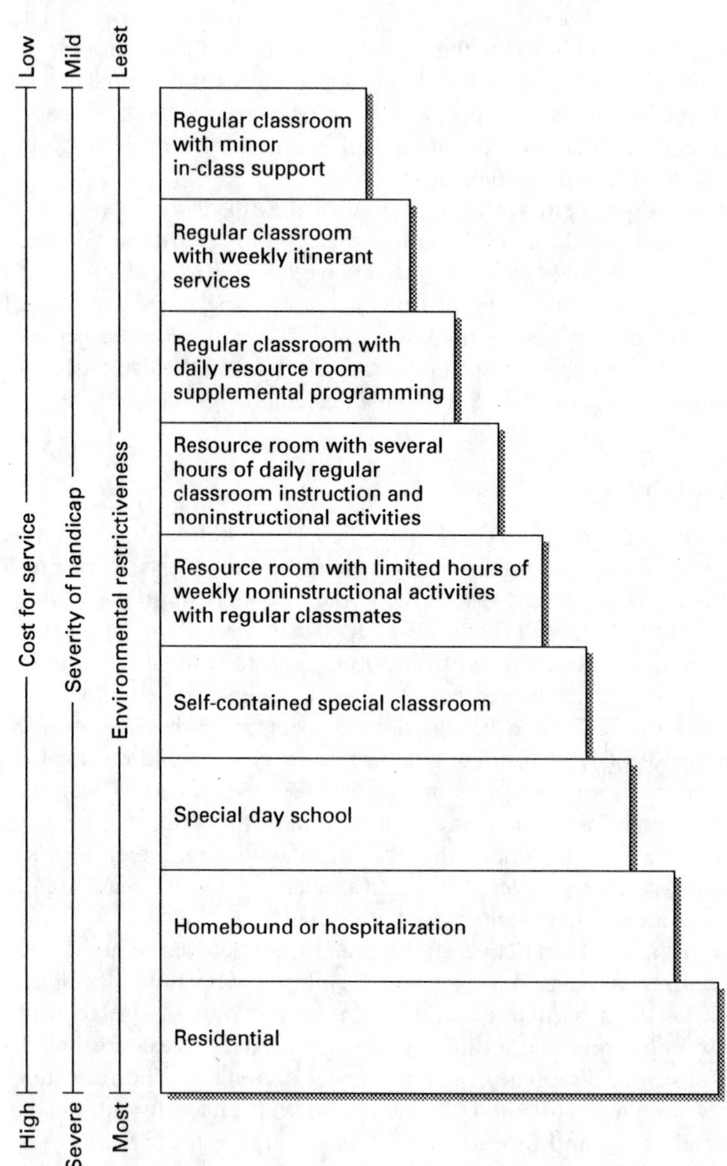

From: C. R. Reynolds and L. Mann, ENCYCLOPEDIA OF SPECIAL EDUCATION. Copyright © 1987 John Wiley & Sons, Inc., New York. Reprinted by permission of John Wiley & Sons, Inc.

Figure 3.2 Flowchart of Consultation-Assessment-Intervention Service System

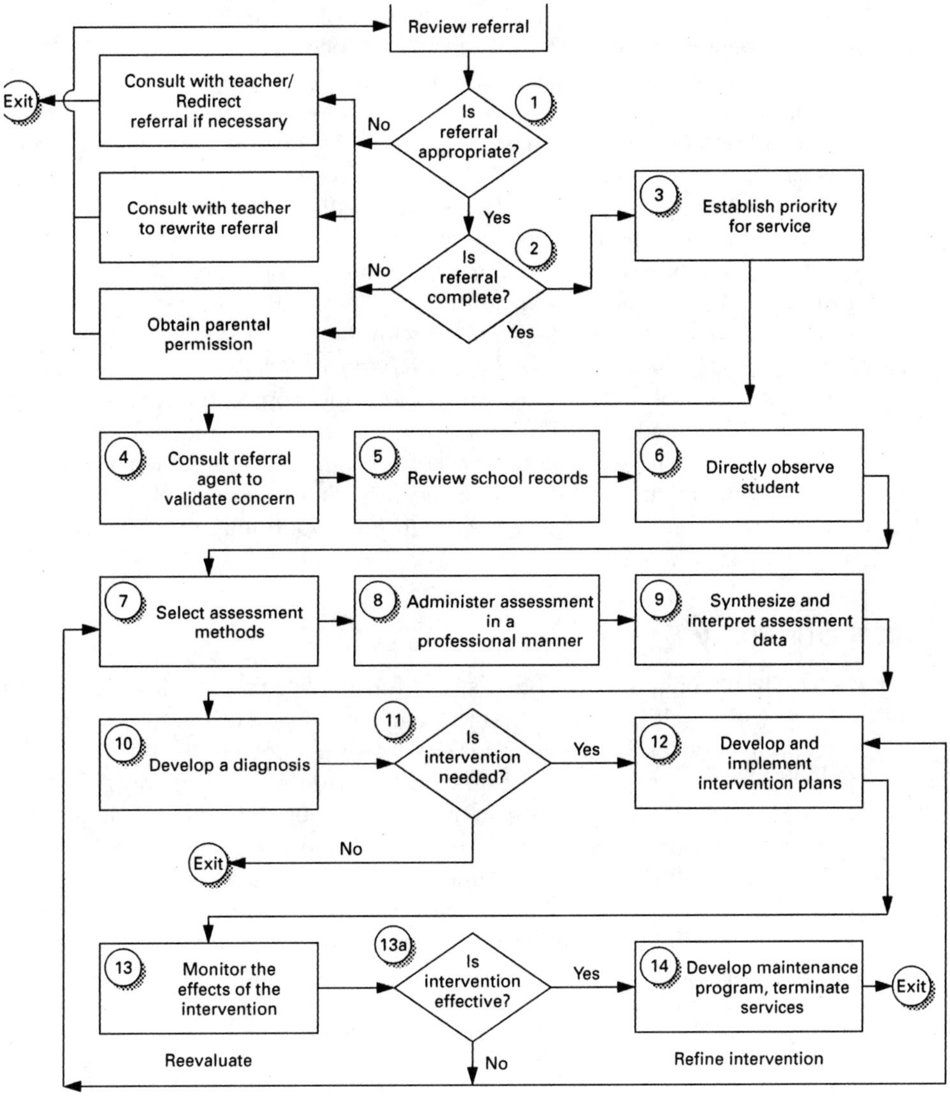

Review referral

1 Is referral appropriate?
No → Consult with teacher/ Redirect referral if necessary → Exit
Yes

2 Is referral complete?
No → Consult with teacher to rewrite referral
No → Obtain parental permission
Yes

3 Establish priority for service

4 Consult referral agent to validate concern

5 Review school records

6 Directly observe student

7 Select assessment methods

8 Administer assessment in a professional manner

9 Synthesize and interpret assessment data

10 Develop a diagnosis

11 Is intervention needed?
No → Exit
Yes

12 Develop and implement intervention plans

13 Monitor the effects of the intervention

13a Is intervention effective?
Yes
No

14 Develop maintenance program, terminate services → Exit

Reevaluate

Refine intervention

From: C. R. Reynolds, et al. (1984) SCHOOL PSYCHOLOGY ESSENTIALS OF THEORY AND PRACTICE. New York: John Wiley & Sons, Inc. Reprinted by permission of the authors.

and the multidisciplinary team designs a program individualized for a child's unique strengths and weaknesses. Occasionally, however, as in all decision-making processes, disagreement arises about what represents the most appropriate educational services. The definition of the term "appropriate" has thus become a major issue in the placement process.

Such disagreements have usually been between parents and the school system. Parents, for example, may want their child to be placed in a special school in another state that has an excellent reputation for handling problems similar to the ones their child is experiencing. The local school system may refuse to pay for placement in such a setting, saying they can provide an appropriate education within the district.

Does a school system have an obligation to provide the best possible education for a child or only an appropriate education? In response to this question, the U.S. Supreme Court sided with the school system in the case of *Hendrick Hudson District Board of Education v. Rowley* (1982). The Court ruled that a school system must provide an appropriate but not necessarily an ideal educational program for a child and that "the requirement that a state provide specialized services to handicapped children generated no additional requirement that the services so provided be sufficient to maximize each child's potential 'commensurate with the opportunity provided to other children'" (*Hendrick,* p. 198).

Chapter Summary

The law has been a double-edged sword for individuals providing services to children with disabilities. For the most part, the laws have been very helpful in securing services for these children. However, they sometimes cause the system to become rigid and inflexible and provide services in ways that may not be optimal. In the present system, children must be evaluated in specific ways and labeled as disabled before they can receive services. Some who need services still do not qualify under the existing guidelines. Many critics of the present system insist that all children who need help should receive it. Opponents of that proposal say a system is necessary to account for the money spent on special education. The prudent psychoeducational specialist will remember that the laws governing special education are useful tools for problem solving and advocating an appropriate education. It is important to understand the laws so that they may be used and applied to the advantage of the children that we serve.

Chapter 4

Basic Statistical Concepts

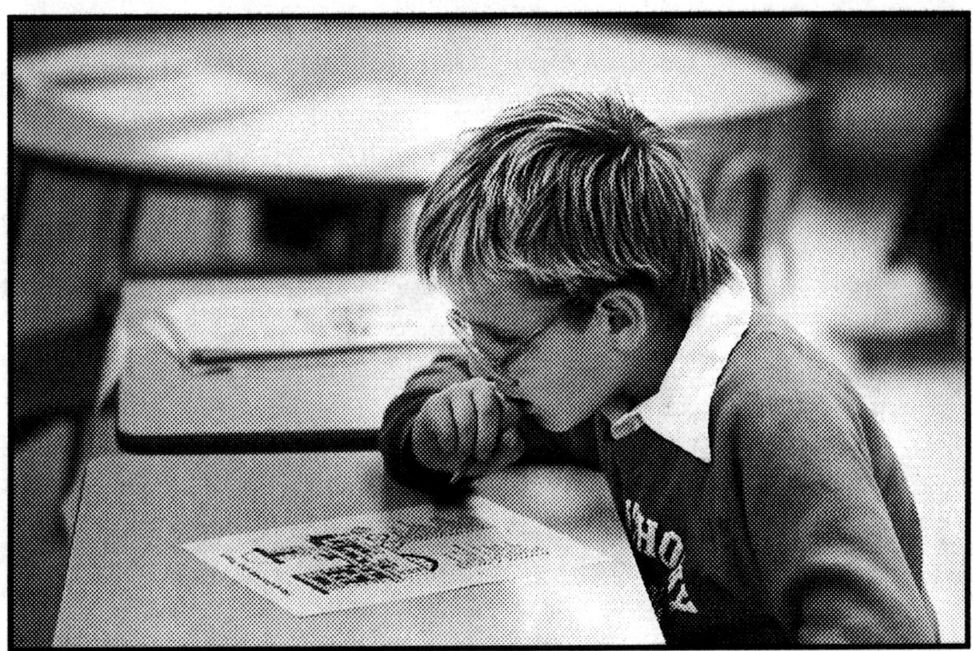

During the early 1980s millions of people throughout the world spent countless hours almost oblivious to events occurring around them. The focus of their rapt attention was the Rubik's Cube, which outsold virtually every other puzzle or game in existence. The Rubik's Cube heightened interest in puzzles of all types, and prompted *Psychology Today* magazine to commission Dr. Robert Sternberg and Janet Davidson (1982) of Yale University to study the types of people who spend their time solving these puzzles. They tested the hypothesis that people who are good at puzzles and brainteasers are more intelligent than those who are not good at solving puzzles.

Sternberg and Davidson discovered that puzzle solving and intelligence (as defined by IQ) were highly correlated, thus suggesting that people who solve certain types of puzzles are more intelligent than people who cannot solve the puzzles. Even more unusual was the fact that the time it took to solve the puzzles had a higher correlation (i.e., a stronger relationship) with IQ than did the number of puzzles solved correctly. The unusual aspect of this finding was that more intelligent people took *longer* to solve the puzzles than less intelligent people. Thus, the higher their IQ, the longer the individual took to solve a puzzle. This certainly seems to go against common sense, because one would expect that bright people solve problems more quickly than individuals with lower intelligence.

What do these results mean? Can we say that practice in solving puzzles causes you to be more intelligent? If someone is a poor problem solver, can we predict that the person is less intelligent? Should we recommend that a course in puzzle solving be introduced in every high school in the country? Why does it take smart people longer to solve puzzles? These and many more important questions can be asked about the findings. This chapter introduces the methods and techniques test developers and statisticians use to answer questions of this kind.

The Methods of Data Analysis

One of Mr. Barton's high school students brought Sternberg and Davidson's *Psychology Today* article to class. Students questioned whether a test of puzzle solving could really indicate intelligence and whether more intelligent people really took longer to solve problems, so Mr. Barton decided to launch an investigation. As a first step, he constructed a 25-item test composed of brain twisters taken from Sternberg and Davidson's article. (Sample items are displayed in table 4.1.) He then administered the test to 20 students and noted the number of puzzles they were able to solve correctly. In addition, he recorded the time required by each student to solve the puzzles. Finally, he obtained the students' IQ scores. All of this information is displayed in table 4.2.

At first glance table 4.2 is a confusing array of numbers. What do all these scores mean? Is IQ related to puzzle-solving ability? Are Mr. Barton's results similar to Sternberg and Davidson's original findings? How do you tell? Some way of summarizing these scores must be found so that we can get an overall picture. In the following sections we introduce some terminology and a process for summarizing and understanding these data. The information will be useful in learning to apply statistical concepts to your own data and for reading research reports, but it is even more important in interpreting the statistical terminology found in tests and test manuals. The discussion begins with an overview of scales of measurement.

Measurement Scales

As a first step in clarifying the data it is important to determine what kinds of measurement scales were used. **Measurement** can be defined as assigning numbers to objects or events according to a set of rules. Clearly, not all types of measurement are the same. Measuring the size of an atom, for example, requires a vastly different type of measurement than measuring a student's knowledge about spelling rules. The types of measurement can be classified within a hierarchy according to the precision of the measurement and the types of arithmetical operations that can be performed. The four types of measurement scales are **nominal** scales, **ordinal** scales, **interval** scales, and **ratio** scales.

Table 4.1 Sample Items from Mr. Barton's Test Questions

1. Water lilies double in area every 24 hours. At the beginning of the summer there is one water lily on a lake. It takes 60 days for the lake to become covered with water lilies. On what day is the lake half-covered?
2. If you have black socks and brown socks in your drawer, mixed in the ratio of 4 to 5, how many socks will you have to take out to make sure of having a pair of the same color?
3. How could two men play five games of checkers and each win the same number of games without any ties?
4. A bottle of wine costs $10. The wine was worth $9 more than the bottle. How much was the bottle worth? (Hint: The answer is not $1.)

Answers

1. Fifty-ninth day
2. Three socks
3. They were not playing with each other.
4. The bottle was worth $0.50, and the wine was worth $9.50.

Adapted from R. J. Sternberg and J. E. Davidson, "The Mind of the Puzzler" in *Psychology Today,* 16:37–44, 1982. Reprinted with permission from Psychology Today Magazine Copyright © 1982 (Sussex Publishers, Inc.)

Nominal Scales

Sometimes the scores assigned to people have a qualitative rather than a quantitative meaning. Qualitative measurement is referred to as nominal scale measurement and represents the least sophisticated level of measurement because the scores are simply used for grouping people, objects, or events into categories. Examples of nominal scales are Democrat-Republican, Chevy-Ford-Chrysler, and girl-boy. Some statisticians claim that nominal measurement is not measurement at all, because the only measurement operation is the judgment of whether something is equal to (=) or not equal to (≠) other members of the category.

Many times nominal data are in the form of numbers, but the numbers still do not imply that something has been measured. For example, a researcher may say Female = 1 and Male = 2. In this case the numbers are much like the numbers on football players' jerseys, and they possess no numerical qualities. It would be inaccurate to say that it takes two females to equal one male. It would be equally inaccurate to average the numbers on football players to determine the winning team. With nominal level measurement, numbers simply refer to the names of objects or people.

Ordinal Scales

The term *ordinal* implies a rank ordering of the characteristic being measured. In a horse race, for example, we indicate which horses came in first,

Table 4.2 Data from Mr. Barton's Test

Student	*Number of Puzzles Solved Correctly*	*Average Amount of Time Spent on Each Puzzle (in seconds)*	*IQ Score*
Tommy	6	101	111
Jane	4	69	90
Linda	5	65	92
Larie	8	114	115
Anita	8	100	108
Sarah	7	64	99
Dustin	8	107	102
Bob	7	90	100
Mary	7	87	107
Katie	6	62	94
Ron	8	105	103
Deb	10	161	121
Mitzi	10	141	141
Wade	7	88	106
Wes	8	106	107
Brendon	8	89	99
Megan	9	121	110
Edna	9	110	118
Bunny	11	161	136
Flo	12	170	182

second, and third; the higher the ranking, the faster the horse. Here the relative magnitude is meaningful in that numbers are assigned according to the amount of the characteristic being measured (e.g., speed in a horse race). If Stefan Edberg, Jimmy Connors, Martina Navratilova, and Ann Landers would play in an imaginary tennis tournament, their rank order of finish should reflect their tennis skill. If Edberg finished first, he would do so because he performed better than Connors, who came in second. If Connors finished second it is likely that he did so because he played better than Navratilova, who finished third. Because Ann Landers is not known for her tennis ability, she would likely finish fourth. Thus, when these individuals are assessed according to their tennis skills, the fact that one received a higher ranking is based on ability. Contrast this with nominal scales, in which the numbers on the football jerseys did not have any meaning in terms of magnitude.

It should be noted that equal intervals do not usually exist between rankings. In the tennis tournament just described, a much greater difference in tennis ability exists between Landers and Navratilova (ranked fourth and third, respectively) than between Connors and Navratilova (ranked second and third, respectively). Similarly, the interval between kindergarten and 2nd grade is greater in terms of the number of basic academic skills learned in that time period than between 10th and 12th grades.

Measurements on an ordinal scale, however, tell us nothing about how much better Edberg was than Connors, only their relative ranking. Ordinal measurements thus may yield deceptive results when manipulated arithmetically. For example, if the director of a tennis tournament decided to make pairings for doubles based on the average ranking of the partners, he might pair ranks 2 and 3 against ranks 1 and 4, giving both teams an average ranking of 2.5. Unfortunately, the magnitude of the difference between Ann Landers (fourth place) and Martina Navratilova (third place) is so great that the pairings would not be equal. The team of Connors and Navratilova would probably be far superior to the Edberg and Landers team.

Interval Scales

Unlike the ordinal scale, equal differences between scores can be treated as equal units when using an interval scale. Interval scale measurement is rare in educational assessment and most common in the physical sciences, when measuring temperature with an ordinary thermometer. The 10-degree difference between the temperatures of 30° F and 40° F is assumed to be the same as the difference between 0° F and 90° F. The zero point in interval measurement, which indicates that zero amount of the attribute exists, is arbitrary. With temperature, for example, the zero point is not the beginning of the scale. Further, when the thermometer reads zero, it is incorrect to say that there is a total absence of temperature.

Ratio Scales

Like the interval scale, in the ratio scale there is equal distance between the variables being measured. The major difference is that with a ratio scale a true, or real, zero point exists. Measurements of height, weight, and length exemplify ratio scales that have a zero point and equal units.

A second difference between ratio and interval scales is the computation of arithmetical operations. Addition and subtraction produce meaningful results with both types of scales. However, multiplication and division yield understandable results only when a true zero point exists, and these operations are appropriate only for ratio level measurement. Thus, it would not be accurate to say that 10° C (Centigrade) is twice as hot as 5° C because temperature is an interval scale. However, it would be correct to say that 10 feet is twice as long as 5 feet, because length is a ratio scale.

Table 4.3 summarizes the major characteristics of each of the four kinds of scales. The scores on Mr. Barton's test would most likely be ordinal data. It would be wrong to say that a child who scores 120 on an IQ test is twice as smart as a child who scored 60. Also, there is no evidence for equal intervals between ranks.

Table 4.3 Characteristics of Measurement Scales

Scale	***Characteristics***
Nominal scale	Mutually exclusive categories
Ordinal scale	Mutually exclusive categories Magnitude
Interval scale	Mutually exclusive categories Magnitude Equal intervals
Ratio scales	Mutually exclusive categories Magnitude Equal intervals Absolute zero point

Frequency Distributions—Organizing the Data

Now that we have some understanding of the type of data with which Mr. Barton was dealing, we can discuss some statistical procedures that will help us interpret the data. The next step in trying to summarize the puzzle-solving data might be for Mr. Barton to construct **frequency distributions** and **graphs.**

The frequency distribution for the number of puzzles solved correctly is presented in table 4.4. First, the scores were ranked from highest to lowest, and then the number of students who achieved each score was tallied. Already the scores are becoming easier to understand. For example, it is apparent that most students tend to score around the middle of the distribution, with a score of 8 being about average. For an even clearer picture of the score distribution, we can draw graphs to represent the data visually. Figure 4.1 displays the number of puzzles solved correctly in the form of a bar graph, or histogram, and figure 4.2 presents the same data using a frequency curve polygon. By looking at the graphs it is easy to compare scores.

Central Tendency—The Mean, Median, and Mode

Three different statistics are used to describe the **central tendency,** or average, of the frequency distribution: the **mean, median,** and **mode.** A measure of central tendency is needed because it is useful to have one point that is representative of the distribution. Perhaps the best-known measure of central tendency is the mean. To calculate the mean you add all the scores and divide by the total number of scores. The procedure used to calculate the mean number of puzzles solved correctly and mean IQ in Mr. Barton's class is presented in table 4.5, which also introduces some basic statistical symbols. Each puzzle-solving score is represented by the letter X. When the 20 Xs are added, this summing process is shown as ΣX; the Greek capital letter sigma, Σ, is a symbol for "sum of the scores that follow." In table 4.5, IQ is

Table 4.4 Frequency Distribution of Puzzles Solved Correctly in Mr. Barton's Test

Score	*Number of Students*
4	I
5	I
6	II
7	IIII
8	IIIII
9	III
10	II
11	I
12	I

Figure 4.1 Bar Graph of the Frequency Distribution of Puzzles Solved Correctly in Mr. Barton's Test

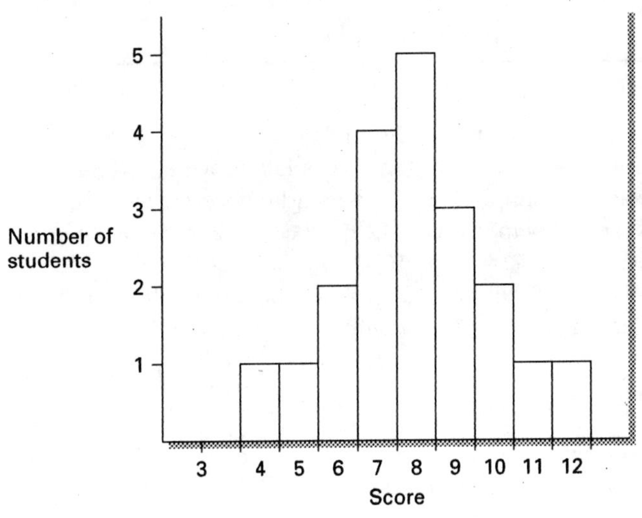

represented by the letter Y, and thus ΣY means to add the Y scores. N simply refers to the number of people in each group, and when divided into ΣX yields the mean (M). Now if the students were to ask Mr. Barton how the class performed on the test, he could simply report the mean, which was 7.9 puzzles solved.

Although the mean is by far the most frequently used measure of central tendency, the median and mode are also reported, especially when data are ordinal or nominal. The mode is the score that occurs most frequently in the distribution. In table 4.2, for example, the score of 8 is the mode, for it occurs

Figure 4.2 Frequency Curve Polygon of Puzzles Solved Correctly in Mr. Barton's Test

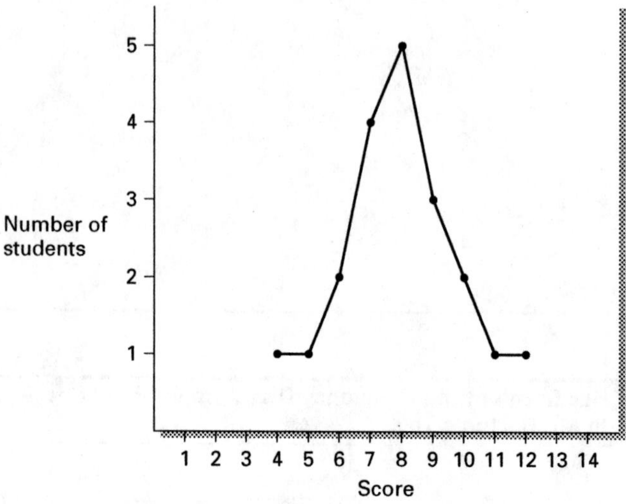

most often. The median is the middle score—the one that divides the distribution in half: 50 percent of the scores fall above it and 50 percent fall below it. For example, suppose a test was administered to seven students who obtained the following scores: 12, 5, 10, 4, 9, 2, 6. If we reorder the scores from low to high (2, 4, 5, 6, 9, 10, 12), it is clear that the median is 6 because as many scores fall below it (2, 4, 5) as above it (9, 10, 12). It is the middle score and represents the 50th percentile.

Variability—The Range and Standard Deviation

To know only a person's raw score is of little value. Knowing where that score falls in relation to the mean is a little more helpful but can still be misleading. Scores are much easier to interpret if both the central tendency and the **variability** of the distribution are determined. Variability refers to the extent to which scores differ from one another. If a test were given and the resulting scores were all the same, as would occur if everybody scored a perfect score, the distribution would have no variability.

Suppose that you have two sets of data: A = 3, 5, 7 and B = 1, 5, 9. Notice that distributions A and B each have the same mean (5) but that they differ in the amount of variability. Distribution A is less variable around the mean than distribution B. Figure 4.3 displays ways in which the relationship between variability and central tendency can vary. Descriptions of two common measures of variability follow.

Table 4.5 **Computation of the Mean Number of Puzzles Solved Correctly and Mean IQ in Mr. Barton's Test**

Student	*Number of Puzzles Solved Correctly (X)*	*IQ (Y)*
Tommy	6	111
Jane	4	90
Linda	5	92
Larie	8	115
Anita	8	108
Sarah	7	99
Dustin	8	102
Bob	7	100
Mary	7	107
Katie	6	94
Ron	8	103
Deb	10	121
Mitzi	10	141
Wade	7	106
Wes	8	107
Brendon	8	99
Megan	9	110
Edna	9	118
Bunny	11	136
Flo	12	182
	$\Sigma X = 158$	$\Sigma Y = 2241$
	$N = 20$	$N = 20$
	$M = 7.9$[a]	$M = 112.05$[b]

$$^{a}M = \frac{\Sigma X}{N} = \frac{158}{20} = 7.9$$

$$^{b}M = \frac{\Sigma Y}{N} = \frac{2241}{20} = 112.05$$

Range

The easiest way to calculate the variability of a distribution, or the **range,** is to subtract the lowest score from the highest score. To calculate the range of IQ scores in Mr. Barton's class (see table 4.5), you would subtract the lowest IQ, 90, from the highest IQ, 182. This yields a range of 92. The range is limited in its ability to reflect the variability of a distribution.

Standard Deviation

An index of the degree of variability in a distribution without the limitations of the range is the **standard deviation.** Understanding standard deviation is prerequisite to understanding and interpreting virtually all standardized tests. Conceptually, the standard deviation is a logical way to measure the variability of a

Figure 4.3 Variations in Normal Distributions

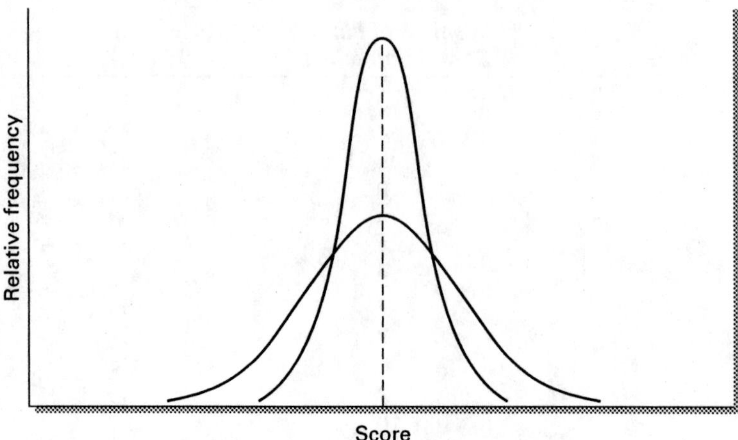

(a) Equal means, unequal standard deviations

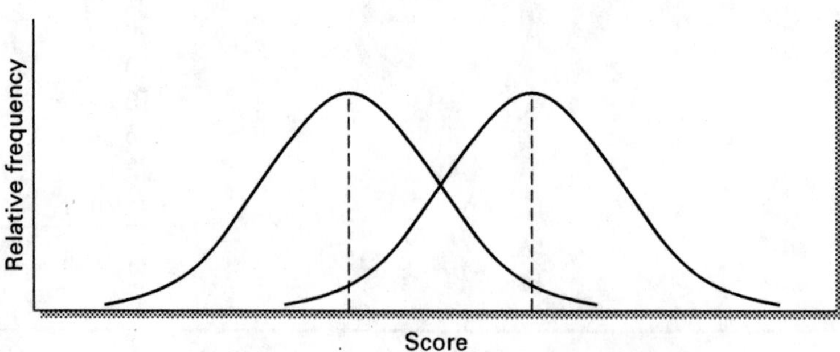

(b) Unequal means, equal standard deviations

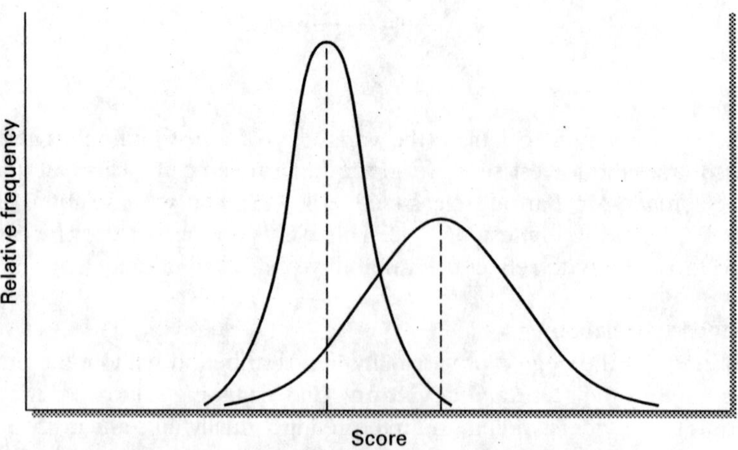

(c) Unequal means, unequal standard deviations

Table 4.6 Computation of the Standard Deviation of the Puzzle Scores in Mr. Barton's Class

Student	*Number of Puzzles Solved Correctly (X)*	*Mean Number of Puzzles Solved Correctly (M)*	*M – M = x*	x^2
Tommy	6	7.9	–1.9	3.61
Jane	4	7.9	–3.9	15.21
Linda	5	7.9	–2.9	8.41
Larie	8	7.9	.1	.01
Anita	8	7.9	.1	.01
Sarah	7	7.9	–.9	.81
Dustin	8	7.9	.1	.01
Bob	7	7.9	–.9	.81
Mary	7	7.9	–.9	.81
Katie	6	7.9	–1.9	3.61
Ron	8	7.9	.1	.01
Deb	10	7.9	2.1	4.41
Mitzi	10	7.9	2.1	4.41
Wade	7	7.9	–.9	.81
Wes	8	7.9	.1	.01
Brendon	8	7.9	.1	.01
Megan	9	7.9	1.1	1.21
Edna	9	7.9	1.1	1.21
Bunny	11	7.9	3.1	9.61
Flo	12	7.9	4.1	16.81

$$SD = \sqrt{\frac{\Sigma x^2}{N}} = \sqrt{\frac{71.8}{20}} = 1.89$$

distribution. If we want to assess the degree to which scores in a distribution differ from one another, it seems logical to base our assessment upon the extent to which scores deviate from the central value of the distribution. That is, one subtracts each score from the mean of the distribution. Table 4.6 shows how this is accomplished for the puzzle scores of the children in Mr. Barton's class.

The first step is to calculate the mean (*M*). Next, each student's score (*X*) is subtracted from the mean. These new scores, symbolized by the lowercase letter *x*, measure the distance of each score from the mean. At this point it may seem plausible simply to find the average variability by adding all of the *x* scores and dividing by the total number of scores. Unfortunately, when you add the distance scores for an average distance score, you will always get a sum of zero, because the mean is the algebraic middle of the distribution. Instead, the distance scores must first be squared and then summed, thus eliminating the negative values. The average deviation of the squared distance scores (x^2) is then calculated as

$$\frac{\Sigma x^2}{N}$$

Since the distance scores were originally squared, this result is in the form of squared units. To return to regular units you calculate the square root. Thus, the standard deviation (SD) is determined as

$$\sqrt{\frac{\Sigma x^2}{N}}$$

The standard deviation for the number of puzzles solved correctly is 1.89. The meaning of this number will become more apparent as you read the next section on the normal curve.

The Normal Curve

The standard deviation is a particularly useful tool when used in conjunction with the normal distribution, or **normal curve.** For example, IQ test scores in the general population tend to conform to a normal distribution (see figure 4.4) with a mean of 100 and a standard deviation of 15. Since IQ scores form a normal distribution, we know that approximately 34 percent of the scores fall between the mean and one standard above the mean. Thus, approximately 68 percent of the population scores between 85 and 115 on IQ tests and approximately 96 percent scores between 70 and 130.

The normal or bell-shaped curve seen in figure 4.4 represents the distribution of such a large number of human attributes that it is used frequently in psychoeducational work, especially in educational measurement. If we were to examine the distribution of people on many physical or psychological attributes (e.g., height, weight, intelligence, and graduate school aptitude), a natural pattern would appear. This pattern is such that most people are about average, a few are moderately above or below average, and even fewer have extremely high or extremely low scores. If we plotted such a distribution it would resemble the familiar normal curve (see figure 4.5).

Every normal curve has a single peak near the middle of the distribution, indicating frequently occurring scores, and then trails off in each direction, indicating that as we move away from the mean, we encounter fewer scores. We can take this a step further and say that the likelihood of obtaining a score near the middle of the distribution is very good but that it is much less likely that people will score at the extreme ends of the distribution. Hence, IQ scores of 100 are fairly common but not many people have scores above 140. Flo, in Mr. Barton's class, whose IQ is 182, is an extremely rare individual.

Figure 4.4 The Normal Distribution of IQ Scores

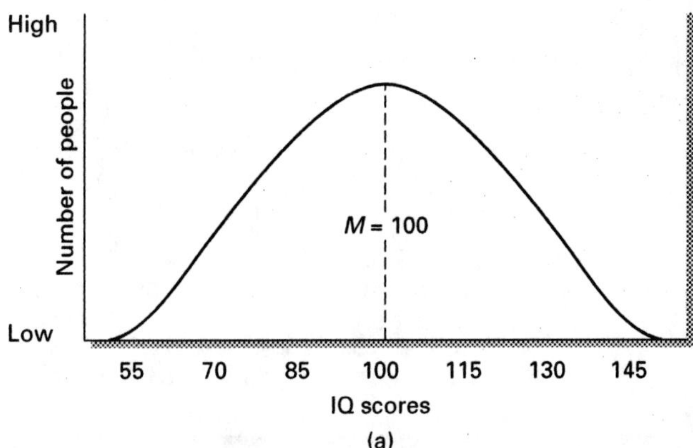

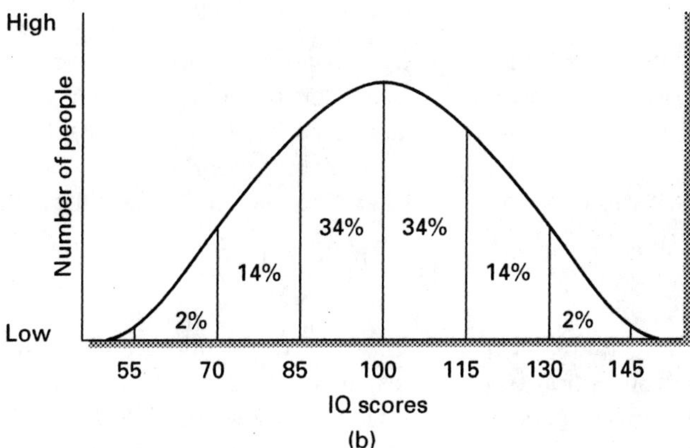

Standard Scores

One of the most frequent uses of the normal curve is to determine the degree to which an individual's score is unusual by comparing it with those of others. For example, many parents of preschoolers believe firmly that their child is "gifted." One such child, Megan, was recently tested with a popular preschool "intelligence" test. She earned a score of 600. Her parents were sure that any child who could score 600 must surely be gifted, and they eagerly awaited an interpretation of the test.

Since intelligence is normally distributed in the population, we can use the theoretical properties of the normal curve to determine whether Megan is

Figure 4.5 The Normal Curve

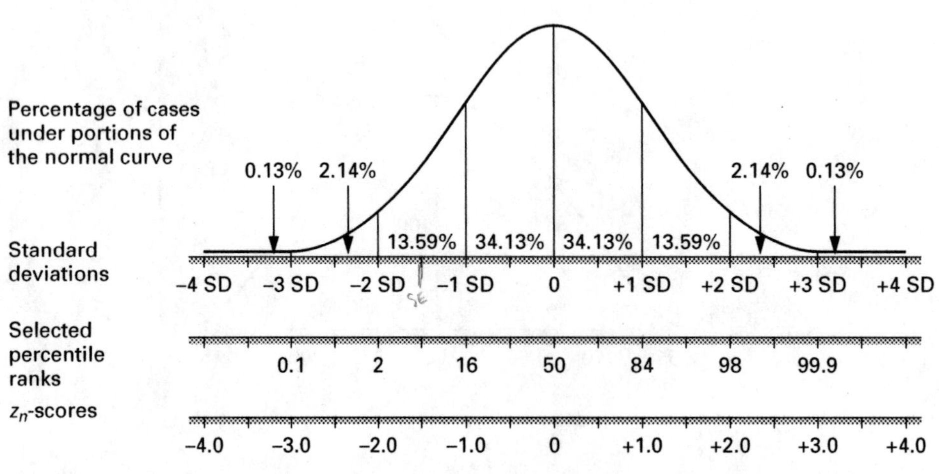

in fact gifted. This is most easily accomplished through the use of a **standard score,** or *z*-score, which indicates the number of standard deviation units a particular raw score is either above or below the mean. Recall that approximately 16 percent of people score one or more standard deviations above the mean. We can convert a raw score to a *z*-score by the following formula:

$$\frac{X - M}{SD}$$

where X = child's score, M = mean of distribution, and SD = standard deviation of distribution. On the test given to Megan, the mean is 500 and the standard deviation is 100. Thus, Megan's *z*-score is determined as follows:

$$z = \frac{600 - 500}{100} = 1.00$$

From her *z*-score it would appear that Megan's performance was above average but not necessarily gifted. Since the *z*-score is in standard deviation units, a score of 1.00 indicates that Megan is one standard deviation above the mean. The normal curve (figure 4.5) shows that one standard deviation above the mean is better than the scores of about 84 percent of the population and thus not really rare. If only those in the top 2 percent of the population are defined as gifted (as is fairly common in education), a *z*-score of 2.00 would be needed for a child to be labeled "gifted." To have a *z*-score of 2.00, Megan would need a raw score of 700:

$$z = \frac{700 - 500}{100} = 2.00$$

Figure 4.6 Mary's Scores on Two Tests

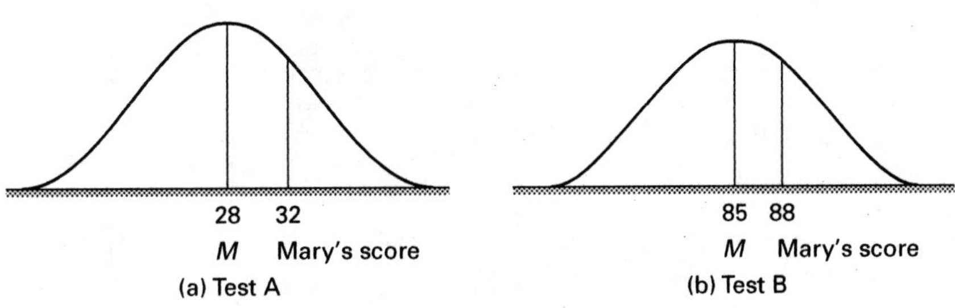

By using a similar procedure with other scores, even though they may have different means and standard deviations, it is possible to determine exactly how extreme a particular score is. If we return to Mr. Barton's data, we can see that Mitzi's *z*-score for the number of puzzles solved correctly ($z = 1.06$) is an above-average score. This score is calculated as follows:

$$z = \frac{10 - 8}{1.89} = 1.058 = 1.06$$

Standard scores are also useful if we have a person's scores on two tests and want to know on which test the individual performed better. The use of standard scores allows us to convert the two tests to a common scale. For example, if Mary scored 32 on Test A, with a mean of 28 and a standard deviation of 4, and she scored 88 on Test B, with a mean of 85 and a standard deviation of 6, which was the relatively better score? Figure 4.6 displays her scores graphically. We can see that her score on Test A is relatively farther from the mean than her score on Test B; that is, a greater percentage of persons scored lower than Mary on Test A than on Test B. Thus, Mary did relatively better on Test A. It would be inefficient to plot distributions of scores on both tests to answer questions of this type. Standard scores can be used to answer such questions more effectively:

$$z\text{-score on Test A} = \frac{32 - 28}{4} = \frac{4}{4} = 1$$

$$z\text{-score on Test B} = \frac{88 - 85}{6} = \frac{3}{6} = .5$$

Since her *z*-score is higher for Test A, it is apparent that she did relatively better on that test.

Percentiles

Percentiles are a more common and understandable way of expressing a person's relative position in a distribution than are standard scores. A percentile is

Figure 4.7 Illustration of a Percentile

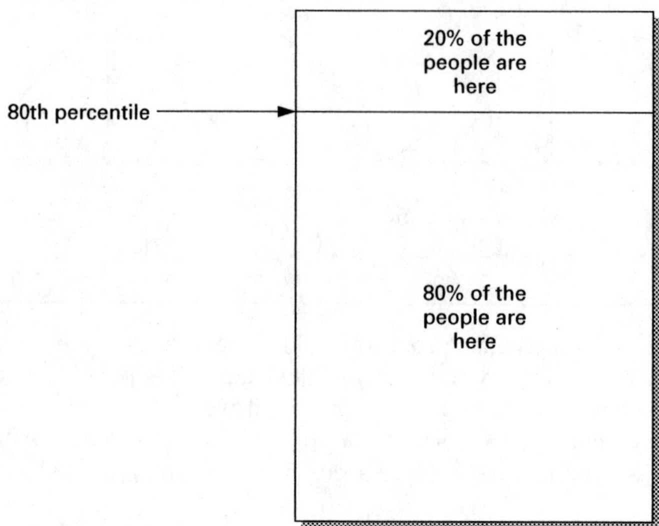

the point on a distribution below which a given percentage of the scores are found. For example, the 44th percentile is the point on the distribution below which 44 percent of the cases fall. By definition, the percentile rank for the median is 50 because 50 percent of the cases fall at or below the median. As another example, a score of 36 on a given test is at the 60th percentile if 60 percent of the scores are below it. On a different test, a score of 36 might be at the 20th percentile because only 20 percent of the cases fall at or below it (see figure 4.7).

Percentiles are popular because they appear easy to understand and interpret and are relatively easy to calculate. However, one problem in understanding and interpreting percentiles is that they are frequently confused with percentages, especially by parents and students. In testing, percentages usually refer only to the percentage of correct or incorrect answers.

Correlation—A Measure of the Relationship Between Two Variables

Let's return to Sternberg and Davidson's (1982) findings that puzzle-solving ability is related to intelligence and that the higher the IQ, the more time taken for puzzle solving. Sternberg and Davidson used **correlation** to assess the relationship between puzzle solving and intelligence. Correlation is simply a measure of how things are related to one another. In this context, "related" means that people who score one way on the puzzle-solving test tend to score in a predictable way on the IQ test. If high scores on one test tend

Table 4.7 Computation of Pearson Product Moment Correlation (*r*) for Mr. Barton's Test

Number of Puzzles Solved Correctly (X)	X^2	*IQ (Y)*	Y^2	*XY*
6	36	111	12,321	666
4	16	90	8,100	360
5	25	92	8,464	460
8	64	115	13,225	920
8	64	108	11,664	864
7	49	99	9,801	693
8	64	102	10,404	816
7	49	100	10,000	700
7	49	107	11,449	749
6	36	94	8,836	564
8	64	103	10,609	824
10	100	121	14,641	1,210
10	100	141	19,881	1,410
7	49	106	11,236	742
8	64	107	11,449	856
8	64	99	9,801	792
9	81	110	12,100	990
9	81	118	13,924	1,062
11	121	136	18,496	1,496
12	144	182	33,124	2,184
$\Sigma X = 158$	$\Sigma X^2 = 1{,}320$	$\Sigma Y = 2{,}241$	$\Sigma Y^2 = 259{,}525$	$\Sigma XY = 18{,}358$

$$r = \frac{N\,\Sigma XY - \Sigma X\,\Sigma Y}{\sqrt{\left[N\,\Sigma X^2 - (\Sigma X)^2\right]\left[N\,\Sigma Y^2 - \left(\Sigma Y^2\right)\right]}}$$

$$r = \frac{20 \times 18,358 - 158 \times 2,241}{\sqrt{\left[20 \times 1,320 - (158)^2\right]\left[20 \times 259.545 - (2,241)^2\right]}}$$

$$r = \frac{13,082}{15,551.52} = .84$$

to correspond with high scores on the other test, the two tests are said to have a *positive correlation*. If high scores on one test tend to correspond with low scores on the other test, the tests are said to have a *negative correlation*. If scores on one test have no relationship to scores on the other test, we say there is *no correlation* between the tests.

The Pearson product moment correlation, symbolized by *r*, is the most common method of assessing the correlation between variables. The correlation coefficient can range from –1.00 to +1.00. The smaller the correlation coefficient, whether positive or negative, the weaker the relationship between variables. Correlations close to zero would mean that little or no relationship

Figure 4.8 Scatterplot of the IQ and Puzzle-Solving Scores of Mr. Barton's Students

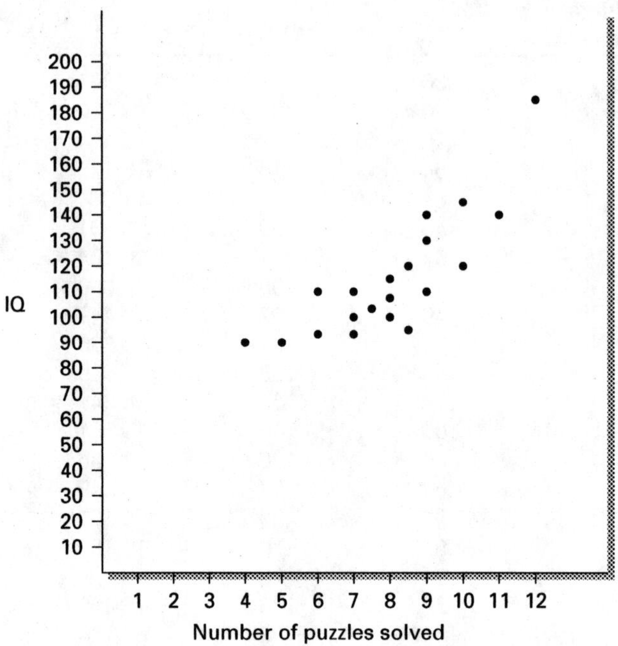

exists between variables. Positive numbers, such as +.87, denote positive relationships and negative numbers, such as –.87, indicate a negative correlation. The positive or negative *sign* of the correlation does not indicate the strength of the relationship, only the direction. Two variables that have a negative correlation coefficient of –.92 would thus be more strongly related than two variables that have a +.36 correlation.

The correlation data for Mr. Barton's experiment are presented in table 4.7. Examine the table closely and try to determine the type of relationship, if any, between puzzle solving and IQ. Those with a sharp eye may be able to detect that a positive relationship exists. However, when analyzing a large number of scores, it is usually difficult to tell by visual inspection the type of relationship between two variables. **Scatterplots** are often used for this purpose. To construct a scatterplot of the data of table 4.7, we plot each pair of X and Y scores as a geometric point (see figure 4.8). This scatterplot represents the puzzle-solving and IQ scores for the 20 students in Mr. Barton's class. It is apparent from the scatterplot that a positive relationship does exist. If the relationship were negative, it would resemble the scatterplot in figure 4.9. Notice that as scores on one test increase, those on the other decreased. However, in figure 4.8, as scores on the IQ test increased, so did puzzle-solving scores.

Figure 4.9 Scatterplot of a Fictitious Negative Relationship

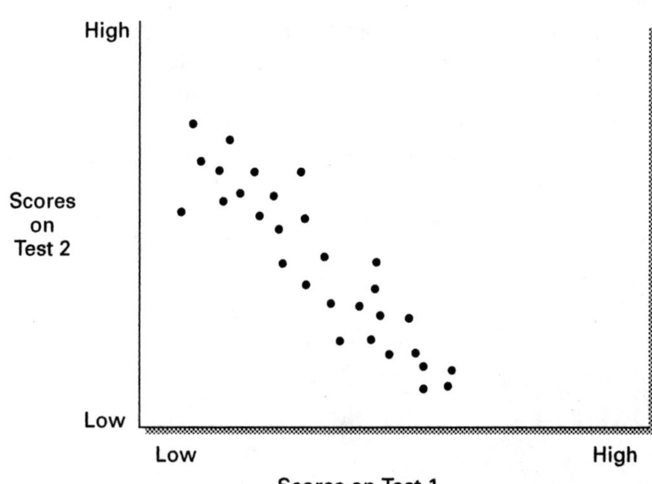

Sternberg and Davidson reported the relatively high positive correlation of .66 between number of puzzles solved correctly and IQ. How would we compute a similar correlation for Mr. Barton's data? Table 4.7 shows the steps for calculating the Pearson product moment correlation, which describes the relationship between the two sets of scores. Note that there $r = .84$, which is higher than the correlation of .66 obtained by Sternberg and Davidson. Mr. Barton was also interested in knowing if those students with higher IQ scores took longer to solve puzzles. Try figuring this out on your own from the data in table 4.2. You should discover that the correlation is .85.

Correlation takes some time and work to understand, but it will help you grasp other concepts in this book. Therefore, although it is not essential to know how to calculate a correlation coefficient, it is important to understand what a correlation means.

Chapter Summary

In this chapter we described a variety of techniques for organizing test scores and other data. Data management techniques are dictated to some extent by the level of measurement used: nominal, ordinal, interval, or ratio. The first step in organizing data is to develop a frequency distribution that specifies how many people received a particular score. Techniques for describing the frequency distribution include those that describe its central tendency (mean, median, and mode) and those that reflect the variability in the distribution (range and standard deviation). Standard scores and percentiles tell how a particular person scored relative to others. The chapter concluded with a discussion of correlation, which assesses the relationship between two variables.

Some people feel that statistics makes everyone the same, that is, it reduces people to numbers and these numbers do not convey the uniqueness of any one person. Although it is true that statistics can be misused, it is important to keep in mind that statistical analyses would not be needed if everyone were the same. It is because of the rich variety among individuals that statistics, when properly understood and used, can be helpful.

CHAPTER 5

Essential Characteristics of Tests: Reliability, Validity, and Norms

The Department of Mathematics at Johns Hopkins University in Baltimore conducted a talent search a few years ago to locate 11th-grade students who showed exceptional promise in math. Teachers in the area were contacted and invited to send their brightest math students to the contest. Julian C. Stanley, director of the Study of Mathematically Precocious Youths at Johns Hopkins University heard about the contest and asked to nominate some children. His was a special case, because the students he had in mind were not in any of his classes and he was obviously not an 11th-grade teacher. His only prior dealings with students had been three years earlier, when he had administered the mathematical part of the College Entrance Examination Board's Scholastic Aptitude Test (SAT-M). Stanley received permission to submit nominees, and eventually 10 of his nominees took the math department's test. The results of the contest were astonishing:

> Among the 51 people who entered the contest, the 10 chosen by Stanley [based on their scores] SAT-M ranked 1, 2, 3, 5.5, 7, 8, 12, 16.5, 19, 23.5.

> Points earned by the top three were 140, 112, and 91. The highest scoring person nominated only by a teacher scored 83. Just 3 of 10 ranks, 2, 5.5, and 19, had also been nominated by their teachers. The No. 1 contestant was not nominated by his teacher. He is quite able mathematically but had been far from the top of the 396 entrants in my March 1972 SAT-M contest. Most of the higher scorers from that testing had already skipped beyond the 11th grade and therefore were not eligible to enter the math department's contest. (The ablest of them, a 16-year-old Hopkins student, had already completed a junior-year course in mathematical analysis with a final grade of A.) (Stanley, 1976, p. 313)

The results were so astounding because teachers who had known their students for almost an entire year could not compete with three-year-old SAT-M scores in selecting the best math talent. In fact, one of the teacher nominees received only two points, whereas the lowest rank of the SAT-M nominees was 23.5 out of 51.

This represents a striking example of how well tests can predict behavior under some circumstances. However, before we conclude that the test was far superior to the teacher in determining talent, let's keep in mind that the contest was really just another test. A cynic would say that the only math talent identified by the test was the ability to take another test.

Not all math tests are as good as the SAT-M; some have inadequate norms and poor standardization, and many do not have any demonstrated validity. How can you distinguish between good tests and poor tests? How can you select a test that is suitable for your purposes? What are some of the characteristics of good tests? This chapter discusses three technical components that contribute to the quality of a test: reliability, validity, and norms.

Reliability

At the Olympics in Mexico City during the summer of 1968, Bob Beamon won a gold medal by broad jumping over 28 feet. This was about 3 feet farther than any human being had ever jumped. Some sports authorities now recognize that jump as the single greatest athletic accomplishment ever. Until much later, no one, including Beamon himself, even came close to equaling that record. If the event is examined objectively, the question must be asked, "Did the jump represent Beamon's true jumping ability or was it a rare fluke?" Since Beamon's jumps before and after the record setter were nowhere close to 28 feet, we may assume the jump was a fluke; that is, a rare combination of factors may have combined and resulted in the record-setting performance. We might conclude that the jump was not an accurate representation of Beamon's jumping ability because it could not be repeated.

An only slightly less rare event occurred in the 1976 Olympics, when Nadia Comenich of Romania scored a perfect 10 points in the gymnastics competition. However, her score did appear to be a much more reliable indicator of her true athletic ability, because the 14-year-old performer repeatedly received ratings of 10 in various other competitions.

Whether we are measuring athletic ability or spelling skill, concern arises about the degree to which the result is a true measure of a person's ability. In the terminology of educational and psychological measurement, this is a concern about **reliability.** Reliability involves the degree to which we get the same result when repeatedly measuring the same thing. Since Nadia Comenich's achievements were repeated and Bob Beamon's were not, we would say that her score was a reliable measure of her gymnastics skill but that his broad jump was not a reliable measure of his jumping ability.

The same kind of logic can be applied to educational and psychological tests. For example, Jill and Toni studied together for a midterm physics exam, and both seemed to know the material equally well. However, when the test was given, Toni scored much higher than Jill. In talking, they discovered some reasons for the difference in scores. Jill had a cold and did not sleep well the night before. Further, she had a bad case of test anxiety and said she had not been able to think clearly. Toni, on the other hand, was feeling great on the day of the test. In addition, some of the examples on the test involved the application of physics problems to automobiles. Since Toni is in an automotive repair class this term and Jill is not, her score, relative to Jill's, could have been enhanced. They both said that they had guessed at some of the answers, but Toni had evidently guessed correctly more often. This illustrates a case in which both students had about the same true ability in physics but extraneous factors caused them to receive different scores.

Learning some basic terminology will allow us to explain what happened to Jill and Toni more precisely. We can divide each of their scores into two parts. The first, and preferably the major, part of their score reflects their knowledge about physics. This score is referred to as a **hypothetical true score.** It is called hypothetical because there is really no way we can determine their actual knowledge of physics. The other part of their scores, or the **error score,** consists of all factors that caused their scores to fluctuate, including guesses, fatigue, and anxiety. Theoretically, it is impossible ever to know a person's true score because some error factor is always present.

Symbolically, we represent a person's score, X, as follows:

$$X = T + E$$

where

$$X = \text{test score}$$

$$T = \text{true score}$$

$$E = \text{error score}$$

This equation, though quite theoretical, represents a most essential concept for the practitioner: *Every score obtained while assessing a child contains some degree of error.* Even the best test may overestimate or underestimate a child's true ability. This is a critical piece of information if important educational decisions are made on the basis of the obtained score. In many states, one criterion for classifying a student as mentally disabled is an IQ score of 69 or below. What if the child scored exactly 69? Given that there is some error in the test score, caution must be exercised in deciding to label the child as retarded. Certainly the error could have worked in the child's favor, and the true IQ may be only 63. However, if the error worked against the child, the true IQ may be closer to 75. In a problem-solving process involving a child's placement, factors such as illness or motivation, which could have affected the test performance and thus inflated or deflated the error component, should be considered.

Test scores are not unalterable facts but instead are subject to error, just as a teacher's judgments are liable to fluctuate. Tests are not the only form of assessment for which reliability must be a concern. Simply observing a child in class is also subject to such problems. If two people were to observe the same child, would they see the same things? Would they agree that a certain behavior occurred or failed to occur? Unless observations are highly structured, two people are likely to disagree about what they saw. Although this chapter will primarily focus on reliability as it applies to standardized tests, the reader should bear in mind that reliability is *always* a concern, whether the assessment takes the form of standardized tests, informal tests, interviews, or observations.

Types of Reliability

You are likely to encounter many of the numerous methods for computing test reliability as you read test manuals. The more common methods include test-retest, equivalent form, split-half, and internal consistency.

Test-Retest Reliability

Recall that reliability refers to the extent to which we get the same result when repeatedly measuring the same thing. A logical way to establish the reliability of a test would then be to measure the same person twice and compare the results. This is precisely what is done in the **test-retest** procedure. Table 5.1 illustrates this process using a kindergarten screening test that was administered to the same 20 children on a Monday and again on the following Friday. (*Note:* Reliabilities are rarely, if ever, computed on only five scores, but only five are utilized here.) Correlations are computed for both sets of scores, yielding the reliability coefficient r_{xx}. This symbol is used to designate reliability because the Pearson product moment correlation r is often used for assessing reliability. The subscript $_{xx}$ refers to the correlation of a test x with itself.

Although the test-retest method is useful, it is used very seldom in the actual computation of reliability, because it can overestimate or underestimate the reliability coefficient. A spuriously high reliability coefficient may be

Table 5.1 Test-Retest Reliability of a Kindergarten Screening Test

Student	Number of Answers Correct: Test	Retest
1	9	10
2	7	6
3	5	1
4	3	5
5	1	3

$$r_{xy} = \frac{N\ \Sigma XY - (\Sigma X)\ (\Sigma Y)}{\sqrt{\left[N\ \Sigma X^2 - (\Sigma X)^2\right]\left[N\ \Sigma Y^2 - (\Sigma Y)^2\right]}}$$

$$r = \frac{150}{\sqrt{(200)(230)}}$$

$$r = .70$$

obtained when the second test is given too soon following the initial testing, because students may recall their first responses and tend to respond in the same way (Blood & Budd, 1972). If the test-retest interval is too long, however, the reliability coefficient may be artificially low, because a person's true score may change during that time as, for example, additional skills may be learned. Another problem with the test-retest method is that having students take the same test twice is an inefficient use of time.

If a test-retest reliability coefficient is reported in a test manual, the interval between testings must also be reported. The evaluation of the length of the interval is a subjective process. If a relatively stable trait, such as intelligence, is being measured, a longer interval may be used. However, when assessing a skill such as arithmetic ability, which can change relatively quickly when learning new material, the value of r_{xx} is likely to be reduced with long intervals.

Equivalent-Form Reliability

If a test of math aptitude is being constructed, one way to assess a person's true ability would be to construct a test using all possible math questions. Of course this is impractical because such a test would contain millions of questions, beginning with simple number recognition and continuing through advanced mathematical theory. Most math tests thus sample only a few of all possible items. If the sample is representative of the larger domain of items, we can generalize from the sample to the domain. Given the extremely large number of potential tests measuring math aptitude, it should be possible to construct several equivalent tests. Each would be a measure of math aptitude, and although they would have different items, each should provide equally good estimates of a person's true score.

Figure 5.1 Analogy of Equivalent-Form Reliability Using Shots at a Bull's-Eye

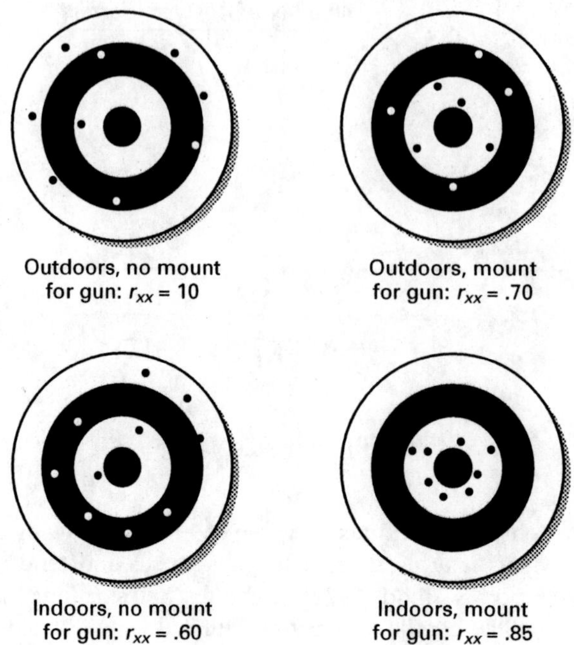

From: PSYCHOLOGY, Second Edition by Henry Gleitman. Copyright © 1991, 1986, by W. W. Norton & Company, Inc. Reprinted by permission of W. W. Norton & Company, Inc.

Using this example, it seems logical to determine correlations between the two alternative forms of the same test as a measure of reliability. This method of reliability computation is referred to as **equivalent-** or **parallel-form reliability.** If the test is reliable, the scores on separate tests should be relatively consistent. Figure 5.1 illustrates this process using an analogy suggested by Gleitman (1981). The bull's-eye represents a person's true score. Each shot aimed at the bull's-eye symbolizes an attempt at measuring a person's true score. When the instrument firing the shots is reliable, each measure will be close to the bull's-eye. However, much more scatter is present when the measurements come from an unreliable source.

Although the use of equivalent forms as a measure of reliability can be more easily justified from a theoretical perspective, this method shares some of the shortcomings of the test-retest method, including requiring students to sit through two test sessions, and determining the appropriate length of the interval between testings. In addition, it is difficult to construct a second form that is truly equivalent, because both tests should have identical means and standard deviations.

Split-Half Reliability

In one sense, the split-half method is identical to the equivalent-forms method. **Split-half reliability** is determined by dividing one test into two parts of equal lengths. One common method of dividing the test is by odd- and even-numbered questions. Each person then receives a score for both sets of questions. The "equivalent forms" in this case are the halves of the same test. The reliability coefficient is derived by determining the correlation between the halves.

A primary difference between this method and equivalent-form reliability is that with this method the length of the test is halved. This can be a problem because longer tests are generally more reliable than shorter ones, because they are less affected by factors that can increase measurement error, such as guessing. The Spearman-Brown formula has been developed to correct for the shorter test length and is reported frequently in test manuals.

Compared with the test-retest and equivalent-form methods of calculating reliability, the split-half approach has the advantage of requiring only one test administration. Because the data are thus available even if the test-retest procedure is used, most test manuals that report reliability will give a split-half reliability coefficient, regardless of other methods used. However, split-half reliabilities may be inflated somewhat because these estimates do not reflect errors of measurement due to changes in the student over time. For example, error related to a student's particularly bad mood on test day would not be reflected with the split-half procedure, because the entire test would probably be affected by the mood.

Internal Consistency

Although split-half reliability measures the **internal consistency** of a test, it is used less often today than the Kuder-Richardson formula 20 (KR-20) and coefficient alpha, which are also derived from a single test. These procedures reflect the degree to which an individual's test performance is consistent from item to item. Under most conditions, both procedures yield roughly consistent results (Lindeman & Merenda, 1979).

The Standard Error of Measurement

The preceding methods of calculating the reliability coefficient help to answer the question, "How consistently do we get the same result when repeatedly measuring the same thing?" Another reliability question deals with the amount of variation expected in a score, or "How much confidence can we place in this score?" This is an important issue in interpreting the meaning of a score. If a person's score is 69, are we reasonably sure that it represents a true score?

The **standard error of measurement** can answer these questions, as the example of Bob Beamon's Olympic broad jump can illustrate. Recall that Beamon made one jump of over 28 feet, a distance much further than he jumped before or since. If we examine his feat more closely, we can see that it was not a reliable measure of how well he could routinely jump. Table 5.2

Table 5.2 Bob Beamon's Broad Jumps Before and After His Olympic Jump

Hypothetical Jumps Before Olympics (feet)	*Hypothetical Jumps After Olympics (feet)*
24	26
23	23
24	24
25	25
25	24
25	24
23	25
26	25
24	26
24	25

presents data on 10 hypothetical jumps Beamon could have made prior to his record jump and 10 jumps he might have made following the Olympics. Figure 5.2 displays a graph of these data. Note that there is some variability in the jumps, perhaps related to factors such as motivation, anxiety, illness, and weather. Notice also that the higher scores in the distribution are statistically rarer. Clearly, then, the 28-foot jump is not representative of his jumping ability. Which distance is representative? Measurement theory dictates that the mean of this distribution is the most logical reflection of Beamon's true jumping ability. Excluding the 28-foot jump, Beamon's mean from table 5.2 is 24.5 feet. Any of the jumps that deviate from this measure of his true jumping ability would be attributable to error. In other words, if Beamon were in perfect condition each time he jumped and if all other factors remained constant, he would always jump the same distance.

If we wanted to measure the variability of Beamon's jumps, the standard deviation would be the appropriate means. In this case the standard deviation would be a measure of the degree to which Beamon's jumps deviated from his true jumping ability. In measurement terminology, the extent to which a particular jump deviates from his true jumping ability is considered error, because Beamon would jump the same distance each time if sources of error did not cause variations. In a sense, the standard deviation would characterize the amount of error in the distribution. This special type of standard deviation is called the **standard error of measurement,** although it is really a standard deviation of measurement error. The standard error of measurement, or SEM, is directly related to the reliability of a test and is calculated as follows:

$$\text{SEM} = \text{SD}_{\text{X}}\sqrt{1 - \text{r}_{\text{XX}}}$$

where

SD_{xx} = standard deviation of obtained scores

r_{xx} = test reliability

Figure 5.2 Graph of Bob Beamon's Olympic Broad Jump and Jumps Before and After

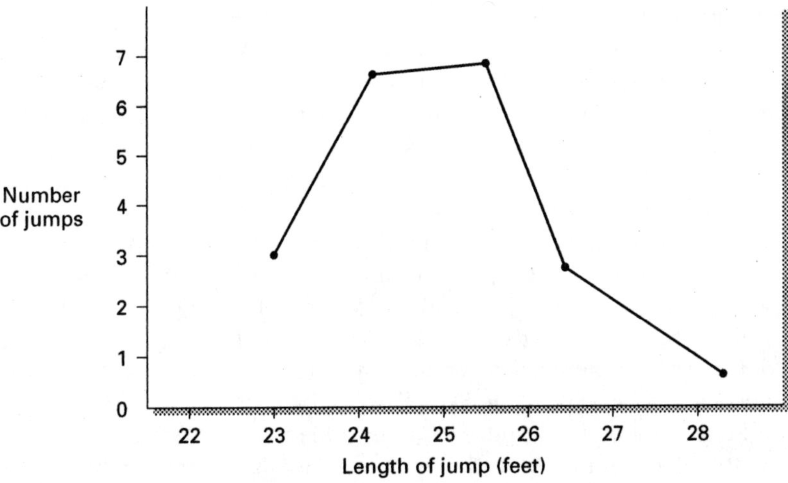

Tests that have higher reliability coefficients have a lower SEM. This means that more confidence can be placed on scores from reliable tests because they have less error. In other words, there is less variability of obtained scores around the true score. However, a relatively larger standard deviation tends to increase the standard error of measurement.

A Practical Use of the Standard Error of Measurement

All test scores contain some degree of error. It is difficult to communicate the concept of test error to laypeople who try to interpret educational and psychological tests. Many tend to believe that a person's obtained score is the true score. In actuality, the person is likely to obtain a *different* score if given the test again. To the extent that a test is reliable, the magnitude of the difference between the two test scores will be small.

The SEM can be used to communicate this rather complex array of information to others in a relatively straightforward manner using **confidence intervals.** A confidence interval provides a range of scores rather than an exact score. Instead of indicating that John has an IQ of 110, we would say that John's IQ is between 105 and 115. In this way, we indicate that his score is probably within 5 points of 110 but not exactly 110. We can increase the precision of our communication by indicating our degree of confidence that the true score will be within the interval. For example, we might say that we are 68 percent confident that John's score is between 105 and 115. We are able to make this type of statement by applying our knowledge of the normal curve. Recall that 68 percent of the cases in a distribution fall within one standard deviation of the mean. When using the SEM, we can say that 68 percent of the time the true score will fall within one SEM of the obtained score (and about 16% of the score would be above and another 16% below the confidence interval).

To establish a confidence interval, the first step is to select the degree of confidence desired. The most commonly used intervals are the 68 percent and the 95 percent confidence levels, because they correspond with one and two standard deviations, respectively. Next, the *z*-score associated with the particular level of confidence is selected. For example, the *z*-score corresponding to the 95-percent confidence level is 1.96. This *z*-score is then multiplied by the SEM to yield one-half of the confidence interval. This one-half interval is then added to and subtracted from the obtained score. An example from the Wechsler Intelligence Scale for Children (WISC-R) (Wechsler, 1974) will illustrate. On the WISC-R, the SEM for children 11.5 years old is 2.96. If a child of that age obtains an IQ score of 100 on the test, the 95 percent confidence level is derived by multiplying the *z*-score corresponding to the 95 percent level (1.96) by the SEM (2.96) to obtain a value of 5.8. Typically, this value is rounded off and then both added to and subtracted from the obtained score. In this example, we would say that we are 95 percent confident the student's score is 100, plus or minus 6. Alternatively, we could say that we are 95 percent certain that the *range* of scores from 94 to 106 contains the child's true IQ. It should be noted that as the confidence interval increases, the band of scores must become wider. However, it is not possible to establish 100 percent confidence boundaries.

Some test users may resist the use of confidence intervals because they make for unduly tenuous statements. However, people do change, and our assessment procedures have not reached a level of precision that enables us to communicate more precisely. To do otherwise misinforms the recipient of test information. The use of confidence intervals may prevent such nonsense as rigidly adhering to a single criterion of 130 IQ for placement in a program for the "gifted" that puts one child who has an IQ of 131 in such a program and denies admission to another child with an IQ of 129. In actuality, the range of true scores for both children overlaps markedly.

Factors Affecting Reliability

The reliability of a test can be affected by a variety of factors. Table 5.3 lists the more common factors that can influence test scores and thus the reliability of a test. Some factors, such as whether a child guesses on questions, are not under the control of the person giving the test. Others, such as ambiguous instructions, can be eliminated by careful test design and administration. In reporting test results to others, it is important to note factors that may have influenced the reliability of the test scores. Motivational lapses in those being tested, for example, are some of the more common reasons given for poor test performances.

Table 5.3 Factors Affecting Test Reliability

I. Lasting and general characteristics of the individual
   1. General skills (e.g., reading)
   2. General ability to comprehend instructions, testwiseness, techniques of taking tests
   3. Ability to solve problems of the general type presented in this test
   4. Attitudes, emotional reactions, or habits generally operating in situations like the test situations (e.g., self-confidence)

II. Lasting and specific characteristics of the individual
   1. Knowledge and skills required by particular problems in the test
   2. Attitudes, emotional reactions, or habits related to particular test stimuli (e.g., fear of high places brought to mind by an inquiry about such fears on a personality test)

III. Temporary and general characteristics of the individual (systematically affecting performance on various tests at a particular time)
   1. Health, fatigue, and emotional strain
   2. Motivation, rapport with examiner
   3. Effects of heat, light, ventilation, etc.
   4. Level of practice on skills required by tests of this type
   5. Present attitudes, emotional reactions, or strength of habits (insofar as these are departures from the person's average or lasting characteristics—e.g., political attitudes during an election campaign)

IV. Temporary and specific characteristics of the individual
   1. Changes in fatigue or motivation developed by this particular test (e.g., discouragement resulting from failure on a particular item)
   2. Fluctuations in attention, coordination, or standards of judgment
   3. Fluctuations in memory for particular facts
   4. Level of practice on skills or knowledge required by this particular test (e.g., effects of special coaching)
   5. Temporary emotional states, strength of habits, etc., related to particular test stimuli (e.g., a question calls to mind a recent bad dream)
   6. Luck in the selection of answers by "guessing"

From R. L. Thorndike, PERSONAL SELECTION, John Wiley & Sons, New York, 1949. Reprinted by permission of John Wiley & Sons, Inc.

Validity

Validity, or the extent to which a test fulfills its function, is the sine qua non of educational and psychological tests. Put another way, a test is valid if it measures what it is supposed to measure. Reliability, you will recall, refers to how consistently and accurately a test measures *something.* What the "something" is really does not matter in determining reliability. Thus, a test can have high reliability and yet not be valid for your particular purpose. Reaction time, for example, can be very reliably measured, but it is not a valid measure of intelligence. Reliability is a necessary, but not a sufficient, condition for validity. This means that a test *must* be measuring a trait or skill consistently *before* it can be considered to measure what it is supposed to measure.

When we measure height, for example, there is little question about the validity of a tape measure for this purpose. However, other concepts are not so easily defined. Suppose we want to measure a child's motivation. Most people would agree that motivation is an important determinant of how a child functions in school. If you think of various children with whom you are acquainted, you can probably categorize some as "motivated" and others as "unmotivated." Now comes the tricky part. What is it about these children that causes you to give them such labels? What specific kinds of behaviors did you think about when you evaluated motivation? How fast the child completes assigned work? Previous work habits? Attitude? How would you construct a test to measure motivation? Would it be capable of measuring motivation in every situation and circumstance? Could it tell you if a child would be motivated in both math and reading?

Obviously, constructing a test to measure a concept such as motivation is a difficult task, and not everyone will agree on the best method for measuring motivation. At the outset, we wish to reinforce Cronbach's (1970) assertion that we cannot ask the general question, "Is this a valid test?" Instead, the question should be rephrased: "Is this a valid test for the purpose for which it is intended?" A test that has been validated for assessing intelligence may be totally useless when used to diagnose neurological problems even though neurological functioning and intelligence may both utilize cognitive processes.

In 1974 a joint committee of the American Psychological Association, the American Educational Research Association, and the National Council on Measurement in Education met to grapple with some of these issues and identified three separate methods for evaluating the validity of a test: content validity, criterion-related validity, and construct validity.

Content Validity

A test is said to have **content validity** to the extent that it is an adequate sample of the attribute, trait, or skill being assessed. The process of content validation consists of the test developer's decision that the items on the test are representative of a specified skill or ability domain. Obviously, an item requesting students to calculate the speed of the moon would be inappropriate on a test of third-grade math ability. A third-grade math test with good content validity should include a representative sample of the types of problems that third-grade children normally encounter. Thus, if a test contains too few items, omits some important aspects of math functioning (e.g., no word problems), or contains subject matter irrelevant to math functioning, its content validity would be reduced.

Most of the commercially available achievement tests are reviewed by experts in the particular subject areas of the tests to determine if their content validity is adequate. Still, each user must determine if the test appropriately measures content for each particular use. If a skill is omitted on a test that is important in a particular situation, then the test may not be valid in that instance. For some tests, such as the BRIGANCE Inventory of Basic Skills, content validity was a major objective in designing the test (BRIGANCE, 1977). Such criterion-referenced tests are designed to assess major skills within a content area. Table 5.4 illustrates the various skills measured by the BRIGANCE.

Cronbach (1970) suggested that "the most general maxim to ensure content validity is this: *no irrelevant difficulty*" (p. 147, italics in original). For example, a student may be perfectly capable of computing the math problems on a test but fail certain items because they are embedded in lengthy paragraphs. Such a test might be more a measure of reading comprehension than computational skill. Test users should be alert to such instances in which irrelevant difficulties may unnecessarily influence test results.

Test users cannot rely on the test name to guide them in selecting an instrument that is valid for their purposes. Three problems that arise in using the test name to judge content validity are called the "jingle fallacy," the "jangle fallacy," and the "jungle fallacy" (Kelly, 1927; Messick, 1984). Test users fall victim to the jingle fallacy when they assume two tests with the same name are measuring similar things. A case in point is the Illinois Test of Psycholinguistic Ability (ITPA) (Kirk, McCarthy, & Kirk, 1968), which is assumed to measure something called "psycholinguistic ability," or, more simply, language functioning. However, as Carroll (1972) pointed out in his analysis of the ITPA:

> It requires some stretching of the meaning to call the ITPA a measure of "psycholinguistic abilities." The title is a misnomer, and users should be cautioned to look carefully at the true nature of the test, which might less misleadingly have been named the "Illinois Diagnostic Test of Cognitive Functioning." From the present title, a potential user might feel justified in expecting it to cover such language skills as reading, writing, and spelling. Actually, tests of these skills were deliberately excluded. (p. 442)

A second example of the jingle fallacy involves two tests that contain measures of spelling ability: the Wide Range Achievement Test-Revised (WRAT-R) (Jastak & Wilkinson, 1984) and the Peabody Individual Achievement Test (PIAT-R) (Dunn & Markwardt, 1970). The WRAT-R spelling test consists of dictating a word and requiring the examinee to write the word from memory. In contrast, the spelling subtest of the PIAT-R requires the child to select the correctly spelled word from four choices. If the technical characteristics of these tests were equal, teachers wishing to predict how well a child will actually spell would choose the WRAT-R because in reality children seldom encounter a multiple-choice spelling situation. Thus, even though the two tests purport to measure spelling achievement, they do not measure the same skills.

A companion to the jingle fallacy is the jangle fallacy, which causes a test user to assume incorrectly that two tests with different names are measuring

Table 5.4 Detailed Range of Skills Assessed by the BRIGANCE® Inventory of Basic Skills

I. Readiness

Test	Title	Test	Title	Test	Title
1	Color recognition	9	Fine motor skills	17	Numeral recognition
2	Visual discrimination	10	Verbal fluency	18	Number comprehension
3	Visual-motor skills	11	Verbal directions	19	Recognition of lower case letters
4	Visual memory	12	Articulation of sounds	20	Recognition of upper case letters
5	Body image	13	Personal data response	21	Writing name
6	Gross motor coordination	14	Sentence memory	22	Numbers in sequence
7	Identification of body parts	15	Counting	23	Lower case letters by dictation
8	Directional/positional skills	16	Alphabet	24	Upper case letters by dictation

II. Reading

Test	Title	Test	Title	Test	Title
A. Word recognition		C-3	Initial consonant sounds visually	C-14	Common endings of rhyming words
A-1	Word recognition grade level	C-4	Substitution of initial consonant sounds	C-15	Suffixes
A-2	Basic sight vocabulary	C-5	Ending sounds auditorily	C-16	Prefixes
A-3	Direction words	C-6	Vowels	C-17	Meaning of prefixes
A-4	Abbreviations	C-7	Short vowel sounds	C-18	Number of syllables auditorily
A-5	Contractions	C-8	Long vowel sounds	C-19	Syllabication concepts
A-6	Common signs	C-9	Initial clusters auditorily	D. Vocabulary	
B. Reading		C-10	Initial clusters visually	D-1	Context clues
B-1	Oral reading level	C-11	Substitution of initial cluster sounds	D-2	Classification
B-2	Reading comprehension level	C-12	Digraphs and diphthongs	D-3	Analogies
B-3	Oral reading rate	C-13	Phonetic irregularities	D-4	Antonyms
C. Word analysis				D-5	Homonyms
C-1	Auditory discrimination				
C-2	Initial consonant sounds auditorily				

different things. Close examination of the Devereux Child Behavior Rating Scale (McDaniel, 1973), which purports to measure child behavior, and the Inferred Self-Concept Scale (Spivack & Seift, 1967), which is supposed to reflect self-concept, illustrate this fallacy. Both instruments ask someone familiar with the child to rate that child's behavior. In addition, both contain a list of behaviors that the rater is to check if applicable to the child being examined. Although these tests have different names, their content is very similar, and in fact the Inferred Self-Concept Scale appears to be more a measure of overt behavior than self-concept.

The jungle fallacy is one to which many test developers fall victim. In this fallacy, two tests that are supposed to measure different things are found to be highly statistically correlated. The correlation is taken as evidence that the two tests are measuring the same thing. The fallacy is in not distinguishing between what is being measured and the instruments used for measuring. Thus, though a test of self-concept and a test of intelligence may be highly correlated, this should not be seen as proof that they are both measuring intelligence or self-concept. Although either of these possibilities *may* be true, a third explanation is that both tests are measuring still another construct, such as social acceptability. When asked to define the concept of intelligence, some individuals have responded that it is what intelligence tests measure. We must draw a distinction between the test, the name of the test, and that which the test is supposed to measure. If the test has construct validity, it defines that construct, although the test developer names it.

Criterion-Related Validity

For a test to have **criterion-related validity,** it must be highly correlated with some other measure or event (i.e., future or concurrent criterion). For example, when tests are given to candidates for medical school admission, there should be a high correlation between test scores and the criterion of success in medical school, because predicting such success is the reason for the test. The criterion validity of such a test would be assessed by computing correlations between the applicants' scores with their actual grades in medical school a year or two later or with another criterion of medical school success.

Most intelligence tests are designed to have good criterion-related validity. With intelligence tests given to children, the most frequent goal is to predict success in school. Jensen (1980) has reported that correlations between intelligence tests and measures of school achievement are generally in the range of .50 to .70, which is relatively high for a single test predicting a complex set of skills. A criterion measure may be available at the time the test is taken, but administering the test is more efficient than measuring the criterion behavior directly. For example, a behavioral measure of neurological dysfunction may not be nearly as accurate as examining the brain directly through a CAT scan, but it is much more time and cost efficient. If the behavioral test and other factors suggest some organic problem, additional testing may be warranted. In such situations, the test serves to predict a criterion (in this case, brain functioning) that is not readily and directly observed.

How successfully do tests predict behavior? In the field of special education, one does not have to look very far to find a very capable individual who was misdiagnosed, on the basis of tests, as someone who would never be a success in school. Predictive validity is not easy to establish; tests that are used to predict behaviors are sometimes wrong, just as predictions of the stock market, longevity, and athletic game results can often be wrong (as we saw in chapter 2). Tests with good predictive validity only help to improve accuracy, not to ensure it.

Construct Validity

Construct validity reflects the extent to which a test is capable of measuring a hypothetical trait, or construct. Tests have been designed to measure a number of constructs, including intelligence, motivation, anxiety, and self-concept. These traits are considered hypothetical because they do not represent observable behaviors that can be seen or measured directly.

To determine if a test has construct validity, we must rely on the theory behind the construct or statistical analyses of test scores. For example, psychological theory holds that there is a strong relationship between anxiety and scores on college exams. This theory predicts that people with a moderate level of anxiety perform best; extremely low levels of anxiety apparently do not provide motivation sufficient to perform well, and high levels of anxiety can interfere with test performance. Tests measuring anxiety could be validated against this prediction if students with high, medium, and low levels of anxiety should perform in the hypothesized ways on college tests.

The problem with a test lacking construct validity is that it may not be measuring the underlying trait. The Peabody Picture Vocabulary Test-R (Dunn & Dunn, 1981), for example, was once used to yield IQ scores. However, since the test measured only receptive vocabulary, we would not be too surprised if people who scored high IQs on the test did not perform as theory says those with high intelligence should perform, because the construct of intelligence is defined narrowly.

Normative Procedures

The third major factor we will consider in the evaluation of tests is the procedure for establishing test norms. Recall that in chapter 4 we used percentiles and *z*-scores to compare one person's score with those of others who had taken the same test, which is necessary because the interpretation of any score on a norm-referenced test requires some means of comparing it with an established point of reference. Test manuals facilitate such interpretation by providing a set of **norms** for use in comparing an individual's scores with those of a representative sample. Tables usually allow a raw score to be con-

Figure 5.3 **Normative Table for Translating Raw Score (RS) to Grade-Equivalent Score (GE) from the Level 2 Test Form of the Wide Range Achievement Test-Revised**

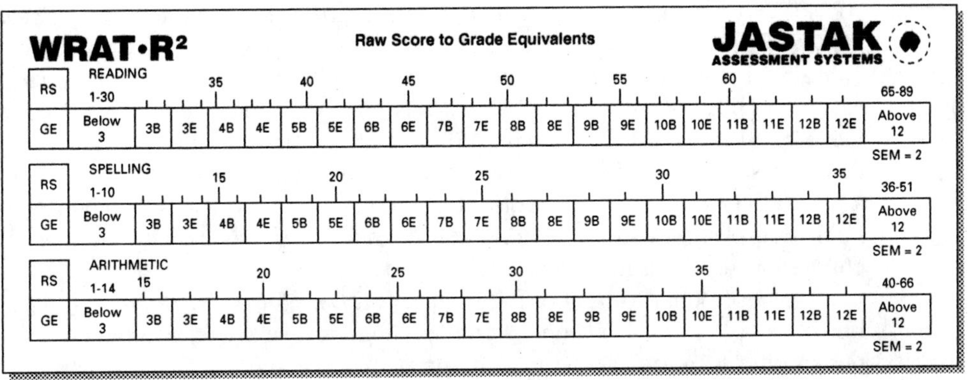

From: S. Jastak and G. Wilkinson, WIDE RANGE ACHIEVEMENT TEST. Copyright © 1984 Jastak Associates, Inc., Wilmington, DE.

verted to one derived in reference to the norm group. A norm table from the Wide Range Achievement Test-Revised is displayed in figure 5.3. From the table it can be determined that a raw score of 45 on the reading subtest is consistent with the performance of a sixth grader. People discussing this score would probably say that the student is reading at the sixth-grade level, since reporting a score of 45 will have little meaning to most people. Because the scores from the norm group are the ones reported most frequently, the characteristics of the normative sample are extremely important in evaluating a test for possible use.

Criteria for Evaluating the Normative Sample

To evaluate the representativeness of the normative sample, one should first determine that the individuals in the norm group are reasonably comparable to those being tested. According to Hills (1976):

> The best clue for [someone] . . . who does not know a lot about sampling procedures is to look for a clear statement of the population, some description of how samples were drawn from the population, and a description of how closely the sample fits the characteristics of the population. If all these things are provided, the user is reasonably safe in assuming that the norms adequately represent the population and were obtained from sound sampling procedures. If the publisher does not give details of how the sample was drawn, how well it fits the population, and so on, but merely speaks of the size of the sample or gives a vague

> description perhaps based on equating this test through another test, etc., be careful. If the results seem strange it may be because the norms are not sound. (p. 130)

This means that information given in the test manual should be quite specific. For example, more than six pages of the Wechsler Intelligence Scale for Children-Revised (WISC-R) manual describe the normative sample alone. Table 5.5 is from this manual and represents the type of detailed information to which Hills was referring. Contrast this level of specificity with the Jordan Left-Right Reversal Test (Jordan, 1980), which contains only the statement that the standardization sample included children from "rural and urban areas, public and private schools, all socioeconomic levels," with little documentation of the precise characteristics of the sample, such as the number of children tested from rural and urban schools.

The representativeness of the sample can be inferred by noting the number of people in each of the following categories: sex, age, community size, geographic location, acculturation, primary language, and socio-economic status. Certainly, it would affect the interpretation of a test of learning abilities if the norm group consisted only of Nashville children or only of children with learning disabilities. A common limitation is the failure to report the ages of the sample. For example, a test may be designed for children from 2 to 10 years of age. However, the test authors may have been unable to test any 2-year-olds. In this situation it is possible to extrapolate statistically how 2-year-olds *might* have scored, although this is a much less accurate method of predicting performance.

In addition to being representative, the normative sample must also be *recent*. The decline of SAT scores of the last decade shows why it is necessary to review and reinterpret norm-referenced scores. When tests are revised or translated into a new language, new norms must be gathered. Since our culture is changing at a rapid pace, we would expect that the way in which people respond to tests would also change.

Should you make comparisons even if the sample is probably unrepresentative? After all, isn't it better to use a poorly normed test than to make decisions without *any* comparative information? Salvia and Ysseldyke (1978) suggest that the answer is a resounding NO!

> It is occasionally argued that inadequate norms are better than no norms at all. This argument is analogous to the argument that even a broken clock is correct twice a day. With 86,400 seconds in a day, remarking that a clock is right twice a day is an overly optimistic way of saying that the clock is wrong 99.99 percent of the time. Inadequate norms do not allow meaningful and accurate inferences about the population. If poor norms are used, misinterpretation follows. (p. 122)

Cronbach (1970) suggests that norms are unimportant only if one is concerned simply with identifying individual differences within a group or a

Table 5.5 **WISC-III Standardization Sample by Age, Race/Ethnicity, and Geographic Region**

		White				*Black*				*Hispanic*				*Other*			
Age	***n***	**North-east**	**North Central**	**South**	**West**	**North-east**	**North Central**	**South**	**West**	**North-east**	**North Central**	**South**	**West**	**North-east**	**North Central**	**South**	**West**
6	200	14.5	21.5	23.5	10.0	1.0	4.0	9.5	0.5	1.0	0.5	4.5	5.0	0.0	1.5	1.5	1.5
7	200	13.0	24.5	19.0	13.0	2.5	4.0	7.5	2.0	1.0	0.5	5.0	5.0	0.5	0.5	0.0	2.0
8	200	14.0	21.0	22.0	12.5	2.5	3.0	8.5	0.5	2.0	0.5	5.0	4.0	1.0	0.5	0.0	3.0
9	200	15.5	21.5	20.5	13.0	1.0	3.5	0.0	1.0	2.0	1.0	4.0	3.5	0.5	0.0	1.5	1.5
10	200	15.5	22.5	19.0	13.5	2.0	3.5	9.0	0.5	1.5	1.5	4.5	3.0	1.0	0.5	1.0	1.5
11	200	16.0	19.5	20.0	15.0	3.0	3.5	8.0	1.0	0.5	1.0	6.0	3.5	0.5	1.0	0.5	1.0
12	200	15.5	22.0	22.0	11.5	2.0	3.5	7.0	0.5	1.0	0.5	5.0	4.5	2.0	0.5	1.0	1.5
13	200	15.0	23.5	18.5	12.5	2.5	2.0	9.5	2.0	0.5	0.5	6.5	4.0	0.5	0.0	0.5	2.0
14	200	15.0	21.5	21.0	12.5	2.5	1.5	10.0	2.0	0.0	1.0	4.5	6.0	0.5	0.5	0.5	1.0
15	200	11.5	23.5	22.0	14.0	1.5	3.0	11.5	0.5	0.5	0.5	4.5	4.5	0.0	0.5	0.5	1.5
16	200	3.0	20.0	23.0	14.0	0.5	3.5	11.5	0.5	0.5	0.5	3.5	6.5	0.0	0.5	0.5	2.0
Total	2200	14.4	21.9	21.0	12.8	1.9	3.2	9.3	1.0	1.0	0.7	4.8	4.5	0.6	0.5	0.7	1.7
U.S. Population[a]		14.0	20.8	22.3	13.0	2.2	3.0	8.9	1.2	1.8	0.8	3.4	4.8	0.6	0.6	0.7	1.9

[a]U.S. population data for children aged 6–16 are from *Current Population Survey,* March 1988. U.S. Bureau of the Census, 1988, Washington, D.C. From *Wechsler Intelligence Scale for Children-Third Edition (WISC-111).*

person's absolute performance. Thus, if the goal is to select the three students in each class most in need of remedial reading, national norms are not needed, for the purpose here is to choose those with the lowest absolute performances.

Alternatives to National Norms

As an alternative to national norms, some test users have developed local norms when the situation dictates the use of a particular test but the norms for that test are not representative of the locale or population being tested. Instances in which a local group is not adequately represented by national norms are not uncommon. Individuals familiar with school districts are aware that even *within* a particular district, the achievement levels of students vary from school to school. Local norms may be helpful when there is a reason to believe national norms should not be applied to a local group. The interested reader is referred to an article by Elliott and Bretzing (1980) for information on the procedures to use in constructing local norms.

Grade-Equivalent Scores

One of the most popular methods of using norms is to translate a person's score into a grade equivalent. This popularity stems from the fact that grade-equivalent scores seem to be simple and easily interpreted by persons unfamiliar with tests. If we say that Tim scored at the third-grade level on a particular test of reading comprehension, people understand our words very quickly; however, they may not have much real understanding. Several such disadvantages argue against the use of grade-equivalent scores. In fact, in June 1980 the Board of Directors of the International Reading Association recommended that test authors and publishers eliminate grade-equivalent scores from their tests.

Critics of grade-equivalent scores have identified three major limitations to their use. First, these scores do not provide equal units of measurement (i.e., they are ordinal rather than interval level measurements). This means that an increase in reading achievement from grade 5.0 to grade 6.0 on a particular test is probably not the same amount of growth as an increase from grade 2.0 to grade 3.0 on the same test. On the original Test of Written Language (Hammill & Larsen, 1990), for example, raw scores on the handwriting subtest range from 0 to 10. A student who earns a raw score of 5 obtains a grade-equivalent score of 4.6. If that test were given one month later and that same student were to earn *one* additional point, the grade-equivalent score for a raw score of 6 would be 7.2. Such a result would give the superficial impression that the student had made nearly three years growth in handwriting ability in only one month!

The second problem with grade-equivalent scores is that the same score may not have the same meaning for students of different ages. For example, a first-grade student and a seventh-grade student who have a grade score of

4.0 may not be equivalent in reading ability. Perhaps the test required only the ability to recognize words. If the task had been reading comprehension, the seventh-grade student, who may have a richer variety of experiences, may be able to comprehend the material at a higher level and thus outperform the first-grade student on the more complex task.

Another problem with grade-equivalent scores is that they are misrepresented by critics of education (Mehrens & Lehmann, 1978). For example, a local school board candidate may alarm parents by indicating that fully 50 percent of the children in the district are functioning below grade level. The truth is that *by definition,* 50 percent of the students *should* be below grade level. A score of 5.0 is used to describe the *average* fifth grader. On a national basis, about 50 percent of the students will be below average and about half will be above average. Some local districts may have a larger percentage above or below average depending on the composition of their student populations.

Sources of Information to Aid in Test Selection

The bulk of this chapter has been devoted to the three most important characteristics to consider when selecting a test: reliability, validity, and norms. Careful attention to these characteristics should increase the likelihood of selecting a good test. In addition to analyzing a test yourself, it is possible to obtain information from other sources. Without any question the most highly regarded source when evaluating tests is the *Buros Mental Measurements Yearbook.* The *Yearbook* functions as a *Consumer Reports* for the testing industry. When selecting a stereo or automobile, many individuals do the best they can to evaluate the potential purchase but then, to be completely sure, they consult experts, who can determine the advisability of the choice by application of their advanced knowledge. This information is often already available in the form of such publications as *Consumer Reports,* which annually assigns experts to evaluate a large number of products. Likewise, the *Buros Mental Measurements Yearbook* contains experts' reviews of virtually every test marketed in the English-speaking world. The *Yearbook* series, which was initiated by Oscar Buros in 1938, has three primary objectives:

1. To provide comprehensive and up-to-date bibliographies of recent tests published in all English-speaking countries.
2. To provide comprehensive and accurate bibliographies of references on the construction, validation, use, and limitations of specific tests.
3. To provide frankly critical test reviews, written by persons of outstanding ability representing various viewpoints, which will help test users to make more discriminating selections of the standardized tests that will best meet their needs.

Yearbook test reviews are indeed "frankly critical," as can be seen in the following Focus on Practice. The quality of the reviews is extremely high for

Focus on Practice

Sample Review from Mental Measurements Yearbook Borman-Sanders Science Test

Carl J. Olson, Assistant Professor of Medical Education, University of Illinois at the Medical Center; Chicago, Illinois.

This test, containing 75 multiple-choice and 25 matching items, allegedly measures the achievement of "elementary principles and facts of physical science with which the elementary school pupil should be familiar."

Despite the catalog claims, the Borman-Sanders is a prime example of a test that measures practically nothing of consequence but does it with high reliability. The failure of the test authors to provide important technical information—such as the distribution of the norming population, the methods used in computing reliabilities, and substantiating evidence to support claims of validity—is important, but it becomes secondary when one reviews the test content.

While the format is awkward and difficult to read, it may be the best feature of the test. It certainly helps to conceal the fact that most of the test items suffer from the molehill-out-of-the-mountain syndrome, asking for what may be the least important information about significant science concepts. In addition to being obsolete, the remainder of the test items are insignificant (e.g., "Inflate a balloon and release it, open end toward you. The principle it exemplifies was worked out by: 1. Sir Isaac Newton 2. Henri Becquerel 3. Alexander Graham Bell 4. J. Bjerknes"), provincial (e.g., "A wild flower sometimes called the 'Kansas City Feather' is really a: 1. sunflower 2. smartweed 3. spiked blazing star 4. snow on the mountain"), and trivial (e.g., "The space capsule of the Redstone rocket that carried the United State's [sic] second astronaut was named: 1. Monarch 2. Angel 3. Liberty bell 4 Trieste").

In all fairness, it must be noted that the multiple-choice items as exemplified above are superior to the matching section of the test.

There is not a single item that requires student cognition above the level of recall or which appears to be relevant to modern science curricula. If the Borman-Sanders has any use, it is as a convenient compendium for instructors of measurement courses. In it they will find examples of nearly every error in test development and construction that it is possible to commit, all arranged in one convenient unattractive package.

two primary reasons. First, only specialists and scholars of the highest caliber are selected to write the reviews. Second, each review is carefully edited, and every fact is checked before it is published. Statements made by reviewers for or against a test are carefully evaluated.

In addition to the reviews, the *Yearbook* also lists virtually every article that investigates the technical qualities of a particular test. For some of the more widely used tests, this can amount to several hundred references. The *Yearbook* can also be used as a catalog to locate various types of tests and their cost. One drawback is that the *Yearbook* is not really a yearbook and in fact is only published every five to seven years. This can mean that a newly published test is not reviewed until several years after it appears. This problem has been partially corrected by putting all test reviews on a national computer network so that they can be obtained through a computer terminal and a telephone hookup at most university libraries.

Reviews of tests are also available in other sources, particularly professional journals such as the *Journal of Educational Measurement, Measurement and Evaluation in Guidance, Journal of Educational Research,* and *Journal of School Psychology.* In choosing a test, one should not rely solely on the advice of experts. Rather, expert advice is most useful concerning the technical adequacy of a test. Whether the test is relevant and valid for the intended purpose can only be decided by the test user.

Chapter Summary

Beginning students in a testing course are often surprised to learn about the shortcomings of commercially available tests. The lesson is similar to learning that many car manufacturers are more often concerned with efficiency than with quality. Thus, the consumer must be prepared to evaluate the quality of tests, rather than relying on the claims of test publishers or the opinions of those who may be less than objective, by assessing a test's reliability and validity and the procedures for establishing test norms.

This chapter also stressed that the entire assessment process contains various degrees of error that may be based in the examiner, the test, the examinee, the teacher observations, the parent reports, and the thinking of the people who use the tests to make decisions. It is the wise student who takes from this chapter a sense of humility born of an awareness of the insufficiency of knowledge.

Part Two

Assessment for Instructional Planning and Curricular Modification

Assessment practice has moved over the last decade from an almost exclusive focus on "What is wrong with this child?" to a focus on "What does this child need?" Diagnosing and labeling a child tells us virtually nothing about what needs to be done to improve the child's functioning. In this section we describe some tools and a process for determining what is causing the problem and what to do about it. Chapters 6 to 8 describe specific "nontest" methods for assessment of children in their natural environment. Chapter 9 presents a model for integrating the problem-solving approach, in a systematic way, into educational decision making. After reading this section, you will have the skills you need for assessing problems without using tests.

CHAPTER 6

Curriculum-Based Assessment

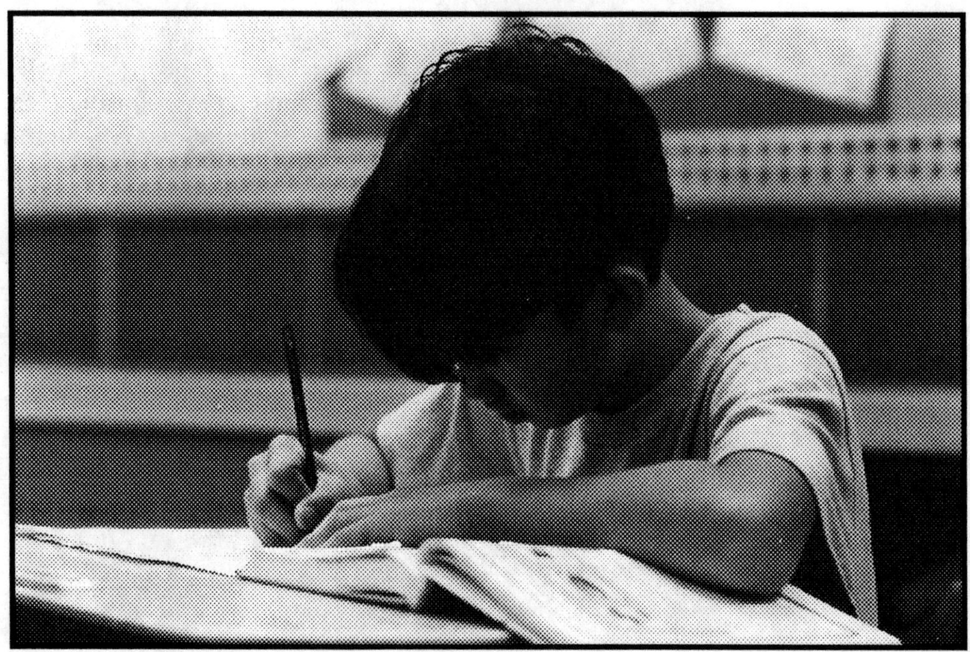

Wanda and Ted Johnson are excited. It's a cool Tuesday evening in early February and they are on their way home after their parent-teacher conference with their son's fourth-grade teacher. Wanda and Ted learned a lot about Timmy's school behavior and his progress in reading and math. Both Wanda and Ted liked Timmy's teacher, Ms. Bailey. She answered questions thoroughly and she seemed to respect the Johnson's ideas. At the end of the meeting, she had thanked them for having Timmy ready for and interested in coming to school every day.

The Johnsons had been most impressed by the fact that Ms. Bailey had given them a series of graphs that gave very specific information about the progress that Timmy was making in reading and arithmetic. In the past (the Johnsons have had two other children attend this elementary school), they had not been given such detailed information about their children's progress (see figure 6.1 later in this chapter for an example of the type of graphs Wanda and Ted were given). Sure, they had seen worksheets and grade cards and lists of mastered objectives, but they had never been given information that so precisely charted Timmy's progress. On many past occasions they had been given results from standardized tests like the California Achievement Test; however, they were not always sure what these results meant and how these results related to their child's specific progress in their local elementary school.

Ms. Bailey explained that the school had started a new program this year called "curriculum-based assessment" to help keep track of the progress of individual students in reading and math. She had been using the program since September and she wanted to share Timmy's results with his parents. "Do you believe it?" said Wanda. "Why, Ms. Bailey was even able to show us how Timmy struggled with his math during the first few weeks of school and that after she had changed her instructional strategies his progress improved dramatically." (Ms. Bailey had changed the skills Timmy was working on when her data revealed that he had not mastered all his basic addition facts. Also, she began rewarding his improvements with free time). "I wonder," said Ted. "Do you think that a program like the one that Timmy is participating in would have helped Susan? She struggled so much with reading in school, maybe. . . ." "No sense crying over spilled milk," mused Wanda. "Let's just be thankful that Timmy's problems with math were spotted early and that he's on the right track for now."

What Is Curriculum-Based Assessment and Why Do We Need It?

The term **curriculum-based assessment** (CBA) means simply measurement that uses "direct observation and recording of a student's performance in the local curriculum as a basis for gathering information to make instructional decisions" (Deno, 1987, p. 41). In the preceding example, Wanda and Ted were given assessment data that showed specifically how Timmy was progressing through the local reading and math curriculum. Later in this chapter we discuss a computer program that allows teachers to do curriculum-based assessment in a manner that yields information similar to that which was given to Wanda and Ted.

The process of CBA has also been referred to as *direct assessment* of academic skills, and many different models of direct assessment have been advanced. These models all have in common the basic assumption that one should test what one teaches. Typically, these approaches have emphasized direct, repeated assessment of academic target behaviors (Lentz, 1988b). In each academic area, *probes* are developed (e.g., brief reading passages, short spelling lists, samples of math items from the curriculum, etc.) and these probes are used to collect data on student performance. The probes are developed from the books and materials that make up the child's curriculum. Hence, CBA provides a structured way to see how well a child performs on the materials the teacher is assigning the class. The assumption is that if we want to know whether children are progressing in reading and writing, then we should observe (or count) their behavior as they read and write in school, and we should collect this data as often as is feasible so that we quickly know whether a child is making progress or falling behind.

A child who has difficulty learning needs to be tested frequently to see if instruction is having the desired effect. Ideally, all children would be tested frequently to assess their rate of learning. If learning is not occurring, then instruction needs to be altered in some way. When a child is tested only once or twice a year (or even once every term), it is impossible to monitor accurately the effects of instruction. Since traditional norm-referenced achievement tests are not designed to be administered repeatedly, these tests cannot be used to monitor a student's progress. A child would become familiar with the items and may show progress if tested again and again, but the gains in test scores would be due to familiarity with the test rather than real gains in achievement.

Despite the apparent simplicity of the notion that one should test what one teaches and test as often as is possible, the process of finding effective and useful forms of curriculum-based measures has yielded many different solutions. Investigators have had different objectives, focused on different aspects of the assessment process, collected differing amounts and types of validity data, and used somewhat different terminology to describe their approaches (see table 6.1).

In addition to those listed in table 6.1, many others (e.g., Becker, Engelmann, Carnine, & Maggs, 1982; Haring, Lovitt, Eaton, & Hansen, 1978; White & Liberty, 1976) have used curriculum probes to assess student performance, develop learning objectives, and measure student progress. The **direct instruction** model developed at the University of Oregon has been one of the most widely used and successful applications of direct or curriculum-based assessment (Becker et al., 1982).

Recently, much attention has been devoted to the technology of curriculum-based measurement (e.g., Deno, 1985; Kramer, 1993; Shinn, 1989) and the use of this technology in monitoring the development of children's basic academic skills (e.g., reading, spelling, written expression, and arithmetic). **Curriculum-based measurement** (CBM) is the name given to one form of curriculum-based assessment that was developed during the early 1980s at the University of Minnesota. The 1980s saw a virtual explosion of research in curriculum-based measurement (Shinn, 1989). Much of the remainder of this chapter is devoted to an analysis of CBM research. Specific examples of potential use in classrooms are provided following a brief explanation of why curriculum-based assessment has become of such importance to education.

Why Curriculum-Based Assessment?

For a number of years, teachers and teacher preparation programs have been criticized for lack of attention to educational measurement (e.g., Kramer, 1993). Many believed that teachers were not well prepared to measure the educational progress of the children with whom they were working. The primary

Table 6.1 Comparison of CBA Models

Comparative Features	*CBM-ID (Gickling & Havertape, 1981)*	*CBM (Deno, 1985)*	*CR-CBA (Blankenship, 1985)*	*CBE (Howell, 1986)*
Relationship to assessment and decision making	Instructional planning	Student progress monitoring	Instructional planning	Instructional planning
Evidence of utility for making other decisions	Indirect monitoring of student progress	Screening, eligibility, program evaluation	No	No
Timing in instructional planning	Ongoing, with most of assessment, *preceding* initial instruction	Ongoing, with most of assessment *after* initial instruction	Pretesting and mastery testing, with most of assessment *preceding* initial instruction	Ongoing, with most of assessment *preceding* initial instruction
Focus of material for monitoring progress	Short term	Long term	Short term	Short term
Test formats	Short duration	Short duration	Varies	Varies
Data on technical adequacy	Content validity, Construct validity	Reliability, criterion-related validity, construct validity	Content validity	Content validity

From: M. R. Shinn, S. Rosenfeld, and N. Knutson, "Curriculum-Based Assessment: A Comparison of Models" in SCHOOL PSYCHOLOGY REVIEW, 18:299–316.

concerns have been that teachers were given little instruction in measurement principles and even less opportunity to practice effective measurement procedures while training to be a teacher. The need to better prepare teachers and to equip them with functional tools for measuring academic progress led many to explore CBA.

An additional reason for the development of CBA was that although it is true that standardized test batteries, criterion-referenced instruments, and informal assessment inventories can be used to measure student achievement and to diagnose strengths and weaknesses, these tools have not been very useful for measuring short-term change in student academic performance (Lentz, 1988b). Teachers needed an effective, efficient tool for measuring whether a child's performance had improved this week, this month, this term.

Finally, there is often a mismatch between the content and sequence in which skills are introduced in a particular school district and the content of achievement tests and inventories. It does no good for an achievement test to tell you that your students have not yet mastered multiplication facts, when you know that you have just this month introduced multiplication to them. Also, it is not uncommon for someone who has tested a child with standardized tests to say something like "Susan appears to be reading at grade level," only to have the classroom teacher say "No way." How can this be? As Jenkins and Pany (1978) have shown (see table 6.2), just because a reading curriculum says that a particular reader is written at a grade 1 or 2 level does not mean that an achievement test will agree that the words used in that reader are grade 1 or grade 2 level material. Furthermore, each achievement test may give a different assessment of the difficulty of the material. Jenkins and Pany selected words from two different levels (grade 1 and 2) of different reading series and then evaluated the "difficulty" (i.e., actually, the grade level) of these words according to a series of achievement tests. As can be seen, a child's "grade level" score in reading may vary dramatically depending on the reading curriculum used in a school and the particular achievement test used to assess the child.

Although the Jenkins and Pany article is somewhat dated now and the tests and reading curriculum listed in table 6.2 have all been revised, Good and Salvia (1988) have found more recently that this type of mismatch remains a problem and that reading curricula and achievement tests are no better matched today than they were a decade ago. Several other investigations have had the same findings (Bell, Lentz, & Graden, 1992; Martens, Steele, Massie, & Diskin, 1995; Shapiro & Derr, 1987). The inability of achievement tests to match the local curriculum severely limits the ability of these tests to provide information of use to teachers, parents, or students. Curriculum-based approaches to assessment were designed to avoid this and other problems by measuring student progress directly from the curriculum in which the student is working. Thus we become more concerned with Johnny or Susan's rate of progress through our curriculum rather than their score on an achievement test

Table 6.2 Grade Equivalent Scores Obtained by Matching Specific Reading Text Words to Standardized Reading Test Words

		MAT			
Curriculum	***PIAT***	***Word Knowledge***	***Word Analysis***	***SORT***	***WRAT***
Bank Street Reading Series					
Grade 1	1.5	1.0	1.1	1.8	2.0
Grade 2	2.8	2.5	1.2	2.9	2.7
Keys to Reading					
Grade 1	2.0	1.4	1.2	2.2	2.2
Grade 2	3.3	1.9	1.0	3.0	3.0
Reading 360					
Grade 1	1.5	1.0	1.0	1.4	1.7
Grade 2	2.2	2.1	1.0	2.7	2.3
SRA Reading Program					
Grade 1	1.5	1.2	1.3	1.0	2.1
Grade 2	3.1	2.5	1.4	2.9	3.5
Sullivan Associates Programmed Reading					
Grade 1	1.8	1.4	1.2	1.1	2.0
Grade 2	2.2	2.4	1.1	2.5	2.5

From: "Standardized Achievement Test: How Useful for Special Education?" by J. R. Jenkins and D. Pany, EXCEPTIONAL CHILDREN, 44, 1978, 448–453.

that is unlikely to match the material we're using in the regular classroom, which may yield a grade level score that is essentially meaningless.

Curriculum-Based Measurement

As indicated earlier, the term *curriculum-based measurement* (CBM) has been most closely associated with the research completed at the University of Minnesota (e.g., Deno, 1985). Deno and his colleagues wanted to develop a technology for assessing student achievement that was reliable and valid, simple and efficient, easily understood, and inexpensive. In short, they wanted something that would be easy to use and that would provide good quality information.

The amount of research and extent of use of CBM during the last 10 years is solid evidence of how well Deno and others have succeeded in achieving these goals. This line of research has led to the existence of a technology where academic probes of 1- to 3-minute duration can be developed from the school curriculum materials, be used by teachers in a reliable manner, and provide accurate indicators of student progress (e.g., Deno, 1985).

Focus on Practice

Using Curriculum-Based Measurement—Specific Directions for Constructing Reading Probes

1. For each book in a basal reading series, the evaluator should select three 150- to 200-word passages (for first through third grades, 50- to 100-word passages)—one from the beginning, one from the middle, and one from the end. This will provide a total of three passages for each book in the basal reading series. To facilitate the scoring process, the evaluator may find it helpful to retype the passage on a separate sheet with corresponding running word counts placed in the right-hand margin.

   For preprimers and primers, shorter passages may be used. In addition, the differentiations between preprimers may not be salient enough to warrant separate probes for each individual book. In these cases, it is recommended that only the last of the preprimer books be used for purposes of assessment.

   Another issue that sometimes emerges is that a basal reading series may have more than one level assigned to a single book (e.g., parts of the Macmillan-R series). Although it is only necessary to assess by book, and not by level, some examiners may wish to create a series of probes for each level within the book. This is a perfectly acceptable practice, but may lengthen the assessment period considerably.

   Passages selected should not have a lot of dialogue, should be text (not poetry or plays), and should not have unusual or foreign words. It is not necessary to select passages only from the beginning of stories within the text.

2. The evaluator should make two copies of each passage selected. One passage will be used for the child to read and the other copy will be used to score the child's oral reading. The evaluator may consider covering your copy with a transparency so that the copy can be reused.

3. *Optional:* For each probe, the evaluator may develop a set of five to eight comprehension questions. These questions should include at least one "who," "what," "where," "why," and inference-type question.

From: E. S. Shapiro, ACADEMIC SKILLS PROBLEMS: DIRECT ASSESSMENT AND INTERVENTION.

For example, simply counting the number of words read correctly from passages selected from a basal reader during brief oral reading sessions provides an excellent indication of a child's progress in reading (Deno, Mirken, Lowry, & Kuehnle, 1980). This process can be completed as little as once or twice a week and still provide reliable data.

In addition to reading, investigation of curriculum probes have been conducted across a variety of academic skill areas including spelling (e.g., Fuchs, Fuchs, Hamlett, & Allinder, 1991), written expression (e.g., Deno, Marston, & Mirken, 1982), and arithmetic (e.g., Fuchs, Fuchs, Hamlett, & Stecker, 1990). Simple measures of academic output such as number of digits (not problems) calculated correctly, letters (not words) correct in spelling, and number of words written are excellent gauges of student learning. Although most investigations have focused on the development of skills in elementary students, more recent research has focused on secondary populations and content areas (e.g., Marston & Tindal, 1995; Tindal & Parker, 1989). CBM research has been disseminated widely, with applications in special (e.g., Germann & Tindal, 1985) and regular (e.g., Marston & Magnusson, 1985) education. Individuals interested in learning more about how to use this exciting technology in areas other than reading are encouraged to read about it in greater detail (e.g., Shapiro, 1996; Shinn, 1989).

One of the most impressive aspects of the research on curriculum-based measurement has been the collection of substantial reliability and validity data. The data obtained in the original Minnesota research, as well as subsequent investigations, suggest that curriculum-based measurement procedures are as psychometrically sound as standardized achievement tests. Deno (1985) has provided validity evidence indicating that curriculum-based measures are better predictors of short-term change than standardized tests and that a variety of CBM measures differentiate between students of different ages and ability levels (see Focus on Research). These graphs may look complex, but all they really show is that "better" students and older students do better on CBM measures. This finding is exactly what one expects and supports the validity of CBM as an accurate measure of reading. In addition, the final graph shows that CBM is a more sensitive measure of reading improvement than other measures.

CBM measures have been applied successfully to screening for program eligibility (e.g., Marston & Magnusson, 1985), placement in curriculum levels (e.g., Deno & Mirken, 1977), and progress monitoring (e.g., Fuchs, 1988). CBM data have been used to differentiate among exceptionalities and place children in special programs (Marston & Magnusson, 1985; Shinn & Marston, 1985). Still others have advanced methods of developing local CBM norms to assist individual school districts in the identification and placement of children in special programs (e.g., Shinn, 1988), and many school districts have moved to implement comprehensive CBM programs. The best feature of CBM, however, is its utility in assisting classroom teachers in determining the effectiveness of instruction (e.g., Fuchs, 1993; Fuchs, Fuchs, & Hamlett, 1989).

Using Curriculum-Based Measurement in Schools

With the explosion in research in curriculum-based assessment and curriculum-based measurement have come many attempts to apply this technology to schools, classrooms, and individual children. Next we examine five different uses of CBM data in educational decision making.

Focus on Practice

Using Curriculum-Based Measurement— Specific Directions for Reading Assessment

Setting of Data Collection

The reading measures must be administered to students individually. Prepare two copies of each passage, a numbered copy for examiner use and an unnumbered copy for the students to read.

Directions

Say to the student: *"When I say 'start,' begin reading aloud at the top of this page. Read across the page* [demonstrate by pointing]. *Try to read each word. If you come to a word you don't know, I'll tell it to you. Be sure to do your best reading. Are there any questions?"*

Say *"Start."*

Follow along on your copy of the story, marking the words that are read incorrectly. If a student stops or struggles with a word for 3 seconds, tell the student the word and mark it as incorrect.

Place a vertical line after the last word read and thank the student.

Count the number of words read correctly and incorrectly.

Scoring

The most important piece of information is the number of words read correctly. Reading fluency is a combination of speed and accuracy.

1. *Words read correctly.* Words read correctly are those words that are pronounced correctly, given the reading context.
   a. The word "read" must be pronounced "reed" when presented in the context of "He will read the book," not as "red."
   b. Repetitions are not counted as incorrects.
   c. Self-corrections within 3 seconds are counted as correctly read words.
2. *Words read incorrectly.* The following types of errors are counted: (a) mispronunciations, (b) substitutions, and (c) omissions. Further, words not read within 3 seconds are counted as errors.
   a. *Mispronunciations* are words that are misread: *dog* for *dig*.
   b. *Substitutions* are words that are substituted for the stimulus word; this is often inferred by a one-to-one correspondence between word orders: *dog* for *cat*.
   c. *Omissions* are words skipped or not read; if a student skips an entire line, each word is counted as an error.
3. *3-Second rule.* If a student is struggling to pronounce a word or hesitates for 3 seconds, the student is told the word, and it is counted as an error.

Screening for Possible Program Eligibility

One use of curriculum-based probes has been to make an initial assessment of which children should be referred for subsequent testing to determine if they are eligible for special education services. Most (Marston & Magnusson, 1985; Shinn, 1989) have advocated a cutoff that would result in any student whose performance was below the median performance for her or his grade to be referred for more extensive testing. Graden, Casey, and Christenson (1985) have also reported on a prereferral system that involved the use of curriculum-based measurement.

There is much to admire in a procedure that uses the data from the local curriculum to determine possible eligibility for special programming. Lentz (1988b), however, has cautioned against the use of CBM in screening, stating that "perhaps determining program eligibility for special education should not be a function for the screening phase, rather should come only after remedial efforts in the regular classroom have failed" (p. 103). Lentz is concerned that we not use CBM to refer children for special education before we try to fix the problem in the regular classroom. Further, we hope that using CBM data for screening does not divert attention from other nonstudent variables (e.g., teacher behavior, parent cooperativeness) that may need to be attended to before the child can begin to achieve in the classroom.

Placement in Curriculum

Using the curriculum that the child is about to encounter in the classroom as an assessment tool to determine the level at which the child is to be placed in the curriculum makes a great deal of sense. Criteria (e.g., correct words per minute) are established following the collection of normative data and performance on curriculum-based samples and are then used to decide where in the curriculum to begin instruction (Germann & Tindal, 1985; Marston & Magnusson, 1985). As was seen in the Focus on Research box, children tend to do better on CBM measures as they move through the grades. Once normative data are established for a particular school or school system, we would be able to place a child at an appropriate level in each subject area based on our knowledge of the student's performance on those same CBM measures.

Obviously, the primary goal of placement in a sequenced curriculum is to facilitate instruction. In addition, measurement data used to determine the point at which instruction is to begin can also be used to measure individual progress toward goals, an objective that is discussed in more detail next.

Monitoring Progress

Clearly, CBA and CBM procedures have been put to many different uses. CBM differs from most other curriculum-based systems in that monitoring

Focus on Research

CBM Validity Data

The graphs printed on the next pages are from a journal article prepared by Stan Deno (1985). The graphs demonstrate the potential usefulness of curriculum-based measurement data and suggest ways that these types of data might be used by teachers. The first graph provides evidence that as students get older and move through elementary school they tend to read more words correctly during a 1-minute reading sample (assuming that the level of reading material is kept constant). This graph also demonstrates that regular education children do best, followed by Chapter 1 and special education students. These findings are exactly what one expects and support the contention that CBM measurement discriminates between individuals of differing ability and developmental levels.

In a similar manner, the next three graphs show that as individuals grow older they get better in reading, as well as math and spelling, as measured by CBM techniques. Although these data are averages from groups of children, these results give us confidence that when we use CBM with a particular child, our results will tell us whether the child is improving or not. Finally, the last graph demonstrates the sensitivity of CBM measures and gives us confidence that we will notice even small improvements in academic behavior if we use curriculum-based measurement. In this graph, data are presented from a 10-week period in which a child was measured weekly with CBM (words read and written correctly) while also given the SAT Reading and Language tests at the beginning and end of the 10-week period. This graph demonstrates that although the child was improving in reading and writing in the local curriculum, this change was not noticed on the standardized achievement tests. Once again, these data suggest that CBM may be a very useful tool for teachers in monitoring short-term change and for providing evidence to parents and teachers of the extent of improvement in children's academic functioning. Clearly, CBM technology is a tool unlike any tool that has ever been available to teachers. It is only a matter of time before this technology is refined and becomes a standard part of a teacher's measurement arsenal.

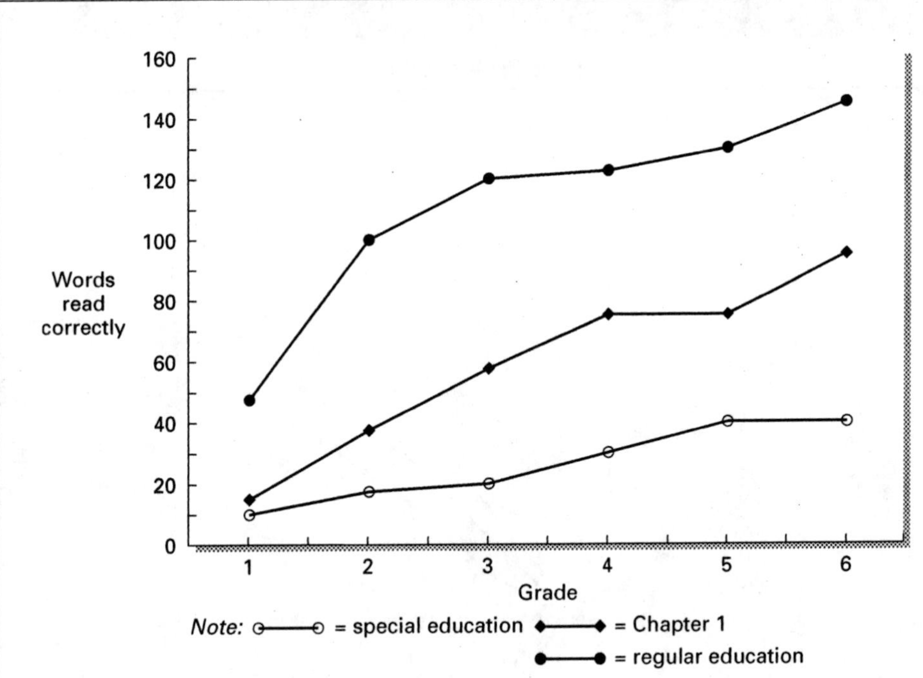

Comparison of Regular Class Chapter 1 and Special Education Students on CBM in Reading

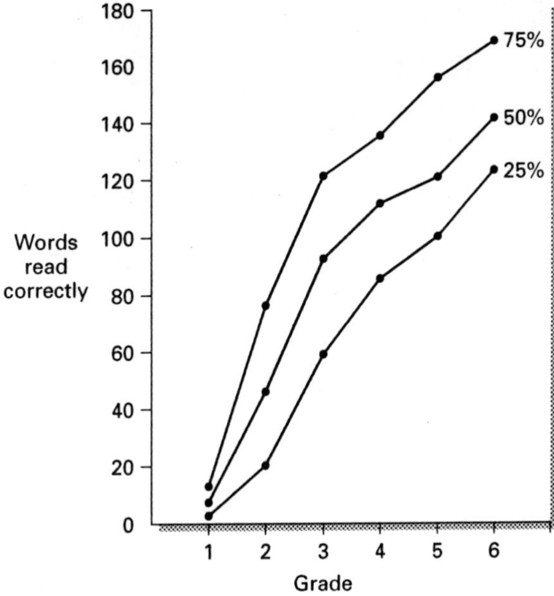

Total Number of Words Read Correctly in 1 Minute from Third-Grade Oral Reading Passage

continued

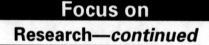

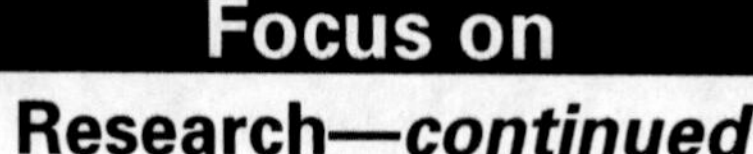

Focus on Research—*continued*

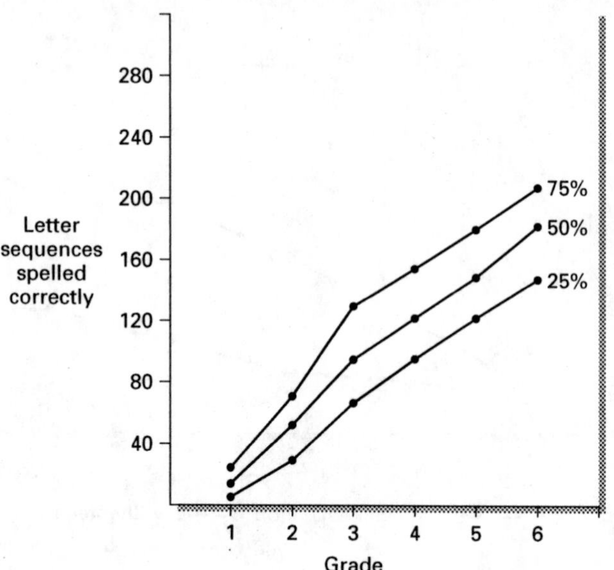

Total Number of Letter Sequences Spelled Correctly During a 3-Minute Spelling Task from Third-Grade Words

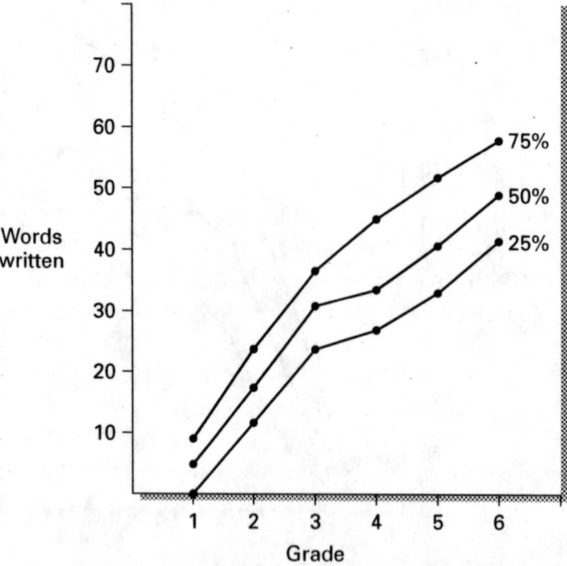

Total Number of Words Written During a 3-Minute Writing Task

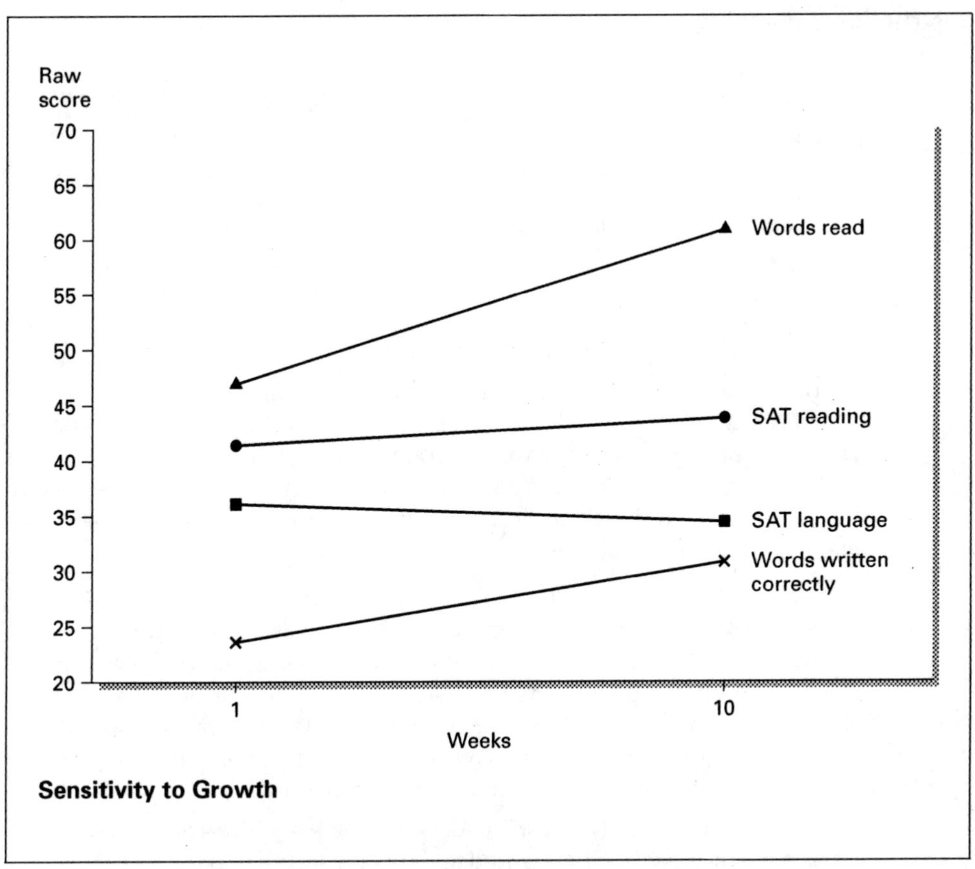

Sensitivity to Growth

student progress is really what the process is all about, as Deno (1985) has stated when describing the rationale and goals of CBM: "Since the purpose of developing the measurement procedures was to place in teachers' hands a simple way to routinely monitor student achievement in the curriculum . . ." p. 221). During the initial development stages of CBM there was little way of knowing the many different applications that CBM would have. It was clear, however, that teachers needed a more effective way to monitor student achievement. Monitoring student progress is how CBM has been most routinely used. Indeed, all of the applications of CBM discussed here (screening, placement in the curriculum, planning, special class placement) involve progress monitoring. Because these data are simple to collect and understand, they also can be very useful in providing feedback to parents as indicated in the opening section of this chapter.

Instructional Planning

Unfortunately, teachers who collect student performance data do not always use these data to evaluate and alter instruction (Baldwin, 1976; White, 1974). Any attempt to use CBM to impact on instructional quality and student performance must consider the need to make the system feasible for teacher use.

Lynn Fuchs and colleagues have completed much research related to these issues. For example, Fuchs, Hamlett, and Fuchs (1990) have developed and evaluated computer software applications of CBM technology "(1) to ensure standardization of the CBM monitoring, (2) to increase the feasibility of the monitoring systems, and (3) to extend the information teachers can derive from measurement" (p. 167). This software is designed to assist teachers in monitoring academic progress in reading, mathematics, and spelling and *to facilitate student achievement.* Due to availability of Apple II computer systems in many schools across the country, the program is available currently only for these computers. Although the CBM implementation strategies vary slightly across the three academic areas, the process of using the software looks something like this:

1. In each of the three academic skill areas, teachers and students have separate disks. Following initial preparation of disks for individual students and orientation to the task, a student sits at the computer and completes a timed task ranging from 1 or 2 minutes for math to 2.5 minutes for reading to 3 minutes for spelling. The computer scores the responses and these data are saved to a student performance graph that is available for both teacher and student to observe.
2. Following collection of baseline data, teachers are instructed to set performance goals for each student. Specific instructions are available for teachers to guide them through the goal-setting process. Teachers may select goals based on data collected during the development of this software (e.g., an average increase of .7 word per week) or their individual knowledge of the student. Teachers are encouraged to set ambitious goals for their students. When teachers view each student's progress, they are able to see both the individual data points and the student's goal line (i.e., the student's hypothesized trend line based on the baseline data and the ultimate goal). Student graphs show data points but not the student's goal line (see figure 6.1).
3. During the school year it is recommended that students use the software once (for regular education students) or twice (for special education students) per week to provide data on the extent of their progress in whatever academic areas are being monitored. Both regular and special education students are able to use the software with little or no teacher monitoring.
4. When teachers use their teacher disk to examine individual student data, they are prompted as follows: (a) Insufficient data for analysis—this may

Figure 6.1 Teacher and Student Graphs from *Monitoring Basic Skills Progress*, by Fuchs, L. S., Hamlett, C., & Fuchs, D., 1990

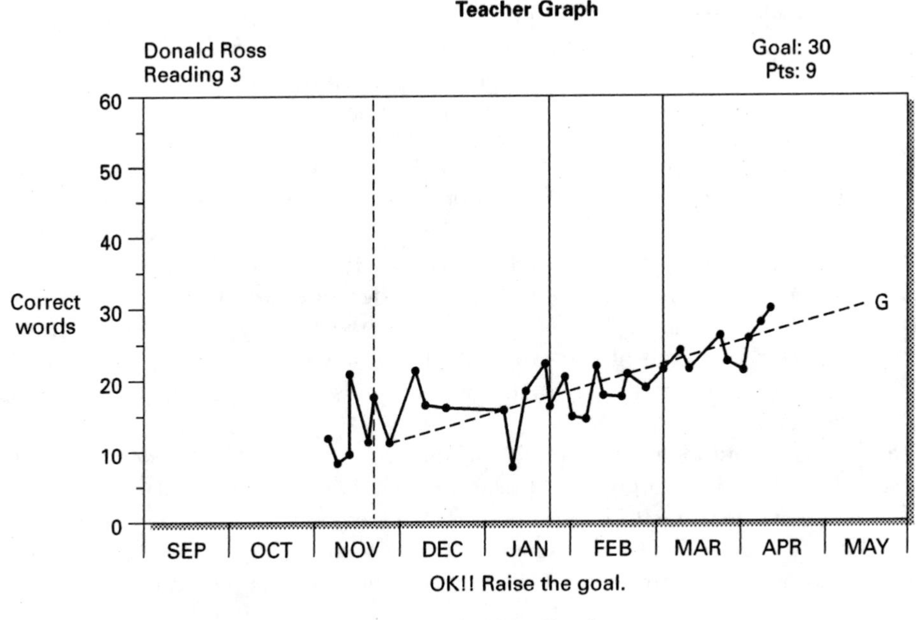

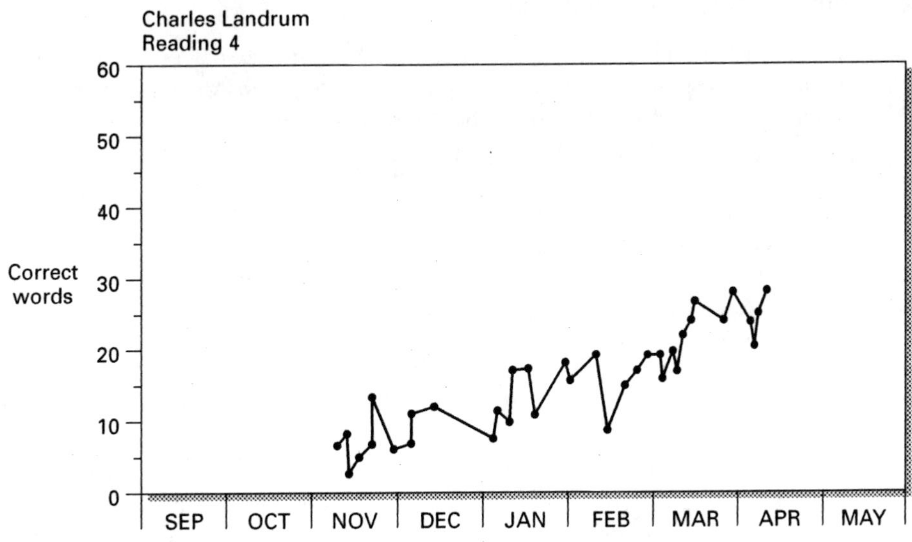

mean that not enough data are available for a decision or that the available data do not suggest any changes; (b) Uh-oh! Make a teaching change; or (c) OK! Raise the goal. The specific prompt depends on the amount of data that has been collected (e.g., Insufficient data . . .) or the match between student performance and the student's goal line. Specific numbers of data points needed to make each type of decision and a simple explanation of the specific decision rules for each type of decision are contained within the program manual.

Obviously, our review of the Fuchs et al. (1990) *Monitoring Basic Skills Progress* program has been very brief. The primary purpose in presenting this information has been as a backdrop for pointing out that the research of these investigators (e.g., Fuchs & Fuchs, 1986) has shown that the simple graphing and inspection of CBM data as described results in student achievement gains. That is, teachers who inspected the graphs of student performance were more likely to have higher levels of student improvement over the course of the study than teachers whose students' performances were not graphed.

Most important, requiring teachers to use standardized decision rules like those in step 4 to guide instruction results in even better outcomes than just allowing teachers to visually inspect student performance data. When teachers are required to either change instructional strategies or raise goals based on computer prompts, student achievement increases (Fuchs et al., 1989).

Placement in Special Programs

Using curriculum-based measurement to assist in the placement of children in special programs is one area where we have some concern. There is little doubt that use of CBM in placement decisions can be an improvement over use of standardized intelligence and achievement data (Salvia & Ysseldyke, 1991). Making eligibility decisions via CBM data may decrease the likelihood that children will be placed in special programs based on assumptions about underlying abilities (e.g., attention span, memory) or personality traits and increase the likelihood that children are placed in programs based on performance data relative to their peers (e.g., Shinn, 1989).

However, we must guard against CBM becoming just another method of classifying children as being learning disabled, slow learners, or mentally disabled. We must be careful that people do not stop the collection of CBM data after children are placed in special programs but continue to monitor progress following the decision to place a child in special education. The goal in making an eligibility decision about a child's qualifications for special education is not to simply place a child in a different program but to provide a greater likelihood that the child will learn. We gain little if we place children in special education but fail to change their instructional programs or monitor their progress.

Chapter Summary

The connection between direct assessment of academic behavior and effective education for children would seem obvious, but alas it has not been so. Although there can be little question that CBA is here to stay, many teachers have little or no exposure or practice with these procedures during their training to become teachers. Most educational measurement texts ignore or gloss over curriculum-based measurement, preferring instead to instruct teachers in the ways to construct good multiple-choice and essay tests. In addition, public education does not have an impressive track record of adopting efficacious procedures in a timely or comprehensive manner (e.g., Bickel & Bickel, 1986; Greer, 1983). We are concerned, therefore, that CBA may be ignored or, perhaps even worse, be used in a manner that perpetuates bad practice.

Attempts to develop curriculum-based academic probes have proven very beneficial and there appears to be multiple applications of these approaches. It has been suggested that although the traditional academic achievement test has many virtues, it does not yield the most appropriate data for learning about a child's short-term progress through the local curriculum series. An alternative perspective was presented in this chapter and data from research on curriculum-based measurement (Deno, 1985) were examined. We believe that in the future a comprehensive academic assessment of a child will include standardized assessment data as well as information that is related to the child's current progress in his or her local curriculum.

Care must be taken so that new procedures are not used to support old, ineffective practices. The data indicating that CBM procedures are more efficient, as reliable and valid, and more cost-effective than traditional measures of academic behavior are encouraging. These data do not suggest, however, that the use of more curriculum-based assessment procedures can be of assistance to a faulty process such as the classification of children. Classification of children into different groups has been a means by which we have attempted to get extra help to some children. CBM should not be used simply as the means to classify, but as a way to increase the potential that a student will be helped and as a way to monitor whether that assistance really does help the student.

Although many questions remain unanswered and problems loom on the horizon, the development of CBM and other curriculum-based assessment strategies offers much to education, teachers, and students. The computer software application described in this chapter has been shown to improve student performance and to provide teachers with accurate assessment of student progress. Teachers and others preparing for careers in education or educational psychology would do well to learn all they can about curriculum-based assessment.

CHAPTER 7

Observation-Based Assessment

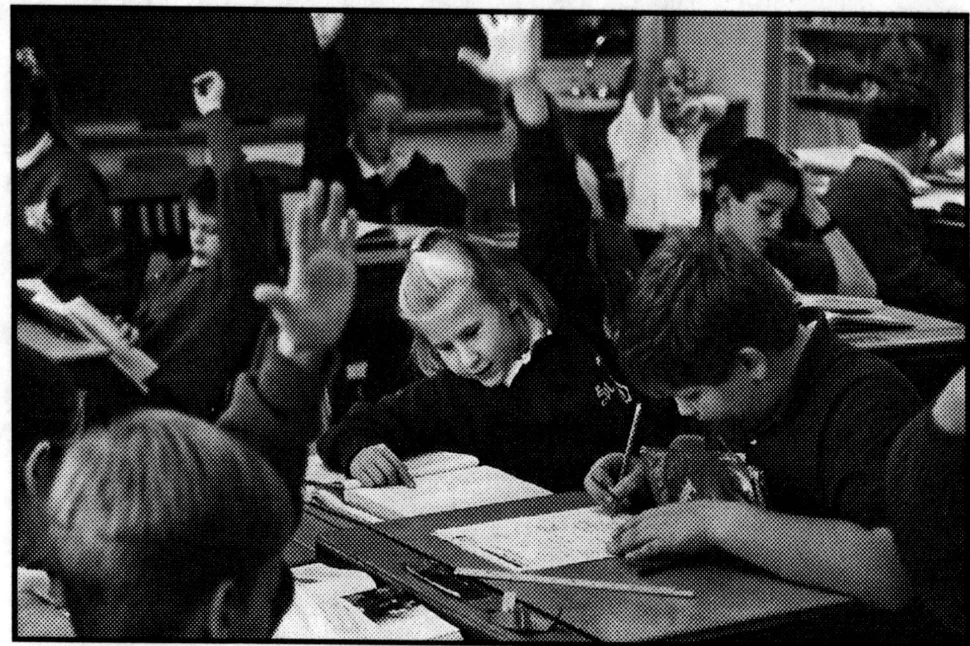

Observation-based assessment (OBA) refers to the systematic recording of observable behaviors of persons in specific situations. Any behavior that can be directly observed can be measured using observational methods. For example, running, jumping, completing math problems, and socially interacting with others represent directly observable behaviors. In contrast, thinking, paying attention, and feeling do not represent directly observable behaviors. Many tests described in this book seek to measure traits and characteristics that are not directly observable. For instance, the intelligence tests described in chapter 12 (e.g., WISC-III, Stanford-Binet, etc.) are designed to measure the trait of intelligence. "Intelligence," however, cannot be directly observed. As such, a child's responses to test items (which are directly observable) are interpreted as indications of the child's "intelligence" (which is not directly observable).

We made a distinction between direct and indirect assessment methods in chapter 1. An additional difference between direct and indirect assessment methods is related to when and where behavior is sampled (Cone & Hawkins, 1977). **Indirect assessment** of behavior (e.g., intelligence tests, perceptual-motor tests, etc.) measures *indications* or *surrogates* of some hypothetical trait or characteristic (intelligence, perception, memory, etc.). Indirect assessment methods can also refer to the measurement of behavior that has already occurred at other times and in other situations. Behavior rating scales and checklists described in chapter 13 represent indirect assessment because these methods rely on a rater's evaluation of behavior that has already occurred.

Direct assessment of behavior refers to the assessment of behavior *at the time and place of its actual occurrence.* Direct assessment differs from a teacher's verbal description or rating of behavior because the teacher's description or rating is based on past performance of behavior in another situation. For example, if a teacher tells you that Frank hit Joe three times, then this represents an indirect assessment of behavior. On the other hand, if you went to the classroom and directly observed Frank hitting Joe three times, then you would have directly observed Frank's hitting behavior.

To summarize, this chapter focuses on the direct assessment of behavior using strategies and techniques that depend on the direct observation of behavior. The key distinction between indirect and direct measurement of behavior emphasized here is whether the behavior is assessed at the time and place of its actual occurrence. Also, behavior assessed using observational methods is not interpreted as an indication of some hypothetical trait or characteristic. Instead, the behavior is interpreted in its own right. Frank hitting Joe would *not* be interpreted as an indication of the trait of aggression. It would be interpreted by the simple description of Frank hitting Joe.

Considerations in Observation-Based Assessment

A number of factors must be considered before using observation-based assessment. These factors include: (a) operational definitions of behavior, (b) the dimension of behavior to be measured, (c) number of behaviors to be assessed, (d) number of observation sessions, and (e) the recording method(s) to be used. Each of these factors is discussed in the following sections.

Operational Definition of Behavior

Most of us use general descriptions of behavior that serve as a type of shorthand in talking about an individual's behavior or behavior patterns. These general descriptions, however, are not particularly useful in communicating with others about children's behavior. Terms such as *learning difficulty, hyperactive,* or *depressed* may mean very different things to different people and as such often create confusion and miscommunication.

An **operational definition** of behavior refers to defining behavior in clear, unambiguous, and explicit terms. These types of definitions are called operational definitions because they specify the operations that will be used in defining a behavior. For instance, an operational definition of the behavior of *noncompliance* might be as follows: *Noncompliance is defined as the student* *not complying with a verbal request or direction from the teacher within five seconds after the request or direction has been given. Examples of verbal requests or directions are being told to sit down, begin work, be quiet, come to the teacher's desk, etc.*

Operational definitions should be *objective, clear,* and *complete* (Kazdin, 1984). Objective means that the definition should refer to observable behaviors and/or environmental events. Operational definitions are clear if they can be read, repeated, and paraphrased by others. Observers should be able to read the definition of behavior and use it to record behavior (Kazdin, 1984). Operational definitions are complete if they specify the boundary conditions for inclusion of behaviors in the definition and delineate behaviors that are not considered part of the definition. Using our definition of noncompliance, the student is considered noncompliant if compliance with any verbal request or direction is not completed within five seconds (inclusionary criteria). However, the student would not be considered noncompliant if the teacher used hand motions or some other nonverbal request or direction (exclusionary criteria).

Dimensions of Behavior

Behavior can be described and measured along four dimensions: (a) frequency, (b) temporality, (c) intensity, and (d) permanent products. The **frequency** of behavior refers to how often a behavior occurs. Examples of behaviors that can be measured along a frequency dimension are the number of correct oral responses to questions, number of temper tantrums in a four-hour period, or number of days absent from school. Frequency measures of behavior are useful if the behavior can be categorized into discrete categories (i.e., Yes, the behavior occurred or No, the behavior did not occur).

Behavior also can vary along a **temporality** dimension. There are two aspects of temporality: *duration* and *latency.* Duration refers to how long a behavior lasts. For example, if the child began homework at 7:00 P.M. and completed homework at 8:00 P.M., the duration of homework behavior would be 60 minutes. Latency describes the amount of time that elapses between an environmental event and a behavior. Using our example of noncompliance, if the teacher instructed the child to sit down (an environmental event) and the child sat down (a behavior) after two minutes, the latency would be two minutes or 120 seconds.

Behaviors can also vary in **intensity.** Intensity refers to the amount of force with which a behavior is performed. Intensity is not as easily measured as frequency or temporality. For example, screaming in class that is heard by a teacher and children five classrooms away has a higher intensity than screaming heard only by teachers and children in adjacent classrooms. Technically, the intensity of screaming in the preceding examples could be objectively measured in decibels, which would reflect differences in the force of the behavior.

Many behaviors leave **permanent products** in the environment. These might be called *behavior by-products.* Examples of permanent products of behavior are number of worksheets completed, number of correct written responses to math problems, number of paper wads in a student's desk, and so forth. You should realize that behavioral by-products are *not* really a measure of behavior, but rather a measurement of the result of behavior. One potential difficulty with using behavioral by-products is determining the person who is responsible for a particular behavior. For example, if graffiti is written on a child's desk, then the teacher must determine which student was responsible for it. As many teachers know, this can be a source of great controversy among teachers and students.

To summarize, using observation-based assessment requires you to decide which behavioral dimension is most relevant to your purpose. These various behavioral dimensions are not unlike the type of evidence used in murder trials to determine guilt or innocence. Admissible evidence in court includes eyewitness testimony ("I saw him shoot the subject with a gun five times"). This describes a frequency dimension. Evidence could also include a duration dimension ("I saw the defendant talking with the subject for five minutes before he shot him"). It might also include a latency dimension ("The defendant stated to the subject that if he did not leave within the next 30 seconds, he would shoot him"). Finally, conviction of guilt in murder trials relies heavily on permanent products of behavior (e.g., a murder weapon, bullets, and a dead body).

Number of Behaviors Assessed

Some children display behavior problems that might be limited to only one or two behaviors. Other children exhibit multiple behavior problems and potentially display an overwhelming number of behaviors that might be observed. An important decision facing the person conducting observation-based assessment is how many behaviors should be observed. This decision is influenced by the nature and severity of the child's behavior problems and the degree of teacher concern with each behavior problem.

It has been our experience in talking with teachers about problem behaviors of children that some teachers will list as many as 5 to 10 behaviors that are problematic in their classrooms. Whereas some children may display 10 or more behavior problems, not all behavior problems are necessarily independent. Some behaviors may be subsets of a larger class of behavior. For example, *noncompliance* represents a class of behaviors that may have a number of behavioral components (e.g., defiance to teachers, cursing, throwing objects, refusing to complete assigned work, etc.).

In deciding the number of behaviors to be observed, it is useful to organize specific behaviors into larger categories for observation purposes. These larger categories containing specific behaviors are known as **response classes** because they describe a "class" or category of behaviors that share some similarities. In our example of noncompliance, we might define this response class by the specific behaviors that make up noncompliance. Thus, cursing, throwing objects, refusing to complete assigned work, and defiance to the teacher would be the behaviors making up the response class of noncompliance.

Some behaviors, however, may be independent from one another and therefore do not belong to the same response class. For instance, a child may exhibit social withdrawal, poor work completion, and temper tantrums. For some children, these behaviors may be unrelated. In these cases, persons conducting observation-based assessment would want to systematically observe all behaviors that may be of concern to teachers. If this is not possible, another strategy would be to have the teacher rank order the behaviors in terms of importance to him or her and the child.

Number of Observation Sessions

Another consideration in using observations is the issue of how many times a child should be observed. The central issue here is the *representativeness* of observations. That is, are the observations collected representative of the child's typical behavior in school? You will recall from chapter 5 that norms for standardized tests should be representative of the children being assessed by tests. In observation-based assessment, the observations you conduct should be representative of the child's behavior. Representativeness of norms for tests is based on groups of children. Representativeness of observations is based on the behavior of a single child.

Observers cannot be present in classrooms every minute of every day. As such, observers must *sample* the behavior of concern to draw valid conclusions from observational data. This sample of behavior must be representative or typical of the child's behavior in the classroom. Some behaviors may be highly atypical or unrepresentative of the child's behavior. This could be due to a variety of factors, such as unusual life events (death in the family, illness, etc.). Other behaviors may occur so infrequently that it might be impossible for an observer to directly assess the behavior.

Recording Method

The type of recording method to be used depends on the dimension of behavior you are interested in measuring. A number of recording methods are designed to assess the four dimensions of frequency, temporality, intensity, and permanent products. The four general categories of recording methods are (a) event-based methods, (b) interval-based methods, (c) time-based methods, and (d) product-based methods.

Event-based recording is designed to measure the frequency of behavior. It refers to the measurement of the number of times a behavior occurs. Event recording is best used with behaviors that are discrete in nature; they have an obvious beginning and end. Behaviors such as number of correct oral responses to questions, number of times a child hits others, or the number of positive comments to others would be examples of behaviors conducive to event recording.

Interval-based methods refer to recording behaviors as occurring or not occurring during specified time intervals. A time unit such as one minute might be divided into six 10-second intervals. The behavior would be observed as occurring or not occurring during each of the six 10-second intervals. For instance, a behavior such as *off-task* might be recorded for one minute. Suppose the student was off-task for three of the six 10-second time intervals. The student's rate of off-task behavior would be 50 percent of the intervals. Interval-based recording methods are best used for behaviors that are continuous and do not have a specific beginning and end.

Time-based recording methods refer to the measurement of the temporal aspects of behavior such as duration, latency, or interresponse times. What is being measured in time-based recording is the temporal aspects of behavior, *not* the number of times a behavior occurs, as in event recording. Remember that duration refers to how long a behavior lasts and is measured in seconds, minutes, or even hours. Latency refers to the *amount of time elapsed* between an environmental event and a behavior and can be measured in time units.

Permanent product recording methods refer to the measurement of actual physical by-products of behavior. Written work, vandalized school property, messy restrooms, and the like are amenable to permanent product recording methods.

Guidelines for Using Recording Methods

The proper use of recording methods requires familiarity with some specific information and rules for measuring behavior. In the following sections, we will present some basic information that should be helpful in using these recording methods.

Event-Based Recording Guidelines

Several guidelines are used in event-based recording, including the behavior or behaviors to be recorded, the number of times the student will be observed, and the length of each recording session. Event recording methods are relatively easy to design. Figure 7.1 shows an example of an event-based recording procedure designed to measure the frequency of inappropriate talking-out behavior in a classroom for one school week. Note that figure 7.1 contains a column for the day of the week, the duration of the observation session, the frequency of the behavior, and the *rate of behavior*. The rate of behavior is simply the frequency of the behavior divided by the amount of time the behavior was observed.

Figure 7.1 Example of a Weekly Event Recording

Name: Joe **Week of:** March 2nd

Observer: Kramer **Teacher:** Jones

Behavioral Definition: Inappropriate talking out which includes verbalizations by the student when teacher or another student is talking.

Day	Observation Time	Frequency	Total	Rate
Monday	8:30–9:00 (30 minutes)	III	3	3/30 = .1
Tuesday	2:00–2:15 (15 minutes)	~~IIII~~	5	5/15 = .33
Wednesday	10:00–11:00 (60 minutes)	II	2	2/60 = .03
Thursday	1:00-1:20 (20 minutes)	~~IIII~~ II	7	7/20 = .35
Friday	9:20–9:45 (25 minutes)	III	3	3/25 = .12
TOTAL			**20**	**20/150 = .13**

$$\text{Rate of Behavior} = \frac{\text{Frequency of Behavior}}{\text{Duration of Session R}} = \frac{F}{D}$$

Rate is a more informative measure of behavior than overall frequency because observation sessions typically vary in terms of time the behavior is observed. To compare the frequency of talking-out behavior from Monday to Friday, only the behavior rates, not the daily frequencies are directly comparable. Teachers can use tally marks or check marks on the blackboard to count the frequency of behavior. This type of event-based recording differs only in that students are able to see a running record of their behavior. Event-based recording used in this way can be conducted on individual students or for the entire class.

An example of using event-based recording for the behavior of an entire classroom would be to define a behavior such as disruptive behavior. If any student in the class exhibited disruptive behavior, a mark would be placed on the board. The total number of marks in a specified period of time would represent the frequency of disruptive behavior for the entire classroom.

A variation of event-based recording that is sometimes useful for teachers is known as a Planned Activity Check (PLACHECK). In using PLACHECK, the teacher defines a behavior such as working quietly. At periodic intervals, the teacher looks and simply counts the number of children engaged in the behavior. For example, if 20 out of 30 children are engaged in the behavior at 10:30 A.M., then about 67 percent of the class would be working quietly. If the teacher uses PLACHECK at 11:00 A.M. and finds that only 10 out of 30 children are working quietly, then only 33 percent of the class would be considered engaging in the behavior. You should realize that PLACHECK is not technically measuring the number of times a behavior occurs, but rather the number of students engaging in that behavior. Figure 7.2 presents a weekly PLACHECK monitoring form for a class of 30 students. Keep in mind the following guidelines when using event-based recording procedures:

1. Only record discrete behaviors; that is, event-based recording should be used only with behaviors that have a discernible beginning and end.
2. Provide a clear and specific operational definition of the behavior to be recorded.
3. Design an event-based recording observation sheet that contains the following information: (a) name of student, (b) behavior to be recorded, (c) operational definition of the behavior, (d) dates and days behavior will be recorded, (e) time and duration of observation sessions, (f) frequency of behaviors, and (g) rate of behaviors. Use figure 7.1 as a guideline.
4. When recording a behavior or behaviors for an entire classroom, decide whether to use tally marks or a PLACHECK method. Use figure 7.2 as a guideline.

Interval-Based Recording Guidelines

Interval-based recording methods involve dividing an observation period into smaller time intervals and recording whether a behavior occurred during that interval. For example, an observation period of 30 minutes might be divided into thirty 1-minute time intervals. The observer would record whether or not the behavior occurred during each of the 1-minute intervals. It is important to remember that the length of the observation interval depends on the frequency of behavior. Thus, behaviors occurring at high frequencies should be measured with *shorter observation intervals,* and behaviors occurring at low frequency should be measured with *longer observation intervals*. The advantage of interval-based recording methods is that the observer does not have to continuously observe and record the behavior. Instead, an observer *samples* the behavior within specified time intervals.

There are four basic types of interval-based recording methods: (a) partial-interval recording, (b) whole-interval recording, (c) point-time sampling, and

Figure 7.2 Example of a PLACHECK Recording Method for a Classroom of 30 Students

Teacher: Smith **Week of:** October 16th

Behavioral Definition: Number of students engaged in academic tasks such as reading, completing written assignments, copying from board, etc.

Time	Monday	Tuesday	Wednesday	Thursday	Friday	Median
9:30	60%	50%	48%	51%	55%	51%
10:15	75%	75%	82%	70%	71%	75%
10:45	62%	72%	70%	69%	75%	70%
11:15	71%	80%	82%	81%	80%	80%

Note: Be sure to count the number of students engaging in the behavior at the time you observe. Divide this number by the total number of students present in class that day and multiply by 100 to calculate the percentage of students engaged in the behavior.

(d) sequential point-time sampling. **Partial-interval recording** involves an observer recording a behavior as occurring if it occurs *at any time* during a specified time interval. For instance, if an observer is recording behavior within 1-minute time intervals and the behavior occurs at any time during the 1-minute interval, then the behavior is recorded as having occurred during that interval. Only one occurrence of a behavior in a specified interval is recorded regardless of how many times the behavior occurred during that interval. If a behavior occurs three or four times during a 1-minute interval, it can only be counted as having occurred *once* during that interval. As such, partial-interval recording may underestimate the frequency of behavior. The purpose of partial-interval recording is to assess whether a behavior occurred during an interval, *not* to assess the overall frequency of the behavior during any particular interval.

Whole-interval recording differs from partial-interval recording in that the behavior must occur *during the entire observation interval.* Using the preceding example, a behavior would have to occur continuously during an entire 1-minute interval to be recorded as occurring. For example, if you are measuring on-task or attending behavior of a student, the student would have to be on-task or attending for the entire 1-minute interval to be considered on-task. Whole-interval recording is more of a duration method than a frequency method in that it is measuring how long a behavior lasts within a specified time interval. Whole-interval recording tends to underestimate the actual durations of behavior.

Point-time sampling refers to recording a behavior as occurring or not occurring at a specific point during an observation interval. Usually an observer records the behavior *at the end of an observation interval.* In the preceding example, a student would be considered on-task only if the behavior was being exhibited at the end (the 60th second) of a 1-minute observation interval. Point-time sampling is less labor intensive for observers because they only have to observe behavior at specific points within observation intervals rather than the entire interval as is the case with partial-interval and whole-interval methods. Point-time sampling is not a particularly accurate method to use with behaviors that are short duration (i.e., the observation method will tend to underestimate occurrences of behavior). In addition, point-time sampling will underestimate the occurrence of behaviors if the observation intervals are too long. Figure 7.3 depicts a general example of an observation sheet that could be used with partial-interval, whole-interval, and point-time sampling recording.

Sequential point-time sampling involves the exact same method as point-time sampling, *except more than one student is observed.* Instead of observing one student at specific points within observation intervals, several students are observed sequentially over observation intervals. Figure 7.4 shows an example of a sequential point-time sampling recording of three students. It is important to remember that students are observed *sequentially* over the entire observation session. That is, Jack is observed first and his behavior is recorded at the end of the first 1-minute observation interval. Next, Joe is observed and his behavior is recorded at the end of the interval. Finally, Steve is observed and his behavior is recorded at the end of that interval. We then go to the next observation interval and observe Jack, Joe, and Steve in the same order and record their behavior. This continues for the entire observation session. The chief advantage of sequential point-time sampling is that we can compare the rates of behavior for different students within the same classroom. Being able to make comparisons among students is sometimes useful information for evaluating students' behavioral improvement and in making referral decisions for special education assessment.

Keep in mind the following guidelines when using interval-based observation methods:

1. Decide which interval-based method to use: partial-interval, whole-interval, point-time sampling, or sequential point-time sampling.
2. The method used will depend, in part, on the frequency of the behavior to be recorded. Point-time and sequential point-time sampling methods tend to underestimate high frequency and/or short duration behaviors. For these types of behaviors, it is probably better to use event-based recording procedures.

Figure 7.3 General Recording Form of Interval-Based Recording

Name: Laura **Date:** Feb. 23rd

Observer: Witt **Teacher:** Smith

Behavioral Definition: Off-task behavior which includes looking away from academic materials, talking to other students, out-of-seat, etc.

Minute	10 sec.	20 sec.	30 sec.	40 sec.	50 sec.	60 sec.	%
1	X	X	X	O	O	O	50
2	O	O	X	X	X	X	67
3	X	X	X	X	X	X	100
4	O	O	X	O	O	X	33
5	X	O	X	X	O	X	67
6	X	O	X	X	O	O	50
7	O	O	X	X	O	X	50
8	X	X	X	X	X	X	100
9	O	O	O	O	O	O	0
10	X	X	O	X	O	X	67

X = Behavior Occurred During Interval
O = Behavior Did Not Occur During Interval

Average % = 58.4%

3. Select the length of the observation interval to be used. Remember that the length of the interval is influenced by the frequency of the behavior. Therefore, high frequency behaviors should have shorter observation intervals (e.g., 10–15 seconds) than low frequency behaviors (e.g., 10–15 minutes).
4. In using sequential point-time sampling, use a criterion to select students for observation. For instance, you might have a teacher nominate the "Best-behaved," "Average-behaved," and "Poorly behaved" students in the classroom. Your observations of the student of concern can be compared with observations of the other three students.

Figure 7.4 Example of Sequential Point-Time Sampling

Students: Joe, Jack and Steve

Observer: Gresham **Observation Time:** 10:00-10:27 A.M.

Behavioral Definition: Disruptive behavior which includes talking out, bothering others, out-of-seat, etc.

X = BEHAVIOR OCCURRED O = BEHAVIOR DID NOT OCCUR

Students	1	2	3	4	5	6	Total
Joe[1]	X	X	O	O	O	X	50%
Jack[1]	O	X	X	O	X	X	67%
Steve[1]	X	O	X	O	O	O	33%
Joe[2]	X	X	X	X	X	X	100%
Jack[2]	O	O	O	O	O	O	0%
Steve[2]	X	X	X	X	X	X	100%
Joe[3]	O	O	O	O	O	O	0%
Jack[3]	X	O	O	O	O	O	17%
Steve[3]	X	X	X	X	X	X	100%

Percent Occurrences:
Joe: 50% Jack: 28% Steve: 78%

Time-Based Recording Guidelines

Time-based recording methods measure the temporal aspects of behavior such as duration and latency. Whereas event- and interval-based recording procedures are measuring the frequency of behavior, time-based methods record either how long a behavior lasts (duration) or elapsed times between environmental events and behaviors (latency).

Duration measures of behavior are obtained by recording the length of time elapsing between the beginning and the end of a behavior. For example, if a student begins talking at 11:00 and finishes talking at 11:05, the duration of the behavior is 5 minutes. Many behaviors are amenable to duration measurement, such as length of time attempting tasks before asking for assistance, length of time sitting in one's seat, and length of time engaged in academic

Figure 7.5 Example of Duration Recording

Name: Frank **Date:** 10/30/92

Observer: Elliott **Situation:** Free time

Behavioral Definition: Temper outbursts defined as yelling, crying, screaming, and/or flapping arms.

Behavior Began	Behavior Ended	Duration
8:45	9:00	15 minutes
9:30	9:35	5 minutes
10:07	10:15	8 minutes
TOTAL		28 minutes

tasks. In using duration recording it is important to clearly record the time the behavior begins and ends. The difference between the beginning and end of a behavior is the behavior's duration. Figure 7.5 depicts an example of a duration recording sheet.

Latency recording involves recording the time elapsing between an environmental event and the initiation of a behavior. Whereas duration recording is measuring how long a behavior occurs, latency is measuring how much time elapses until the beginning of a behavior. Latency recording is appropriate for many types of behaviors in classrooms that involve instructions, directions, or commands (e.g., sit down, clean up your desk, answering questions presented orally, etc.). Figure 7.6 presents an example of a latency recording sheet.

Keep in mind the following guidelines when using time-based recording procedures:

1. Decide what temporal dimension of behavior you wish to measure: duration or latency.
2. If you are interested in how long a behavior lasts, use duration recording.
3. If you are interested in compliance-type behaviors (i.e., compliance with instructions, directions, or commands), use latency recording.
4. Be sure to record the starting time and the ending time for duration or latency recording.

Product-Based Recording Guidelines

Permanent product recording describes the measurement of the by-products of behavior. Unlike event-based, interval-based, or time-based methods, perma-

Figure 7.6 Example of Latency Recording

Name: Steve **Date/Day:** 4/12/Monday

Observer: Gresham **Situation:** Reading group

Behavioral Definition: Compliance with teacher instructions or directions.

Time Instruction Given	Time Behavior Began	Latency
9:00	9:01	60 seconds
9:31	9:33	120 seconds
10:05	10:10	300 seconds
11:14	11:15	60 seconds
12:01	12:10	540 seconds
TOTAL		1080 seconds

Median = 120 seconds

nent products measurement involves the measurement of actual *physical products.* Examples of physical by-products of behavior are worksheets completed, written homework, number of words written correctly, number of math problems solved correctly on written tests, and so forth. Permanent product recording represents an easier means of measurement than other recording procedures and products can be collected and stored for future reference. You should note, however, that permanent products are *traces* or *results* of behavior rather than behaviors themselves.

Reliability in Observation-Based Assessment

Chapter 5 stressed that tests must be reliable to be of practical value in assessment. Recall that reliability refers to the degree to which we obtain the same result when repeatedly measuring the same thing. Reliability is just as important in observation-based assessment as it is in standardized testing.

The central meaning of reliability in observation-based assessment is the degree to which two observers viewing the same behavior at the same time agree with each other. Another term used to refer to reliability in observation-based assessment is **interobserver agreement.** Suppose you and another observer went to a classroom to observe a student's out-of-seat behavior. Using event recording, you observed the behavior as occurring 10 times and the other observer recorded it as occurring 12 times. These observations were obviously less than perfectly reliable. Does this mean you were wrong? Does this mean that the other observer was wrong? Not necessarily. For example, your recording of 10 could be accurate. On the other hand, the other observer's recording of 12 could be accurate.

Methods for Calculating Interobserver Agreement

The method used for calculating estimates of interobserver agreement depend on the type of recording method used. The following methods are recommended for calculating interobserver agreement for event-based, interval-based, and time-based methods. Reliability estimates are not of great concern in permanent product measurement because the actual physical products exist.

Event-Based Agreement

To assess the interobserver agreement of event recording, the following formula may be used: **Smaller Frequency/Larger Frequency** × **100 = % Agreement.** For example, you observed the frequency of out-of-seat behavior as occurring 10 times. Another observer recorded the frequency of the same behavior as occurring 12 times. The percentage agreement is 10/12 × 100 = 83%.

Interval-Based Agreement

Interval-based reliability estimates are computed by comparing the observations of two observers on an interval by interval basis. The number of agreements and the number of disagreements are computed and entered into the following formula: **Number of Agreements/Number of Agreements + Number of Disagreements.** For example, in ten 1-minute observation intervals there were eight agreements and two disagreements. The percentage agreement would be 8/(8 + 2) × 100 = 80%. This formula can be used for partial-interval, whole-interval, point-time sampling, and sequential point-time sampling methods.

Time-Based Agreement

All time-based recording methods use the same basic formula for computing interobserver agreement. This formula involves dividing the shorter recorded time by the longer recorded time and multiplying by 100 to compute percentage of agreement. The basic formula is: **Shorter Recorded Time/Longer Recorded Time** × **100 = % Agreement.** In computing duration agreement estimates, the following formula should be used: **Shorter Duration/Longer Duration** × **100 = % Duration Agreement.** For computing latency agreement, the formula is: Shorter Latency/Longer Latency × 100 = Latency Agreement. To compute interresponse time agreement: **Shorter Interresponse Time/Longer Interresponse Time** × **100 = Interresponse Time Agreement.** Figure 7.7 presents examples of computing interobserver agreement estimates for event-based, interval-based, and time-based recording procedures.

Figure 7.7 Basic Formulas for Calculating Interobserver Agreement

Event-Based Recording

%Agreement = Smaller Number/Larger Number × 100

Example: 15/20 × 100 = 75%

Interval-Based Recording

$$\%\text{Agreement} = \frac{\text{Number of Agreements}}{\text{Number of Agreements} + \text{Number of Disagreements}} \times 100$$

Example: 20/20 + 5 × 100 = 20/25 × 100 = 80%

Time-Based Recording

%Agreement = Shorter Time/Longer Time × 100

Example: 30 seconds/32 seconds × 100 = 93.8%

Focus on Practice

How to Observe Classroom Behavior

Do you believe everything that everyone tells you? If not, then you might want to consider seeing things for yourself. This section describes a simple process for observing behavior in the classroom.

Why observe? First, you *can't* really believe everything that the teacher tells you. Teachers who refer a child tend to overestimate the severity of behavior problems. Second, a behavior, such as talking out, may function very differently depending on context, and only a highly trained specialist can evaluate the function of the behavior. Talking out of context may function to get peer attention and in another context may function as self-stimulation for the student or to gain teacher attention. The intervention you design *must* be different in each of these cases. Third, observation is conducted to assess not only child behavior but also *teacher* behavior or classroom conditions that may be contributing to the child's behavior. If you rely exclusively on teacher's self-report, approximately zero percent of teachers will report their own contributions to the behavior problems.

10 Steps to Conducting Classroom Observations

The conduct of classroom observation involves 10 essential components. Each of these components are described.

1. **Definition(s) of the target behavior(s).** The first step is to define the target behaviors. One good way to decide what is appropriate behavior in the

continued

Focus on Practice—*continued*

classroom is to use the classroom rules posted by the teacher. However, teachers' rules are frequently not well operationalized. Even more frequently, teachers have no rules posted. If that is the case, then you can utilize some standard observational categories. A simple system will consist of the following:

On-task: Eye contact with teacher or task and performing the requested task.
Verbal off-task: Inappropriate verbalization or making sounds with object, mouth, or body.
Motor off-task: Student fully or partially out of assigned seat without teacher permission, or playing with objects.
Passive off-task: Student not engaged with assigned task and passively waiting, sitting, daydreaming, etc.

Occasionally, a student will exhibit unusual behaviors that would not be picked up using a standard coding system. In these cases, you will need to define the behavior yourself. For example, a child with Tourette's disorder who exhibits verbal and motor tics may require a special "tic" category.

2. **Observation of the teacher's interaction with the target student.** Frequently, student behavior is a function of teacher reaction to the behavior. Hence, examining teacher behavior is an essential aspect of any classroom observation. Examples follow:

   Positive teacher attention: Positive comments, smiling, touching, or gesturing directed toward target student.
   Negative teacher attention: Reprimands, negative consequences, or negative gestures directed toward target student.
   Neutral teacher attention: Teacher attends to student but there is neither negative nor positive valence associated with the attention (e.g., teacher looks at student).

3. **Class activity.** The basic activity in which the class is engaged should be noted on the observational form. Some examples follow:

   teacher directed whole class activity
   teacher directed small group activity
   independent seat work
   other

4. **Observation interval.** To structure the observation period, an *interval* observation system is most often used. Hence, if you observe for 20 minutes, the entire observational period would be broken down into many smaller intervals. The lengths of these smaller intervals depends on the type and frequency of the behavior being observed. For example, if you are observing a high-frequency behavior, you would choose a small interval (10 seconds).

Alternatively, if you are observing a low-frequency behavior such as fighting, you would choose a longer interval.

5. **Alternative measures.** Although the interval recording (described above) is useful in most cases, it is occasionally necessary to monitor some behaviors using different methods. The two methods most commonly used as an alternative to interval recording are event and duration systems.

   Event recording allows you to note *every* instance of a behavior. Students who are self-abusive, for example, may strike themselves 20 to 30 times in 30 seconds. An interval system would not accurately convey the intensity of the behavior.

   Duration recording allows one to note how long a behavior occurs. A child who has trouble paying attention, for example, may be on-task and off-task several times during a 30-second interval, but using an interval system would be marked as off-task only once. With duration recording, you simply record the length of time the child is either off-task or on-task.

6. **Observe a peer for comparison.** To determine whether the behavior you observe is a problem, you can compare the target student's behavior with a "normal" peer. To accomplish this, you simply record the behavior of a peer in the classroom using the same system you chose for the target student. You should choose the same-sex peer who has been nominated by the teacher as "normal." This can help you in consulting with the teacher because you can present the data for the target student and the comparison student.

7. **Class scan check.** To characterize the classroom context, it is beneficial to conduct periodic (i.e., every 3–5 minutes) classroom scans. The purpose here is to note relevant features of the classroom environment. In particular, it is important to determine the degree to which other students in the classroom are on-task, following teacher's directions, etc. The scan is an *informal* procedure that will end up later in your notes to help you characterize the classroom. It is informal in that there is no need to precisely quantify the amount of on-task activity. For example, you could provide a rough estimate of the percentage of students who are on-task.

8. **Necessary equipment.** At a minimum, classroom observations require the following equipment:

   Wristwatch—watch with second hand needed to monitor intervals and length of observation sessions.
   Observation form—see figures 7.3 or 7.4, for example.
   Stopwatch—to monitor duration.

9. **Calculation of the data.** It is useful to determine the percentage of time a student is on-task. To accomplish this, you divide the number of on-task intervals by the total number of intervals observed and multiply by 100 as follows:

$$\frac{\text{\# of on-task intervals}}{\text{total intervals observed}} \times 100$$

continued

Focus on Practice—*continued*

10. **Interpretation and report of the data.** To summarize and report the data, you should begin by describing the context of the observation. Here you can report observations from a classroom scan check and you can note ongoing classroom activities during observation (e.g., teacher-directed small-group activity). Next, you can report the percentage of on-task behavior for the target students and tell how this contrasts with the comparison student. The idea is to determine whether the target student exhibited behavior that is markedly different from the norm or from what would be reasonably expected in that particular classroom context.

    What follows is an example of how to report data:

    Kevin was observed for 30 minutes during Mrs. Wickstrom's English class. During the observation session, the class was engaged in teacher-directed large group instruction. In a classroom where students were generally very well behaved, Kevin's behavior was quite noticeable. He was off-task approximately 88% of the time. This off-task behavior consisted of mostly verbal off-task and motor off-task behaviors. That is, he was talking and out of his seat a great deal. By comparison, a peer nominated by Mrs. Wickstrom as being "normal" was only off-task 7% of the time.

For classification of a student as behavior disordered, at least three different observation sessions should be used. The reason for observing on multiple occasions and preferably multiple settings is to increase the validity of your results.

Threats to Interobserver Agreement

There are several threats to the agreement between two observers in using observation-based assessment. Kazdin (1977) discussed three major threats to reliable measurement of behavior: (a) observer drift, (b) observer reactivity, and (c) observer bias.

Observer drift refers to the fact that observers may change the definition of behavior over time. That is, observers may tend to "drift" away from the original definition of the behavior. For example, the original definition of out-of-seat behavior may have specified that if the child's buttocks did not contact the chair, he or she would be considered out of seat. After a period of time, one observer may begin to count as out of seat only those instances when the child stands up, whereas the other observer stays with the original definition. This "drifting" away from the original definition by one observer will obviously have the effect of decreasing the agreement between the two observers.

Observer reactivity describes the fact that observers will tend to be *more reliable* in their observations if they know their agreements are being checked by someone else. In this sense, observers are "reacting" to outside monitoring by improving the accuracy with which they record behavior. This might also suggest that observations are less reliable when interobserver agreements are never checked, which would make assessment data less accurate (Wolery, Bailey, & Sugai, 1988).

Observer bias refers to the effects of expectations or biases that might influence the accuracy of measurement. For example, if observers expect high rates of behavior to occur based on a teacher's verbal description, they may record higher frequencies of the behavior than if they had not talked with the teacher before the observation. Expectation biases can have a substantial influence on the reliability of measurement using observation-based methods (Kazdin, 1977).

Guidelines for Improving Observer Agreement

Several steps can be taken to improve the degree of agreement between observers. Wolery et al. (1988) offer the following guidelines:

1. Define the behavior to be counted in clear, operational terms.
2. Be sure to clearly and specifically describe the procedures to be followed in observing behavior and follow these procedures closely.
3. Practice the observation system *before* conducting the actual observations.
4. Immediately record the observational data. Do not wait until a later time to record the data.
5. Use equipment such as stopwatches, beepers, or videotapes to improve accuracy.
6. Periodically review the observation procedures and definitions of behavior.

Chapter Summary

Observation-based assessment represents a direct form of assessment in which an individual's behavior is measured at the *time* and *place* of its occurrence. Unlike standardized tests and rating scales, observational assessment evaluates ongoing behavior in the situation of interest (e.g., classrooms, playgrounds, etc.). Observational assessment requires an observer to be present in these situations to systematically observe and record behavior.

Several considerations in using observational assessment were discussed. One, it is critical that behaviors being observed are operationally defined. Operational definitions describe the operations involved in measuring behavior in clear and specific terms. Two, the dimensions of behavior to be assessed must be specified. Behavioral dimensions include frequency (how often a behavior occurs), a temporal dimension (duration or latency), an intensity dimension (the force of a behavior), and a permanent product dimension (by-products or effects of behavior). Three, the number of behaviors to be observed is an important consideration. Some behaviors are interrelated and form what is known as a response class. Specific behaviors within a response class can be used to define that response class. Four, the number of observation sessions is an important consideration because one must ensure a representative sample of a student's behavior. Five, the observation recording method used corresponds to the dimension of behavior to be assessed. Event-based and interval-based methods (e.g., partial-interval, whole-interval, and point-time sampling) are used to measure the frequency dimension of behavior. Duration, latency, and interresponse times are used to measure the temporal dimension of behavior. Behavioral by-products or behavioral effects are used to measure the permanent products dimension.

Reliability was described as being as important in observational assessment as it is in test-based assessment. Reliability was defined as the degree to which two observers viewing the same behavior at the same time agree with one another. Various methods for calculating reliability or interobserver agreement were discussed. Different methods were described for event-based, interval-based, and time-based observation methods.

Finally, three threats to obtaining reliable estimates of behavior were discussed. Observer drift referred to the tendency of some observers to change or "drift" from the original operational definition of behavior. Observer reactivity described the effects of observers being monitored for accuracy in their recording of behavior. Observer bias is the effects of expectations or preconceived biases on the reliability of observational data.

Focus on Research

Systematic Screening for Behavior Disorders: Observation Codes

The Systematic Screening for Behavior Disorders (SSBD) (Walker & Severson, 1992) is described in chapter 13 as a useful approach to measuring problem behaviors of students in grades 1 to 6. The SSBD is described as a "multiple-gating" procedure in that it contained a series of progressively more expensive and precise assessments or "gates." The first gate consists of teacher nominations and the second gate consists of teacher ratings of nominated children. The third gate utilizes direct behavioral observations of students' school adjustment.

The third gate uses two measures of school adjustment using direct observations. The first measure is Academic Engaged Time (AET), which measures the amount of time a student is academically engaged during classroom instructional periods. AET is operationally defined as follows (Walker & Severson, 1992): *AET means that the student is appropriately engaged in working on assigned material that is geared to her/his ability and skill levels. While academically engaged, the student is: (a) attending to the material and the task, (b) making the appropriate motor responses, (e.g., writing, computing), (c) asking for assistance (where appropriate) in an acceptable manner, (d) interacting with the teacher or classmates about academic matters, or (e) listening to teacher instructions and directions.* Nonexamples *of AET would include such things as not attending to the assigned task, breaking classroom rules (out of seat, talking out, disturbing others, etc.) or daydreaming.*

AET represents a *duration measure* of behavior in that it assesses the amount of time a student is academically engaged. For example, if a student is observed from 9:00 to 9:15, the observer starts a stopwatch when the student meets the definition of academic engagement and stops the watch when the student is not academically engaged. The total elapsed time at the end of the 15-minute observation period represents the total amount of time the student was academically engaged. This number is converted to a percentage by dividing the elapsed time of academic engagement by the total amount of time observed and multiplying by 100. For example, if the student was academically engaged for 5 out of 15 minutes, the percentage of academic engagement would be 33 percent. Figure 7.8 presents the AET recording form.

The second observation measure in the SSBD is the Peer Social Behavior Code (PSB), which measures the quality, level, and distribution of student's social behavior during free-play settings (e.g., playgrounds). The PSB uses a partial interval recording method in which five categories of behavior are observed and coded: (a) Social Engagement, (b) Participation, (c) Parallel Play, (d) Alone, and (e) No Codeable Response. The PSB intervals are 10 seconds in length and a behavior is recorded if it occurs at any time during the 10-second interval. A total of 6 minutes and 40 seconds of data can be recorded per observation session. Figure 7.9 shows the PSB recording form and figure 7.10 shows the PSB observation summary sheet. Note that the frequency of each behavior is converted to a percentage and averaged over two observation sessions. Two observation sessions are used to ensure a representative sample of behavior.

The following operational definitions are given for each of the PSB codes:

Social Engagement: Refers to an exchange of social signals between two or more children that involve either verbal or nonverbal interaction. Social engagement is coded when the target child is physically oriented toward another child (or children), is exchanging social signals of a reciprocal, purposeful nature with them, and/or produces verbal behavior in some form during the recording interval.

Participation: This is coded when the target child is participating in a game or activity (with two or more children) that has a clearly specified and agreed upon set of rules. Examples would be kickball, four-square, dodgeball, soccer, basketball, tetherball, hopscotch, and so forth. Nonexamples include tag, jump rope, follow the leader, and other unstructured games.

Parallel Play: This is coded when the target child is engaged in some activity within 5 feet of another child, but is not interacting (either verbally or nonverbally) with him or her. Although the activities the children are engaged in may be identical, the target child and other pupil(s) are behaving independently

continued

Figure 7.8 Systematic Screening for Behavior Disorders AET Recording Form

Systematic Screening for Behavior Disorders ACADEMIC ENGAGED TIME (AET) RECORDING FORM*

Student Name ____________________ School ____________________ Grade ____

Teacher Name ____________________ Observer ____________________

Reliability Observer ____

SESSION #1

Date ____________________

Time Start __________ Time Stop __________ Length of Session __________

__________ ÷ __________ = __________ x 100 = __________

Time on Stopwatch | Length of Session | AET | % AET

Convert time to total # of seconds (i.e., minute equals 60 seconds) before computing. Divide time on stopwatch by total time observed.

Classroom Activity During Observation

____

____

SESSION #2

Date ____________________

Time Start __________ Time Stop __________ Length of Session __________

__________ ÷ __________ = __________ x 100 = __________

Time on Stopwatch | Length of Session | AET | % AET

Convert time to total # of seconds (i.e., minute equals 60 seconds) before computing. Divide time on stopwatch by total time observed.

Classroom Activity During Observation

____

____

Total Time Engaged for Sessions 1 & 2 = __________ seconds = __________ Total AET

Total Time Observed for Sessions 1 & 2 = __________ seconds

Average Percent AET for Sessions 1 & 2 = Total AET _____ x 100 = __________ Percent AET

Figure 7.9 SSBD Recording Form for Peer Social Behavior

Systematic Screening for Behavior Disorders PEER SOCIAL BEHAVIOR RECORDING FORM*

Student Name ____________________ Teacher Name ____________________

School ________________________ Grade ______ Observer ______________

Reliability Observer ____________________ Date _________ Time Start _____

Time Stop ______ Length of Session __________________

Interval Number	+ - SE	+ - P	✓ PLP	✓ A	• ✓ N
0-1					
2					
3					
4					
5					
6					
7					
8					
9					
10					
11					
12					
13					
14					
15					
16					
17					
18					
19					
20					

Interval Number	+ - SE	+ - P	✓ PLP	✓ A	• ✓ N
21					
22					
23					
24					
25					
26					
27					
28					
29					
30					
31					
32					
33					
34					
35					
36					
37					
38					
39					
40					

continued

Focus on Research—*continued*

Figure 7.10 SSBD Peer Social Behavior Observation Summary Sheet

Systematic Screening for Behavior Disorders
PEER SOCIAL BEHAVIOR
OBSERVATION SUMMARY SHEET*

Student Name ______________________

School ______________________ Grade ________

Dates Observed ______________ and ______________
Session #1 Session #2

	Number of Intervals*	Observation #1**	Number of Intervals*	Observation #2**	Average of 1 and 2
1. Social Engagement (SE)	____	____%	____	____%	____%
2. Participation (P)	____	____%	____	____%	____%
3. Parallel Play (PLP)	____	____%	____	____%	____%
4. Alone (A)	____	____%	____	____%	____%
5. No Codeable Response (N)	____	____%	____	____%	____%
6. Social Interaction (SI)	____	____%	____	____%	____%
7. Negative Interaction (NI)	____	____%	____	____%	____%
8. Positive Interaction (PI)	____	____%	____	____%	____%
9. Total Positive Behavior	____	____%	____	____%	____%
10. Total Negative Behavior	____	____%	____	____%	____%

* Enter the number of intervals recorded for each category.

** Enter the percentage of time spent for each category by dividing the total number of intervals that you observed during the observation session into the intervals recorded under different categories and multiplying by 100.

of each other. Examples of parallel play would include playing in a sandbox next to another child, running in a group, or sitting on a swing set with one or more students. A child engaged in self-talk (i.e., verbal behavior not directed toward anyone else) would be coded parallel play if the child met the other conditions of the Parallel Play category. Note: The target child need not be engaged in an activity similar to that of the children around him or her. For example, the child may be climbing a fence near (within 5 feet of) a sandbox where others are playing.

Alone: This is coded when the target child is not within 5 feet of another child, is neither socially involved nor socially engaged, and is not participating in a game or structured activity with other children. Examples would include sitting, standing, shooting baskets, kicking balls off walls, and so forth. A child engaged in self-talk (i.e., verbal behavior not directed toward anyone else) would be coded Alone if the child met the other conditions of the Alone category.

No Codeable Response: This is recorded when the target child's playground behavior cannot be accurately coded in one of the above five categories, e.g., the child is out of view or talking to an adult during recess. This category is coded only if there is no codeable behavior for an entire interval.

Comment on the SSBD Observation Measures

To the author's knowledge, the SSBD, AET, and PSB observation measures represent the only well-standardized measures of behavior using observation-based assessment. Unlike the observation-based assessment measures described in this chapter, the SSBD observation measures can be compared with a representative sample of students. The SSBD measures were standardized on more than 1,200 students in six states representing the northeastern, midwestern, southern, and western regions of the United States. Percentile and T scores are available for the AET and PSB categories. The SSBD Technical Manual presents extensive evidence for the reliability and validity of the SSBD observational measures.

CHAPTER 8

Performance-Based Assessment

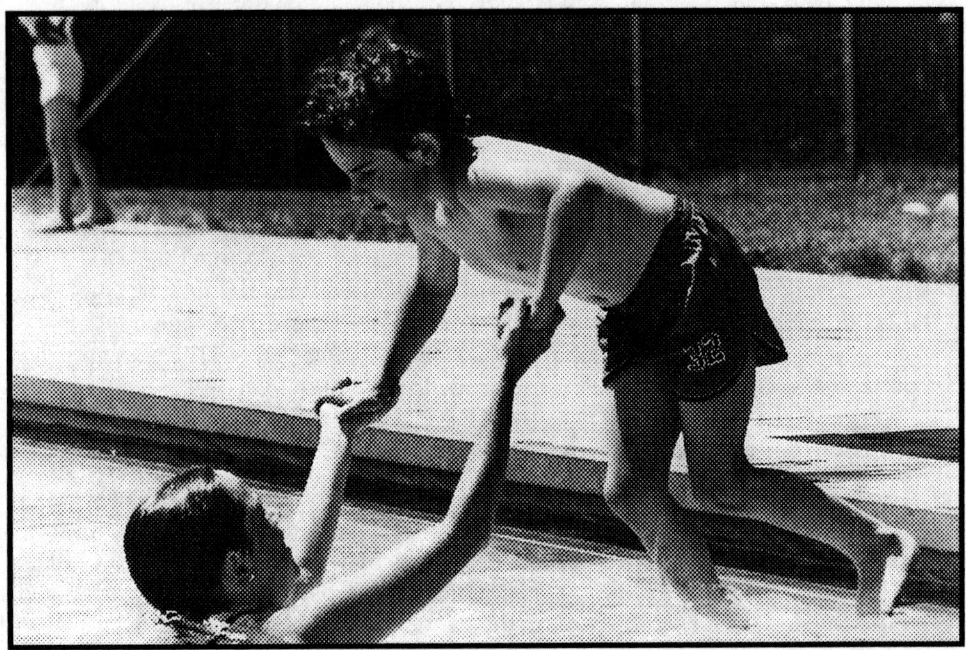

Recall watching the summer Olympics on television, in particular, the diving competitions. Try to visualize one of your favorite competitors *performing* a dive. Remember what the diver did: She slowly walked to the end of the board or platform, stood still for a few seconds to compose herself and visualize the dive she was about to do, and then she launched into the dive, twisting and turning through the air, and finally entering into the water with almost no splash. The crowd applauded, the diver swam to the side of the pool, and then the camera focused on a group of expert judges who each, in a matter of seconds, provided a score for the dive. In most cases, the judges' scores were nearly identical. This is an amazing result given that the dive took less than 3 seconds from beginning to end and the dive itself was a complicated series of physical maneuvers.

The description of the Olympic diving competition, although different from a typical classroom activity, serves as a useful illustration of many of the important features of a performance assessment. First, the diver, like a learner in a classroom, must *demonstrate* she can apply her knowledge and skills *by actually doing or creating something* (e.g., a backward double somersault) that is valued and purposeful. Second, the diver's performance is *observed* by judges, or in the case of a classroom, a teacher. Third, these judges use preestablished *criteria to score* the diver's performance, which in turn, provides the diver with feedback. These criteria are based on a set of *performance standards* developed by experts in diving and increase the likelihood that the judges' scores will be consistent or reliable. Finally, the scores are used to determine how well the diver did in comparison to other divers who competed in the same competition.

Our diving example was devised to highlight essential features of any formal performance assessments. In the remainder of this chapter, we examine performance assessment and compare it with other assessment methods we have introduced in earlier chapters. We envision performance assessment as an important supplement to other types of assessment. Therefore, after clarifying terms commonly used to describe performance assessments, we provide two classroom examples of such assessments and several additional examples of scoring criteria or rubrics. We discuss scoring criteria for mathematics and written communication to highlight key development and usage issues. Finally, we examine potential advantages and disadvantages of performance assessments based on research and our experiences so that you can make informed decisions about using it to supplement other types of assessments.

Definitions and Core Concepts

Performance assessment is defined as "testing methods that require students to create an answer or product that demonstrates their knowledge or skills" and can take many forms, including conducting experiments, writing an extended essay, or doing mathematical computations (U.S. Office of Technology Assessment [OTA], 1992). Performance assessment is best understood as a continuum of assessment formats ranging from the simplest student-constructed responses to comprehensive demonstrations or collections of work over time. Whatever format, common features of performance assessments involve (a) students' construction rather than selection of a response, (b) direct observation of student behavior on tasks resembling those commonly required for functioning in the world outside school, (c) illumination of students' learning and thinking processes along with their answers, and (d) the use of predetermined scoring criteria to score the student's performance and provide him or her feedback.

Coutinho and Malouf (1992) noted in their seminal article on performance assessment of students with disabilities that writers have used a variety of terms (e.g., authentic, portfolio, alternative) to refer to assessment methods featuring student-generated responses. The term *performance* emphasizes a *student's active generation of a response* and highlights the fact that the response is observable, either directly or indirectly via a permanent product, whereas the term *authentic* (which perhaps is used as often as is performance) refers to the nature of the *task* and *context* in which an assessment occurs. The authenticity dimension of assessment has become a very salient issue for at least two reasons. First, most educators assume the more realistic or authentic a task is, the more interesting it is to students. Thus, students' motivation to engage in and perform a task is perceived to be much higher than on tasks where they have trouble seeing the relevance to real-world problems or issues. Second, for educators espousing a competence-based or an outcomes-oriented approach to education, it is important to focus assessments on complex sets of skills and conditions that are like those to which they wish to generalize their educational efforts. *Portfolio* assessment is an approach to documenting individuals' skills and competencies by assembling previously completed work samples and other permanent products (e.g., classroom tests, standardized tests, videotaped presentations, pictures of projects, audiotapes of reading, etc.) produced by the individuals. In many cases, products resulting from performance assessments are collected in portfolios.

The term *performance* is consistently used by most authors discussing statewide, on-demand assessments where students must produce a detailed response; the term *authentic* is used more often by educators to describe teacher-constructed or teacher-managed classroom assessment tasks that students must perform. We prefer to use performance assessment rather than authentic assessment; however, any serious discussion of educational assessment must consider the key dimensions implicit to both terms.

Figure 8.1 highlights the performance and authenticity dimensions of the emerging conceptualization of educational assessment tasks (Elliott, 1994). It also indicates that a common third dimension of a valid assessment task is that the content assessed represents the content taught. Collectively, figure 8.1 synthesizes three key dimensions that educators want to manipulate in their assessments of students' achievement: *student response, nature of the task,* and *relevance to instruction.* As indicated in the figure, assessment tasks can be characterized as varying in the degree to which they are *performance in nature* (e.g., low performance: filling in a bubble sheet or selecting the best answer by circling a letter; high performance: writing and presenting a report of research or conducting a scientific experiment in a lab), *authentic* (e.g., low authenticity: reading isolated nonsense words or writing a list of teacher-generated spelling words; high authenticity: reading a newspaper article or the directions for installing a phone answering system or writing a letter to a friend using words that are important to the student), and *aligned with curriculum outcomes* (e.g., low alignment: facts and concepts are taught, but application is assessed; high alignment: application of facts and concepts are taught and assessed). Many educators are searching for assessments that are relatively high on all three dimensions. That is, they want highly authentic or real-world tasks that clearly are connected to their instructional curriculum and require students to produce, rather than select, a response. Conceptually, such tasks would lie within the HIGH circle in figure 8.1.

Performance assessment of students' achievement is not entirely new to many educators. For example, educators in the areas of physical education,

Figure 8.1 The Relationship Among Performance, Authenticity, and the Classroom Curriculum in an Assessment Task

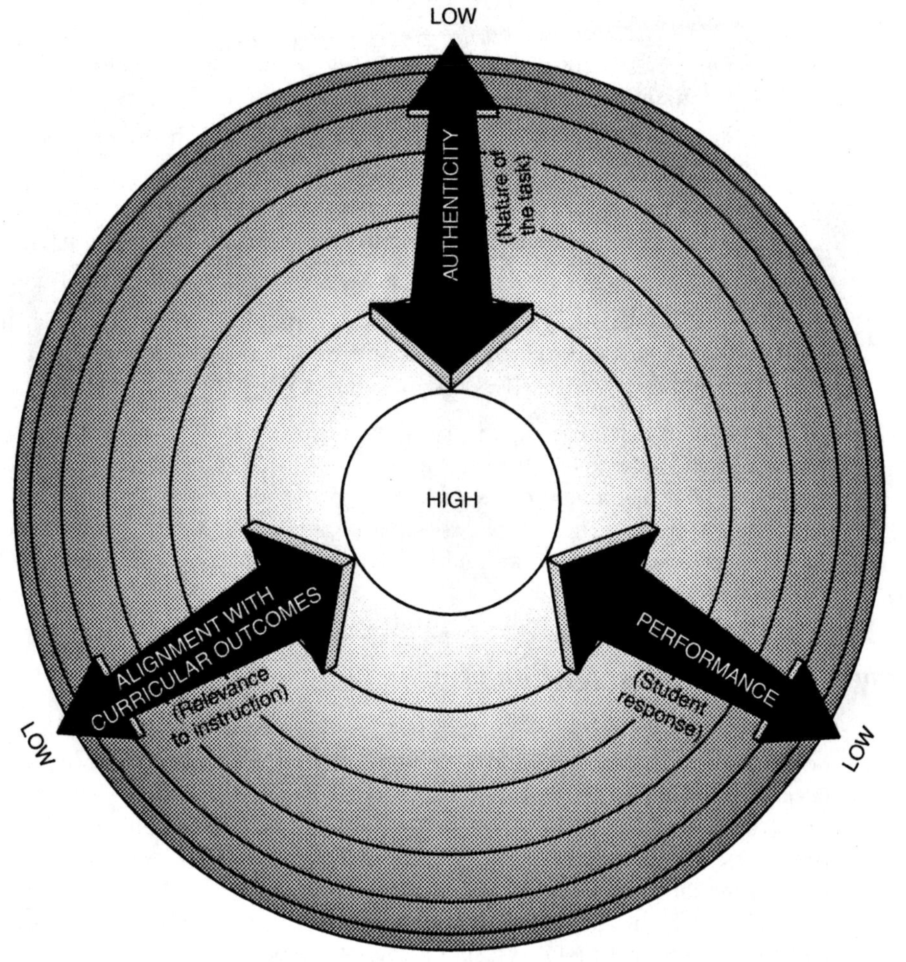

art, music, and vocational and technological arts all use, to a large extent, students' products or performances to determine whether the learning objectives of a class have been met. What is new is (a) the use of this form of assessment in the "core" curricular areas of math, science, language arts, and social studies, (b) the use of scoring criteria or rubrics to influence and interpret performances, and (c) the encouragement of students to conduct self-assessments. Thus, many educators already use some "weak" forms of performance assessment; that is, they (a) ask students to apply their knowledge and skills by producing a product and (b) provide students feedback about their performances in the form of grades. Besides these two traditional elements of performance assessment, the new, instructionally "stronger" forms of performance assessment take steps to influence students' performances by doing the following:

1. Selecting assessment tasks that are clearly aligned or connected to what has been taught
2. Sharing the scoring criteria for the assessment task with students prior to working on the task
3. Providing students clear statements of standards and/or several models of acceptable and exemplary performances prior to their attempting a task
4. Encouraging students to complete self-assessments of their performances
5. Interpreting students' performances by comparing them with consensus standards that are developmentally appropriate, as well as possibly comparing them with other students' performances.

As conceptualized here, the stronger forms of performance assessment interact in visible ways with instruction that precedes *and* follows an assessment task. This approach to assessment emphasizes the point that the central purposes of most educational assessments are to facilitate communication among key educational stakeholders—teachers, students, and parents—and to guide instruction!

Why Performance Assessment?

Assessment of students' academic functioning is a fundamental part of educational decision making and has become one of the focal issues of educational reform in the 1990s. Leading educators and consumers want assessment methods to cover content indicative of "important" educational outcomes, cause students to use higher-order thinking skills, apply their knowledge, and inform teaching (Linn, 1993; Stiggins, 1992; Wolf, LeMahieu, & Eresh, 1992). Many educators are dissatisfied with existing standardized multiple-choice or true-false tests because they believe they place too much emphasis on facts and basic concepts while downplaying the application of knowledge and skills. Policymakers and many educators also want assessments to be nonbiased and accessible to all learners. Thus, we have challenging agendas for excellence, equity, and accountability in the assessment of students' knowledge and skills.

Some educators (e.g., Archbald & Newmann, 1988; Wiggins, 1993) have promoted performance assessment as offering a flexible, authentic method of assessing learning and educational outcomes while enhancing the development of clearer academic standards for all learners. Many advocates of performance assessment hope that authentic/performance assessments will be *reactive* and influence instructional activities in the classroom. That is, they believe if teachers use assessments that require students to produce something that is valued in the real world, something that is meaningful, then teachers will be more likely to adjust their curriculum to focus on real-world outcomes that are highly valued. Many state-level performance assessment projects currently underway seem to be counting on the fact that their assessment instruments (and scoring criteria) will be reactive. This issue of reactivity in assessment is not new, at least not to those familiar with behavioral assessment and the behavior change research (Kazdin, 1974). In most assessment situations, assessors work hard to reduce or eliminate reactivity effects on the person being assessed. In the case of performance assessment, however, advocates are hoping that consumers (teachers and parents) of assessment results will react—that is, they will change their expectations about assessment outcomes and scoring criteria, which in turn will lead to improved student learning. In many ways with performance assessments, teachers are being encouraged to "teach to their tests" by aligning their curriculum and instruction with their assessments.

From a classroom-based perspective, performance assessments would appear to allow more flexibility in the administration of tasks and offer an increased number of pathways for a learner to demonstrate command of knowledge and skills required to accomplish a task. From an empirical perspective, a paucity of evidence exists concerning the functioning of a wide range of students on performance assessments, whether the tasks are part of an on-demand large-scale assessment program or at the classroom level. Given that at least 40 states in the United States currently are involved in the use or development of some form of statewide, on-demand performance assessment instruments (Thurlow, 1994), it seems that information about the use of performance assessments with all students is needed to guide the actions of educators who want to improve assessment and education. Not everyone is enthusiastic about the potential of performance assessments to impact instruction and provide for quality assessments of students' learning. Several measurement experts (e.g., Mehrens, 1992; Stiggins, 1991) have recommended that we proceed with the use of performance assessment with great caution because of the limited reliability and validity evidence.

Examples of Classroom Performance Assessments and Guidelines for Use

During the past several years, numerous books and manuals have been published that provide examples of performance assessment materials and guidelines for developing these assessments (e.g., Blum & Arter, 1996; Herman, Aschbacher, & Winters, 1992). There are not published sets or kits of performance assessment tasks at this time, nor should there be. The power of alternative assessments, like performance assessment, lies in their ability to be constructed by teachers or other professionals so they are aligned with instruction and provide information to learners and teachers about the learners' accomplishment of important competencies or outcomes. In effect, performance assessments are a method or means for collecting information about and judging the proficiency of students' learning. Thus, the pieces of a good performance assessment should include the following: an authentic task; a set of objective scoring criteria that can be used to describe the performance and/or products resulting from the performance; a set of performance standards that provide information about the overall quality of the performance and products; and an opportunity to work on and complete the task under conditions that are as realistic as possible. To illustrate these components, let's first turn to a performance assessment that one of us designed with a fourth-grade teacher to evaluate students' spelling competencies. After that, we examine an oral presentation scoring guide that has been used to assess the speaking skills of students in grade 2 through graduate school.

Performance Spelling

Performance spelling was designed to increase students' use of spelling words to communicate and to advance their writing skills (Elliott & Bischoff-Werner, 1995). This approach to spelling is individualized to each student, encourages active parent involvement in selecting words and studying, has public scoring criteria that all students know and use, and has a scoring and progress monitoring system that students manage. This system has been used by many elementary and early middle school teachers and requires each student to select 5 target words and their teacher to select 5 target words for a total of 10 words per week (Olson, 1995). The selected words (actually the number of which is arbitrary) should be words the student is interested in using in written communications with others and for school work assignments. Students study these words from Friday, over the weekend if they wish, until the next Thursday, when they are tested by writing each spelling word and a sentence correctly using the word. All students have a copy of the scoring requirements for this weekly test; these requirements focus on four areas of spelling and writing (see figure 8.2).

As indicated in figure 8.2, students' spelling tests focus on accuracy, usage, punctuation, and legibility of writing. Each of these areas of functioning has a set of prespecified scoring criteria, and in turn, the scoring criteria are used to establish performance standards. For example, with regard to the area of usage, students are required to compose a sentence using the target word appropriately. Usage is evaluated using a 3-point scale, where a 0 = not used or used incorrectly, a 1 = acceptable basic use, and a 2 = elaborative use (i.e., enriched vocabulary and language use, adjectives, etc.). After each of 10 sentences are scored, an overall usage score can be determined and characterized via the following performance standards: Exemplary = 90–100%, Satisfactory = 50–89%, and Inadequate = 0–49%. A similar logic, although varying in criteria and scales, is used to score the students' accuracy, punctuation, and legibility areas.

Figure 8.2 Performance Spelling Scoring Criteria and Standards

SPELLING: SCORING CRITERIA AND STANDARDS

Accuracy	(0-1)	0 = incorrect spelling 1 = correct spelling
Exemplary 90-100%, Satisfactory 70-89%, Inadequate 0-69%		
Usage	(0-2)	0 = not used or used incorrectly 1 = acceptable basic use 2 = elaborative use (enriched vocabulary and language use, adjectives, etc.) Example: ate (0) He had ate books. (1) My dog ate his food. (2) She ate the delicious meal her father prepared.
Exemplary 90-100%, Satisfactory 50-89%, Inadequate 0-49%		
Punctuation	(0-3)	0 = no beginning capital letter or ending mark 1 = either beginning OR ending 2 = both beginning and ending 3 = both, plus additional punctuation (quotation marks, commas, etc.)
Exemplary 90-100%, Satisfactory 67-89%, Inadequate 0-66%		
Legibility	(0-2)	0 = generally illegible (majority) 1 = acceptable 2 = cursive, no trace overs
Exemplary 90-100%, Satisfactory 50-89%, Inadequate 0-49%		

Students use a progress-monitoring graph to record their own scores for each week in each of the four areas (see figure 8.3). Over the course of a year, students progress from writing 10 separate sentences to writing a paragraph with the 5 words they picked and another paragraph with the 5 words selected by the teacher. Eventually, students are required to use all 10 words in a thematically focused paragraph. These paragraphs are still scored using the accuracy, usage, punctuation, and legibility criteria. Olson (1995) reported that students at all skill levels could successfully participate in performance spelling and when compared with students in other spelling programs (such as basal series), those in the performance spelling program, on average, actually (a) spelled more words and more difficult words and (b) wrote much more on a weekly basis. Teachers familiar with the performance spelling approach see it as more than a weekly spelling test, rather they commonly characterize it as a language arts program and opportunities for students to apply their knowledge of spelling and English grammar.

Figure 8.3 Performance Spelling Progress Graph

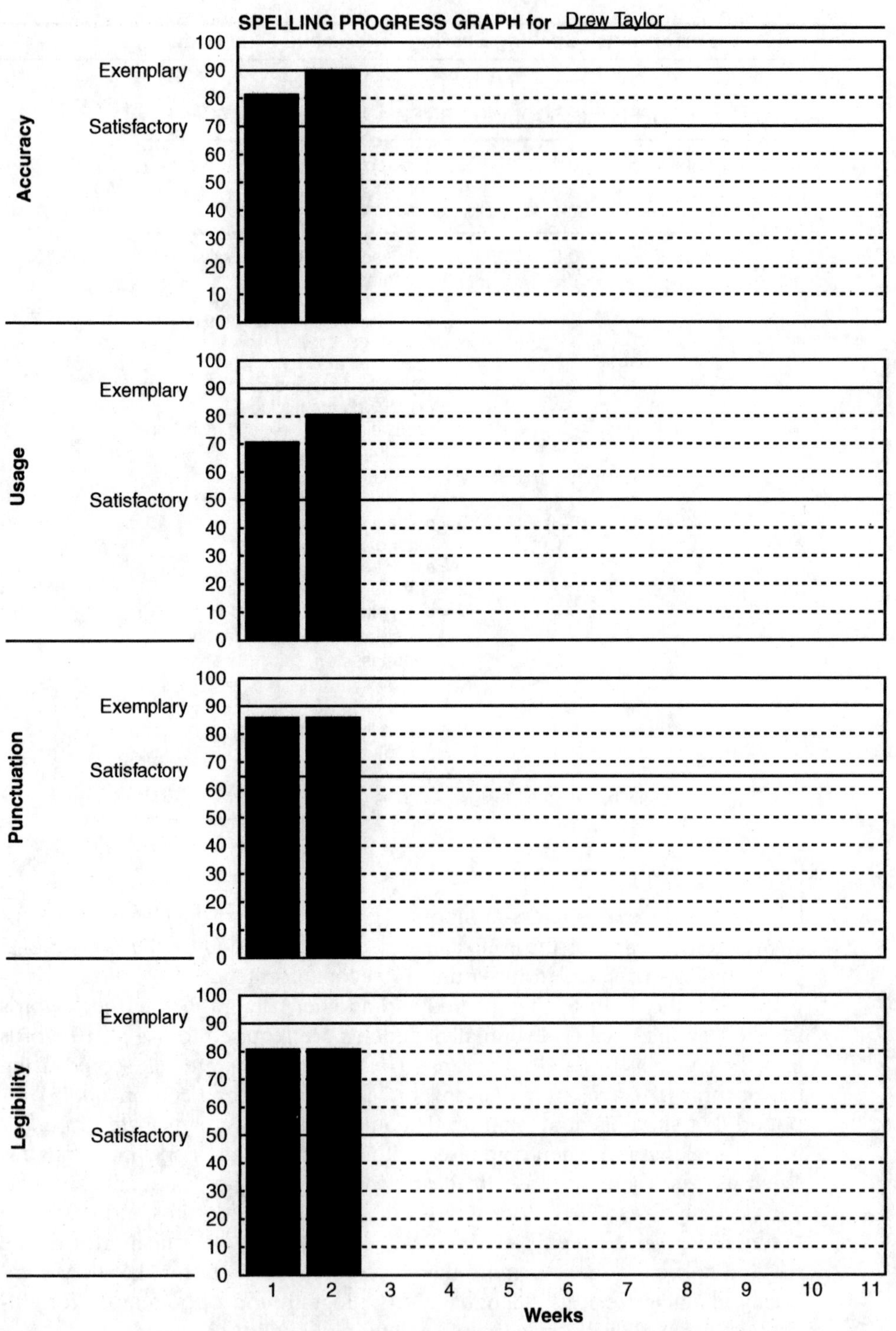

This example of performance spelling highlights several important characteristics of strong performance assessments. First, they are connected to the curriculum and are authentic with regard to the work they require students to create. Second, preestablished scoring criteria are available and understood by students prior to participating in the task. The scoring criteria in this example represent an *analytic approach* to scoring, whereby a skill area is broken down into subcomponents. Third, the scoring criteria can be used to build performance standards that communicate to students their level of proficiency in a skill or content area. Finally, teachers can use the results of the test to plan the next week's instructional focus for students, and students can monitor their own progress within specific skill areas over time.

Let's next examine another example of a performance assessment and focus on the development of scoring criteria. Good scoring criteria are critical to successfully scoring and communicating with students about their work.

Oral Classroom Presentation

Oral presentations or speaking skills are part of many learning activities and projects in classrooms grades 1 through 12, and yet there are no formal tests of oral presenting skills. What you say in a presentation is always important, and in some classes, *how* you say it is also highly valued. How would you evaluate an oral presentation? What behaviors or skills make an excellent presentation?

The first step in developing a performance assessment is to have a clear instructional purpose and vision of the desired outcome(s) of the assessment. Once you have this picture or model of an excellent performance or product, you need to identify the subcomponents or subparts of the outcome and describe them in objective terms so they can be observed by two or more people. Some typical aspects of a good presenter include speaking clearly and at an appropriate rate, making eye contact with the audience, understanding the topic, answering questions, and presenting information in an organized manner. These typical aspects can be more generally characterized as physical expression, vocal expression, verbal expression, and knowledge of the subject matter. In addition, some teachers place importance on time management skills and the use of materials to support an oral presentation.

Assuming you agree that these are reasonable characteristics or dimensions of an oral presentation, how would you develop scoring criteria that are objective and meaningful to students? In figure 8.4 we have listed each of these major components of an oral presentation along with various subcomponents that could be directly observed while a student did his or her presentation. Do you agree that these six components and the related subcomponents could be used to directly observe and describe a student if he or she were given an opportunity to do a brief presentation in front of a class? If not, how would you modify these descriptions so they could be used as scoring criteria?

Figure 8.4 Oral Presentation Scoring Criteria

ORAL PRESENTATION SCORING CRITERIA

Each of the behaviors or skills listed below will be evaluated using a 4-point scale where 4 = Mastered, 3 = Competent, 2 = Minimally Acceptable, and 1 = Poor. These ratings will be the basis for a written summary of your presentation.

I. Physical Expression
- _____ A. Maintained eye contact with audience
- _____ B. Positioned so everyone can see you and materials on board/screen

II. Vocal Expression
- _____ A. Spoke in a steady, clear voice
- _____ B. Spoke loudly to be heard by entire audience
- _____ C. Paced words and varies tone to emphasize points

III. Verbal Expression
- _____ A. Used precise words to convey meaning
- _____ B. Avoided unnecessary repetition
- _____ C. Organized information logically
- _____ D. Summarized main points at conclusion
- _____ E. Answered questions directly

IV. Knowledge of Subject Matter
- _____ A. Presented and used facts accurately
- _____ B. Integrated information meaningfully
- _____ C. Demonstrated understanding of the problem or topic
- _____ D. Explained the conclusions or results clearly
- _____ E. Critically evaluated study

V. Time Management
- _____ A. Materials and setting organized
- _____ B. Used time well

VI. Support Materials
- _____ A. Used materials to support major points
- _____ B. Provided materials that supplemented presentation

Notes: ____

____

Once a set of knowledge or behavioral components are determined for a given performance task, the teacher or evaluator must decide on which dimension(s) to evaluate each component. Most human behaviors can be characterized along dimensions of *frequency* (e.g., never-sometimes-very often-almost always-always) and *quality* (e.g., poor-fair-good-excellent). (See table 8.1 for examples of some additional dimensions that educators commonly use to characterize gradations in students' performances or work products.)

Table 8.1 Quantitative and Qualitative Dimensions Commonly Used to Characterize Students' Performances or Products

Frequency (Never-Sometimes-Very Often-Almost Always-Always)
Quality (Poor-Fair-Good-Excellent)
Development (Not Present-Emerging-Developing-Accomplished-Exceeding)
Usage (Unused-Inappropriate Use-Appropriate Use-Exceptional Use)
Amount (None-Partially-All)
Percentage (0%–25%–50%–75%–100%)
Accuracy (Totally Incorrect-Partially Correct-Totally Correct)
Effort (Not Attempted-Minimal Effort-Acceptable Effort-Outstanding Effort)

In the case of an oral presentation, we often have used a combination of frequency and quality to provide students comprehensive feedback about their performances. Consequently, we have used four levels of proficiency (e.g., 1 = poor, 2 = minimally acceptable, 3 = competent, and 4 = mastered) to indicate overall performances for each skill. Figure 8.5 illustrates the use of this oral presentation scoring criteria and the narrative feedback summary that was provided to a student about his oral presentation.

This example of a performance assessment of an oral presentation illustrates several key aspects about the development and use of scoring criteria. First, it is possible to break a task down into many specific behaviors or characteristics. There is a point, however, that the list of behaviors or characteristics becomes too long and cumbersome to use. Teachers rarely have the time to observe a large number of performance criteria for each student. Detailed performance criteria are useful only when the observer has the time to carry out focused observations of a single student and when each criterion is essential for successfully completing a larger task. Thus, for classroom performance assessments to be manageable and meaningful, a balance must be established between specificity and practicality of the scoring criteria. The key to accomplishing this balance is an ongoing process whereby the criteria are evaluated and refined to ensure only the essential criteria are used. This usually results in a shorter, more clearly defined set of criteria. Figure 8.6 represents a shortened version of the oral presentation criteria, which was modified after the original version was used a couple of times.

General Guidelines for Developing Performance Criteria

Scoring criteria are perhaps the most instructionally relevant aspects of a performance assessment because teachers can use them to signal important skills and competencies to students *prior to* their work and use them to *communicate feedback* to them once they have completed their work. Thus

Figure 8.5 Examples of Completed Oral Presentation Rating Scale with Narrative Feedback Summary

ORAL PRESENTATION SCORING CRITERIA

Each of the behaviors or skills listed below will be evaluated using a 4-point scale where 4 = Mastered, 3 = Competent, 2 = Minimally Acceptable, and 1 = Poor. These ratings will be the basis for a written summary of your presentation.

I. Physical Expression
- 4 A. Maintained eye contact with audience
- 4 B. Positioned so everyone can see you and materials on board/screen

II. Vocal Expression
- 4 A. Spoke in a steady, clear voice
- 4 B. Spoke loudly to be heard by entire audience
- 4 C. Paced words and varies tone to emphasize points

III. Verbal Expression
- 4 A. Used precise words to convey meaning
- 4 B. Avoided unnecessary repetition
- 3 C. Organized information logically
- 2 D. Summarized main points at conclusion
- 4 E. Answered questions directly

IV. Knowledge of Subject Matter
- 4 A. Presented and used facts accurately
- 3 B. Integrated information meaningfully
- 4 C. Demonstrated understanding of the problem or topic
- 4 D. Explained the conclusions or results clearly
- NA E. Critically evaluated study

V. Time Management
- 4 A. Materials and setting organized
- 1 B. Used time well

VI. Support Materials
- 4 A. Used materials to support major points
- 4 B. Provided materials that supplemented presentation

Notes: 65/72 pts. = "Competent" with room for improvement. Please see summary.

based on the spelling and oral presentation examples of performance assessments, it is possible to offer the following guidelines for writing performance criteria:

1. Identify the steps or features of the task to be assessed by (a) observing others do the task or by imagining yourself completing it and/or (b) inspecting an excellent example of a finished product.
2. List the important criteria that you would ideally use to judge the performance or product.

Figure 8.5 ***continued***

PRESENTATION FEEDBACK

Presenter: Joe
Date: February 27, 1997
Topic: The Relationship Between Observations and Ratings
Time limit: 15 minutes

Comments
I enjoyed listening to your presentation on Tuesday -- you were well organized and clearly understood the thesis you presented. The attached rating scale documents my analysis of your presentation according to six categories. You will note that you achieved top ratings for 14 of 19 skills (no rating for "Critically evaluated study" because it was not appropriate for this presentation). The two skill areas where I believe you could improve the most are: Used time well and Summarized main points at conclusion. I realize time constraints played some role in limiting what you could say, but you spent too much time on the Method and too little time on the Results and Discussion, and because you ran out of time, you could not provide a good summary of the main points. Perhaps the entire issue here is the limited time you had, however, you knew the time constraints well in advance of the presentation. You spoke quite clearly, used your support materials very well, and provided a clear context for understanding the study.

Recommendations
1. Provide a handout or overhead with a graphic or flowchart documenting the Method. The details of the Method are not as important as the Results, so feature Results information and let the audience question you about how you got them.

2. Consider starting with an orienting question that engages the audience, for example "What is the relationship between direct observations and ratings of a child's behavior?" or "How can we increase the agreement between observations and ratings of students' behavior?"

3. Monitor your own time throughout the presentation so you are not surprised to learn you have only 5 minutes left.

4. Provide a handout with a concise summary of your Results and Conclusion. (By the way, I know you had a handout, but I did not get one. Please provide me a copy at your convenience.)

OVERALL SCORE = 65/72 (92%) Grade = AB Rater: S.N. Elliott

3. Keep the number of performance criteria small enough so they can be observed and judged in a reasonable time period.
4. Express the criteria in terms of observable student behavior or product characteristics. Avoid vague and ambiguous terms such as "correctly" or "appropriately."
5. Arrange the criteria in the order in which they are likely to be observed, to facilitate recording and communication.
6. Select dimensions on which each criterion will be rated. Consider dimensions such as frequency, amount, quality, or accuracy and develop descriptions for three to five anchor points.

Figure 8.6 Shortened Version of the Oral Presentation Rating Scale

ORAL PRESENTATION SCORING CRITERIA

Each of the behaviors or skills listed below will be evaluated using a 4-point scale where 4 = Mastered, 3 = Competent, 2 = Minimally Acceptable, and 1 = Poor. These ratings will be the basis for a written summary of your presentation.

I. Physical Expression
   ____ A. Maintained eye contact with audience

II. Vocal Expression
   ____ A. Spoke loudly to be heard by entire audience
   ____ B. Paced words and varies tone to emphasize points

III. Verbal Expression
   ____ A. Used precise words to convey meaning
   ____ B. Organized information logically
   ____ C. Summarized main points at conclusion

IV. Knowledge of Subject Matter
   ____ A. Presented and used facts accurately
   ____ B. Integrated information meaningfully
   ____ C. Demonstrated understanding of the problem or topic
   ____ D. Explained the conclusion or results clearly

V. Time Management
   ____ A. Used time well

VI. Support Materials
   ____ A. Used materials to support major points
   ____ B. Provided materials that supplemented presentation

Notes: ____

____

With this background on writing scoring criteria, or **rubrics** as many teachers call them, let's examine scoring criteria that have been used in statewide or schoolwide assessments of students' knowledge and skills. Examples like those we discuss next often serve as useful models for individuals; instead of starting from scratch in designing a rubric for written communications, mathematics, or science, consider the advantages and disadvantages of each of the following scoring criteria.

Written communication example

Figure 8.7 provides an example of an evolving analytic rubric for scoring students' written products. As you can see, it covers five characteristics of writing (i.e., organization, sentence structure, usage, mechanics, and format) and uses a 5-point quality scale ranging from a score of 1 (generally poor quality

Figure 8.7 Analytic Scoring Criteria for a Written Communication

Criteria for Analytical Scoring

	1	2	3	4	5
Organization	Little or nothing is written. The essay is disorganized, incoherent, and poorly developed. The essay does not stay on the topic.		The essay is not complete. It lacks an introduction, well-developed body or conclusion. The coherence and sequence are attempted, but not adequate.		The essay is well-organized. It contains an introductory supporting and concluding paragraph. The essay is coherent, ordered logically, and fully developed.
Sent. Str.	The student writes frequent run-ons or fragments.		The student makes occasional errors in sentence structure. Little variety in sentence length or structure exists.		The sentences are complete and varied in length and structure.
Usage	The student makes frequent errors in word choice and agreement.		The student makes occasional errors in word choice or agreement.		The usage is correct. Word choice is appropriate.
Mechanics	The student makes frequent errors in spelling, punctuation, and capitalization.		The student makes an occasional error in mechanics.		The spelling, capitalization, and punctuation are correct.
Format	The format is sloppy. There are no margins or indentations. Handwriting is inconsistent.		The handwriting, margins, and indentations have occasional inconsistencies—no title or inappropriate title.		The format is correct. The title is appropriate. The handwriting, margins, and indentations are consistent.

Source: Adams County School District #12. 11285 Highline Dr., Northglenn. Colo. 80203

work) to a score of 5 (generally high quality work). Descriptions are used to "anchor" rating points 1, 3, and 5. Raters are encouraged to compare a student's work on each dimension with the description that best characterizes the work, and thus assign a rating from a 1 to a 5 for each dimension. Descriptive anchors have yet to be developed for points 2 and 4. As this type of scoring rubric is used, a teacher typically could select a couple of examples of students' work that represent various levels of performance such as "poor" (should have ratings of 1 on all five dimensions), "acceptable" (should have ratings of 3 or 4 on all five dimensions), and "outstanding" (should have ratings of 5 on all five dimensions). These papers serve as models or anchor papers that other raters could use to practice scoring and to "calibrate" their scoring to increase the likelihood for agreement among raters.

Mathematics scoring rubric

Mathematics has been the subject matter most frequently talked about by educators interested in performance assessments. This is probably the result of the NCTM (National Council of Teachers of Mathematics) *Curriculum and*

Evaluation Standards (1989) and the importance given to mathematics in recent educational policy reforms at the national and state levels. Consequently, many educators have developed scoring rubrics; not surprisingly, there are some very different formats for organizing these rubrics or scoring guides (see figures 8.8 and 8.9). The scoring guide in figure 8.8 is organized around four fundamental competencies: understanding a problem; use of mathematical procedures; mathematical problem solving; and communicating mathematically. The definitions of each of these four competency areas provides a scorer with information concerning the general evidence that is necessary to make a decision about the extent to which the competence is exhibited. A scorer must review a student's work and rate each area using a 5-point scale with descriptive anchors for points 1, 3, and 5. For example, with regard to the Understanding the Problem competence area, a scorer would look for evidence in a student's work that shows he or she has made connections between the problem situation, the relevant (but not irrelevant) information provided, and a logical response. If the student's answer lacks these connections or is inconsistent or unrelated to the problem/question, then a scorer should rate it a 1. If the student's response indicates he or she was able to extract the essence of the problem but was unable to solve it correctly, then a scorer should rate it a 3. Finally, when the student's response shows that he or she used all the relevant information and connected this information to mathematical concepts to generate a viable solution to the problem, a scorer should rate it a 5. With the rubric in figure 8.8, it appears that ratings of 2 or 4 are used to characterize responses that are not complete but show some understanding of a portion of the problem.

The mathematical scoring guide illustrated in figure 8.8 could be used for a wide range of mathematical problems. It represents an *analytical* set of scoring criteria that emphasizes relative ratings with some diagnostic value. This type of scoring criteria can be used quite efficiently to score many products and provides a general communication framework that focuses on four important areas of mathematical functioning.

The scoring rubric in figure 8.9 looks very different from that in figure 8.8, yet upon close inspection you will find similar criteria that call for evidence of understanding the problem (e.g., "shows understanding of underlying mathematical concepts, procedures, and structures" and "examines and satisfies all essential conditions of the problem"), uses mathematical procedures (e.g., "appropriately applies mathematics to the situation"), uses problem-solving strategies (e.g., "solution and work is efficient and shows . . . reflection and checking of work"), and communicates mathematically (e.g., ". . . unambiguous and insightful explanation" and "presents strong supporting arguments with examples . . ."). The rating scale and descriptive anchors represent a hierarchy of proficiency ranging from a 0 for "no attempt" to a 4 for "exemplary response."

The mathematics scoring rubric exhibited in figure 8.9 characterizes a *holistic* approach to scoring and has been used in statewide or district-level

Figure 8.8 Analytic Scoring Criteria for Mathematics

Student Name________________________________ **Date**____________________

UNDERSTANDING THE PROBLEM: Scoring Guide

Understanding the problem includes the ability to interpret the problem and select appropriate information to apply a strategy for solution. Evidence of understanding the problem is communicated through making connections between the problem situation, relevant information, and logical/reasonable responses.

5 **FULL CONCEPTUAL UNDERSTANDING:** The student used all relevant information, connected to mathematical concepts with appropriate models or symbols, to solve the problem.

4

3 **PARTIAL CONCEPTUAL UNDERSTANDING:** The student was able to extract the "essence" of the mathematics in the problem but was unable to use this information to solve the problem.

2

1 **LACK OF CONCEPTUAL UNDERSTANDING:** The student's answer was inconsistent or unrelated to the problem/question.

MATHEMATICAL PROCEDURES: Scoring Guide

Mathematical procedures deals with the student's ability to demonstrate appropriate use of mathematics. Evidence of procedural knowledge is provided in the mathematics the student chooses to use and their ability to select and apply the appropriate procedures correctly.

Mathematical procedures includes the various numerical algorithms in mathematics that have been created as tools to meet specific needs in an efficient manner. It encompasses the abilities to read and produce graphs and tables, execute geometric constructions, perform noncomputational skills such as rounding and ordering, verify and justify the correctness of a procedure using concrete models or symbolic methods, and extend or modify procedures to deal with factors inherent in the problem setting.

5 **FULL USE OF MATHEMATICAL PROCEDURES:** The student used mathematical principles efficiently while justifying the solution.

4

3 **PARTIAL USE OF MATHEMATICAL PROCEDURES:** The student was not precise in using mathematical terms, principles, or procedures.

2

1 **LACKS USE OF MATHEMATICAL PROCEDURES:** The student used unsuitable methods, imprecise language, or senseless manipulation of data in his/her attempted solution.

Figure 8.8 ***continued***

PROBLEM SOLVING STRATEGIES: Scoring Guide

Problem solving requires the use of many skills which are often used in certain combinations before the problem is solved. A combination or sequence of skills used in working toward the solution is referred to here as a strategy. Strong student responses should demonstrate the ability to use problem-solving skills/strategies and demonstrate good reasoning that lead to a successful resolution of a problem.

5 **EVIDENCE OF THOROUGH/INSIGHTFUL USE OF SKILLS/STRATEGIES:** The skills and strategies used show some evidence of insightful thinking to explore the problem.

4

3 **EVIDENCE OF ROUTINE OR PARTIAL USE OF SKILLS/STRATEGIES:** The skills and strategies used did have some focus but clarity was limited.

2

1 **LIMITED EVIDENCE OF SKILLS/STRATEGIES:** The skills and strategies used lacked a central focus and the details were sketchy or not present.

MATHEMATICAL COMMUNICATION: Scoring Guide

Effective communication is essential to learning and knowing mathematics. Mathematical communication is demonstrated by the use of symbols and terms which attach specific, and sometimes different, meaning to common words. In assessing the student's ability to communicate mathematically, particular attention should be paid to both the meanings they attach to the concepts and procedures of mathematics and also their fluency in explaining, understanding, and evaluating the ideas expressed in mathematics.

5 **CLEAR, COMPLETE COMMUNICATION:** The student gave a completed response with clear, coherent, unambiguous, and elegant explanations.

4

3 **PARTIAL OR INCOMPLETE COMMUNICATION:** The student completed the problem but the explanation was unclear, inconsistent or not complete.

2

1 **LIMITED OR LACK OF COMMUNICATION:** The student's explanation was not understandable or not present.

Comments ______________________________

____

____

Rater ______________________________

Figure 8.9 Holistic Scoring Rubric for Mathematics

Mathematics Scoring Rubric

4 **Exemplary Response**
- 4.1 Complete in every way with clear, coherent, unambiguous and insightful explanation
- 4.2 Shows understanding of underlying mathematical concepts, procedures, and structures
- 4.3 Examines and satisfies all essential conditions of the problem
- 4.4 Presents strong supporting arguments with examples and counterexamples as appropriate
- 4.5 Solution and work is efficient and shows evidence of reflection and checking of work
- 4.6 Appropriately applies mathematics to the situation

3 **Competent Response**
- 3.1 Gives a fairly complete response with reasonably clear explanations
- 3.2 Shows understanding of underlying mathematical concepts, procedures, and structures
- 3.3 Examines and satisfies most essential conditions of the problem
- 3.4 Presents adequate supporting arguments with examples and counterexamples as appropriate
- 3.5 Solution and work show some evidence of reflection and checking of work
- 3.6 Appropriately applies mathematics to the solution

2 **Minimal Response**
- 2.1 Gives response, but explanations may be unclear or lack detail
- 2.2 Exhibits minor flaws in underlying mathematical concepts, procedures, and structures
- 2.3 Examines and satisfies some essential conditions of the problem
- 2.4 Draws some accurate conclusions, but reasoning may be faulty or incomplete
- 2.5 Shows little evidence of reflection and checking of work
- 2.6 Some attempt to apply mathematics to the situation

1 **Inadequate Response**
- 1.1 Response is incomplete and explanation is insufficient or not understandable
- 1.2 Exhibits major flaws in underlying mathematical concepts, procedures, and structures
- 1.3 Fails to address essential conditions of the problem
- 1.4 Uses faulty reasoning and draws incorrect conclusions
- 1.5 Shows no evidence of reflection and checking of work
- 1.6 Fails to apply mathematics to the situation

0 **No Attempt**
- 0.1 Provides irrelevant or no response
- 0.2 Copies part of the problem but does not attempt a solution
- 0.3 Illegible response

performance assessments to provide a summary of a student's work on a series of problems. The scoring and interpretation framework illustrated here is consistent with a standards-based accountability approach where students' work is compared with a general descriptive performance standard. For this scoring rubric or the one in figure 8.8 to be very effective as instructional feedback, samples of work that are representative of each performance level (i.e., exemplary, competent, minimal, etc.) would most likely need to be provided to effectively communicate with students the ways their work could be improved.

Which approach to scoring is better, analytic or holistic? It depends! That is, in keeping with what we have stated in earlier chapters, it depends on the *purpose of the assessment.* The pattern of results from an analytic scale provides useful feedback about the relative strengths and weaknesses of an individual student and possibly about the instructional program. However, despite the fact that one of the qualities of a good analytic scale is that each dimension be distinct, the subscales or dimensions assessed are often highly interrelated. Under such circumstances, the diagnostic value of subscale performance is diminished. Holistic scoring is usually faster than analytic scoring. When the purpose of the assessment is to primarily provide information for program accountability and for identifying students who may be at risk of not achieving fundamentals, holistic scoring is often preferred.

An emerging approach in the performance assessment scoring arena is the concurrent use of holistic and analytic scoring criteria. This takes more time, of course, since the approach first involves scoring all students' work holistically, then rescoring—using an analytic scoring guide—the tasks of those students who did poorly. The dual goals of program accountability and diagnostic feedback to students who are having learning difficulties is served well by this combined holistic-analytic approach.

Scoring, Interpreting, and Reporting Results

Stiggins (1994) asserted that there are three critical issues in developing scoring criteria: (a) the level of detail needed in assessment results, (b) the manner in which results will be recorded, and (c) who will do the observing and evaluating. We have already examined some aspects concerning the level-of-detail issue via the discussion of analytic versus holistic scoring approaches. As previously noted, both approaches require explicit performance criteria. Your choice of scoring approach should be decided by how you plan to use the results. If you need a rather precise detailed account of functioning, you would develop an analytic set of scoring guidelines. Conversely, if you are interested in a general picture of functioning, then a holistic approach will serve your purpose. Although there is no consensus on this, Stiggins recommends that when a holistic score is needed "it is best obtained by summing analytical scores, by simply adding them together. Or, if your vision of . . . academic success suggests that some analytical scales are more important than others, they can be assigned a higher weight (by multiplying by a weighting factor) before summing" (p. 196). It may also be acceptable to add a rating scale that reflects an "overall impression" to a set of analytical score scales, if the user can define how the whole is equal to more than the sum of the individual parts of performance.

With regard to recording of results from performance assessments, we have emphasized the use of *rating scales* that characterize performances or products on a continuum of frequency or quality. This approach allows scorers to record their observation of a skill or dimension and at the same time indicate their judgment of the quality of it. A simpler, but often less informative, approach to recording results is the use of a *checklist*. As the name indicates, scorers are simply required to check whether a skill or dimension of a performance or product was observed. To illustrate the difference in a checklist and rating scale approach to recording, look back at the oral presentation scoring criteria illustrated in figure 8.4. This set of criteria could be used as a simple checklist or, when the 4-point scale of proficiency is applied, as a rating scale recording method. The checklist version of the criteria would be quicker to complete, but some qualitative information would be missing. For example, even in a poor oral presentation a speaker might make eye contact with the audience when he or she is first introduced and when finished. Thus, using a checklist approach, the criterion of "Maintained eye contact with the audience" would most likely get checked as observed. But if the rating scale were applied, it probably would get scored a 2 to indicate a "minimally acceptable" level of the skill.

A final approach to recording performance assessment results is to use an anecdotal record. This involves writing some detailed descriptions of a student's performance or the product he or she produced. This allows for richer portraits of the student's achievement but requires more time. The use of anecdotal records is a good adjunct method to either checklists or rating scales and should be encouraged when the purpose of the assessment is primarily to provide students feedback about an important set of skills that soon will be "exercised" again in learning activities. Anecdotal records are particularly helpful during the early stages in the development of a performance assessment task. By examining their notes, scorers often discover important skills or dimensions of functioning that should become part of a more formalized set of criteria with rating scales.

The interpretation of any performance or product involves *subjective judgments*. Professional judgments guide every aspect of the design and development of any assessment, and performance assessments in particular. For years, many experts in the assessment community have looked at performance assessments with skepticism because of the potential impact of scorer subjectivity. The possibility of bias or inaccurate scores has rendered this approach to assessment too risky or unreliable for some users. Recently, however, assessment experts and educators have realized that carefully trained performance assessment users can use this method effectively. (Interestingly, behavioral psychologists have used observation-based assessment methods for decades and have demonstrated high levels of interrater and intrarater reliability and validity for an array of observation systems—see chapter 7, "Observation-Based Assessment," for more information.) In many cases where educators are interested in collecting evidence on complex achievement outcomes, assessors have few or no choices but to use performance assessments. Therefore, it is very important that users work to make performance assessments as objective as possible by doing the following:

1. Clearly stating the purpose for an assessment
2. Being explicit about the assessment target and the key elements of a sound performance
3. Describing the key elements as scoring criteria
4. Sharing the scoring criteria with students in terms they understand
5. Practicing to use the criteria and then monitoring their consistent use of the criteria with actual student products or performances
6. Double-checking (using other raters) to ensure bias does not enter into the assessment process.

The Use of Multiple Scorers and Student Self-Assessment

The last point in the preceding list, about the use of other raters to monitor scoring for bias or inaccurate judgments, is very important and is a practice that most educators probably do not routinely do and often openly resist. With explicit scoring criteria that have been preestablished, in many cases, and the assessment of permanent products (e.g., written reports, mathematical solutions to story problems, audio and videotapes of performances, etc.), it is convenient to invite others (i.e., teachers, parents, and students themselves) to score an assessment. In the performance spelling approach discussed earlier in this chapter, all the students' weekly spelling tests were scored first by parent volunteers and then double-checked by the students themselves. Few discrepancies in scores were ever reported, thus the scoring criteria were deemed highly objective and could be used with high reliability. In addition to the "psychometric" confidence gained from having others score an assessment, the learner appears to benefit from scoring his or her own work. First, more students seem to internalize or understand the characteristics of good work, as defined by their teacher, if they are involved in discussing performance criteria and in scoring. Second, students gain a more personal sense of their strengths and weaknesses, especially when analytic scoring criteria are used. Finally, getting students to be responsible for evaluating their own work with established scoring criteria provides them the opportunity to review and reflect on their work—something that does not routinely happen in busy classrooms or in the homes of many students.

In conclusion, many teachers are finding that by using the scoring criteria (they produced with the express purpose of scoring students' work) as part of their preinstruction expectations about good work, they are effectively improving their instruction and aligning their curricular activities with their assessments. They are also having more conversations with students about what it means to produce good work. Thus, explicit scoring criteria developed for performance assessments have, in many cases, stimulated CIA (i.e., curriculum-instruction-assessment) connections in classrooms.

Comparison of Performance Assessment with Other Assessment Methods

The potential for using performance assessment to evaluate students' classroom learning is perhaps better understood by comparing it with other forms of classroom assessments. Table 8.2 provides direct comparisons of four assessment methods (objective test, essay test, oral questions, and performance assessments) on eight characteristics.

In this summary table, performance assessment is characterized as criterion-referenced, focusing on both process and products in an answer, scored by multiple raters possibly including the student himself or herself, often individualized, and often involves a range of modes of responding (e.g., pencil-and-paper, videotape, group reports, graphic materials). The characteristics of performance assessment that are considered an advantage in the daily classroom-based assessment of a student may be a disadvantage when it comes to classifying a student for possible inclusion in a special program. Thus, a thorough understanding of the qualities of the various assessment methods is needed when considering the purpose of any assessment activity. Clearly, in some situations, especially those situations requiring a norm-referenced interpretation and interval scales of measurement, traditional assessments may fit the needs of an assessor better than performance assessments. In others, especially those with a priori competence criteria and requiring low-inference analyses of the application of knowledge and skills by professional judges, performance assessment may be better suited.

Several educators have noted that performance assessment shares some common attributes with curriculum-based assessment (CBA) (Elliott & Fuchs, 1997; Shapiro & Elliott, in press). CBA and performance assessment are similar but complementary assessment methods. That is, both CBA and performance assessment are concerned about the alignment between what is taught in a curriculum and what gets assessed; however, CBA focuses on *mastery of discrete skills in core content* areas whereas performance assessment focuses on *application of skills to complex, authentic tasks that often require integration of knowledge and skills from several areas.* Shapiro and Elliott (in press) have suggested that CBA and performance assessments are feasible and desirable alternatives to more traditional, norm-referenced methods of academic assessment. Indeed, CBA and performance assessments can collectively provide a means for preplacement evaluation, determine accuracy of student placement within curriculum material, assist in the development of strategies for academic

Table 8.2 Comparison of Various Types of Assessment

	Objective Test	*Essay Test*	*Oral Question*	*Performance Assessment*
Purpose	Sample knowledge with maximum efficiency and reliability	Assess thinking skills and/or mastery of a structure of knowledge	Assess knowledge during instruction	Assess ability to translate knowledge and understanding into action
Typical Exercise	Test items: Multiple-choice True/false Fill-in Matching	Writing task	Open-ended question	Written prompt or natural event framing the kind of performance required
Student's Response	Read, evaluate, select	Organize, compose	Oral answer	Plan, construct, and deliver original response
Scoring	Count correct answers	Judge understanding	Determine correctness of answer	Check attributes present, rate proficiency demonstrated, or describe performance via anecdote
Major Advantage	Efficiency—can administer many items per unit of testing time	Can measure complex cognitive outcomes	Joins assessment and instruction	Provides rich evidence of performance skills
Potential Sources of Inaccurate Assessment	Poorly written items, overemphasis on recall of facts, poor test-taking skills, failure to sample content representatively	Poorly written exercises, writing skill confounded with knowledge of content, poor scoring procedures	Poor questions, students' lack of willingness to respond, too few questions	Poor exercises, too few samples of performance, vague criteria, poor rating procedures, poor test conditions

Influence on Learning	Overemphasis on recall encourages memorization; can encourage thinking skills if properly constructed	Encourages thinking and development of writing skills	Stimulates participation in instruction, provides teacher immediate feedback on effectiveness of teaching	Emphasizes use or available skill and knowledge in relevant problem contexts
Keys to Success	Clear test blueprint or specifications that match instruction, skill in item writing, time to write items	Carefully prepared writing exercises, preparation of model answers, time to read and score	Clear questions, representative sample of questions to each student, adequate time provided for student response	Carefully prepared performance exercises; clear performance expectations; careful, thoughtful rating; time to rate performance

From: R. J. Stiggins, "Design and Development of Performance Assessments." EDUCATIONAL MEASUREMENT: ISSUES AND PRACTICE, 1987 6,3, p. 35.

problem remediation, provide a means for setting Individualized Education Plan (IEP) short- and long-term goals, provide a method for monitoring student progress and performance across time, provide an empirical method for determining intervention effectiveness, provide a potential strategy for screening, and offer accountability for teachers and psychologists in making eligibility decisions. These methods appear to be highly acceptable to school personnel (Elliott & Kratochwill, 1996), and CBA measures have shown increasing use by school psychologists over the past decade (Shapiro & Eckert, 1993).

It is important to emphasize, however, that CBA and performance assessments provide a methodology for different purposes than published norm-referenced tests and thus are not designed to replace them. Traditional academic assessment methods offer excellent, psychometrically sound measures to make between student and other nomothetic comparisons. Indeed, although CBA and performance assessment measures also can be used in this way, they do not offer the psychometric sophistication of more traditional tests. CBA and performance assessment measures can provide clear and direct links to instructional processes, something not typical of published norm-referenced tests.

Overview of Research on Performance Assessments and Implementation Issues

An examination of the published research literature on performance assessment provides limited information about critical issues in the assessment of students with disabilities or students at risk for learning difficulties. Performance assessments reportedly are used frequently by regular classroom teachers with individual students and recently by many state departments of education to monitor the status of learning at the school, district, and state levels. Although special educators have supported its use in the assessment of students with disabilities because of its perceived flexibility and alignment with curriculum (Choate & Evans, 1992; Coutinho & Malouf, 1992; Taylor, Tindal, Fuchs, & Bryant, 1993), we were unable to locate any published, databased reports of performance assessment being used by psychoeducational personnel to assess students for special education classification or placement. Accounts of the reliability of scoring procedures have dominated the databased studies, although several researchers have investigated the effects of race and gender—topics concerning equity and test validity quite relevant to the use of performance assessments with students with learning problems. In addition, recently completed work by Elliott and Kratochwill (1996) provides a comparative analysis of mildly disabled and nondisabled students on a large-scale performance assessment in mathematics and language arts.

Students with Different Ethnic and Cultural Backgrounds

Several teams of researchers have been interested in how students of different abilities and ethnic backgrounds function on performance assessment tasks.

Baxter and colleagues (Baxter, Shavelson, Herman, Brown, & Valadez, 1993) developed assessments from hands-on instructional activities in mathematics and examined their reliability and validity for obtaining individual achievement data for Anglo and Latino sixth graders. They concluded that tasks were the major source of unreliability and that many tasks (e.g., at least six) were needed to get a dependable measure of students' mathematics achievement. With respect to validity, Baxter and colleagues suggested that performance assessments measure different aspects of mathematics achievement than do traditional multiple-choice tests, and they differentiated students who have been taught in hands-on curricula from those in traditional curricula. Ethnic group comparisons indicated Anglos scored higher, on average, than Latinos on all achievement measures. The magnitude of the difference varied by the curricular experience of the students. For students in traditional curricula, qualitative analysis indicated Anglo and Latino students approached the problems similarly, made the same types of errors, and employed the same problem-solving strategies.

Kopriva and colleagues (Kopriva, Lowrey, & Martois, 1994) noted that most performance-type items are language intensive and hypothesized that English Language Learners (ELL) would experience more difficulty than English-speaking classmates. Kopriva et al. interviewed a sample of fourth graders in California using the math and writing scales from the California Learning Assessment System (CLAS). Students were administered either the English or Spanish (translated) version of the math and/or writing assessment, using a silent or read-aloud administration format. All other directions and procedures for administering this assessment were the same as those employed during the regular statewide administration of the CLAS.

After the assessments, a sample of low-, mid-, and high-performing students and their teachers were interviewed with their test booklets in front of them. Teachers reported that the problems assessed were appropriate; however, a large percentage of them reported that their students would have difficulty reading the instructions silently. In a CLAS statewide special study, mathematics scores tended to be rather low, with a mean of 1.3 out of 4 possible for the open-ended questions, and 2.9 correct out of 7 possible for the multiple-choice section. Kopriva and colleagues interpreted the low, flat scores as related to the lack of integrated, ongoing opportunities for students to experience these types of problem-solving items. Students who were interviewed reported overwhelmingly that they were required to respond to open-ended questions such as those on CLAS only once in a while or never. Yet, more than half of the lowest functioning students "preferred the open-ended format over the close-ended format, citing freedom to explain most often as their reason why" (Kopriva et al., 1994, p. 7).

Students with Mild Disabilities

Elliott and Kratochwill (1996) summarized results of an investigation concerning the use of a statewide performance assessment with students with disabilities.

Their ethnically diverse sample included 184 fourth-, eighth-, and tenth-grade students, of which 92 were identified as disabled. The students' performances were compared on a language arts and a mathematics performance assessment instrument and a standardized multiple-choice knowledge and concept test. The major objective of the investigation was to gain an understanding of how students with mild disabilities reacted to on-demand performance tasks. On both the math and language arts tasks, students with and without mild disabilities scored, on average, below the preliminary "proficiency" criteria described for the tasks. Students with disabilities, however, consistently scored 1/2 to 2/3 standard deviations below that of nondisabled classmates. Correlations between students' scores on the performance assessment tasks and the state's multiple-choice knowledge and concepts test were moderate (.36 to .68).

Following the completion of the tests, Elliott and Kratochwill interviewed a subsample of students. Students with disabilities indicated lower satisfaction with the performance tasks than their nondisabled cohorts. However, overall, the students with disabilities reported that the performance tests showed what they could do and were interesting to complete. Teachers involved in the administration of the performance tasks also were interviewed to provide additional data on testing accommodations and the functioning of students with disabilities on performance tests. Teachers indicated the performance assessment tasks were useful but generally difficult for all students. Teachers at all grade levels noted that a range of testing accommodations were made for students with disabilities on both the math and language arts performance tasks and that their testing accommodation efforts provided them insights into ways to accommodate future instructional tasks. Typical testing accommodations included increased time to complete tasks, assistance reading instructions, and modification of the test setting to diminish distractions.

The results of the Elliott and Kratochwill study provide evidence that students with mild disabilities can meaningfully participate in on-demand performance assessments with minimal accommodations. Their level of performance is similar to that found with more traditional multiple-choice achievement tests; however, students' posttest interviews indicated that they generally found the PA tasks more interesting and useful in representing what they know.

Status of Performance Assessment and Potential Barriers to Its Use

Practically speaking, performance assessment is an appealing approach for many educators, especially those interested in current reforms featuring outcome competencies and standards. The primary basis for our knowledge about performance assessments comes from statewide and national assessments, where data are analyzed in group fashion for accountability purposes and where student samples often have not been representative because of the relatively low participation rates for students with disabilities. From these assessment programs, the following trends have been observed: (a) significant differences in scores among students grouped on variables of disability and race, (b) moderate correlations between performance-based and multiple-choice tests of achievement, (c) high interrater agreements among scorers of performance assessments, (d) high content validity, but more limited subject matter coverage than typically found on multiple-choice tests, (e) greater language demands for performance assessments than for multiple-choice items, (f) student satisfaction with performance assessment tasks comparable to or greater than with multiple-choice tests and belief that performance assessments do a better job of showing what students have learned, and (g) across all students, lower performance assessment scores than on other forms of assessment, suggesting the tasks are more difficult.

Barriers to the use of performance assessments with individual students who may be having difficulty learning come in several forms. Examples include: (a) a paucity of psychometric evidence about performance assessments for the purpose of making diagnostic and placement decisions about individual students, (b) a limited number of educators and school-based professionals with technical knowledge about performance assessment; that is, how to develop them, reliably score them, and use the results to guide instruction, (c) no widely published case studies of students to illustrate the use of performance assessments in the educational decision-making process, (d) the fact that performance assessments are interpreted within a criterion-referenced rather than a norm-referenced framework, limiting the utility of the information for formal classification decisions, (e) the fact that performance assessments have not been developed to assess discrete, basic skills, limiting their potential to provide diagnostic information for skill-oriented remediation programs, and (f) the role of strong professional judgments in decision making, which is frequently questioned on grounds of accuracy and subjectivity.

Chapter Summary

Advances in the use of performance assessments will continue concurrently with the study of the validity of these assessment methods. Given the existing knowledge base, it is recommended that results from performance assessments be conceptualized as supplemental to traditional assessment results when making classification decisions. Achievement and learning evidence resulting from performance assessments, particularly those that are aligned with a student's curriculum, would appear to be highly relevant to decisions concerning educational placements and instructional interventions. The burgeoning interest in performance assessments highlights many educators' desire to have assessments comprised of tasks that they understand and that emphasize the application of knowledge, while not having the negative valence frequently associated with tests such as IQ tests. More research and feedback from educators is needed to determine whether performance assessments can fulfill this desire.

CHAPTER 9

Integrating Problem Solving into Educational Decision Making

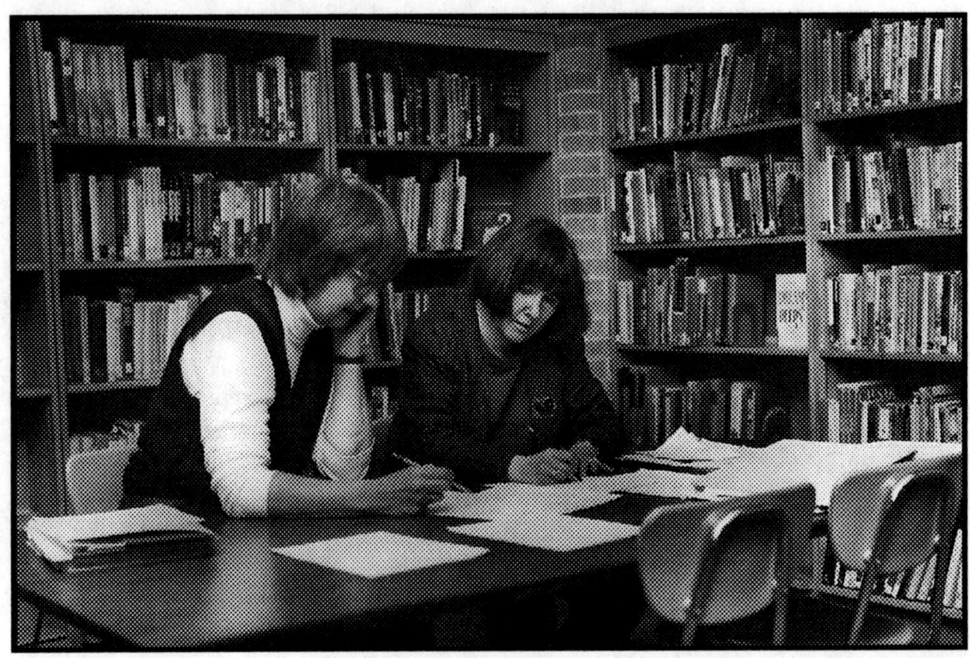

At this point in your study, assessment may appear more complicated than you initially thought. One does not simply give a test, get a test score, and know what to do to benefit the child. In this chapter, we will put it all together. That is, we will integrate many of the assessment steps presented previously into a single framework for problem solving to meet the needs of learners experiencing difficulty. Reducing problem solving to its simplest form will also help you to understand all of the interrelated concepts, decisions, and actions that are a part of the problem-solving model presented in this chapter. In figure 9.1, the fundamental question associated with each step is presented. All of the assessment activities are directed toward finding answers to these questions. The purpose of this chapter is to integrate the kinds of instructional and administrative placement decisions made in schools into this process. We will spend most of the chapter untangling the issues related to each step by integrating the problem-solving model with instructional and ad-

Figure 9.1 Problem-Solving Steps in Educational Decision Making

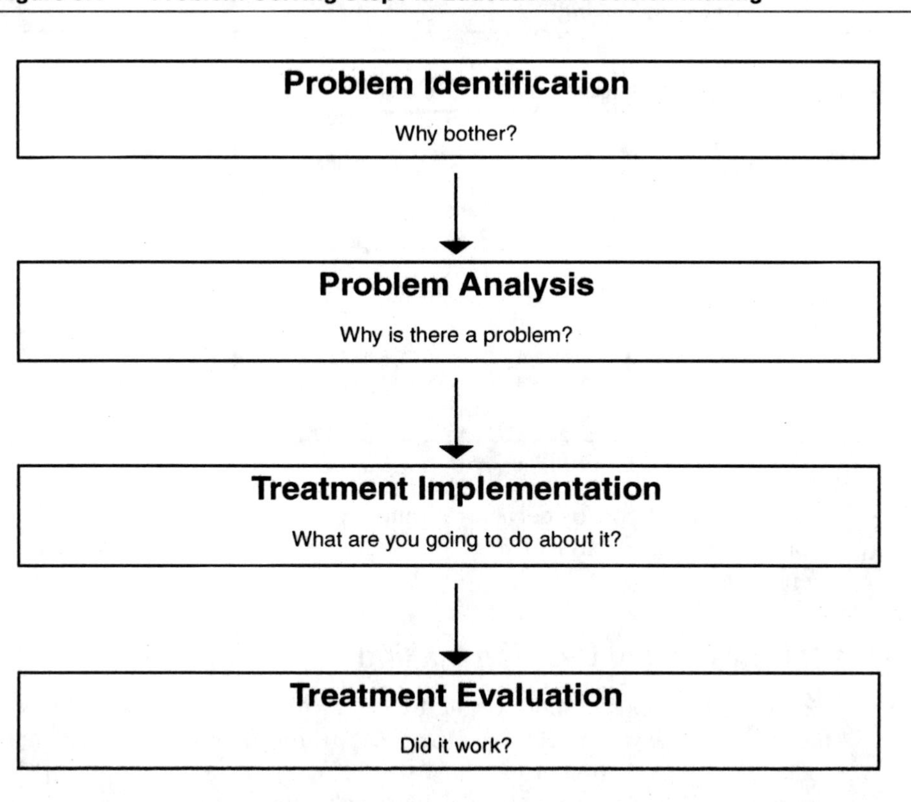
Problem Identification
Why bother?
Problem Analysis
Why is there a problem?
Treatment Implementation
What are you going to do about it?
Treatment Evaluation
Did it work?

ministrative placement decisions. The last part of the chapter will be devoted to issues that are unique to the areas of reading and math.

Problem Solving and Educational Decision Making

The process of integrating educational decisions, including decisions about instruction and managing behavior as well as administrative decisions about where students are placed, into the problem-solving model involves analyzing (a) our objectives for students, (b) where students perform relative to those objectives (answering the question "Why bother?"), (c) factors over which we have control (answering the questions "Why is there a problem?" and "What are you going to do about it?"), and (d) how available resources can be used to help solve the problem (answering the question "Did it work?"). Figure 9.2 presents each step of a two-phase model of problem solving. The two phases reflect the two broad categories of decisions educators make about students: instructional and administrative or classification

Figure 9.2 The Two-Phase Model of Applying Problem Solving for Educational Decision Making

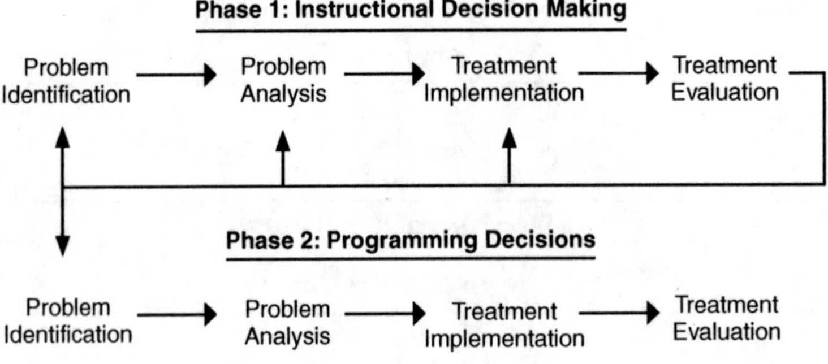

decisions. Each type of decision requires problem solving. This model is a more expanded version of a model described by special educator Stanley Deno (1989).

Phase 1: Instructional Decision Making

Figure 9.3 describes in more detail the key factors associated with Phase 1 of the problem-solving model. In this phase, instructional decision making, the focus is on how a teacher can help the child. Problem solving is applied to the instructional decisions that teachers make about students, specifying objectives and outcomes, planning instruction according to students' learning needs, monitoring pupil progress, and evaluating the effectiveness of instruction. Problem solving in this phase involves the teacher, should involve the parent, and may involve other consultants (e.g., a special education teacher, school psychologist, speech pathologist, etc.). If Phase 1 is successful, then the problem can be resolved in the classroom, and Phase 2, classification (programming decisions), will not be necessary.

Ideally, teachers will use the techniques described here on an ongoing basis to resolve small problems before they become large ones. However, many times procedures will be used as part of prereferral interventions (Graden, Zins, & Curtis, 1988). It is also desirable for the teacher to make modifications that are minimally intrusive in the classroom and that are maximally effective at improving student learning. If initial efforts are unproductive, the process can be repeated until an effective intervention is developed.

Even under these circumstances, some students may need more long-term interventions. Phase 2 is intended to address these students' needs. In some circumstances, a multidisciplinary team (MDT) may need to consider more restrictive interventions like special education placement (which involves differ-

Figure 9.3 Phase 1: Instructional Decision Making

Problem Identification	Problem Analysis	Treatment Implementation	Treatment Evaluation
• Specify the curricular objective(s) • Describe the student's expected functioning • Assess student performance relative to the objective(s) • Evaluate the discrepancy between actual and expected functioning	Consider likely reasons for why the student is not at the expected level of functioning: 1. Doesn't want to do it... 2. Needs more time doing it... 3. Doesn't know how to do it... 4. Hasn't had to do it... 5. It's too hard...	Ongoing progress monitoring with reliable and valid measures that reflect student progress in the curricular objective(s)	Describe student performance relative to the objective(s) Evaluate discrepancy: Reduced? • Continue? • Fade? Persistent? • Poor problem identification? • Wrong hypothesis? • Poor treatment implementation? • Not strong enough?

ent levels of intensity). We will discuss each of the steps in Phase 1 in detail, pointing out the factors that need to be considered at each step of problem solving. We will highlight the subject areas of reading and math separately because they are so common and require discussions unique to each.

Problem Identification

We described the problem identification stage in the first chapter as the process of defining the behavior in observable terms. In the classroom, defining the behavior involves specifying the curricular objective that the student is expected to meet. The curricular objective, as defined by the local school district's curriculum, is *the* standard for performance. It describes what the school district expects of its students. For example, most school districts expect that children will be able to count, to sequence numbers, and to compute single-digit addition problems before they leave first grade. A child who was in third grade who could not perform these activities would have a problem because there is a big difference between where the child *is* and where the child is *expected to be*. The curricular objectives are intended to reflect the kinds of skills that students are expected to have to participate productively in society. Therefore, describing what book students are supposed to be in is not specifying the curricular objective. Rather, specifying the curriculum means describing student outcomes in observable terms in instructional materials: reading words with vowel diphthongs, doing long-division math problems, writing paragraphs with proper syntax, grammar, and punctuation, and so on. The challenge for teachers is to express these curricular objectives in measurable terms so that they can assess a student's performance (e.g., "Students will write the correct time to the quarter hour when shown an analog clock"). The objectives must be large and meaningful enough to describe important outcomes but small enough to allow for calibrating expected outcomes (Howell et al., 1993).

The curricular objective describes our expectations for student performance. A problem arises when a discrepancy exists between what we expect and how a student is actually functioning. Identifying the problem consists of describing the discrepancy between actual student functioning and expected student functioning (Deno, 1989; Howell et al., 1993). Having specified the curricular objective, we now describe actual student functioning (e.g., "When given a worksheet containing 20 analog clocks showing time to the quarter hour, Timmy wrote 3 correct answers"). By having observable and measurable objectives and observable and measurable statements of student functioning, we know where the child is and where the child needs to be and we can now generate individual goal statements for students (e.g., "When given a worksheet containing 20 analog clocks showing time to the quarter hour, Timmy will write 19 correct answers"). The goals that we have for students must be tied to the curriculum.

Problem Analysis

The challenging part of problem analysis is sorting through all of the possible, *relevant* factors that are adversely affecting student learning. There are only a small number of factors over which we have control. We don't have control over birth trauma. Yet birth trauma may be a contributing factor. We don't have control over a child's IQ or socioeconomic status. Therefore, we can do little about how students are functioning before they arrive in our classrooms; we must take them as they are. It may be interesting to learn about those factors, but spending time discussing them may actually be a deterrent to problem solving if it hinders us from considering things over which we *do* have control and that *can* have positive effects for students. We do have control over some very powerful factors that affect student learning and that can change the direction of a student who has typically experienced chronic school failure (Greenwood, Hart, Walker, & Risley, 1994).

Predicting which interventions will work is difficult, so an efficient process is needed to avoid wasting valuable time. Therefore, some guidance is needed about which hypotheses are most likely to help us solve the problem. For this, past experience is informative. After reviewing more than 40 years of learning research, we reduced all of the factors known to affect student academic learning to the five most common reasons. In simplest terms, the top five reasons students do poorly are (a) they don't want to do it, (b) they need more time doing it, (c) they don't know how to do it, (d) they haven't had to do it before, or (e) it's too hard. It is possible to take comfort in the fact that there is a finite number of reasons for poor student performance, each of which is well supported by empirical research and each of which has implications for designing instructional modifications. These reasons will provide a starting point for developing interventions. Interestingly, even if the initial concern is behavioral (e.g., the student is out of seat, disrupting the class, etc.), these five reasons are a good place to start. The reason many children act out is often related to academic problems. Besides, the goal of problem solving is to help students learn. Students will learn by doing reading, math, writing, and so on. On the other hand, if students are "on-task" (e.g., sitting quietly at their desk), they are not necessarily learning. Finally, if there are simple things that teachers do naturally (e.g., modeling, correcting errors, etc.) that work, academic interventions will be easier to carry out than complicated behavioral interventions. Therefore, targeting academic skills makes the most sense in many cases.

Teachers shouldn't expect to have to go through this problem-solving process for every student, nor could they do so realistically. Some students, however, require more individualized problem solving because they are not progressing academically. We have a professional obligation to meet those students' needs. Yet educators must be efficient in their problem-solving approach: Some students will require less intensive modifications than others. Therefore, the most efficient thing to do is to assume the easiest reasonable hypothesis first, try out an intervention, and monitor and evaluate outcomes. If that approach doesn't work, try something more time intensive and continue until something works. We believe that being more efficient in this manner is likely to have better benefits for students. Easier solutions are more likely to be implemented consistently; harder solutions are cumbersome for teachers and support personnel and are less likely to be implemented. Therefore, the "reasonable hypotheses" are in order from those requiring the simplest intervention to those requiring the most intense instructional intervention (see figure 9.4). The research supporting each of these hypotheses is discussed in the following box.

We next describe each reasonable hypothesis by looking at Terry, a fifth grader in Mr. McGowen's class. Terry has consistently received poor grades on his writing assignments. He writes very little in any assignment (e.g., journal, essays, content papers such as science and social studies, etc.). Mr. McGowen and Terry's parents are very concerned and want to improve Terry's writing skills.

What is the cause of his poor performance in writing? First, we will test the possibility that Terry is able to write well but merely doesn't want to do it (Reason #1). To do this we can compare his performance during exercises when he is offered an incentive versus exercises when he is not offered an incentive. Initially, Terry is asked what he would like to work for; Mr. McGowen and Terry's parents could arrange to offer Terry incentives for

Figure 9.4 Problem Analysis: "Reasonable Hypotheses" for Academic Deficits

Problem Analysis: "Reasonable Hypotheses" for Academic Deficits

REASON #1: The student doesn't want to do it...

- The student is not motivated to respond to the instructional demands.

REASON #2: The student needs to spend more time doing it...

- The student spends an insufficient amount of time actively responding to curricular materials.

REASON #3: The student needs more help...

- The student receives insufficient feedback to learn the target skill.
- The student displays poor accuracy in the target skill(s).
- The student displays poor fluency in the target skill(s).
- The student does not generalize use of the skill(s) to the natural setting and/or to other materials/settings.

REASON #4: The student hasn't had to do it before...

- The instructional demands do not promote mastery of the curricular objective(s).

REASON #5: It's too hard...

- The student's skill level is poorly matched to the difficulty level of the instructional materials.

---

writing more on his papers, thereby providing a test of the first hypothesis. Also, someone on the MDT could work individually with Terry and see if his writing improved when motivated. If Terry's writing performance improves dramatically in response to the incentives, Mr. McGowen and Terry's parents now know that Terry is able to write, he simply lacks the motivation to do so. Terry's writing performance may not improve. In that case, Mr. McGowen and Terry's parents need to test other possibilities.

They may hypothesize that he has had insufficient time to practice writing (Reason #2). Terry may not be fluent in writing because he has not practiced enough. Mr. McGowen could increase the amount of time that Terry spends writing by, say, 10 minutes a day. After a period of monitoring, they

Focus on Research

Integrating Research into Practice: A Note on Student Learning in Classrooms

This discussion describes the conceptual rationale and empirical support for the five reasonable hypotheses outlined in figure 9.4. The first reasonable hypothesis (i.e., the student doesn't want to do it) is based on a distinction between performance and skill deficits. The next two reasonable hypotheses (2 and 3) are based on the learner's individual instructional needs as they master skills. The last two reasonable hypotheses (4 and 5) are based on the effects of instructional materials on student learning. Each hypothesis can be linked to the kinds of things that teachers can modify in the classroom—incentives, planning and delivery of instruction, and instructional materials.

Performance Versus Skill Deficit

The first line of investigation should be to examine whether the student is actually not able to do the skill (a skill deficit) or whether the student is able to do the skill but "just doesn't want to" (a performance deficit). Lentz (1988a, p. 354) describes the distinction in the following manner: "*Skill* problems will require interventions that produce new behavior; *performance* problems may require interventions involving manipulation of 'motivation' through contingency management." If we are working from a simplest to hardest hypothesis framework, the easiest hypothesis is to assume that the student can perform the skill, they just aren't doing it. Students' motivation and performance (i.e., increasing active participation and decreasing disruptive behaviors) have been strengthened through incentives for reading (Ayllon & Roberts, 1974; Staats & Butterfield, 1964; Staats, Minke, Finley, Wolf, & Brooks, 1964) and math (Broughton & Lahey, 1978). If a student fails to respond to incentives for increased academic performance, it means either that we used the wrong incentives or the student doesn't have the skills to perform the task and needs help.

The Instructional Hierarchy

How much help students need depends on their level of skill mastery. A learner goes through a sequence of stages before he or she is able to use the skill proficiently over time (Daly, Lentz, & Boyer, 1996; Haring et al., 1978; Howell et al., 1993). Through effective instruction, the learner first becomes accurate in the performance of the skill. At this stage, the instructor models use of the skill and observes the learner, giving feedback about performance—praising accurate use of the skill and correcting errors. Once the learner is accurate, he or she must become fluent in the use of the skill. So it's not enough to know that "4 × 2 = 8."

continued

Focus on Research—*continued*

For the skill to be useful in the future (e.g., with long division), the learner must be able to respond rapidly when presented with the problem. Practice is what improves skill fluency. Accurate and fluent skill use then allows the learner to generalize the skill across time, across settings, and across other skills (Daly et al., 1996; Daly, Martens, Killmer, & Massie, 1996; LaBerge & Samuels, 1974; Wolery et al., 1988).

Instruction is based on strategies for first improving accuracy, then fluency, and finally generalization. If we are problem solving and the objective is to find the easiest strategy in the most efficient manner, we will alter the order in our search for reasonable hypotheses. It's easiest to assume that the student simply needs more practice (i.e., has poor skill fluency). If that hypothesis doesn't work out, we will assume that the student needs more modeling and error correction (i.e., has poor skill accuracy and fluency). If you still haven't found an effective solution, you then assume that the student needs a lot of modeling, error correction, and practice across different instructional materials (i.e., has poor skill accuracy, fluency, and generalization). Using the heuristic notion of an "instructional hierarchy" developed by Haring et al. (1978), Daly et al., (1996) showed that, in many studies, the effectiveness of instructional strategies for improving student accuracy and fluency could be predicted based on the instructional strategies used (e.g., modeling versus practice). Strategies that incorporate modeling, prompting, and error correction can be expected to improve accuracy. Strategies that incorporate practice and reinforcement for rapid responding can be expected to improve fluency. Please note that other instructional hierarchies have been developed in the last century. Haring et al.'s (1978) model is particularly useful because it can do more than explain patterns of results; it allows us to predict which interventions are most likely to be effective based on the components of instruction and where students are at in the learning sequence. In a demonstration of the predictive power of this particular instructional hierarchy, Daly and Martens (1994) accurately predicted the pattern of results of three reading interventions based on the instructional strategies incorporated by each.

Instructional Assignments and Tasks

When we are examining the instructional tasks and assignments as possible factors related to poor student performance, there are at least two reasons why they may be hindering student learning: either they are not helping the student to practice actual skill use (Vargas, 1984) or they are too difficult (Gickling & Armstrong, 1978; Gickling & Rosenfield, 1995). Practicing the skill means that instructional materials provide enough examples and nonexamples of the target skill so students know when to use the skill (Englemann & Carnine, 1991). For instance, if you are teaching colors to preschool students, you want to be sure to present enough examples of red using lots of different shapes so that students don't confuse the color red with the shape of the objects you are using. Practicing the skill also means that students need to know how to get the correct answer in order to respond correctly. Although this may appear obvious, many instructional materials let students get the correct answer for the wrong reason (Vargas, 1984). For instance, Bill knows how to fill out his vocabulary worksheets by looking at the number of blanks where he is supposed to write the response and counting the number of letters in each of the vocabulary words. Bill isn't learning his vocabulary words. He has devised an ingenious strategy for getting the right answer without knowing it for the right reasons (even if he is working harder to get the right answer in this way).

You might consider that the instructional materials are too difficult. Gickling and Armstrong (1978) improved students' accuracy of assigned work and on-task behavior by changing instructional materials to ensure that they weren't too difficult or too easy. When students are instructed at their instructional level, they are more likely to generalize what they've just learned to other similar instructional materials (Daly, Martens, 1996). The importance of the effects of task difficulty on student learning cannot be overstated. Unfortunately, teachers often have learners with multiple skill levels in their classrooms and changing instructional materials to match everyone's instructional level is a difficult task and is one of the last things that they may resort to. For this reason, we put it at the bottom of the list of reasonable hypotheses. However, if instructional changes based on the other factors don't work, teachers will be hard-pressed to insist that they don't want to change the difficulty level of the materials.

can examine Terry's performance to see if he is writing better. If so, Terry merely needed extra time devoted to writing. If not, either 10 minutes a day was not enough practice or we can assume that he doesn't know how to write well and needs help (Reason #3).

If Terry needs help, it means either that he needs more feedback or that his accuracy is so poor that he needs more modeling and prompting in order to write better. To give more feedback, Mr. McGowen will have to tailor assignments to check on Terry's writing more frequently so that he can praise instances of good writing and correct errors more often. If this doesn't work, Mr. McGowen will need to come up with strategies for modeling good writing skills (e.g., giving Terry examples of good writing with explanations of the features of the good writing samples), prompting Terry to write well (e.g., reminding Terry how to organize the structure of a paragraph, how to come up with more diverse adjectives, etc.), and perhaps explicitly teaching Terry strategies for writing better. If Mr. McGowen finds that Terry is responding well to more feedback and/or modeling, he will have to investigate to determine whether Terry's writing is improving across different assignments. We can't assume that the teaching strategies that improve student learning under one set of conditions will lead to improvements under other conditions: Terry may not generalize his newly learned skills. If this is the case, Mr. McGowen will need to help Terry to use the strategies across writing assignments until he observes generalized improvement in Terry's writing.

If all else fails, there will be a need to consider the instructional materials and the kinds of tasks that students are given (Reason #4). It may be that students can complete the assignments without actually knowing how to use the skill. For instance, if Emily's spelling instruction involves selecting the correctly spelled word (e.g., *analytical*) from three alternatives (e.g., "(a) *analitical,* (b) *analytical,* and (c) *annalytical*), Emily is not learning to spell the word. She is learning how to select it from alternatives. Or take the case of Bill (described in the preceding box) who has figured out that if he pays attention to the filled-in spaces next to the blank spaces on his vocabulary worksheets, he can write the correct word without even reading the definition. In Terry's case, Mr. McGowen must scrutinize the writing assignments to determine whether they actually have Terry practice writing the way that he will need to be able to write in the future (e.g., essays, correspondence, etc.), assignments that are consistent with curricular objectives. If this line of thinking doesn't lead to a fruitful solution, Mr. McGowen should consider that the writing assignments may be too difficult for Terry (Reason #5). He will need to change his instructional demands so that Terry is able to practice writing on simpler assignments with some success. Mr. McGowen may actually not have Terry write a three-page essay in a week's time but might expect Terry to write a number of individual paragraphs to practice organizing paragraphs, using modifiers, writing grammatically correct sentences, and so on.

We've taken you through a series of hypotheses that educators can consider when problem solving about students. It is not suggested that you implement these hypotheses rigidly in a fixed pattern if you have information to suggest that one or more of them is more or less likely. Instead, these are merely guidelines for hypotheses that you can consider in order of complexity. The objective is to gather enough information about student functioning and the natural environment to lead you to possible solutions. Your hypotheses should lead you to solutions that you can implement reasonably in the classroom. We will describe some tried and true (i.e., empirically validated) solutions in the areas of reading and math at the end of the chapter.

Treatment Implementation

Regardless of the modifications that are made, it is crucial to monitor outcomes to determine whether the modification is improving student learning. Direct measures of academic performance (reading, writing, math, etc.) over time must be used. This represents the process of formative evaluation during the first phase of the Treatment Implementation stage of the problem-solving

Figure 9.5 Implementing an Intervention

Questions to Consider...	Answers:
• How do you increase the chances that the intervention is being used?	Use a script!
• How do you know that the intervention is being implemented?	Use a script!
• How do you know that it was effective?	Continuous Progress Monitoring

Intervention Script
for
Small Group

Date: ______________

Participants: Mrs. Rosen, Elizabeth, Lauren, Jimmy, & Karen
Time: During partner reading (10:00–10:25)
Materials: Phonics book and copies for all group members

______________ Read one page of the story aloud.
______________ Have the group read the page aloud.
______________ Have one child read the page aloud.
______________ If the student does not read the word within 3 seconds or mispronounces a word, say the word.
______________ At the end of the page, have the student reread sentences with words read incorrectly in them.
______________ Continue in this manner until the entire story is read.

model (figure 9.2). It is also strongly suggested that you measure whether the modification is actually being done. It's possible that the correct solution is being used, it's just not being done correctly. Perhaps the intervention is too cumbersome and requires modification. It would be a grave error to conclude that an intervention was not effective when it wasn't implemented properly. Hence, it would be helpful to know if it wasn't being done in order that modifications can be made so that it will get done. One way to monitor whether the treatment is being used is to create a "script" or a list of procedures that describes in detail the steps, materials, time of day, and other relevant information about implementing the intervention (Ehrhardt, Barnett, Lentz, Stollar, & Reifin, 1996). An example of a script is presented in figure 9.5. By having individuals check off steps completed, the script can serve the purpose of (a) reminding those with responsibilities to follow through and (b) verifying that the intervention was actually carried out.

Treatment Evaluation

In evaluating the intervention, it is necessary to consider a series of questions. First, has the discrepancy (described in the first step) been reduced? Has the student met the goal? If the answer is yes, then you have to consider whether it is necessary to continue the intervention to maintain student progress or whether it is time to reduce the extra support. The answer to this question is an empirical one: There is no way to know in advance. Your answer will be determined in part by how difficult it is to maintain the extra modification(s) and how independently you believe the student can function. If you do decide to fade the extra support, it is important to continue to monitor progress in order to verify that a discrepancy no longer exists.

If the intervention was not effective, there are several possible reasons. There is a good chance that you did not identify the problem clearly enough at the start (Kratochwill & Bergan, 1990). If this is a possibility, go back and scrutinize how well you defined the problem. Another possible reason for poor outcomes may be that you have chosen the wrong hypothesis. You may have hypothesized that the student merely needed more practice when in fact their accuracy was poor. Alternately, the intervention may have been ineffective because it wasn't used correctly or as frequently as intended. Finally, it's possible that you chose the right intervention; it just wasn't used enough times to produce positive effects. You will notice that each of these possibilities takes you back to a previous step. We recommend strongly that if the intervention was not effective, you cycle back through the problem-solving process until you find something that is effective. Remember that these initial interventions provide assessment information. Importantly, you will learn some things that do and do not work. One outcome is that you know what works but doing the intervention requires too much work. Hence, more resources or even special education services may be required to continue the necessary modifications.

Phase 2: Programming Decisions

In a small number of cases, the intervention warranted by the problem is too difficult to be addressed with only the resources available in the general education classroom. For these children, Phase 2 of the problem-solving model—classification, or programming—is needed (see figure 9.6). This type of problem solving is almost entirely administrative. From chapter 2 we know that a lot of error is associated with traditional psychoeducational practices. Even if we assume that there are psychological profiles (e.g., learning disabled, emotionally disturbed, etc.), which itself is a stretch from what we actually know, identifying students with any degree of accuracy is equivalent to crap shooting: sometimes the numbers roll the way we would like them to and sometimes they don't. Perhaps a more professionally honest approach is to examine administratively how much help is available to go around and

Figure 9.6 Phase 2: Programming Decisions

Problem Identification	Problem Analysis	Treatment Implementation	Treatment Evaluation
• Examine responsiveness to intervention • Describe performance relative to peers	• Examine resources required to make modifications • Examine ranking on norm-referenced tests to determine eligibility • Formulate an Individualized Education Plan	Ongoing progress monitoring with reliable and valid measures that reflect student progress in the IEP goals	Describe student performance relative to the objective(s) Evaluate discrepancy: Reduced? • Continue? • Fade? Persistent? • Poor problem identification? • Wrong hypothesis? • Poor treatment implementation? • Not strong enough?

whose needs can be met with the help that is available. As we describe this phase of problem solving, the emphasis will be on (a) using the data from previous problem solving, (b) making projections for the needed level of services based on the intensity of the problem and the availability of resources, and (c) monitoring progress continuously.

Problem identification at the level of programming, or making classification decisions, involves examining how responsive the student was to previous intervention and where the student stands compared with same-age peers after intervention. If we have tried several solutions and the child proves resistant to intervention, then and only then is it appropriate to consider special education services (Gresham, 1991b). We may administer standardized, norm-referenced tests (of the type to be described in the next section of the book) to describe student functioning compared with a nationally normed sample of same-age peers. The effects of error on decision making at this level are greater. Perhaps problem solving at the first phase was too abbreviated and an effective and reasonable solution was missed. Perhaps the norm-referenced test results penalized the child because he or she was instructed in a curriculum that didn't overlap sufficiently with the test (Good & Salvia, 1988). It is essential to be very sure of the decision before proceeding to the next level. The discussion at this stage should focus on finding convincing reasons to rule out easier solutions (e.g., the student didn't get as much help as he or she needed in the classroom).

When analyzing a problem at this level of decision making, educators need to decide which classroom placement is best suited to meet the instructional and management needs of the student. This decision should be based on problem-solving information from prior attempts to resolve the problem in the student's current classroom placement. An important factor in this level of decision making is ensuring that the student is receiving educational programming in the least restrictive environment necessary. Because of the persistence of categorical disability classifications (e.g., learning disabled), it is also necessary to examine student functioning on norm-referenced tests (cognitive abilities, adaptive behavior, achievement, etc.) to determine whether students qualify for services. Because of all the problems inherent in psychoeducational assessment, we recommend that you use the tests only as indicators of student ranking on reading, math, aptitude, and so on. Indeed, some states like Iowa are discarding this level of problem solving, eschewing the need for traditional psychoeducational assessment. If the student meets eligibility criteria, it is necessary to create an Individualized Education Plan (IEP). This process is simplified by virtue of all of the previous work that went into developing goal statements and planning instructional modifications. When adhering to the problem-solving model, the IEP generated can be thought of as a "smart" IEP, one that is informed by previous problem-solving efforts and one that emphasizes curricular objectives that the student must master.

Implementing and evaluating the intervention involves the same processes as in the previous phase of problem solving—ongoing progress monitoring with systematic decision making. These processes meet the due process requirements for students with IEPs and constitute best practices. In fact, because special education programming is essentially an intrusive intervention by virtue of its restrictiveness, the need for careful adherence to formative evaluation and good instructional decision making is heightened.

Now that you've seen the scope of problem solving across both instructional and administrative decision making, we would like to turn our attention to issues unique to the areas of reading and math achievement. Although the same process is applicable to both, each requires different efforts related to developing instructional objectives and generating interventions.

Issues in Application to Reading Problems

Specifying the Curricular Objective: Two Approaches to Specifying Objectives

Reading presents unique challenges to describing instructional objectives. It's a complex activity that requires the student to have linguistic and decoding strategies that must be integrated to produce fluid reading that allows the reader to understand what he or she is reading. Scope and sequence charts, which are available in most school districts' curricula, usually contain a broad array of very specific objectives (e.g., "reads vowel diphthongs") along with other objectives that are less precisely specified (e.g., "extracts the meaning from age appropriate texts"). It is the teacher's responsibility to teach students so that they master the objectives. Consequently, at least one part of teaching will be devoted to teaching a series of objectives, presumably ordered by difficulty level throughout the school year. These objectives can be described as "subskills." Really, however, the ultimate objective is for the student to read the curricular materials fluently and with comprehension for that grade level by the end of the school year.

With respect to assessing outcomes, the question is, does the teacher monitor outcomes on subskills (e.g., vowel diphthongs) or on global objectives (e.g., reading the curricular texts fluently and with comprehension)? Monitoring subskills means that the teacher is changing assessment materials and procedures each time he or she begins working on a new objective. Monitoring specific subskills also means that it's not possible to get the big picture: Is the student's overall reading skill improving over time? Fuchs and Deno (1991) recommend measuring general outcomes like oral reading fluency rather than subskills for a couple of reasons. First, if teachers are changing assessment procedures and materials frequently, the reliability and validity of the assessment techniques will be unknown. Also, with a more global indicator like oral reading fluency it's possible to estimate student progress over time. Therefore, when problem solving about a student having difficulty learning to read, it's probably best to use a good global indicator of the curricular objective like oral reading fluency that is tied to the curriculum (i.e., using curricular materials).

Analyzing Problems in Reading: Linking Hypotheses to Instructional Modifications

Earlier in the chapter, we described five reasonable hypotheses for why students don't do well. This section provides examples of specific reading interventions that have been shown to be effective at improving students' reading skills. Figure 9.7 contains hypotheses with the names of interventions that can be linked to each of the hypotheses. It's beyond the scope of this chapter to describe the interventions in detail. However, we will describe in general terms how investigators have improved students' reading skills with each of the interventions.

Once again, the first step is to determine whether the student has a skill or performance deficit. Lovitt, Eaton, Kirkwood, and Pelander (1971) improved students' oral reading fluency by offering incentives for reading faster (intervention #1). If offering incentives doesn't help to improve a student's reading, we need to consider the possibility that the student needs help: They have a skill deficit. It may be that the student merely needs to practice

Figure 9.7 Linking Hypotheses to Interventions in Reading

Academic Interventions in Reading Identified by Presumed Function of the Behavior

Reasonable Hypothesis	Possible Interventions
Performance Deficit: The student is not motivated to respond to the instructional demands	Increase interest in improving responding: 1. Contingent Reinforcement
Skill Deficit:	
Student displays poor fluency and generalization in target skill(s)	Increase practice/drill: 2. Modified Repeated Readings
Student displays poor accuracy, fluency, and generalization in target skill(s)	Increase modeling and error correction: 3. Listening Passage Preview + Error Correction (Phrase Drill)
Student does not generalize use of the skill to other materials/settings	Instruct the student to generalize use of the skill: 4. Listening Passage Preview across passages (including generalization passage)
Student's skill level is poorly matched to the difficulty of the instructional materials	Increase student responding using better matched instructional levels: 5. Identify student's accuracy and fluency across instructional materials

to improve his or her fluency. For example, Rashotte and Torgesen (1985) improved students' oral reading fluency by having them repeatedly read instructional passages and giving them feedback about their performance after each reading (intervention #2). This task was not as boring as it may appear. After a month of daily repeated readings, half of the students asked to continue the repeated readings sessions.

If repeated practice doesn't help to improve a student's reading, then perhaps students are not accurate in their reading and would benefit from modeling and error correction. Daly and Martens (1994) found that reading passages to students (Listening Passage Preview) was more effective at increasing students' oral reading fluency than (a) word list training or (b) having students practice reading passages by themselves. Because students make a lot of errors when they are just becoming accurate, a good error correction strategy is in order. Students' reading errors can be corrected in several ways. Having students practice accurately reading error words in sentences appears to be the most effective procedure (Howell et al., 1993; Martens, Witt, Daly, & Vollmer, in press). O'Shea, Munson, and O'Shea (1984) improved students' reading by having them repeatedly read sentences containing words that they had previously missed. It stands to reason that an intervention that contains modeling of accurate and fluent reading (by reading passages to students) and good error correction (practicing words accurately in sentences) will have strong, positive effects on a student's reading if they have poor accuracy (Lentz, 1988a).

For all of these interventions, it is crucial to assess the effects across time and across reading materials. We may help students to read a passage or two really well, but if it doesn't help their reading in other texts and if they are not retaining what they learned over time, we have to work to help the student generalize the skills. The most straightforward way to do this in reading is to continue to provide good instruction across passages: modeling, error correction, and repeated practice by using passages that have a lot of similar words will help students to generalize (intervention #4) (Daly, Martens, et al., 1996; Rashotte & Torgesen, 1985).

What if the student is still not reading better? In this case, it is reasonable to assume that the instructional materials may be too difficult and that the student's skill level is poorly matched to the difficulty of the instructional materials. Daly, Martens, et al. (in press) found that when they instructed students having difficulty learning to read in materials that were well matched to the students' skill levels and in materials that were difficult for the students, the students read better in texts that had a lot of the same words as those used for instruction. Surprised? Probably not. However, we expect that teachers who have numerous students will have difficulty changing instructional materials to meet everybody's "instructional level." Therefore, we suggest this as a last alternative. If nothing else works, move the student's placement in the curriculum.

Issues in Application to Math Problems

Specifying the Curricular Objective: The Sequence of Learning Arithmetic Skills as the Basis for Assessment

Learning arithmetic skills follows a logical and orderly sequence. A knowledge of this sequence of skills is essential for defining expectations for student performance. We will discuss two approaches by which these skills have been described and organized: (a) scope and sequence charts, and (b) learning hierarchies.

Scope and Sequence Charts

Scope and sequence charts, such as the one presented in table 9.1, list the skills students need to know (scope) along a timeline in the order according to which they are usually taught (sequence). Many teachers derive their weekly and even daily lesson plans by using scope and sequence charts to

Table 9.1 Scope and Sequence Chart for Mathematics

Grade	*Skills Acquired*
Kindergarten	Rote counting to 10 Use whole numbers in serial order Begin cardinal numbers, ordinal numbers Begin reading numerals One-to-one matching Addition as joining of sets
Grade 1: First Half	Rote counting to 100 Read and write whole numbers through 50 Place value at tens place Equivalent/nonequivalent sets Know meaning of signs –, +, and = Addition and subtraction as inverse functions Solving missing addend problems Using 0 in subtraction
Grade 1: Second Half	Rote counting beyond 100 Counting by fives, twos, tens Odd and even numbers Signs (&) Read and write to 99 Begin fractions 1/2, 1/3, 1/4 Addition combinations through 19 Addition of two-digit numbers with 2 or 3 addends through 99 (no carrying) Subtract two-digit numbers to minuends of 19 or less Multiples of 10 (2 tens = 20, 3 tens = 30)
Grade 2: First Half	Place value to hundredth place Addition two-digit numerals with 3 or 4 addends with sums less than 100 (no carrying) Subtract two-digit numerals (no borrowing) Understand division as separation of set into equivalent sets
Grade 2: Second Half	Count by ones, twos, fives, tens, hundreds, through 999 Odd-even numbers Read and write numerals through 999 Write numerals in expanded notation Introduce carrying (regrouping) Subtraction involving borrowing at the tens, hundreds places with numerals including 0 Begin combination of multiples of 2, 3, 4, and 5 with products of 0–25 Know meaning of x and y Begin division problem with same facts as above.
Grade 3: First Half	Count and write to 1,000 Place value for thousands Equivalent fractions for 1/2, 1/4, 1/3 Roman numerals to XII Addition of three-digit numerals with carrying Subtraction facts with combinations of 0–19 Introduce $\sqrt{\ }$ for division

Grade 3: Second Half	Read and write numerals with dollars and cents Rounding of numbers Fractions 1/6, 1/8 Roman numerals through XXX Addition up to seven digits Begin addition of fractions with like denominators, with sums less than 1 Subtraction of 4–7 digits with borrowing Multiplication through 9 × 9 Multiplication of two- or three-digit factors by one factor with or without carrying Division with combination through 9 × 9
Grade 4: First Half	Read and write whole numbers to 9,999 Roman numerals through C Understand concepts of 1/2, 1/4, 1/3 as equivalent sets of groups of objects, as well as congruent parts of a whole
Grade 4: Second Half	Read and write numerals to million Place value for million Learn names *numerator* and *denominator* Multiplication of two-digit numeral by two-digit multipliers Division with two-digit divisor Fractional parts, fifths, sevenths, ninths
Grade 5: First Half	Relationship between improper fractions and mixed fractions Write improper and mixed fractions Add three- or four-digit numbers of 2–6 addends Add fractions with like denominators Subtract like and mixed fractions with like denominators Multiply three-digit numbers by two-digit multipliers Two-digit divisors with 5–9 in one's place
Grade 5: Second Half	Decimals and place value Add decimal fractions Add fractions with unlike denominators Subtract five-digit numerals, fractional numbers, mixed numbers from whole numbers Multiplication with multiples of 100
Grade 6: First Half	Learn to express numbers by using exponents Vocabulary: *power, squared, cubed* Add and subtract fractions with unlike denominators Multiplication with three-digit multipliers Multiplication of fractional numbers with proper fractions, whole numbers, and improper fractions Division of fractional numbers
Grade 6: Second Half	Relate percent to ratio, fractions, and decimals Add positive and negative numbers Multiplication with decimals and decimal fractions Division of decimal fractions

focus on specific aspects of major skills. Note that the same skills reappear at different levels for review or more sophisticated application. Scope and sequence charts are useful in assessment for defining the curricular objectives that students are expected to master.

Learning Hierarchies

Learning hierarchies are a second approach to organizing skill sequences. Although both learning hierarchies and scope and sequence charts list skills in an ordered sequence, they differ in that (a) learning hierarchies are typically much more detailed and specific than scope and sequence charts, and (b) learning hierarchies specify a skill that a student will be required to learn and then list the behaviors the child must acquire before successfully performing the skill in question. Table 9.2 presents a series of objectives from a learning hierarchy that was used to teach the concept of number. Note the differences between the wording and specifications of these objectives versus those in the scope and sequence chart in table 9.1.

Another difference between scope and sequence charts and learning hierarchies is that learning hierarchies do not specify the time periods for the acquisition of skills. This represents a philosophical as well as a practical difference. Scope and sequence charts are constructed in a manner consistent with many stage theories of child development in which children are thought to be ready to learn certain concepts at certain ages. On the other hand, learning hierarchies are derived from a behavioristic notion that children who have learned all the prerequisite skills for a specific learning objective are ready to learn the next objective regardless of age. Whatever one's theoretical beliefs, learning hierarchies are an invaluable asset in the assessment of children's learning problems. A detailed discussion of the hierarchies is beyond the scope of this chapter, because to present a learning hierarchy that encompasses the same range of skills as the scope and sequence chart presented in table 9.1 could require several hundred pages. The interested reader is instead referred to an excellent book entitled *The Analysis of Behavior in Planning Instruction* (Holland, Soloman, Doran, & Frezza, 1976).

Analyzing the Problem in Math: Linking Hypotheses to Instructional Modifications

Numerous strategies can be used for improving students' math skills, some of which are better matched to particular hypotheses about why a student is not doing well in math. Because it is beyond the scope of this text to describe interventions for all of the hypotheses described in figure 9.4, we will describe a few that have been shown repeatedly to produce strong effects. First, let's consider whether the student's poor performance may be the result of a performance deficit. We've seen that incentives can be effective at improving student performance. Another strategy for improving students' motivation that is even simpler is offering choices of assignments. Students' on-task

Table 9.2 Objectives of the Curriculum for Teaching the Concept of Number from a Learning Hierarchy

Units 1 and 2: Counting and One-to-One Correspondence

A. The child can recite the numerals in order.
B. Given a set of movable objects, the child can count the objects, moving them out of the set as he counts.
C. Given a fixed ordered set of objects, the child can count the objects.
D. Given a fixed unordered set of objects, the child can count the objects.
E. Given a numeral stated and a set of objects, the child can count out a subset of stated size.
F. Given a numeral stated and several sets of fixed objects, the child can select a set of size indicated by numeral.
G. Given two sets of objects, the child can pair objects and state whether the sets are equivalent.
H. Given two unequal sets of objects, the child can pair the objects and state which set has more.
I. Given two unequal sets of objects, the child can pair objects and state which set has less.

Units 3 and 4: Numerals

A. Given two sets of numerals, the child can match the numerals.
B. Given a numeral stated and a set of printed numerals, the child can select the stated numeral.
C. Given a numeral (written), the child can read the numeral.
D. Given several sets of objects and several numerals, the child can match numerals with appropriate sets.
E. Given two numerals (written), the child can state which shows more (less).
F. Given a set of numerals, the child can place them in order.
G. Given numerals stated, the child can write the numeral.

Unit 5: Comparison of Sets

A. Given two sets of objects, the child can count sets and state which has more objects or that sets have same number.
B. Given two sets of objects, the child can count sets and state which has less objects.
C. Given a set of objects and a numeral, the child can state which shows more (less).
D. Given a numeral and several sets of objects, the child can select sets which are more (less) than the numeral: given a set of objects and several numerals, the child can select numerals which show more (less) than the sets of objects.
E. Given two rows of objects (not paired), the child can state which row has more regardless of arrangement.
F. Given three sets of objects, the child can count sets and state which has most (least).

Table 9.2 *continued*

Unit 6: Seriation and Ordinal Position

A. Given three objects of different sizes, the child can select the largest (smallest).
B. Given objects of graduated sizes, the child can seriate according to size.
C. Given several sets of objects, the child can seriate the sets according to size.
D. Given ordered sets of objects, the child can name the ordinal position of the objects.

Unit 7: Addition and Subtraction (Sums to 10)

A. Given two numbers stated, set of objects, and directions to add, the child can add the numbers by counting out two subsets then combining and stating combined number as sum.
B. Given two numbers stated, set of objects, and directions to subtract, the child can count out smaller subset from larger and state remainder.
C. Given two numbers stated, number line, and directions to add, the child can use the number line to determine sum.
D. Given two numbers stated, number line, and directions to subtract, the child can use the number line to subtract.
E. Given addition and subtraction word problems, the child can solve the problems.
F. Given written addition and subtraction problems in form: $\begin{array}{r}x\\ \underline{+y}\end{array}$ or $\begin{array}{r}x\\ \underline{-y}\end{array}$; the child can complete the problems.
G. Given addition and subtraction problems in form: $x + y = \square$, or $x - y = \square$; the child can complete the equations.

Unit 8: Addition and Subtraction Equations

A. Given equation of form $z = \square + \Delta$, the child can show several ways of completing the equation.
B. Given equation form of $x + y =\ \ +$, the child can complete the equation in several ways.
C. Given equations of forms $x + y = z +$ and $x + y =\ \ + z$, the child can complete the equations.
D. Given equations forms of $x + \square = y$ and $\square + x = y$, the child can complete the equations.
E. Given complete addition equation (e.g., $x + y = z$), the child can write equations using numerals and minus sign (e.g., $z - x = y$) and demonstrate relationship.
F. Given counting blocks and/or number line, the child can make up completed equations of various forms.

From: L. B. Resnick et al. "Task Analysis in Curriculum Design: A Hierarchically Sequenced Introductory Mathematics Curriculum" in JOURNAL OF APPLIED BEHAVIOR ANALYSIS 6:684–685, 1973. Published by the Society for Experimental Analysis of Behavior, Inc. Reprinted with permission of the author.

behavior has been improved by giving students choices of instructional activities (Dunlap et al., 1994), a strategy that can be easily adapted to math instruction. Interestingly, in some of this research students displayed high rates of on-task behavior on the very assignments that they refused to do previously. The difference was that they were allowed to choose among several instructional assignments during seatwork. When they got to choose the assignment, their compliance and on-task behavior improved.

If incentives fail to improve student performance, there are some strong, time-honored interventions that increase the rate of student responding while increasing the rate of teacher feedback (praise and error correction) for student responding. Heward (1994) describes two interventions that teachers can readily adapt to large- and small-group math instruction: choral responding and response cards. When teachers have all of the students respond in unison to math problems using **choral responding,** everyone is participating in all of the guided practice problems. As a teacher develops his or her skills with this technique, he or she can tune in to individual students to determine whether they are responding accurately. Another way to assess whether students are accurate and to provide immediate feedback is through the use of **response cards.** Teachers can have students write out answers to problems on slates or a laminated surface and hold them up so that the teacher can scan every student's response. Both strategies are simple to implement (although we recommend that you review Heward's recommendations for how to implement each most efficiently). Few strategies are as quick and efficient in alerting the teacher to students who are learning the lesson.

Finally, in this category of intervention, one form of intervention that is both efficient and highly effective is "reciprocal peer tutoring" (Fantuzzo & Rohrbeck, 1992). We refer you to the work of Fantuzzo and his colleagues for the details of how to implement reciprocal peer tutoring (Fantuzzo, King, & Heller, 1992; Fantuzzo, Polite, & Grayson, 1990). **Reciprocal peer tutoring** involves pairing students who are having difficulty with math, giving them assignments, assigning roles of tutor and student, agreeing on incentives for accurate work and on-task behavior, and having the tutors prompt their peer to write the correct response. The tutor presents math problems on flash cards and the student writes the answer on a sheet of paper. If the student does not write the correct answer, the tutor has the student correct his or her response. If the student is incorrect on a second try, the teacher can help and the student can have a third try. The peers alternate roles. A growing number of investigations have shown that this simple tutoring strategy can improve students' math skills (Fantuzzo et al., 1992; Fantuzzo et al., 1990).

As with reading, if a student has poor accuracy in math objectives, two teaching strategies that are called for include modeling and error correction. One intervention that incorporates both modeling and feedback with error correction is called "Cover-Copy-Compare" (Skinner, Turco, Beatty, & Rasavage,

1989). The teacher provides the student with an answer sheet along with a blank assignment sheet. The student is instructed to look at the problem on the answer sheet with the correct response, cover the correct response, write the correct answer on the assignment sheet, and compare his or her response to the right answer to check for accuracy. Cover-Copy-Compare incorporates both modeling for correct responses and feedback (including error correction when the student writes the wrong response) for accuracy of responding.

None of the interventions described here create excessive burdens for the classroom teacher; all can be implemented flexibly with the assistance of support personnel and instructional assistants; and all increase active student responding.

Chapter Summary

Although the problem-solving model is simple and straightforward when reduced to its simplest terms (figure 9.1), implementing it becomes complex very quickly in the face of the numerous decisions that we make about students and their functioning in classrooms. The model that we presented in this chapter divided problem solving into two phases. The first phase involves looking at modifications that can be made in the classroom setting. We tried to provide guidelines for this process in broad brushstrokes, highlighting the core elements of assessment and intervention. The decisions that are made in this phase are low-inference decisions that are more readily reversible. Thus, if an intervention is not effective, it is possible to go back to examining how the problem was defined, what factors were thought to affect student performance, and/or whether the intervention was actually done. It may be necessary to modify the instructional intervention several times until the right strategy is found. It is crucial to know what works and what doesn't work for individual students. Educators do this by being systematic in their problem solving when confronted with a student who is not as academically or socially competent as his or her peers. Routinely gathering outcome data is essential for accountable practice and good problem solving.

Educators can reduce the error rate in decision making by adhering to Phase 1 of the problem-solving model and proceeding to Phase 2 only when they have sufficient evidence that it is not possible to meet the students' needs with the resources available in the classroom setting. The Phase 1 problem-solving data should be used to guide this decision-making process. Finally, if students are classified, educators are responsible to ensure that this intrusive level of intervention is producing good benefits for the student. In other words, the same rules about monitoring special education outcomes apply. This is especially important because, contrary to popular belief that special education is a panacea for students with learning difficulty (expressed in statements like "If we could only get the child some services . . ."), special education services have not been shown to be effective for students on average and have even been shown to be harmful for many students (Kavale, 1990).

In chapter 1 we stressed the need for developing a professional model for assessment. Your model will guide you in the standards that you have for assessment practices. To develop those standards, you must understand the relationship between assessment and decision making. It is critical to evaluate what you know and what you need more information about. This chapter can serve as a reference point for evaluating how well you do problem solving and what additional information, training, and resources you need to do it even better in the future.

Part Three

Examining the Technical Characteristics of Commonly Used Norm-Referenced Tests

In Part Three we examine six major areas in which children function: academic achievement, language, cognitive abilities, behavior, adaptive behavior, and perceptual-motor skills. Within each of these areas we provide an evaluation of commonly used tests and assessment techniques.

Given the number of tests available, only the most frequently used or most reliable and valid are reviewed. Many of the most commonly used tests, however, are inadequate and should never have been published. We discuss why such tests are conceptually, technically, or functionally flawed and suggest alternatives.

Ironically, it is with standardized tests that you are most likely to err in your decision making. Why? Because such tests with their technical manuals and all the supporting data *seem* to provide incontrovertible evidence, the test user may have an undeserved level of comfort with the scores. Reading this section will help you learn why it is important to avoid falling into that trap.

Chapter 10

Academic Achievement: Reading and Mathmatics

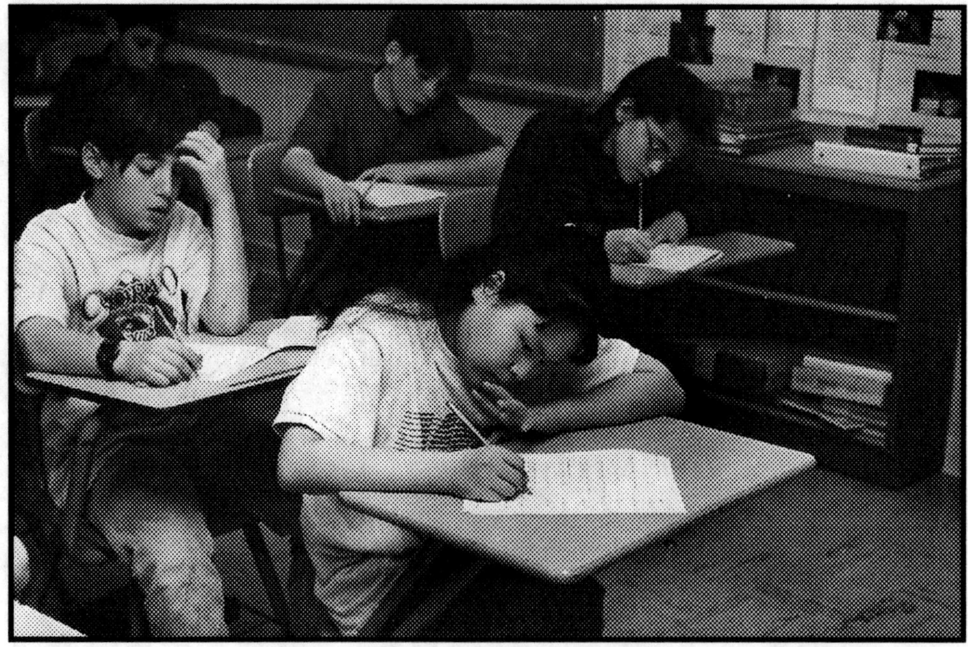

The scene is a familiar one. A teacher stands at the front of the classroom, a packet of test booklets held firmly in hand. In a few minutes she will break the seal on the packet of booklets and hand one to each student. She has placed a small clock on her desk so that students will be aware of how much time they have left on each section of the test. During the administration of the test she will also record the time remaining on the chalkboard. The students are sitting quietly, their pencils primed for action. They have been told that during the next few days they will be taking a number of different kinds of tests in reading, mathematics, and language arts. Although they may suspect that the test results will be reported to their parents, they are unaware of the many other uses for the results of standardized achievement batteries.

School districts all across the country set aside a certain number of days each year to administer achievement batteries. Indeed, many large school districts have separate departments that devote a great deal of time to the administration, interpretation, and dissemination of the results of such tests (see

Focus on Practice: The National Association of Test Directors). Although these tests are given routinely, there is considerable misunderstanding about their appropriate use.

Criticism of achievement batteries has focused on their validity (Wright & Piersel, 1987). A frequent complaint concerns their potential for underestimating the ability of individuals from minority cultures. These are important criticisms. The manner in which achievement batteries have been used (and abused) has also come under close scrutiny. For example, suppose in the case cited at the beginning of the chapter, the teacher worked within a school district that in the past year had taken a good deal of criticism because the students' average test scores were the lowest in five years and were lower than those in most other districts in the state. Administrators, feeling the pressure to "do something," met behind closed doors to discuss two plans for raising the scores. One of the strategies is designed to elevate individual scores while the other will eliminate some low scores; in both cases the score of the "average" student will go up. More specifically, the tactics include:

1. Coaching students in the weeks before the test. This coaching, or "teaching to the test," would involve using class time to practice answering items similar to those on the actual test. Although school officials do not know the exact items that will appear on the test, they do have a good idea of the types that will be sampled as a result of studying the publisher's objectives for the test.
2. Excluding special education students from the testing. The school officials argue that these students have already been extensively tested to qualify for special services and that little can be gained from further testing.

These strategies would most probably increase the average scores for each grade level, and thus the average score for the entire district would be higher than those from previous years. What is to be gained, however, if test scores are raised but no longer accurately reflect the knowledge level of a particular child or the average performance of children within the district? As Anastasi (1981) states, "a test score is invalidated . . . when a particular experience raises the score without appreciably affecting the behavior domain that the test samples" (p. 1087). In the preceding example, the school officials would be raising scores without modifying students' knowledge, thus invalidating the test. Although activities similar to those just described have taken place in some schools, they are certainly not standard practice. There is, however, a real potential for abuse when test score data have high stakes involving the allocation of resources and public perceptions of schools' effectiveness.

In this chapter, we examine the foundations of general achievement batteries, methods of utilizing the data obtained from them, a small sample of these tests, and some commonly used reading and math achievement tests. In the first part, the tests presented are designed to measure more than one achievement area (e.g., reading and math, social studies and science). The last part of the chapter is devoted to domain-referenced achievement tests of reading and math.

Focus on Practice

The National Association of Test Directors

Although the example of a fictional school district's approach to achievement batteries is not very flattering, most school districts do use data obtained from such tests in an appropriate fashion. The National Association of Test Directors (NATD) is a group of individuals (typically the coordinators of evaluation or assessment from large school districts) interested in learning the best ways to use tests within the public schools. They are exploring which tests have been found useful across the nation, the desirability of testing every student every year, and the most effective means of reporting scores to parents. During a recent meeting of the NATD (which took place at the 1987 annual meeting of the American Education Research Association) the agenda of items for future study included:

1. The desirability of developing a national, cooperative item bank for school systems designing their own achievement tests.
2. The effects of competency testing.
3. The merits of the national standardization of tests.
4. Methods of reporting district test results to the public.
5. Use of grade-equivalent scores by publishers, educators, and the public.
6. Strategies for test selection.
7. Methods of evaluating achievement in social studies and science.
8. Computer scoring of tests.
9. Use of standardized tests to determine school effectiveness, teacher effectiveness, and principal effectiveness.

Thus, although our example focused on the misuse of testing practices, clearly, individuals and groups such as the NATD are working to improve their use in the schools.

The Development and Use of Achievement Batteries

An **achievement battery** is a collection of tests from different subject areas that have been integrated into one test battery. Achievement batteries are often confused with aptitude tests, and both tests do measure, to some extent, prior learning. Achievement tests typically are samples of rather specific knowledge domains such as elementary mathematics, geography, and/or American history before 1865, whereas aptitude tests have a much broader pool of information from which to choose. It is important to remember, however, that both types of tests involve measurement of what an individual has learned. An aptitude test is not administered in a vacuum and the things that someone has learned/not learned in the past (e.g., the importance of double-checking an answer) cannot help but influence how they will do on a test of "aptitude" or "intelligence."

Selection of an appropriate instrument depends on careful analysis of (a) the purpose of the assessment, (b) the content and technical properties of the instruments being considered, and (c) the match between them. In other chapters we have emphasized the necessity of evaluating the technical adequacy of tests and the extent to which a variety of instruments meet this need. However, no understanding of reliability or validity will compensate for a failure to analyze carefully the purpose of the assessment. Questions related to the goals and objectives of a testing program must be answered before, not after, testing. For example, why is an achievement battery being considered? How will the results be used? Are you interested in receiving diagnostic information for students in special programs or only in reporting the results from a reliable, norm-referenced test to state and federal agencies? Has the match between the content of the school district's curriculum and the content of the test been evaluated? This type of planning must be completed before one begins to consider specific instruments: No test is capable of correcting for insufficient or inadequate planning. Since a general purpose of assessment is to make decisions about students' functioning, planning assessment means selecting tests that give the most accurate, reliable, and valid information necessary for the decision that you need to make.

It is also important to note that the label a test author or publisher applies to an achievement battery (e.g., The All-Purpose Achievement Test) or a particular subtest (e.g., reading) is, in and of itself, not an indication of the validity of that test for measuring the variable indicated by the title. A thorough analysis of the content is a necessary part of determining whether a test is qualified for the kind of decision that you must make. Later in this chapter a number of achievement batteries are discussed, but we now turn to a closer examination of the specific issues that must be considered before beginning an evaluation of achievement batteries.

Survey Versus Diagnostic Tests

Achievement batteries generally fall into one of two categories: screening (also called survey) or diagnostic tests. Many group tests designed for use with all students are used as screening tests in special education. Screening batteries are designed to provide a general estimate of current levels of academic achievement across a wide range of skill levels and carry with them the many problems described in chapter 2 resulting in frequent errors in decision making. Often, these tests contain a limited sample of problems from a particular content area. Survey tests typically are norm-referenced and administered to determine an individual's relative standing within a group. These tests generally are not designed to be aids in the development of specific educational programs. Instead, survey batteries are intended to provide a gross,

Focus on Research

The National Assessment of Educational Progress

How does student achievement today compare with that of previous generations, and what changes will occur during the next few decades? How good is the American educational system? There appears to be as many answers to these queries as there are people to ask. In just the last few years numerous groups (e.g., the Carnegie Foundation National Commission on Excellence in Education) have filed reports on the current status of the American educational system.

The National Assessment of Educational Progress (NAEP) was developed to monitor how the knowledge and skills of American schoolchildren changed over time (Ebel, 1966; Merwin, 1966; Tyler, 1966). In addition to written tests in 10 areas (literature, science, social studies, writing, citizenship, music, mathematics, reading, art, and vocational education), interviews, observations, questionnaires, and performance items have been included in the NAEP assessment strategy. The tests were first administered in 1969 at four age levels: 9, 13, 17, and 23 to 35. Plans were for the tests to be readministered to new groups periodically.

Over the last two decades the NAEP has undergone significant changes (Johnson, 1992). Current goals for the NAEP include both providing a national census on academic performance *and* trying to identify reasons for changes in scores. Innovative assessment strategies were developed with plans for the 1992 testing to include more extensive use of writing samples, oral interviews, and portfolio assessment (Mullis, 1992).

During the past few years, ETS and numerous professional journals (e.g., *Journal of Educational Measurement*) have published thousands of pages detailing the strategies and results of previous NAEP testing. Although it is beyond the scope of this brief report to summarize all of the findings, it is fair to say that these data have not indicated that American education should be a model for the world. NAEP results are often cited as evidence that American schoolchildren know less than children in most other developed countries. Deficiencies in math and science education have been of special concern to those who see America falling behind in the race to be a leader in new technology and innovation. Many reasons have been proposed for the apparent failure of American education to keep pace with the rest of the world and much disagreement about the cause and cure of this problem exists. One thing is clear, however, is that the NAEP provides information about the achievement of American schoolchildren in an ongoing, systematic manner that is not available from other sources.

overall picture of an individual's current level of achievement and as such are a reasonable first step in the assessment of academic skills. Therefore, they cannot be used for instructional planning, as they yield only a student's ranking compared with a sample of peers.

Sometimes, because of prior testing or background information, an examiner may need more specific information about an individual's skills. Diagnostic achievement batteries are designed to identify specific strengths and weaknesses in a variety of academic skills, such as reading, arithmetic, and spelling. A particular content area (e.g., reading) is typically subdivided into skill areas (in this case, word recognition, word analysis, and vocabulary). Although many educators use these tests to interpret individual student's mastery of basic skills in specific areas, the small number of items, the novelty of the assessment setting, and the probable lack of overlap with instructional material make interpretation based on them quite susceptible to error.

Group Versus Individual Administration

Achievement batteries can also be categorized as either group or individually administered. Group tests are typically given to entire classes at one time. Group tests also require less training in administration techniques than do most individual tests. Although individual tests cannot routinely be given to groups, a group test may be administered to one student, provided that it is administered in the standardized fashion. Some individual tests are poorly constructed or sample only a limited amount of content (e.g., the Wide Range Achievement Test-III), whereas some group tests have been meticulously developed and sample from an extensive variety of academic areas (see table 10.1). Nonetheless, all such tests must be scrutinized for (a) their reliability and validity, (b) the reliability and validity of the decisions that they lead to, and (c) the degree to which they contribute meaningfully to problem solving when students don't do well.

We examined in chapter 2 some of the common practices with these tests and the inherent problems that result from their use. However, because of their continued use for classification decisions, we will examine the technical characteristics (i.e., reliability and validity) of some of the more common tests of general achievement and tests of reading and math. Consider this an exercise in evaluating norm-referenced tests based on the information provided in their respective technical manuals. As a result of this discussion, you will also be knowledgeable about the technical characteristics of individual tests in the event that you are called on to use assessment data derived from them in a decision about a student.

General Achievement Tests

Many different achievement batteries are available for inspection and use. Some of the most widely used tests of achievement are discussed next,

Table 10.1 Widely Used Group-Administered Comprehensive Achievement Batteries

Battery	*Grades*	*Subject Areas*
Iowa Tests of Basic Skills (Forms G and H) (Hieronymus et al., 1986)	K.1–1.5	Listening, Vocabulary, Word Analysis, Language, Mathematics
	K.8–1.9	Listening, Vocabulary, Word Analysis, Reading, Language, Mathematics
	1.7–2.6	Vocabulary, Word Analysis, Reading Comprehension, Spelling, Mathematics Concepts, Mathematics Problems, Mathematics Computation, Listening, Capitalization, Punctuation, Usage and Expression, Visual Materials, Reference Materials, Social Studies, Science
Note: At older grade levels not all subject areas need be administered to all children as subtests are divided into Basic, Complete, and Complete Plus Supplemental batteries of tests. Schools may choose whichever battery they believe best meets their need.	2.5–3.5	Vocabulary, Word Analysis, Reading Comprehension, Spelling, Mathematics Concepts, Mathematics Problems, Mathematics Computation, Listening, Capitalization, Punctuation, Usage and Expression, Visual Materials, Reference Materials, Social Studies, Science
	3–9	Vocabulary, Word Analysis, Reading Comprehension, Spelling, Mathematics Concepts, Mathematics Problems, Mathematics Computation, Listening, Capitalization, Punctuation, Usage and Expression, Visual Materials, Reference Materials, Supplemental Social Studies/Science Test
Metropolitan Achievement Tests (Seventh Edition) (Prescott, Balow, Hogan, & Farr, 1992) (Survey Battery)	K.0–K.5	Reading, Mathematics, Language, Total
	K.5–1.9	Reading, Mathematics, Language, Total
	1.5–2.9	Reading, Mathematics, Language, Basic Total, Science, Social Studies, Complete Total
	2.5–3.9	Reading, Mathematics, Language, Basic Total, Science, Social Studies, Complete Total
Note: At older grade levels some subject areas (e.g., Reading) contain a number of different subtests (e.g., at grades 3.5–4.9 Reading consists of vocabulary, word recognition, reading comprehension, and total reading).	3.5–4.9	Reading, Mathematics, Language, Basic Total, Science, Social Studies, Complete Total, Research Skills
	5.0–6.9	Reading, Mathematics, Language, Basic Total, Science, Social Studies, Complete Total, Research Skills
	7.0–9.9	Reading, Mathematics, Language, Basic Total, Science, Social Studies, Complete Total, Research Skills
	10.0–12.9	Reading, Mathematics, Language, Basic Total, Science, Social Studies, Complete Total, Research Skills

Table 10.1 *continued*

SRA Achievement Series (Forms 1 and 2) Science Research Associates, 1987) *Note:* At all age levels some subject areas (e.g., Mathematics) contain a number of different subtests (e.g., at grades 6.5–8.5 Math consists of math computations, math concepts, math problem solving). The Verbal, Nonverbal, and Total tests are referred to as Educational Ability Scales.	K.5–1.5	Reading, Mathematics, Composite, Verbal, Nonverbal, Total
	1.5–2.5	Reading, Mathematics, Composite, Verbal, Nonverbal, Total
	2.5–3.5	Reading, Mathematics, Language Arts, Composite, Verbal, Nonverbal, Total
	3.5–4.5	Reading, Mathematics, Language Arts, Composite, Verbal, Nonverbal, Total
	4.5–6.5	Reading, Mathematics, Language Arts, Reference Materials, Social Studies, Science, Composite, Verbal, Nonverbal, Total
	6.5–8.5	Reading, Mathematics, Language Arts, Reference Materials, Social Studies, Science, Composite, Verbal, Nonverbal, Total
	8.5–10.5	Reading, Mathematics, Language Arts, Reference Materials, Social Studies, Science, Composite, Verbal, Nonverbal, Total
	9.0–12.9	Reading, Mathematics, Language Arts, Reference Materials, Social Studies, Science, Survey of Applied Skills, Composite, Verbal, Nonverbal, Total
Stanford Achievement Test (Ninth Edition) (The Psychological Corporation, 1996)	1.5–2.5	Reading, Mathematics, Language, Spelling, Listening, Environment, Basic Battery, Complete Battery
	2.5–3.5	Reading, Mathematics, Language, Spelling, Listening, Environment, Basic Battery, Complete Battery
Note: At all grade levels some subject areas (e.g., Language) contain a number of different subtests (e.g., at grades 3.5–4.5 Language consists of mechanics, expression, and total scores).	3.5–4.5	Reading, Mathematics, Language, Listening, Spelling, Study Skills, Science, Social Studies, Listening, Using Information, Thinking Skills, Basic Battery, Complete Battery
	4.5–5.5	Reading, Mathematics, Language, Listening, Spelling, Study Skills, Science, Social Studies, Listening, Using Information, Thinking Skills, Basic Battery, Complete Battery
	5.5–6.5	Reading, Mathematics, Language, Listening, Spelling, Study Skills, Science, Social Studies, Listening, Using Information, Thinking Skills, Basic Battery, Complete Battery
	6.5–7.5	Reading, Mathematics, Language, Listening, Spelling, Study Skills, Science, Social Studies, Listening, Using Information, Thinking Skills, Basic Battery, Complete Battery
	7.5–8.5	Reading, Mathematics, Language, Listening, Spelling, Study Skills, Science, Social Studies, Listening, Using Information, Thinking Skills, Basic Battery, Complete Battery
	8.5–9.9	Reading, Mathematics, Language, Listening, Spelling, Study Skills, Science, Social Studies, Listening, Using Information, Thinking Skills, Basic Battery, Complete Battery

although options from which to choose are extensive and growing (see e.g., Kramer & Conoley, 1992).

BRIGANCE® Diagnostic Inventory of Basic Skills

Overview and Purpose

The Diagnostic Inventory of Basic Skills, or DIBS (BRIGANCE®), was the first of a series of individually administered, criterion-referenced diagnostic tests (e.g., Diagnostic Inventory of Early Development-Revised, Diagnostic Comprehensive Inventory of Basic Skills, and Diagnostic Inventory of Essential Skills) originally developed by Albert H. Brigance (1977). The inventories are similar in purpose and format but differ in the assumptions about the performance level of the individual being assessed. The specific skills tested on each inventory differ, although there is some overlap. The DIBS is designed for students achieving in the kindergarten through sixth-grade levels, and its author has identified its five specific purposes:

1. to assess basic readiness and academic skills in key subject areas from the kindergarten to sixth-grade level;
2. to provide a systematic performance record, expressed in grade-level terms, for diagnosis and evaluation;
3. to define instructional objectives in precise terms to measure a student's performance in a given subject area;
4. to determine a student's level of achievement, readiness to advance, or need for improvement; and
5. to guide the teacher in designing an instructional program to meet the specific needs of the student (Brigance, 1977).

The DIBS assesses skills in four general areas: readiness, reading, language arts, and math. Each of these domains is broken into a number of skill (and subskill) areas, with the items arranged in order of difficulty. Table 10.2 presents the skill areas in the Readiness and Reading domains. As this table indicates, the DIBS attempts to provide comprehensive diagnostic information on a variety of skills.

The comprehensive nature of the DIBS has contributed to its widespread use, as has its ease and flexibility of administration. Directions are clear and are printed on each page of the examination material. Examiners are encouraged to modify the procedures in any manner they deem appropriate to determine whether students have mastered particular skills. Depending on the age, skill level, distractibility of the child, and the amount of information desired, administration can take from 10 minutes to a few hours spread across a couple of days.

Standardization Sample and Norms

The DIBS is criterion-referenced, and little normative data are reported in the manual.

Table 10.2 Readiness and Reading Skills Assessed in BRIGANCE® Diagnostic Inventory of Basic Skills

Readiness

Color recognition
Visual discrimination
Visual-motor skills
Visual memory
Body image
Gross motor coordination
Identification of body parts
Directional/positional skills
Fine motor skills
Verbal fluency
Verbal directions
Articulation of sounds
Personal data response
Sentence memory
Counting
Alphabet
Number recognition
Number comprehension
Recognition of lowercase letters
Recognition of uppercase letters
Writing name
Numbers in sequence
Lowercase letters in sequence
Uppercase letters in sequence

Reading

Word recognition
Word recognition grade level
Basic sight vocabulary
Direction words
Abbreviations
Contractions
Common signs

Reading
Oral reading list
Reading comprehension level
Oral reading rate

Vocabulary
Context clues
Classifications
Analogies
Antonyms
Homonyms

Word analysis
Auditory discrimination
Initial consonant sounds auditorily
Initial consonant sounds visually
Substitution of initial consonant sounds
Ending sounds auditorily
Vowels
Short vowel sounds
Long vowel sounds
Initial clusters auditorily
Initial clusters visually
Substitution of initial cluster sounds
Digraphs and diphthongs
Phonetic irregularities
Common endings of rhyming words
Suffixes
Prefixes
Meaning of prefixes
Number of syllables auditorily
Syllabication concepts

Data Obtained

Based on their performance, individuals are considered to have either mastered or not mastered the skill assessed in each sequence. In addition, grade-level information is provided for many of the subtests based on the author's attempts to "text-reference" the DIBS. That is, many commonly used texts, word lists, developmental scales, and the like were examined to determine the level at which a particular skill is typically first introduced or expected. No summary or overall achievement level scores are provided.

Reliability and Validity

No information related to the reliability and little validity data are reported in the test materials. A major drawback to the DIBS is the lack of specific details about its development and refinement.

Summary

Perhaps the greatest disadvantage to the DIBS is the lack of specific information about the development of the scale and the author's failure to provide any reliability data. As a result, it is not possible to know how reliable test results are, or how reliable the decisions about student performance are. Because the reliability of a test is also an integral part of its validity, it is not possible to assess how valid the DIBS is for educational decision making.

California Achievement Tests

Overview and Purpose

The California Achievement Tests, or CAT (CTB/McGraw-Hill, 1985), is one of a number of widely used group-administered, comprehensive achievement batteries currently available for use in public schools (see table 10.1). The CAT (Forms E and F) is a series of comprehensive tests that measure skills in seven areas: Reading, Spelling, Language, Mathematics, Study Skills, Science, and Social Studies. Not all tests are administered at all levels and some tests (e.g., science and social studies) are optional (Airasian, 1989). The CAT assesses skills at 11 overlapping grade levels (K–12). Table 10.1 shows that many group achievement tests have divided their tests into grade levels that overlap. The overlap in grade levels makes it easy to assess children at their functional level rather than their assigned grade level. The CAT has two forms (E and F) for the eight oldest age groups. Brief, optional pretests are available for teachers who want to estimate a child's functional level prior to administering a form of the CAT. Both norm-referenced (national and local) and criterion-referenced information are available with the CAT.

Standardization Sample and Norms

The CAT was standardized on a stratified national sample of approximately 300,000 students in grades K to 12 during the fall and spring of the 1984–85 school year. Stratification variables included type of school (public or Catholic), geographic region, social class/SES, and size of school district and community type (rural, urban, suburban). An attempt was made to provide adequate representation of disabled and minority populations.

Data Obtained

The CAT may be hand-scored or returned to the publisher for scoring. A variety of derived scores are available: grade equivalents, percentiles, normal curve equivalents, scale scores, anticipated achievement scores, and category objective scores. Information provided by the test publisher to assist in the interpretation of results appears adequate, although the test publisher has been criticized for not having enough information available for users who need to understand appropriate uses of test scores (Wardrop, 1989).

Reliability and Validity

Reliability estimates are provided for each subtest at each level. Extensive information is presented on the internal consistency (KR-20) of the CAT, and these estimates appear to be uniformly high. Test-retest figures for the subtests are consistent with internal consistency estimates (generally .86 or above). Most validity data on the CAT are related to content validity. Objectives for the CAT were developed following a review of curriculum guides from various state departments of education and large cities as well as the objectives of other achievement tests. Test items were developed by professional item writers and care was taken to eliminate those items that appeared to be biased in any fashion.

Summary

The CAT is a well-standardized, reliable achievement battery for testing school-age children. Its development began approximately a half century ago, and the current edition of the battery is an excellent example of a well-constructed, group-administered test. Although billed as a comprehensive test, the CAT focuses on the evaluation of basic academic skills (reading, mathematics, and language arts). The adequacy of the test's category objectives and the value of criterion-referenced results in helping teachers plan instruction remain unknown.

Kaufman Test of Educational Achievement (Comprehensive Form)

Overview and Purpose

The Kaufman Test of Educational Achievement, or K-TEA (Kaufman & Kaufman, 1985), is designed to measure school achievement of children from 6 years, 0 months, to 18 years, 11 months. It is individually administered and is available in two forms. The Brief Form assesses the global areas of Reading, Mathematics, and Spelling; a Battery Composite score is also available. The Comprehensive Form assesses the areas of Mathematics Applications, Reading Decoding, Spelling, Reading Comprehension, and Mathematics Computation; Reading Composite, Mathematics Composite, and Battery Composite scores are also available. Although there are a number of similarities between the two forms (e.g., in how they are presented to individuals and the information in their manuals), the content does not overlap. A decision about whether the Brief or the Comprehensive Form is used depends on the amount and type of information desired on an individual child (e.g., screening versus diagnostic). A description of the Comprehensive Form follows. According to the K-TEA manual, the administration of the test takes from 20 to 30 minutes for first graders and from 55 to 65 minutes for eleventh and twelfth graders. The K-TEA may be administered by educational and psychological personnel skilled in testing as well as "technicians" and paraprofessionals with proper training. It is suggested that the interpretation of the results requires more skill than does the administration and that interpretation should be the responsibility of trained personnel. The subtests on the Comprehensive Form include:

1. Mathematics Applications—60 items presented orally and assessing a wide variety of concepts and applications of mathematical principles
2. Reading Decoding—60 items involving identification of letters and pronunciation of words
3. Spelling—50 items that the examiner reads aloud and uses in a sentence, with the student then writing the word
4. Reading Comprehension—50 items requiring oral answers to questions related to paragraphs the subjects have read. Some items also require gestural or oral responses to printed sentences
5. Mathematics Computation—60 written items ranging from simple addition and subtraction to algebraic computations

The Comprehensive Form allows for extensive error analysis of an individual's mistakes on any of the five subtests. For example, in Mathematics Computation, the subskill areas include Basic Addition, Regrouping Addition, Basic Subtraction, Regrouping Subtraction, Multiplication, Division, Fractions, Advanced Addition, Advanced Subtraction, Algebraic Equations, and Square Roots and Exponents. Reading Comprehension has two subskill areas, Literal Comprehension and Inferential Comprehension.

Standardization Sample and Norms

Standardization of the Comprehensive Form took place during two separate nationwide administrations in the spring and fall of 1983. Approximately 2,500 students (1,400+ in the spring and 1,000+ in the fall) participated in the standardization. An attempt was made to select a representative national sample based on U.S. Census Bureau data. The samples were stratified within each grade level (approximately 100 per grade for both spring and fall) by race or ethnic group, sex, socioeconomic status (educational attainment of parents or other adults living in the household), and geographic region. No systematic attempt to include special education students was made, although permission slips for participating in the standardization were given to special education students. That is, these students were provided an opportunity to participate, but no record was kept of the number who returned permission slips.

Data Obtained

The K-TEA provides standard scores, with a mean of 100 and a standard deviation of 15 (although there is some variability in the exact means and standard deviations on each subtest and composite at each grade), grade equivalents, age equivalents, percentile ranks, stanines, and normal curve equivalents.

Reliability and Validity

Mean split-half reliability coefficients ranged from .90 (Mathematics Computation) to .95 (Reading Decoding) for the subtests and .94 (Mathematics Composite) to .98 (Battery Composite) for the composites. Test-retest reliability estimates (N = 172, retest interval of 1 to 35 days) are reported for grades 1 to 6 and 7 to 12. For the lower grades, estimates ranged from .83 (Mathematics Computation) to .95 (Spelling/Reading Decoding) for the subtests and .93 (Mathematics Composite) to .97 (Battery Composite) for the composites. For the higher grades, estimates ranged from .90 (Reading Comprehension) to .96 (Spelling) for the subtests and .94 (Reading Composite) to .97 (Battery Composite) for the composites.

Standard errors of measurement (SEM) are reported and generally range from about 2 standard score points for the Battery Composite to 3 to 5 points for the individual subtests. Reading Composite SEMs are generally about 3 points, whereas Mathematics Composite SEMs generally are 3 to 4 points.

Validation of the K-TEA was a sequential process involving assessment of content validity, construct validity, and concurrent validity. A content blueprint for the K-TEA was developed by its authors, members of the publisher's staff, and curriculum consultants. The large number of items originally considered were reduced through various types of analyses (both conventional as well as the Rasch-Wright item response techniques). After national samplings some items were eliminated either because they failed to fit the Rasch-Wright model or because of evidence of bias. Evidence for construct validity is provided in that as children grow older and experience more schooling, their K-TEA scores tend to improve. Internal consistency estimates for the five subtests ranged from .77 to .85 (by grade level). Evidence of concurrent validity is provided through correlations between the K-TEA scores of some of the standardization sample with either the Kaufman Assessment Battery for Children (K-ABC), Wide Range Achievement Test (WRAT), Peabody Individual Achievement Test (PIAT), or Peabody Picture Vocabulary Test-Revised (PPVT-R). Comparisons also were made between K-TEA scores and three group achievement batteries: Stanford Achievement Test, Metropolitan Achievement Tests, and Comprehensive Tests of Basic Skills. The large amount of information collected in these comparisons indicate that, in general, the K-TEA subtests and composites appear to measure the same abilities as similar subtests and composites on other academic tests.

Summary

The K-TEA appears to be a psychometrically sound achievement battery. The standardization process is exemplary in its attention to detail. The test provides norm-referenced information. Interpretation is limited to describing students' ranking compared with other same-age or same-grade students on the global domains. Unfortunately, the information cannot be used for instructional decision making because it assesses only global domains such as reading comprehension with a limited number of items that overlap to varying degrees with different reading curricula.

Peabody Individual Achievement Test-Revised

Overview and Purpose

The Peabody Individual Achievement Test-Revised, or PIAT-R (Markwardt, 1989), is an individually administered, norm-referenced achievement battery. The Peabody Individual Achievement Test was originally published in 1970. Designed as a screening or survey measure, the PIAT-R provides an overview of scholastic attainment in six content areas: Mathematics, Reading Recognition, Reading Comprehension, Spelling, Written Expression, and General Information. The test takes approximately 60 minutes to administer and is normed for grades K to 12. Only the Written Expression subtest is timed; however, on the other subtests examiners are warned to give individuals enough time to respond but not to wait an "unlimited time" for them to answer. The subtests include:

1. Mathematics—100 multiple-choice items ranging from matching and visual discrimination at the lower levels to trigonometry at the upper levels
2. Reading Recognition—100 items including 16 multiple-choice "readiness" questions (e.g., matching letters) and 84 words to be read aloud
3. Reading Comprehension—82 questions requiring the individual to read a sentence silently and to pick the one picture from four different choices that best illustrates the meaning of the sentence
4. Spelling—100 multiple-choice items requiring a range of skills from identification of printed letters to the spelling of words read by the examiner
5. Written Expression

   Level 1 assesses writing readiness skills with 19 items, requires the child to write his or her name, copy letters, and write letters, words, or sentences in response to dictation;

   Level 2 consists of a 20-minute period in which the individual is asked to write a story about a picture
6. General Information—100 open-ended questions testing general knowledge in science, social studies, fine arts, humanities, and recreation

The manual is clearly written, and the record booklet is easily used. The administration of the PIAT-R is generally easy to learn, although individuals familiar with the original PIAT will need to acquaint themselves with the changes and additions before attempting to administer this test.

Standardization Sample and Norms

The original standardization sample consisted of 1,563 students kindergarten through 12th grade, most of whom attended public schools (91.4%). An additional 175 kindergarten children were tested the following fall to provide data for beginning kindergarten students. The sample was stratified according to geographic region, race/ethnic group, and socioeconomic status based on the "most current Census information available." Between 98 and 148 children were sampled at each of the 13 grade levels in the sample. Children in special education classes were not included in the standardization.

Data Obtained

The PIAT-R provides grade equivalents, age equivalents, percentile ranks, stanine scores, normal curve equivalents, and standard scores by grade or age (with a mean of 100 and a standard deviation of 15) for each of the subtests and composite scores (Total Reading and Total Test) except for those in the written language area. For written language, grade-based stanines are provided and a developmental scaled score is available for Level 2. An optional written language composite score (Spelling + Written Expression) is also available.

Reliability and Validity

Test-retest, split-half, Kuder-Richardson, and item response estimates of reliability were obtained for the PIAT-R (except for the written expression subtest and scores). The median split-half reliabilities for all subtests evaluated were above .90 (range .92–.98). Both Kuder-Richardson (KR-20) and item response estimates of reliability were high, with median estimates above .94 for all subtests at all ages and grades. Fifty individuals in kindergarten as well as grades 2, 4, 6, and 8 were retested at intervals of two to four weeks after original testing to assess test-retest reliability. Median test-retest reliabilities are reported as .96 for the Total Test, .84 for Mathematics, .96 for Reading Recognition, .88 of Reading Comprehension, .88 for Spelling, and .91 for General Information. The median standard error of measurement for standard scores (mean of 100 and standard deviation of 15) is reported for both grade and age norms. These figures indicate median SEM estimates as approximately 2.0 points for the total test and range from 2.4 to 4.1 for the subtests. Reliability for the Written Expression-Level 1 subtest was calculated using interrater, internal consistency, and test-retest procedures. Although interrater reliabilities were high (.88–.95), more modest estimates were obtained with internal consistency (.61–.69) and test-retest (.56) procedures. Written Expression-Level 2 reliabilities were determined using interrater, internal consistency, and alternate form estimates for the two forms (i.e., the two different picture prompts—A/B). Median interrater reliabilities were .58/.67 for the two prompts, internal consistency estimates of .86/.88 were obtained for the total sample, and test-retest estimates ranged from .44 to .61.

Two types of validity information are presented in the PIAT manual: content and construct. Content validity was established by extensive review of curriculum materials to aid in item development. In addition, experts in the various areas were asked to evaluate the extent to which the test material was representative of the curricula of various grade levels and the specific content domain (e.g., mathematics) to be tested. The use of time review, item analysis, and content experts in the test development process is detailed in the test manual and appears very thorough. Construct validity was based on correlations between scores on the PIAT-R and both the original PIAT and the Peabody Picture Vocabulary Test-Revised (PPVT-R). These results suggest moderate overlap between these tests as would be expected. Factor analysis was also used to assess construct validity and yielded a three-factor solution, generally supportive of test validity (Benes, 1992; Rogers, 1992).

Summary

The PIAT-R continues to be widely used in screening academic skill development in spite of the problems associated with this practice. Although the multiple-choice format appears to be useful for children with language or physical disabilities, this is not the format curricula usually required for producing knowledge (i.e., spontaneously verbalizing the response), limiting the generalizations that we can draw about how well individuals can verbally produce answers spontaneously. Substantial reliability and validity information has been collected, although more data assessing concurrent validity are needed. One might say that the PIAT-R provides a rough measure of academic competence across a number of important academic skill areas. Given the potential long-lasting consequences of norm-referenced assessment for classification, however, educators should seek more than just a rough estimate of students' skills before making important decisions about student placements.

Wide Range Achievement Test-3

Overview and Purpose

The WRAT-3 is an individually administered test of reading, spelling, and arithmetic achievement (Wilkinson, 1993). Each of the academic areas has one subtest with two alternate forms ("BLUE" and "TAN" forms). The test makers report that it takes approximately 15 to 30 minutes to administer the WRAT-3. The test is purported "to measure the codes which are needed to learn the basic skills of reading, spelling, and arithmetic" (p. 10).

Standardization Sample and Norms

The test was standardized on a sample of 4,433 individuals ranging in age from 5 years, 0 months to 74 years, 11 months. The authors attempted to configure the standardization sample by age, regional residence, gender, ethnicity, and socioeconomic level so as to match 1990 U.S. Census data.

Reliability and Validity

The authors report three types of reliability: internal consistency (coefficient alpha), alternate forms, and test-retest. The reported coefficient alphas for individual subtests range from .69 to .96. The median coefficient alphas range from .85 to .95 over all of the combined scores and individual subtest scores across all three areas—reading, spelling, and arithmetic. The median correlation for alternate forms in reading is .92 (range = .87 to .99 across all ages), in spelling is .93 (range = .86 to .99 across all ages), and in math is .89 (range = .82 to .99 across all ages). Test-retest samples were gathered for 142 individuals from the norm group (ages 6 to 16). Using standard scores, uncorrected correlation coefficients ranged from .84 to .95 across combined and individual subtest scores in reading, spelling, and arithmetic.

As evidence of content validity, the test authors report item and person separation scores averaging 1.0 and .98, respectively. Although these data suggest that items were selected to represent easy, hard, and "in-between" (i.e., of moderate difficulty) items at each age level, they do not necessarily indicate that the test items are representative of "the words in the English language for reading and spelling and the arithmetic computation problems taught in Kindergarten through high school for arithmetic" (p. 176). Indeed, given the small number of words that appear on the test and varying curricula that exist across school districts, content validity can only be judged in each local situation. It hardly seems likely, however, that a test can be judged as having content validity across all possible test administrations.

The test authors present test correlations with age (in months) that range from .52 to .58, median intercorrelations among subtests of .66 to .87 across all age groups in the standardization sample, correlations ranging from .51 to .74 for each form (Blue and Tan) with the global scales of the Wechsler Intelligence Scale for Children-III, and correlations ranging from .28 to .63 for the combined areas with the global scales of the Wechsler Adult Intelligence Scale-Revised. The authors also reported uncorrected correlations ranging from .66 to .92 for each form and combined score in reading, spelling, and arithmetic with the previous edition of the WRAT, the WRAT-R. Correlations of combined scores with the California Test of Basic Skills (4th ed.), the California Achievement Test (Form E), and the Stanford Achievement Test ranged from .41 to .87.

Summary

In short, the WRAT-3 correlates moderately with just about anything, reducing our confidence that (a) we can discriminate well between achievement areas using the test scores and (b) we are obtaining a good global measure of achievement. Perhaps the most telling piece of evidence that should be a caveat itself is the percentage differentiation that the authors obtained among groups of students previously classified as "gifted," "learning disabled," "educably mentally handicapped," and "normal." WRAT-3 scores led to agreement in classification for 85 percent of the "gifted" group, 72 percent of the "learning disabled" group, 83 percent of the "educably mentally handicapped" group, and 56 percent of the "normal" group. In other words, for each of the three diagnostic categories (gifted, learning disabled, and educably mentally handicapped), there is at least one case of disagreement for every three to four cases of agreement, an extremely high error rate for a decision of weighty consequence. Agreement for the group classified as "normal" is just above chance levels. It appears that the WRAT-3 has little diagnostic utility for instructional or classification decisions.

Woodcock-Johnson Psychoeducational Battery-Revised

Overview and Purpose

The Woodcock-Johnson Psychoeducational Battery-Revised, or WJ-R (Woodcock & Johnson, 1989), is a comprehensive, multiple-skill battery designed to assess cognitive skills and achievement. The WJ-R is individually administered to individuals from 3 to 80 years of age. The complete battery contains 39 tests, or measures, organized into two parts: Cognitive Ability and Academic Achievement. There are 21 tests for evaluating cognitive ability and 18 tests for assessing academic achievement. Both the cognitive and achievement parts of the test are further divided into standard and supplemental batteries. The achievement battery has two alternate forms (A and B). The number of tests administered to a particular individual is a function of the person's age and the purpose of the assessment (e.g., reading comprehension would not be administered to a typical 3-year-old, or an examiner may wish to test only cognitive abilities or achievement or a subsection of these skills). As would be expected, the time needed to administer the WJ-R depends on the purpose of the assessment, the age and responsiveness of the examinee, and the number of tests to be administered.

The WJ-R is both a revised and an expanded version of the original Woodcock-Johnson. For example, changes include new tests added to the cognitive and achievement batteries, individual items revised and reordered on some subtests, and more sample items added to some subtests. As mentioned, the achievement battery now has two parallel forms (A and B). Individuals familiar with the previous edition will note that the WJ-R no longer includes tests of interests. According to the authors, the uses of the revised Woodcock-Johnson include diagnosis, determination of discrepancies among academic and cognitive abilities, program placement, planning individual programs, guidance, assessment of growth, program evaluation, research, and psychometric training.

Standardization Sample and Norms

The WJ-R was standardized on 6,359 subjects (the majority, or 3,245, were in school at the time) in more than 100 communities throughout the United States. The sample was stratified on the basis of 1980 and later U.S. Census data according to the following subject and community variables: sex, race, geographic region, and community size. For adults, these variables were also considered: funding source of college and university being attended (for the college sample), type of college, education, occupational status, and occupation. The manual states that "Severely handicapped students" were not included in the sample; however, the term was not defined. Nor were students with less than one year of experience with English included in the sample.

Data Obtained

Although the WJ-R is organized into subtests, the basic units of analysis are the cluster scores, or scores earned on groups of subtests. The WJ-R yields a variety of derived scores including cluster scores, percentile rankings, age and grade equivalents, and relative mastery indexes. Scoring the WJ-R may be the most difficult task associated with the test. According to Cummings (1985), in his review of the original Woodcock-Johnson Psychoeducational Battery:

> Once the instrument has been administered, the process of obtaining derived scores is somewhat arduous. There are numerous score transformations and sums to be added. Consider the process of obtaining a percentile rank for a child's verbal ability cluster. The raw score is transformed to a part score, the part scores are totaled to obtain a cluster score, the average age score for the child's chronological age is found in a table and then subtracted from the obtained cluster score in order to arrive at the cluster difference score, and finally a table is consulted to determine the examinee's percentile rank. For Parts I and II of the battery, this procedure must be completed 13 times. (p. 1760)

Scoring of the current revision is just as difficult and examiners are encouraged to use the computer-based scoring system available from the test publisher (written expression must be hand-scored). Scoring itself may be a significant source of error.

Reliability and Validity

Split-half reliabilities for subtest scores and cluster scores are reported and are generally excellent. Median reliabilities on the achievement battery are all above .86 for subtests and .94 for clusters. No test-retest comparisons are reported (except for Writing Fluency, in which split-half estimates were inappropriate), and thus no evidence on the effects of stability over time is available. Extensive concurrent and predictive validity data are reported in the manual. The WJ-R serves as an excellent model for the reporting of test validity data. Correlations with a number of intellectual measures (e.g., the K-ABC), achievement tests (e.g., K-TEA, PIAT, WRAT-R), and related tests are reported. A major shortcoming is that no specific information is presented to support the uses of the WJ-R that have been identified by the authors. It is therefore not clear that the WJ-R can be useful, accurate, or valid for educational decision making.

Summary

The WJ-R, as an individually administered battery of tests, is relatively easy to administer, adequately standardized, has acceptable reliability estimates for obtaining student rankings, but is difficult to score. Our experience with the written language subtests suggests that these subtests can be especially difficult to score reliably. In a relatively short period this test has had a significant impact on achievement testing and today is one of the most popular individually administered batteries with school-age populations. The inclusion of measures of cognitive ability and achievement within an individually administered battery is an innovative and positive feature. Coverage of such a broad age range also makes the WJ-R an attractive instrument.

The Wechsler Individual Achievement Test

Overview and Purpose

The Wechsler Individual Achievement Test (WIAT) is a norm-referenced test of reading, mathematics, language, and writing skills for students in grades kindergarten through 12th grade (The Psychological Corporation, 1992). It contains eight subtests and takes 30 to 50 minutes to administer for students in grades kindergarten through second grade and 55 to 60 minutes to administer for students in grades 3 through 12, according to the test makers. They claim: "It is particularly suitable for investigating ability-achievement discrepancies in children aged 6:0 to 16:11 because its normative sample is linked to that of the WISC-III" (p. 7).

Standardization Sample and Norms

The standardization sample was made up of 4,252 children in age groups ranging from 5 through 19 years of age enrolled in kindergarten through grade 12. It contained approximately equal numbers of males and females with approximately equal numbers of students at each age and grade level. Using 1988 U.S. Census data, the test makers created a stratified sample that contained proportional numbers of different ethnic groups with proportional representation of four geographical regions (Northeast, North Central, South, and West). Finally, they include information about parent education level across the different groups.

Reliability and Validity

Reliability evidence is presented in the form of split-half, test-retest, and interscorer. The average split-half correlations across ages range from .81 to .92 for subtests and .90 to .97 for composites (corrected with the Spearman-Brown prophecy formula). Test-retest estimates were gathered for a smaller sample of students in grades 1, 3, 5, 8, and 10; they range from .68 to .94 for subtests and .78 to .96 for composites. Interscorer agreement data are provided for only four subtests, subtests that "require more judgment in scoring and are thus more likely to result in scorer error" (p. 144). An average correlation of .98 was obtained for Reading Comprehension and Listening Comprehension. Intraclass correlations were calculated for the Oral Expression subtest (average .93) and the two prompts for the Written Expression subtest (Prompt 1 average correlation = .89; Prompt 2 average correlation = .79). A lot of discussion is devoted to score difference interpretation across composite scores. However, there is no discussion of the *reliability* of decision scores, which (as we saw in chapter 2) is always lower than the individual reliabilities of the subtests used in the calculation of the difference scores (Barnett & Macmann, 1992b).

With respect to content validity, the authors explain, "Of all of these steps, the one most critical to content validity was the process of matching the content, that is, items, of each subtest to the curriculum objectives represented in the subtest." The critical question, however, is whether school curricula contain the subtest curriculum objectives from the WIAT. Construct validity was estimated through intercorrelations of subtests, correlations with other Wechsler scales (WPPSI-R, WISC-III, and the WAIS-R), examining group differences, and a study that examined correlations with other achievement tests. Subtest intercorrelations range from .39 to .63; composite intercorrelations range from .59 to .91. Correlations with the Stanford Achievement Test, Seventh Edition Plus; Iowa Test of Basic Skills, Form G; and California Achievement Tests, Form E across measures ranged from .71 to .77 in reading, .67 to .78 in math, and .72 to .75 in spelling.

Most correlations with other commonly used individually administered achievement tests were in the .70s to .80s. Generally lower correlations were obtained with group-administered achievement tests and student grades. The manual also presents descriptive profiles of the results for samples of various groups (i.e., children in gifted programs, children with mental retardation, children with emotional disturbance, children with learning disabilities, children with attention-deficit hyperactivity disorder, and children with hearing impairments) but does not provide any information about accuracy or consistency of profiles.

Summary

The WIAT is likely to become a popular testing instrument for at least two reasons. First, the Wechsler name will probably attract a lot of educators because of the time honored role that the various Wechsler tests have developed in psychological testing. Second, the link to the WISC-III standardization sample will probably appeal to those who calculate ability-achievement discrepancies. Unfortunately, such comparisons represent one of the most unreliable and tenuous practices that exists in psychological testing. The sudden availability of this measure may have the consequence of proliferating questionable test interpretation practices rather than improving them. In the next section, we move from general achievement tests to tests that assess specific areas of academic functioning (e.g., reading, math).

Assessment of Reading

What Is Reading?

Asking "What is reading?" may seem simplistic, but numerous definitions of reading have been proposed by experts (see, e.g., Chall, 1967; Gibson &

Reading is more than looking at written words!

"Wait! Wait! . . . Cancel that, I guess it says 'helf.' "

"The Far Side" cartoon by Gary Larson is reprinted by permission of Chronicle Features, San Francisco, CA.

Levin, 1975); for example: Reading is recognizing letters that make words; reading is sounding out a sequence of sounds to make words; reading is identifying words and understanding what the author is trying to say (Guerin & Maier, 1983). For our purposes, *reading is defined as a self-directed process of extracting information from written or printed symbols.* This definition is narrower than many and is influenced by the writings of Harris (1970), Gibson and Levin (1975), and Gillet and Temple (1990).

Gillet and Temple (1990), in their comprehensive volume on reading, discussed the "many sides" of reading and in so doing emphasize the critical

Focus on Practice

Sight-Word Vocabulary

The English language is made up of thousands of words, yet, quite logically, beginning readers generally are exposed to a subset of 300 to 400 high-frequency words. Such a corpus of words is often referred to as a sight-word vocabulary. Regardless of the reading series and instructional approach used to teach reading, almost all young readers are exposed to words such as *to, we, up, big, dog,* and *girl.* Several published lists of high-frequency words from the first, second, and third grades exist, such as the Dolch Basic Sight Vocabulary List, the BRIGANCE® Basic Sight Vocabulary, and the Durrell Word Frequency List. Below are 50 words extracted from these lists:

to	that	like	father	run
the	are	did	come	name
in	up	her	from	over
and	they	baby	here	day
at	me	but	just	ride
we	go	with	if	where
see	mother	will	or	look
on	was	dog	make	home
not	box	what	blue	school
said	had	no	green	pets

For most children, the identification of these words requires practice and illustrative examples. By third grade these words should be read rapidly with very few errors. You might informally assess several young children to determine the development of their sight-word vocabulary.

role that reading plays in the development of a person and a country. For example, they see reading as: a language ability, a set of perceptual abilities, a literary act, an automatized psychomotor act, a political issue, a matter of self-worth, a pressing economic issue, a critical instructional concern, and an outcome of self-directed discovery learning. We cannot investigate all these perspectives on reading here. We agree, however, that reading is one of the most important aspects of schooling and when a student has trouble reading, it requires expert assessment and remedial attention.

The Development of Reading

Learning to read occurs in three general stages labeled **prereading, decoding,** and **comprehension.** Each of these stages is characterized by the acquisition of several subskills that collectively contribute to efficient reading.

Prereading Stage

Broadly defined, the prereading stage occurs between birth and the time a child can recognize and decode words. In normal children, the latter usually begins around 5 or 6 years of age. Sensory skills such as hand-eye coordination and sound discrimination are considered prerequisites to reading. A narrower and more practical approach to identifying prereading skills has been advocated by Venesky (1976), who suggested that the following five actions are involved in decoding:

1. attending to letter order
2. attending to letter orientation
3. attending to word detail
4. matching sounds
5. blending sounds

Once children master these skills, they should be able to recognize words and thus move developmentally into the decoding stage.

Decoding Stage

This stage or period of reading development usually is the focus of reading instruction during the first three or four years of school. Often referred to as the "learning to read" stage, it primarily involves the refinement of sound blending skills and the acquisition of rules concerning word structure such as silent letter conventions, vowel conventions, and syllabification.

Current approaches to teaching decoding skills stress a combination of phonics and language experience methods. Phonics emphasizes letter sound relationships, and the language experience approach emphasizes the relationship of decoding words to a child's general language experiences. Basal reading materials typically combine these two approaches to the task of teaching reading. Table 10.3 illustrates abbreviated instructional objectives by grade level for a typical basal reading series.

Comprehension Stage

The ultimate goal of reading is comprehension, or extracting meaning from what is read. Thus, this last, broad stage of reading development is often referred to as the "learning from reading" stage. The reading skills and activities in this stage can be classified as literal, or direct, comprehension and inferential, or indirect, comprehension. Literal comprehension involves remembering written information. Inferential comprehension is much more complex and requires a reader to piece together information and go beyond what is written to make it meaningful. Both literal and inferential comprehension require good attention skills, memory ability, and some prior knowledge of a topic.

Focus on

Research

Dyslexia: A Confusing Term

The term *dyslexia* is commonly used to describe any reading disorder that is not the result of organic defect, low intelligence, emotional disturbance, or environmental deprivation. Knowing what dyslexia is not, however, is only half the story. Several researchers have described various subtypes of dyslexia characterized by deficits in word-analysis skills, configuration and orientation of letters and words, or a combination of these two problems. These difficulties are experienced by many developing readers and should not and cannot be reliably used to formulate a diagnosis of dyslexia because the research literature on dyslexia is replete with definitional problems. Researchers have simply chosen to define and measure dyslexia in so many different ways that the term has virtually lost a specific meaning. At best, the word "dyslexia" means a possible reading problem!

White and Miller's (1983) research supports our position about the construct of dyslexia. They investigated the use and meaning of the term *dyslexia* by examining 45 studies reported in the *Journal of Learning Disabilities.* They concluded that a major weakness in the studies was the inadequate definition of dyslexia, which ultimately negates the generalization and often the replication of the research. Those who read such research should be cautioned that at this time, both research and practice concerning dyslexia should be questioned.

From: "Dyslexia: A term in search of a definition," by M. White and S. R. Miller (1983) THE JOURNAL OF SPECIAL EDUCATION 17(1), 5–10.

Factors That Influence the Development of Reading

The research on reading indicates that numerous factors influence the development of reading. In this section, we identify and briefly review the effect of major noninstructional and instructional factors, both of which should be considered in any assessment of a reading problem.

Noninstructional Factors

Noninstructional factors are those that cannot be controlled by a teacher, including characteristics of the learner such as sex or auditory ability. A sex difference has historically been identified in reading achievement, with girls outperforming boys (Dwyer, 1973). Such assertions, however, are based on published reports at least 20 years old. Fry and Lagomarsino (1982) believe that the sex difference in reading achievement in regular classrooms is rather

Table 10.3 Curriculum Sequence Chart for a Typical Basal Reading Series

Grade	***Skills Acquired***
Kindergarten	Identify sounds and pictures Express ideas in complete verbal sentences Understand meaning of words such as *above* and *far* Understand concepts of size, small; etc. Recognize and identify colors Organize objects into groups Match forms Understand beginning concepts of number
Grade 1	Recognize letters of alphabet; can write and give sound Auditory and visual perception and discrimination of initial and final consonants Observe left to right progression Recall what has been read Aware of medial consonants, consonant blends, digraphs Recognize long sounds of vowels; root words; plural forms; verb endings *-s, -ed, -d, -ing;* opposites; pronouns *he, she* Understand concept of synonyms, homonyms, antonyms Understand simple compound words Copy simple sentences, fill-ins
Grade 2	Comprehension and analysis of what has been read Identify vowel digraphs Understand variant sounds of *y* Identify medial vowels Identify diphthongs Understand influence of *r* on preceding vowel Identify three-letter blends Understand use of suffix *-er* Understand verb endings (for example, *stop, stopped*)
Grade 3	Recognize multiple sounds of long *a* as in *ei, ay, ey* Understand silent *e* in *-le* endings Understand use of suffix *-est* Know how to change *y* and *i* before adding *er, est* Understand comparative and superlative forms of adjectives Understand possessive form using *s* Use contractions Identify syllabic breaks
Grade 4	Recognize main and subordinate parts Recognize unknown words using configuration and other word attack skills Identify various sounds of *ch* Recognize various phonetic values of *gh* Identify rounded *o* sound formed by *au, aw, al* Use and interpret diacritical markings Discriminate among multiple meanings of words

Table 10.3 ***continued***

Grade 5	Read critically to evaluate Identify digraphs *gn, mb, bt* Recognize that *augh* and *ough* have round *o* sound Recognize and pronounce muted vowels in *el, al, le* Recognize secondary and primary accents Use of apostrophe Understand suffixes *-al, -hand, -ship, -ist, -ling, -an, -ian, -dom, -ern* Understand use of figures of speech: metaphor, simile Ability to paraphrase main idea Know ways paragraphs are developed Outline using two or three main heads and subheadings Use graphic material
Grade 6	Develop ability for critical analysis Recognize and use Latin, Greek roots, such as *photo, tele, graph, geo, auto* Develop generalization that some suffixes can change part of speech such as *-ure* changing an adjective to noun (*moist-moisture*) Understand meaning and pronunciation of homographs Develop awareness of shifting accents

From: INFORMAL ASSESSMENT IN EDUCATION (pp. 245–246), by Gilbert R. Guerin and Arlee S. Maier, 1983, Palo Alto, CA: Mayfield Publishing Company. Copyright © 1983 Mayfield Publishing Company. Reprinted by permission.

meager and is disappearing. More boys than girls may be labeled "reading disabled," but sex will not account for much of the difference in first-grade or third-grade reading achievement.

The relation between reading achievement and auditory acuity, however, is fairly strong. Deaf children rarely learn to read well (Gibson & Levin, 1975). Correctly identifying letters by name involves visual discrimination, and many researchers have found that a child's ability to recognize and name letters before or during kindergarten is a very good predictor of first-grade and primary reading achievement (see e.g., deHirsch, Jansky, & Langford, 1966). On the other hand, intelligence, as typically measured, is a rather weak predictor of progress in learning to read.

Instructional Factors

Time on-task, classroom management, and size of reading group are all instructional factors that influence learning to read. Wyne and Stuck (1979) worked with second- and third-grade students who were reading below grade level. After an eight-week program to increase task-oriented behavior during reading, they found that reading achievement was positively influenced by the amount of time a student spent actively learning to read. A more recent investigation by Gaskins (1988) reported that poor readers spent "an alarming amount of time in unproductive ways" (p. 751). Gaskins noted that it was not uncommon for teachers to allow 5 to 10 minutes of reading group time to elapse before instruction began and to use a significant portion of reading time dealing with disciplinary and management tasks. Anderson, Evertson, and Brophy (1979) found that a teacher who can structure, maintain, and monitor classroom activities will facilitate higher reading performances. Good (1979) reported that small-group instruction, compared with individualized programs, appears to yield higher reading achievement for first- and second-grade students.

Typical Reading Problems

Reading problems usually are manifested in children in three ways: (a) ineffective decoding or word attack strategies, (b) inconsistent comprehension, and (c) a negative attitude toward reading. Clearly, problems in any of these areas will likely affect the others. Therefore, early and ongoing evaluation of reading progress is desirable.

Word attack problems often are evidenced by mispronunciations of letter sounds, omissions of syllables, and substitutions of sounds. Some of the most pervasive problems are the result of the failure to learn the long and short vowel sounds and the rules of word construction that provide cues to syllabification. In addition, efficient word attack ability requires a large sight-word vocabulary (e.g., *the, on, at, to, out, go*) and knowledge of prefixes (e.g., *pre-*, *post-*, *a-*, *re-*,) and suffixes (e.g., *-ing, -ed, -ly, -ish, -ful*).

Difficulties with comprehension directly follow from flawed word attack skills. However, even when one can accurately read every word in a sentence, comprehension is not ensured. Reading rate, memory, background knowledge, and perspective are all critical influences on reading comprehension. For young readers, among whom literal comprehension is usually stressed, reading rate and memory are probably the most salient. However, as readers mature, the importance of background knowledge and perspective increases. For example, read the following paragraph:

> Rocky slowly got up from the mat, planning his escape. He hesitated a moment and thought. Things were not going well. What bothered him most was being held, especially since the charge against him had been weak. He considered his present situation. The lock that held him was strong but he thought he could break it. He knew, however, that his timing would have to be perfect. Rocky was aware that it was because of his early roughness that he had been penalized so severely—much too severely from his point of view. The situation was becoming frustrating; the pressure had been grinding on him far too long. He was being ridden unmercifully. Rocky was getting angry now. He felt he was ready to make his move. He knew his success or failure would depend on what he did in the next few seconds. (Anderson, Reynolds, Schallert, & Goetz, 1977, p. 372)

Depending on your background and experience, you probably understood this passage to be about either a convict planning his escape or a wrestler plotting his moves to break a tough hold. A reader's background, which is largely measured through language proficiency and fund of words, thus plays an important role in comprehension. Obtaining such basic information is fundamental to administering and interpreting reading tests. If you believe you have a good command of this basic knowledge, you are ready to begin an examination of reading tests.

Reading Tests

More than 175 published reading tests were in circulation as of early 1989, according to *The Tenth Mental Measurements Yearbook* (Conoley & Kramer, 1989). Because it would be impossible to discuss each of these tests here, we have selected a small number to examine in detail either because of their popularity or because they represent a particular type of test (such as group administered/individually administered, or norm-referenced/criterion-referenced). We first document the various reading skills each test purports to measure and then discuss their technical adequacy.

Reading Skills and Selected Reading Tests

Carnine and Silbert (1979) developed a three-part model of reading instruction that is useful for examining the content of reading tests. Specifically, they hypothesized that the important elements of reading could be described as units, skills, and knowledge base. *Units* form a hierarchy beginning with single words and continuing to entire passages. *Skills* begin with sounding out letters and increase in complexity to include inferential comprehension and evaluation actions. The hierarchy for *knowledge base* begins with simple vocabulary and increases to sophisticated vocabulary.

This three-part model can be used to describe and compare the content of 10 popular reading tests (see table 10.4). Table 10.4 indicates that no single test samples all reading behaviors. For example, the California Achievement Tests (CTB/McGraw-Hill, 1985), and the Metropolitan Achievement Tests, Seventh Edition (Prescott, Balow, Hogan, & Farr, 1992) are both widely used group tests that cannot assess oral reading but rather sample a broad range of decoding and comprehension behaviors. Tests such as the Gates-McKillop-Horowitz Reading Diagnostic Tests (Gates, McKillop, & Horowitz, 1981) and the Nelson-Denny Reading Test (Brown, Bennett, & Hanna, 1981), which were developed for two very different age groups, focus on decoding and comprehension, respectively.

The Technical Adequacy of Reading Tests

As emphasized in chapter 5, reliability, validity, and norms are important indicators of the quality of a test. However, table 10.5 reveals that not one of

Table 10.4 Reading Skills Sampled by Selected Reading Tests

	Decoding																Comprehension																
	Units						Skills							Knowledge			Units					Skills							Knowledge				
	Letter Sounds	Letters	Letter combination	Syllables	Words	Phrases	Sounding out	Sight reading	Breakdown of large words	Accuracy	Fluency	Oral reading	Silent reading	Oral language	Word familiarity	Syntax	Words	Phrases	Sentences	Paragraphs	Passages	Literal	Inferential	Sequencing	Summarization	Simplification	Critical reading	Study skills	Syntax	Semantics	Facts	Logic	Schema
California Achievement Tests (CTB/McGraw-Hill, 1985)	x	x	x	x	x	x	x	x	x				x	x	x		x	x	x	x		x	x				x			x		x	
Metropolitan Achievement Tests (Prescott, Balow, Hogan & Farr, 1992)																																	
Surveys	x	x	x		x	x	x	x					x	x	x		x	x	x	x	x	x	x		x					x		x	
Instructional	x	x	x	x	x	x	x	x	x					x	x	x	x	x	x	x	x	x	x		x	x		x		x			
Peabody Individual Achievement Tests-Revised (Markwardt, 1989)		x			x			x		x		x	x	x	x		x	x	x			x								x			
Gates-McKillop-Horowitz Reading Diagnostic Tests (Gates & McKillop, 1981)	x	x	x	x	x	x	x	x	x	x	x	x		x	x	x																	
Diagnostic Reading Scales (Spache, 1972)	x	x	x	x	x	x	x	x		x	x	x	x	x	x	x	x	x	x	x		x	x	x							x		
Nelson-Denny Reading Test (Brown, Bennett, & Hanna, 1981)					x	x	x	x		x	x	x	x	x	x	x	x	x	x	x	x	x	x						x	x	x	x	
TERA-2 Test of Early Reading Ability (Reid, Hresko, & Hammill, 1989)		x																															
Degrees of Reading Power (The College Board, 1981)																	x	x	x	x	x	x											
Woodcock Reading Mastery Tests-Revised (Woodcock, 1987)		x			x	x		x					x	x	x	x	x	x	x	x	x	x		x					x	x			
Gates-MacGinitie Reading Tests (MacGinitie, 1978)			x	x	x	x	x						x	x	x		x	x	x	x	x	x	x							x	x	x	

Table 10.5 Reliability, Validity, and Norms for Selected Reading Tests

	Reliability				Validity	Norms	
Test*	Test-Retest	Parallel Form	Internal Consistency	Standard Error of Measurement	Criterion Validity	Sample	Representativeness
California Achievement Tests	None	.54–.90	.76–.97	Yes	None	200,000: grades K–12; national representation	Excellent
Metropolitan Achievement Tests Survey	N/A	N/A	.85–.96	Yes	.55–.82	550,000: grades K–12; national representation	Excellent
Instructional	N/A	N/A	.88–.95	Yes	N/A		Excellent
Peabody Individual Achievement Tests-Revised	.95	None	.97	Yes	None	1,563 ages 5–18, national representation	Adequate
Gates-McKillop-Horowitz Reading Diagnostic Tests	.94	None	None	No	.68–.96	600: grades 1–6	Inadequate
Diagnostic Reading Scales	.30–.96	None	.87–.96	Yes	.13–.77		
Nelson-Denny Reading Tests	None	.69–.92	None	Yes	None	25,000: grades 9–16	Excellent
Tests of Early Reading Ability-2	.79	None	.78–.98	Yes	.52–.66	1,184: ages 3–7; national representation	Excellent
Degrees of Reading Power	None	.86–.91	None	Yes	.70–.84	34,000: grades 4–12; national representation	Excellent
Woodcock Reading Mastery Tests-Revised	None	.16–.94	.84–.99	Yes	None	6,089: grade K through 75 yrs	Adequate
Gates-MacGinitie Reading Tests	.77–.89	.77–.94	.88–.94	No	.88–.91	6,500: grades 1–12; national representation	Adequate

*For sources of tests see table 10.4.

Note: "None" means the information is relevant and desired but not provided, whereas "N/A" means the information is not applicable.

the 10 standardized reading tests in the sample provides data on all seven of the basic evaluative indexes. This should cause you to choose any reading test with caution, given that these 10 are among the most frequently used. In all cases, users must consult a test's technical manual for details about its psychometric characteristics.

Woodcock Reading Mastery Tests-Revised

The Woodcock Reading Mastery Tests-Revised (WRMT-R), a revised version of the 1973 WRMT, is a comprehensive battery of tests measuring several important aspects of reading ability. The WRMT-R consists of six tests and a two-part supplementary checklist that all can be individually administered to persons kindergarten through age 75 years. Two alternate forms of the test are available (Forms G and H), both of which are accompanied by a comprehensive and well-organized test manual.

Content

The most comprehensive form (G) of the WRMT-R consists of 905 items that are the result of a validation process, which started with expert nominations and ended with a systematic statistical examination. The items are organized into six subtests that are divided into three clusters: Readiness Cluster, Basic Skills Cluster, and Reading Comprehension Cluster.

The Readiness Cluster includes a Visual-Auditory Learning subtest (134 items that measure how well an individual can form associations between visual stimuli and oral responses) and a Letter Identification subtest (51 items that measure an individual's ability to name various forms of uppercase and lowercase letters). A Supplementary Letter checklist that presents letters in the style of many beginning reading materials is also included in the Readiness Cluster.

The Basic Skills Cluster includes Word Identification and Word Attack subtests. The Word Identification subtest includes 106 items arranged in increasing difficulty and is designed to measure a person's ability to identify words in isolation. The Word Attack subtest consists of 45 items also arranged in order of difficulty. The items on the subtest are either nonsense words (e.g., *wug*) or words with a very low frequency of usage. The goal of the subtest is to measure a person's ability to apply phonic and structural analysis skills with unfamiliar words. Figure 10.1 is a copy of the Word Attack Error Inventory that can be used to facilitate interpretation of a person's performance on the Word Attack subtest. An examination of the Pronunciation column provides an overview of the sounds students will be tested on.

The Reading Comprehension Cluster is composed of two tests: Word Comprehension and Passage Comprehension. The Word Comprehension test consists of three subtests: Antonyms, Synonyms, and Analogies. Each of these subtests is intended to measure a person's reading vocabulary at a different level of processing. The Antonyms subtest is purported to measure

Figure 10.1 Word Attack Error Inventory Completed on the Woodcock Reading Mastery Tests-Revised for Rosa, a Sixth-Grade Student

WORD ATTACK ERROR INVENTORY

Directions: Circled numbers refer to item numbers in the Word Attack test. For each Sound Category or Syllable, shade the circles representing the subject's errors on the target sound or target syllable. (Include as errors any items that the subject was administered, but did not respond to.) Draw a line through the circles for any items that were not administered.

Final Word Attack item administered 36

Single Consonants and Digraphs

Sound Category	Pronunciation	Spellings	Additional Spelling Examples[a]
1	b	● b- ● -b	(21) buf- (36) -bet ~~(38) bef~~
2	ch	(24) ch- ● -ch	~~(45) cher~~
3	d	(1) d- (16) d- (24) -d ● -d-	(26) tad- (29) ad-
4	f	(4) -ff (8) f-	(21) buf- (36) -ful ~~(38) bef~~
5	g	(9) g- (12) -g ● g- ● g-	● cig-
6	h		(19) -hip
7	hw	(18) wh-	
8	j	~~(44) ge~~	(29) -jex ~~(38) sodge~~
9	k		(33) -k-d (34) -nk
10	kw	~~(43) qu~~	
11	l	(28) l-	(36) -ful ~~(38) lib~~
12	m	● -m ● -m	(36) man- ~~(38) mot~~ ~~(38) bem~~
13	n	(6) n- (6) -n (7) -n (20) n- (34) kn- ~~(43) gn~~	(19) vun- ~~(45) pno~~
14	ŋ	(31) -ng	(26) -ing (36) -cing-
15	p	(2) -p ● p- (13) p- (15) -p (28) -p	(19) -hip
16	r	(4) r- (10) r- ~~(37) wr~~	
17	s	(11) -ss (22) s- ~~(44) c~~	(36) cig- (36) -cing- ~~(38) sodge~~
18	sh	(17) sh-	
19	t	(9) -t (14) -t	(21) -ty (26) tad- (36) -bet
20	th	(25) th- ~~(42) the~~	
21	v	~~(41) v~~	(19) vun-
22	w	(14) w-	(27) tw-
23	ks		(29) -jex
24	y	(31) y-	
25	z	● z-	~~(38) trans~~ ~~(42) l-e~~

Consonant Blends

Sound Category	Pronunciation	Spelling (Individual pronunciations are enclosed in parentheses.)
26	Two-consonant blends	(3) -ft (15) pl- (16) -d's (dz) (23) -c-d (st) (25) -n't (27) tw- ● -n't ● -k-d (kt) ● -nk (ŋk) ~~(43) l-e (la)~~
27	Three-consonant blends	(23) str-

Vowels

Sound Category	Pronunciation	Spellings	Additional Spelling Examples[a]
28	a	(2) a- (4) -a- (6) -a- ● -a- ● -a- (24) -a- ● -a-	(26) tad- (29) ad- (36) man-
29	e	● -e- ● -e-	(29) -jex (36) -bet ~~(38) bem~~
30	i	(3) i- ● -i- ● -i-	● -hip (26) -ing ● cig-
31	o	(11) o- (12) -o-	~~(38) mot~~ ~~(38) sodge~~ ~~(40) mon~~
32	u	(7) u- (16) -u-	(19) vun- (21) buf- ~~(40) glus~~
33	ā	(8) -ay (23) -a-e- ● -ai- (33) -a-e- ~~(37) ey~~	
34	ē	(1) -ee (14) -ea-	(21) -ty
35	ī	(18) -ie ● -igh (22) -y ~~(43) i-e~~	
36	ō	(13) -oe	~~(45) pno~~ ~~(45) mo~~
37	aw	~~(41) au~~	
38	oi	● -oi-	
39	o͞o	(10) -oo	
40	ou	● -ou- ~~(43) ou~~	
41	er	● -ir- ~~(44) yr~~	~~(40) mer~~ ~~(45) cher~~

Multisyllable Words

Syllable	Pronunciation	Spelling	Syllable	Pronunciation	Spelling	Syllable	Pronunciation	Spelling
42	vun	(19) vun-	52	man	(36) man-	61	mon	~~(40) mon~~
43	hip	● -hip	53	sin	(36) -cing-	62	glus	~~(40) glus~~
44	buf	(21) buf-	54	fel	● -ful	63	te	~~(40) te~~
45	tē	(21) -ty	55	baf	~~(38) baf~~	64	mer	~~(40) mer~~
46	tad	(26) tad-	56	mot	~~(38) mot~~	65	nō	~~(45) pno~~
47	iŋ	(26) -ing	57	bem	~~(38) bem~~	66	mō / mōk	~~(45) -mo- / -moch-~~
48	ad	(29) ad-	58	tranz	~~(38) trans~~	67	cher / er	~~(45) -cher / -er~~
49	jeks	(29) -jex	59	lib	~~(38) lib~~			
50	sig	● cig-	60	soj	~~(38) sodge~~			
51	bet	● -bet						

[a]Shade the circles for the additional examples only if the subject makes an error on the *target sound*.

ability to read a word (e.g., *good*) and then respond orally with a word opposite in meaning (e.g., *bad*). The Synonym subtest requires reading a word (e.g., *pretty*) and then stating another word similar in meaning to the presented word (e.g., *beautiful*). The Antonyms and Synonyms combined contain 67 items. The Analogies subtest is the most difficult of the Word Comprehension subtests. It requires reading a pair of words and ascertaining the relationship between the words and then reading the first word of a second pair and using the same relationship to supply a new word to complete the analogy appropriately. For example, *he-she boy-*_______ or *milk-drink apple-*_______. The Passage Comprehension test contains 68 items that are purported to measure a person's ability to study a short passage—usually two or three sentences long—and to identify a key word missing from the passage. This type of task is referred to as a **modified cloze procedure** and requires a variety of comprehension and vocabulary skills. Figure 10.2 illustrates the skills assessed by two subtests from the WRMT-R.

The WRMT-R has retained many of the features of the original WRMT; however, several content and administrative changes should be noted. First, the Readiness Cluster was created. Second, the Word Comprehension test was expanded to include antonyms and synonyms, and vocabulary in the content areas of science, mathematics, social studies, and humanities can now be evaluated. Third, the number of sample items has been increased in some tests to facilitate student performance. And, four, the normative sample of the test was extended to include college/university and adult groups.

Administration and Scoring

Administration of the WRMT-R requires attention to details, a thorough reading of the test manual, and general test administration experience. The WRMT-R manual provides an excellent chapter on administration with supporting self-training checklists and sample exercises.

The administration of the full scale requires, on average, 45 minutes. The test materials are well designed and feature an easel-like kit that can be positioned so that a subject can see only the stimulus items while the examiner can see both the instructions and correct answers.

The items on the test have been arranged from easiest to most difficult, except on the Visual-Auditory Learning subtest. Such an arrangement results in a power test and allows one to establish both basal and ceiling levels. By using Starting Point guidelines, an examiner tries to begin at a level of difficulty that can ensure early successes on items without seeming too simple for the examinee. The goal is to establish a basal level of six or more consecutive items passed and a ceiling level of six consecutive items failed. The use of basal and ceiling rules permits the examiner to estimate the score that would have been obtained if every item on the test had been administered to a subject. When computing the test raw score, the examiner assumes that all items below the basal would have been answered correctly, and that all items above the ceiling would have been answered incorrectly.

Figure 10.2 Sample Items from the Word Comprehension and Word Attack Subtests of the Woodcock Reading Mastery Tests-Revised

**WORD COMPREHENSION SAMPLE ITEMS—
DO NOT RECORD ON THE RESPONSE FORM**

Point to the first sample item and say: **Listen carefully and finish what I say** (point to each of the three words and the blank space, in turn, while reading the item).

A dog walks; a bird . . . (pause). (*flies*) If the subject gives an incorrect response or does not respond, read the item again, completing it with the correct word.

Continue with the remaining sample items in the same manner (point to each word as the item is read to the subject):

One is to two as three is to . . . (pause). (*four, six*)
He is to she as boy is to . . . (pause). (*girl*)
Grass is to green as snow is to . . . (pause). (*white*)

dog—walks	**bird—**
one—two	**three—**
he—she	**boy—**
grass—green	**snow—**

**WORD ATTACK SAMPLE ITEM—
DO NOT RECORD ON RESPONSE FORM**

Say: **I want you to pronounce some words that are not real words. I want you to tell me how they sound.** Point to "tat." **How does this word sound?**

Sample: **tat**

If the subject incorrectly responds to "tat," point to "tat" and say it clearly. Do not pronounce any other words during the Word Attack Test.

Proceed to the next page and begin the test. Continue testing until the subject has missed five or more consecutive words, or has responded to Item 50.

How do these words sound? Point to each word if necessary. If the subject fails to respond in a few seconds, encourage a response. If the subject still fails to respond, continue the test by pointing to the next word.

1. ift (ift)*	**2. bim** (bim)	**3. ut** (ət)	**4. rayed** (rād)	**5. kak** (kak)
6. aft (aft)	**7. nen** (nen)	**8. ab** (ab)	**9. tash** (tash)	**10. wip's** (wips)

*Pronunciation symbols used by permission of the publishers of the Merriam-Webster Dictionaries. See test manual for further explanation.

Each item on the WRMT-R is worth one raw score point. With the exception of the Visual-Auditory Learning and Word Comprehension subtests, the raw score on a subtest is the sum of the correct answers given plus a score of 1 for every item in the test below the basal. The WRMT-R provides users with an array of derived scores as a result of raw scores on the various subtests and clusters and the level of interpretation one desires. Figure 10.3 provides a picture of the four levels of interpretation for WRMT-R performances and lists the types of scores rendered. A detailed discussion of these various scores is beyond the scope of this chapter. Suffice it to say that the WRMT-R provides users with both norm-referenced and criterion-referenced results based on a large (N = 6,089) nationally representative sample of individuals from 60 communities in the United States.

Reliability and Validity

The overall reliability and validity of the WRMT-R are summarized in table 10.5. The test's manual provides good documentation of internal consistency and standard errors of measurement as evidence of the various subtest reliabilities. Median split-half reliability coefficients for all WRMT-R subtests exceed .84, with the average being in the .90 range. The validity data for WRMT-R are mostly correlations with other tests (i.e., concurrent validity) of reading and cognitive abilities. Generally, the WRMT-R correlates highly (r > .80) with tests such as the Wide Range Achievement Test—Reading subscale, Peabody Individual Achievement Test—Reading subscale, and Iowa Test of Basic Skills—Total Reading. The author also provides a rational case for the content validity of the instrument and provides some intercorrelational data on WRMT-R subscales, which are asserted to support the instrument's construct validity. In summary, the reliability and validity of the Woodcock Reading Mastery Tests-Revised meets basic technical characteristics expected of tests used to rank student performance compared with a normative sample of same-age peers.

Test of Early Reading Ability-2

According to the test makers, the Test of Early Reading Ability-2 (TERA-2) "measures children's ability to attribute meaning to printed symbols, their knowledge of the alphabet and its functions, and their understanding of the conventions of print" (Reid, Hresko, & Hammill, 1989, p. 1). As such, the test is intended to aid educators in identifying children who are significantly different from their peers, document children's progress in learning to read, serve as a research tool in research on early literacy, and "giving direction to instructional practice." The TERA-2 is a 46-item test with rules for where to begin and where to end based on a child's age and number correct as they proceed through the administration of the test. There are two forms of the test (Forms A and B).

Figure 10.3 Hierarchy of Interpretive Information Available from the Woodcock Reading Mastery Tests-Revised

	Basis	Type of Information
Level I. Analysis of errors	Individual item responses	Description of a subject's performance on precisely defined skills
Level II. Level of development	Sum of item scores	Raw score *Rasch ability score (test W score, subtest part score, cluster W score) Grade equivalent Age equivalent
Level III. Quality of performance[a]	Performance on a reference task	*W-difference score (DIFF) Instructional range Relative Performance Index (RPI)
Level IV. Standing in a group	Deviation from a reference point in a group	Rank order *Standard score Percentile rank

Note: Scores marked with asterisks are the most suitable for statistical analysis.
[a]Another example of a Level III score is the Snellen Index for visual acuity.

Standardization Sample and Norms

The test was standardized on a sample of 1,454 children from 15 states representing a wide range of geographical locations and roughly proportional representation to U. S. population data for sex, residence, race, and ethnicity. Children in the standardization sample were 3 to 9 years of age.

Reliability and Validity

The manual describes three types of reliability evidence: internal consistency (coefficient alpha), Rasch Analysis, and test-retest with alternate forms. The average internal consistency estimate for Form A across all age levels was .91 (range = .78 to .98). The average internal consistency estimate for Form B across all age levels was .90 (range = .80 to .94). A Rasch Analysis indicated good "inter-item" reliabilities for both forms and good item fit. Test-retest data with alternate forms were obtained for 49 students ages 7 to 9 years.

After partialing out the influence of age, a correlation of .79 was obtained for the raw scores.

The authors argue that the TERA-2 has content validity because "special care was taken to select items that were representative of the subject matter being assessed and that required a variety of responses" (Reid et al., 1989, p. 27). They go on to argue, however, that interpreting content validity is a subjective process, stating, "Only if the selection of items is consistent with the theoretical orientation of the examiner will the examiner agree that the test measures the construct under question" (p. 28). We, however, disagree that content validity is "a question of personal preference" (p. 28). Content validity is substantiated by showing that test items match curricular goals and objectives, not educators' theoretical orientations or personal preferences. The test makers argue that the test has construct validity because raw score averages increase with age, correlations of .84 were obtained between ages and raw scores on both forms, and average standard score differences of 14.7 and 11.2 were obtained between the standardization sample and a sample of 22 children classified as learning disabled (ages 6 to 9). Finally, correlations ranging from .37 to .59 with the BSSI-D are reported. Unfortunately, no information is provided on what the BSSI-D is. It is unclear what the correlations mean.

Summary

After reviewing the test manual, one is underwhelmed by the paucity of data on the test and left to wonder what kinds of decisions can be made with confidence about students based on test results. The leap of faith required to make inferences from students' test behavior and scores to the constructs that it is intended to represent (i.e., constructing meaning from print, knowing the alphabet and its function, and discovering the print conventions) is akin to leaping from one side of the Grand Canyon in hopes of landing on the other side. The TERA-2 is not adequate for either instructional or classification decisions.

Assessment of Mathematics

Louise had *dyscalculia*[1] or at least that is what her parents had been told by her new teacher in a meeting at school on a day less than a week ago that was filled with bewilderment and sadness. However, her 12-year-old brother, Todd, diagnosed her as normal in less than an hour and "cured" her even more quickly. And Todd was right!

Louise, a fifth grader, was never an outstanding student in any subject but had always "gotten by." In fifth grade she seemed to be falling behind the rest of her class and thus was referred to the school diagnostic team. The results of an evaluation indicated that she had average intelligence (i.e.,

[1] *Dyscalculia* is a term originally used in medicine to indicate the virtual loss of mathematical ability after head trauma and was "borrowed" by some educators to describe arithmetic learning disorders.

Figure 10.4 Sample Problems from Louise's Arithmetic Test

$$\begin{array}{r} 3 \\ \times 2 \\ \hline 6 \end{array} \quad \begin{array}{r} 5 \\ \times 7 \\ \hline 35 \end{array} \quad \begin{array}{r} 6 \\ \times 6 \\ \hline 36 \end{array} \quad \begin{array}{r} 9 \\ \times 8 \\ \hline 72 \end{array}$$

$$\begin{array}{r} 12 \\ \times 2 \\ \hline 24 \end{array} \quad \begin{array}{r} 14 \\ \times 2 \\ \hline 48 \end{array} \quad \begin{array}{r} 42 \\ \times 3 \\ \hline 86 \end{array} \quad \begin{array}{r} 33 \\ \times 2 \\ \hline 96 \end{array}$$

she achieved a Full Scale score of 103 on the Wechsler Intelligence Scale, WISC-III) and that in reading and spelling she was performing at an average level (i.e., at the 51st percentile). However, the testing in arithmetic suggested she was approximately two years below grade level, at the 14th percentile for her age. Based on this information, the diagnostic team recommended that Louise be given special help for her problems in arithmetic. In an attempt to involve the parents in the evaluation of their child, the school had furnished them with a copy of the arithmetic quiz on which Louise had performed so poorly.

The quiz was a norm-referenced test that contained a separate test form for each specific grade level; Louise took the fifth-grade form. One evening Todd picked up Louise's quiz and began to examine its content and her responses. He noticed that many test items required multiplication (as would be expected for a test of fifth-grade mathematics) and that Louise had missed a large proportion of these items (not to mention the division items). Eight of the multiplication problems from the test are presented in figure 10.4. From the first four problems on the test it was immediately obvious to Todd that his sister knew her multiplication facts. After all, she was capable of correctly multiplying 9 times 8. However, when she attempted to multiply anything but two 1-digit numbers, she was almost always wrong.

Neither norm-referenced test scores nor the number of correct answers on a teacher-made quiz tell why an answer is right or wrong but only whether something *is* right or wrong. Todd, on the other hand, was a curious youngster who wanted to know what Louise was doing wrong. Maybe there was some pattern to her errors. Working under the assumption that she knew her multiplication facts, Todd decided that either she was careless or some problem existed with the process she was using to multiply. He soon discovered that there was, in fact, a problem with her process: She was multiplying digits within one factor. Thus, to get an answer of 86 from the product of 42 times 3, Louise would first multiply 3 times 2 to get 6. Then, she would mistakenly multiply 4 times 2 to get 8. Her errors and her "dyscalculia" were related to this problem.

Testing can have positive and negative motivational side effects.

MATH TEST TODAY
WARREN
"I THOUGHT THERE WAS SUPPOSED TO BE SAFETY IN NUMBERS."

Courtesy of James Warren. Reprinted by permission.

Todd quickly called Louise into the living room and instructed her in the appropriate process of multiplication. Later, her parents shared this information with her teacher and the evaluation team members. The problem was resolved without much alteration in Louise's school routine.

This hypothetical example illustrates two important points relative to the assessment of arithmetic skills. First, it is important to go beyond test scores and examine the content of the test and the processes children use in responding to items. Second, arithmetical ability is not simply some general capacity that one has or does not have. Instead, it is composed of a series of clearly observable skills. A major goal in mathematics assessment is to find exactly where in the sequence a child fails. This specific information is highly relevant, because instruction should logically be directed toward the next skill in the sequence.

Standardized Diagnostic Tests of Arithmetic

We will examine two diagnostic arithmetic tests from the many tests now available. An expanded list of these tests plus three other commonly used tests is presented in the skills-by-assessment instrument matrix in table 10.6.

KeyMath Diagnostic Arithmetic Test-Revised

Overview and Purpose

The KeyMath Diagnostic Arithmetic Test-Revised (Connolly, 1988) is an individually administered instrument used with children in kindergarten through

Table 10.6 Diagnostic Arithmetic Tests by Skills Assessed

	Operations						Application				Scores				Other	
Instrument	**Add**	**Subtract**	**Multiply**	**Divide**	**Fractions**	**Symbols**	**Money**	**Time**	**Measurement**	**Word Problems**	**Grade Equivalent**	**Age**	**Percentiles**	**Scaled Scores**	**Administration Time**	**Grade Range of Skills Tested**
Buswell-John Diagnostic Test for Fundamental Process in Arithmetic (Buswell & John, n.d.)	x	x	x	x											15–20 min.	1–6
Diagnostic Mathematics Inventory (Gessell, 1977)	x	x	x	x												1.5–8.5
Diagnostic Test of Arithmetic Strategies (Ginsburg & Matthews, 1984)															80 min.	1–6
ENRIGHT® Diagnostic Inventory of Basic Arithmetic Skills (Enright, 1983)	x	x	x	x	x						x				not stated	1–6
KeyMath Diagnostic Arithmetic Test (Connolly, Nachtman, & Pritchett, 1976)	x	x	x	x	x	x	x	x	x	x	x				30 min.	K–8
Stanford Diagnostic Mathematics Test (Beatty, Madden, Gardner, & Karlsen, 1976)	x	x	x	x	x	x	x	x	x	x	x		x	x	approx. 90 min.	1.5–12
Steenburgen Diagnostic-Prescriptive Math Program (Steenburgen, 1978)	x	x	x	x	x										10–20 min.	1–6
Test of Early Mathematics Ability-2 (Ginsburg & Baroody, 1990)	x	x	x			x	x			x		x	x		20 min.	preschool 1–3
Test of Mathematical Abilities-2 (Brown, Cronin, & McEntire, 1994)	x	x	x	x	x	x	x	x	x	x	x	x	x	x	1 hr., 15 min.	3–12

ninth grade. Each of the two forms of the instrument contains 14 subtests that are categorized into three major areas: Basic Concepts, Operations, and Applications. The test is designed primarily for diagnosing difficulties in arithmetic.

The author estimates that the instrument requires approximately 30 minutes to administer. The manual is well organized and provides detailed directions for administration. In addition to the manual and an easel kit containing the test, the other major component is an individual test record form that can be used to profile subtest scores. Although this record form is relatively simple to use once you become familiar with it, at first glance it appears extremely complex and may discourage some test users.

Standardization Sample and Norms

The technical procedures utilized in the standardization of the KeyMath-R are among the best of all the diagnostic arithmetic tests. The test was normed on a sample of 1,798 children in kindergarten through ninth grade. This sample was stratified with care according to geographic region, grade, sex, socioeconomic status, and race. Item difficulty and reliability estimates are based on highly sophisticated procedures that are representative of the care with which the instrument was constructed.

Data Obtained

The KeyMath-R purports to offer four levels of interpretation:

- Level 1—Total Test Performance. At the most general level, the KeyMath-R provides age- and grade-equivalent scores representing a child's overall test performance compared to other children of the same age. *Caution* must be used in score interpretation at this level because the KeyMath-R is a measure of the same format as those that have been shown to lead to a high percentage of decision errors.
- Level 2—Area Performance. The test makers assert that relative strengths and weaknesses among the test's three broad areas of Basic Skills, Operations, and Applications can be determined. *Even more caution* must be used in this kind of score interpretation: Large differences in scores between the three intercorrelated factors are more likely due to error than to "true" differences.
- Level 3—Subtest Performance. The KeyMath-R provides a system for profiling a subject's strengths and weaknesses across each of the 14 subtests. This kind of interpretation is *contraindicated* because of the high levels of error associated with small numbers of items on subtests and their shared common variance (which increases the likelihood that large discrepancies are a result of error).
- Level 4—Item Performance. The test developers claim that it is possible to examine each individual item to ascertain the actual skills a student is lacking. This kind of interpretation is also *contraindicated* for the same reasons stated above.

Administration

The KeyMath-R is constructed in an easel format. With the easel, a child is presented the test stimulus and the examiner is shown the test question. Administration procedures are quickly learned, and the author states that the instrument can be administered by paraprofessionals who may lack formal training in testing. Obviously, the test must be interpreted by someone who is familiar with the mathematics curricula of elementary schools and who has some background in testing and measurement.

Reliability and Validity

Reliability data reported in the manual include that derived from alternate-form, split-half, and item response theory procedures. Remarkably, the authors obtained alternate-form data on approximately one-third of the standardization sample. The correlations between alternative forms of the test ranged from .50s to .70s for subtests to approximately .90 for the total test. Split-half coefficients were even higher with reliability based on the total test in the low to middle .90s.

Although the reliability of the test as a whole is good to excellent, the reliability for some subtests, including some major ones such as fractions, addition, subtraction, and division, are well below minimal standards at some age levels. As would be expected, most reliability problems occur at the lower grade levels.

Major improvements have been made for the KeyMath-R (over the original KeyMath) in the reporting of validity studies. Generally the KeyMath-R correlates moderately with other standardized tests of arithmetic achievement, including the Comprehensive Tests of Basic Skills and the Iowa Tests of Basic Skills. The Comprehensive Tests of Basic Skills correlated .66 with the total score on the KeyMath-R and the total score for the Iowa Tests of Basic Skills correlated .76. We judge the content validity of the test to be reasonably good for a norm-referenced mathematics test. However, it is highly unlikely that the content validity will be acceptable for instructional planning or assessment for intervention, given the small number of items for any individual math skill measured by the test. The procedures used to develop the test resulted in a comprehensive instrument that assesses a relatively wide range of arithmetic skills.

Summary

The KeyMath-R is a well-organized test for the assessment of arithmetic skills in children in elementary and junior high school. Although some technical properties of the test are below minimal standards, it can provide useful information to teachers and other consumers. Overall this appears to be the best instrument on the market.

Diagnostic Test of Arithmetic Strategies

Overview and Purpose

One of the few math tests that takes advantage of the recent research pertaining to mathematical computation and thinking in children is the Diagnostic

Test of Arithmetic Strategies, or DTAS (Ginsburg & Mathews, 1984). Unlike many other tests in this area, the focus of this test is on the identification of correct and incorrect strategies (i.e., processes) rather than correct and incorrect answers to problems. Whereas a test such as the KeyMath-R may suggest that a child has a deficiency in, for example, subtraction, the DTAS is designed to provide reasons for that weakness.

Administration of the DTAS requires a different kind of thinking by the examiner than is needed for most norm-referenced tests. The primary difference is the degree to which the examiner must be flexible, as a passage from the manual suggests:

> The identification of strategies and methods requires flexible questioning. The examiner should feel free at any time to ask questions designed to reveal how children solve particular problems. Questions like, "How did you get that answer?" or "How did you do it?" are always appropriate on the DTAS. Similarly, such techniques as telling the child, "Pretend that you are the teacher and tell me how to work the problem," may also be effective and should be encouraged. The examiner should feel free to improvise on the directions to some degree. (Ginsburg & Mathews, 1984, p. 10)

The authors suggest the test can be administered by anyone "reasonably experienced" in using tests in education, language, or psychology. We disagree. Much of the rich array of information that can be derived from the DTAS would be lost if it were administered by someone unfamiliar with testing in arithmetic. We believe that the test should be administered by a teacher, psychologist, or educational diagnostician. The DTAS is designed for children experiencing difficulty with addition, subtraction, multiplication, or division. Thus, it is appropriate for most children in grades 1 through 6 and some older children who have deficiencies in basic arithmetic processes. The instrument is divided into four subtests, one for each basic arithmetic computational skill; each section requires approximately 20 minutes to administer. Generally, only one subtest is administered per session.

Standardization Sample and Norms

No data pertaining to the standardization sample or norms are provided with the DTAS, presumably because the purpose of the test is to identify processes, not to compare performances of children of the same age.

Data Obtained

Each of the four subtests is scored in three major areas: (a) setting up the problem, (b) written calculation, and (c) informal skills. Detailed directions and assistance are provided for scoring each area.

Within each subtest, the section devoted to setting up the problem helps the examiner determine whether a child has mastered some of the mechanics of arithmetic. These mechanics include writing digits and aligning numbers appropriately for arithmetical operations. For example, if a child were told to add 84 plus 3, each of the numbers would have to be written correctly and the 4 in 84 would have to be aligned with the 3 on the bottom.

The written calculation section examines whether the child obtained the correct answer to each problem, whether some standard method or an idiosyncratic method was used to obtain the answers, whether there were number fact errors, and whether any "bugs" (incorrect processes) or "slips" (simple errors usually involving a lack of attention) were consistently used for computation. Scoring for "bugs" is a fascinating aspect of the test. Examiners are provided with a considerable amount of instruction of "bug hunting," as table 10.7 shows.

The informal skills section assesses the specific type of strategy used by a child to obtain a particular answer. For example, a child who is asked to add 4 plus 5 may use her fingers to count the correct answer, thus using the strategy of counting rather than the preferred strategy of long-term memory of addition facts.

The DTAS does not yield traditional scores such as percentiles or grade equivalents. Instead, the test describes a child's specific skills and the computational processes and strategies used. This type of information is highly relevant for instructional planning but is less useful for placement decisions.

Reliability and Validity

Reliability data are not present in the manual, which is a serious omission and a cause for concern. The fact that the publisher suggests a flexible administration format may actually decrease reliability. In addition, scoring the test is a complex procedure, and one cannot know whether different examiners would reach the same conclusions about a particular child.

No validity data are provided. At the least, the authors should have incorporated a thorough analysis of content validity to demonstrate that the DTAS adequately samples all relevant computational processes.

Summary

Despite the lack of adequate standardization and validation data, the DTAS does hold promise for the diagnostician. Its primary advantage over virtually all other tests is the degree to which it assesses arithmetical processes. By assessing the strengths and weaknesses with such processes, it may be possible to determine why a child is failing. With reasons for the problem known, instructional remedies should not be far behind.

Test of Math Abilities-2

Overview and Purpose

The Test of Math Abilities-2, or TOMA-2 (Brown, Cronin, & McEntire, 1994), is a recently revised edition of the Test of Math Abilities. Like its predecessor, it is designed to assess skills in computations and story problems and to provide related information about "attitudes, vocabulary, and general cultural

Table 10.7 Directions for Locating "Bugs"

The DTAS provides direct measures of key bugs. Problems 5 and 6 are designed to identify Bug A *addition like multiplication* as in the following

32	21
+ 7	+ 6
109	87

On problem 5 the child does: "2 + 7 = 9, and then 3 + 7 = 10 so that the answer is 109." On problem 6, the child does "6 + 1 = 7 and then 2 + 6 = 8, so the answer is 87."

Problems 7 and 8 are chiefly designed to test Bug B *zero makes zero* as in

26	30
+20	+42
40	70

On problem 7 the child reasons: "6 + 0 = 0, 2 + 2 = 4, so the answer is 40." By the same logic, problem 8 gives an answer of 70.

Problems 9 and 10 are designed to identify Bug C *add from left to right,* which results in

2		1
81	or	81
+45		+45
18		27
3		1
92	or	92
+43		+43
18		36

Using this bug on problem 9 the child reasons: "8 + 4 is 12; put down the 1 and carry the 2: 2 + 1 + 5 is 8; so the answer is 18." Or on problem 9 the child may put down the 2, carry the 1, and get 27 as the answer. By the same logic, the answer to problem 10 will be 18 or 36. Of course this bug may be used on other problems.

From: Ginsburg, H. P. and Matthews, S. C. (1984) DIAGNOSTIC TEST OF ARITHMETIC STRATEGIES. Austin, TX: PRO-ED. Reprinted by permission.

applications of mathematical information" (p. 1). This revision of the TOMA continues to remain unique in going beyond an assessment of the mastery of basic arithmetic skills to measure also factors that are thought to affect math performance, such as a child's attitude toward the subject. The instrument is designed for students who range in age from 8–0 through 18–11.

The TOMA-2 has five subtests, which reflect various components of mathematical functioning and attitudes.

1. *Computation.* This subtest, which assesses students' mastery of arithmetical computations, consists of 30 problems ranging from addition to writing in scientific notation (e.g., $[x + y]\ [x - y] =$ _____).
2. *Story problems.* This subtest presents verbal descriptions of 25 problems that require arithmetical solutions (e.g., "Tom has 1 yellow boat. He has 1 red car. He has 1 blue car, too. How many cars does Tom have?").
3. *Vocabulary.* To assess knowledge of mathematics vocabulary, in this subtest students are asked to write definitions for words such as *dozen, calendar, binomial,* and *irrational number.*
4. *General information.* This 30-item subtest is intended to assess student's application of math to everyday problems (e.g., "How many pennies are in a dime?" "Why can a canceled check be your receipt?").
5. *Attitude toward math.* This subtest, now a supplemental subtest (i.e., not used in calculating a global math score), is comprised of 15 statements with which students must agree or disagree. (For example: "It's fun to work math problems.")

Very little specialized training is required to administer the TOMA-2. Directions for administration and scoring are clearly presented in the manual and can be followed by anyone reasonably familiar with educational and psychological tests. Each of the subtests requires from 10 to 25 minutes, with the total testing time ranging from 1 hour to 1 hour and 47 minutes. The authors also point out that the test can be administered in a group format.

Standardization Sample and Norms

The TOMA-2 was standardized on a sample of 2,082 students from 26 states. The revision includes substantially more students in the sample with a broader range of geographical representation. The authors took care to create a sample that is comparable to the U.S. population on variables such as gender, race, ethnicity, and disability. The sample was comprised of students ranging in age from 8 to 18.

Data Obtained

Norms are provided in terms of standard scores and percentiles for each of the five subtests, with separate norms for each of the 11 age levels. Thus, users access the norm table for a particular child's age and determine percentiles or standard scores for each subtest. The number of items has been increased for most of the subtests in this revision.

Reliability and Validity

Two forms of reliability data, internal consistency and test-retest stability, are reported in the manual. Internal consistency coefficients averaged across age levels are above .80 for all subtests. Figures for test-retest reliability were somewhat lower, with correlation coefficients (averaged across ages 10 to 14) ranging from .70 for Attitude Toward Math to .92 for the Math Quotient. To support the content validity of the test, the authors present a logical analysis of the role of each subtest in general mathematical ability and an empirical item analysis suggesting acceptable discriminative power for items. The degree to which test items sample adequately the broad content of most mathematics curricula is still questionable, however, given the (still) small number of items on such important subtests as Computation. The TOMA-2 has moderate-to-low positive correlations with the KeyMath Diagnostic Arithmetic Test, the math subtest from the Peabody Individual Achievement Test, the math subtest from the Wide Range Achievement Test, and the SRA Achievement Series. Most of the correlations with these tests were in the .30s and .40s. The test authors infer construct validity because test scores are highly correlated with age and grade level.

Summary

The major use of the TOMA-2 continues to be as a test of computational accuracy. In this role it continues to be only mediocre. However, if math anxiety, vocabulary, or application to real life events are thought to influence math performance, then the TOMA-2 may provide tentative information about whether these factors contribute to the problem. Scores from any of the subtests should be considered only as a rough screening because of very limited sampling of skills. Indeed, the math curriculum in which students are being instructed may provide more examples of student performance in important objectives than those sampled by the TOMA-2, leaving one to question whether the time involved in administering the test will produce additional benefit beyond looking at the student's actual work or asking them directly about what is difficult about math.

Chapter Summary

Achievement batteries are receiving increased attention as educators, legislators, and the public become concerned with measuring "minimal competency," or the extent to which individuals have mastered the content of a particular area. Within the public schools, such attention has generally been focused on the testing of high school seniors and teachers, not to make a comprehensive assessment of their knowledge but rather to make sure that they have obtained a minimal level of competency to function in society or in the classroom. Achievement batteries will continue to play a part in the process.

This area will continue to be an important one as schools and states attempt to develop evaluation programs to ensure that students have learned and teachers can teach. Achievement batteries will most certainly play a significant role in such evaluations, although many questions about their use have been raised in this text and elsewhere. Many have even questioned whether *any* tests can measure competence. The movement toward curriculum-based assessment techniques discussed elsewhere in this text (e.g., see chapter 6) also offers hope for a better understanding of what it means to be competent in a particular academic skill area. Debates will continue, but in the interim many states already have mandated that teachers and students must be tested to determine minimal competence.

Unfortunately, in the haste to develop programs to test minimal competence, many poor tests and testing practices have been used. One of the most persistent problems facing individuals has been how to establish the cutoff scores that determine who passes and who fails the test (Livingston & Zieky, 1982). In the past, three basic approaches have been used (Wise, 1985). The first is to adopt cutoff scores used at other locations for the same test. The second is to collect preliminary scores for a limited period and then to use them to establish a cutoff. The third approach is to form a panel of "experts" in the area you are evaluating (e.g., teacher education) and have them systematically assess the test items to determine cutoff scores.

The first approach is clearly the simplest. However, this will not work if a test has been developed for local use, if others have not used the test, or if different cutoffs have been used in different places. Finally, this approach may cause legal problems if you cannot justify the score you have established. Imagine trying to justify your decision not to let students graduate from high school because their scores fell below a cutoff that was established in another state or part of the country!

In the second approach, local data could be used to establish the cutoff scores, although there remains the problem of establishing the number of individuals who should pass and fail. For example, it may be decided that the lowest 20 percent of the examinees will fail a given test. But what happens if the quality of the people passing and failing the test changes from year to year? In the first year you may be content that the lowest 20 percent failed, but in subsequent years you may feel that the 20 percent cutoff is discriminating against people who are truly competent or letting incompetent people slip through. In either case, how do you know what level of performance signifies competence?

In the third approach, the use of a panel of experts has the advantage of requiring panel members to directly judge the minimal level of basic skills required to pass certain test items. There is, however, no guarantee that the experts will arrive at an acceptable or useful cutoff.

The development of basic competency tests and the establishment of cutoff scores are not easy tasks. Although the answers are not simple, we can be assured that with the push for excellence in education, minimal competency tests will be with us for the foreseeable future. The unfortunate consequence is that many of these popular measures are inadequate for individual instructional decision making. They give us a student's global ranking on knowledge domains, but they don't target specific areas for further investigation or intervention, ultimately limiting their utility in helping those students most at risk for not demonstrating competency.

CHAPTER 11

Language

Language is the currency of learning. The ability to receive and send spoken messages is critical to academic and social success. Some children experience significant delays or deficits in language skills and often require special services to benefit from schooling. This chapter briefly reviews language development and describes methods for assessing basic language abilities in schoolchildren. Interested readers are referred to sources such as Lahey (1988) or Bates, O'Connell, and Shore (1987) for more comprehensive treatments of language development and disorders.

Fundamentals of Language

Definitions of Language

The function of language is to communicate. The essence of communication is the ability to share one's thoughts, feelings, and experiences with other people. Thus, in any communication, there is a sender and receiver who are embedded in a physical and social context. As conceptualized here, characteristics of the sender, the receiver, and the communication context influence the meaningfulness of a communication. Nevertheless, the use and understanding of language are the main factors in successful communication. Language has been defined differently by numerous investigators. Two representative definitions are:

> Language is a system of signs and the possible relations among them which, together, allow for the representation of an individual's experience of the world of objects, events, and relations. (Bloom, 1975, p. 249)
>
> Languages are composed of speech sounds, syllables and sentences, and meaning is largely conveyed by the properties and particular use of these units. (Menyuk, 1971, p. 15)

Bloom's definition emphasizes the *communication* aspect of language, whereas Menyuk's stresses the *structural* aspects of language. According to Lamberts (1979), these definitions have four components in common:

1. *Symbols* that represent experiences
2. Symbol combinations that convey meaning
3. *Vocal sounds* that produce the meaning
4. Interpersonal dimensions to communication that are separate from the code

As a result, Lamberts (1979) recommends the following targets for assessment: (a) vocabulary (the size of the child's symbol set); (b) grammar (knowledge of *rules* for symbol combination); (c) speech sounds (ability to produce sets of phonemes); and (d) competence in interpersonal *uses* of language.

Components of Language and Normative Development

Although numerous definitions of language exist, there is high agreement that language has four main components: phonology, morphology, syntax, and semantics.

Phonology is the sound system of language. The ability to perceive and reproduce sounds is the basis for speech. English has about 45 speech sounds, or phonemes, which is why English sounds are significantly more diverse than the 26 letters in the alphabet. Children normally demonstrate mastery of the English sound system by the age of 6 or 7. As some guideposts, one can expect a child to master the phonemes *b, t, d, k, g* and all vowels by age 4, and *r, l, th, ar, bl, br,* and *pr* by age 7. By about age 3, children demonstrate knowledge of which sound combinations are typical of their language (Menyuk, 1972).

Words are composed of phonemes and form a second basic unit of language commonly referred to as **morphology.** Thus, words, or morphemes, are the smallest elements in language that have meaning. Inflection, root words, suffixes, and prefixes are all morphological components of words. Children use morphological clues in language to derive meaning. For example, *jump* indicates the action of a child, whereas *jumped* indicates both the action and that it already happened. A good command of morphology is invaluable in analyzing words and developing comprehension skills.

Another basic component of language is **syntax,** or the rules for joining words to form sentences. Children's language learning progresses from the establishment of simple, one-proposition sentences ("Mommy come") through the gradual completion of the grammatical elements of a proposition ("Mommy is coming") to the combination of two or more propositions ("Mommy is coming home and will play") and finally to forming complex sentences ("Mommy is coming home and will play after she makes supper"). Most linguists agree that by age 5 children normally develop their basic oral syntactic ability.

We expect 2-year-olds to verbalize approximately 150 words, to name familiar people, and to use verbs but not correctly with subjects. By the age of 5, the normal child's vocabulary will have increased to approximately 1,600 words and will contain adverbs, adjectives, prepositions, and conjunctions used in sentences of six or more words.

A final component of language is **semantics,** or comprehension of the meanings and interrelationships of words as they are used in sentences and paragraphs. Besides learning a lexical, or dictionary, definition of a word, children must learn how words derive meaning when used in a sentence. A solid understanding of syntax is essential to adequate semantic development, since the same word can often be used meaningfully as a noun, verb, and adjective. For example, the word *swimming* can be used as follows:

1. *Swimming* (noun) is one of my favorite sports.
2. He is *swimming* (verb).
3. The *swimming* (adjective) club will have a meeting on Saturday.

Given such complexity, it should not be surprising that the development of semantics is a slow, error-filled process.

Development of the major components of language (phonology, morphology, syntax, and semantics), however, is not enough for successful communication. One must also learn how to use language appropriately within context, which is known as **pragmatics.** Van Hattum (1980) defined pragmatics as the "rules governing the use of language by an individual in context" (p. 300). In assessing the meaning of language within a social context, one must consider factors such as (a) the age and sex of the speaker and listener, (b) the relationship between the speaker and listener (e.g., parent to child, sibling to sibling), (c) the prior knowledge or past experiences of the speaker and listener, (d) the physical setting of the communication, and, finally (e) the purpose of the message. Thus, a comprehensive evaluation of a child's language skills involves several linguistic and extralinguistic factors and provides educators and psychologists with significant challenge. In the next sections, we identify typical language and speech problems in children and outline general considerations for conducting language assessments.

Language Versus Speech Disorders

Central to competently assessing any domain of behavior is knowledge of desired behaviors. Guerin and Maier (1983) developed a Spoken Language Screening form that summarizes most language skills necessary for educational success (see table 11.1). Close examination of this table shows that assessment of language functioning is generally characterized by three domains: receptive, inner, and expressive (see figure 11.1); each will be discussed in a later portion of this section. Let's now briefly examine speech problems that often accompany and occasionally confound a language assessment.

Speech disorders are commonly classified as either articulation, voice, or fluency disorders. Individuals assessing children's language skills must be generally knowledgeable of speech problems so that they recognize what is and is not a language problem and can make appropriate referrals to speech and language pathologists.

Articulation is the process of producing speech sounds. **Articulation disorders,** by far the most common speech problem, include the addition, subtraction, omission, or distortion of speech sounds (see table 11.2). Functional articulation disorders result from faulty learning, whereas organic disorders are due to abnormalities of the speech mechanism. Common organic articulation disorders in children are **apraxia** (deficits in performing voluntary movements of the speech mechanism) and **dysarthria** (impairment of both the reflexive and voluntary components of the speech mechanism). Variations in pitch, loudness, or vocal quality may be considered **voice disorders.** These characteristics of voice are influenced by the speaker's age and sex. Descriptions of voice disorders are presented in table 11.2. **Fluency disorders** of speech are characterized by difficulties of sequence, duration, rate, and rhythm. Fluent speech is a smooth synthesis of sounds. Probably the most common and obvious fluency disorder is stuttering, which is characterized by sound repetitions, sound prolongations, and broken words. Other types of relatively rare fluency errors also are summarized in table 11.2.

Language Assessment Considerations

Formal Assessment

Both formal and informal assessment methods are available for screening the language skills of children; full speech and language examinations usually require the specialized knowledge of speech and language pathologists. Strategies for the formal assessment of language have evolved from tests of articulation and phonology to measures of language structure and content to the current emphasis on pragmatics.

Table 11.1 Spoken Language Screening Form

Category	*Above Average 0*	*Average 1*	*Below Average 2*
I. Receptive Language			
1. Volume of voice	____	____	____
2. Understands gestures	____	____	____
3. Remembers directions	____	____	____
4. "Reads" picture stories	____	____	____
5. Response time to questions or direction	____	____	____
6. Listening vocabulary	____	____	____
7. Enjoys listening to books	____	____	____
8. Interprets anger or teasing from others	____	____	____
II. Inner Language			
9. Amount of general knowledge	____	____	____
10. Gets "point" of story or discussion	____	____	____
11. Understands directions or demonstrations	____	____	____
12. Sense of humor	____	____	____
13. Sticks to topic	____	____	____
14. Can predict what will happen next	____	____	____
15. Can summarize story	____	____	____
16. Can do simple mental arithmetic	____	____	____
III. Expressive Language			
17. Pronunciation	____	____	____
18. Speed of speech	____	____	____
19. Speaks in complete sentences	____	____	____
20. Uses words in correct order	____	____	____
21. Uses correct word in conversation	____	____	____
22. Ability to recall names for objects or people	____	____	____
23. Can repeat a story	____	____	____
24. Participates in class discussions	____	____	____

Score:

27 or less	Satisfactory performance.
28–35	Child should be watched and language abilities checked on a periodic basis.
36 or more	Thorough evaluation needed.

From: INFORMAL ASSESSMENT IN EDUCATION (pp. 189–190), by Gilbert R. Guerin and Arlee S. Maier, 1983, Palo Alto, CA: Mayfield Publishing Company.

Figure 11.1 Domains of the Language Process

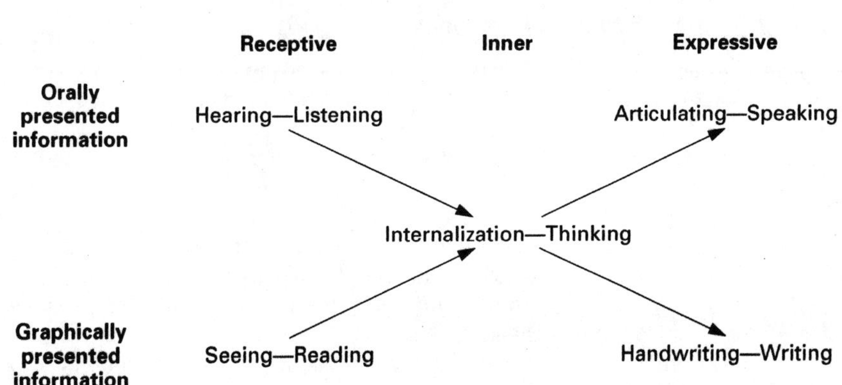

Formal measures of language typically have used one or more of five types of tasks, which have been characterized by Bryen and Gallagher (1983) as the following:

1. Elicited imitation (child repeats a list of phrases or sentences spoken by an examiner)
2. Object manipulation (child moves objects as evidence of understanding a direction or a story)
3. Picture identification (child points to the pictures that show a stimulus object or situation given by the examiner)
4. Language completion (child supplies a missing word or otherwise finishes an incomplete linguistic structure)
5. Spontaneous language sample (child's spontaneous language is transcribed by an examiner)

An informal language assessment provides a rich source of data to supplement standardized tests and can utilize many of the preceding tasks.

An important issue in the formal assessment of language is the representativeness of language sampled. In many testing situations, language behavior is artificially separated from a meaningful context, so it is distorted or represents a very small portion of a child's repertoire of linguistic competence. When this occurs, an inaccurate evaluation can result, and thus it is desirable to supplement any formal measure of language with direct observations, teacher/parent interviews, and spontaneous language samples (i.e., informal assessment).

A second important consideration is the differentiation of **receptive** and **expressive** language. Clearly, language involves both the ability to receive messages and to express messages; however, during the assessment of a child's language skills, it is often desirable to focus on subskills such as reception and

Table 11.2 Speech Disorders

Disorder	***Type of Errors***	***Description***
Articulation	Addition	Adding a sound or sounds to a word, as in *rutin* for *ruin.*
	Substitution	Substituting a sound or sounds for a sound or sounds in a word, such as in *tat* for *cat.*
	Omission	Omitting a sound or sounds from a word, as in *uck* for *truck.*
	Distortion	Distorting the sound or sounds in a word.
Voice	Hypernasality	Allowing excessive air to pass through the nasal cavity.
	Denasality	Allowing too little air to pass through the nasal cavity, so the student sounds as though he or she has a head cold.
	Hoarseness	Deep, harsh voice. Student sounds as though he or she has a cold.
	Intensity	Using the inappropriate loudness of speech. This varies with situations. For example, it is appropriate to be loud at a sporting event but not in a library.
	Frequency	Using the inappropriate pitch of speech. Appropriateness varies with a person's age and sex.
Fluency	Repetitions	Repeating sounds, syllables, or words, as in *my-my-my-my-my wagon.*
	Prolongations	Prolonging sounds in a word, as in *sssssssssing.*
	Blocks	Pausing before or after a sound, as in *b . . . all.*
	Circumlocutions	Talking around feared words, as in "I live on the avenue between First and Third Avenues," for "I live on Second Avenue."
	Starters	Using various words or phrases to start sentences or phrases in hopes of avoiding stuttering. Examples include *and then, you know,* and *I mean.*

From Bruce A. Bracken, *The Psychoeducational Assessment of Preschool Children,* 2/e.

expression. Tasks that do not require a verbal response, such as picture identification or object manipulation, stress comprehension or receptive language, whereas elicited imitation and language completion tasks are primarily measures of expressive language. Of course, expressive skills require some foundation of receptive skills, but there is much controversy among linguists about the degree to which children's receptive language is more advanced than their expressive language (Ingram, 1974; Lahey, 1988). We have set forth three pragmatic points that are relevant to the assessment of children's receptive and expressive language, regardless of the outcome of the theoretical controversy:

1. Assessment of language abilities should consider both receptive and expressive skills. Tasks in which a child is required to perform an action

(e.g., pointing to a picture) are tapping receptive skills, whereas tasks in which the child describes something or repeats or completes a statement tap expressive abilities.

2. Many standardized language tests assess only receptive or only expressive abilities. Thus either multiple tests or informal methods should be used to achieve a balanced assessment of both types of skills.
3. Teachers often overestimate a child's linguistic abilities because of correct responses to instructions and classroom verbalizations. This occurs because the classroom provides a rather predictable context with many models and nonverbal cues that enhance some receptive skills; when removed from such a setting, the child's receptive skills may suffer. Therefore, in any assessment of receptive and expressive language, it is desirable to minimize extralinguistic cues such as teacher gestures or facial expressions, written instructions, and peer models.

Informal Assessment

Before reviewing several standardized tests of language, let us focus on some informal methods and tasks that can and should supplement any assessment of language competence. Approaches to informal language assessment can be divided into two categories: structured, nonstandardized tasks and spontaneous samples of language.

Structured, Nonstandardized Tasks

A wide variety of structured, nonstandardized tasks of informal assessment have grown out of research on language. These include tasks to assess (a) means-ends relations, (b) sentence imitation, (c) egocentric listening, (d) grammatical structures, and (e) comprehension of temporal relations, anaphoric pronouns, and questions. Leonard, Perozzi, Prutting, and Berkley (1978) outlined strategies by which informal assessment methods can be reliably developed with many such tasks. Bryen and Gallagher (1983) also provided excellent guidance to an examiner of young children's language. Samples of their work in developing structured, nonstandardized assessment procedures from the literature is illustrated in table 11.3.

Spontaneous Samples of Language

Informal assessment through spontaneous samples of language involves transcribing and analyzing episodes of communication. This method has two advantages over more formalized, structured approaches to assessment; namely, the availability of both a sizable body of normative data on spontaneous language production and more natural, less artificial, language samples (e.g., Kretschmer & Kretschmer, 1978). The potential features for analysis include phonological production, vocabulary, sentence length and structure, word uses, and pragmatics such as turn-taking, initiation of conversation, and

Table 11.3 Structured, Nonstandardized Assessment Procedures

Target Language Aspect	*Materials Needed*	*Response Paradigm*[a]	*Procedures*
Object use/play (Chappell & Johnson, 1976; Sinclair, 1970)	Common objects (e.g., cup, doll, pillow, hairbrush, ball, mirror, spoon, plastic phone)	*OM*	1. Place objects in groups of three in front of the child. Observe interaction. Does child interact with the object exploratively, functionally, or symbolically? 2. If child does not spontaneously interact with objects, hand the child one object at a time. Observe and note quality of interaction, as above. 3. Follow-up with verbal directives at a symbolic level (e.g., *Make dolly sleep on the pillow.*)
Early language comprehension (Bloom, 1973; Brown, 1973; Weiss & Lillywhite, 1976)	Contexts of commonly occurring activities	*NC*	1. Using commonly occurring activities, present simple sentences or words that relate to the context (e.g., at the door say, *bye-bye*). Observe and note child's response. 2. Use same procedure as in 1, but *not* in the same context in which that activity typically occurs (e.g., at a table say, *Want to go bye-bye?*). Observe and note the influence of context on language comprehension.
Early language production (Bloom, 1973; Brown, 1973)	Familiar objects or toys	*S & A*	1. Place familiar toys/objects in front of child, one at a time. Engage child in play. Record any utterances child makes and the context. Analyze the semantic categories used by child (e.g., agent, action, criterion, recurrence).

			2. If no spontaneous utterances, try eliciting utterances by asking early *wh-* questions (e.g., What's this? What's the ball doing? Where's the ball?).
Reference descriptions semantic features (Clark, 1973a; Katz & Fodor, 1963)	Common objects (e.g., nail, envelope, ball) and a list of words without a specific reference (e.g., *animal, toy, hungry, arithmetic*)	*D*	1. Ask the child to "tell you all about" the object presented. Probe, saying *"Tell me more."* 2. After using the referent words, ask child to tell you about the words without referents. Probe. 3. Record responses and analyze semantic features used to describe each word (function, name, attributes, class inclusion).
Semantic features at the sentence level (Clark, 1973a; Katz & Fodor, 1963)	List of sentences, some of which are anomalous (violate semantic categories): 1. *She is my brother.* 2. *My mother has no children.* 3. *The candy eats Carol.* 4. *My dog writes nice stories.* 5. *The liquid became an odorless audience.* 6. *The sun danced lightly through the clouds.*	*J,A,D*	1. After reading each sentence, ask whether sentence is a good (makes sense) or bad sentence; then ask why it is a good (or bad) sentence. Have child correct "bad" sentences. Record all responses. 2. Note what factors influenced child's judgments. Note child's explanations and ability to correct anomalous sentences. Note differences, if any, between tacit and explicit language knowledge.
Specific grammatical structures (Bliss et al., 1977; Menyuk, 1969; Potts et al., 1979)	Short stories, with or without accompanying pictures, which focus on particular grammatical structures. Example 1—copula and deletion of past tense marker in main verb; *Carol got a rag,*	*SC*	Construct or obtain short stories that tap structures of interest. Where appropriate, have pictures which provide needed content clues. Read each story, having the child complete it. Note the child's response for

Table 11.3 *continued*

Target Language Aspect	***Materials Needed***	***Response Paradigm***[a]	***Procedures***
	and what she did next _______ (*was wipe it up* versus *wiped it up*) (Potts et al., 1979, p. 33) Example 2—count or mass nouns; *Look at the sandbox. There's lots of sand and lots of toys on it. Joe said, "There's no room for me in my sandbox, there's so many* _______ *(toys, things). And there's so much* _______ *(sand, junk)."* (Potts et al., 1979, p. 69)		semantic relevance, correctness of syntactic structures, and awareness of the rules for dialogue.
Comprehension of anaphoric pronoun *it* (Chipman & deDardel, 1974)	Flattened cake of clay, one box containing 5 marbles, one with 20 marbles, one clear box (empty), one tray on which is displayed chocolate divided into demarcated squares on bar of plasticine	*OM*	Present appropriate materials saying: (1) *There is the clay. Give it to me.* (2) *There is a box with five marbles.Give it to me.* (3) *The chocolate is there. Give it to me.* Note the child's comprehension of the pronoun *it.*
Comprehension of temporal connectives *before, after, until* (Barrie-Blackey, 1973)	Dolls and dollhouse; sentences containing various subordinate clauses beginning with *before, after,* or *until* (e.g., *Daddy lies down after he comes in. Mommy sits down before Daddy comes in. Daddy stands up until Mommy sits down.*)	*OM*	Sentences are said to the child who acts them out using the toys.

Comprehension of connectives and propositional logical relations (Paris, 1973)	Paired pictures (e.g., Developmental Learning Materials (DLM). Sequential Picture Cards) related to accompanying sentences in four different truth forms: true-true, true-false, false-true, false-false. Compound sentences containing the following connectives: *and* (conjunction), *but* (conjunction), *both—and* (conjunction), *neither—or* (disjunction), *either—or* (disjunction), *if—then* (conditionality), *if—and only if then* (biconditionality)	*A*	Picture pairs are displayed and the descriptive sentence is read. The child must decide if the description was true or false (e.g., *The boy is riding the bicycle and the dog is lying down.*)
Comprehensions of *wh*-questions—*who, why, when,* and *how* (Cairns & Hsu, 1978) Comprehending ongoing	Brief videotapes or films of family life, including a father, a mother, a teenage sister, a 6-year-old brother, and a dog. Questions of the following six types: *Who* subject (e.g., *Who bugged the boy?*) *Who* object using progressive aspect (e.g., *Who was the Daddy feeding?*) *Who* object using *do* support (e.g., *Whom did the boy feed?*) *Why* (e.g., *Why did the dog eat the sandwich?*) *When* (e.g., *When did the girl feed the dog?*) *How* (e.g., *How did the girl feed the dog?*)	*A*	After being introduced to each character by a photograph which remains on display, the child watches a taped segment and then is asked the six types of questions. Administer directions on the made-up scripts

Table 11.3 ***continued***

Target Language Aspect	*Materials Needed*	*Response Paradigm*[a]	*Procedures*
discourse (Glucksberg & Krauss, 1967)	Crayons and drawing paper or paste and cut-out construction paper of different sizes, colors, and shapes. A "make pretend" script of a fantasy story which the child will draw following your directions of the script or dictation of the script; or directions about the cut-out shapes that the child will follow to construct a design, mask, or scene. Script sentences should vary in complexity, have an ongoing coherent theme, and utilize, where appropriate, anaphoric pronouns. Example 1: *Hi, I'm Mary Martian from Mars. As you know, I'm a little purple Martian with red, round eyes, a square head, and green pointed ears.* Example 2: *Through the window of my spaceship I can see your planet earth. It has a big round yellow sun and blue clouds. It has trees, flowers, and birds.*	*OM*	to the child in two or three sentences at a time. Encourage the child to make his picture story (or design) exactly like the story you tell. If possible, have child retell the story or design. Analyze child's picture to determine if he was able to accurately process elaborate ongoing language. This includes expanded NP's, anaphoric pronouns.

From: Linda J. Hargrove and James A. Poteet, *Assessment in Special Education: The Education Evaluation.*

[a]Response paradigms: A, answers to stimulus questions; D, descriptions; J, judgments about grammaticality; NC, natural content; OM, object manipulations; PI, picture identification; S, spontaneous language; SC, story completion.

Focus on Practice

Assessment of the Language Proficiency of Latino(a) Students

At present, 9 percent of the U.S. population is estimated to be Latino(a). By the year 2020, the Latino(a) population is expected to surpass the Black cohort to become the largest minority group in the nation (Bouvier & Davis, 1982). Presently, many Latino(a) children have limited English proficiency.

Because language proficiency is so intimately linked to academic success, the question of differentiating Latino(a) students experiencing a language disorder from a bilingual, cross-cultural difference is a crucial one for educators and language specialists. For example, a Latino(a) student functioning adequately in Spanish but poorly in English is qualitatively different from a Latino(a) student who is functioning poorly in both languages. The latter case is indicative of an actual language or communication disorder for which speech or language services are probably needed.

Several English- and Spanish-language proficiency tests are available, including the Woodcock Language Proficiency Battery-English Form (Woodcock, 1980) and its Spanish version, the Bateria Woodcock de Proficiencia en el Idioma-Version en Espanol (Woodcock, 1981); the Expressive One-Word Picture Vocabulary Tests in Spanish and English (Gardner, 1983); and the Test for Auditory Comprehension of Language, also in Spanish and English (Carrow-Woolfolk, 1973).

As observed by Langdon (1989), one must go well beyond standardized tests in the assessment of Latino(a) students. She points to the need to rule out the effects of numerous factors that influence language. For example, Langdon suggests it is important to know the length of residence in the United States, a student's attendance record at school, the types of classrooms a student has been instructed in, the student's health and development, and how the student uses language. To facilitate the assessment of Latino(a) students in California, Langdon developed an assessment protocol. This protocol is reprinted here and should help you conceptualize an assessment plan that will more fairly and effectively facilitate your work with Latino(a) students who may be experiencing language difficulties.

A Model Speech and Language Assessment Protocol for Students With Limited English Proficiency

I. Reason for Referral: A brief description of the teachers' and parents' concerns and perceptions about the language problem.

II. Background Information:

- Family: Child's place of birth; number of siblings; sibling position; languages spoken at home, by whom, and for what proportion of the time; parental occupation; parents' education; whether parents have language problems; whether child is any different from his or her siblings; child's level of comprehension and expression at home; storytelling or story reading at home; language of media programs; family activities during free time; child activities at home; length of residence in country.

continued

Focus on Practice—*continued*

- Health: Gestational, birth, neonatal history; developmental milestones; medically related conditions, hospitalizations; hearing; vision.
- School History: Impressions from previous teachers; attendance; results from academic testing; types of programs attended; grades and performance; modifications of regular program; any other test results.

III. Testing: Description of discrete point tests in both languages; language samples taken in a variety of contexts (familiar topics, explaining rules of games, retelling stories, creating hypothetical situations), and interacting with a variety of people; complete assessment of language proficiency in each language; full description of where testing and language samples were done.

IV. Discussion:

- Language Proficiency: Comparisons between languages in different areas; which areas are stronger in each language; the influence of the student's experiences in each language; the impact of all this on academic performance; the degree and impact of primary or secondary language loss.
- Language Development: Status of basic interpersonal communication skills (BICS) and cognitive academic language proficiency (CALPS) in each language; status of CALP in the primary language when English was introduced (see Mercer, 1979); breaks in language exposure; integration of language data with intellectual and academic data; comparison of student with peers who have similar linguistic and school-based experiences.
- Language Samples: Transcribed excerpts in both languages; descriptions of contexts where these were taken; fluency variables (pauses, hesitations, and repetitions); pragmatic skills (turn-taking, and staying on topic); code switching patterns; dialect; articulation; syntax, grammar, and complexity of sentences; voice quality and resonance; status of oral peripheral mechanism.
- Behaviors: Observations on the one-to-one interactions across contexts.
- Eligibility: Rationale for determining eligibility or noneligibility.

V. Goals and Objectives:

- School Based: How each is linguistically appropriate; in which language the intervention should take place; answer to the "reason and referral"; suggestions for teachers on how to help the student.
- Home Based: Summarize these to parents in a letter (in the primary language); specific suggestions for helping the student at home.

Readers interested in the development and assessment of English language skills in Hispanic children are referred to a comprehensive review by Wilen and Sweeting (1986) and to an entire issue of *Exceptional Children* focusing on "Meeting the Multicultural Needs of the Hispanic Students in Special Education" guest edited by Fradd, Figueroa, and Correa (1989).

Table 11.4 Other Frequently Used Language Tests

Test Name	***Date***	***Author***	***Publisher***
Arizona Articulation Proficiency Scale	1970	J. Fudala	Western Psychological Services
Carrow Elicited Language Inventory	1974	E. Carrow	Learning Concepts
Expressive One Word Picture Vocabulary Test	1979	M. Gardner	Academic Therapy Publications
Illinois Test of Psycholinguistic Abilities	1968	S. Kirk, J. McCarthy, & W. Kirk	University of Illinois Press
Northwestern Syntax Screening Test	1971	L. Lee	Northwestern University Press
Phonological Process Analysis	1979	F. Weiner	University Park Press
Test of Adolescent Language-2	1987	D. Hammill, L. Brown, S. Larsen, & L. Wiederholt	Pro-Ed
Test for Auditory Comprehension of Language-Revised	1985	E. Carrow-Woolfolk	DLM Teaching Resources
Test of Written Spelling-2	1986	S. Larsen & D. Hammill	Pro-Ed

listening skills. (For detailed systems for analyzing spontaneous language samples, see Engler, Hannah, & Longhurst, 1973; Miller, 1981.) Engler and colleagues provided a method for analyzing patterns of language used by children to determine linguistic constructions. This analysis determines deviant or absent linguistic structures and can be used to plan specific remedial interventions. Informal assessment is also important because it allows the examiner to assess how a child uses language in the natural context. Increasingly, an understanding of how a child uses language in his or her normal daily routine appears essential to understanding whether a child has a language disability and what should be done about it if she or he does (Damico, 1985). Readers interested in a more comprehensive coverage of informal language assessment are referred to Bryen and Gallagher (1983), and Guerin and Maier (1983). We will now evaluate six commonly used standardized measures of language. Other popular standardized tests of language skills are listed in table 11.4.

Standardized Language Tests

Fluharty Preschool and Language Screening Test

Overview and Purpose

The Fluharty Preschool and Language Screening Test, or FPLST (Fluharty, 1978), is designed to identify preschool children (2 to 6 years of age) in need of comprehensive speech and language evaluations. The test is individually administered and generally takes less than 10 minutes to complete. Thirty-five items compose the total test and are divided into three sections:

1. Section A—requires the identification of 15 common objects and is designed to assess vocabulary and articulation
2. Section B—measures receptive language abilities through nonverbal responses to 10 sentences
3. Section C—requires the oral repetition of 10 short sentences and is an attempt to measure expressive language

Standardization Sample and Norms

The FPLST was standardized on 2,147 children from four racial and ethnic backgrounds, three socioeconomic classes, and several geographic areas. More specific data on the exact composition of the standardization sample are included in the manual in tabular form, although no mention is made of its representatives of the population at large.

Data Obtained

Children receive four scores (identification, articulation, comprehension, and repetition). A child "fails" the test if any of the four scores falls below the cutoff scores, which, according to the manual, were determined by correlating scores from the FPLST with scores from the Peabody Picture Vocabulary Test (Dunn, 1965), the Goldman-Fristoe Test of Articulation (Goldman & Fristoe, 1972), and the Northwestern Syntax Screening Test (Lee, 1971). However, the derivation of the cutoff score is not explained.

Reliability and Validity

Test-retest reliability coefficients were obtained by retesting 50 of the children in the standardization sample six weeks after the initial testing. Pearson correlations ranged from .95 to .99 for the four scores. Five speech pathologists estimated interrater reliability. Ten children from the standardization sample were retested and the five speech pathologists scored their responses. Interrater reliability ranged from .87 to 1.00 for the four scores.

Validity is reported in the test manual by indicating the correlation between a child's performance on the FPLST (pass/fail) and the outcome of a more comprehensive speech evaluation (needs therapy/does not need therapy). A Pearson correlation was calculated on the basis of data from 211 children and equaled .90. At one level the validity data can be criticized, because the Pearson Product Moment correlation statistic is not the appropriate procedure for estimating the relationship between two dichotomous variables. More importantly, specific figures are needed on the number of children who were correctly identified as needing therapy to evaluate the efficacy of the test as a screening measure. Finally, no information is provided on how the determination of whether a child needed speech therapy was made (e.g., what test was used and who made the determination).

Summary

The FPLST is a simple screening instrument. Reliability and validity data are not known because the procedures used to determine them are not well explained and seem inappropriate, decreasing even further the confidence that we can have in test results. Thus, the ultimate value of the test must be questioned.

Goldman-Fristoe Test of Articulation

Overview and Purpose

More than a decade after its initial development the Goldman-Fristoe Test of Articulation, or GFTA (Goldman & Fristoe, 1986), remains very popular. Designed to evaluate a child's ability to articulate or produce the sounds of speech, the GFTA is divided into three sections: Sounds-in-Words, Sounds-in-Sentences, and Stimulability. Consonant sounds and blends are elicited in words and sentences (Sounds-in-Words and Sounds-in-Sentences), followed by an attempt to stimulate correct pronunciation of all misarticulated sounds (Stimulability). The first two sections of the GFTA help to determine the content of any remedial activity, and the final section aids in the assessment of a child's receptivity and ability to profit from instruction. The GFTA is individually administered.

Standardization Sample and Norms

The major difference between the current and previous version of this test was the addition of normative data for the 2- to 6-year-old population. Eight hundred and fifty-two children (200 in each of four age groups) comprised the standardization sample of 2- to 6-year-olds and the sample appears representative of the larger population (Mowrer, 1989). Norms from the school-aged group (6 to 16) were derived from 38,802 subjects who had participated in the National Speech and Hearing Survey (Hull et al., 1971), although the exact process used to develop normative data is not clear (Mowrer, 1989).

Data Obtained

Percentile ranks are available for the Sounds-in-Words section. The most appropriate use of the GFTA, however, is as a criterion-referenced measure of children's ability to produce different sounds.

Reliability and Validity

Reliability for the GFTA is reported as percentage of agreement. For example, to assess interrater reliability, eight speech pathologists evaluated 37 children on two separate occasions (one-week interval) and reliability was reported as the number of times they agreed divided by the number of times they agreed plus the number of times they disagreed. Interrater reliability for presence or absence of an error on the Sounds-in-Sentences subtest is reported as 94 percent, and for the Sounds-in-Words subtest, the figure is 89 percent. Interrater comparisons for the specific type of error were also made; here the percentage of agreement figures are 86 percent and 89 percent, respectively. Unfortunately, the percentage-of-agreement method of calculating interrater agreement tends to yield spuriously high percentages. The use of the median as a measure of central tendency, which tends to discount the value of extreme scores, has also been criticized. Similar agreement values (88–91%) were obtained for interrater and intrarater reliability estimates; however, these figures are subject to the same criticisms as above. No data on age or backgrounds of subjects in the reliability studies were provided.

No validity data are presented. No attempt was made to relate the GFTA scores to other standardized measures of articulation. For a test that is often used in criterion-referenced assessment such as the GFTA, content validity is most critical. The test seems to include a thorough sampling of speech sounds, but documentation of content validity by the test authors would be helpful.

Summary

The GFTA may provide an estimate of children's ability to articulate sounds in a variety of word positions and contexts (in words and sentences). Interrater reliability data appear barely adequate, and the test seems to sample thoroughly the content it purports to measure, although evidence in the manual for both reliability and validity is sketchy.

Peabody Picture Vocabulary Test-Revised

Overview and Purpose

The Peabody Picture Vocabulary Test-Revised, or PPVT-R (Dunn & Dunn, 1981), is a revision of the original Peabody Picture Vocabulary Test. The PPVT-R is a measure of receptive vocabulary, and, according to its authors, "it is not, however, a comprehensive test of general intelligence, instead it measures only one important facet of general intelligence: vocabulary" (p. 2). This statement is important, because the original PPVT was described as a test of intellectual ability and yielded "IQ" scores. The PPVT-R is untimed and generally takes between 10 and 15 minutes to complete. The test has two forms (Form L and Form M), both containing 175 test items and 5 training items. It can be administered to individuals between the ages of 2.5 and

40. During administration, the examiner reads a stimulus word aloud, and individuals are required to pick the picture (from four choices) that best depicts that word. Members of minority cultures and women appear in nonstereotypical roles in the pictures of the PPVT-R (McCallum, 1985).

Standardization Sample and Norms

The PPVT-R was standardized on a national sample of 4,200 children and youths (ages 2.5 to 18) and 828 adults (ages 19 to 40). The sampling procedure was based on data from the 1970 U.S. census. Stratification variables for the younger sample included age, sex, geographic region, occupation of major household wage earner, ethnicity, and community size. Stratification variables for the older sample included age, sex, geographic region, and occupation. Although both of the standardization groups appear to be representative when compared with 1970 census data, the standardization for the younger group was clearly more comprehensive.

Data Obtained

Raw scores (number correct between basal and ceiling) may be transformed to stanines, age equivalents, standard scores (with a mean of 100 and a standard deviation of 15), or percentile ranks.

Reliability and Validity

Split-half, immediate test-retest with alternate forms, and delayed test-retest with alternate forms reliability data are presented in the test manual. Median split-half reliabilities of above 80 are reported for both forms. Median reliabilities during immediate retests (*N* = 642) are reported as .82 for raw scores and .79 for standard scores. Median delayed retest reliabilities (*N* = 962) equal .78 for raw scores and .77 for standard scores.

No data on the validity of the PPVT-R are included in the manual. Published data confirm that the alternate forms are equivalent and that the PPVT-R generally yields lower scores than did the original PPVT (see, e.g., Bracken & Prasse, 1981). The PPVT-R also tends to yield lower scores than frequently used measures of cognitive ability such as the Wechsler Intelligence Scale for Children-Revised (Bracken, Prasse, & McCallum, 1984; Davis & Kramer, 1985).

Summary

The PPVT-R is an easy-to-use and appropriately standardized test of receptive (or hearing) vocabulary. The reliability data indicate that if used for individual decision making, there will be a lot of errors. There is no evidence of validity of the measure as presented with the authors. Therefore, educators do not know what the test is actually measuring. Furthermore, recent data indicate that the scores on the PPVT-R tend to be lower than those for either earlier versions of this test or commonly used measures of intellectual ability.

Clinical Evaluation of Language Fundamentals-3

Overview and Purpose

The test authors describe the CELF-3 as "an individually administered instrument for the identification, diagnosis, and follow-up evaluation of language skill deficits in children, adolescents, and young adults ages 6 through 21" (Semel, Wiig, & Secord, 1995, p. 1). The authors claim that it is a measure of content (semantics) and form (phonology, syntax, and morphology), but not of use (pragmatics); but that it is also useful for discriminating receptive and expressive skills in individuals ages 6 through 21. It contains 11 subtests, but administration of only 6 subtests is necessary at any given age level to be able to compute Receptive, Expressive, and Total Language scores. Receptive subtests include Concepts and Directions, Sentence Structure, Word Classes, Semantic Relationships, and Listening to Paragraphs. Expressive subtests include Word Structure, Recalling Sentences, Formulated Sentences, Sentence Assembly, and Word Associations. An optional subtest—Rapid, Automatic Naming—is also included.

Standardization Sample and Norms

The standardization sample was stratified according to the following variables: age, gender, race/ethnicity, geographic region, and parent education level. The standardization sample included more than 3,300 children, adolescents, and young adults. There were roughly equal proportions of individuals by geographical region, 200 individuals per age group from ages 6 to 16, and 50 per age group from ages 17 to 21. Gender was divided evenly (50% female and 50% male) and the stratification by race/ethnicity and parental education of primary caregiver mirrors 1980 U.S. Census data.

Data Obtained

The test produces subtest standard scores, Receptive and Expressive Language standard scores, and a Total Language score as well as percentile ranks, normal curve equivalents, and stanines for subtest and composite standard scores.

Reliability and Validity

Three types of reliability data are presented: internal consistency reliability coefficients (coefficient alpha), test-retest, and limited interrater correlations for subtest raw scores. The internal consistency reliability coefficients (coefficient alpha) range from .54 to .91 for subtests, and from .84 to .95 for the composite scores (Receptive, Expressive, and Total Language). Test-retest estimates were obtained for ages 7, 10, and 13, ranging from .45 to .91 for subtests and .77 to .94 for composite scores. The manual also describes interrater correlations for subtest *total raw scores* (and not item by item agreement) on only two subtests: Formulated Sentences and Word Associations (with ranges from .70 to .98 for samples from three different ages—6, 11, and 16). This limited analysis is especially problematic because almost half of the subtests require "some familiarity with dialectal differences or variations of the individual being tested" (Semel et al., 1995, p. 54).

In support of the content validity of the measure, the authors argue that the language domains that the CELF-3 is intended to measure have good empirical support. Specifically, they say, "The language skills sampled by CELF-3 (e.g., morphology, syntax, semantics) are well documented in the literature addressing language disorders and competent language use . . ." (Semel et al., 1995, p. 59). One is left to judge on empirical and logical grounds how well the actual test and test items are good, accurate, and complete indicators of these different constructs. Unfortunately, without highly specialized knowledge in this area, professionals will not be able to do so adequately. In describing the construct validity of the measure, the authors appear to (accurately) limit the very diagnostic utility of the measure that was highlighted at the beginning of the manual by saying, "These fundamental elements of language cannot be evaluated independently or out of context. Form (syntax, morphology, and phonology) content (semantics), and memory, as well as receptive and expressive domains of language, cannot be separated and examined independently of each other. Although it is still of value to report separate composite scores for receptive and expressive language, the two are obviously highly related to each other, and it would be risky to interpret them outside of the context of the whole test" (Semel et al., 1995, pp. 60–61). What is unclear is how it is "still of value to report separate composite scores . . ." given that language is a complex phenomenon with many interrelated parts.

Intercorrelations of subtests, classification agreements between school-based diagnoses of learning disability and test-based diagnoses of learning disability, correlations with the previous version of the CELF (i.e., the CELF-R), correlations of the CELF-3 with a preschool version of the CELF, and correlations with a commonly used aptitude test (i.e., the WISC-III) are presented as empirical support for the construct validity of the measure. Like many other measures of its kind, moderate correlations and poor agreement rates for the diagnostic category of learning disabled were obtained across all areas. Subtest intercorrelations for subtest standard scores range from .31 to .63. There was 71.3 percent agreement of LD or Non-LD for 136 cases with prior school-based identification as LD or Non-LD. Correlations with the CELF-R range from .42 to .75 for the subtests and .72 to .79 for composite scores. Using a sample of 101 6-year-old children, correlations of .29 to .63 were obtained between the CELF-3 and the CELF-Preschool. Correlations of composite scores for a sample of 203 children and adolescents (ages 6, 9, 12, and 15) with the WISC-III ranged from .70 to .75 on the Verbal scale, .56 to .60 on the Performance scale, and .71 to .75 on the Full Scale IQ.

Summary

The primary drawback to the CELF-3 is that it does not examine pragmatic language functioning. The tasks isolate skills from the kinds of environments where children use language. Therefore, inferences drawn from the results must be tentative and need further confirmation through observation in the natural environment.

Test of Early Language Development-2

Overview and Purpose

According to its manual, the Test of Early Language Development-2, or TELD-2 (Hresko, Reid, & Hammill, 1991), is a device for assessing the early development of oral language in the areas of expressive and receptive language, syntax, and semantics. Administration of the test is simple and explained well in the manual. It includes 136 items divided into two alternate forms of 68 items and is administered individually in approximately 15 to 40 minutes. Children are required to repeat words and sentences, answer questions, and respond to a set of pictures.

Standardization Sample and Norms

The TELD-2 was standardized on a sample of 1,329 children in 30 states. The sample was stratified on the basis of age, sex, geographic region, race, ethnicity, rural versus urban residence, and occupation of parents. Data presented in the manual support the authors' contention that this sample compares favorably with national census figures.

Data Obtained

Raw scores can be converted to percentiles, age equivalents, and two types of standard scores: quotients with a mean of 100 and a standard deviation of 15 and NCE scores. The authors correctly caution users against an overreliance on age-equivalent scores due to the psychometric shortcomings of age-equivalent scores.

Reliability and Validity

Reliability data are reported in terms of internal consistency and test-retest estimates. All internal consistency figures (coefficient alpha) exceed .90. Test-retest reliability for immediate (.98) and delayed (.97) retesting are excellent. Content, criterion-related, and construct validity of the TELD-2 are discussed in the test manual. Data on item selection, sampling, and discrimination appear to support the claim of content validity for the TELD-2. Criterion-referenced validity was established by correlating TELD-2 scores with (a) similar language measures and (b) the original TELD. Correlations with similar tests yielded moderate correlations .47 to .66, suggesting that the TELD-2 may measure similar, but not completely overlapping, content. As might be expected, the TELD and TELD-2 scores are highly correlated (.96/.97 between the TELD and two forms of the TELD-2). Construct validity was established by correlating TELD-2 scores with scores from tests of intelligence and academic achievement. These comparisons indicate that the TELD-2 does appear to be more closely related to language measures than to other types of tests.

Summary

The TELD-2 appears to be a quick, easy-to-administer overall measure of language ability in young children. The manual provides a clear and detailed explanation of the rationale and appropriate use of the test. Psychometric characteristics are stronger than most other measures in this area and a significant improvement over the previous edition.

Test of Written Language-3

Overview and Purpose

The Test of Written Language-3, or TOWL-3 (Hammill & Larsen, 1996), was designed to provide a comprehensive assessment of written language skills in children from 7 to 17 years of age. Subtests include Vocabulary, Spelling, Style, Logical Sentences, Sentence Combining, Contextual Conventions, Contextual Language, and Story Construction. The TOWL-3 is designed for either group or individual administration and requires approximately 90 minutes to complete. Administration and scoring are difficult but are well explained in the manual. The test authors claim that the results of the TOWL-3 are described as appropriate for identifying students who perform below their peers, determining specific strengths and weaknesses, documenting progress, and conducting research.

Standardization Sample and Norms

The TOWL-3 was standardized on 2,217 students in 25 states. A comparison between the normative group and U.S. population data in terms of gender, place of residence, race, ethnicity, geographic distribution, family income, educational attainment of parents, and disability status is presented in the manual. The sample does appear representative in these areas. New to this edition is an attempt to control for socioeconomic status, educational level of parents, and inclusion of children with disabilities in the sample.

Data Obtained

Raw scores on the TOWL-3 may be transformed to percentile ranks or standard scores. Subtest standard scores have a mean of 10 and a standard deviation of 3, whereas the composite scores (Contrived Writing, Spontaneous Writing, and Overall Written Language) have a mean of 100 and a standard deviation of 15. Grade and age equivalents are reported in the manual in spite of their extreme limitations and frequent misinterpretation.

Reliability and Validity

Internal consistency, alternate forms, test-retest, and interscorer figures are reported. Coefficient alpha and split-half measures of internal consistency are at .91 or above for the composite scores (Contrived Writing, Spontaneous Writing, and Overall Writing). Coefficient alphas (averaged across age levels) range from .69 to .91 for both test forms. The subtest Contextual Conventions has the poorest evidence of internal consistency. The test authors also present similar internal consistency data for selected subgroups from the standardization sample. Alternate form reliability data drawn from the entire normative sample are reported. Correlations (averaged across age levels) were all .80 or above except for the Contextual Conventions subtest (for which a correlation of .71 was obtained). Test-retest with alternate forms was undertaken by testing 27 children in grade 2 and 28 students from grade 12 from Austin, Texas. The period of time between being tested with the two forms of the test was two weeks and the test composite and the composites appear to yield stable scores (.83 or above). The reliability evidence for many of the subtests falls below .80 on at least one form for at least one grade level (i.e., Vocabulary, Style, Logical Sentences, Contextual Conventions, Contextual Language, and Story Construction). Unfortunately, the one reported test of interscorer reliability involved only two scorers. Although these estimates of interscorer reliability are high, this comparison is not a good measure of whether professionals in the field will be able to score the test in a reliable manner. Information on content, criterion-related, and construct validity is reported in the test manual. Under content validity, the manual thoroughly discusses the rationale for the test content and the manner in which it was selected. Correlations between the TOWL-3 and a variety of other tests were used as an index of criterion-related and construct validity. These comparisons appear to support the authors' claim that the test does measure skills related to written language.

Summary

The updated version of the TOWL remains one of the best instruments for obtaining global rankings of individual students' written language skills. The test takes a long time to administer and is more difficult to learn to score than some other tests, but the manual does provide thorough instructions. In fact, the manual serves as an excellent model in its description of what the test does and does not accomplish.

Woodcock Language Proficiency Battery-Revised

Overview and Purpose

The Woodcock Language Proficiency Battery, or WLPB (Woodcock, 1991), contains 13 tests organized into three areas: oral language, reading, and written language. The battery can be administered to individuals from 2 to 90 years of age and requires about an hour and a half for an experienced examiner. In reality, the WLPB-R is a portion of the Woodcock-Johnson Psychoeducational Battery-Revised (WJ-R; Woodcock & Johnson, 1989) that has been repackaged and distributed as a separate test of language ability. According to the manual, the WLPB-R can be used for evaluating English as a Second Language, diagnosis, program placement, individual program planning, guidance, evaluating gains in language development, program evaluation, training students about testing, and research.

Standardization Sample and Norms

The normative sample for the WLPB-R included 6,359 subjects stratified on the basis of sex, race, occupation, geographic location, and type of community. It should be noted that this norm group is the sample that participated in the norming of the WJ-R and is not a separate norming of the WLPB-R. As was indicated in the review of the WJ-R (see chapter 10), the process of subject selection was excellent.

Data Obtained

Raw scores on the WLPB-R may be converted into a number of other scores, including percentile ranks, age equivalents, standard scores, normal curve equivalents, and relative mastery indexes. If an examiner has not tired of the scoring process after calculating all of these scores, intra-English discrepancy scores can be completed that allow for an assessment of the degree of difference among the three areas of English assessed with this test: oral language, broad reading, and broad written language. Calculating scores on the WLPB-R is no easy matter and can take a great amount of time.

Reliability and Validity

Internal consistency, interrater reliability, and test-retest reliability are reported in the test manual. As with the original WJ-R from which it was developed, the WLPB-R appears to yield reliable scores and to be internally consistent. Development, selection, and sequencing of items for the WLPB-R was exemplary. In addition, a number of criterion (i.e., concurrent) validity studies are presented in the manual. The inclusion of these studies is a significant improvement over the original edition of the WLPB when the user was simply referred to the validity studies on the original Woodcock-Johnson Psychoeducational Battery as evidence of the validity of the WLPB. The criterion validity studies with tests like the Boehm Basic Concept Scales, the PPVT-R, the K-ABC, Stanford-Binet IV, and various other achievement and special ability tests support the general contention that the WLPB-R measures a similar construct (i.e., language functioning). These studies involved few subjects and restricted age ranges and a more definitive statement about the test's value will be possible following the collection of additional validity data.

Summary

The major value of the WLPB-R appears to be its comprehensiveness. It includes a variety of skill areas, assesses these areas in a thorough manner, and covers a wide age range. Examiners will find the administration, scoring, and interpretation of this test somewhat more cumbersome than most standardized tests. The WLPB-R appears psychometrically sound; however, a clear indication of its potential awaits the collection of more comprehensive validity data. It is fair to say that the WLPB-R appears to have promise for applications to some educational decision making.

Chapter Summary

Language is a rich and complex area of human functioning. A commonly accepted way of dividing up language into vocabulary, rules, vocal sounds, and interpersonal communication skills was described early in the chapter. This division has constituted the customary way that language has been assessed. Two consistent features occur across most of the language tests that we have reviewed: (a) they are quick and simple to administer, and (b) they yield a "score." Herein constitutes the allure of language tests. There has been an unfortunate emphasis on the evaluation of each of these important language skills in isolation (e.g., in a one-on-one setting with an unknown adult testing for articulation skills) and a neglect of (a) how young children integrate these areas to produce language, and (b) the environmental circumstances in which the young children display language (i.e., the home and classroom settings).

We describe this emphasis as unfortunate because assessing language in isolation may ultimately do a disservice to the children being served. First, professionals may end up spending a lot of time screening children's language, a practice that produces a lot of errors (as we saw in chapter 2). Second, this extra time screening children individually means time lost on other professional activities. For instance, language specialists could spend time helping to strengthen the curriculum and instruction in settings where children's language functioning affects their performance by consulting with teachers and parents (e.g., preschool) (Adelman, 1982). Excellent examples of fruitful activities for educators include what Wolery, Bailey, and Sugai (1988) refer to as "capitalizing on naturally occurring events and routines," strategies like the *mand-model procedure, incidental teaching,* and *naturalistic time delay.* (See also Barnett & Carey [1992] for discussions of these procedures.)

The bottom line is that the best first step in the practice of assessment of language is to *not* begin with assessment, but to spend time strengthening the language training skills of important intervention agents like parents and teachers. The next step is to examine students' language functioning in natural settings like the classroom and the home. To do this, however, educators need to have a clear idea of what to look for. One strategy that can guide assessment in this area is called *template matching* (Barnett & Carey, 1992). The reader is referred to Ager and Shapiro (1995) and Barnett and Carey (1992) for descriptions of the procedures. Briefly, template matching is a process involving observation of typical peers to examine how proficient they are in using language strategies as a basis for generating goals for students having difficulty with language and using effective teaching strategies to promote competence in these areas. If a child still proves resistant to intervention and curricular modification, it may then be necessary to isolate language skills to provide remediation in particular areas. Following this approach, the decision to examine language skills in isolation on a norm-referenced test will be based on a lot of accumulated information about attempts to address the problem in the natural setting.

CHAPTER 12

Cognitive Abilities

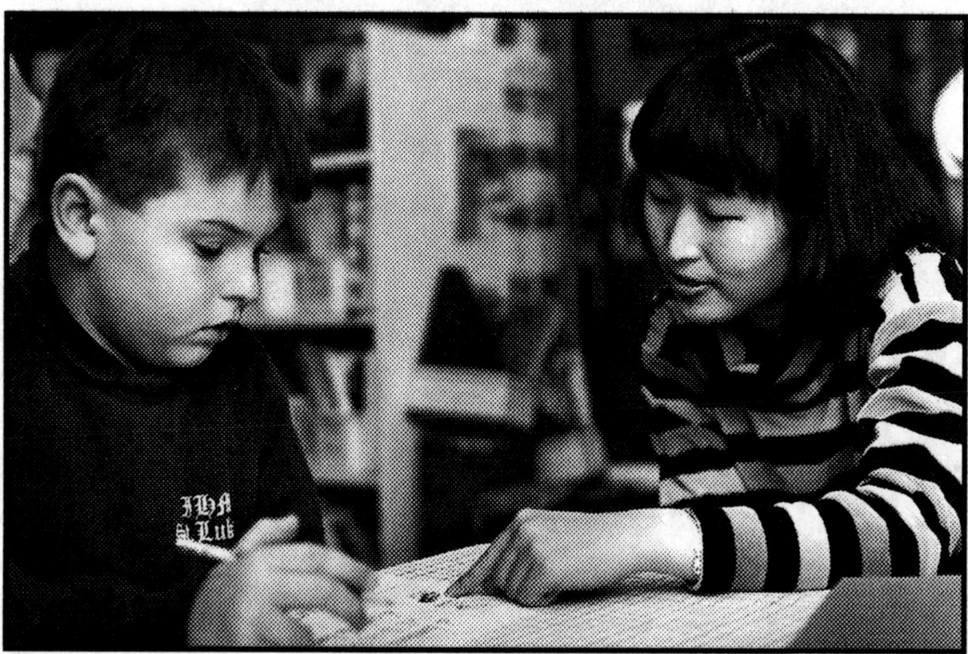

A young school psychologist, Dr. Bailey, approaches a fifth-grade classroom. She knocks on the door and is greeted warmly by the teacher. The teacher turns toward her class and asks Ted to come to the door. Ted knows Dr. Bailey is there to see him. He worked with her last Wednesday, and she has come back to work with him again this week. During the next 60 minutes Ted and Dr. Bailey will be together in a quiet room adjoining the school library. During this time Ted is asked to answer a number of questions (e.g., What is the capital of France? From what animal do we get veal? What is 65 – 11? How are concrete and asphalt alike?) and to complete a variety of timed tasks (e.g., Put these pictures in the correct order to tell a good story; Copy these designs; Tell me what important part is missing from this picture; Put this puzzle together).

At the end of the testing session, Ted is tired. He has tried to do his best, and Dr. Bailey congratulates him for his effort. Ted knows that he answered some questions correctly and that he missed some of the harder ones. Dr. Bailey accompanies Ted back to his classroom, thanks him and his teacher, and then returns to her office to score Ted's responses. In approximately

15 minutes she will have calculated Ted's IQ score according to the directions provided by the developer of the test she administered.

Scenes similar to the one described occur many thousands of times across this country every year. Intelligence tests are just one of many different kinds of tests administered to schoolchildren during the typical evaluation process. Is IQ testing a worthwhile exercise? Here is what some noted scholars have had to say about intelligence and IQ tests:

> The IQ test has also played an important part in the American school system—especially in assigning lower class and minority children to dead-end classes for those with mild mental disabilities. (Kamin, 1981)
>
> A person's level of g [i.e., *general* intelligence] has ramifications for everyday life—in school, at work, and in personal matters. Because a standard IQ score is usually a good measure of g, it efficiently tells us something important. (Herrnstein, 1982)
>
> IQ is a questionable measure of general intelligence and a minor determination of success. (Robinson, 1973)
>
> IQ jointly with scholastic performance predicts more of the variance among persons in adult occupational status and income than any other known combination of variables, including race and social class or origin. (Jensen, 1980)
>
> If . . . the impression takes root that these tests really measure intelligence, that they constitute a sort of last judgment on the child's capacity, that they reveal "scientifically" his predestined ability, then it would be a thousand times better if all the intelligence testers and all their questionnaires were sunk without warning in the Sargasso Sea. (Lippmann, 1976)
>
> The outstanding success of scientific measurement of individual differences has been that of the general mental test. Despite occasional overenthusiasm and misconceptions and the fact that the established tests are rendered obsolescent by recent conceptual advances, the general mental test stands today as the most important technical contribution psychology has made to the practical guidance of human affairs. (Cronbach, 1970)

Who is correct? Should these tests that purport to measure cognitive abilities and general intelligence be abolished or are they useful tools for understanding people? Why is the debate so intense? Although there is much debate among experts about the value of intelligence tests, the general public appears to believe that intelligence does play a role in the behavior and decision making of individuals.

The tests discussed in this chapter have sometimes been referred to as "mental tests," tests of "general ability" or "academic aptitude," "intelligence tests," or tests of "cognitive abilities." We will attempt to make clear the many important issues related to intelligence testing through careful review and analysis of fact and fiction. Toward that end we examine the origins and current status of the mental testing movement, explore many of the issues surrounding the use of these tests in our society, discuss a number of the most widely used measures of intelligence, and conclude with a brief discussion of the future directions.

Historical Approaches to the Definition and Measurement of Intelligence

Early Efforts

The study of intelligence can be clearly traced to 19th-century attempts to measure individual differences in a wide variety of human characteristics. It has been claimed that this testing movement was an essential part of the establishment of psychology as a separate discipline (see, e.g., Sattler, 1988). Three major contributors to these early efforts were Sir Francis Galton in England, Wilhelm Wundt in Germany, and J. McKeen Cattell in the United States. Galton developed psychophysical measurements such as strength of push and pull, breathing capacity, keenness of the senses, and mental imagery. His efforts in the study of individual differences led to the development of a psychometric laboratory at the International Exposition in England in 1884 and to his designation as the "father" of the testing movement (Shouksmith, 1970).

Wundt opened the first psychological testing laboratory in Leipzig, Germany, in 1879. He utilized the early work of Galton and others but took a slightly different approach. He attempted to identify general laws governing behavior rather than to measure the extent of individual variation among humans. Cattell, who gave us the term *mental tests,* imported these techniques to the United States. Procedures to measure factors such as sensory acuity, strength of grip, sensitivity to pain, and memory for dictated consonants characterized his efforts to assess individual differences and later to measure individual mental skills. The tests used by these pioneers were not very useful in predicting behavior (e.g., a good sensory acuity score did not translate to good academic achievement) and seem primitive by today's standards. These early approaches did, however, serve as a foundation for future research and moved intellectual measurement out of the realm of speculation and clinical judgments and into the world of scientific measurement.

Early 20th-Century Approaches: The Search for Relevance

Around the turn of the century in France, Alfred Binet became interested in studying complex mental processes. His findings were similar to those previously cited and supported the notion that simple sensory discriminations and physical attributes had little relation to general mental functioning. In 1905 the Minister of Public Instruction in France wanted a test that would assist school personnel in determining which students were *not* capable of achieving in the regular classroom. In response to the minister's request, Binet and his associate, Theodore Simon, developed and published the Binet-Simon Scale. Revised in 1908, the scale's major contributions were that it was pragmatic in development, used complex tasks as test items, ranked items in order of difficulty and grouped them according to age levels, measured general mental ability rather than separate mental faculties, included careful instructions for administration, and exhibited some concern with normative data. Further, student test scores were shown to be related to academic performance. The Binet-Simon Scale was designed to predict school achievement and did a fairly good job of it.

Following the introduction of this scale in the United States, the testing movement began to flourish. It appears, however, that the intentions of those who brought these scales to the United States were not so benevolent. Lewis Terman, the person who translated the Binet into English, creating the first "Stanford-Binet," wrote that members of non-Caucasian groups had lower levels of intelligence and that:

> Children of this group should be segregated in special classes. . . . They cannot master abstractions, but they can often be made efficient workers. . . . There is no possibility at present of convincing society that they should not be allowed to reproduce, although from a eugenic point of view they constitute a grave problem because of their unusually prolific breeding. (1916, as cited in Lewontin, Rose, & Kamin, 1984)

Unfortunately, these tests were used for more than predicting achievement and led to disastrous social consequences for many individuals (see Lewontin et al., 1984; and Kamin, 1974 for fascinating reviews of the dark origins of IQ testing in the English-speaking world).

Although a significant advance over previous efforts, the Binet-Simon Scale and its subsequent revisions had problems. One of the most persistent criticisms was related to its age-scale format; that is, tests were selected for inclusion at various age levels based on the difficulty of the tests, and different tasks were included at different age levels. The result was a great deal of heterogeneity of item content (see figure 12.1) for representative items across age levels. Thus, interpretation of an individual's performance on the Binet was difficult because of the varied item content and because measurements of individuals of different ages were not strictly comparable. (If all this talk about the structure and design of the Binet is a little fuzzy, don't be discouraged. This test has been confusing people for years!)

Enter David Wechsler, who took a different approach to the development of an intelligence test. Wechsler wanted to find tasks that would measure various cognitive abilities and could be used across a wide range of age levels. He studied a variety of tests available and developed 11 subtests, which he used to form the Wechsler Bellevue Intelligence Scale, designed for use with adults. The same subtests were administered to all individuals, making interpretation of performance and comparison across individuals (or intraindividual comparisons across time, etc.) easier. This test led to the development of the Wechsler series of intelligence tests (Wechsler Primary and Preschool Scale of Intelligence [WPPSI], Wechsler Intelligence Scale for Children [WISC],

Figure 12.1 Early 20th-Century Approaches: The Search for Relevance

Year III

Credit—6 tests × 1 month or 4 tests × 1 1/2 months

1. Stringing Beads—the examiner models the stringing of beads on a shoestring and the child is asked to "play this game."
2. Picture Vocabulary—naming pictures of common objects.
3. Block Building—bridge-building a bridge of three blocks modeled by the examiner.
4. Picture Memories—finding animal pictures hidden by the examiner.
5. Copying a Circle—three trials of copying a circle.
6. Drawing a Vertical Line—one trial drawing a vertical line just like the one drawn by the examiner.

A. Repeating 3 Digits—repeating 3 digits in sequence.

Year VIII

Credit—6 tests × 2 months or 4 tests × 3 months

1. Vocabulary—children are asked to provide the definitions of words.
2. Memory for Stories: The Wet Fall—children are asked a series of questions based on a story read by the examiner.
3. Verbal Absurdities I—a series of absurd or foolish situations are presented and the child asked to tell, "What's foolish about this?"
4. Similarities and Differences—describing the similarities and differences of two things.
5. Comprehension IV—a series of general comprehension questions to which the examinee must respond.
6. Naming the Days of the Week—naming the days of the week.

A. Problem Situation I—incomplete situations are presented, followed by questions which require the child to infer what is happening in the scene.

Superior. Adult III

Credit—6 tests × 6 months or 1 test × 9 months

1. Vocabulary—providing definitions of words.
2. Proverbs III—explaining the meaning of words.
3. Opposite Analogies IV—analogies are provided with the final word in the analogy supplied by the subject.
4. Orientation: Direction III—analyzing distance and direction based on information provided by the examiner.
5. Reasoning II—individual is presented brief problem and given 5 minutes to solve it (without pencil and paper).
6. Passage II: Tests—repeating the main ideas of a brief passage read by the examiner.

A. Opposite Analogies—same as above.

From: STANFORD-BINET INTELLIGENCE SCALE 1973: NORMS EDITION by L. M. Terman and M. A. Merrill. 1973. Boston: Houghton Mifflin. These Stanford-Binet materials are also included in the Fourth Edition. Authors of this revision are Elizabeth Hagen, Jerome M. Sattler, and Robert L. Thorndike.

Wechsler Adult Intelligence Scale [WAIS]). Today, the current revisions of the Wechsler tests are the most widely used measures of cognitive functioning in educational and clinical settings. Later we will examine one of these instruments, the WISC-III, and the subtest format that Wechsler developed.

Recent Developments

Both Binet and Wechsler wanted to develop a test instrument that would be useful in the clinical and educational assessment of individuals. Although both men conceptualized intelligence as a complex and multifaceted phenomenon, their tests yielded global intelligence scores that suggested a more unified view of intelligence. Many individuals lost sight of the fact that the Binet-Simon and Wechsler scales contained a variety of tasks tapping many different abilities and instead focused on the comprehensive IQ scores these tests yielded. The question of whether intelligence is a single ability or a collection of multiple abilities has received the attention of theorists and researchers during the last 50 years.

The best-known proponent of the former approach was Charles E. Spearman (1927), who set forth a **two-factor theory** of intelligence. He hypothesized that performance on intelligence tests resulted from a general factor (*g*) and a group of specific factors that varied from test to test. Spearman is sometimes viewed as a single-factor theorist due to his emphasis on the importance of *g*, which he said is involved in all problem solving and is especially important in complicated mental activities. Specific factors, on the other hand, are unique to a particular activity or test. A major implication of this theory was that although specific factors must be considered, the primary goal of intellectual measurement should be the construction of tests that measure *g*. Why? Because if we develop tests that are good measures of this general factor that influences performance on all tasks, we should be better able to predict how an individual will do on tasks in the future.

Louis L. Thurstone (1938) and J. P. Guilford (1967) have been more closely identified with the **multifactor theory** approach. Both believed that intelligence could not be reduced to a unitary factor such as *g*. Thurstone developed the Primary Mental Abilities Test to measure what he felt to be the primary mental abilities (such as verbal skills, perceptual speed, inductive reasoning, word fluency, and rote memory), and Guilford developed a three-dimensional Structure of Intellect Model (see figure 12.2) that organized intellectual factors hierarchically. Both approaches assumed that a model of intellectual functioning must include a variety of fairly broad factors if it is to account for the complexity of mental activity.

Within the last decade, two other explanations of intelligence have gained increased attention. The first is based on the work of Alexsadr Luria and has been expanded by J. P. Das and his colleagues (Das, Kirby, & Jarman, 1979; Jarman & Das, 1977). This model has been referred to as simultaneous/successive processing, and later in the chapter we look at a new test based on

Figure 12.2 Guilford's Three-Dimensional Structure of Intellect Model

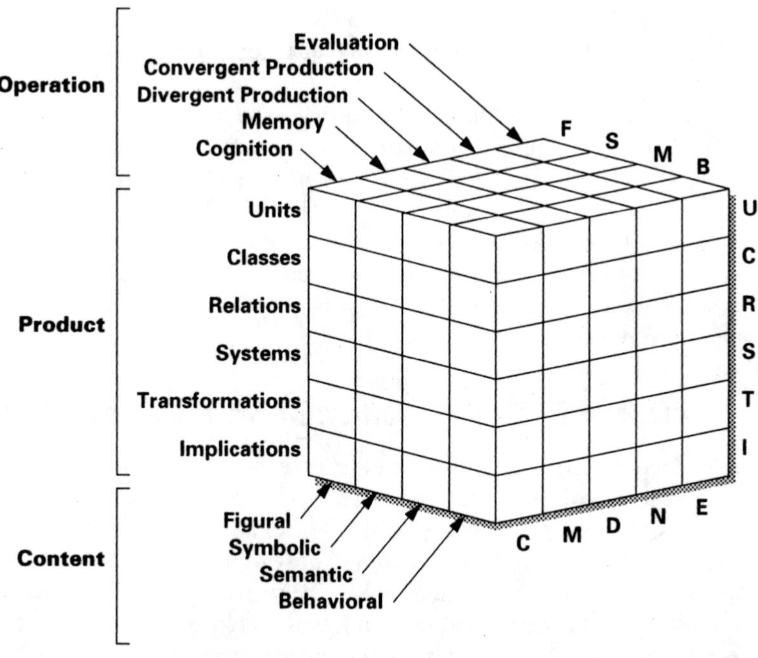

From J. P. Guilford, *The Nature of Human Intelligence.* Copyright © 1967 McGraw-Hill, New York. Reprinted with permission.

this theoretical model. Simply stated, this model suggests that individuals process information primarily in one of two ways—simultaneously or successively. In the former, problem solving and decision making involve the simultaneous integration of a variety of stimuli. Information is processed in a holistic manner, as when people are asked to recognize faces, solve mazes, and complete puzzles. In the successive mode, stimuli are arranged in sequence and dealt with one at a time. Decisions are reached by processing information in an orderly, sequence-dependent fashion (e.g., remembering a series of digits or words in the proper order). The usefulness of this model and its ability to increase our understanding of human behavior remain to be determined.

More recently, Sternberg (1984) has postulated a "triarchic theory" of intelligence that is composed of three components. The first component emphasizes the ability of individuals to organize, plan, and carry out activities (these skills have sometimes been referred to as metacognitive abilities); the second component focuses on the individual's experience with novel, complex problems; and the third component concentrates on intelligence as it relates to the external world. Sternberg believes that conventional intelligence tests have worked as well as they have because the tasks represented on them involve many of the abilities emphasized in his first two subtheories. He suggests, however, that intelligence tests are imprecise measures of these abilities and further, that we must consider the ability of individuals to adapt to their particular environment to have a complete definition of intelligent behavior.

As we indicated at the beginning of this section, questions about the nature of intelligence have occupied the thoughts and research efforts of many people during the last century. We do not mean to imply that this concern began in the late 19th century, for the quest began long before. Furthermore, we have only touched on the work of some of the most important contributors to this effort. Next we examine certain crucial issues related to the application of measures of cognitive ability by professionals in educational and mental health settings.

The Assessment of Cognitive Ability: Critical Issues and Concerns

Intelligence testing has gained widespread acceptance in the United States. This is true among not only measurement experts, many psychologists, and educators but also the general public. For example, parents have become increasingly concerned with providing the optimal environment for their infants and preschoolers to maximize intellectual potential, and as children grow older teachers and parents often want to know their child's IQ score. A trip to your favorite bookstore is likely to reveal a number of books concerned with "increasing your child's IQ" or "testing your own intelligence in 15 minutes by asking yourself only four simple questions." This growing fascination with IQ measurement has not occurred without concern. Before analyzing the most widely used tests of cognitive ability, let's first explore a few of the most critical issues associated with the measurement of intelligence.

Stability of IQ

As a result of the popularization of intelligence tests and the intelligence testing movement, numerous misconceptions about the nature of intelligence developed and were fed by overzealous testers and a misinformed public. One of the most pervasive ideas, which became solidly entrenched in public opinion, was the notion that an infant was born with a certain amount of "intelligence" that did not change as the child grew older. As with many myths, this one was supported with a grain or two of truth. In general, most research has suggested that IQ tests do *tend* to yield scores that are *fairly* stable. However, this same research indicates that IQs are more stable over shorter as opposed to longer periods and more stable for older children and adults than for children under 6 years of age. A good deal of evidence indicates that IQ scores obtained before children enter kindergarten or first grade are not highly reliable. No one knows exactly to what extent intelligence scores can be altered through environmental manipulation. Although studies of the late 1960s and early 1970s (e.g., the Milwaukee Project) reported that intensive early intervention in children's lives was capable of producing incredible increases in measured IQ, such studies have been severely criticized (see, e.g., Sommer & Sommer, 1983). Despite this criticism, most experts would agree that enriched environments are better than impoverished ones for fostering intellectual development.

Data on the relative stability of IQ can be deceiving and must be interpreted with care. When looking at the IQ scores of large groups of individuals, we can make the general statement that most of those within the group would receive similar scores if retested. However, it is not at all unusual for particular individuals to show a great deal of variability in their scores. Changes of 8, 10, 15, or even 30 IQ points are not unheard of, and each author of this text has tested children who exhibited these types of changes. This potential for intraindividual difference in IQ scores during different testing sessions means that when examining test results, we must not assume that a child who obtained an IQ in a certain range of intelligence will always remain in that range.

Bias in Cognitive Ability Testing

No issue related to the assessment of cognitive abilities has generated as much or as heated debate as the question of whether IQ tests are biased against individuals from minority cultures. Discussions in the popular press have vehemently assailed most aptitude and achievement tests as being unfair to children from backgrounds that are different from those of most middle-class White Americans (Herrnstein, 1982). Although we have no data other than our perceptions, we believe that most students enter our classes convinced that standardized tests are unfair, inaccurate indicators of the abilities of individuals from minority populations. Numerous researchers have investigated the issue of bias in mental tests, with the greatest amount of attention focused on the differences between the performance of Blacks and Whites (e.g., Jensen, 1980). Some have turned to the courts for help in determining whether IQ tests are biased and whether they should be used in the assessment of minority children, but the courts have not been consistent in their findings (*Larry P. v. Riles,* 1986; *PASE v. Hannon,* 1980).

Many different types of test bias have been identified, and these have been discussed at length by both proponents and opponents of cognitive ability testing. Table 12.1 lists and defines the most common types of test bias that have been studied. As Brown (1983) has indicated, there is no universally accepted definition of bias but most definitions hold that

> a test can be considered biased if it differentiates between members of various groups (for example, between men and women or between blacks and whites) on bases other than the characteristic being measured.

Table 12.1 Types of Test Bias

Type	*Definition*
Mean Differences	Average scores for various groups (such as black, white, and Hispanic or rich and poor) are different
Item/Content Bias	Portions of test content are biased in a manner that differentially affects the performance of certain groups (such as black and white, or men and women)
Factor Analysis	The factors (for example, verbal abilities or attention) being measured are different for various racial, cultural, or economic groups
Predictive Validity	Scores predict with varying levels of confidence for different groups
Social Consequences	Tests are misused or misinterpreted to justify restrictive social policies
Selection Ratios	Test results are used in ways that cause particular groups to be over- or underrepresented in special classes or certain diagnostic categories (for example, mentally disabled)

Adapted from D. Reschly, "Concepts of Bias in Assessment and WISC-R Research with Minorities" in H. Vance and L. F. Wallbrown (eds.) WISC-R RESEARCH INTERPRETATION, pp. 87–94. Copyright © 1980 by the National Association of School Psychologists. Adapted by permission of the publisher.

> That is, a test is biased if its content, procedures, or use result in a systematic advantage or disadvantage to members of certain groups over other groups and if the basis of this differentiation is irrelevant to the test purpose. (p. 224)

An examination of the research and writings related to bias in cognitive ability testing reveals that the issues are very complex, not easily resolved, and complicated by the emotional intensity with which individuals have advanced their arguments in this area. Consider the following factors, and you will understand why testing bias has come to be such an emotional topic:

1. Our society has long discriminated against African Americans and members of other minority groups through a variety of overt and covert mechanisms. Slavery, exclusionary voting laws, separate educational systems, racial slurs, and the like have all occupied a place in this abhorrent, unfortunate history. Although discrimination continues to exist at unacceptable levels, many public and private institutions have committed themselves to the establishment of equal opportunity for all.
2. Intelligence testing has been popular in this country since the introduction of the Binet scales. African Americans, for example, have consistently obtained average scores that are approximately one standard deviation (15–16 IQ points) below the average score of Whites. Some

have used this type of information to argue for the existence of genetic differences between the races (e.g., Jensen, 1980). Others have suggested that environmental factors are more crucial in the development of intelligence (e.g., Kamin, 1981), but there is little disagreement with the fact that average scores do differ among racial and ethnic groups.

3. The most widely used tests of cognitive ability have been developed by Whites, published by Whites, and made money for Whites. Furthermore, these tests are used to estimate and predict performance in a society that is dominated by the White culture. A good deal of evidence indicates that White society has used the results of these tests to justify discriminatory laws and practices (McPherson, 1985).

Given society's attention to the issue of equality, the different performances on IQ tests by different groups, and the fact that the history of these tests has been dominated by Whites, it is not surprising that so many believe so strongly that these tests must be biased against minorities and in favor of Whites.

In fact, little evidence supports the belief of bias in intelligence tests. First, although it is true that Blacks average lower intelligence scores than Whites, this is not enough information to conclude that the tests are biased, especially when socioeconomic status is considered. The tests may be biased, but first we must determine if the differences in scores reflect true differences in the ability being measured. Tests are designed to discriminate—to tell good spellers from poor ones, to predict success or failure in graduate school or in a job as a bank teller, and to determine those who have learned the material in history class and those who have not. Simple differences in average scores alone do not prove that bias exists. The fact that you may consistently obtain lower scores than a friend in history class does not mean that the instructor or the tests are biased. Other factors must be studied to reach that conclusion. In the case of intelligence tests, we must investigate their content, construct, and predictive validity. That is, we have to examine whether the test items are biased in favor of one group, whether the test measures the same abilities for all groups, and whether the test predicts equally well for all groups.

The technical evidence overwhelmingly indicates that the vast majority of items used on tests such as the Wechsler and Binet are not biased, that these tests tend to measure the same factors (verbal, perceptual, performance, quantitative, or the like) and predict success equally well for all racial groups (Reynolds, 1982). This last point is critical. It is important to remember that IQ tests do not measure the amount of some innate, immutable ability that we all possess but do provide a general measure of expected school achievement, just as they were designed to do in the early 1900s. The evidence on predictive validity suggests that whether someone is African American, Caucasian, or Latino does not really matter: An individual with an IQ score of 60 from a reliable test is at risk of failing in most every public educational system, and an individual with a score of 140 is likely to do well in that same system.

The research indicates that these tests, although not perfect predictors, are not biased and that race has nothing to do with the accuracy with which these tests predict. Therefore, when we say that the difference in the average IQ scores of Blacks and Whites is not due to test bias, we are not asserting that Blacks are less intelligent but that they are more likely to experience problems in our educational system. Nor does the failure to find bias in these tests explain why one group obtains higher scores than another, and whether that difference is due to a biased school system, cultural deprivation (or advantages), or, as some have asserted, genetic differences. We only know that the tests do a fair job of what they were designed to do—predict school achievement.

Although we conclude that most intellectual or cognitive ability tests are not biased, these instruments have clearly not always been used in a nonbiased fashion. Many have argued that early immigration restrictions were in part based on the data showing that certain ethnic groups scored lower than others on IQ tests (McPherson, 1985). Because the term *intelligence* has been misused by so many people and because there is such widespread misunderstanding of what these tests are designed to do, it has been easy for some individuals to use differences in the average scores of various racial groups as confirmation of racist ideology.

It may be true that most intelligence tests are free of bias; it is also true that these tests have been used to discriminate. To see that these tests are used fairly and judiciously, they must be revised frequently to make sure that they reflect the most advanced understanding of the nature of cognitive abilities and that they utilize appropriate methodologies for assessing cognitive skills. As we will soon see, however, bias may not be the biggest problem facing tests of cognitive abilities.

Treatment Validity and Educational Applications

Our review of the measurement of cognitive abilities has revealed that some commonly held beliefs about negative aspects of these testing instruments can be called into question. We have concluded that most measures of intellectual or cognitive ability yield reliable results, that they are reasonably good predictors of achievement levels, and that they are essentially free of bias. This last factor has been especially satisfying to those who have suggested that most of these tests validly estimate the cognitive abilities of minority populations.

We cannot help but wonder, however, if there is not a more subtle, more damaging problem in how these tests have been used in educational, clinical, and vocational settings (Witt & Gresham, 1985). We are specifically speaking of the question of **treatment validity,** of the ability of a test to lead to better treatments, such as more effective educational programs or better counseling or teaching strategies (Gresham, 1992). Although many have tried, there simply is no clear evidence that test results yielded by general measures of intelligence can be directly translated into effective educational or clinical programs (Kramer, Henning-Stout, Ullman, & Schellenberg, 1987).

It is important to remember that although these types of tests were developed to provide educators with general predictions of success in the educational system, they were not designed to enable educators or psychologists to design effective remedial strategies for individual children. Although we can be relatively confident that children who score in the superior (or gifted) range of intelligence will do better in school than those who score in the intellectually disabled range, we cannot design individualized educational programs for either gifted or mentally disabled children based on their particular pattern of scores or their overall intelligence test performance. The tests were not designed for that purpose, and attempts to make them into tools for specific instructional planning have failed miserably (Kramer et al., 1987).

Measures of Cognitive Ability

What we have called "measures of cognitive ability" have typically been referred to as "tests of intelligence." Instruments developed early in the history of the testing movement (e.g., the Wechsler series of tests) retain the term *intelligence* in their titles. Newer instruments are titled somewhat differently. Is the search for a new name a reaction to all the controversy over intelligence tests and the true meaning of the term *intelligence,* or the result of the realization that we must move beyond attempts to measure the hypothetical construct of intelligence? Both explanations are probably at least partly true, as is the realization by publishers that tests that do not mention intelligence in their titles have a better chance of being effectively marketed. Whatever the reason, many different tests purport to measure cognitive abilities: short tests, long tests; individual tests, group tests; comprehensive tests, specific tests; tests for infants, tests for children and adolescents, tests for adults, and so on.

Wechsler Intelligence Scale for Children-III

Overview and Purpose

In recent years the most widely administered test of cognitive ability with school-age children has been the Wechsler Intelligence Scale for Children-Revised (WISC-R) (Wechsler, 1974). The original WISC was designed as a downward extension of the adult intelligence scale that David Wechsler had developed (the Wechsler Bellevue Intelligence Scale) while working at Bellevue State Hospital. Originally published in 1949, the WISC was first revised in 1974 and became the WISC-R following the revision. In 1991 the WISC-R was revised and reappeared as the WISC-III. The general format and item content on the WISC-III remain similar to earlier editions of this test. This is not to suggest, however, that there have not been numerous changes with the current version of the WISC. For example, the pictures used are larger, updated, and better reflect ethnic diversity. Symbol Search is a new subtest and new rules for subtest administration (e.g., establishing ceilings) have been introduced on many subtests.

The WISC-III is individually administered by a qualified examiner (who is usually a psychologist with several advanced assessment courses and more than 500 hours of supervised experience) in 60 to 90 minutes. The WISC-III is designed for children from 6 to 17 years of age and aims to provide a global measure of intelligence that taps "many different mental abilities, which all together reflect a child's general intellectual ability" (Wechsler, 1991, p. 1). The test is comprised of 13 subtests, 6 in the Verbal Scale and 7 in the Performance Scale. All instructions are given orally and all subtests on the Verbal Scale require oral responses. Performance subtests have time limits, and in some cases bonus points are provided for quick, accurate responses. Arithmetic is the only timed subtest on the Verbal Scale. The 13 subtests are examined in more detail in the following sections.

Verbal Scale

1. Information—30 questions requiring general knowledge of facts
2. Similarities—19 pairs of words requiring an indication of how the items are similar
3. Arithmetic—24 (timed) arithmetic problems requiring a response without the aid of paper and pencil
4. Vocabulary—30 words requiring definitions or synonyms
5. Comprehension—18 problem situations requiring solutions or an understanding of social rules
6. Digit Span—forward and backward repetition of digits

Performance Scale

1. Picture Completion—30 drawings of common objects, all of which require the identification of a missing essential element
2. Coding—symbols such as vertical lines and circles are to be matched to specific numbers according to a key available for the individual to review and examine
3. Picture Arrangement—a series of pictures requiring placement in a logical, ordered sequence
4. Block Design—12 abstract designs to be copied using two-colored blocks
5. Object Assembly—5 jigsaw puzzles of common objects requiring assembly
6. Symbol Search—a series of paired groups of symbols with the child scanning each group to assess whether or not a target symbol appears in the search group

7. Mazes—8 mazes requiring a child to mark the way out without being blocked

Verbal and Performance subtests are to be administered in alternating order unless the needs of the child dictate otherwise. Mazes, Symbol Search, and Digit Span are considered supplemental tests and generally are not included in the calculation of the IQ scores, unless one of the regular subtests is omitted or "spoiled" because of improper administration or disruption. Symbol Search may only be substituted for the Coding subtest.

Not all items on the WISC-III are administered to each child. Each subtest has specific rules about where to begin and end, depending on the age or assumed ability of the child. The specificity of administration and scoring directions provided in the manual generally are considered assets of the Wechsler series of tests (in addition to the WISC-III, the Wechsler Preschool and Primary Scale of Intelligence-Revised, and the Wechsler Adult Intelligence Scale-Revised). Wechsler originally divided his tests into verbal and performance sections based on his conceptualization of intelligence, and he placed subtests that he believed involved primarily verbal or performance abilities into each domain. Many subsequent factor analytic studies (see, e.g., Kaufman, 1979) have generally supported the verbal/performance organization of the test.

Standardization Sample and Norms

The WISC-III remains a model of standardization procedures. It was standardized on 2,200 children selected to be representative of the U.S. population based on data gathered in 1988 by the U.S. Bureau of the Census. The sample was stratified on the basis of geographic region, age, gender, parent education, and race/ethnicity. Data were gathered in 31 states. Two hundred children (100 boys and 100 girls) were tested at each of 11 different ages, with the median age at each age level being the sixth month of that age range.

Data Obtained

Raw scores on each subtest are first changed into normalized standard scores (scaled scores) with a mean of 10 and a standard deviation of 3. Tables of scaled scores and their raw score equivalents are provided for each four-month age interval (e.g., 6-0 to 6-3, 6-4 to 6-7, 6-8 to 6-11 all the way to 16-8 to 16-11). The scaled subtest scores are then added and converted into deviation IQs (standard scores) for the Verbal, Performance, and Full Scales. Verbal Scale IQ, Performance Scale IQ, and Full Scale IQ each has a mean of 100 and a standard deviation of 15. A child's "test-age" for each subtest can be obtained, and a mean or median test-age for each of the scales can be calculated. With this revision, the examiner is also able to calculate four "factor-based scores," including Verbal Comprehension, Perceptual Organization, Freedom from Distractibility, and Processing Speed. These scores also have a mean of 100 and a standard deviation of 15. The factor-based scores are the result of previous analyses with the WISC-R (e.g., Kaufman, 1979) and factor analysis of the standardization data from the WISC-III. Although the author attempts to validate a four-factor solution as indicated above, only the Verbal Comprehension and Perceptual Organization factors receive strong empirical support (e.g., Little, 1992). New norms have been introduced to encourage examiners to determine strengths and weaknesses among individual subtests.

Reliability and Validity

Subtest reliabilities (split-half and test-retest) are very good, ranging from .69 to .87 and .57 to .89, respectively. Average Verbal Scale, Performance Scale, and Full Scale IQ reliability estimates are all above .90. Retest coefficients (with a range of 12 to 63 days between testing) were obtained by testing 353 individuals across 6 of the 11 different age groups. Average gains of 2 to 3 IQ points on the Verbal Scale, 12 to 13 points on the Performance Scale, and 7 to 8 points on the Full Scale were reported for the test-retest sample. The manual includes, for each age level, the standard error of measurement for each subtest as well as for the Verbal, Performance, and Full Scale scores. Interscorer agreement for the subtests is very high, with reliability coefficients above .90 for all subtests evaluated.

Much of the information related to validity presented in the WISC-III manual has to do with earlier research on the WISC-R. For example, correlations between the WISC-R and other tests in the Wechsler series (Wechsler Preschool and Primary Scale of Intelligence [WPPSI] and Wechsler Adult Intelligence Scale [WAIS]) yield similar correlation coefficients (a range of .70–.90) for age ranges in which the tests overlap. Studies comparing WISC-R scores and other intellectual tests such as the Stanford Binet IV and the K-ABC have yielded correlation coefficients in the .70 to .90 range.

Scores on the WISC-III have also been compared with the more recent revisions of the tests in the Wechsler series (i.e., the WPPSI-R, the WAIS-R, and the WISC-R). As might be expected, most correlations are above .85 among these similar tests. The correlations among the Performance Scales on these tests provide the smallest correlation coefficients whereas the Full Scale scores generate the highest coefficients. Intercorrelations among the individual subtests and the correlations of each subtest with the IQ scores also are reported in the manual. The WISC-III is similar to the WISC-R in that IQ scores appear to be moderately related to achievement based on correlations between the WISC-III and measures of academic achievement. Scaled scores (Verbal, Performance, and Full Scales) obtained from the WISC-III can be expected to be lower than the same scores obtained from the WISC-R. Examiners can expect differences of about 5 points for the Full Scale score and from 2 to 7 points for the Verbal and Performance Scale scores, respectively.

Summary

From a technical perspective, the WISC-III is a sound instrument. Although recently revised, preliminary information suggests that it will be widely used and that obtained scores will be moderately related to school achievement.

The Wechsler tests are the standard against which other measures of cognitive abilities have been judged for the last three decades. Revised and restandardized in 1974 and again in 1991, the format and many items on the WISC-III are unchanged from the original WISC published in 1949. Pictures and some items have been updated and new norms provided. Much has been learned about the nature of cognitive abilities in the last 30 years and yet the design and purpose of the WISC-III has changed little. Many of the problems associated with earlier editions do not seem to have been addressed with the current revision of this test.

Stanford-Binet Intelligence Scale IV

Overview and Purpose

The original Binet-Simon Scale discussed earlier in the chapter has gone through a number of revisions during the last half century. Most practitioners were familiar with the 1973 edition of the test, the Stanford-Binet Intelligence Scale (SBIS), which served as the standard for intelligence testing for so many years (Terman & Merrill, 1973). Recently, the SBIS has undergone substantial modification and restandardization (Thorndike, Hagen, & Sattler, 1986). The following Focus on Practice and figure 12.3 detail certain ways that the test has been altered through the years. Although many item types that were present in previous editions have been retained, the current organization differs radically from previous editions. This difference is made more apparent by comparing the descriptions in the Focus on Practice and figure 12.3 with figure 12.1.

According to its authors (Thorndike et al., 1986, p. 2), the SBIS is designed to meet the following objectives:

1. To help differentiate between students who are mentally disabled and those who have specific learning disabilities
2. To help educators and psychologists understand why a particular student is having difficulty in school
3. To help identify gifted students
4. To study the development of cognitive skills of individuals from ages 2 to adult

The test is individually administered, covers ages 2 to adult, and includes items that are grouped into 15 tests assessing four broad areas of cognitive functioning: Verbal Reasoning, Quantitative Reasoning, Abstract/Visual Reasoning, and Short-Term Memory. Descriptions of the subtests and their appropriate age ranges follow.

Verbal Reasoning

1. Vocabulary (2-0 through adult)—46 items, the first 14 being picture vocabulary with the remainder requiring oral responses

Focus on Practice

Stanford-Binet—Past and Present

Although the scales and most of the items in the 1986 edition of the Stanford-Binet are new, users will recognize some familiar items that have been revised to be in accord with current test standards and to improve testing procedures. For example, figure 12.3 shows the evolution of two item types. The card used to measure the examinee's knowledge of parts of the body illustrates an increased sensitivity to issues of ethnicity and gender. The rosy-cheeked boy used in the 1937 edition wore a short red jacket, shorts, and black patent-leather shoes. The blue-eyed girl in the 1973 edition had blond hair tied with a pretty pink ribbon. By contrast, the child in the 1985 edition is drawn with facial features, dress, and hair that *minimize* gender and racial characteristics. The Bead Memory subtests, which also originated in the 1937 edition, required the examiner to create simple bead chains. The new test uses photographs as the stimuli, which eliminates the need for examiners to create sample chains and results in increased standardization of administrative conditions.

Figure 12.3 The Development of Two Stanford-Binet Subtests

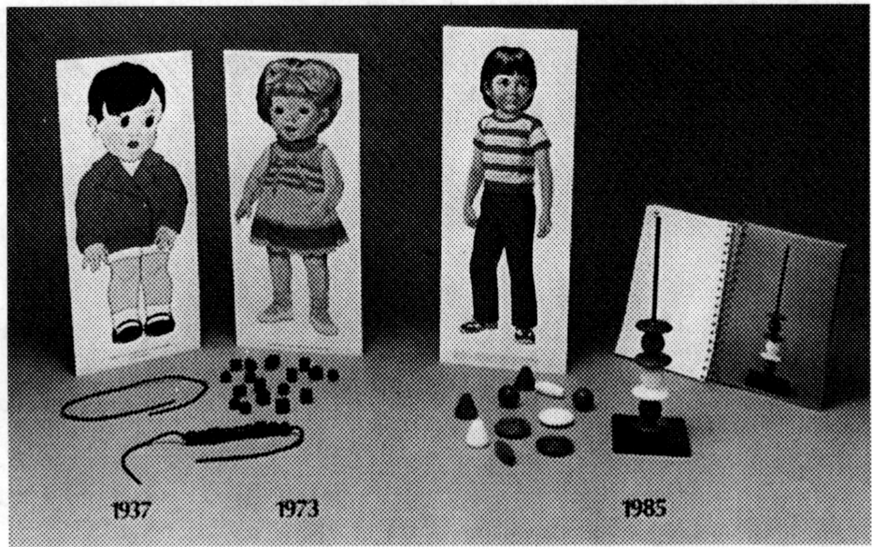

From: Elizabeth Hagen, Jerome M. Sattler, and Robert L.Thorndike, STANFORD-BINET INTELLIGENCE SCALE, 4th edition. Riverside Publishing Company, Chicago, IL 1986. Reproduced with permission of The Riverside Publishing Company, Chicago, IL.

2. Comprehension (2-0 through adult)—42 items, the first six requiring the identification of various body parts on a picture card of a child (see Focus on Practice and figure 12.3), with subsequent questions requiring verbal responses
3. Absurdities (2-0 through 17-11)—32 items requiring the determination of what is wrong or silly in each picture
4. Verbal Relations (10-0 through adult)—18 items requiring a description of how the first three of four words are related but different from the fourth word

Quantitative Reasoning

1. Quantitative (2-0 through adult)—40 items assessing a broad range of arithmetic skills through tasks ranging from counting blocks to orally presented word problems
2. Number Series (5-0 through adult)—26 items requiring the discovery of the "certain rule," according to which a number sequence is arranged and the naming of the numbers that come next
3. Equation Building (10-0 through adult)—18 items requiring rearranging numbers and arithmetic signs into a true equation

Abstract/Visual Reasoning

1. Pattern Analysis (2-0 through adult)—42 items requiring duplication of patterns presented via either a form board, an examiner's model, or pictured cube patterns
2. Copying (2-0 through 17-11)—28 items requiring the use of blocks to copy block designs or pencil and paper to copy line drawings
3. Matrices (5-0 through adult)—26 items requiring the determination of an appropriate shape, design, letter, or the like to fill a blank spot in a matrix
4. Paper Folding and Cutting (10-0 through adult)—18 items requiring the study of pictures describing a paper-folding and cutting sequence to determine how a piece of paper would look after being folded and cut

Short-Term Memory

1. Bead Memory (2-0 through adult)—42 items requiring the identification of colored bead shapes exposed by the examiner for two seconds or the duplication of bead designs depicted on stimulus cards exposed for five seconds
2. Memory for Sentences (2-0 through adult)—42 items requiring the repetition of orally presented phrases or sentences or both
3. Memory for Digits (6-0 through adult)—26 items requiring the repetition of a series of digits either as stated (11 items) or in reverse order (12 items)
4. Memory for Objects (5-0 through adult)—14 items in which examinees are shown a number of pictures of common objects, one at a time.

> Examinees are then shown a picture containing many different pictures and asked to identify the pictures shown previously, in the correct order.

As indicated previously, not all items within a particular test nor all tests are administered to each individual. The starting point for each examinee is determined by the results of the vocabulary test, and all tests are to be administered in a prescribed order depending on the subject's age and ability.

Standardization Sample and Norms

The standardization sample was stratified on the basis of data from the 1980 U.S. Census and included the following variables: geographic region, community size, ethnic group, age, and gender. The manual indicates that socioeconomic status was monitored through indexes of parental occupation and educational attainment. Approximately 200 to 300 (range of 194 to 460) individuals were tested within each of 17 age groups.

Data Obtained

Raw scores for each test are converted to Standard Age Scores (SAS), which have a mean of 50 and a standard deviation of 8. The SAS within each area are summed and an Area SAS derived. The Area SAS can be summed to determine a Composite SAS score. Both Area SAS and Composite SAS have a mean of 100 and a standard deviation of 16. If fewer than four areas are used to determine the Composite SAS, the examiner is cautioned to calculate a Partial Composite score.

Reliability and Validity

Data related to internal consistency estimates and test-retest reliability are presented in the SBIS technical manual. Median KR-20 reliabilities for the individual tests range from .94 (Paper Folding and Cutting) to .73 (Memory for Objects). Standard error of estimate (SEM) figures generally range between 2 and 3 for each age group. Internal consistency estimates are usually lower for (a) younger children and (b) the Short-Term Memory tests. Reliability estimates for the Area SAS generally were above .80, with most above .90 (SEM 2.8–7.2). Composite score reliabilities were all above .95 (SEM 1.6–3.6). Two groups (5-year-olds and 8-year-olds), totaling 112 children, were retested within two to eight months of the original testing to determine test-retest reliability. Test-retest estimates for 5-year-olds and 8-year-olds were as follows: individual tests: .56 to .78 and .28 to .86, respectively; Area SAS: .71 to .91 and .51 to .90, respectively; and Composite SAS: .91 and .90, respectively.

The only validity information presented with the SBIS is related to construct validity. Factor analytic studies tend to support the test as a measure of general cognitive ability. The rationale for the placement of each of the subtests within separate areas is sound, with the least amount of support for those within the Abstract/Visual Reasoning subtest. Correlations with other measures of cognitive ability also tend to support the construct validity of the SBIS (most correlation coefficients were above .60). The highest correlations were obtained with older samples (such as the Wechsler Adult Intelligence Scale Revised [WAIS-R]) and the lowest generally with younger samples (such as the Wechsler Preschool and Primary Scale of Intelligence [WPPSI]). The manual suggests that the SBIS will not be a useful measure with 2- and 3-year-old children of below-average abilities due to floor effects on a number of tests. Data from samples of exceptional children indicate that the SBIS does yield Composite SAS consistent with the children's identified areas of exceptionality (e.g., high scores for gifted children). No information related to the use of the SBIS in educational planning or treatment is presented in the manual.

Summary

For many years the SBIS was synonymous with the very notion of intelligence testing in the United States (Boring, 1950). The reasons given for the reorganization and the inclusion of specific tests are not substantial, and the descriptions of specific tests and the presumed abilities involved in each are inadequate. Although the authors do occasionally provide cautions regarding the limitations of the current SBIS, there is little evidence that it meets any of the four original objectives of the test. Research that has appeared since the publication of the test appears to support the test as a reliable measure of general cognitive ability (i.e., intelligence) (e.g., Lamp & Kron, 1990; Rothlisberg & McIntosh, 1991), although the specific factor structure of the test is less clear (e.g., Gridley & McIntosh, 1991; Thorndike, 1990). Much more study is required before its strengths and limitations can be adequately assessed.

Kaufman Assessment Battery for Children

Overview and Purpose

The Kaufman Assessment Battery for Children, or K-ABC (Kaufman & Kaufman, 1983) is an individually administered, multisubtest battery designed to provide information on the intellectual and achievement abilities of preschool and elementary school children between the ages of 2.5 and 12.5. The K-ABC breaks intellectual functioning into two distinct styles of information processing: sequential and simultaneous. In the sequential (or successive) mode, stimuli are arranged in sequence, and decisions are reached by processing information in an orderly (i.e., one at a time), sequence-dependent fashion. In the simultaneous mode, information is arranged in a simultaneous fashion, and the decision-making process proceeds in an integrated, holistic manner. The K-ABC, at least as it relates to mental processing, is not designed to measure what or how much a child knows but rather how that child goes about knowing. Stated differently, the K-ABC attempts to assess intellectual ability by asking questions about how a child approaches problem solving and information processing and places less importance on previously learned information. The K-ABC Mental Processing subtests (the Sequential and Simultaneous Scales combined) were designed to minimize the importance of verbal skills to make the test as fair as possible for individuals from diverse cultural backgrounds. In fact, smaller black–white discrepancies in standard scores (3–8 points) have been reported for the K-ABC than for most popular intelligence tests.

The K-ABC is composed of three scales (Sequential Processing, Simultaneous Processing, and Achievement) and 16 subtests. The specific composition of each scale and the design and age range of each subtest is as follows:

Sequential Processing Scale

1. Hand Movements (2 through 12-5)—21 items requiring the repetition of a series of hand movements in the correct order
2. Number Recall (2-6 through 12-5)—19 items requiring recall of numbers from 2 to 8 in sequence
3. Word Order (4-0 through 12-5)—20 items requiring subjects to point to pictures of common objects in the same order as the objects were named by the examiner

Simultaneous Processing Scale

1. Magic Window (2-6 through 4-11)—15 pictures presented by rotating a wheel so that only a portion is visible at any one time, requiring children to name the object pictured
2. Face Recognition (2-6 through 4-11)—15 items requiring the identification of one or two faces from those in a group
3. Gestalt Closure (2-6 through 12-5)—25 items requiring the identification of incomplete ink-blot drawings of common objects
4. Triangles (4-0 through 12-5)—18 items requiring the copying of abstract designs using several rubber triangles
5. Matrix Analogies (5-0 through 12-5)—20 items requiring the selection of a picture or design that best completes an analogy
6. Spatial Memory (5-0 through 12-5)—21 items requiring recall of the location of pictures on a page
7. Photo Series (6-0 through 12-5)—17 items asking subjects to organize an array of photographs illustrating an event and then to order the photographs in their proper time sequence

Achievement Scale

1. Expressive Vocabulary (2-6 through 4-11)—14 pictures requiring identification
2. Faces and Places (3-0 through 12-5)—35 pictures of famous persons, places, or fictional characters requiring identification

3. Arithmetic (3-0 through 12-5)—38 items requiring number identification, multiplication, division, and rounding
4. Riddles (3-0 through 12-5)—32 items requiring the identification of the items or concepts referred to in riddles
5. Reading/Decoding (5-0 through 12-5)—38 items ranging from letter identification to word recognition
6. Reading/Understanding (7-0 through 12-5)—24 items requiring the acting out of commands given in sentences

No child takes more than 13 subtests, and not all items within a subtest are administered. Explicit instructions are provided to determine where to begin testing as well as the criteria for discontinuing a subtest.

Standardization Sample and Norms

Two thousand children, (100 for each six-month age group between the ages of 2.5 and 12.5) were in the standardization group. Stratification variables included age, sex, geographic region, socioeconomic status (determined by parental education), race or ethnic group, community size, and educational placement (to ensure adequate representation of children with disabilities). In addition, to allow specific race and parental education comparisons, sociocultural norms were established by the additional testing of 496 black and 119 white children.

Data Obtained

Raw scores on each subtest are first changed into normalized standard scores. Subtests on the Sequential and Simultaneous Scales have a mean of 10 and a standard deviation of 3. Subtests on the Achievement Scale have a mean of 100 and a standard deviation of 15. The scores from the subtests on each scale are then totaled and transformed into a Sequential Processing Scale score, a Simultaneous Processing Scale score, a Mental Processing Composite score (Sequential plus Simultaneous scores), and an Achievement Scale score, each with a mean of 100 and a standard deviation of 15. A Nonverbal Scale score, with a mean of 100 and a standard deviation of 15, can be calculated as an estimate of the intellectual potential of individuals with language or communication problems. In addition to these scores, tables allow the examiner to generate information such as national percentile rank, sociocultural percentile rank, age equivalents, confidence intervals, and subtest (or scale) strengths and weaknesses for most of the subtest and scale scores.

Reliability and Validity

Internal consistency reliabilities (presented for both preschool and school-age children, respectively) for the subtests (.72–.89 and .71–.92, respectively) and global scales (Sequential: .90 and .89, respectively; Simultaneous: .86 and .93, respectively; Mental: .91 and .84, respectively; Achievement: .93 and .97, respectively; and Nonverbal: .87 and .93, respectively) are very good. Test-retest reliabilities were obtained by retesting a portion of the standardization sample at each of three different ages (2-6 to 4-11: N = 84; 5-0 to 8-11: N = 92; 9-0 to 12-5: N = 70) for the subtests (.62–.87; .61–.98; and .59–.94, respectively) and global scales (median coefficient = .88).

Extensive information, covering more than 40 pages, related to construct, predictive, and concurrent validity accompanies the K-ABC. Evidence for construct validity is good, with factor analytic studies typically identifying two separate factors (interpreted as simultaneous and sequential factors). In addition, moderate correlations (.36–.76) between K-ABC standard scores and WISC-R Full Scale IQ scores have been obtained (with the K-ABC Achievement Scale–WISC-R Full Scale correlation generally the highest). Both predictive and concurrent validity studies suggest the relationship of the K-ABC with various achievement scales. Regardless of whether there was a delay of 6 to 12 months between the administrations of tests (predictive validity) or whether the tests were administered at the same time (concurrent validity), the results indicate moderate correlations between the Simultaneous, Sequential, and Nonverbal Scales and achievement test scores (typically .30s–.50s); and slightly higher correlations when the Mental or Achievement Scales were reported (.40s–.80s). Although no long-term predictive validity studies are currently available, they will be important in evaluating the test's usefulness. It will be especially interesting to see if the K-ABC predicts achievement equally well for Blacks and Whites in light of the small Black–White differences in obtained test scores.

Summary

The K-ABC has received widespread attention since its introduction. Hailed by its publishers as the most innovative and useful entrant into the cognitive assessment arena in the last half century, the test has not avoided substantial and pointed criticism (Bracken, 1985; Page, 1985). The K-ABC is psychometrically sound, has very good standardization, is attractively presented, and is relatively easy to learn and use. However, the major questions remain to be resolved over whether the theoretical model on which the test is based is sound and whether the test ultimately aids in the treatment process. To date, there is no sound evidence that the results from this test can be used to plan educational programming.

Columbia Mental Maturity Scale

Overview and Purpose

The third edition of the Columbia Mental Maturity Scale, or CMMS (Burgemeister, Blum, & Lorge, 1972) was originally designed to estimate the "general reasoning ability" of physically disabled and nonverbal children between the ages of 3 years, 6 months, and 9 years, 11 months. The CMMS contains

92 items, each printed on a 6-by-19-inch card that features three to five color or black-and-white drawings of figural and pictorial symbols such as shapes, common objects, abstract designs, dots, and body parts. Children are asked to examine each card and identify the one image that does not relate to any of the others. Correct responses require the formulation of an explicit rationale for determining the relationships among the pictures. No time limit is imposed on the child; however, the examiner is instructed to encourage a response after 20 to 25 seconds.

The CMMS is individually administered and takes approximately 15 to 20 minutes to complete. It differs from the other individually administered instruments we have examined in that it assesses a very limited range of cognitive abilities: classifying, discriminating, and perhaps reasoning. However, since it requires only nonverbal, pointing responses, it has been useful in the assessment of children with a variety of disabilities.

Standardization Sample and Norms

The 1972 CMMS was standardized on 2,600 children from 25 states. The sampling procedure was designed to ensure a representative national sample based on the 1960 census data, with the stratification variables including geographic region, race, parental occupation, age, and sex. The design and execution of the norming process for the CMMS is excellent.

Data Obtained

An Age Deviation Score (ADS) with a mean of 100 and a standard deviation of 16 can be calculated for each child completing the CMMS. In addition, a Maturity Index, or mental age score, can be obtained by determining the age group in the standardization sample that most closely corresponds to a child's performance.

Reliability and Validity

Test-retest reliability and internal consistency estimates (split-half reliability) are provided in the CMMS manual. Test-retest figures were calculated on a group of approximately 100 children at each of three ages and ranged from .84 to .86. Split-half estimates ranged from .86 to .91. The standard error of measurement is given as 5 to 6 ADS points (depending on the age group). Validity for the CMMS was established by correlating scores with results from achievement and ability tests. Correlations with achievement scores ranged from .31 to .61 (Stanford Achievement Test) and with mental tests from .62 to .69 (Otis-Lennon Mental Ability Test) and .67 (SBIS).

Summary

As a test of cognitive abilities, the CMMS is limited because it does not sample a broad range of skills. The test, however, has traditionally been used to estimate the intellectual potential of individuals who have difficulty responding verbally.

McCarthy Scales of Children's Abilities

Overview and Purpose

The McCarthy Scales of Children's Abilities, or MSCA (McCarthy, 1972) was developed to measure general intellectual development in children between the ages of 2.5 and 8.5. Before this test, psychologists and educators wanting to assess the abilities of this age group had been limited in their choices to the SBIS or the WPPSI. With the publication of the MSCA it was hoped that psychologists and educators would have a single instrument for measuring several aspects of cognitive and motor abilities in preschool and early elementary school children.

The MSCA is individually administered, like the WISC-III, SBIS, and K-ABC, and requires training and supervised experience for proper use. It has a wide variety of "gamelike and nonthreatening" tasks that are organized into 18 subtests and six scales. The six scales, Verbal, Perceptual-Performance, Quantitative, General Cognitive, Memory, and Motor are discussed in greater detail below.

1. **Verbal Scale.** As on the WISC-III, this scale is designed to assess the ability of the subject to understand, process, remember, and problem solve with the English language. Subtests include Pictorial Memory, Word Knowledge, Verbal Memory, Verbal Fluency, and Opposite Analogies. In addition to measuring an individual's receptive and expressive language abilities, the Verbal Scale assesses attentional, short-term memory, and reasoning abilities.
2. **Perceptual-Performance Scale.** The seven subtests on this scale are designed to evaluate an individual's nonverbal problem-solving skills and visual-motor coordination. Subtests include Block Building, Puzzle Solving, Tapping Sequence, Right-Left Orientation (ages 5 and above), Draw-A-Design, Draw-A-Child, and Conceptual Grouping.
3. **Quantitative Scale.** A unique feature of the MSCA is the Quantitative Scale, which is designed to provide an index of the ability to use and remember numerical symbols and concepts. Its subtests include Number Questions, Numerical Memory, and Counting and Sorting. In addition to math skills, the ability of children to attend, concentrate, and hold material in short-term memory is important on this scale.
4. **General Cognitive Index (GCI).** This index includes the 15 subtests that are part of the Verbal, Perceptual-Performance, and Quantitative Scales. Although not referred to as an IQ score, the GCI is defined as an overall measure of a child's "cognitive functioning" (McCarthy, 1972).

5. **Memory Scale.** This scale is composed of four subtests aimed at assessing auditory and visual short-term memory—Pictorial Memory, Tapping Sequence, Verbal Memory, and Numerical Memory—which all appear on other MSCA scales.
6. **Motor Scale.** This scale includes five subtests designed to measure fine and gross motor skills: Leg Coordination, Arm Coordination, Imitative Action, Draw-A-Design, and Draw-A-Child (the last two also appear on the Perceptual-Performance Scale).

Standardization Sample and Norms

The standardization group was based on a national sample, stratified on the following variables: age, sex, color, geographic region, and father's occupation. Urban-rural residence was also included as an "informal selection variable." The standardization sample size at each of 10 ages (each half year from 2.5 to 7.5, plus 8.5), ranged from 100 to 106, making a total of 1,032 cases. In general, the design and execution of the standardization process for the MSCA are considered excellent.

Data Obtained

Standard scores (referred to as Indexes) are computed for each scale. The GCI has a mean of 100 and a standard deviation of 16. Each of the remaining scale indexes has a mean of 50 and a standard deviation of 10.

Reliability and Validity

The manual provides internal consistency measures as well as stability coefficient and standard errors of measurement for each of the six scales (at all 10 age levels in the standardization sample). Split-half reliability for the GCI (r = .93) and the other scales (.79–.88) is very good. The average standard error of measurement for the GCI is 4 points. Stability coefficients of the MSCA, with a 30-day test-retest interval, are .90 for the GCI and range from .69 to .89 for the other scales.

Both concurrent and predictive validity are referred to in the manual. Concurrent validity was established by correlating the MSCA Scale Indexes with IQ scores obtained on the WPPSI and SBIS. Correlations ranged from .45 to .91 (median r = .75), if one excludes the scores from the Motor Scale Index (r ranged from .02–.10). Predictive validity was established by comparing the MSCA scores of 35 children with their scores obtained four months later on the Metropolitan Achievement Test; correlations ranged from .34 to .54. A number of other validity studies have been published in recent years, and the concern has been raised that the MSCA seems to underestimate the intellectual abilities of children identified as learning disabled.

Summary

The MSCA is a well-designed, psychometrically sound instrument for assessing the cognitive abilities of young children. Most children find the test interesting

Focus on Research

Defining Intelligence

There is an intuitive appeal to the method used by Robert Sternberg of Yale University in New Haven to define and describe intelligence. He began with the assumption that the usual definitions developed by and for experts were often "rarefied abstractions, unconnected with real people or real life. And formal IQ tests seem unfair or beside the point" (Sternberg, 1982, p. 30). His approach was simply to ask laypeople how they define intelligence or intelligent behavior.

Sternberg first asked people to list behaviors that were embodied in the terms *intelligence, academic intelligence, everyday intelligence,* and *unintelligence.* From the responses he developed a master list of 250 relatively unique behaviors that characterize either intelligent or unintelligent people. Next, Sternberg and his associates had another group of individuals rate each of the 250 behaviors on a 1-to-9 scale to indicate relative importance of each characteristic to an "ideally intelligent person." To determine whether laypeople differed from experts in their notions of intelligence, the behaviors were also rated by a number of university professors who specialized in the study of intelligence or intelligence testing.

Laypeople viewed intelligence as composed of three broad facets: practical problem-solving ability, verbal ability, and social competence. Surprisingly, the laypeople and the experts did not differ a great deal in their views of intelligence. There were, however, three areas of difference. First, laypeople tended to have a broader view of intelligence. What experts study in terms of intelligence and the content of IQ tests comprises only a portion of the broad array of characteristics that laypeople associated with the concept of intelligence. Second, laypeople tended to emphasize the importance of intelligence in *inter*personal relationships in a *social* situation, whereas the experts tended to stress *intra*personal competence and an *individual* context. For example, laypeople were more likely to associate "acts politely" with intelligence, and experts stressed behaviors such as "reasons logically and well." Third, the scientists considered motivation to be much more central to the concept of intelligence than did laypeople. Thus characteristics such as "displays dedication and motivation in chosen pursuits" were rated highly by the experts.

A remarkable aspect of this research was the use of the 250 behaviors as a measure of intelligence. The list of behaviors was used as a means for individuals to rate themselves. People were instructed to rate the degree to which each of the 250 behaviors was characteristic of themselves. The scoring was based on how closely a person's responses resembled those of someone considered to be ideally intelligent. Thus, it was not possible to falsify the results by rating oneself high on the desirable characteristics. Results of the rating scale correlated about as well with IQs as other more traditional tests of intelligence, which suggests a kind of validity.

The appeal of this approach is that it allows society or the culture, not so-called experts or intelligence tests, to define intelligence. Obviously, Sternberg's method is but one of hundreds of approaches to defining and measuring intelligence.

and enjoyable, although the material on the test is becoming somewhat dated. A good deal of evidence suggests that the MSCA yields lower scores for children with learning disabilities and who are mentally disabled (Nagle, 1979) than do other frequently administered tests of cognitive ability. Perhaps a more significant concern is that the MSCA's design is based on a rather traditional conceptualization of intelligence (i.e., verbal-performance) that seems dated by today's standards.

Chapter Summary

What is this thing called intelligence? Is it a single ability that affects all cognitive activity? Is it something we all have to a greater or lesser extent? Or is it a collection of abilities and thus more appropriate for us to consider its relationship to specific skills like verbal and performance abilities or simultaneous and successive processing? Or, is it time for a new definition?

Sternberg (1979) argues that it is indeed time for a novel approach, some new ideas, a little fresh air. He suggests that we view intelligence as a prototype, an ideal model. This approach would argue that instead of formulating theories, developing tests to fit our theories, and testing individuals on our measures of cognitive ability (to confirm our theories!), we should move in a different, almost opposite direction. Sternberg would have us start by asking: What are the characteristics of intelligent people? How do they behave? How do they think? As we proceed, we would first answer the questions intuitively, based on our observations and experience (the intelligent person is a good planner and organizer, has excellent abstract reasoning skills, and is able to think logically), and only after we have developed some ideas about the intelligent person (our prototype) should we begin to research the nature of the abilities we have identified.

At this point Sternberg would have us ask: What is abstract reasoning? How do people demonstrate it? What are its components? What is the nature of logical thinking and what are the psychological mechanisms that underlie it? Are the types of people we have identified as intelligent really better planners, and if so, on what types of tasks? He would also have us ask how these skills relate to an individual's ability to adapt to the environment. Are the same skills important in all environmental settings, or are there important interactions between environment and ability of which we must remain aware? This approach has been referred to as **componential analysis** because it is designed to identify the critical components of intelligence that relate to performance as well as knowledge acquisition, transfer, and retention (Sternberg, 1984). Componential analysis has received a great deal of attention and has been the focus of intensive research. Will componential analysis improve our ability to develop educational interventions for children? How will the psychologists of the next century view our efforts? Will our work seem as primitive to them as the efforts of Galton and Wundt seem to us?

Finally, it should be apparent that we believe there are many potential problems with the use of intelligence tests. As part of a comprehensive battery of tests, intellectual tests can provide limited information of use. When interpreted inappropriately or as a sole measure of a person's abilities, test results can easily be misinterpreted and mistakes can lead to unfortunate and even disastrous consequences for children. Many of these tests seem outdated in terms of current understanding of how best to help children achieve and learn. As Cantor (1990) has stated, "Regardless of the sophistication of theory and structure, modern measures of intelligence lack treatment utility and thus, fail to address the desired outcomes of psychoeducational assessment-potential intervention strategies" (p. 443). Although intelligence tests continue to play a substantial role in the assessment of children, these tests are likely to continue to fade in importance unless it can be shown that they possess treatment validity and are important tools in making a difference in the lives of children.

CHAPTER 13

Assessment of Social, Behavioral, and Emotional Problems: The Use of Behavior Rating Scales and Inventories

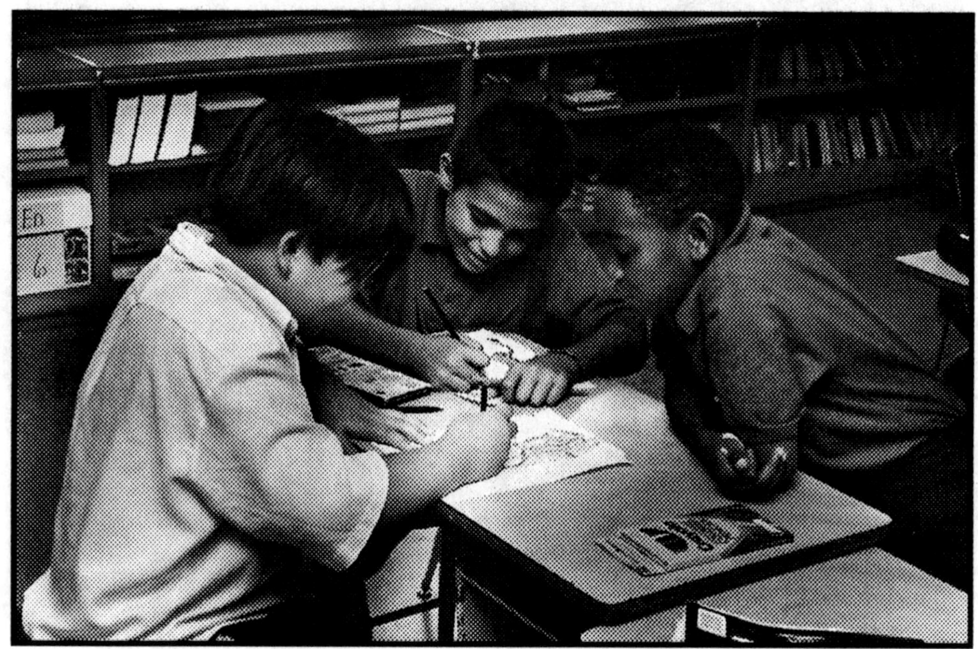

Teachers' judgments of students' classroom social behavior and academic competence are among the primary bases for referrals for psychoeducational services (Hoge, 1983). Teacher and parent judgments are summary, evaluative conclusions based on samples of behavior observed over a period of time. Behavior rating scales and inventories are the most common methods for quantifying teacher and parent judgments (Carlson & Lahey, 1983; Edelbrock, 1988; Gresham, 1985).

This chapter presents the rationale behind the use of behavior rating scales and inventories to assess children's social and academic behaviors. Specific behavior rating scales will be discussed and advantages and disadvantages of each will be described. More importantly, the intelligent use of behavior rating scale information in the problem-solving process will be described with specific recommendations regarding how to get the most information out of behavior ratings from parents and teachers. Before discussing the rationale and method of behavior rating scale assessment, we present a list of assumptions that should be kept in mind when using and interpreting behavior rating scale information.

Assumptions Regarding Behavior Rating Scales

Assumption 1: Ratings are summaries of observations of the relative frequency of specific behaviors.

One student may exhibit cooperative behavior three times a day, whereas a second student performs the same behavior once a day. Although these students exhibit different rates of behavior, when their teacher is asked to rate how often the behavior occurs, the teacher may characterize both students on a rating scale as exhibiting the behavior with equal frequency. In short, the precision of measurement with rating scales is relative, not absolute, and needs to be supplemented by more direct methods of assessment such as direct observation procedures discussed earlier.

Assumption 2: Ratings of behavior are evaluative judgments affected by the environment and a rater's standards for behavior.

An individual's behavior may change depending on the situation. Such variability has led researchers to characterize many behaviors as situationally specific rather than as traits or permanent characteristics of the individual (Achenbach, McConaughy, & Howell, 1987; Kazdin, 1979). In addition to environmental influences, behaviors deemed important in one setting may be largely determined by the standards of behavior established by the adult or adults who regulate the setting. Because both the rater's standards for behavior and the situation will influence the actual rating, one should use multiple raters (e.g., teachers, parents, and students) in the assessment process. These multiple raters observe the student's behavior in many situations and settings. The composite picture of a student given two or three raters may be clearer and more accurate than the picture obtained by a single rater.

Assumption 3: The social validity of behaviors assessed and possibly treated should be understood.

Socially valid behaviors are those behaviors that society considers important, encourages, and reinforces. The social validity of a behavior is reflected in the *importance* attributed to it by society or adults who regulate specific settings in which the child functions. Social validity can also refer to the *tolerance* of a given behavior in a given setting. Problem behaviors such as fighting, inattention, disruptive behavior, shyness, and so forth are tolerated to different degrees by different persons in different settings. For example, being quiet and shy may be tolerated in church but not in situations requiring verbal communication and social interaction. Being assertive may be tolerated by parents at home but not by teachers at school. Thus, in interpreting and using behavior ratings, it is important to consider the tolerance levels of certain behavior held by raters in specific settings.

Assumption 4: Multiple raters of the child's behavior may agree only moderately.

This statement is based on three facts. First, many behaviors are situationally specific. Second, all measures of behavior are made with some degree of error. Third, rating scales use rather simple frequency response categories for quantifying behaviors that may vary widely in their frequency, intensity, and duration. The work of Achenbach et al. (1987) provides empirical support for this position. Moderate agreement should not be taken as an indictment of the use of multiple raters. Rather, it suggests that different raters perceive behaviors in various settings differently. Collectively, such ratings may tell us more about a child than only one rater from one setting.

These four assumptions regarding behavior rating scales represent important considerations in using this type of assessment methodology. It is important to recognize that the results one obtains from behavior rating scales are joint reflections of actual child behavior and the behavior standards and tolerance levels of persons completing the ratings (Edelbrock, 1988; Gresham & Elliott, 1990).

Technical Considerations in Behavior Rating Scales

How are behavior rating scales constructed? The construction of behavior rating scales varies according to a number of factors, including what is to be assessed, response scaling, how items are selected, scoring, and standardization (Edelbrock, 1988). Each of these technical considerations will be described briefly to give readers a flavor of how behavior rating scales are constructed and the various criteria used in constructing different scales.

Content Assessed

Behavior rating scales assess a variety of content areas, including childhood psychopathology, social skills, depression, hyperactivity, anxiety, and many others. Some behavior rating scales assess a number of the aforementioned areas and other scales focus on only one or two content areas. Items for behavior rating scales may come from a variety of sources. These sources might include clinical case records, experts (e.g., psychologists, psychiatrists, mental health professionals, etc.), school records, and the research literature. These items may be revised, rewritten, or discarded based on the readability and clarity for rating purposes. Edelbrock (1988) indicated that good items for behavior rating scales are written in terms of overt, easily observable events, behaviors, or characteristics.

Scaling

Behaviors on behavior rating scales must be quantified in some way to have some meaning. Response scaling may include two-point (e.g., Yes/No; Agree/Disagree; Present/Absent), three-point (e.g., Never/Sometimes/Frequently), four-point, and even five-point scales. As mentioned earlier, behavior rating scales attempt to measure behavior *relatively* rather than in *absolute* terms. Raters are typically not asked to report on the specific number of times a given behavior occurs or an estimate of its duration or intensity.

Building a Behavior Rating Scale

There are two basic approaches to constructing or building behavior rating scales. The first approach is called the **empirical** approach because the final items appearing on the scale are selected on empirical or quantitative grounds. Most behavior rating scales are constructed on the basis of a statistical procedure known as **factor analysis.** In factor analysis, items belonging to a factor (or scale) are retained if they correlate highly with that factor or scale. Items showing little or no correlation with a particular factor or scale are either deleted from the final version or are moved to another factor with which they highly correlate.

The second approach to building a behavior rating scale is termed the **rational** approach. In a rational approach, behaviors on rating scales are selected on the basis of theoretical notions of what behaviors tend to co-occur. There is no basis, other than rational considerations, for including or excluding specific behaviors from behavior rating scales constructed in this manner. Edelbrock (1983) indicated that behavior rating scales constructed using a rational approach have less descriptive validity and less predictive power than empirically derived behavior rating scales.

Normative Characteristics

The standardization and normative characteristics of behavior rating scales exhibit a great deal of variability. Some behavior rating scales have no normative data and, as such, are limited in the types of comparisons that can be made. Behavior rating scales that do have normative data vary in terms of how the norms are stratified. For example, scales may be stratified according to sex, age, disability group membership, or a combination of demographic characteristics. The decision of whether to stratify behavior rating scales according to certain demographic variables depends on whether the variable influences the scores obtained from behavior rating scales. Thus, if sex, age, or disability status influence scores derived from behavior rating scales, then the scale is typically stratified according to these variables. Chapter 5 provides a more complete discussion of norming and standardization of tests.

Informant Considerations

A key issue in using behavior rating scales is who the informant should be in completing the rating scale. Typically, informants are teachers, parents, and children themselves. Some behavior rating scales are for teachers only, others for parents only, others for children only, and still others utilize all three informants. Some informants are in a better position to rate certain behaviors than others. For instance, teachers are in a better position to rate attention span, classroom behaviors, social interactions in school settings, and the like. Parents, on the other hand, are likely to be more knowledgeable about behaviors such as sleep disturbances, sibling interactions, mealtime behaviors and so forth.

The best practice in using behavior rating scales is to employ multiple informants to rate the same child's behavior (Achenbach et al., 1987; Edelbrock, 1983; Gresham & Elliott, 1990). Multiple informants can provide a more complete view of a child's behavior across situations and settings. By using multiple informants, one can discern which behaviors tend to occur across a variety of situations and which behaviors appear to be situationally specific. This information can be of use in classification decisions as well as for intervention planning.

Review of Selected Behavior Rating Scales

Social Skills Rating System

Overview and Purpose

The Social Skills Rating System (SSRS) (Gresham & Elliott, 1990) provides a broad, multirater assessment of student social behaviors that can affect teacher-student relations, peer acceptance, and academic performance. The SSRS documents the perceived frequency and importance of behaviors influencing the student's development of social competence and adaptive functioning at school and at home. The SSRS components include three behavior rating forms (teacher, parent, and student versions) and an integrative assessment and intervention planning record. Teacher, parent, and student forms elicit information about a student from the viewpoint of the informant. Teacher and parent forms are available for three developmental levels: preschool, grades K through 6, and grades 7 through 12. The SSRS uses teacher, parent, and student rating scales to sample three domains of *social skills, problem behavior,* and *academic competence.*

The Social Skills Scale has five subscales:

1. *Cooperation,* which includes behaviors such as helping others, sharing materials, and complying with rules and directions;
2. *Assertion,* which includes behaviors such as asking others for information, introducing oneself, and responding to the actions of others;

3. *Responsibility,* which includes behaviors that demonstrate ability to communicate with adults and regard for property or work;
4. *Empathy,* which includes behaviors that show concern and respect for others' feelings and viewpoints; and
5. *Self-Control,* which includes behaviors that emerge in conflict situations, such as responding appropriately to teasing and in nonconflict situations that require taking turns and compromising.

The Problem Behavior Scale has three subscales:

1. *Externalizing Problems,* which are inappropriate behaviors involving verbal or physical aggression toward others, poor control of temper, and arguing;
2. *Internalizing Problems,* which are behaviors indicating sadness, anxiety, and poor self-esteem; and
3. *Hyperactivity,* which are those behaviors involving excessive movement, fidgeting, and impulsive reactions.

The Academic Competence domain concerns student academic functioning. This domain, as measured by the SSRS, consists of a small, yet critical, sample of relevant behaviors. Items are rated on a five-point scale that corresponds to percentage clusters (1 = lowest 10%, 5 = highest 10%). This domain includes items measuring reading and mathematics performance, motivation, parental support, and general cognitive functioning. This scale appears on the teacher form at the elementary and secondary levels. Table 13.1 summarizes the scales and subscales of the SSRS across different informants and levels.

Standardization Sample and Norms

The SSRS was standardized on a national sample of 4,170 children using their self-ratings as well as ratings of children made by 1,027 parents and 259 teachers. The sampling plan was designed to obtain approximately equal numbers of male and female students and a sufficient number of students at each grade level to ensure response stability. Grade placement was used throughout the statistical analyses as a convenient and practical substitute for age. The SSRS standardization sample was stratified according to sex, grade, ethnic representation, geographic region, and community size. The standardization sample contained 50.6 percent females and 49.4 percent males. Approximately 27 percent of the sample consisted of minority students (Black, Hispanic, etc.) compared with about 31 percent minority population based on the U.S. Census. Approximately 12.4 percent of the sample was from the Northeast, 29.3 percent from the North Central region, 44.3 percent from the South, and 14 percent from the West. About 35 percent of the sample came from the central city, 47 percent from suburban or small-town areas, and 18 percent from rural areas.

Table 13.1 SSRS Scales and Subscales Across Forms, by Level

	Teacher Form			*Parent Form*			*Student Form*	
	Preschool Level	**Elementary Level**	**Secondary Level**	**Preschool Level**	**Elementary Level**	**Secondary Level**	**Elementary Level**	**Secondary Level**
Social Skills								
Cooperation	X	X	X	X	X	X	X	X
Assertion	X	X	X	X	X	X	X	X
Responsibility	—	—	—	X	X	X	—	—
Empathy	—	—	—	—	—	—	X	X
Self-Control	X	X	X	X	X	X	X	X
Problem Behaviors								
Externalizing	X	X	X	X	X	X	—	—
Internalizing	X	X	X	X	X	X	—	—
Hyperactivity	—	X	—	—	X	—	—	—
Academic Competence								
(No subscales)	—	X	X	—	—	—	—	—

X = Included on the form indicated.

From: SOCIAL SKILLS RATING SYSTEM (SSRS) by Frank M. Gresham and Stephen N. Elliott

Data Obtained

Four types of scores are available from the SSRS: raw scores, descriptive behavior levels, standard scores, and percentile ranks. Raw scores are based on the results of three-point ratings of social skills and problem behavior (0 = Never occurs, 1 = Sometimes occurs, and 3 = Very Often occurs) for the Social Skills and Problem Behavior Scales. All social skills items are rated on two dimensions: frequency and importance. The inclusion of an importance dimension allows raters to specify how important each social skill is for classroom success (teacher ratings), for their child's development (parent ratings), and for the student's relationships with others (student ratings). Figure 13.1 shows how these dual frequency and importance ratings are made on the SSRS. Raw scores for the teacher ratings of Academic Competence are based on five-point ratings of students relative to his or her classmates (1 = Lowest 10%, 2 = Next Lowest 20%, 3 = Middle 40%, 4 = Next Highest 20%, and 5 = Highest 10%).

Subscale and scale raw scores are translated into behavior levels for the Social Skills and Problem Behavior Scales and Subscales. These behavior levels for each scale and Subscale are labeled *Fewer* (one standard deviation or greater below the mean raw score of the standardization sample), *Average* (within one standard deviation above or below the standardization sample mean), and *More* (greater than one standard deviation above the standardization sample mean). Since each item on the Social Skills and Problem Behaviors Scales represents a specific behavior, the words *Fewer, Average,* and *More* can be directly interpreted as referring to amounts, or frequencies of behavior.

For the Academic Competence Scale, students who are viewed by teachers as more academically capable than the majority of students in the standardization sample are assigned an *Above Average* behavior level, whereas students who are viewed by teachers as less academically capable than the majority of students in the standardization sample are assigned a *Below Average* behavior level. Standard scores with a mean of 100 and a standard deviation of 15 are available on the SSRS for the Social Skills, Problem Behaviors, and Academic Competence Scales. No standard scores are computed for the SSRS subscales. In addition, national percentile ranks are available for the SSRS scales (Social Skills, Problem Behaviors, and Academic Competence). Separate norms are used for males and females, for preschool, elementary, and secondary students, and for disabled and nondisabled students at the elementary level.

Reliability and Validity

The SSRS manual presents extensive evidence for the reliability and validity of the scales. Internal consistency estimates for the SSRS across all forms and levels yielded a median coefficient alpha for the Social Skills Scale of .90, whereas it was .84 for the Problem Behaviors Scale, and .95 for the Academic Competence Scale. Overall, these coefficients indicate a relatively high

Figure 13.1 Portions of the Teacher Elementary Questionnaire Showing Frequency Ratings and Scoring of the Social Skills Subscales for Andrew, a Hypothetical Case

FOR OFFICE USE ONLY How Often?			**Social Skills**	How Often?			How Important?		
C	A	S		Never	Sometimes	Very Often	Not Important	Important	Critical
		1	1. Controls temper in conflict situations with peers.	0	(1)	2	0	1	2
	1		2. Introduces herself or himself to new people without being told.	0	(1)	2	0	1	2
	1		3. Appropriately questions rules that may be unfair.	0	(1)	2	0	1	2
		0	4. Compromises in conflict situations by changing own ideas to reach agreement.	(0)	1	2	0	1	2
		1	5. Responds appropriately to peer pressure.	0	(1)	2	0	1	2
	1		6. Says nice things about himself or herself when appropriate.	0	(1)	2	0	1	2
	1		7. Invites others to join in activities.	0	(1)	2	0	1	2
1			8. Uses free time in an acceptable way.	0	(1)	2	0	1	2
1			9. Finishes class assignments within time limits.	0	(1)	2	0	1	2
	1		10. Makes friends easily.	0	(1)	2	0	1	2
		0	11. Responds appropriately to teasing by peers.	(0)	1	2	0	1	2
		0	12. Controls temper in conflict situations with adults.	(0)	1	2	0	1	2
		1	13. Receives criticism well.	0	(1)	2	0	1	2
	1		14. Initiates conversations with peers.	0	(1)	2	0	1	2
1			15. Uses time appropriately while waiting for help.	0	(1)	2	0	1	2
1			16. Produces correct schoolwork.	0	(1)	2	0	1	2
4	6	3							
C	A	S	SUMS OF HOW OFTEN COLUMNS						

FOR OFFICE USE ONLY How Often?			**Social Skills (cont.)**	How Often?			How Important?		
C	A	S		Never	Sometimes	Very Often	Not Important	Important	Critical
	0		17. Appropriately tells you when he or she thinks you have treated him or her unfairly.	(0)	1	2	0	1	2
		1	18. Accepts peers' ideas for group activities.	0	(1)	2	0	1	2
	0		19. Gives compliments to peers.	(0)	1	2	0	1	2
1			20. Follows your directions.	0	(1)	2	0	1	2
2			21. Puts work materials or school property away.	0	1	(2)	0	1	2
		1	22. Cooperates with peers without prompting.	0	(1)	2	0	1	2
	1		23. Volunteers to help peers with classroom tasks.	0	(1)	2	0	1	2
	2		24. Joins ongoing activity or group without being told to do so.	0	1	(2)	0	1	2
		1	25. Responds appropriately when pushed or hit by other children.	0	(1)	2	0	1	2
0			26. Ignores peer distractions when doing class work.	(0)	1	2	0	1	2
1			27. Keeps desk clean and neat without being reminded.	0	(1)	2	0	1	2
1			28. Attends to your instructions.	0	(1)	2	0	1	2
1			29. Easily makes transition from one classroom activity to another.	0	(1)	2	0	1	2
		1	30. Gets along with people who are different.	0	(1)	2	0	1	2
6	3	4							
C	A	S	SUMS OF HOW OFTEN COLUMNS						

degree of scale homogeneity. Subscale internal consistency estimates were lower and showed more variability across forms. Median correlations for the Social Skills and Problem Behaviors Subscales were all between .78 and .84. The median subscale internal consistency estimate was .81.

Test-retest reliability of the SSRS was measured by having samples of teachers, parents, and students from the elementary standardization sample rate the same students four weeks after their original standardization ratings. The temporal stability of teacher ratings was .85 for Social Skills, .84 for Problem Behaviors, and .93 for Academic Competence. Parent stability estimates were .87 for Social Skills and .65 for Problem Behaviors. The test-retest estimate for Student Social Skills ratings was .68.

The SSRS manual presents a number of studies investigating the construct, criterion-related, and content validity of the scale. For example, the SSRS Social Skills Scale and Subscales correlate highly with other measures of social skills such as the Walker-McConnell Scale of Social Competence and School Adjustment (Walker & McConnell, 1988) and the Social Behavior Assessment (Stephens, 1978). The SSRS Problem Behaviors Scale and Subscales show moderate to high correlations with the Child Behavior Checklist (Achenbach & Edelbrock, 1983) and the Harter Teacher Rating Scale (Harter, 1985). In addition, the SSRS Social Skills, Problem Behaviors, and Academic Scales reliably differentiate mildly disabled (e.g., learning disabled, behavior disordered, and mildly mentally disabled) students from nondisabled students.

Summary

The SSRS is a well-designed, well-constructed, and well-researched multirater approach for measuring social skills, problem behaviors, and academic competence for children between the ages of 3 to 18 years. The SSRS has a representative national standardization and extensive evidence for reliability and validity. One of the most attractive features of the SSRS is its utility in selecting target behaviors for intervention purposes, a feature uncommon to most behavior rating scales.

Child Behavior Checklist and Profile

Overview and Purpose

The Child Behavior Checklist (CBCL) (Achenbach & Edelbrock, 1983) is a 138-item scale designed to record the behavioral problems and social competencies of children ages 4 through 16 years. The CBCL is a multirater behavior rating scale that utilizes teacher, parent, and child ratings. The CBCL consists of 118 items covering specific behavior problems that are rated by teachers, parents, and children (ages 11–18 years) on a three-point scale (0 = Not True, 1 = Somewhat or Sometimes True, 2 = Very or Often True). Twenty additional items are not included on the CBCL, assessing social competence with respect to school performance, social relations, and the amount and quality of the child's participation in hobbies, activities, and sports.

Table 13.2 Examples of Narrow-Band Factors Under Broad-Band Factors of the Child Behavior Checklist

Externalizing Problems

Aggressive
Delinquent
Hyperactive
Sex Problems
Cruel

Internalizing Problems

Depressed
Social Withdrawal
Somatic Complaints
Uncommunicative
Schizoid
Obsessive Compulsive

These later items will provide a global sense of school/community adjustment. The CBCL is scored as The Child Behavior Profile that provides a graphical representation of item responses across domains.

The CBCL assesses two *broad-band* domains of childhood and adolescent behavior problems and a number of *narrow-band* behavior problems contained within these broad-band domains. The broad-band factors are *Externalizing Problems* and *Internalizing Problems.* The various narrow-band factors under each of these broad-band domains are contained in table 13.2 and the Child Behavior Profile is presented in figure 13.2.

Standardization Sample and Norms

The CBCL was standardized on more than 1,300 children and adolescents between the ages of 4 to 16 years. Separate norms are available for boys and girls within three broad age groups: (a) 4 to 5 years, (b) 6 to 11 years, and (c) 12 to 16 years. The normative sample for the parent version of the CBCL, however, is based on a geographically restrictive sample, as virtually all cases came from Washington, D.C., Maryland, and Virginia. For the parent version, 80 percent of the sample were White, 19 percent were Black, and 2 percent other. For the teacher version of the CBCL (N = 1,100), the sample came from three geographic regions (East, South, and Midwest). In this sample, 77 percent were White and 23 percent were Black. Sex and age were the two variables that accounted for the most variance in CBCL scores and, as such, norms were stratified according to these two variables. Socioeconomic status, occupation of head of household, type of community, and other demographic variables accounted for little variance in CBCL scores.

Figure 13.2 Behavior Problem Portion of a Hand-Scored Teacher Profile Completed for 12-Year-Old Raymond

Internalizing — 1991 TRF Profile - Boys 12–18 — Externalizing

%ILE	I WITHDRAWN	II SOMATIC COMPLAINTS	III ANXIOUS/ DEPRESSED	IV SOCIAL PROBLEMS	V THOUGHT PROBLEMS	VI ATTENTION PROBLEMS	VII DELINQUENT BEHAVIOR	VIII AGGRESSIVE BEHAVIOR	T	Score
		17	35	25	15			49		ID# 040491
	17		33	24		39	17	47		IN: Raymond.trf
		16			14				95	Boy AGE: 12
		15	31	23	13	38	16	45		DATE FILLED:
	16	14	30	22				44		04/04/91
			29		12	37		43	90	BY: Teacher
		13	28	21	11		15	42		CARDS 02,03
	15	12	26	20		36		41		AGENCY 23
				19	10		14	40	85	
	14	11	24	18	9	35		39		# ITEMS 34
		10	23	17			13	37		TOTSCORE 41
			22		8	34			80	TOT T 58
	13	9	21	16	7		12	35		INTERNAL 21
		8	19	15		33		34		INT T 68++
		7			6			33	75	EXTERNAL 7
%ILE	12		17	14	5	32	11	32		EXT T 55
		6	16	13				31		++ Clinical
98	11	5	15	12	4	31	10	30	70	+ Borderline
	9	3		9	3	27	7	23		
				8		26		21		
93			10		2	25		20	65	
	7	2	8			23	6	17		
	5		7	5		20	4	13		
84			6	4		19		12	60	
	4		5	3	1	16	3	9		
	3		4	2		13	2	7		
69			3			12			55	
	2		2					4		
	1			1		7		2		
50	0	0	0-1	0		0-6	0	0-1	50	

OTHER PROBLEMS

I WITHDRAWN

- 2 42. Rather BeAlone
- 0 65. Won't Talk
- 0 69. Secre-tive
- 2 75. Shy
- 0 80. Stares
- 0 88. Sulks
- 1 102. Under-active
- 2 103. Sad
- 1 111. With-drawn
- **8 TOTAL**
- **65 T SCORE**

II SOMATIC COMPLAINTS

- 0 51. Dizzy
- 1 54. Tired
- 0 56a. Aches
- 0 56b. Head-aches
- 0 56c. Nausea
- 0 56d. Eye
- 0 56e. Skin
- 0 56f. Stomach
- 0 56g. Vomit
- **1 TOTAL**
- **57 T SCORE**

III ANXIOUS/ DEPRESSED

- 2 12. Lonely
- 0 14. Cries
- 0 31. FearDoBad
- 0 32. Perfect
- 0 33. Unloved
- 1 34. OutToGet
- 1 35. Worthless
- 1 45. Nervous
- 1 47. Conforms*
- 0 50. Fearful
- 0 52. Guilty
- 2 71. SelfConsc
- 1 81. HurtCrit*
- 0 89. Suspic
- 2 103. Sad
- 1 106. AxPleas*
- 1 108. Mistake*
- 1 112. Worries
- **14 TOTAL**
- **69 T SCORE**

IV SOCIAL PROBLEMS

- 1 1. Acts Young
- 0 11. Clings
- 2 12. Lonely*
- 0 14. Cries*
- 0 25. NotGet Along
- 0 33. Unlove*
- 1 34. OutTo Get*
- 1 35. Worth-less
- 0 36. GetHurt*
- 0 38. Teased
- 0 48. NotLiked
- 1 62. Clumsy
- 1 64. Prefers Young
- **7 TOTAL**
- **64 T SCORE**

V THOUGHT PROBLEMS

- 0 9. Mind Off
- 0 18. Harms Self*
- 0 29. Fears*
- 0 40. Hears Things
- 0 66. Repeats Acts
- 0 70. Sees Things
- 0 84. Strange Behav
- 0 85. Strange Ideas
- **0 TOTAL**
- **50 T SCORE**

VI ATTENTION PROBLEMS

- 1 1. Acts Young
- 2 2. Hums*
- 0 4. Finish*
- 1 8. Concentr
- 0 10. SitStill
- 0 13. Confuse
- 1 15. Fidget*
- 1 17. DaDream
- 0 22. Direct*
- 0 41. Impulsv
- 1 43. Nervous
- 0 49. Learng*
- 0 60. Apath*
- 0 61. Poor School
- 1 62. Clumsy
- 0 72. Messy*
- 1 78. Inatten*
- 0 80. Stares
- 0 92. UnderAch*
- 0 100. Tasks*
- **9 TOTAL**
- **53 T SCORE**

VII DELINQUENT BEHAVIOR

- 0 26. NoGuilt
- 0 39. Bad Compan
- 0 43. LieCheat
- 0. 63. Prefers Older
- 0 82. Steals
- 0 90. Swears
- 1 98. Tardy*
- 0 101. Truant
- 0 105. Alcohol Drugs
- **1 TOTAL**
- **53 T SCORE**

VIII AGGRESSIVE BEHAVIOR

- 1 3. Argues
- 0 6. Defiant*
- 0 7. Brags
- 0 16. Mean
- 0 19. DemAttn
- 0 20. DestOwn
- 0 21. DestOthr
- 0 23. DisbSchl
- 0 24. Disturbs*
- 0 27. Jealous
- 0 37. Fights
- 0 53. TalksOut*
- 0 57. Attacks
- 0 67. Disrupts*
- 0 68. Screams
- 1 74. ShowOff
- 0 76. Explosive*
- 0 77. Demanding
- 1 86. Stubborn
- 1 87. MoodChng
- 0 93. TalkMuch
- 0 94. Teases
- 0 95. Temper
- 0 97. Threaten
- 2 104. Loud
- **6 TOTAL**
- **55 T SCORE**

OTHER PROBLEMS

- 0 5. ActOppSex
- 0 28. EatNonFood
- 0 30. FearSchool
- 1 44. BiteNail
- 1 46. Twitch
- 0 55. Overweight
- 0 56h. OtherPhys
- 1 58. PickSkin
- 0 59. SleepClass
- 0 73. Irresponsb
- 1 79. SpeechProb
- 0 83. StoresUp
- 0 91. TalkSuicid
- 0 96. SexPreocc
- 0 99. TooNeat
- 0 107. DislkSchl
- 0 109. Whining
- 0 110. Unclean
- 0 113. OtherProb

*Not on Cross-Informant Construct

Data Obtained

The parent, teacher, and youth self-report versions of the CBCL yields three types of scores: raw scores, T scores (M = 50, s = 10), and percentile ranks. As mentioned earlier, separate norms and scores are available for males and females in three broad age groupings (4–5 years, 6–11 years, and 12–18 years). T scores and percentile ranks are calculated for the broad-band domains of Externalizing and Internalizing problems and each narrow-band factor with the Externalizing and Internalizing domains.

Reliability and Validity

The CBCL has extensive evidence for reliability and validity. Test-retest reliability estimates for the parent and teacher versions of the CBCL were .91 and .89, respectively (median). Interrater reliabilities between teachers were .57 and between mothers and fathers .64. The relatively lower interrater reliabilities between teachers and parents is most likely a function of the situational specificity of behavior rather than the unreliability of the rating scales (Achenbach et al., 1987).

Validity evidence for the CBCL is based on numerous investigations using both the parent and teacher versions. The CBCL correlates with observational measures of children's behavior in classroom settings, behavior ratings using other behavior rating scales, and it reliably differentiates among regular and special education students, clinic-referred and nonreferred students, and among diagnostic subgroups of emotionally disturbed children (Edelbrock, 1988).

Summary

The CBCL represents a norm-referenced, reliable, and valid measure of childhood psychopathology. The major advantage of the CBCL, like the SSRS, is its incorporation of a multirater approach to assessing children's behavior. One drawback of the CBCL is its length (i.e., 118 items for the parent version and 113 items for the teacher version). The CBCL is used primarily to identify and classify children's behavior problems. Individual behaviors on the CBCL may be targets of intervention, but the technical manual provides little discussion of how the CBCL can be linked to intervention strategies.

Revised Behavior Problem Checklist

Overview and Purpose

The Revised Behavior Problem Checklist (RBPC) (Quay & Peterson, 1983) is an 89-item behavior rating scale for children between the ages of 6 to 18 years. The RBPC represents a revision and extension of the original 55-item Behavior Problem Checklist (Quay & Peterson, 1983), which has been used in more than 100 published studies with a variety of populations (for a comprehensive review see Quay, 1983). The scale was designed to be completed by adults familiar with a target child or adolescent and may include parents, teachers, or direct service child-care workers.

The RBPC comprises six factors or dimensions of problem behaviors: (a) Conduct Disorder, (b) Socialized Aggression, (c) Attention Problems-Immaturity, (d) Anxiety-Withdrawal, (e) Psychotic Behavior, and (f) Motor Excess. A child receives a weighted raw score on each factor, which may then be compared with data derived from empirical investigations of the scale. Examples of behaviors for each dimension are as follows:

1. *Conduct Disorder:* Child is disruptive, annoys others, fights, and blames others.
2. *Socialized Aggression:* Child stays out late at night, has bad companions, and is loyal to delinquent friends.
3. *Attention Problems-Immaturity:* Child has short attention span and poor concentration, is distractible, and has trouble following directions.
4. *Anxiety-Withdrawal:* Child feels inferior, self-conscious, fearful, and anxious.
5. *Psychotic Behavior:* Child uses repetitive speech, parrots others' speech, and expresses far-fetched ideas.
6. *Motor Excess:* Child is restless, hyperactive, squirms, fidgets, and unable to relax.

Standardization Sample and Norms

According to the manual, four samples were used to generate item statistics and factor analyses of the RBPC. Sample I consisted of 276 cases in two private psychiatric residential facilities. This sample consisted of males (72%) and females (28%) between the ages of 5 years, 5 months and 22 years, 11 months, with a mean of 15 years and a standard deviation of 3 years. Sample II consisted of 198 cases who were rated by their parents (mostly mothers) at the time of their admission to either an inpatient or outpatient psychiatric facility. The ages ranged from 3 to 21 years with a mean age of 11 years, 6 months and a standard deviation of 4 years. Sample III included 172 students in a special school for children with developmental disabilities. No ages were reported for this sample. Sample IV consisted of 114 students attending a private school for children with learning disabilities. They had a mean age of 10 years with a standard deviation of 2 years.

In sum, the available standardization data were based on 760 cases, which were exclusively "clinical" or pathological groups. The manual does provide some data from 566 "normal" children in public schools in New Jersey and South Carolina in grades 1 through 5. This sample, however, is inadequately described in terms of raters, demographic characteristics, and other relevant criteria for standardized tests and rating scales. Further, the manual does not provide standard scores or percentile ranks but instead relies on weighted raw scores. Given the nature of the standardization sample, the RBPC is inappropriately used as a norm-referenced instrument to identify behavior problems of the general school-age population.

Data Obtained

Each item on the RBPC is scored on a three-point scale (0 = Not a Problem, 1 = A Mild Problem, and 2 = A Severe Problem). The maximum score on any scale is twice the number of items on that scale, whereas the minimum score is zero. For example, the Conduct Disorder Scale, with 22 items, has a maximum raw score of 44 and a minimum score of zero. The Motor Excess Scale, with 5 items, has a maximum raw score of 10 and a minimum score of zero. All scores of the RBPC are weighted raw scores that are summed for each scale or factor. Standard scores cannot be derived from the RBPC in its current form.

Reliability and Validity

The manual provides evidence for internal consistency and interrater reliability. The coefficient alphas for each of the six scales are as follows: (a) Conduct Disorder = .94, (b) Socialized Aggression = .84, (c) Attention Problems/Immaturity = .92, (d) Anxiety/Withdrawal = .82, (e) Psychotic Behavior = .72, and (f) Motor Excess = .75. The only interrater reliability evidence was based on staff members in residential facilities and ranged from .85 (Conduct Disorder) to .52 (Anxiety/Withdrawal), with a median interrater reliability coefficient of .58. No data concerning test-retest reliability are reported. Quay (1983) states that "it is, of course, reasonable to assume that much of the concurrent, predictive, and construct validity already established for the Behavior Problem Checklist (Quay & Peterson, 1983) can be generalized to the RBPC" (p. 247). However, this is not necessarily true, because the RBPC represents a new scale and as such must establish reliability and validity in its own right. The only validity evidence provided for the RBPC is factorial validity and group differentiation in which "normal" children were differentiated from "clinical" samples. To date, the RBPC has a paucity of validity data to support its use.

Summary

The RBPC is a poorly standardized behavior rating scale that has limited evidence for reliability and validity. The fact that the original Behavior Problem Checklist has extensive reliability and validity evidence does not necessarily ensure that the RBPC will assume the same psychometric features. However, the RBPC can be used to identify teachers' behavioral concerns for individual students, particularly from a criterion-related framework. In addition, teachers may be asked to rate several students in their classroom, and these ratings can be compared.

Systematic Screening for Behavior Disorders

Overview and Purpose

The Systematic Screening for Behavior Disorders (SSBD) (Walker & Severson, 1992) is a multiple-gating screening device for the identification of children with behavior disorders. The SSBD is known as a "multiple-gating" device because it contains a series of progressively more expensive and precise assessments or "gates." The SSBD utilizes a combination of teacher nominations, teacher rating scales, and direct observations of classroom and playground behavior to identify children for placement in programs for the behaviorally disordered.

The first gate of the SSBD uses teacher nominations, in which teachers are asked to identify three students in their classes that match two profiles or types of behavior patterns. The first pattern is known as *externalizing*, which refers to all behavior problems that are directed outwardly, by the child, toward the external social environment. Externalizing behavior problems are "behavioral excesses" in that they occur too often. Examples of externalizing behavior problems are defying teachers, aggressive behavior, noncompliance with teacher directions, arguing, and so forth (Walker & Severson, 1992). The second pattern is known as *internalizing,* which refers to all behavior problems that are directed inwardly and that represent problems with self. Internalizing behavior problems are known as "behavioral deficits" (i.e., they refer to behaviors that occur too infrequently). Examples of internalizing behavior problems are not talking with other children, not participating in games or activities, being shy, having low or restricted activity levels, and so forth.

The second gate of the SSBD involves the use of teacher ratings of externalizing and internalizing behavior patterns. Teachers are asked to rate the three children ranked the highest on externalizing problems and three children ranked the highest on internalizing problems (for a total of six students). Teachers rate these children on a Critical Events Checklist that assesses whether a student has exhibited any of 33 externalizing and internalizing behavior problems within the past six months. The second rating involves the Combined Frequency Index, which measures how often the student exhibits specific adaptive and maladaptive behaviors. Those students exceeding the normative criteria in the second gate of the SSBD are then independently assessed in gate three.

In gate three of the SSBD, a school professional (e.g., school psychologist, guidance counselor, social workers, etc.) assesses students on two measures of school adjustment using direct observation procedures. The first measure is known as *academic engaged time* (AET), which is recorded during independent seatwork periods. The second measure is the *peer social behavior observation,* which measures the quality and nature of students' social behavior during recess periods. Students exceeding normative criteria on these two measures are considered to "pass" gate three and are referred for a formal assessment of behavior disorders. Figure 13.3 presents a graphical display of the multiple-gating procedure used by the SSBD.

Standardization Sample and Norms

The SSBD was nationally standardized on 4,500 cases on the Stage Two measures and approximately 1,300 cases on the Stage Three measures. These

Figure 13.3 Multiple-Gating Assessment Procedure for Identification of Students with Behavior Disorders

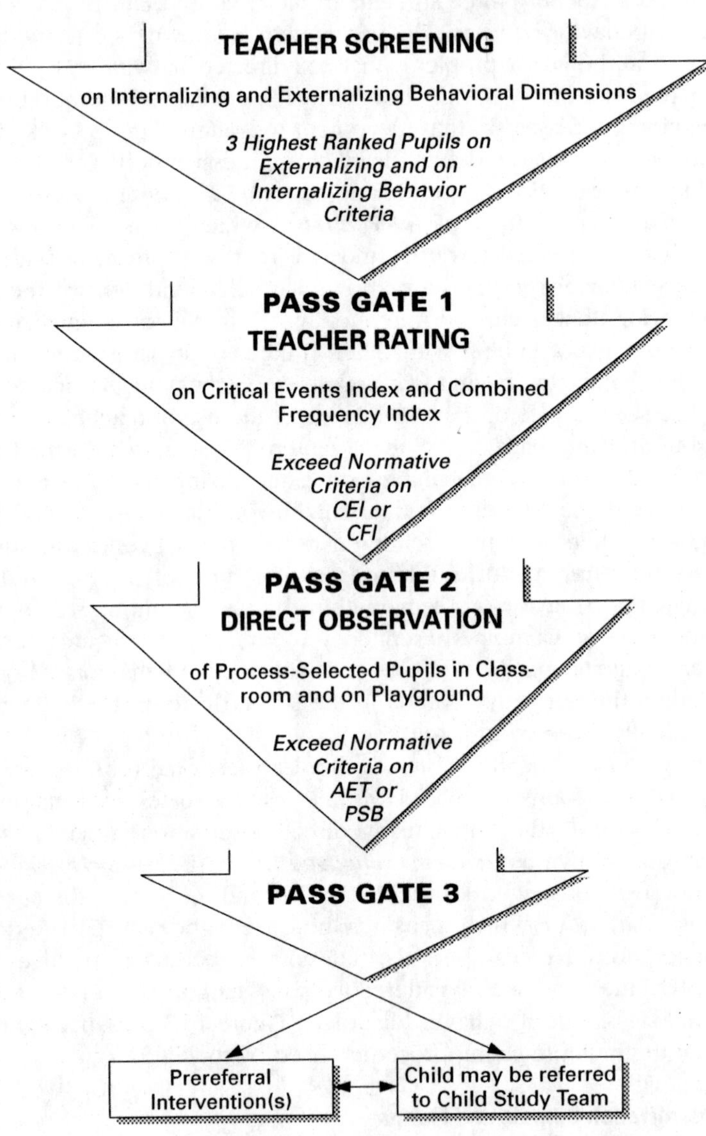

cases were collected from 18 school districts in eight states: Oregon, Washington, Utah, Illinois, Wisconsin, Rhode Island, Kentucky, and Florida. The standardization sample included both White and non-White students and a broad representation of students from low socioeconomic status. The SSBD appears to have an adequate standardization sample for the purposes for which it is to be used.

Data Obtained

The SSBD uses raw scores, T scores, and percentile ranks for the various measures. These scores are based on separate norms for males and females, grade levels (e.g., grades 1–6 and grades 4–6, depending on the measure), internalizers, externalizers, and nonranked students. Explicit criteria based on these normative data are used to "pass" a student through a particular gate.

Reliability and Validity

The SSBD has extensive evidence for reliability and validity. Three types of reliability are presented: test-retest, internal consistency, and interrater. The mean one-month test-retest reliability for Stage One measures (i.e., teacher nominations) was .79 for externalizers and .72 for internalizers. Test-retest reliabilities for Stage Two measures were .81 for the Cumulative Frequency Index (CFI) (adaptive behavior rating scale) and .90 (maladaptive behavior rating scale). Internal consistency estimates of the CFI adaptive and maladaptive behavior rating scales were .94 and .92, respectively. The average interitem correlations for the adaptive and maladaptive behavior rating scales were .59 and .49, respectively. Interrater reliability was not established for the Stage Two measures; however, interrater reliability for the Academic Engaged Time measure ranged from 90 to 100 percent. For the Peer Social Behavior observation, the interrater reliabilities ranged from 80 to 90 percent.

The SSBD technical manual presents a large amount of data supporting the validity of the measure. Included in this discussion is evidence for content, construct, concurrent, and discriminant validity. For example, the SSBD correlates with measures of behavior problems, social skills, and sociometric status. It reliably differentiates behaviorally disordered students from nondisordered students as well as distinguishes among externalizers, internalizers, and nonreferred students.

Summary

The SSBD is a well-conceptualized and well-researched instrument designed for the identification of students with behavior disorders. Its multiple-gating procedure represents an efficient method of identifying students with behavior problems and is designed to save time and money in the assessment process. We feel that the SSBD serves as one of the best examples of how assessment methods (teacher nominations, teacher ratings, and direct observations of behavior in naturalistic settings) can be combined to identify students in need of special services and to identify target behaviors for intervention. In our opinion, there is no better instrument for the screening and identification of students with behavior disorders.

Student Self-Concept Scale

Overview and Purpose

The Student Self-Concept Scale (SSCS) (Gresham, Elliott, & Evans-Fernandez, 1992) is a 72-item group or individually administered multidimensional measure of self-concept. The SSCS provides a norm-referenced measure of self-concept for children and adolescents in grades 3 through 12 and documents the perceived *confidence* and *importance* of specific behaviors influencing the development of students' self-concepts.

The SSCS conceptualizes self-concept as being multidimensional in nature in that individuals categorize their self-perceptions into facets or domains (e.g., academic, social, etc.). The SSCS defines self-concept as an individual's perception that he or she can perform certain behaviors that will result in certain outcomes. Self-concept is multidimensional and is determined by an individual's feelings of efficacy in performing certain behaviors and the importance of these behaviors for that individual. The following subscales and composite scales are measured on the SSCS:

1. *Academic Self-Concept Subscale.* This subscale measures students' confidence in being able to perform behaviors that are academic in nature (e.g., reading, math, etc.) or academically related (e.g., listening to the teacher, following directions, etc.).
2. *Social Self-Concept Subscale.* This subscale measures students' confidence levels in the social domain (e.g., playing with others, sharing with others, etc.).
3. *Self-Image Self-Concept Subscale.* This subscale measures general self-concept and taps students' global perceptions of who they are (e.g., proud of self, well liked by others, etc.).
4. *Confidence Composite Scale.* This scale is a composite obtained by adding the Academic, Social, and Self-Image Subscales.
5. *Outcome Academic Subscale.* This subscale measures students' perceptions that certain academic behaviors will result in certain academic outcomes (e.g., "If I study hard, I will make good grades in school").
6. *Outcome Social Subscale.* This subscale measures students' perceptions that certain social behaviors will result in certain social outcomes (e.g., "If I take turns in games, others will want to play with me").
7. *Outcome Self-Image Subscale.* This subscale measures students' perceptions that certain self-perceptions will result in certain outcomes (e.g., "If I am proud of who I am, I will get along better with others").

8. *Outcome Composite Scale.* This scale is a composite obtained by summing the Academic, Social, and Self-Image Subscales.
9. *Lie Scale.* This scale measures the degree to which students are attempting to present unrealistic levels of social desirability or "faking good" responses (e.g., "I like everyone I know," "I never get mad," etc.). Importance scores are also available for Academic, Social, and Self-Image Subscales.

Standardization Sample and Norms

The SSCS was standardized on a national sample of 3,586 elementary and secondary school students from 19 states. The standardization sample closely approximated the U.S. student population in terms of gender, race, geographical region, and urbanization, with a special emphasis on obtaining sufficient representation of special education students. Males and females were evenly represented both across the sample and within each grade level, with 49 percent being males and 51 percent being females. Approximately 16 percent of the standardization sample were students with disabilities (e.g., learning disabilities, behavior disorders, mild mental disabilities), which represents a slightly higher percentage of students with disabilities than the U.S. student population (i.e., 11%).

Norms were stratified by broad age groupings (elementary and secondary) and by gender. Gender was a particularly important stratification variable as females obtained higher scores in academic and social domains across virtually all grade levels, whereas males obtained higher scores in self-image across virtually all grade levels.

Data Obtained

Three different types of normative scores were derived for the SSCS. One is the percentile rank, the other is a standard score with a mean of 100 and a standard deviation of 15, and the last is a descriptive behavior level score. Both percentile rank and standard scores are derived for the Confidence Subscales (Academic, Social, and Self-Image), the Composite Self-Concept, and the Outcome Composite Scales. Descriptive behavior levels are available for the three Outcome Subscales (Academic, Social, and Self-Image). Descriptive behavior levels consist of three levels labeled *High, Average,* and *Low.* These levels were determined by the means and standard deviations of the subscales. For instance, the Average category lies within the range one standard deviation around the mean, whereas the High and Low categories fall beyond one standard deviation above and below the mean, respectively. Descriptive behavior levels, like percentile ranks and standard scores, are computed separately by gender and grade level.

Reliability and Validity

The SSCS technical manual provides extensive evidence for reliability and validity. In terms of reliability, both internal consistency and test-retest reliability evidence is reported. Internal consistency estimates range from .89 to .92 for the Composite Confidence ratings and .79 to .82 for the Composite Outcome ratings. The median coefficient alpha reliability was .90 and .81 for the Composite Confidence and Composite Outcome Scales, respectively.

Subscale internal consistency estimates were lower, based largely on the fewer numbers of items on which these estimates were based. These subscale coefficient alphas ranged from .72 to .84 with a median internal consistency estimate of .78 for elementary students and .81 for secondary students.

Test-retest reliability estimates were based on samples of students at elementary and secondary levels completing the SSCS on two separate occasions separated by approximately four weeks. For SSCS Confidence Subscale ratings, the median stability coefficient was .68 for elementary students and .77 for secondary students. Composite Confidence ratings were slightly more stable with coefficients of .73 and .84 for elementary and secondary students, respectively.

The SSCS technical manual provides a large number of studies supporting the content, construct, social, and criterion-related validity of the scale. The SSCS correlates moderately to highly with other established measures of self-concept such as the Piers-Harris Children's Self-Concept Scale (Piers, 1984) ($r = .40$), Tennessee Self-Concept Scale (Roid & Fitts, 1988) ($r = .59$), Self-Description Questionnaire-1 (Marsh, 1988) ($r = .76$), and Coopersmith Self-Esteem Inventory (Coopersmith, 1981) ($r = .54$). The SSCS also correlates with the Social Skills Rating System (SSRS) (Gresham & Elliott, 1990), with correlations between the SSCS Composite Confidence score and SSRS subscales ranging from .37 to .48. SSCS scores also showed moderate negative correlations with the Child Behavior Checklist-Self-Report Form (CBCL) (Achenbach & Edelbrock, 1987). The correlation between the SSCS Composite Confidence score and CBCL Total Problems scores was –.60, suggesting that self-concept is inversely related to behavior problems in children. The SSCS also reliably differentiates between children with learning disabilities and children without learning disabilities. For example, significant differences were found between these groups on the Academic and Social Subscales using both Confidence and Outcome ratings as well as the Composite Scales.

Summary

The SSCS provides users several unique features to facilitate more comprehensive assessment and intervention services for children experiencing difficulties in self-concept. One, the SSCS provides norms based on a large, representative sample for boys and girls in grades 3 to 12. Two, the SSCS is theoretically based, which provides more specific, behavioral information regarding a child's self-concept. Three, consistent with recent theoretical advances in the study of self-concept, the SSCS provides a multidimensional measure of self-concept. Four, the SSCS represents the first self-concept scale to utilize joint ratings of confidence and importance for each behavior on the scale. The inclusion of importance ratings facilitates intervention planning for children and adolescents having problems in self-concept.

The SSCS offers a useful means for assessing and treating self-concept problems. The multidimensional nature of the scale allows users to distinguish self-concept problems across important domains such as academic and social and to separately assess students' levels of outcome expectations. Finally, unlike many self-concept scales, the SSCS provides an empirical means of detecting invalid profiles by the inclusion of a Lie Scale to measure social desirability of responding to items.

Other Behavior Rating Scales

Far too many behavior rating scales are available to conduct a comprehensive review of each scale. In the foregoing sections, we have reviewed what we believe to be the most well-researched and/or most frequently used behavior rating scales used with school-aged children and adolescents. The following paragraphs review other behavior rating scales used with special children to assess a variety of problem behaviors and social competencies.

Behavior Assessment System for Children

The most promising scale released in the last few years is the Behavior Assessment System for Children (BASC; Reynolds & Kamphaus, 1992) which attempts to provide for a *comprehensive* assessment of behavior using multiple methods and multiple informants. Although the instrument is too new for research independent of the test developers to have emerged in sufficient quantity, the technical data in the test manual are impressive. The system can be used to assess both adaptive and maladaptive behavior in children aged 4 to 18 years. A unique feature of the system is that it includes not only rating scales, with parent, teacher, and child self-report versions, but also structured observation and the collection of a developmental history.

Technical adequacy of the BASC is adequate with reliability and validity. The parent scale has reliability coefficients that dip into the mid to upper .70s, which is less than ideal for diagnostic decisions. The system does include some adaptive as well as maladaptive items, but there is a lack of overlap in behaviors from scale to scale within the system.

A relative strong point, compared with other instruments, is the inclusion of a behavioral observation system. The good news is that observation was included. The bad news is that the manual provides little technical support for using the system. Further, there is a lack of systematic procedures for integrating information from the observation with the rating scales.

The BASC has already generated a great deal of interest among practitioners. Given the breadth of the instrument, the technical sophistication with which it was developed, and the technical support available to users, the BASC is likely to become a frequent choice for practitioners who seek to assess the social emotional functioning of children.

Conners Rating Scales

The Conners Parent Rating Scale and Conners Teacher Rating Scale (Conners, 1985) represent two rating scales designed to identify behavior problems in school-age children and adolescents between the ages of 3 and 17 years. The Conners Parent Rating Scale (CPRS) is a 93-item scale that assesses eight domains of problem behavior: Fearful-Anxious, Hyperactive-Immature, Restless-Disorganized, Conduct Disorder, Antisocial, Obsessional, Psychosomatic, and Learning Problem-Immature. Each behavior is rated on the CPRS on a four-point scale and these raw scores are transformed into T scores (M = 50, s = 10). A brief version of the CPRS called the Abbreviated Parent Questionnaire is based on 10 items/behaviors that assess hyperactivity. This "Hyperactivity Index" is used frequently as part of an assessment of Attention Deficit Hyperactivity Disorder.

The Conners Teacher Rating Scale (CTRS) (Conners, 1985) is designed to measure problem behavior in children between the ages of 4 and 12 years. The CTRS is a 39-item behavior rating scale, which was standardized only on Canadian children. The CTRS measures six domains of problem behaviors: Daydreams-Attendance Problem, Asocial, Overindulgent, Conduct Problem, Emotional-Overindulgent, and Anxious-Passive. Behaviors on the CTRS, like the CPRS, are rated on a four-point scale. T scores (M = 50, s = 10) are calculated from the raw scores of each of the six factors on the scale. Like the parent version, the CTRS has a 10-item "Hyperactivity Index" called the Abbreviated Teacher Questionnaire. Normative data are available for this scale for children ages 3 to 17 years.

The CPRS and CTRS are used less frequently than other behavior rating scales discussed in this chapter. However, the Abbreviated Parent and Teacher Questionnaires that assess hyperactivity are used often in research and clinical practice to assist in the diagnosis of Attention Deficit Hyperactivity Disorder. Research with the Conners Scales suggests that they have adequate reliability and validity for use as screening devices to identify behavior problems in children and adolescents. Unlike the Social Skills Rating System and the Child Behavior Checklist, the Conners Scales were standardized on separate normative samples, thus not allowing for direct comparisons between parent and teacher ratings of the same children.

Walker-McConnell Scale of Social Competence and School Adjustment

The Walker-McConnell Scale of Social Competence and School Adjustment (W-M) (Walker & McConnell, 1988) is a 43-item teacher rating scale that assesses children's social skills in kindergarten through sixth grade. The W-M assesses three domains of social skills: Teacher-Preferred Social Skills, Peer-Preferred Social Skills, and School Adjustment. The W-M scale was standardized on a sample of more than 1,800 children from 18 states. The technical manual provides extensive evidence for reliability (e.g., internal consistency, test-retest, and interrater) and validity (e.g., content, construct, discriminant, factorial, and criterion-related). This scale covers a much narrower age range than the Social Skills Rating System (Gresham & Elliott, 1990) and utilizes only one type of rater (i.e., the teacher). In spite of this, the W-M scale is a reliable and valid measure of elementary-aged children's social skills.

Focus on Research

Is Behavior Situationally Determined or Cross-Situational? Implications from Research Using Behavior Rating Scales

Different schools of thought exist regarding whether behavior is determined by situational factors or by internal personality characteristics that are cross-situational. For example, certain psychodynamic theories (e.g., psychoanalysis) suggest that behavior is determined by personality traits that remain constant across a variety of situations. On the other hand, environmental theories (e.g., applied behavior analysis) maintain that behavior is determined largely by situational and setting factors and, thus, is situationally specific.

To help answer this age-old question, Achenbach, McConaughy, and Howell (1987) reviewed 119 studies that used multiple informants completing behavior rating scales to assess the degree of consistency among informants' ratings of emotional/behavioral problems of children between the ages of 1.5 and 19 years of age. These authors computed correlations between different pairs of informants to assess the level of agreement or consistency in ratings. Specifically, ratings from parents, teachers, mental health workers, observers, peers, and self-reports of children were compared.

Achenbach et al. (1987) sought to answer the following questions in their analysis:

1. Is there any consistency between and among informants?
2. If so, how much?
3. Does consistency among informants vary with the type of informant and child characteristics such as age, sex, type of problem, and severity of problem behavior?
4. What are the implications for assessment practice in data showing high or low levels of consistency among different informants?

Findings

1. Correlations among informants playing similar roles with respect to children (e.g., pairs of parents, pairs of teachers, pairs of mental health workers, etc.) were higher than correlations between informants playing different roles with respect to children (e.g., parents and teachers, teachers and mental health workers, peers and observers, etc.).

continued

Focus on Research—*continued*

2. Based on 119 studies, the mean correlations between informant were as follows:

Similar Role Correlations

a. Parents/Parents: $r = .59$

b. Teachers/Teachers: $r = .64$

c. Mental Health Worker/Mental Health Worker: $r = .54$

d. Observer/Observer: $r = .57$

e. Peer/Peer: $r = .73$

Mean $r = .61$

Different Role Informants

a. Parent/Teacher: $r = .27$

b. Parent/Mental Health Worker: $r = .24$

c. Teacher/Mental Health Worker: $r = .34$

d. Observer/Teacher: $r = .42$

e. Observer/Parent: $r = .27$

f. Peer/Teacher: $r = .44$

g. Self/Peer: $r = .26$

h. Self/Teacher: $r = .20$

i. Self/Parent: $r = .25$

j. Self/Mental Health Worker: $r = .27$

Mean $r = .30$

3. There was no significant difference between correlations obtained from mothers' versus fathers' ratings of boys versus girls and clinical versus non-clinical samples.
4. Higher correlations were found between informants for externalizing problems than for internalizing problems. Mothers and fathers, however, showed no differences in their ratings of externalizing and internalizing problems of their children.

Implications for Assessment Practice

1. These informants are likely to vary in their effects on children. Different informants are needed for different settings and situations.
2. The low correlation between children's self-ratings and other informants such as parents, teachers, and mental health workers indicate that children's self-reports cannot be substituted for reports by other informants.

3. The relatively low correlations among informants *do not necessarily* suggest that the measures used to collect information (i.e., behavior rating scales) are unreliable or invalid. Rather, it may suggest that different informants contribute valid, but different information.
4. In using behavior rating scales, one must ensure that a representative sample of ratings is taken from various informants having similar and different roles with respect to children. The presence or absence of consistency in these informants' ratings may help in the design, implementation, and evaluation of interventions to change behavior.

From: T. Achenbach, S. McConaughy, and C. Howell, Child/Adolescent Behavioral and Emotional Problems: Implications of Cross-Informant Correlations for Situational Specificity, PSYCHOLOGICAL BULLETIN, 101:213–232. Copyright © 1987 by the American Psychological Association. Adapted with permission.

Walker Problem Behavior Identification Checklist

The Walker Problem Behavior Identification Checklist (WPBIC) (Walker, 1983) is a 50-item checklist designed to identify behavior problems in children in grades 4 through 6. It is composed of observable, operational statements about classroom behavior that were furnished by a representative sample of elementary school teachers. The WPBIC assesses five categories of problem behavior: Acting Out, Withdrawal, Distractibility, Disturbed Peer Relations, and Immaturity. Each behavior on the scale is rated on a 4-point scale and yields a weighted raw score. These weighted raw scores are transformed to T scores (M = 50, s = 10). The WPBIC manual provides evidence for internal consistency and test-retest reliability. However, internal consistency data are provided only for the total score and not the five subscales. Validity evidence includes predictive, content, construct, and content validities. The greatest drawback of the scale is that it was not standardized on a representative sample of children and therefore scores obtained may not be comparable to other samples.

Chapter Summary

Summary of Behavior Rating Scales

Behavior rating scales represent useful, economical, reliable, and valid approaches for assessing social skills and problem behaviors of children and adolescents. They can be used for screening purposes, for classification purposes, and can be of great assistance in identifying target behaviors for intervention. It should be pointed out, however, that behavior rating scales *should not* be used in isolation for any of these purposes. Like other assessment strategies discussed in this book, one must always use multiple types of assessment to get a complete picture of children and their behavior.

You will recall that many of the behavior rating scales discussed in this chapter utilized multiple informants (e.g., parents, teachers, and children). A somewhat complex question is, How is one to interpret the information from multiple informants for a single child? One way of answering this question is based on the principle of **multiple operationalism** (Campbell & Fiske, 1959; Gresham, 1985). That is, behavior can be defined or operationalized from different perspectives. For example, a parent may define arguing with peers as a form of assertive behavior, whereas a teacher may view this same behavior as aggressive behavior. Thus, the parent and the teacher have defined or "operationalized" this behavior in different ways. Does this mean that whatever method we used to measure behavior is invalid? The lack of agreement between the parent and the teacher in this case could be due to a variety of factors. For example, the same behavior may be viewed as assertion in one setting (e.g., a baseball game) and as aggression in another setting (e.g., the classroom). In this case, the *situation,* not the behavior, may lead adults to define behaviors differently. In using behavior rating scales, it is important to consider and assess the situational determinants of behavior.

Another commonly encountered phenomenon in using multiple informants for behavior rating scales is when one informant rates the behavior as not occurring and the other informant rates the behavior as occurring very often. For instance, a parent may rate the behavior of temper tantrums as never occurring, whereas the teacher may rate this same behavior as occurring frequently. At first blush, this would seem to indicate complete disagreement and a lack of validity of the scale used to measure the behavior of temper tantrums. Another possibility might be that the behavior is *situationally specific* in that it never occurs in the home (perhaps because it has been punished in that setting) but occurs frequently at school (perhaps because it has been reinforced with attention from the teacher and peers). Thus, the explanation for the apparent disagreement between informants in this case has to do with situational factors and *not* any psychometric characteristics of the rating scale.

Social Validity

One type of validity that is important to the use of behavior rating scales is termed **social validity** (Gresham, 1985). Social validity (Wolf, 1978) refers to the determination of the applied or social importance of exhibiting certain behaviors in particular situations. Wolf (1978) has suggested that social validation occurs on three levels: (a) determining the *social significance* of behavior, (b) determining the *social acceptability* of interventions to change behavior, and (c) determining the *social importance* of the effects produced by interventions. The notion of social validity is important in the use and interpretation of data from behavior rating scales, particularly the concepts of social significance and social importance. Social significance refers to behaviors that are considered by authoritative adults as being significant (as opposed to trivial) behaviors for children. In terms of problem behaviors, socially significant behaviors are behaviors that deviate from or occur more frequently than the typical behaviors exhibited by a child's peers. In terms of prosocial behaviors, these behaviors would occur less frequently than those of a representative sample of a child's peers.

One way of assessing whether or not a behavior is socially significant is to use social comparisons. Social comparisons involve the identification of the referred child's peers who are similar in age and demographic variables but differ in performance of certain behaviors. The behavior of the referred child can be compared with a child's peers by using well-standardized and representatively normed behavior rating scales to assess whether the behavior significantly deviates from the behavior of the child's peers. For example, if a child receives a T score of 70 (i.e., two standard deviations above the mean) on an aggression subscale of a behavior rating scale, then one can conclude that the child is significantly more aggressive than his or her peers whose mean score would be 50. This T score of 70 would indicate that 98 percent of the children on whom the scale was normed had lower scores on aggression than the referred child. As such, one might conclude that this child's aggressive behavior constituted socially significant behavior.

Social importance addresses the question, Does the quantity and quality of behavior change make a difference in the child's functioning? In other words, do the changes in behaviors subsequent to an intervention bring the behavior into tolerable/acceptable limits? Social comparisons can be used to assess the social importance of behavior change using normative data from behavior rating scales. For example, if the above child's T score of 70 on aggression was reduced to a T score of 50 by an intervention, then one could conclude that the intervention had a socially important effect on behavior. That is, the intervention brought the child's aggressive behavior into an average range.

Social validity represents an important consideration in using behavior rating scales. Without representative norms, it is difficult to establish with confidence that behaviors assessed represent socially significant behaviors. Without representative norms, one would have great difficulty in determining whether or not an intervention produced socially important effects.

Putting It Together

The following sample case report (see Focus on Practice) illustrates the principle of good assessment practice for behavior problems in the classroom. In reading this report, try to identify the important principles discussed in this chapter for using behavior rating scales. Pay particular attention to how the results of behavior rating scales are combined with other assessment methods and how an intervention plan was developed and evaluated.

Focus on Practice

Integrating Assessment Information from Multiple Informants

Investigators of the social behavior of children have noted differences in behavior across various settings. It is not unusual, for example, for a child to demonstrate the ability to join a group of neighborhood friends, but to be quite reluctant to approach a group of classmates at school. Thus, a respect for the situationally specificity of an individual's social behavior is an important consideration when assessing a person.

The Social Skills Rating System (SSRS) (Gresham & Elliott, 1990) discussed in this chapter provides a means of integrating information from multiple raters of a child's social behavior. This is accomplished by using the Assessment-Intervention Record (AIR), which provides: (a) a format for documenting background information, (b) a means for analyzing and synthesizing multirater assessment data, (c) documentation of social behavior strengths and weaknesses, (d) a functional system for classifying social skills deficits tied to a model for developing intervention plans, and (e) a summary report to guide further assessments and interventions.

Case Illustration

To illustrate the various functions of the AIR, the information on Andrew Taylor, a 9-year-old boy living with both parents, is presented (see figure 13.4a). Andrew's SSRS multirater data were summarized and integrated (see pages 2 and 3 of the AIR presented in figures 13.4b and c). Andrew's Graphic Profile Summary illustrates both agreement and disagreement among raters. Andrew's teacher and his mother both believe that Andrew has *fewer* social skills than his peers in the comparison groups. Andrew's own ratings of his social skills were on the low side of average. A review of the Social Skills Subscales, however, reveals some disagreements.

Andrew's mother rated Andrew low in Assertion skills. Andrew's teacher did not feel that Andrew was particularly low in Assertion skills, but that he did have a lack of Self-Control skills. Andrew also rated himself low in Self-Control skills, but his mother did not. Andrew's teacher and his mother also agreed that, in general, Andrew did not have an unusual number of Problem Behaviors, although they both thought he had some externalizing problems.

The patterns of agreements and disagreements among raters provides a basis for consultation and offers directions for clarifying the apparently diverse views of some of Andrew's behaviors (see figures 13.4 e–g). For example, is the teacher trying to get Andrew to be more controlled while the mother is trying to have him become more assertive? Do these two people have contradictory goals for Andrew? These questions could be explored in discussions with Andrew's mother and teacher to assist in the identification of common behavior-change goals for Andrew.

In summary, the overall ratings of Andrew's behavior by his teacher and his mother showed below-average performance of a number of important social skills when compared with a national sample of same-sex peers. These interindividual data in the form of standard scores and percentile ranks could be used alone, to identify Andrew as a child needing further evaluation, or they could be used in conjunction with other assessment information to explore the possibility of a formal classification requiring special services. Andrew's complete AIR follows. It details global ratings social skills and problem behaviors as well as specific behaviors from multiple informants. In addition, it provides specific recommendations for intervention planning to remediate Andrew's social skills deficits.

Figure 13.4a Page 1 of the *Assessment-Intervention Record* Completed for Andrew, a Hypothetical Case

Teacher Form
Parent Form
Student Form

Social Skills Rating System

Assessment-Intervention Record

Frank M. Gresham and Stephen N. Elliott

Student Information

Name Andrew Taylor Date of Birth 6 (Month) 22 (Day) 80 (Year)

Sex: ☐ Female ☒ Male Ethnic Group (optional) ______ Age 9 (Years) 6 (Months)

Grade and School 4th / Prairieview

Parents' or guardians' names

1. Nelson Taylor Address 58 Shoeman Circle
   Phone 603-274-8139
2. Ann Taylor Address same
   Phone ______

Teacher's name Bentler

Reason for referral Has difficulty controlling his temper and frequently gets into arguments with a classmate. Generally, poor interactions with peers.

Social Skills Assessment

Record the SSRS forms that have been completed and by whom. Also list any other methods of assessing the student's behavior that have been completed and will be summarized on page 6 of this report.

SSRS	Date Completed	Rater
Teacher Form	12-1-89	Jane Bentler
Parent Form	12-5-89	Ann Taylor
Student Form	12-5-89	Andrew Taylor

Other assessment methods Classroom and playground observations, Walker Problem Behavior Checklist, brief interview and role-play session with Andrew (12-10-89).

Figure 13.4b Standard Score Summary, Page 2 of the *Assessment-Intervention Record,* Completed for Andrew

Standard Score Summary

Instructions

Copy the standard score, the percentile rank, the standard error of measurement, the confidence level and the standard score confidence band from the individual Teacher, Parent, and Student questionnaires in the appropriate spaces below.

If you wish to see a graphic summary of these results, complete the Graphic Profile Summary on page 3.

	Teacher	*Parent*	*Student*
SOCIAL SKILLS			
Standard Score	84	79	89
Percentile Rank	14	8	23
SEM	± 4	± 5	± 6
Confidence Level	68% ☒ 95% ☐	68% ☒ 95% ☐	68% ☒ 95% ☐
Confidence Band (standard scores)	80 to 88	74 to 84	83 to 95
PROBLEM BEHAVIORS			
Standard Score	113	100	
Percentile Rank	81	50	
SEM	± 5	± 5	
Confidence Level	68% ☒ 95% ☐	68% ☒ 95% ☐	
Confidence Band (standard scores)	108 to 118	95 to 105	
ACADEMIC COMPETENCE			
Standard Score	109		
Percentile Rank	73		
SEM	± 3		
Confidence Level	68% ☒ 95% ☐		
Confidence Band (standard scores)	106 to 112		

Description of Subscales

SOCIAL SKILLS

The SSRS is designed to evaluate the frequency and the importance of **Social Skills** in five areas. These areas are:

Cooperation: behaviors such as helping others, sharing materials, and complying with rules and directions

Assertion: initiating behaviors, such as asking others for information, introducing oneself, and responding to the actions of others, such as peer pressure or insults

Responsibility: behaviors that demonstrate ability to communicate with adults and regard for property or work

Empathy: behaviors that show concern and respect for others' feelings and viewpoints

Self-Control: behaviors that emerge in conflict situations, such as responding appropriately to teasing, and in nonconflict situations that require taking turns and compromising

Figure 13.4c Graphic Profile Summary, Page 3 of the *Assessment-Intervention Record,* Completed for Andrew

Graphic Profile Summary

Instructions

The relationships among teacher, parent, and student ratings for the scales and subscales can be made readily apparent. Transfer the results from each questionnaire to the profile below. Simply make X's in each box for each form. (See sample below.) You may wish to use different colors for Teacher, Parent, and Student Forms. An example of a completed profile is shown in Chapter 3 of the SSRS Manual. If you need more specific statistical information for the scales, refer to page 2 of this Record.

Scales

SOCIAL SKILLS

	Teacher	Parent	Student	
More				More
Average			X	Average
Fewer	X	X		Fewer

PROBLEM BEHAVIORS

	Teacher	Parent	
More			More
Average	X	X	Average
Fewer			Fewer

ACADEMIC COMPETENCE

Teacher	
	Above Average
X	Average
	Below Average

Subscales

	Cooperation			Assertion			Self-Control			Responsibility	Empathy	
	Teacher	Parent	Student	Teacher	Parent	Student	Teacher	Parent	Student	Parent	Student	
More												More
Average	X	X	X	X		X		X		X	X	Average
Fewer					X		X		X			Fewer

	Externalizing		Internalizing		Hyperactivity		
	Teacher	Parent	Teacher	Parent	Teacher	Parent	
More	X	X					More
Average			X	X	X	X	Average
Fewer							Fewer

SAMPLE:

Example of Fewer, Average, and More ratings

		MORE X
	AVERAGE X	
FEWER X		

PROBLEM BEHAVIORS

The SSRS Teacher and Parent Forms provide frequency ratings of potential **Problem Behaviors** in three areas at the elementary level and two areas at the preschool and secondary levels. These areas are:

Externalizing: behaviors involving verbal or physical aggression toward others, poor control of temper, and arguing

Internalizing: behaviors indicating anxiety, sadness, loneliness, and poor self-esteem

Hyperactivity: behaviors involving excessive movement, fidgeting, and impulsive reactions (elementary level only)

ACADEMIC COMPETENCE

The SSRS Teacher Forms also include a nine-item scale of **Academic Competence.** Ratings of reading, mathematics, motivation, and parental support are included in this scale.

Figure 13.4d Analysis of Social Behaviors, Page 4 of the *Assessment-Intervention Record,* Completed for Andrew

Analysis of Social Behaviors

Identifying Social Skills Strengths and Weaknesses and Interfering Problem Behaviors

The Standard Score Summary and the Graphic Profile Summary have enabled you to identify a student's overall strengths and weaknesses. Before planning interventions for these general weaknesses, an analysis of the behaviors represented by the items in the subscales is needed. This analysis should focus on those social skills that have been identified as general strengths ("more than") or general weaknesses ("fewer than"). **Importance** ratings, as well as **Frequency** ratings must be used for this analysis. You will need to examine the questionnaires to complete this analysis. A sample case identifying a student's strengths and weaknesses is given in Chapter 4 of the SSRS Manual.

Social Skills Strengths are defined by Frequency ratings of 2 and Importance ratings of 1 or 2.

Social Skills Performance Deficits are mild deficits and are defined by Frequency ratings of 1 and Importance ratings of 2.

Social Skills Acquisition Deficits are moderate to severe deficits and are defined by Frequency ratings of 0 and Importance ratings of 1 or 2.

Problem Behaviors are those behaviors of an externalizing, internalizing, or hyperactive nature that can interfere with the acquisition or performance of social skills. Any item on the Problem Behaviors subscales that receives a Frequency rating of 2 may suggest an interfering problem behavior.

Social Skills Strengths (Frequency = 2, Importance = 1 or 2) Review the SSRS questionnaires to identify items that characterize social skills strengths. Enter a brief description of the items in the appropriate section below. List one or two behaviors rated as strengths from each subscale if that subscale is rated "More." Remember, the subscales are designated: C = Cooperation, A = Assertion, R = Responsibility, E = Empathy, S = Self-Control.

	Teacher Form	Parent Form	Student Form
1	Puts materials away	Attends to speakers	Smiles, waves, nods to others
2	Joins ongoing activity	Volunteers to help with	Asks others before using things
3		tasks	Feels sorry when bad things
4		Answers phone correctly	happen
5		Completes household tasks	Does homework Acknowledges compliments

Comments on social skills strengths

Andrew is attentive to most academic tasks and seems to care about his schoolwork. He also is very involved with activities and needs no help in joining others to play or work. In many ways he has good leadership skills, but often gets upset if he doesn't get his way.

Figure 13.4e Analysis of Social Behaviors, Page 5 of the *Assessment-Intervention Record*, Completed for Andrew

Social Skills Performance Deficits **(Frequency = 1, Importance = 2)** Review the SSRS questionnaires to identify items that characterize social skills performance deficits. Enter a brief description of the items in the appropriate section below. If possible, list one or two behaviors rated as performance deficits from each subscale that has a Behavior Level of "Fewer."

	Teacher Form	Parent Form	Student Form
1	Controls temper with peers	Keeps room clean	Makes friends easily
2	Finishes within time limits	Responds when hit or pushed	Tells others when upset
3	Receives criticism well	Makes friends easily	Disagrees with adults without fighting
4	Uses time while waiting	Avoids trouble situations	Active in school activities
5	Responds when hit by others	Controls temper when arguing Reports accidents	Controls temper when people are angry at him

Comments on social skills performance deficits Control of temper with adults, learning to communicate when he's upset, and talking out problems need improvement.

Social Skills Acquisition Deficits **(Frequency = 0, Importance = 1 or 2)** Review the SSRS questionnaires to identify items that characterize social skills acquisition deficits. Enter a brief description of the items in the appropriate section below. If possible, list one or two behaviors rated as acquisition deficits from each subscale that has a Behavior Level of "Fewer."

	Teacher Form	Parent Form	Student Form
1	Responds to teasing by peers	Invites others to home	Ignores classmates
2	Compromises in conflict situations	Starts conversations	Tells new people name
3	Tells you when treated unfairly	Self-confident in situations	Asks friends to help with problems
4	Gives compliments		Talks over problems with classmates
5	Ignores distractions Controls temper with adults		

Comments on social skills acquisition deficits The most serious area concerns his control of his temper and his teasing of peers. Needs work on talking things out with his peers.

Problem Behaviors **(Frequency = 2)** Review the SSRS questionnaires to identify items that characterize problem behaviors. From those Behavior Levels rated "More," list in the appropriate section below all behaviors from each subscale that have a Frequency rating of 2. Remember, the subscales are designated as: E = Externalizing , I = Internalizing , H = Hyperactivity.

	Teacher Form	Parent Form
1	Threatens or bullies others	Threatens or bullies others
2	Talks back when corrected	Talks back to adults when corrected
3	Gets angry easily	
4	Is easily embarrassed	
5		

Comments on problem behaviors Consensus is that Andrew doesn't take criticism well and often is seen as threatening or bullying others when he doesn't get his way.

Figure 13.4f Summary of Additional Assessment Information, Page 6 of the *Assessment-Intervention Record,* Completed for Andrew

Summary of Additional Assessment Information

Use this page to summarize other assessments of this student.

Direct observations—school A 30-minute observation during Math & free time indicates 80% on task for math & appropriate behavior during free time. A 30-minute observation on playground indicates negative peer interactions: 2 name-calling incidents & 2 pushing situations where Andrew started it. Date 12-9-89

Direct observations—home No opportunity

Date

Sociometric measures not done

Date

Teacher interview None

Date

Parent interview None

Date

Student interview He acknowledges having a hard time getting along with 2 boys in his class. He recognizes that he has a "short temper" and probably argues more than he should. He doesn't think he has any academic problems. He likes school and his teacher. Date 12-10-89

Role plays He indicates he is aware of appropriate alternatives to pushing and arguing with peers who disagree with him. He shows he can walk away, express displeasure, and knows how to compromise. Date 12-10-89

Other behavior ratings Walker PBIC total score of 58; no scale scores indicative of serious problems, although Acting Out score of 64 and several behaviors identified by parents are a concern to teachers—see forms for details. Date 12-10-89

Achievement or cognitive measures No need to assess; doing well academically.

Date

Self-concept or self-efficacy measures Not assessed

Date

Previous intervention outcome data None

Date

Figure 13.4g Intervention Plan Summary, Page 8 of the *Assessment-Intervention Record,* Completed for Andrew

Intervention Plan Summary

In this section, summarize your intervention plans. Describe the desired outcome behaviors, the procedures for obtaining these behaviors, the materials and personnel involved, and the method of evaluating results. Each of these components of an Intervention Plan is discussed in Chapter 4 of the SSRS Manual.

Short-Term Objectives

Target behavior(s) (A) Respond appropriately to teasing (B) Control temper when peers disagree with him

Desired outcome behavior(s) (A) Politely acknowledge dislike of teasing by peers whenever teasing occurs. (B) Express his position and disagreement calmly without physical threats

Critical setting or situations for change At school, in class and on playground

Intervention Procedures

Procedure for maintaining strengths Reinforce cooperation/compliance involved in the completion of tasks (both academic and at home)

Procedure for promoting skill acquisition Use modeling with coaching and behavioral rehearsal to teach new ways of responding to teasing and controlling temper

Procedure for increasing skill performance Use verbal praise to reinforce Andrew when he appropriately responds to teasing, and for each day he doesn't lose his temper

Procedure for reducing problem behaviors Try DRO to reduce bullying; if he doesn't respond quickly use response cost or time-out

Procedure for facilitating generalization Involve parents by sending a note home weekly and implement a self-monitoring report card system

Intervention Resources

Reinforcers for target child (1) Free time on computers at school (2) Parent-provided weekly night out (3) comic books

Instructional or intervention materials No special materials needed

Intervention personnel School psychologist and playground monitor

Intervention Evaluation

Change in SSRS ratings Examine Self-Control ratings by Parents, Teachers, and Andrew himself after six to eight weeks

Mainstreamed-peer comparisons ______

Outcome interviews with significant adults In addition to parents and teachers, interview playground monitor and school psychologist

Intervention and Follow-up Evaluation Dates

Intervention begins 1-7-90 Intervention projected to end 3-15-90 Actual ending ______

Intervention evaluation completed ______ Re-evaluation of target behavior(s) ______

CHAPTER 14

Adaptive Behavior

The community of Guadalupe is located on the outskirts of Phoenix and Tempe in central Arizona. It is inhabited almost exclusively by Yaqui Indians who migrated from Mexico. For the most part, the residents live in poverty—many live in huts with dirt floors and have neither water nor electricity. Children growing up in Guadalupe often speak a mixture of Yaqui, Spanish, and English. Their cultural values encourage cooperation over competition and quality of work over speed of work. Because of economic pressures, many children drop out of school at the legal minimum age and begin working.

The culture and values of the residents of Guadalupe are quite different from those of the officials of the Tempe school district, in which Guadalupe is located. Not unlike many other suburban school systems, in the Tempe schools value is placed on achievement, timely completion of work, and preparation for college. Many middle-class children come to school knowing their English alphabet and numbers; many Guadalupe children lack these skills. Many of those who teach children from Guadalupe have White middle-class values and White middle-class expectations for their students.

When children deviate markedly from these expectations, there is a good chance they will be referred for psychological and educational evaluation.

In the early 1970s large numbers of Guadalupe children were failing in the Tempe classrooms, and referrals for special education were occurring at an alarming rate. Many of these children were diagnosed after taking standardized intelligence tests administered in English. These tests often contained items that require good facility with the English language or are timed. On the basis of the teachers' referral and the testing, many of the children were diagnosed as mentally disabled and placed in special education classrooms *even though many were reported to function quite normally in their home environment.* Upon learning of this, a group of concerned citizens in Guadalupe filed suit in federal court (*Guadalupe Organization v. Tempe Elementary School District,* 1972) and successfully barred the school district from continuing these practices. Numerous similar suits were filed in other parts of the country because children, primarily those from minority cultures, who functioned well outside of school were labeled as mentally disabled because of poor performance in school. One result of these suits was a broadening of the criteria used in schools for classifying mental disabilities. Instead of relying solely on in-school behavior and performance on the intelligence test, it was mandated that the evaluation of someone suspected of having a mental disability include an assessment of out-of-school behavior as well. This out-of-school behavior has been referred to as **adaptive behavior.**

What Is Adaptive Behavior?

Although the term applies to the behavior of children with a variety of disabilities (especially children with a behavioral disability), adaptive behavior is best understood within the context of defining a mental disability. The most commonly used definitions are those developed by the American Association of Mental Retardation (AAMR). Prior to the establishment of guidelines by the AAMR, which were formalized in 1959, mental disabilities were defined almost exclusively in terms of a score on an intelligence test. Individuals who scored significantly below were considered to have a mental disability. The AAMR definition of mental disabilities has gradually changed since first appearing in 1961 (Grossman, 1973, 1977, 1981; Heber, 1961), primarily in the use of a wider range of criteria for defining the condition. The 1961 definition broadened the previous definition based on testing. "Mental retardation refers to subaverage general intellectual functioning which originates during the developmental period and is associated with impairment in adaptive behavior" (Heber, 1961, p. 3). A subtle change in wording occurred in 1973: "Mental retardation refers to significantly subaverage general intellectual functioning existing concurrently with deficits in adaptive behavior, and manifested during the developmental period" (Grossman, 1973, p. 11). Although adaptive behavior is mentioned in both definitions, the latter made it quite clear that adaptive behavior must coexist. The 1981 AAMR definition (Grossman, 1981) suggested that mental retardation should be defined by means of a clinical process in which not only IQ but also adaptive behavior, social developmental history, and current functioning in a variety of settings are considered. Adaptive behavior thus became an integral component of the definition of a mental disability. In the most recent definition advanced by AAMR (AAMR, 1992), there has been a further deemphasis on intelligence tests and a corresponding increase in emphasis on adaptive behavior.

But exactly what is adaptive behavior? Several definitions have been offered, but perhaps the most widely accepted is the one advanced by the AAMR:

> Adaptive behavior is defined as the effectiveness or degree with which an individual meets the standards of personal independence and social responsibility expected for age and cultural group. Since these expectations of adaptive behavior vary for different age groups, deficits in adaptive behavior will vary at different ages. These may be reflected in the following areas.
>
> During infancy and early childhood in:
>
> 1. Sensory-motor skills development;
> 2. Communication skills (including speech and language);
> 3. Self-help skills;
> 4. Socialization (development of ability to interact with others); and
>
> During childhood and early adolescence in:
>
> 5. Application of basic academic skills in daily life activities;
> 6. Application of appropriate reasoning and judgment in mastery of environment;
> 7. Social skills (participation in group activities and interpersonal relationships); and
>
> During late adolescence and adult life in:
>
> 8. Vocational and social responsibilities and performances.
>
> The skills required for adaptation during childhood and early adolescence involve complex learning processes. This involves the process by which knowledge is acquired and retained as a function of the experiences of the individual. Difficulties in learning are usually manifested in the academic situation but in evaluation of adaptive behavior, attention should focus not only on the basic academic skills and their use, but also on skills essential to cope with the environment, including concepts of time and money, self-directed behaviors, social responsiveness, and interactive skills. (Grossman, 1977, pp. 11–14)

This definition has two important components. First, it suggests that adaptive behavior must be evaluated relative to the social context in which it occurs. Thus, such behavior is not an immutable property of the individual but instead differs from culture to culture. Second, an individual who behaves adaptively must exhibit skills consistent with his or her age. In younger children this requires the development of skills necessary for independent functioning (e.g., self-help and communication skills). Older children and adults must assume personal and social responsibility and maintain themselves independently, especially in an economic sense.

As noted, AAMR has recently developed new recommendations for the assessment of mental disabilities. The definition includes a marked elaboration of the concept of adaptive behavior. Specifically, the AAMR definition of a mental disability requires the assessment of 10 subareas of adaptive behavior (see table 14.1). Although adaptive behavior has been further delineated, evaluators who attempt to follow the lead of the AAMR will be faced with new problems, not the least of which is the lack of instruments to assess all 10 areas. This will likely mean that more than one instrument would be used to assess adaptive behavior and the comparison of subtests from different instruments has numerous technical problems.

Essentially the new AAMR definition of a mental disability requires that a person have subaverage intellectual functioning and deficits in two or more areas of adaptive skills. Given the high correlation between IQ scores and academic functioning, anyone who has a subaverage score on an IQ test will also almost certainly score low on a test of academic skills. Given that the new definition also considers subaverage intelligence to be an IQ score of less than 75, as compared with 70 in the old definition, it appears to be a definition that will allow more children to be classified.

Although the AAMR standards have never been legally binding on schools, they often do foreshadow changes in the law. Also, the standards are used frequently by school-based assessment specialists to justify actions surrounding classification and diagnosis of a mental disability. Hence, the standards merit a thorough understanding.

Reasons for Assessing Adaptive Behavior

Although now a routine part of school evaluation of a child who may have a mental disability, the assessment of adaptive behavior was uncommon in public schools 20 years ago. Adaptive behavior assessment is now included in evaluations for a number of reasons, and we will begin with the most important.

The Law Requires the Assessment of Adaptive Behavior

The delivery of services to disabled children has been significantly influenced by legislation and the courts. The area of adaptive behavior is no exception. The most obvious reason for the increase in adaptive behavior assessments is the numerous lawsuits filed on behalf of children who were diagnosed as having a mental disability even though they functioned adequately outside of the classroom. Certainly, the assessment of adaptive behavior is warranted on other grounds, but without the force of law, such assessment would be far

Table 14.1 Adaptive Behavior Subdomains of Functioning

1. Communication: Language development, inclusive of both nonsymbolic or preverbal and symbolic or verbal communication (speech, augmentative communication, and nonverbal symbolic communication such as manual signing or symbol use). Communicative skills include, for example, the ability to express oneself with or without the use of symbols and to communicate a request for an object or action, a greeting, a request for attention, a comment, a protest or rejection, an awareness of interrupted activity, attention to object or activity, and acceptance. Higher level skills in communication (e.g., writing a letter) would also relate to functional academics (see the following).
2. Self-Care: Skills involved in toileting, eating, dressing, hygiene, and grooming.
3. Home Living Skills: Skills related to functioning within a home, which include clothing care, housekeeping, yard maintenance, food preparation and cooking, planning and budgeting for shopping, home safety, and daily scheduling. Related skills include orientation and behavior in the home and nearby neighborhood, communication of choices and needs, social interaction, and application of functional academics in the home.
4. Social Skills: Skills related to social exchanges with other individuals, including initiating, interacting, and terminating interaction with others, receiving and responding to pertinent situational cues, recognizing feelings, providing positive and negative feedback, self-regulating one's own behavior, being aware of peers and peer acceptance, gauging the amount and type of interaction with others, assisting others, forming and fostering of friendships and love, coping with demands from others, making choices, sharing, understanding honesty and fairness, and displaying appropriate social-sexual behavior.
5. Community Use: Skills related to the use of community resources appropriately, including traveling in the community, grocery and general shopping at stores and markets, purchasing or obtaining services from other community businesses (gas stations, repair shops, doctor and dentist's offices, etc.), attending church, using public transportation and public facilities like schools, libraries, parks and recreational areas, and streets and sidewalks, and theaters and other cultural places and events. Related skills include behavior in the community, communication of choices and needs, social interaction, and the application of functional academics.
6. Self-Direction: Skills related to making choices, learning and following a schedule, initiating activities appropriate to the setting, conditions, schedule, and personal interests, completing necessary or required tasks, seeking assistance when needed, and resolving problems confronted in familiar and novel situations, and demonstrating appropriate assertiveness and self-advocacy skills.
7. Health and Safety: Skills related to maintenance of one's health in terms of eating, illness, identification, treatment and prevention, basic first aid, sexuality, physical fitness, basic safety, considerations (e.g., following rules and laws, use of seat belt, street crossing, interaction with strangers, seeking assistance), regular physical and dental checkups, and personal habits. Related skills include behavior in the community, communication of choices and needs, social interaction, and the application of functional academics.

continued

Table 14.1 ***Continued***

8. Functional Academics: Cognitive abilities and skills related to learning at school that also have direct application in one's life (e.g., writing, reading, basic practical math concepts, basic science as it relates to awareness of the physical environment and one's health and sexuality, geography, and social studies). It is important to note that the focus of this skill area is not on grade-level academic achievement but rather on the acquisition of academic skills that are functional in terms of independent living.
9. Leisure: The development of a variety of leisure and recreational interests (i.e., self-entertainment and interactional) that reflect personal preferences and choices and, if the activity will be conducted in public, that reflect age and cultural norms. Skills include choosing and self-initiating interests, using and enjoying home and community leisure and recreational activities alone and with others, playing socially with others, taking turns, terminating or refusing leisure or recreational activities, extending one's duration of participation, and expanding one's repertoire of interests, awareness and skills. Related skills include behaviors in the leisure and recreational setting, communication of choices and needs, social interaction, application of functional academics, and mobility skills.
10. Work: Skills related to holding a part- or full-time job or jobs in the community in terms of specific job skills, appropriate social behavior, and related work skills (e.g., completion of tasks; awareness of schedules; ability to seek assistance, take criticism, and improve skills; money management, financial resources allocation and the application of other functional academic skills; and skills related to going to and from work, preparation for work, management of oneself while at work, and interaction with coworkers).

From T. Oakland and D. Goldwater, "Assessment and Intervention for Mildly Retarded Children" in G. Phye and D. Reschly, *School Psychology: Perspectives and Issues,* p. 147. Copyright © 1979 Academic Press, Orlando, FL.

less common today. It would be easy to assume that court intervention in the educational system is an unwarranted intrusion and that educators know best how to assess and educate disabled children. However, in many instances, court decisions have taken what was simply good educational practice and made it the law.

The *Guadalupe* case provides an illustration. The apparent practice in the Tempe schools in the early 1970s was to administer highly verbal intelligence tests in English to children whose primary language was not English. The scores derived from these tests were a major determinant in whether the child was diagnosed as having a deficit in intellectual functioning, even if that child seemed normal to people in his or her community. The plaintiffs in *Guadalupe* argued that school assessment practices were inappropriate. The court agreed and required the assessment of adaptive behavior outside of school as well. Further, the court stipulated that results of intelligence tests could not be the sole basis for classifying children as having a mental disability. From the perspective of a professional psychologist or educator, it is difficult to disagree with the court's ruling because it is consistent with good educational practice!

As cases similar to *Guadalupe* became more numerous, the assessment of adaptive behavior was incorporated into more and more federal and state legislation governing the education of disabled children. Perhaps the most important of these developments was that the assessment of adaptive behavior was incorporated into the Education for All Handicapped Children Act of 1975, P.L. 94–142 and, more recently, the Individuals with Disabilities Education Act (IDEA). The bottom line is that individuals who assess children who might be classified as mentally disabled under IDEA must incorporate an index of adaptive behavior into the assessment process.

Reduction of Bias in Assessment Processes

It is incumbent on professionals who collect and utilize test data to be as fair as possible when identifying a child with a deficit in intellectual functioning. The problems are compounded when evaluating a child from a minority culture. In many cases the content of some tests is especially difficult for such children, even though, as we have stated, the tests are unbiased. Often language problems, cultural differences, and economic factors contribute to differences among racial and ethnic groups. Including a measure of adaptive behavior in the assessment process can help differentiate children whose cultural differences account for low IQ scores. Adaptive behavior is, by definition, the ability to perform in line with *cultural* expectations. *Every* normally functioning 6-year-old can reasonably be expected to take care of his or her self-care needs. However, whether the same child knows which animal gives milk or what skis are depends on a number of sociocultural factors.

Assessment Provides Information on What Skills Need to Be Taught

Intelligence tests can be used for classification and diagnostic decisions, but they are much less useful in providing a parent or teacher with information about *what* to teach. On the other hand, most adaptive behavior scales are composed of checklists or ratings, and respondents indicate whether a child can or cannot perform or how well she or he performs a particular skill. A typical item might assess the extent to which a child is capable of getting dressed without assistance. Perhaps the child can put the clothing on but cannot button buttons or snap snaps. Logically, performing these skills will be appropriate educational goals.

A slightly different approach is to view the age-appropriate skills on a measure of adaptive behavior as goals that must be accomplished before a child can be integrated into the community at a level consistent with societal expectations. Some measures of adaptive behavior provide lists of directly teachable behaviors.

Measures of Adaptive Behavior

The selection of an adaptive behavior assessment instrument that is appropriate for a given child in a specific situation requires careful study. However, few of the scales measure all components of adaptive behavior and some are appropriate only for certain ages. Well over a hundred such instruments are available. We will describe a small sample of what we consider to be the most important. A slightly wider selection is profiled in table 14.2.

Vineland Adaptive Behavior Scales

Overview and Purpose

The purpose of the Vineland Adaptive Behavior Scales (Sparrow, Balla, & Cicchetti, 1984) (VABS) is to assess disabled and nondisabled individuals from birth to adulthood in four behavior domains: Communication, Daily Living, Socialization, and Motor Skills. Three versions of the scales exist, including the Survey Form, which has 297 items; the Expanded Form, which has 577 items; and the classroom edition, which has 244 items. Administration requires that someone familiar with the child be interviewed. The technical information pertaining to the VABS pertains primarily to the Survey Form.

Standardization Sample and Norms

The VABS was standardized on 3,000 individuals ranging in age from birth to 18 years, 11 months. The stratification of the sample is very good with respect to all major demographic variables, including age, geographic region, parental education, race or ethnic group, community size, and educational placement.

Norms are provided in a number of different forms for a wide variety of populations. A useful feature is that standard score equivalents are available for the raw scores for each behavior domain and for overall functioning. This latter score, the Adaptive Behavior Composite Standard, has a mean of 100 and a standard deviation of 15, thus facilitating comparisons with intelligence tests. Other available norms include percentile ranks and stanines, age equivalent scores, and maladaptive level scores for the optional Maladaptive Behavior domain. Supplemental norms are provided for comparison of older individuals up to age 40 as well as those who are emotionally disturbed, hearing impaired, and visually impaired.

Data Obtained

The VABS yields scores for the Communication domain (including subdomain scores for Receptive, Expressive, and Written Language), the Daily Living domain (including subdomain scores for Personal, Domestic, and Community Living), the Socialization domain (including subdomain scores for Interpersonal Relationships, Play and Leisure Time, and Coping Skills), and the Motor Skills domain (including subdomain scores for Gross and Fine

Table 14.2 Measures of Adaptive Behavior

Instrument	Behavior Assessed: Physical Developmental Sensory Motor and Locomotion	Self-Direction	Language and Communication	Vocational and Occupation	Economic	Social	Self-Help, Independent Functioning, and Self-Maintenance	Behavioral Environment: With Peers	in School	In the Family	In the Community	Mixed	Population Type and Size: Age Range	Clinical	School	Purpose: Screening	Placement	Programming	Examiner: Teacher	Diagnostician	Paraprofessional	Respondent: Teacher	Parent/Family	Child	Reliability and Validity: Data Available	Scores: Percentile	Scaled Score	Administration Time
AAMD Adaptive Behavior Scale-School Edition (Lambert & Windmiller, 1981)	x	x	x	x	x	x	x				x		3–17		x		x	x	x	x	x	x	x		Yes	x	x	45 minutes to 1 hour
Adaptive Behavior Inventory for Children (Mercer & Lewis, 1978)				x	x	x	x	x	x	x	x		5–11		x		x			x	x		x		Yes	x	x	1 hour
Camelot (Foster, 1974)	x	x	x	x	x	x	x						2–adult	x		x	x	x	x	x	x	x	x		Yes			1 hour
Children's Adaptive Behavior Scale (Richmond & Kicklighter, 1980)		x	x	x	x	x	x						5–10		x	x	x			x				x	Yes	x		30 minutes
Social and Prevocational Information Battery		x	x	x	x	x	x						junior–senior high school	x		x	x	x	x		x			x	Yes	x		1–2 hours
Vineland Adaptive Behavior Scale (Sparrow et al., 1984)		x	x	x	x	x	x						birth–18 yr. 11 mo.	x	x		x				x	x	x		Yes			20 minutes

From T. Oakland and D. Goldwater, "Assessment and Intervention for Mildly Retarded Children" in G. Phye and D. Reschly, SCHOOL PSYCHOLOGY: PERSPECTIVES AND ISSUES, p. 147. Copyright © 1979 Academic Press, Orlando, FL.

Motor Skills). The Adaptive Behavior Composite Standard is based on functioning in each of the four behavior domains and reflects overall adaptive behavior. The Maladaptive Behavior domain indicates the extent to which the frequency of someone's inappropriate behavior is significantly different from that of the normative group.

Reliability and Validity

Reliability of the VABS appears to be adequate for the four behavior domains and poor to adequate for the subdomains. Median split-half reliability coefficients across ages ranged from .83 for the Motor Skills domain to .90 for the Daily Living domain. Interrater reliability for the domains were lower and ranged from .62 to .78. The reliability of the subdomains is very questionable for some age groups.

Validity data are somewhat sparse. Existing data do suggest the instrument is moderately correlated with other adaptive behavior scales and predictably has relatively low correlations with intelligence tests. A large number of validation studies will no doubt appear over the next few years.

Summary

The VABS is one of the better adaptive behavior tests available. Its psychometric properties are as good or better than those of any other instrument. In addition, it is one of the more useful instruments for making intervention programming decisions.

Social and Prevocational Information Battery

Overview and Purpose

A variety of tests assess the adaptive behavior of children who are 12 years old and younger. However, the range of instruments that assess someone who is in junior or senior high school is much more limited. The Social and Prevocational Information Battery, or SPIB (Halpern, Raffeld, Irvin, & Link, 1975), is one of the most comprehensive scales available for adolescents.

Although it is not billed as an adaptive behavior scale, the SPIB attempts to comprehensively assess the skills needed to develop personal and social responsibility. More specifically, it is designed to assess five areas widely regarded as central to the community adjustment of students with mild mental disabilities.

1. *Economic Self-Sufficiency.* Tests in this domain measure a student's skills in banking, budgeting, and purchasing. Individual items focus on understanding money, establishing a checking account, and paying bills.
2. *Employability.* This section contains items that assess job-related behaviors and job-search skills. The job-related behaviors include how to get along with a boss, how to ask for help, and how to interact with the public. Job-search skills such as completing employment applications and interviewing are also assessed.

3. *Family Living.* This area measures skills related to home management and physical health. A student is questioned about putting out accidental fires, washing clothing, and handling minor illnesses and injuries.
4. *Personal.* This domain assesses knowledge of personal hygiene and grooming, such as showering and changing clothing.
5. *Communications.* This domain exclusively tests the ability to read and interpret functional signs such as ENTER, EXIT, MEN, and POISON.

The SPIB contains a total of 277 items, which are orally administered to one or more students who mark their responses on answer sheets. Because the response format is true-false or picture selection, students are not penalized for reading difficulties. Testing requires three sessions (preferably on separate days) lasting approximately one hour each. The directions for administering the SPIB are highly structured and well organized.

Standardization Sample and Norms

The SPIB was standardized on a sample of 906 junior and senior high school students, stratified according to school size and geographic region. Unfortunately, the entire sample was taken from Oregon. The students were all diagnosed as mildly mentally disabled (mean IQ = 68) and ranged in age from 14 to 20 years. The test manual indicates that the majority of the sample group was Caucasian but does not provide actual numbers of various ethnic groups. Separate norms are provided for students in junior high (grades 7 to 9) and senior high (grades 10 to 12). Since the reference group was entirely diagnosed as mildly mentally disabled students, a student who scores at the 50th percentile is average with respect to the norm group and *not* with respect to the general population.

Data Obtained

By using the norms, raw scores can be converted into percentiles for each of the major areas measured by the SPIB.

Reliability and Validity

Two forms of reliability data are reported for the SPIB: internal consistency and test-retest. For both types, reliability was in the mid-.80s for total test scores. Such figures are good for the total test score.

Several types of validity data are discussed in the manual. Predictive validity was examined by comparing the scores of graduating seniors with counselor ratings of the students one year later. The results of this comparison suggested that the SPIB predicts community adjustment reasonably well. Correlations between the SPIB and IQ scores from both the WISC indicated a moderate positive relationship.

Correlations between individual subtests on the SPIB and Full-Scale IQ scores ranged from .37 to .51, with a median of .49. This suggests that whatever the SPIB is measuring is somewhat similar to what IQ tests measure; in part this is to be expected, for the positive adaptive behavior of adolescents with mild mental disabilities does require some of the skills measured by intelligence tests.

Summary

The SPIB is designed to assess skills associated with the ultimate community adjustment of junior and senior high school students. It is one of the few useful measures of the adaptive behavior of adolescents, for predictive validity data suggest the instrument does adequately predict personal and social adjustment in a community setting.

Adaptive Behavior Inventory for Children

Overview and Purpose

It is important to know that the Adaptive Behavior Inventory for Children (ABIC) was developed by a sociologist, Jane Mercer, and her colleagues (Mercer & Lewis, 1978). Her socioecological perspective is that a child's adaptive behavior can be evaluated only in relationship to the role expectations of the family, the community, the peer group, the school, and the economy and self-maintenance roles. The ABIC is an outgrowth of the research by Mercer and others into the processes used to diagnose individuals as having a mild mental disability (Mercer, 1970). Because she concluded from her data that available tests inadequately measured adaptive behavior, she developed a comprehensive assessment system—the System of Multicultural Pluralistic Assessment (SOMPA)—of which the ABIC is an integral part.

The ABIC can be best understood by reference to the unique rhetoric of Mercer (1979):

> Adaptive behavior is conceptualized as achieving an adaptive fit in social systems through the development of interpersonal ties and the acquisition of specific skills required to fulfill the task functions associated with particular roles. . . . The preschool child's experience is limited mainly to the family and neighborhood. Therefore, questions in the ABIC for young children are concerned mainly with roles in the family and in the immediate neighborhood and peer group. As the child moves into the social system of the school, there are questions concerning performance in nonacademic school roles and interaction with peers at schools. . . . As the child grows older, the child assumes more community roles, ranges over a larger geographic territory, learns to function in earner and consumer roles, and assumes greater responsibility for protection of his or her own health and welfare. The developmental sequencing is reflected in the sequencing of ABIC items. (p. 93)

The ABIC consists of 242 questions that are administered in an interview to either a caretaker who knows the child well or, preferably, a parent. It yields scores for six scales: Family, Community, Peer Relations, Nonacademic

School Roles, Earner/Consumer, and Self-Maintenance. Optimally, the interview takes place in the child's home and is conducted by someone with whom the parent or other caretaker is comfortable. Thus, interviewers are instructed to wear simple clothing that is similar to that worn by those in the same social class as the parent or caretaker. The interview should also be conducted in the primary language of the home. School districts that use the ABIC often find it useful to train paraprofessionals who already fit into a particular social system in the administration of the SOMPA.

Items are structured to assess the *frequency* with which a child performs certain activities. A typical item in terms of format and degree of vagueness of wording is: "Does [name of child] take telephone and other messages correctly and give them to the right person? 1. Sometimes; 2. Regularly; or 3. Never." Respondents are repeatedly asked to distinguish between words such as *sometimes, often, occasionally,* and *frequently.* Since these words may have different meanings to various respondents, the significance of the test results is also called into question. Another problem is that the interviewer must read *all* items appropriate for a child's age, even if the answer is known before the question is asked. Thus, an interviewer sitting in a house with a dirt floor, no electricity, and no running water may feel uncomfortable asking the parent about the child's television habits when obviously there is no television in the home.

Standardization Sample and Norms

The ABIC was standardized on a stratified random sample of 2,085 California schoolchildren. The sample was stratified according to age, gender, ethnic group (there were equal numbers of Whites, Blacks, and Hispanics), and community size. Sample selection appears to have been more carefully conducted than for the other measures of adaptive behavior.

Norms are provided for children aged 5 years, 0 months to 11 years, 11 months. This age span was divided into three-month intervals, with separate norm tables provided for each. The norms are used to convert raw scores into scaled scores for each of the six areas assessed by the ABIC.

Data Obtained

Scoring procedures for the ABIC contain some built-in safeguards to help ensure its validity. The most prominent of these is a Veracity Scale, which contains 24 items that involve activities performed only by older adolescents and would not be at all typical of the 5- to 11-year-old children for whom the ABIC is designed. The validity of a child's scores are questioned if high scores are obtained on too many of these high-level skills. The number of times the respondent answered "don't know" to questions represents another validity check. It is assumed that too many responses of this type suggest that the respondent doesn't know the child well enough to give reliable results!

Raw scores for each of the six scales of the ABIC are converted to scaled scores, which correspond closely to percentiles. A more global indicator of adaptive functioning can be obtained by simply averaging the six scaled scores. The primary use for data obtained from the ABIC is to assist in classification decisions.

Reliability and Validity

Two types of reliability data are available for the ABIC. First, the split-half procedure was utilized to assess reliability using the entire standardization sample. This analysis indicated that reliability was generally above .75 for the six scales and above .95 for the Average Scaled Score across all age groups for which the instrument is appropriate.

Second, the interrater agreement between individuals who heard the same interview was measured at workshops designed to train people to use the ABIC. Near the end of the training, workshop participants listened to an interview conducted by the instructor. Each participant scored the interview independently, and the degree to which the scores differed was assessed. Across a series of 10 such interviews, with different parents and in different communities, there was very high interobserver agreement. The technical manual for the ABIC contains little information relevant to its validity. In fact, Mercer (1979) states that traditional psychometric methods are inappropriate for the validation to the ABIC:

> For example, it would not be logical to validate the mother's report of the child's performance in the peer group with the teacher's report of peer group performance since neither the mother nor the teacher are members of the peer group. Likewise, it would be even less defensible to "validate" the mother's report of the child's family role performance against the teacher's responses to the questions in the Family Scale. The validity of the ABIC is judged by its ability to reflect accurately the extent to which the child is meeting the expectations of the members of the social systems covered in the scales, not by its correlation with teacher judgments, school performance, or performance on measures of achievement tests, aptitude tests, or "intelligence" tests. (p. 109)

Just how to assess whether the ABIC actually reflects the degree to which the child is meeting societal expectations is not known. Lacking such a methodology, other researchers have applied more traditional psychometric criteria to the test (Oakland, 1979). Their research suggests that the correlation between cores on the ABIC and either intelligence tests or achievement tests is so low as to indicate that the ABIC is relatively independent of either intelligence or achievement. This suggests that the ABIC cannot be used in predicting progress in school. Mercer would probably not be surprised by this finding, given that the purpose of the ABIC is to predict acceptance by a social system rather than success in school. Currently, we know of no research indicating how the ABIC is related to other adaptive behavior instruments.

Because of the lack of research on the ABIC, it is impossible to determine exactly what the instrument is measuring. Studies do suggest what it is not measuring (intelligence and school achievement). Until whether it measures some aspect of adaptive behavior that would be useful in schools can be established, its use for this purpose is highly suspect.

Summary

The ABIC was designed from a socioecological perspective to try to improve the process of diagnosing children with mild mental disabilities in elementary school children. Because its primary purpose is as a diagnostic instrument, the ABIC is less useful for developing educational plans. However, given the lack of suitable validity data, its use even for diagnostic purposes is questionable. The ABIC has the potential to be a very useful addition to the list of measures for assessing adaptive behavior, but full potential of this instrument must await additional research.

Children's Adaptive Behavior Scale

Overview and Purpose

Unlike most other measures of adaptive behavior, the Children's Adaptive Behavior Scale, or CABS (Richmond & Kicklighter, 1980), is designed to assess *directly* a child's ability to perform adaptively. Administration of the CABS is similar to the procedure used with individually administered intelligence tests in that the "testing" is conducted by a qualified examiner in a one-to-one setting. During the process the child is asked to perform various tasks and to respond to questions in five major domains:

1. *Language Development.* This area assesses "socially essential, rather than desirable, levels of development" (Richmond & Kicklighter, 1980, p. 5). Although its primary focus is oral expressive language (e.g., the child is asked to name something that can be eaten), some items require the child to read and write.
2. *Independent Functioning.* This domain attempts to measure the extent to which a child can assume responsibility for tasks encountered daily during normal living. Children are asked questions such as, "Why should you brush your teeth?"
3. *Family Role Performance.* This area assesses how well a child is capable of coping with the normal demands of a home environment. Items focus on the family ("How many people are in your family?") and duties usually performed at home (e.g., "Tell me two ways to cook an egg.").
4. *Economic-Vocational Activity.* This area assesses knowledge of working, earning, and spending. A majority of the items pertain to money concepts, money usage ("About how much does a small can of Coke cost?"), and vocational concepts ("Where does a nurse usually work?").
5. *Socialization.* This domain assesses the degree to which a child interacts appropriately with others.

The CABS is designed to be used with children from 5 to 10 years of age. Since the instrument is directly administered, third-party interviews are not required. This may be an advantage, especially in the light of indications that the information elicited from a third party may be subject to bias (Coulter & Morrow, 1978). Administration requires approximately 30 minutes, which is considerably less than is needed for many other measures of adaptive behavior.

Standardization Sample and Norms

The standardization group for the CABS consisted of only 250 mildly mentally disabled children in South Carolina and Georgia. Norms were included at each age level. Although the authors indicate that the test is appropriate for children 5 years of age, no 5-year-olds were included in the sample.

Because the standardization inadequately represents the national population, the authors recommend that users construct local norms. A possible source of confusion in the use of the norms is that they are referenced to a group of children with mild mental disability. The instrument is interpreted by comparing an individual's domain scores with the age norms for the reference group. If there is close correspondence between the child and the reference group, the child is presumed to display adaptive behavior consistent with a diagnosis of mild mental disability. Unfortunately, it is unclear just how close to the norms a child must be for this diagnosis. Likewise, it is not clear how far above the mean for mildly mentally disabled children a child must be for his or her adaptive behavior to be considered inconsistent with such a diagnosis.

Data Obtained

The data obtained from the CABS are in the form of age-equivalent scores for each of the five major domains. The authors indicate that the domains are relatively independent and suggest using five domain scores diagnostically. Thus, they recommend that a child who scores well in the Socialization domain but performs poorly on the Language domain may be a candidate for language programming. This practice, however, is fraught with the difficulties discussed in chapter 2.

Reliability and Validity

Internal consistency reliability coefficients were reported for a sample of 250 mildly mentally disabled children and ranged from a low of .63 for Language Development and Socialization to a high of .83 for Independent Functioning. Reliability coefficients in this range suggest that using the CABS for making important decisions is a questionable practice.

Although the CABS is designed to reflect adaptive behavior, there is some question of whether it may be more highly associated with intelligence than is desirable and to a greater degree than other measures of such behavior. Part of the problem is that because with the CABS a child is evaluated in a one-to-one setting, we must *infer* that behavior in that setting reflects how the child actually performs outside the testing situation. For example, many items on the CABS assess whether a child *knows* how to perform under given circumstances. It is thus assumed that there is a correspondence between knowing and *doing*. However, it is possible, and in fact probable, that such a relationship does not exist in many instances.

Correlations between the CABS total score and the Wechsler Intelligence Scale for Children-Revised (WISC-R; Wechsler, 1974) are .57 for Verbal IQ, .33 for Performance IQ, and .51 for Full-Scale IQ. This would suggest the CABS has a relatively strong relationship to assessed aptitude, especially verbal aptitude. Such a relationship has disturbing implications. Recall that a primary reason for assessing adaptive behavior is to prevent children with language problems from being inappropriately labeled as having a mild mental disability. With the verbal format of the CABS, however, the true adaptive functioning of children with poor language skills may be markedly underestimated. Contrast this with the ABIC, which has near-zero correlations with IQ test scores (Mercer & Lewis, 1978).

Additional evidence that the CABS is measuring something different from other measures of adaptive behavior is that the correlations between CABS and other instruments are low to moderate; the test authors reported that such correlations were statistically significant in 42 of 60 possible comparisons. However, most of these correlations were below .40, suggesting the two instruments are not highly related.

Summary

The CABS is unique in being a *direct* measure of adaptive functioning in children. However, because of sketchy reliability data and validity studies that suggest moderate correlations with verbal IQ test scores, the CABS should be used only in conjunction with measures of adaptive behavior that rely on third-party interviews. In such cases the CABS can broaden the range of skills examined in a comprehensive assessment of adaptive behavior.

Problems and Issues in the Assessment of Adaptive Behavior

The strong need to assess adaptive behavior that arose during the early 1970s resulted in the proliferation of well over 100 scales and checklists (Meyers, Nihira, & Zetlin, 1979), some of which have been reviewed here. With this new technology came the inevitable need to evaluate the effects of more than a decade of research and practice. Thus, we conclude our discussion of adaptive behavior by reviewing two of the most important issues that have evolved in the assessment of adaptive behavior.

Declassification of Students

The most pressing practical problem that has resulted from the use of adaptive behavior instruments is that some children who once qualified for special education placement because of a mild mental disability are no longer eligible. Before we began assessing adaptive behavior, children needed markedly low scores on *only* intelligence tests to be placed in special programs. Now they need low scores on both intelligence tests and measures of adaptive behavior, which is less likely to occur. The declassification of students that may result can produce exceedingly difficult situations. For example, a multidisciplinary team may learn that a particular child has an IQ test score of 69, which is consistent with a diagnosis of mild mental disability, but has scored in the normal range on an adaptive behavior scale. If the IQ test score is at all predictive of functioning, the child will have difficulty succeeding in school. However, since the child has normal adaptive behavior, a diagnosis of mild mental disability may be contrary to state laws and regulations governing disabled children.

One possible outcome for a child who performs consistent with a diagnosis of mild mental disability on a measure of intelligence but who has average adaptive behavior is that no special education is provided at all. This is perhaps the most conservative legal option available. An alternative is to ignore the information concerning adaptive behavior and place the child in a special education program. Perhaps the most satisfying option is to develop and provide alternate programming for children who are comprehensively disabled rather than those who have difficulty only at school. Unfortunately, such alternatives are not widely available.

It is ironic that the declassification issue arose because of "do-gooders" on one side who wanted to provide special education services to children with mild mental disabilities and "do-gooders" on the other side who wanted to prevent abuses such as "the six-hour retarded child" (i.e., a child who is considered to have a mental disability for the six hours spent at school but functions well outside of school in his or her home and community—see President's Committee on Mental Retardation, 1970). This issue exemplifies the type of legalistic game-playing that is unfortunately all too common in current special education practice. This "hardening of the categories" often prevents the provision of services to children who really need them. The real culprit here is the education system—those administrators and school boards who believe that children must be diagnosed before receiving services. However, if children who function poorly in school can be offered a continuum of special services, there would be no need to debate the diagnosis of a particular child. Instead, the debate would center around what type of services to provide.

Relationship Between Adaptive Behavior and Intelligence

What is the optimal relationship between instruments that measure adaptive behavior and those that assess intelligence? Should there be a strong relationship or no relationship at all? Do adaptive behavior instruments actually measure some construct that everyone agrees is adaptive behavior? The answers to these questions are anything but straightforward. The problem is compounded

Focus on Practice

Declassification—A Suggestion from Dan Reschly

How adaptive behavior is conceptualized and measured along with the available special education service options will have a significant influence on the classification/placement decisions that are made. I suggest that the adaptive behavior dimension for school-age children be conceptualized as two separate components. One component should involve performance in the public school setting with primary emphasis on academic achievement in the classroom. The other component should be role performance in social systems outside of the public school such as the home, neighborhood, and community. Separating the adaptive behavior dimensions into two components is advisable because recently published data suggest that adaptive behavior in academic settings and social role performance outside of school are largely unrelated for many students. . . .

The different combinations of adaptive behavior and intelligence have implications for classification and placement decisions. Adaptive Behavior-School (AB-S) should be based on a complete educational evaluation including observation in the classroom, examination of samples of daily work, teacher interview, and the results of individually administered standardized achievement tests. Adaptive Behavior-Outside School (AB-OS) should be based on information from formal inventories . . . or informal data collection procedures.

Of particular interest are the children who exhibit the pattern of very low intelligence, very low AB-S, and normal AB-OS. A major current dilemma is whether these children should be classified and placed in special education programs. Such children are "six-hour retarded children" almost by definition. If they are classified and placed in special education programs, we will almost inevitably overrepresent minority children. In my view these children should be served in special education programs in most instances because they do, in fact, have extreme educational needs that are typically beyond the scope of regular classroom instruction. The solution of "delabelling" these children doe not address these needs. However, the segregated special class for the mildly mentally disabled, which has often been the placement used because in many cases it was the only alternative, is an equally inappropriate solution.

Defining the classification system would be beneficial in resolving this dilemma. The terms *comprehensive* and *quasi* are probably as objectionable as the term *mental retardation*. Using terms like *educational retardation, educationally handicapped,* or some other term that is as behaviorally descriptive as possible of the quasi-retarded pattern would be preferable. Greater refinement in the classification system is useful only if there are implications for placement decisions and educational programming. The change suggested may have such implications.

continued

Focus on Practice—*continued*

The "quasi-retarded" do need special services. However, if special education services are to be provided, the objectives should be oriented toward specific academic needs rather than broad social competencies. In most instances the resource program involving remedial and compensatory tutorial services is a more appropriate option rather than the special class. Special class programs for the mildly retarded have traditionally placed considerable emphasis on broadly defined social competencies and "functional" academic skills (O. Kolstoe, 1976, *Teaching Educable Mentally Retarded Children,* 2nd ed., New York: Holt, Rinehart and Winston). This emphasis is clearly appropriate for the comprehensively disabled but is probably misdirected for most of the quasi-retarded. With few exceptions the quasi-disabled, if placed in special education, should be placed in resource programs.

Using the resource option for the quasi-retarded would alleviate many of the concerns expressed by federal district courts in the placement litigation. This amount of time spent outside of the educational mainstream is minimized by the resource option, thus reducing the very proper concern about racial segregation. Placement in the resource option regardless of classification used may have the additional advantage of being less stigmatizing. Analysis of outcome data must, of course, be the ultimate criteria against which this or any other classification/placement system must be validated.

The following flowchart summarizes Reschly's recommended approach to assessing adaptive behavior and making classification and instructional placement decisions.

because both intelligence and adaptive behavior are hypothetical constructs that are difficult to measure. We will approach this issue of how the two constructs are related by examining first how they are different and then how they are alike.

There are several differences between instruments that assess adaptive behavior and those that assess intelligence. First, adaptive behavior scales are most concerned with everyday behaviors, whereas intelligence tests seek to reflect thinking processes. Because of this, adaptive behavior instruments tend to focus on common or typical behaviors and intelligence tests are concerned primarily with a child's potential. Thus, intelligence tests assess verbal and quantitative learning and higher-order thinking skills, whereas adaptive behavior instruments reflect the degree to which a child can adapt to environmental demands. In sum, IQ scores are secured by a process that samples the child's best possible performance and that interprets the results through a trait system, with a presumption of stability in the obtained scores. That is, a

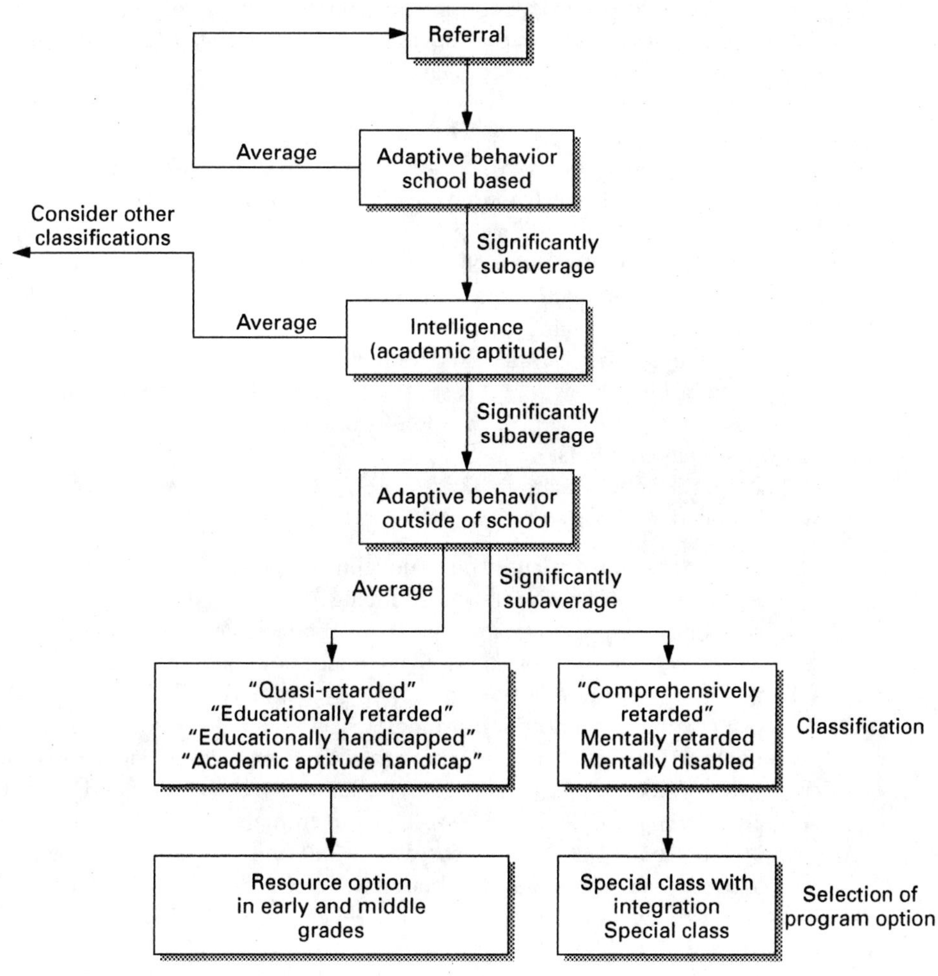

From "Assessing Mild Mental Retardation: The Influence of Adaptive Behavior, Sociocultural Status and Prospects for Nonbiased Assessment" by D. J. Reschly in THE HANDBOOK OF SCHOOL PSYCHOLOGY (pp. 209–242) by C. R. Reynolds and T. B. Gutkin (eds.) Copyright © 1982 John Wiley and Sons, Inc. Reprinted by permission of John Wiley and Sons, Inc.

child's behavior during test administration is assumed to be reflective of enduring traits, an assumption that is weakened by the actual variability of students' behavior in the same testing situations across time and measures. In contrast, adaptive behavior scales secure descriptions of everyday adaptations without necessarily determining best possible performances; in some scales, little or no regard for trait inference is intended. Further, the data on adaptive behavior measurement deny any unitary or general factor (Meyers et al., 1979, p. 434).

Despite the difference between instruments that assess adaptive behavior and intelligence, some adaptive behavior scales have very high correlations (up to .83) with intelligence tests. Thus, one would expect the constructs to be somewhat similar. In one review, adaptive behavior/IQ correlations ranged from a low of .09 for the ABIC to a high of .83 for the old Vineland Social Maturity Scale (Doll, 1965). Such a wide range of correlations results from the types of skills measured by various adaptive behavior instruments and the manner in which they are measured. Scales with a preponderance of items that assess communication skills and cognitive development generally have higher correlations with IQ tests than those that focus on self-help skills and independent functioning. Likewise, adaptive behavior instruments that are directly administered to the child rather than to a third-party informant have higher correlations with IQ tests because the format of the items, the skills assessed, and the method of administration more closely approximate those on IQ measurements.

What should be the relationship between IQ and adaptive behavior? This answer has been summarized by Lambert and Windmiller (1981):

> There is an obvious relationship between adaptive behavior and intelligence. Children with higher levels of intelligence generally learn to perform independent skills sooner, are able to assume greater responsibility, and have a greater capacity for social adjustment than children with lower levels. Yet, it is also true that there are mentally retarded and developmentally delayed children who do not have high levels of intelligence but who show potential for high levels of adaptive behavior. Such a discrepancy indicates that low to moderate correlations between adaptive behavior and intellectual functioning would be expected. An instrument designed to measure adaptive behavior should yield scores that indicate it assesses a dimension or construct that is separate from but related to intelligence since both measures provide evidence of psychological development. (p. 75)

Chapter Summary

Our review of adaptive behavior has summarized the major factors influencing assessment theory and practice in this area. However, several major issues were not resolved. For example, what is adaptive behavior? What is the *best* way to assess it? Are there reliable instruments for measuring adaptive behavior? What do we do with the declassified child? We will be better able to address these questions as research continues to accumulate.

Currently, however, measurement of adaptive behavior is difficult at best. Because of the fluctuations in children's everyday adaptations, it may not be possible to develop a measure that will predict adaptive behaviors across situations and time; however, it is possible to ensure that those measures that are constructed have a truly representative norm sample and high internal consistency. Furthermore, those who use measures of adaptive behavior must be sure that they select those instruments that are in the best interest of children.

Chapter 15

Perceptual-Motor Skills and Abilities

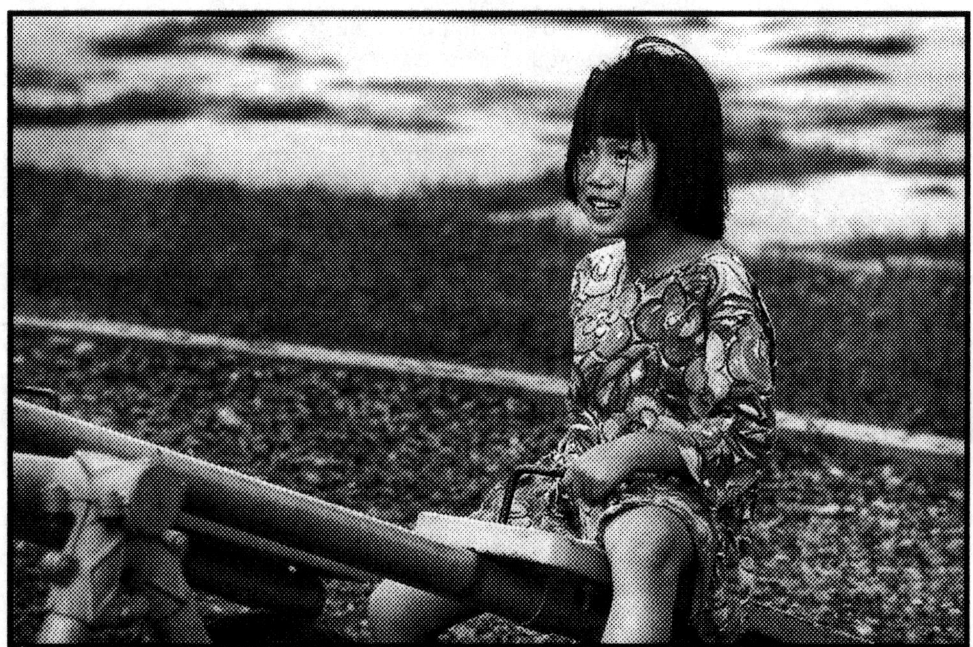

Perceptual-motor skills are viewed by many persons as being important prerequisites to the acquisition and performance of academic skills. These skills are termed *perceptual* because they involve the attention to and interpretation of information gained from the senses (e.g., vision, hearing, touch, etc.). These skills are called *motor* because they involve the execution of physical movements involved in the performance of either fine motor (writing, drawing, etc.) or gross motor (e.g., walking, skipping, jumping, etc.) behaviors. An individual's ability to translate perceptual information into motor responses is known as **perceptual-motor integration.**

Children who perform poorly on tests of perceptual-motor skills are sometimes labeled as having a "perceptual-motor dysfunction" and are placed in specialized curricula designed to remediate these dysfunctions. As such, some educational programs focus on teaching or remediating perceptual-motor skills rather than academic deficits.

The practice of teaching perceptual-motor skills, or what is called **perceptual-motor training,** is questionable given that research has not shown that such training is effective in enhancing basic academic skills (Kavale & Mattison, 1982; Myers & Hammill, 1982). It appears from a careful review of the literature that improving a child's performance on perceptual-motor tests may improve perceptual-motor functioning, but it does not improve reading, arithmetic, or language skills. This holds true regardless of the child's characteristics (e.g., sex, race, and socioeconomic status), the types of perceptual-motor programs used, the grade levels trained, or the quality of the research designed to investigate perceptual-motor training programs (Kavale & Mattison, 1982).

Another use of perceptual-motor tests is in the diagnosis of brain dysfunction or neurological damage. **Neuropsychologists,** psychologists specializing in the assessment of brain-behavior relationships, believe that poor performances on tests of perceptual-motor tests indicate some sort of damage or dysfunction to the central nervous system (Haak, 1989; Reynolds & Fletcher-Janzen, 1989; Telzrow, 1989). These neurological dysfunctions are thought to be reflected in perceptual-motor test performances. For the neuropsychologist, many causes of children's poor academic performances can be traced to brain dysfunction, which is assessed by perceptual-motor tests.

Performance on perceptual-motor tests may be influenced by factors other than neurological dysfunction (unreliability, sensory deficits, motor dysfunctions, etc.). More importantly, there is little justification for using tests of perceptual-motor skills to diagnose brain damage or other forms of neurological dysfunction (Reschly & Gresham, 1989). The simple fact is that *there is not a one-to-one correspondence between perceptual-motor test performance and neurological status.*

If the research does not support the practice of assessing and training perceptual-motor skills and if the research concerning neuropsychological interpretations of perceptual-motor test performance is questionable, then why do we devote an entire chapter to this area? Our rationale is simple: *Perceptual-motor tests are among the most frequently used, misused, and abused tests in school settings.* Surveys have consistently shown that certain perceptual-motor tests rank only second in their frequency of use in the schools (Goh, Telzrow, & Fuller, 1981; Reschly, Genshaft, & Binder, 1987). We believe that readers of this text should become intelligent consumers of this frequently practiced form of assessment and question misinterpretations of perceptual-motor test results.

The purposes of this chapter are to (a) provide an overview of basic principles of perception; (b) review selected tests of perceptual-motor skills; (c) discuss the relationships among perceptual impairments, learning, and neurological status; (d) review research regarding perceptual-motor training programs; and (e) provide an alternative strategy for assessing perceptual-motor skills.

Fundamentals of Perception

In this section, we provide a context for understanding perceptual-motor assessment and describe how this type of assessment came to prominence in the evaluation of children with learning problems. Perceptual-motor assessment, like most other forms of assessment, relies heavily on theoretical and conceptual underpinnings. Therefore, knowledge of these issues is a prerequisite for understanding perceptual-motor assessment techniques.

Perception is the meaning or interpretation of information received through our senses. The way we perceive something depends primarily on two things: (a) the physical features of a stimulus and (b) the way we organize information (Woolfolk, 1987). Because there are five senses, there are theoretically five types of perception. In school settings and in perceptual-motor testing, two types of perception are emphasized: **visual perception** and **auditory perception.**

Physical features of visual stimuli can vary across the dimensions of size, shape, color, clarity, and complexity. Physical features of auditory stimuli can vary along dimensions of pitch, loudness, complexity, and similarity/dissimilarity of sounds. Organization of sensory information depends on the quantity and quality of stored information and concepts as well as an individual's level of cognitive development.

Familiar stimuli are perceived more readily than unfamiliar stimuli. When confronted with an unfamiliar stimulus, we tend to classify that stimulus into a category that is closest to our stored information and concepts. For example, if we have never seen a crocodile but are familiar with alligators, we would probably classify crocodiles as alligators. Similarly, young children familiar only with horses might classify donkeys, mules, and zebras as horses.

Perception and Attention

A critical aspect of perception is **selective attention.** Selective attention refers to the ability to select from an array of competing stimuli those stimuli that are relevant to the task at hand. Another way of defining perception is the selective attention to sensory input and the interpretation of that information as a function of stored information and concepts and the current qualitative level of cognitive development (Wyne & O'Connor, 1979).

Selective attention becomes crucial in learning tasks because the typical classroom has a variety of competing and often confusing stimuli, such as noise from other classrooms, whispering, and sounds from the heating system. Obviously, if one could not ignore these distractions, it would be difficult to learn.

Attention is a complex concept, although teachers frequently refer to attention during instruction. When a teacher says, "Frank, pay attention!" because Frank is looking out of the window during reading instruction, how do we know that he is paying attention if he redirects his eyes to his book? The only way to know is to ask him a question regarding the task in which he is supposedly engaging. If he answers correctly, he must be paying attention. However, he could answer correctly because he had learned the answer earlier. Alternatively, Frank could answer incorrectly because the question was unclear or poorly asked. It should thus be apparent that attention is a complex,

Perceptual-motor skills are important to survival, yet the way they have been traditionally assessed in schools has not yielded valuable instructional information.

difficult construct because it describes an unobservable process that cannot be directly observed; it must be inferred by observing changes in behavioral performances. Similarly, the only way we can measure perception is by the same process of inferring it through observable behaviors.

Principles of Perceptual Organization

The assessment of perceptual-motor skills began in the early 1900s with the work of gestalt psychologists such as Max Wertheimer, Kurt Koffka, and

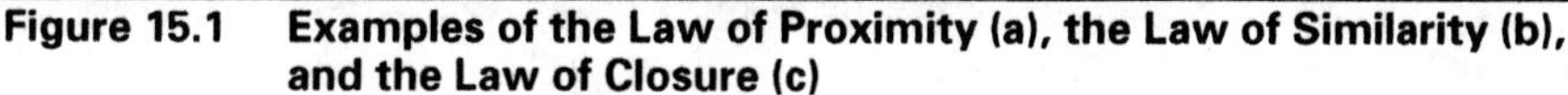

Figure 15.1 Examples of the Law of Proximity (a), the Law of Similarity (b), and the Law of Closure (c)

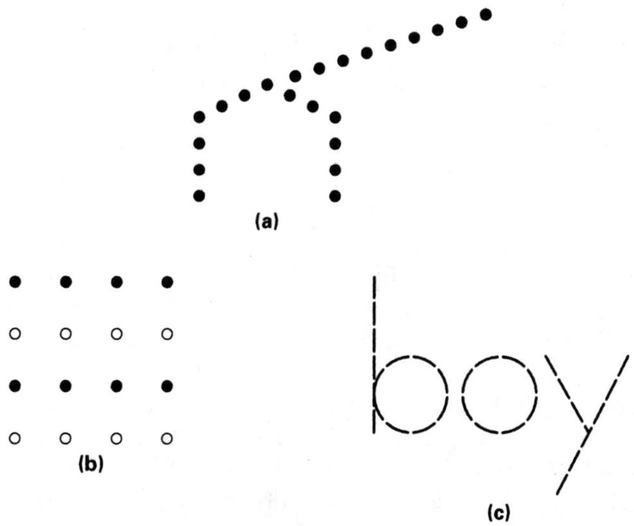

Wolfgang Kohler (McConnell, 1989). The gestalt school of psychology can be defined by the statement "The whole is greater than the sum of its parts." That is, a perceived stimulus has greater meaning to an individual than do its component parts. The basic assumptions of gestalt psychology are called **principles of perceptual organization.** The three basic laws most relevant in the assessment of perceptual-motor skills are (a) the law of proximity, (b) the law of similarity, and (c) the law of closure.

The **law of proximity** states that groups of objects are formed by elements close to one another in space or time. For example, separate notes played in rapid succession compose a melody in music. Similarly, separate printed stimuli on a page compose words that in turn compose sentences and paragraphs. Figure 15.1a depicts the law of proximity.

The **law of similarity** states that similar items tend to be perceived in groups. For example, a football team wearing orange jerseys and white pants would be perceived as one group and another team wearing white jerseys and yellow pants would be perceived as another group. Figure 15.1b illustrates this principle, with filled circles and the open circles each being perceived as separate groups.

Finally, the **law of closure** states that parts of a stimulus that are not presented will be filled in by the perceptual system. For example, if static on your radio interrupts a familiar song at random intervals, your perceptual system will tend to fill in or complete the missing melody and lyrics. Figure 15.1c shows an example of this law using the word *boy*.

The Relationship Between Perceptual Impairments and Learning

The work of the gestalt psychologists set the stage for the clinical application of gestalt principles in the assessment of perceptual impairments. Kurt Goldstein (1939, 1948) was a pioneer in the assessment of brain-injured adults. Goldstein based much of his work on soldiers with demonstrable brain injuries acquired during World War I. Further application of these principles was evident in the work of Heinz Werner and Alfred Strauss, who worked with mentally retarded, autistic, and brain-injured children in the 1940s (Strauss & Lehtinen, 1947).

Central to Werner's and Strauss's assumptions regarding learning problems were **perceptual disorders,** particularly **figure-ground disturbances.** A figure-ground disturbance refers to the tendency to confuse an object with its background. Normally, when we perceive a stimulus (e.g., a painting), we tend to focus on the main object and its details and tend to ignore much of the background. In a figure-ground disturbance, some individuals will focus on or be distracted by details of the background and ignore the figure. In other words, a figure-ground disturbance is "not being able to see the tree for the forest." This relates back to the idea of selective attention discussed earlier in this chapter. That is, persons with a figure-ground disturbance tend to focus on irrelevant aspects of a stimulus (the ground) and not on relevant aspects of that stimulus (the figure).

In the 1960s a new term was introduced to describe children who had no demonstrable sensory impairments and were not mentally disabled but still had difficulty learning. Kirk (1963) labeled these children **learning disabled,** and many of their characteristics were similar to those first described in the 1940s by Werner and Strauss in discussing brain-injured children. Assessment procedures that focus on the measurement of perceptual functioning were stimulated by and continue to be fueled by concern for children with learning disabilities.

Tests of Perceptual-Motor Skills

The majority of tests of perceptual-motor skills on the market today do not merit review because of their psychometric inadequacy (reliability, validity, and normative samples). The following discussion is limited to a small sample of commonly used tests of perceptual-motor functioning.

Our position, which is supported in the following test reviews, is that tests of perceptual-motor skills should *never be used to diagnose or to develop remediation strategies.* There are other ways of collecting more useful information than perceptual-motor tests currently available on the market. Table 15.1 de-

Table 15.1 Questions to Be Asked Before Assessing Perceptual-Motor Skills

1. Do I wish to assess perception, perceptual-motor integration, or both?
2. Am I interested in a particular perceptual skill (e.g., discrimination, figure-ground, closure, or in overall perceptual ability)?
3. Is the measure appropriate for the prospective sample (i.e., are the children physically able to respond, and is the test too easy or too difficult)?
4. Is the measure reliable enough to be used for educational purposes (i.e., as the basis for an educational classification decision)?
5. Are the data derived from the test worth the time and effort of administering and scoring the test?
6. Are there any data that support the relationship between performance on the test and academic performance in the classroom? If so, how strong is this relationship and to what extent can it be generalized across samples (i.e., the external validity of the data)?
7. Are there more direct ways of assessing the skill (e.g., through the use of curriculum-based assessment methods)?

Adapted from: D. Hammill and N. Bartel, TEACHING CHILDREN WITH LEARNING AND BEHAVIOR PROBLEMS. Allyn & Bacon, Boston, MA, 1975.

picts some relevant questions developed by Hammill and Bartel (1975) that should be asked before assessing perceptual-motor skills in the schools. These questions are important because, unfortunately, many professionals administer tests of perceptual-motor skills more out of habit than out of thoughtful consideration of what is assessed and why.

Bender Visual Motor Gestalt Test

Overview and Purpose

The Bender Visual Motor Gestalt Test (Bender Gestalt) was developed by Loretta Bender, a physician, to differentiate brain-damaged from non-brain-damaged adults. Bender (1938) used nine geometric designs published by Wertheimer in 1923 to illustrate the principles of gestalt psychology. Each design is printed on a 4-by-6-inch white card and presented in a specified sequence to an examinee, who is asked to copy all nine designs on a sheet of 8½-by-11-inch white paper. The accuracy of the reproduced design is evaluated by relatively objective scoring criteria.

According to Koppitz (1975), the Bender Gestalt is a test of **visual-motor integration** because it requires the examinee to integrate what is perceived visually with the fine motor responses required to reproduce the designs. It should be noted that some persons may perform poorly on the Bender Gestalt yet not have a visual perception problem. For example, someone who has extremely poor fine motor coordination may be misdiagnosed as having difficulty in visual perception when the problem is simply one of fine motor coordination; Koppitz warns against such simple-minded misinterpretations. This is particularly problematic with individuals with cerebral palsy and children with developmental disabilities.

Standardization Sample and Norms

The most frequently used normative sample and scoring system for children was developed by Koppitz (1975). The Bender Gestalt was originally standardized on 975 children between the ages of 5 and 11. The sample was not geographically representative of the U.S. population, since 83 percent were from the Northeast, 15 percent from the West, and only 2 percent from the South. Koppitz's standardization sample was somewhat more representative with respect to race, with 86 percent being Caucasian, 8.5 percent African American, 4.5 percent Latino, and 1 percent Asian. Koppitz did not attempt to stratify the sample according to socioeconomic status (SES) and suggests that SES may not be an important variable in performance on the Bender Gestalt. This claim, however, is not substantiated by other research, which suggests that Bender Gestalt performances do vary by SES level (Buckley, 1978).

Data Obtained

In school settings, the most commonly used scoring is a relatively objective system known as the Koppitz Developmental Bender Scoring System (Koppitz, 1964). Four types of errors (Koppitz, 1975) are scored with this system:

1. *Distortion of shape.* Distortion of the figure by drawing parts in disproportionate size or substituting angles for curves or circles for dashes or dots. Distortion of shape is scored for Figures A, 1, 3, 5, 6, 7, and 8 for a total of 10 points.
2. *Rotation.* Rotation of any part of the figure by 45 degrees or more. Rotation errors are also scored if the subject draws the figure correctly but rotates the stimulus card. Rotation errors are scored for Figures A, 1, 2, 3, 4, 5, and 8 for a total of 8 points.
3. *Integration.* The failure to connect two parts of a figure, the crossing of two lines at an incorrect place, the failure to cross two lines, or the omission or addition of rows or dots. Integration errors are scored for Figures A, 2, 3, 4, 5, 6, and 7 for a total of 9 points.
4. *Perseveration.* The increase, prolongation, or continuation of the number of units in the design. Perseveration is scored for Figures A, 1, 2, and 6 for a total of 3 points.

A total of 30 errors can be made on the nine designs. The total number of errors a child makes is compared with the appropriate age-level norms in the Koppitz (1975) manual. The error score is then converted into a percentile ranking, which can be used to interpret the child's test performance.

Reliability and Validity

Koppitz (1975) reported both interrater and test-retest reliability, or stability, for the Bender Gestalt. Interrater reliability studies reported in the manual ($N = 23$)

show that the reliabilities range from .79 to .99 with a median of .90. These high reliabilities suggest that raters agreed in the total number of errors they scored on the test. The objective scoring criteria probably account for these high agreement estimates.

The manual reports nine test-retest reliability studies, with stability coefficients ranging from .50 to .90 and averaging .71. Unfortunately, more than half of these studies were conducted with kindergarten children. The mean reliability of .71 suggests that the Bender Gestalt is not stable enough to use in making important decisions for children.

Convincing empirical evidence is not presented in the manual to support Koppitz's (1975) claim that the Bender Gestalt is a measure of visual motor integration. In other words, there is little evidence for the construct validity of the test, although the manual does report the results of correlational studies between the Bender Gestalt and measures of achievement, intelligence, and visual perception.

Evidence for the test's criterion-related validity is presented in the manual, mostly in the form of correlations between the total test score on the Bender Gestalt and measures of academic achievement. The manual lists 54 studies in which the Koppitz-scored Bender Gestalt has been compared with measures of school achievement. Fifty of these studies have been conducted with children in kindergarten through third grade. The validity coefficients in the 54 studies ranged from –.13 to –.58, with a median concurrent validity coefficient of –.23. The direction of these correlations is negative because Koppitz scores are based on the number of errors (i.e., the lower the number of errors, the higher the achievement score). Based on the data presented in the manual, the Bender Gestalt is not a strong predictor of academic achievement; on the average, it accounts for only 5 percent of the variance in academic achievement.

The manual also reports eight correlations between the Bender Gestalt and various measures of intelligence. Validity coefficients in these studies ranged from –.19 to –.60, with a median validity coefficient of –.22, which indicates poor prediction of intellectual functioning, and thus directly contradicts Koppitz's (1975) claim that "the Bender Gestalt can be used with some degree of confidence as a short nonverbal intelligence test for young children" (p. 47). By definition, a correlation of –.22 does not inspire a high degree of confidence and indicates that the Bender Gestalt (scored according to Koppitz) does not adequately measure the construct of intelligence in even the broadest and most liberal interpretation of that concept. As discussed in chapter 12, there are more valid ways of measuring intelligence than the Bender Gestalt.

Summary

The Bender Gestalt is by far the most frequently used test of perceptual-motor functioning, and, because of its simplicity and ease of administration, it is also one of the most frequently misused and abused tests. The reliability of the Bender Gestalt is too low for making any kind of placement decision, yet the test is often inappropriately used to diagnose children as brain damaged, perceptually handicapped, or emotionally disturbed (Salvia & Ysseldyke, 1991). Validity of the Bender Gestalt is likewise not well established. It has not been demonstrated that the test measures the construct of "visual-motor integration," and it has been found to be a very poor predictor of academic achievement and intelligence. In summary, the Bender Gestalt is, in the words of Koppitz (1975), "one of the most overrated, most misunderstood, and most maligned tests currently in use" (p. 2).

Developmental Test of Visual-Motor Integration

Overview and Purpose

Like the Bender Gestalt, the Developmental Test of Visual-Motor Integration (VMI) (Beery, 1982) is a test that requires a child to copy geometric designs from stimulus cards and is scored on a correct/incorrect basis for each design. The VMI is designed for children between the ages of 4 and 13 years and is similar in many respects to the Bender Gestalt.

Standardization Sample and Norms

The VMI was standardized in 1981 on approximately 3,000 children between the ages of 3 years and 19 years. Like the Bender Gestalt, little data are reported in the manual to suggest that the normative sample for the VMI was representative of the U.S. population on variables such as race, geographic region, socioeconomic status, or occupational status of parents.

Data Obtained

The VMI utilizes four types of scores: raw scores, standard scores, age equivalents, and percentile ranks. Standard scores for the VMI are expressed as scale scores having a mean of 10 and a standard deviation of 3.

Reliability and Validity

The VMI manual reports data on three types of reliability: *interrater reliability, test-retest reliability,* and *internal consistency reliability*. Unfortunately, all reliability data reported in the manual are based on an earlier edition of the VMI (1964). Interrater reliabilities for the VMI are similar in magnitude to those of the Bender Gestalt, ranging from approximately .60 to .99 with a median interrater reliability coefficient of .93. Test-retest reliability, or stability, coefficients ranged from about .60 to .90 with a median stability coefficient of approximately .80. The median internal consistency reliability for the VMI was approximately .79. Few data are reported in the manual to support the validity of the VMI as a test of visual-motor integration. Like the reliability data, all validity data reported in the 1982 VMI manual are based on the 1964 version of the test. The VMI does show a higher correlation with academic achievement (reading) than does the Bender Gestalt (r = .50) and intelligence (median r = .48).

Summary

The VMI is designed to be a test of visual-motor integration like the Bender Gestalt. The VMI and the Bender Gestalt have many similarities in terms of administration, scoring, and interpretation. The VMI shares with the Bender Gestalt the dubious honor of having an inadequately described and represented standardization sample and a paucity of empirical data attesting to the validity of the test. One advantage the VMI has over the Bender Gestalt is its reliability, which tends to be somewhat higher.

Goldman-Fristoe-Woodcock Test of Auditory Discrimination

Overview and Purpose

The Goldman-Fristoe-Woodcock Test of Auditory Discrimination, or GFW (Goldman, Fristoe, & Woodcock, 1980), was designed as a measure of speech-sound discrimination skills in persons between the ages of 4 and adulthood. The GFW has two subtests: (a) Quiet Subtest and (b) Noise Subtest. Both are individually administered by tape recordings. An individual is presented with four pictures and must select the one that corresponds to the word spoken on the tape. Pictures depict items with names that have some sound similarity but at least one major sound difference.

Standardization Sample and Norms

The GFW was standardized on 745 subjects ranging from 3 to 84 years of age. The standardization sample was not geographically representative of the U.S. population, with individuals coming from only three states (New Jersey, Minnesota, and Tennessee). The manual presents no information regarding their ethnicity, socioeconomic status, or other important demographic characteristics. In short, the GFW norms are based on an unrepresentative sample.

Data Obtained

Scoring is straightforward and consists of counting the number of errors made by the examinee. Error scores are converted to T scores, which have a mean of 50 and a standard deviation of 10 for each subtest. The manual also reports a supplementary method scoring that differentiates errors by certain kinds of words, such as voiced and unvoiced sounds. Separate norms using this method are not presented.

Reliability and Validity

The manual reports internal consistency reliability coefficients of .79 for the Quiet Subtest and .68 for the Noise Subtest. Coefficients of this magnitude suggest some problem in internal consistency, which in turn suggests that error contributes a great deal to scores obtained on the GFW. The manual indicates that these low coefficients are due to the relatively few items on each subtest. Although this is a statistically viable explanation, it does not increase confidence in the test. Furthermore, the small number of items calls into question the adequacy of content sampling, which then leads one to question the content validity of the test. Validity evidence for the GFW reported in the manual shows correlations of .60 (Quiet Subtest) and .52 (Noise Subtest) with the Stanford Binet Intelligence Scale, but lower correlations with measures of receptive language such as the Peabody Picture Vocabulary Test (.15 for the Quiet Subtest and .00 for the Noise Subtest). In our opinion, the GFW does not adequately discriminate individuals who have good or poor auditory discrimination abilities.

Summary

The GFW is a poorly standardized, technically inadequate measure of auditory discrimination abilities under quiet and noisy background conditions. Although a noise subtest does represent a more ecologically valid condition for testing learning because most classrooms have some background noise at most times, the background noise for the GFW appears to be a school cafeteria. The GFW should not be used to make classification or placement decisions because of poor normative characteristics, low reliability, and a dearth of validity data.

Illinois Test of Psycholinguistic Abilities

Overview and Purpose

The Illinois Test of Psycholinguistic Abilities (ITPA) (Kirk et al., 1968), developed for children between the ages of 2 years, 4 months, and 10 years, 3 months, is designed to measure students' skills in understanding, processing, and producing verbal and nonverbal language. Although it was partially designed to represent a linguistic theoretical model, Carroll (1972) stated that "it requires some stretching of meaning to call the ITPA a measure of psycholinguistic abilities" (p. 42).

The ITPA is composed of 10 regularly administered individual tests and two optional subtests. According to the technical manual (Paraskevopoulos & Kirk, 1969), the psycholinguistic model on which the test is based attempts to relate those functions whereby the intentions of one person are transmitted either verbally or nonverbally to another person (expressive language) and the other person receives and interprets these intentions (receptive language). Specifically, the ITPA was designed to measure an individual's ability to comprehend, remember, and express stimuli that are presented visually or auditorily. The ITPA is presented in this chapter because its 11 subtests represent a number of abilities measured by many other tests of perceptual-motor functioning. The 11 ITPA subtests and examples of items from each are presented in table 15.2.

Standardization Sample and Norms

The ITPA was standardized on 963 children between the ages of 2 years, 7 months, and 10 years, 1 month. The standardization sample was not

Table 15.2 Description and Examples of the ITPA Subtests

Auditory Reception: This test assesses the child's ability to derive meaning from verbally presented material. Since the receptive rather than the expressive process is being sampled, the response throughout is kept at the simple level of a "yes" or "no," either verbally or with a nod or shake of the head. The test contains 50 items.

Typical Items

"Do dogs eat?"

"Do dials yawn?"

"Do carpenters kneel?"

Auditory Association: This test taps the child's ability to relate concepts presented orally. In this test, the requirements of the auditory receptive process and the vocal expressive process are minimal, while the organizing process of manipulating linguistic symbols in a meaningful way is tested by verbal analogies of increasing difficulty. There are 42 orally presented sentence completion items.

Typical Items

"I cut with a saw; I pound with a ________."

"A dog has hair; a fish has ________."

Visual Association: The organizing process in this channel is tapped by a picture association test with which to assess the child's ability to relate concepts presented visually. The child is presented with a single stimulus picture surrounded by four optional pictures, one of which is associated with the stimulus picture. The child is asked, "What goes with this?" (pointing to the stimulus picture). "Which one of these?" (pointing to the four optional pictures). The test contains 20 items of the simpler form and 22 visual analogies.

Verbal Expression: The purpose of this test is to assess the ability of the child to express his [*sic*] own concepts vocally. The child is shown four familiar objects, one at a time (a ball, a block, an envelope, and a button), and is asked, "Tell me all about this." The score is the number of discrete, relevant, and approximately factual concepts expressed.

Manual Expression: This test taps the child's ability to express ideas manually. This ability is assessed by a gestural manipulation test. In the test, 15 pictures of common objects are shown to the child one at a time and he [*sic*] is asked to, "Show me what to do with a ________." The child is required to pantomime the appropriate action, such as dialing a telephone or playing a guitar.

Grammatic Closure: This test assesses the child's ability to make use of the redundancies of oral language in acquiring automatic habits for handling syntax and grammatic inflections. There are 33 orally presented items accompanied by pictures which portray the content of the verbal expressions. The pictures are included to avoid contaminating the test with difficulty in the receptive process. Each verbal item consists of a complete statement followed by an incomplete statement to be finished by the child. The examiner points to the appropriate picture as he [*sic*] reads the given statements.

Typical Items

"Here is a dog; here are two ________."

"The dog likes to bark; here he is ________."

continued

Table 15.2 ***continued***

Auditory Closure: This is basically a test of the organizing process at the automatic level. It assesses the child's ability to fill in missing parts which were deleted in auditory presentation and to produce a complete word. There are 30 items ranging in difficulty from easy words to more difficult ones.

Typical Items

"airpla /"

"ta / le / oon"

" / ype / iter"

Sound Blending: This test provides another means of assessing the organizing process at the automatic level in the auditory-vocal channel. The sounds of a word are spoken singly at half-second intervals, and the child is asked to tell what the word is. At one end of the scale it has been made applicable to younger children by including pictures, thus making the task less open-ended. At the upper levels the test has been extended by including nonsense words.

Typical Items

"type(pause)wri(pause)iter"

"ta(pause)ble"

"wa(pause)ter(pause)me(pause)llon"

Visual Closure: This test assesses the child's ability to identify a common object from an incomplete visual presentation. There are four scenes, presented separately, each containing 14 or 15 examples of a specified object. The objects are seen in varying degrees of concealment. The child is asked to locate and point to all examples of a particular object within 30 seconds.

Typical Items

"Find as many fish as you can."

"Find as many hammers and nails as you can."

Auditory Sequential Memory: This test assesses the child's ability to reproduce from memory sequences of digits increasing in length from two to eight digits. This test differs from the Digit Span subtest from the WISC-R in that the digits are presented at the rate of two per second instead of one per second. The more rapid presentation makes the task easier, which is necessary for two- and three-year-old children.

Typical Items

"4-2"

"3-1-7"

"7-4-8-5-1-3-6-2"

Visual Sequential Memory: This test assesses the child's ability to reproduce sequences of nonmeaningful figures from memory. The child is shown each sequence of figures for five seconds and then is asked to put corresponding chips of figures in the same order. The sequences increase in length from two to eight figures.

Adapted from J. N. Paraskevopoulos and S. A. Kirk, THE DEVELOPMENT AND PSYCHOMETRIC CHARACTERISTICS OF THE REVISED ILLINOIS TEST OF PSYCHOLINGUISTIC ABILITIES, 1969, University of Illinois Press, Urbana.

geographically representative of the United States because all children came from around Urbana, Illinois, and Madison, Wisconsin. The authors stated in the technical manual that children were primarily selected on the basis of "the practical requirements of accessibility and because of suitability to the requirements of being middle class communities" (Paraskevopoulos & Kirk, 1969, p. 57). This lack of representation is a serious problem because curriculum emphasis in local schools can easily affect ITPA scores, and research indicates that ITPA scores are clearly modified by instruction.

The standardization sample included only those children demonstrating "average intellectual functioning," "average school achievement," and "average characteristics of personal-social adjustment." This is perplexing, however, because the ITPA was designed as a diagnostic instrument primarily for children encountering learning difficulties. Yet because these children were systematically excluded from the standardization sample, there are no scores in the sample with whom the scores of children with learning problems can be compared. In fact, children's learning problems may well be diagnosed as being more serious than they actually are because their scores are being compared with a sample with atypically high achievement scores and cognitive functioning. In addition, because only middle-class children were included in the standardization sample, the test is vulnerable to claims of bias against lower class and minority children.

In summary, the ITPA norms are based on a sample that is highly restrictive in terms of geographic region, socioeconomic status, minority group representation, and the inclusion of the full range of scores for comparison purposes, particularly of children with learning difficulties. The ITPA is a poorly standardized test. In fact, the standardization of the ITPA could serve as a handy compendium for violations of virtually every principle of standardization and norms construction discussed in chapter 5 of this text.

Data Obtained

Three types of derived scores can be obtained from the ITPA: (a) scale scores for each subtest, with a mean of 36 and a standard deviation of 6; (b) the psycholinguistic ages (PLAs) for each subtest, which are similar to a mental age or age equivalent; and (c) psycholinguistic quotients (PLQs), which are ratio scores (PLA/CA 100), similar to ratio IQ scores. There are a number of statistical problems with the use of PLAs and PLQs, including unequal standard deviations at each age group, which render scores incomparable from one age to another. For example, a PLQ of 90 at age 4 represents the 50th percentile, whereas this same score at age 10 years is at the 31st percentile. Chapter 4 of this text provides a more comprehensive discussion of the problems in using age and grade equivalents and ratio IQ scores. The technical manual also provides tables for *intraindividual* comparisons in which performances on a given subtest can be compared with the median performance over all ITPA subtests. However, the reliabilities of the subtests are so low that it is unwise to make comparisons among or between them and the total score.

Table 15.3 Median Internal Consistency and Five-Month Test-Retest Reliability Coefficients for ITPA Subtests[a]

Subtest	*Internal Consistency*	*Test-Retest*
Auditory Reception	.88	.46
Visual Reception	.80	.29
Auditory Association	.80	.67
Visual Association	.79	.45
Verbal Expression	.65	.47
Manual Expression	.76	.46
Grammatic Closure	.67	.61
Auditory Closure	.65	.44
Sound Blending	.85	.47
Visual Closure	.60	.63
Auditory Sequential Memory	.82	.74
Visual Sequential Memory	.74	.31
Composite	.90	.77

Adapted from J. N. Paraskevopoulos and S. A. Kirk, THE DEVELOPMENT AND PSYCHOMETRIC CHARACTERISTICS OF THE REVISED ILLINOIS TEST OF PSYCHOLINGUISTIC ABILITIES, 1969, University of Illinois Press, Urbana.

[a]Coefficients are collapsed across age levels and are not corrected for restriction in intelligence range.

Reliability and Validity

The manual extensively presents reliability data, including test-retest, internal consistency, and interscorer reliability. Table 15.3 shows median internal consistency and five-month test-retest reliability coefficients across all age levels for all subtests. As can be seen in this table, the stability of the majority of subtests for the scale is less than adequate. The internal consistency reliabilities are, for the most part, below acceptable standards, with Verbal Expression (r = .65), Visual Closure (r = .60), and Auditory Closure (r = .65) the least internally consistent subtests. In sum, the ITPA does not possess an adequate level of reliability on which to base placement decisions for children. Most subtests are neither internally consistent nor sufficiently stable to ensure accurate measurement of the skills purportedly assessed by the scale.

The ITPA technical manual is virtually devoid of validity data. Thus, little evidence exists to support the statement that the test measures the construct of psycholinguistic abilities. As Carroll (1972) pointed out, almost half of the subtests could be completed by individuals who had never acquired *any* language system. Calling the ITPA a measure of psycholinguistic ability is a misnomer, because it measures only a small fraction of skills that might be considered linguistic. For example, reading, writing, and spelling are clearly language (linguistic) skills, but they were excluded from the ITPA on the premise that the scale was designed to measure basic cognitive skills not attained through schooling.

The technical manual presents no evidence for the criterion-related validity of the ITPA in predicting academic achievement. The ITPA has moderately positive correlations with Stanford-Binet IQ scores, although these correlations may be depressed because of the restricted range of the sample tested.

Summary

The ITPA is a poorly standardized and questionable instrument for measuring psycholinguistic abilities of children. The subtests have relatively low reliabilities and the test's validity has not been clearly established. The unrepresentative standardization sample creates a problem analogous to a situation in which one wishes to define shortness on the basis of a group of persons who are of average height or tall. If you only measure persons who are of average height or tall (relative to the general population), then average-height persons will be defined as short. Given this fallacious means of norms construction coupled with the unreliability of ITPA subtests and the paucity of validity data, the ITPA should not be used for placement or diagnostic decisions for children with learning problems.

Perceptual-Motor Training

As mentioned at the beginning of this chapter, many educators and psychologists believe that a direct relationship exists between perceptual-motor development and academic achievement. Between 1936 and 1970, perceptual-motor programming unquestionably became the most widely used method of assessing and teaching children with learning problems (Hallahan & Cruickshank, 1973). A spate of tests were developed to diagnose perceptual-motor problems and to generate perceptual-motor training programs to remediate these problems (Wallace & Larsen, 1978).

A basic tenet of perceptual theory is that impairment in perceptual-motor skills will significantly interfere with learning, especially learning to read. Underlying this assumption is the hypothesis that a strong relationship exists between measures of perceptual-motor skills and academic achievement. In fact, however, there is *not* a strong relationship between perceptual-motor skills (as measured by tests of perceptual-motor functioning) and academic achievement (as measured by tests of academic achievement) (Wallace & Larsen, 1978).

Studies investigating the relationships between auditory perception skills (Hammill & Larsen, 1974b), visual perception skills (Larsen & Hammill, 1975), and psycholinguistic processes (Hammill & Larsen, 1974a) with academic achievement have been extensively reviewed. Collectively, these studies provide little empirical data to support the assumption that perceptual ability is related to academic achievement (see Focus on Research).

Myers and Hammill (1976) reviewed 105 studies and found little support for the continued use of perceptual-motor training to facilitate academic achievement of school-age children. We must therefore ask what problem one is trying to solve when perceptual-motor tests are administered? We have no simple answer to this question, although we have several hypotheses. Perhaps the use of perceptual-motor tests is promulgated by the testing industry. A basic principle of marketing is that as long as a product is kept before the public's eye, it will be consumed. A brief perusal of testing catalogues suggests that testing companies are not decreasing their marketing of perceptual-motor tests.

Another hypothesis is that some individuals want to attribute learning difficulties to causes intrinsic to the person (e.g., a perceptual-motor dysfunction). Using this logic, one is able to assign a label to a problem that becomes an explanation for the existence of the problem. Thus, if the inability of some children to read, compute, or use language appropriately is attributed to "perceptual-motor deficits" or "psycholinguistic processing dysfunction," assessment of these children will focus on perceptual and processing abilities that are the presumed "causes" of poor achievement. Perceptual-motor assessment, therefore, continues in spite of what we consider to be overwhelming empirical evidence to the contrary (for a review, see Myers & Hammill, 1976).

Finally, we believe many persons are simply unaware of the research findings regarding perceptual-motor and psycholinguistic training programs. The conceptual appeal of these programs coupled with the simplicity of assessing certain perceptual-motor skills may lead many into pseudoexplanations of a child's poor achievement. In this sense, saying something (even though it may be inaccurate) about the cause of Johnny's inability to read is less aversive than saying "I don't know."

The Level of Inference Problem in Assessment

Our review of perceptual-motor assessment has been negative for what we consider to be obvious reasons that pertain to the poor normative samples of most perceptual-motor tests, the relatively poor reliability and validity evidence for these measures, and the lack of a demonstrated relationship between perceptual-motor skills and academic achievement. A major problem with all of these measures, in our opinion, is the high level of inference required to interpret performance on these instruments. **Level of inference** refers to the relationship between behavior actually observed and the interpretation or meaning attributed to that behavior. The level of inference can range on a continuum from simple, straightforward, precise descriptions of what was seen or observed (no inference) to quite abstract and remote interpretations of the meaning of that behavior (high inference).

Figure 15.2 provides examples of the different levels of inference that might be used with Danny's copying of a design from the Bender Gestalt. Each of the interpretations has appeared in the literature on the Bender Gestalt or similar perceptual-motor assessment devices. The level of infer-

Figure 15.2 Five Levels of Inference for Danny's Bender

Danny's Bender

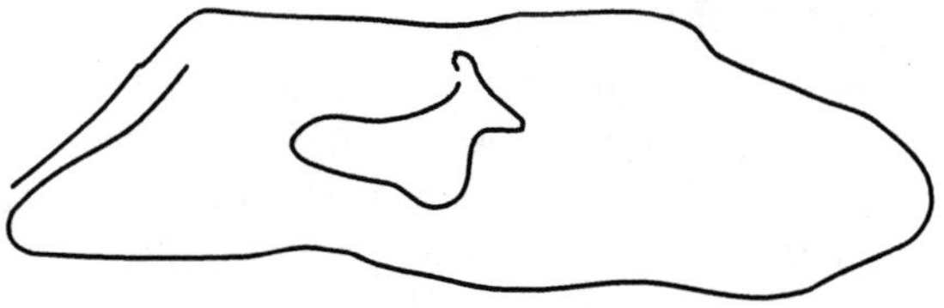

Level I: A straightforward description of behavior (e.g., "Danny could not accurately copy these geometric figures.")

Level II: Naming the skill that presumably underlies the behavior (e.g., "Danny has poor visual-motor skills.")

Level III: Suggestion of immaturity or developmental lag (e.g., "Danny's drawing appears to be immature, suggesting that his overall pattern of development is uneven.")

Level IV: Conclusions about underlying neurological status (e.g., "Danny appears to have neurological dysfunction, particularly in the right parietal lobe of the brain.")

Level V: Indication of underlying personality dynamics or conclusions about emotional status (e.g., "Danny's psychosexual stage of development appears to be rather primitive in view of his inability to correctly reproduce a relatively simple geometric figure that is believed to evoke information on psychosexual status or development.")

ence varies from a straightforward description, "Danny could not accurately copy these geometric figures" (Level I), to a suggestion of underlying personality dynamics or conclusions about emotional status, "Danny's psychosexual stage of development appears to be primitive. . . ." (Level V).

There are several problems with highly inferential interpretations of performance on perceptual-motor tests. One, little empirical data support the inferences made from such tests (Reschly & Gresham, 1989). Two, the alleged variables involved (such as processing and perceptual dysfunctions) cannot be directly observed nor is there hard evidence that the presumed condition actually exists. Three, in virtually all instances there are no treatments or interventions that directly deal with underlying problems of academic deficiencies. We do not deny that individuals with severe neurological problems may draw "poor" Bender designs, but we cannot find any clear-cut evidence that knowing about Bender errors helps one to teach children with learning difficulties.

Focus on Research

Recent Attempts at Ability Training

Special educators have experienced a great deal of difficulty in deciding how best to teach problem learners. Logic would appear to indicate that if one could identify the learner's strengths and weaknesses, one could teach to the strengths and avoid the weaknesses. Unfortunately, research has not supported this process.

Educators and psychologists attempting to identify learner strengths and weaknesses began to talk about underlying learning processes or abilities such as visual sequential memory, auditory discrimination, and visual closure. However, these and other similar so-called abilities merely represent reifications of constructs. That is, these terms do not represent anything concrete but are merely abstractions. When used often enough, these abstractions begin to be discussed and used as if they were real entities (e.g., "she is an auditory learner," or "he needs training to increase his auditory discrimination").

This approach to assessment and teaching is called the ability training model. It rests on the assumptions that learning "abilities" exist, that they can be reliably measured, and that they can be enhanced by training. Extensive research over the past 15 years, however, offers little support for these assumptions (Hammill & Larsen, 1974b; Myers & Hammill, 1982; Ysseldyke, 1973; Ysseldyke & Mirkin, 1982). First, there is little evidence that these so-called abilities even exist. Second, attempts to measure these "abilities" have resulted in some of the most psychometrically inadequate tests on the market today (see the test reviews in this chapter). Thus there is little proof that these "abilities," even if they do exist, can be reliably measured. Finally, there is little evidence that training these "abilities" can improve school performance.

A basic assumption of the ability training model is the existence of aptitude by treatment interactions (ATIs) (Cronbach & Snow, 1977). ATI research has focused more on certain treatments (i.e., teaching strategies) than in others. For example, the statement that a student is a "visual learner" is a statement about a student's aptitude. The statement that the child needs a "whole-word" reading program is a treatment statement. The statement that visual learners will learn more in a whole-word reading program than in a phonics-based program is a statement about an aptitude by treatment interaction.

In special education there is widespread popular belief in the presence of ATIs. Although logic would seem to indicate that ATIs exist, empirical research on teaching has not supported this. Cronbach and Snow (1979) comprehensively reviewed ATI research and concluded that there are no solidly established ATI relations. Thus the age-old adage applies here: "I am an empiricist because

continued

logic is only as strong as its assumptions." The assumptions on which ATIs are based are faulty. As such, teaching strategies based upon ATIs will necessarily be faulty as well.

It would be difficult to find a special educator or school psychologist who does not talk in terms of "aptitudes" or "abilities." The use of these terms is widespread to the point of being epidemic. Although this terminology is a convenient way to label behavior, the terms represent mentalistic fictions used as pseudoexplanations of a child's difficulty in learning academic materials.

Direct Assessment of Perceptual-Motor Skills

Tests of perceptual-motor functioning have a number of conceptual and empirical problems and rely on the use of highly inferential interpretations, which are often unjustified. What are the alternatives to this type of assessment? Our recommendation is relatively simple and straightforward. We suggest the direct assessment of skills with stimuli or materials that the child must use in the classroom setting. We also suggest that the child's performance using these stimuli or materials be interpreted using Level I inference depicted in figure 15.2. For example, we may be interested in whether Danny has adequate visual-motor ability. We could assess this in basically two ways. One, we could present geometric figures (e.g., Bender Gestalt designs) and ask him to copy them from cards. Two, we could present numerals and letters and ask Danny to copy them either from the board or from a workbook. Which strategy would have the most direct relevance for classroom performance? We would obviously opt for the latter, because numerals and letters, not irrelevant geometric designs, are the stimuli with which children must become proficient.

Another example may be instructive. We have heard interpretations of perceptual-motor performance such as this: "Danny had difficulty in reproducing the Bender designs as he achieved a developmental age of only 5 years. His scale score on the Coding subtest of the WISC-III corroborates his poor visual-motor abilities. Taken together, these performances would suggest Danny will have great difficulty in copying from the board and in performing written work at his desk such as reading and math skill sheets."

We consider this type of interpretation to be superfluous. If one wanted to make a prediction about Danny's ability to (a) copy from the board and (b) complete reading and math skill sheets, it would seem logical to assess these behaviors directly. To do this, we might take Danny into his classroom (after school or at recess), have him sit in his assigned seat, and ask him to copy from the board. We could also ask Danny's teacher for representative reading and math skill sheets and ask him to complete these tasks in his classroom. If Danny performed these tasks adequately, what would be the point of knowing his scores on the Bender Gestalt or the WISC-III Coding subtest? Our interest in Danny is not whether he can copy meaningless designs but whether he can perform the tasks required of him in the classroom.

Suppose that Danny could not copy from the board or complete the skill sheets. Does this mean that the Bender Gestalt and WISC-III performances support the conclusion that a visual-motor problem exists? Not necessarily. Our interpretation would be consistent with the Level I inference presented in figure 15.2. That is, "Danny had difficulty in copying geometric designs, copying from the board, and completing reading and math skill sheets." Of course, one will never have to deal with the problem of inconsistencies in performances on perceptual-motor tests and direct assessment if one utilizes only one type of assessment strategy. We strongly prefer to use direct assessment of academic skills in the classroom setting, using the stimuli and materials that the child confronts daily.

The potential of direct assessment of so-called perceptual-motor skills is virtually limitless and depends on the nature of the materials being used in the classroom for a particular child. The chief advantage of this form of assessment is that it has direct relevance for that child in the classroom. We provide a much more detailed discussion of direct assessment approaches in chapter 6, "Curriculum-Based Assessment."

Chapter Summary

The available research suggests that assessment based on a traditional perceptual-motor model has neither high reliability nor validity and has little to do with diagnosing or remediating learning problems. Moreover, better methods of assessment have been developed to accomplish the same goals that perceptual-motor tests purportedly fulfill. This chapter has addressed the widespread use of tests of perceptual-motor functioning and the belief that direct assessment using lower inference techniques is preferable.

Tests of perceptual-motor functioning have little or nothing to do with the problem-solving process. That is, stating that a child has a deficit in visual-motor perception, auditory discrimination, or psycholinguistic processing does not lead to the design, implementation, or evaluation of interventions to solve a child's academic difficulties.

References

A

Achenbach, T., & Edelbrock, C. (1983). *Manual for the child behavior checklist and revised child behavior profile.* Burlington, VT: University of Vermont Department of Psychiatry.

Achenbach, T., & Edelbrock, C. (1987). *Manual for the youth self-report and profile.* Burlington, VT: University of Vermont Department of Psychiatry.

Achenbach, T., McConaughy, S., & Howell, C. (1987). Child/adolescent behavioral and emotional problems: Implications of cross-informant correlations for situational specificity. *Psychological Bulletin, 101,* 213–232.

Adelman, H. S. (1982). Identifying learning problems at an early age: A critical appraisal. *Journal of Clinical Child Psychology, 11,* 255–261.

Ager, C. L., & Shapiro, E. S. (1995). Template matching as a strategy for assessment of and intervention for preschool students with disabilities. *Topics in Early Childhood Special Education, 15,* 187–218.

Airasian, P. W. (1989). [Review of the *California Achievement Tests*]. In J. C. Conoley & J. J. Kramer (Eds.), *Tenth mental measurements yearbook* (pp. 126–128). Lincoln, NE: Buros Institute of Mental Measurements.

Airasian, P. W. (1991). *Classroom assessment.* New York: McGraw-Hill.

American Association on Mental Retardation. (1992). *Mental retardation: Definition, classification, and systems of supports.* Washington, D.C.: Author.

American Educational Research Association, American Psychological Association, & the National Council on Measurement in Education (1985). *Standards for educational and psychological testing.* Washington, DC: American Psychological Association.

Anastasi, A. (1981). Coaching, test sophistication, and developed abilities. *American Psychologist, 36,* 1086–1093.

Anderson, L. M., Evertson, C. M., & Brophy, J. E. (1979). An experimental study of effective teaching in first grade reading groups. *Elementary School Journal, 79,* 193–222.

Anderson, R. C., Reynolds, R. E., Schallert, D. L., & Goetz, E. T. (1977). Frameworks for comprehending discourse. *American Educational Research Journal, 14,* 367–381.

Archbald, D. A., & Newmann, F. (1988). *Beyond standardized testing: Assessing authentic academic achievement in the secondary school.* Reston, VA: National Association of Secondary School Principals.

Arter, J. A., & Jenkins, J. R. (1979). Differential diagnosis prescriptive teaching: A critical appraisal. *Review of Educational Research, 49,* 517–555.

Ayllon, T., & Roberts, M. D. (1974). Eliminating discipline problems by strengthening academic performance. *Journal of Applied Behavior Analysis, 7,* 71–76.

Ayres, R. R., & Cooley, E. J. (1986). Sequential versus simultaneous processing on the K-ABC: Validity in predicting learning success. *Journal of Psychoeducational Assessment, 4,* 211–220.

Ayres, R. R., Cooley, E. J., & Severson, H. H. (1988). Educational translation of the Kaufman Assessment Battery for Children: A construct validity study. *School Psychology Review, 17,* 113–124.

B

Baldwin, V. (1976). Curriculum concerns. In M. A. Thomas (Ed.), *Hey don't forget about me* (pp. 64–73). Reston, VA: Council for Exceptional Children.

Barnett, D. W., & Carey, K. T. (1992). *Designing interventions for preschool learning and behavior problems.* San Francisco, CA: Jossey-Bass Publishers.

Barnett, D. W., & Macmann, G. M. (1992a). Aptitude-achievement discrepancy scores: Accuracy in analysis misdirected. *School Psychology Review, 21,* 494–508.

Barnett, D. W., & Macmann, G. M. (1992b). Decision reliability and validity: Contributions and limitations of alternative assessment strategies. *The Journal of Special Education, 25,* 431–452.

Bates, E., O'Connell, B., & Shore, C. (1987). Language and communication in infancy. In J. D. Osofsky (Ed.) *Handbook of infant development.* New York: Wiley.

Baxter, G. P., Shavelson, R. J., Herman, S. J., Brown, K. A., & Valadez, J. R. (1993). Mathematics performance assessment: Technical quality and diverse student impact. *Journal of Research in Mathematics Education, 24,* 190–216.

Becker, W., Englemann, S., Carnine, D., & Maggs, A. (1982). Direct instruction technology—making learning happen. In P. Karoly & J. Steffen (Eds.), *Advances in child behavior, behavior analysis and therapy* (pp. 151–206). Columbus, OH: Charles E. Merrill.

Beery, K. E. (1982). *Revised administration, scoring, and teaching manual for the Developmental Test of Visual-Motor Integration.* Cleveland, OH: Modern Curriculum Press.

Bell, P. F., Lentz, F. E., & Graden, J. L. (1992). Effects of curriculum-test overlap on standardized achievement test scores: Identifying systematic confounds in educational decision making. *School Psychology Review, 21,* 644–655.

Bender, L. (1938). *The Bender Visual Motor Gestalt Test for Children.* New York: American Orthopsychiatric Association.

Benes, K. M. (1992). [Review of the *Peabody Individual Achievement Test-Revised*]. In J. J. Kramer & J. C. Conoley (Eds.), *Eleventh mental measurements yearbook* (pp. 649–652). Lincoln, NE: Buros Institute of Mental Measurements.

Bennett, R. E., & Shepard, M. J. (1982). Basic measurement proficiency of learning disability specialists. *Learning Disability Quarterly, 5,* 177–184.

Bersoff, D. N. (1983a). Social and legal influences on test development and usage. In B. Plake. *Buros/Nebraska symposium on measurement and testing* (Vol. 1. pp. 126–161). Hillsdale, NJ: Lawrence Erlbaum Associates.

Bersoff, D. N. (1983b). The legal regulation of school psychology. In C. R. Reynolds & T. B. Gutkin (Eds.), *The handbook of school psychology* (pp. 1104–1138). New York: John Wiley.

Bickel, W. E., & Bickel, D. D. (1986). Effective schools, classrooms, and instruction: Implications for special education. *Exceptional Children, 52,* 489–500.

Blankenship, C. S. (1985). Using curriculum-based assessment data to make instructional decisions. *Exceptional Children, 52,* 233–238.

Blood, D. F., & Budd, W. C. (1972). *Educational measurement and evaluation.* New York: Harper & Row.

Bloom, L. (1973). *One word at a time.* The Hague: Mouton.

Bloom, L. (1975). Language development. In F. D. Horowitz (Ed.), *Review of child development research* (Vol. 4). Chicago: University of Chicago Press.

Blum, R. E., & Arter, J. A. (1996). *A handbook for student performance assessment in an era of restructuring.* Alexandria, VA: ASCD.

Boring, E. G. (1950). *A history of experimental psychology* (2nd ed.). New York: Appleton-Century-Crofts.

Bouvier, L. F., & Davis, C. B. (1982). *The future racial composition of the United States.* Washington, DC: Demographic Information Services Center for the Population Reference Bureau.

Bracken, B. A. (1985). A critical review of *The Kaufman Assessment Battery for Children (K-ABC). School Psychology Review, 14,* 21–36.

Bracken, B. A., & Prasse, D. P. (1981). Alternate form reliability of the PPVT-R for white and black EMR students. *Educational and Psychological Research, 1,* 151–154.

Bracken, B. A., Prasse, D. P., & McCallum, R. S. (1984). Peabody Picture Vocabulary Test-Revised: An appraisal and review. *School Psychology Review, 13,* 49–60.

Brigance, A. (1977). *Diagnostic Inventory of Basic Skills.* North Billerica, MA: Curriculum Associates.

Broughton, S. F., & Lahey, B. B. (1978). Direct and collateral effects of positive reinforcement, response cost, and mixed contingencies for academic performance. *Journal of School Psychology, 16,* 126–136.

Broussard, C. D., & Northup, J. (1995). An approach to functional assessment and analysis of disruptive behavior in regular education classrooms. *School Psychology Quarterly, 10,* 151–164.

Brown, F. G. (1983). *Principles of educational and psycholgical testing* (3rd ed.). New York: Holt, Rinehart & Winston.

Brown, J., Bennett, J., & Hanna, G. (1981). *Nelson-Denny Reading Test.* Chicago: Riverside.

Brown, R. (1973). *A first language: The early stages.* Cambridge, MA: Harvard University Press.

Brown, V. L., Cronin, M. E., & McEntire, E. (1994). *Test of Mathematical Abilities-2.* Austin, TX: PRO-ED.

Brown v. Board of Education, 347 U.S. 483 (1954).

Bryen, D. N., & Gallagher, D. (1983). Assessment of language and communication. In K. D. Paget & B. A. Bracken (Eds.), *The psychoeducational assessment of preschool children.* New York: Grune & Stratton.

Buckley, J. (1978). The Bender Gestalt Test: A review of reported research with school-age subjects, 1966–1977. *Psychology in the Schools, 15,* 327–338.

Burgemeister, B. B., Blum, L. H., & Lorge, I. (1972). *Columbia Mental Maturity Scale* (3rd ed.). New York: Harcourt Brace Jovanovich.

Buros, O. K. (Ed.). (1961). *Tests in print.* Highland Park, NJ: Gryphon Press.

Buros, O. K. (Ed.). (1972). *Seventh mental measurements yearbook.* Highland Park, NJ: Gryphon Press.

Buros, O. K. (Ed.). (1978). *Eighth mental measurements yearbook.* Highland Park, NJ: Gryphon Press.

C

Campbell, D., & Fiske, D. (1959). Convergent and discriminant validation by the multitrait-multimethod matrix. *Psychological Bulletin, 56,* 81–105.

Cantor, A. (1990). A new Binet and old promise: A mismatch between technology and evolving practice. *Journal of Psychoeducational Assessment, 8,* 443–450.

Carlson, C., & Lahey, B. (1983). Factor structure of teacher rating scales. *School Psychology Review, 12,* 285–292.

Carnine, D., & Silbert, J. (1979). *Direct instruction reading.* Columbus, OH: Charles Merrill.

Carroll, J. B. (1972). A review of the *Illinois Test of Psycholinguistic Abilities.* In O. K. Buros (Ed.), *Seventh mental measurements yearbook.* Highland Park, NJ: Gryphon Press.

Carrow-Woolfolk, E. (1973). *Test for Auditory Comprehension of Language.* Hingman, MA: Teaching Resources.

Chall, J. S. (1967). *Learning to read: The great debate.* New York: McGraw-Hill.

Chappell, G. E., & Johnson, G. A. (1976). Evaluation of cognitive behavior in the young nonverbal child. *Language, Speech, and Hearing Services in Schools, 1,* 17–74.

Choate, J. S., & Evans, S. S. (1992). Authentic assessment of special learners: Problem or promise? *Preventing School Failure, 37,* 6–9.

Cone, J., & Hawkins, R. (Eds.). (1977). *Behavioral assessment: New directions in clinical psychology.* New York: Brunner/Mazel.

Conners, K. (1985). *The Conners Rating Scales: Instruments for the assessment of childhood psychopathology.* Unpublished manuscript, Children's Hospital National Medical Center, Washington, D.C.

Connolly, A., Nachtman, W., & Pritchett, E. (1976). *Manual for the Keymath Diagnostic Arithmetic Test.* Circle Pines, MN: American Guidance Service.

Conoley, J. C., & Kramer, J. J. (Eds.). (1989). *The tenth mental measurements yearbook.* Lincoln, NE: University of Nebraska Press.

Coopersmith, S. (1981). *Self-esteem inventories.* Palo Alto, CA: Consulting Psychologists Press, Inc.

Coulter, A., & Morrow, H. (1978). *The concept and measurement of adaptive behavior.* New York: Grune & Stratton.

Coutinho, M., & Malouf, D. (1992, November). *Performance assessment and children with disabilities: Issues and possibilities.* Washington, DC: Division of Innovation and Development, U.S. Department of Education.

Cronbach, L. J. (1970). *Essentials of psychological testing.* New York: Harper & Row.

Cronbach, L. J., Gleser, G. C., Nanda, H., & Rajaratnam, N. (1972). *The dependability of behavioral measures.* New York: Wiley.

Cronbach, L. J., & Snow, R. E. (1977). *Aptitudes and instructional methods.* New York: Irvington.

CTB/McGraw-Hill. (1985). *The California Achievement Tests.* Monterey, CA: Author.

Cummings, J. A. (1985). [Review of *Woodcock-Johnson Psychoeducational Battery*]. In J. V. Mitchell, Jr. (Ed.), *Ninth mental measurements yearbook* (Vol. 2, pp. 1759–1762). Lincoln, NE: Buros Institute of Mental Measurements.

D

Daly III, E. J., Lentz, F. E., & Boyer, J. (1996). The instructional hierarchy: A conceptual model for understanding the effective components of reading interventions. *School Psychology Quarterly, 11,* 369–386.

Daly III, E. J., & Martens, B. K. (1994). A comparison of three interventions for increasing oral reading performance: Application of the instructional hierarchy. *Journal of Applied Behavior Analysis, 27,* 459–469.

Daly III, E. J., Martens, B. K., Kilmer, A., & Massie, D. (1996). The effects of instructional match and content overlap on generalized reading performance. *Journal of Applied Behavior Analysis, 29,* 507–518.

Das, J. P., Kirby, J. R., & Jarman, R. F. (1979). *Simultaneous and successive cognitive processes.* New York: Academic Press.

Davis, S. E., & Kramer, J. J. (1985). Comparison of the PPVT-T and WISC-R: A validations study with second-grade students. *Psychology in the Schools, 22,* 29–32.

deHirsch, D., Jansky, J. J., & Langford, W. S. (1966). *Predicting reading failure.* New York: Harper & Row.

Deno, S. (1985). Curriculum-based measurement: The emerging alternative. *Exceptional Children, 52,* 219–232.

Deno, S. L. (1986). Formative evaluation of individual

student programs: A new role for school psychologists. *School Psychology Review, 15,* 358–374.

Deno, S. L. (1987). Curriculum-based measurement. *Teaching Exceptional Children, 20,* 41.

Deno, S. L. (1989). Curriculum-based measurement and special education services: A fundamental and direct relationship. In M. R. Shinn (Ed.), *Curriculum-based measurement: Assessing special children* (pp. 1–17). New York, NY: The Guilford Press.

Deno, S. L., Marston, D., & Mirken, P. K. (1982). Valid measurement procedures for continuous evaluation of written expression. *Exceptional Children, 48,* 368–371.

Deno, S. L., & Mirken, P. K. (1977). *Data-based program modification: A manual.* Reston, VA: Council for Exceptional Children.

Deno, S. L., Mirken, P. K., Lowry, L., & Kuehnle, K. (1980). *Relationships among simple measures of reading and performance on standardized achievement tests* (Research Report No. 20). Minneapolis: University of Minnesota Institute for Research on Learning Disabilities.

Diagnostic and Statistical Manual of the American Psychiatric Association, Fourth Edition (DSM-IV-R).

Doll, E. A. (1965). *Vineland Social Maturity Scale.* Circle Pines, MN: American Guidance Service.

Dunlap, G., DePerczel, M., Clarke, S., Wilson, D., Wright, S., White, R., & Gomez, A. (1994). Choice making to promote adaptive behavior for students with emotional and behavioral challenges. *Journal of Applied Behavior Analysis, 27,* 505–518.

Dunn, L. M. (1965). *Peabody Picture Vocabulary Test.* Circle Pines, MN: American Guidance Service.

Dunn, L. M., & Dunn, L. M. (1981). *Peabody Picture Vocabulary Test-Revised.* Circle Pines, MN: American Guidance Service.

Dunn, L. M., & Markwardt, F. C. (1970). *Peabody Individual Achievement Test.* Circle Pines, MN: American Guidance Service.

Dwyer, C. A. (1973). Sex differences in reading: An evaluation and a critique of current theories. *Review of Educational Research, 43,* 455–468.

E

Eaves, R. C., & McLaughlin, P. A. (1977). A systems approach for the assessment of the child and his environment: Getting back to basics. *Journal of Special Education, 2,* 99–111.

Ebel, R. L. (1966). Some measurement problems in a national assessment of educational progress. *Journal of Educational Measurement, 3,* 11–17.

Ebel, R. L. (1975). Educational tests: Valid? Biased? Useful? *Phi Delta Kappan, 57,* 83–89.

Edelbrock, C. (1983). Problems and issues in using rating scales to assess child personality and psychopathology. *School Psychology Review, 12,* 253–299.

Edelbrock, C. (1988). Informant reports. In E. Shapiro & T. Kratochwill (Eds.), *Behavioral assessment in schools* (pp. 351–383). New York: Guilford Press.

Education for All Handicapped Children Act of 1975. (1977). *Federal Register, 197,* 42474–42518.

Education of the Handicapped Amendments, Public Law 99–457 Federal Register. (1989). *Public Law 99–457.* page 26320.

Ehrhardt, K., Barnett, D. W., Lentz Jr., F. E., Stollar, S. A., & Reifin, L. H. (1996). Innovative methodology in ecological consultation: Use of scripts to promote treatment acceptability and integrity. *School Psychology Quarterly, 11,* 149–168.

Elliott, S. N. (1991). Authentic assessment: An introduction to a neobehavioral approach to classroom assessment. *School Psychology Quarterly, 6,* 273–278.

Elliott, S. N. (1994). *Creating meaningful performance assessments: Fundamental concepts.* Reston, VA: CEC.

Elliott, S. N., & Bischoff-Werner, J. (1995). *Performance spelling.* Madison, WI: Wisconsin Center for Education Research.

Elliott, S. N., & Bretzing, B. H. (1980). Using and updating local norms. *Psychology in the Schools, 17,* 196–201.

Elliott, S. N., & Fuchs, L. S. (in press). The utility of curriculum-based measurement and performance assessment as an alternative to intelligence tests. *School Psychology Review.*

Elliott, S. N., & Kratochwill, T. R. (1996). *Outcomes and reactions of students with disabilities to a statewide performance assessment program.* Madison, WI: Wisconsin Center for Education Research.

Elliot, S. N., Kratochwill, T. R., Littlefield, J., & Travers, J., (1996). *Educational Psychology: Effective teaching, effective leaning.* Madison, WI: Brown & Benchmark.

Elliott, S. N., & Piersel, W. C. (1982). Direct assessment of reading skills: An approach which links assessment to intervention. *School Psychology Review, 11,* 257–280.

Englemann, S., & Carnine, D. W. (1991). *Theory of instruction: Principles and applications* (2nd ed.). New York: Irvington.

Engler, L., Hannah, E., & Longhurst, T. (1973). Linguistic analysis of speech samples: A practical guide for clinicians. *Journal of Speech and Hearing Disorders, 38,* 192–204.

Enright, B. E. (1983). *ENRIGHT Diagnostic Inventory of Basic Arithmetic Skills.* North Billerica, MA: Curriculum Associates.

F

Family Educational Rights and Privacy Act (FERPA), P. L. 93–380, 20 U.S.C.A., 45 C.F.R.

Fantuzzo, J. F., King, J. A., & Heller, L. R. (1992). Effects of reciprocal peer tutoring on mathematics and school adjustment: A component analysis. *Journal of Educational Psychology, 84,* 331–339.

Fantuzzo, J. F., Polite, K., & Grayson, N. (1990). An evaluation of reciprocal peer tutoring across elementary school settings. *Journal of School Psychology, 28,* 309–323.

Fantuzzo, J. W., & Rohrbeck, C. A. (1992). Self-managed groups: Fitting self-management approaches into classroom systems. *School Psychology Review, 21,* 255–263.

Fenton, K. S., Yoshida, R. K., Maxwell, J. P., & Kaufman, M. T. (1979). Recognition of team goals: An essential step toward rational decision-making. *Exceptional Children, 45,* 638–644.

Fluharty, N. B. (1978). *Fluharty Preschool Speech and Language Screening Test.* Hingham, MA: Teaching Resources.

Fry, M., & Lagomarsino, L. (1982). Factors that influence reading: A developmental perspective. *School Psychology Review, 11,* 239–250.

Fuchs, L. S. (1988). Effects of computer-managed instruction on teachers' implementation of systematic monitoring programs and student achievement. *Journal of Educational Research, 81,* 294–304.

Fuchs, L. S. (1993). Enhancing instructional programming and student achievement with curriculum-based measurement. In J. J. Kramer (Ed.), *Curriculum-based assessment: Examining old problems, evaluating new solutions* (pp. 65–103). Lincoln, NE: Buros Institute of Mental Measurements.

Fuchs, L. S., & Deno, S. L. (1991). Paradigmatic distinctions between instructionally relevant measurement models. *Exceptional Children, 57,* 488–500.

Fuchs, L. S., & Fuchs, D. (1986). Effects of systematic formative evaluation on student achievement: A meta-analysis. *Exceptional Children, 53,* 199–208.

Fuchs, L. S., Fuchs, D., & Hamlett, C. (1989). Effects of alternative goal structures within curriculum-based measurement. *Exceptional Children, 55,* 429–438.

Fuchs, L. S., Fuchs, D., Hamlett, C., & Allinder, R. M. (1991). Effects of expert system advice within curriculum-based measurement on teacher planning and student achievement in spelling. *School Psychology Review, 20,* 49–66.

Fuchs, L. S., Fuchs, D., Hamlett, C., & Stecker, P. M. (1990). The role of skills analysis in curriculum-based measurement in math. *School Psychology Review, 19,* 6–22.

Fuchs, L. S., Hamlett, C., & Fuchs, D. (1990). *Monitoring basic skills progress* (computer program). Austin, TX: PRO-ED.

G

Gardner, M. F. (1979). *Expressive One-Word Picture Vocabulary Test.* Novato, CA: Academic Therapy Publications.

Gardner, M. F. (1983). *Upper-Extension Expressive One-Word Picture Vocabulary Test.* Novato, CA: Academic Therapy Publications.

Garwood, S. G., & Sheehan, R. (1989). Designing a comprehensive early invention system: The challenge of Public Law 99–457. Texas: PRO-ED.

Gaskins, R. W. (1988). The missing ingredients: Time on task, direct instruction, and writing. *The Reading Teacher, 41,* 750–755.

Gates, A. I., McKillop, A. S., & Horowitz, E. C. (Eds.). (1981). *Reading Diagnostic Tests.* New York: Teacher's College Press.

Germann, G., & Tindal, G. (1985). An application of curriculum-based assessment. The use of direct and repeated measurement. *Exceptional Children, 52,* 244–265.

Gibson, E. J., & Levin, H. (1975). *The psychology of reading.* Cambridge, MA: The MIT Press.

Gickling, E. E., & Armstrong, D. L. (1978). Levels of instructional difficulty as related to on-task behavior, task completion, and comprehension. *Journal of Learning Disabilities, 11,* 32–39.

Gickling, E. E., & Havertape, J. (1981). *Curriculum-based assessment (CBA).* Minneapolis, MN: National School Psychology Inservice Training Network.

Gickling, E. E., & Rosenfield, S. (1995). Best practices in curriculum-based assessment. In A. Thomas & J. Grimes (Eds.), *Best practices in school psychology III* (pp. 587–596). Washington, DC: The National Association of School Psychologists.

Gillet, J. W., & Temple, C. (1990). *Understanding reading problems: Assessment and instruction* (3rd ed.).

Glenview, IL: Scott, Foresman.

Ginsburg, H. P., & Mathews, S. C. (1984). *Diagnostic Test of Arithmetic Strategies.* Austin, TX: PRO-ED.

Goh, D. S., Telzrow, C. J., & Fuller, G. B. (1981). The practice of psychoeducational assessment among school psychologists. *Professional Psychology, 12,* 696–706.

Goldman, R., & Fristoe, M. (1972). *Goldman-Fristoe Test of Articulation.* Circle Pines, MN: American Guidance Service.

Goldman, R., & Fristoe, M. (1986). *Goldman-Fristoe Test of Articulation.* Circle Pines, MN: American Guidance Service.

Goldman, R., Fristoe, M., & Woodcock, R. (1980). *The Goldman-Fristoe-Woodcock Test of Auditory Discrimination.* Circle Pines, MN: American Guidance Service.

Goldstein, K. (1939). *The organism.* New York: American Book Company.

Goldstein, K. (1948). *After-effects of brain injuries in war.* New York: Grune & Stratton.

Good, R. H., III, & Kaminski, R. A. (1996). Assessment for instructional decisions: Toward a proactive/prevention model of decision-making for early literacy skills. *School Psychology Quarterly, 11,* 326–336.

Good, R. H., III, & Salvia, J. (1988). Curriculum bias in published norm-referenced reading tests: Demonstrable effects. *School Psychology Review, 17,* 51–60.

Good, R. H., III, Vollmer, M., Creek, R. J., Katz, L., & Chowdri, S. (1993). Treatment utility of the Kaufman Assessment Battery for Children: Effects of matching instruction and student processing strength. *School Psychology Review, 22,* 8–26.

Good, T. L. (1979). Teacher effectiveness in the elementary school. *Journal of Teacher Education, 30,* 52–64.

Graden, J. L., Casey, A., & Christenson, S. (1985). Implementing a prereferral system, part I: The model. *Exceptional Children, 51,* 377–387.

Graden, J. L., Zins, J. E., & Curtis, M. J. (Eds.). (1988). *Alternative educational delivery systems: Enhancing instructional options for all students.* Washington, DC: National Association of School Psychologists.

Greenwood, C. R. (1991a). A longitudinal analysis of time, engagement, and achievement in at-risk versus non-risk students. *Exceptional Children, 57,* 521–535.

Greenwood, C. R. (1991b). Classwide peer tutoring: Longitudinal effects on the reading, language, and mathematics achievement of at-risk students. *Journal of Reading, Writing, and Learning Disabilities International, 7,* 105–123.

Greenwood, C. R., Delquadri, J., & Hall, R. V. (1984). Opportunity to respond and student academic performance. In W. L. Heward, T. E. Heron, J. Trapp-Porter, & D. S. Hill (Eds.), *Focus on behavior analysis in education* (pp. 58–88). Columbus, OH: Charles Merrill.

Greenwood, C. R., Hart, B., Walker, D., & Risley, T. (1994). The opportunity to respond and academic performance revisited: A behavioral theory of developmental retardation and its prevention. In R. Gardner III, D. M. Sainato, J. O. Cooper, T. E. Heron, W. L. Heward, J. W. Eshleman, & T. A. Grossi. (Eds.), *Behavior analysis in education: Focus on measurably superior instruction* (pp. 213–224). Pacific Grove, CA: Brooks/Cole Publishing Co.

Greenwood, C. R., Terry, B., Marquis, J., & Walker, D. (1994). Confirming a performance-based instructional model. *School Psychology Review, 23,* 652–668.

Greer, R. D. (1983). Contingencies of the science and technology of teaching and prebehavioristic research practices in education. *Educational Researcher, 12*(1), 3–9.

Gresham, F. M. (1985). Behavior disorder assessment: Conceptual, definitional, and practical considerations. *School Psychology Review, 14,* 495–509.

Gresham, F. M. (1991a). Alternative psychometrics for authentic assessment? *School Psychology Quarterly, 6,* 305–309.

Gresham, F. M. (1991b). Conceptualizing behavior disorder in terms of resistance to intervention. *School Psychology Review, 20,* 23–36.

Gresham, F. M. (1992). Misguided assumptions of DSM-III: Implications for school psychological practice. *School Psychology Quarterly, 7,* 79–95.

Gresham, F. M., & Elliott, S. N. (1990). *Social Skills Rating System.* Circle Pines, MN: American Guidance Service.

Gresham, F. M., Elliott, S. N., & Evans-Fernandez, S. (1992). *Student Self-Concept Scale.* Circle Pines, MN: American Guidance Service.

Gresham, F. M., & Witt, J. C. (in press). Utility of intelligence tests for treatment planning, classification, and placement decisions: Recent empirical findings and future directions. *School Psychology Quarterly.*

Gridley, B. E., & McIntosh, D. E. (1991). Confirmatory factor analysis of the Stanford Binet: Fourth Edition for a national sample. *Journal of School Psychology, 29,* 237–248.

Grossman, H. (Ed.). (1973). *Manual on terminology and classification in mental retardation* (Special Publication No. 2). Washington, DC: American Association on Mental Deficiency.

Grossman, H. (1977). *Manual on terminology and classification in mental retardation* (rev. ed.). Washington, DC: American Association on Mental Deficiency.

Grossman, H. (1981). *Manual on terminology and classification in mental retardation.* Washington, DC: American Association on Mental Deficiency.

Guadalupe Organization v. Tempe Elementary School District, 71–435, District Court for Arizona, January 1972.

Guerin, G. R., & Maier, A. S. (1983). *Informal assessment in education.* Palo Alto, CA: Mayfield.

Guilford, J. P. (1967). *The nature of human intelligence.* New York: McGraw-Hill.

H

Haak, R. A. (1989). Establishing neuropsychology in a school setting: Organization, problems, and benefits. In C. Reynolds & E. Fletcher-Janzen (Eds.), *Handbook of clinical child neuropsychology* (pp. 489–502). New York: Plenum.

Hackola, S. (1992). Legal rights of children with attention-deficit disorder. *School Psychology Quarterly, 7,* 285–297.

Hallahan, D. D., & Cruickshank, W. M. (1973). *Psychoeducational foundations of learning disabilities.* Englewood Cliffs, NJ: Prentice-Hall.

Halpern, A., Raffeld, P., Irvin, L. K., & Link, R. (1975). *Social and Prevocational Information Battery.* Monterey, CA: CTB/McGraw-Hill.

Hammill, D. D., & Bartel, N. R. (1975). *Teaching children with learning and behavior problems.* Boston: Allyn & Bacon.

Hammill, D. D., & Larsen, S. C. (1974a). The effectiveness of psycholinguistic training. *Exceptional Children, 7,* 429–436.

Hammill, D. D., & Larsen, S. C. (1974b). The relationship of selected auditory perceptual skills and reading ability. *Journal of Learning Disabilities, 7,* 429–436.

Hammill, D. D., & Larsen, S. C. (1990). *Test of Written Language-2.* Austin, TX: PRO-ED.

Hammill, D. D., & Larsen, S. C. (1996). *Test of Written Language-3.* Austin, TX: PRO-ED.

Hargrove, L. J., & Poteet, J. A. (1984). *Assessment in special education: The education evaluation.* Englewood Cliffs, NJ: Prentice-Hall.

Haring, N. G., Lovitt, T. C., Eaton, M. D., & Hansen, C. L. (Eds.). (1978). *The fourth R: Research in the classroom.* Columbus, OH: Charles E. Merrill.

Harris, A. J. (1970). *How to increase reading ability.* New York: David McKay.

Harter, S. (1985). *Manual for the Self-Perception Profile for Children.* Denver, CO: University of Denver.

Hartman, A. (1978, October). Diagrammatic assessment of family relationships. *Social Casework,* pp. 465–476.

Hawkins, R. P. (1979). The functions of assessment: Implications for selection and development of devices for assessing repertoires in clinical, educational, and other settings. *Journal of Applied Behavior Analysis, 1,* 97–106.

Heber, R. (1961). *A manual on terminology and classification in mental retardation.* Washington, DC: American Association on Mental Deficiency.

Hendrick Hudson District Board of Education v. Rowley. 347 U.S. 483 (1982).

Hendrick Hudson District Board of Education v. Rowley, 458 U.S. 176, 179 (1982).

Herman, J. L., Aschbacher, P. R., & Winters, L. (1992). *A practical guide to alternative assessment.* Alexandria, VA: ASCD.

Herrnstein, R. J. (1982). IQ testing and the media. *The Atlantic Monthly, 6,* 68–74.

Heward, W. L. (1994). Three "low-tech" strategies for increasing the frequency of active student response during group instruction. In R. Gardner III, D. M. Sainato, J. O. Cooper, T. E. Heron, W. L. Heward, J. W. Eshleman, & T. A. Grossi. (Eds.), *Behavior analysis in education: Focus on measurably superior instruction* (pp. 283–320). Pacific Grove, CA: Brooks/Cole Publishing Co.

Hieronymous, A. N., Linquist, E. F., Hoover, H. D., et al. (1986). *Iowa Test of Basic Skills.* Chicago: Riverside.

Hills, J. R (1976). *Measurement and evaluation in the classroom.* Columbus, OH: Charles E. Merrill.

Hobbs, N. (Ed.). (1975). *Issues in the classification of children.* San Francisco: Jossey-Bass.

Hoge, R. D. (1983). Psychometric properties of teacher-judgment measures of pupil aptitudes, classroom behaviors, and achievement levels. *Journal of Special Education, 17,* 401–429.

Holland, J. G., Solomon, C., Doran, J., & Frezza, D. A. (1976). *The analysis of behavior in planning instruction.* Reading, MA: Addison-Wesley.

Howell, K. W. (1986). Direct assessment of academic performance. *School*

Psychology Review, 15, 324–335.

Howell, K. W., Fox, S. L., & Morehead, M. K. (1993). *Curriculum-based evaluation: Teaching and decision making* (2nd ed.). Belmont, CA: Brooks/Cole Publishing Co.

Howell, K. W., Kaplan, J. S., & O'Connell, C. Y. (1979). *Evaluating exceptional children: A task analysis approach.* Columbus, OH: Charles E. Merrill.

Hresko, W. P., Reid, D. K., & Hammill, D. D. (1991). *Test of Early Language Development-2.* Austin, TX: PRO-ED.

Hull, F. M., et al. (1971). The National Speech and Hearing Survey: Preliminary results. *Journal of the American Speech and Hearing Association, 13,* 501–509.

I

Individuals with Disabilities in Education Act (IDEA). 20 U.S.C. Section 1400 (1990).

Ingram, D. (1974). The relationship between comprehension and production. In R. L. Schieffelbusch & L. L. Lloyd (Eds.), *Language perspective—Acquisition, retardation, and intervention.* Baltimore: University Park Press.

J

Jarman, R. F., & Das, J. P. (1977). Simultaneous and successive synthesis and intelligence. *Intelligence, 1,* 151–169.

Jastak, S., & Wilkinson, G. S. (1984). *Wide Range Achievement Test-Revised.* Wilmington, DE: Jastak Associates.

Jenkins, J. R., & Pany, D. (1978). Standardized achievement tests: How useful for special education. *Exceptional Children, 44,* 448–453.

Jensen, A. R. (1980). *Bias in mental testing.* New York: The Free Press.

Johnson, E. G. (1992). The design of the National Assessment of Educational Progress. *Journal of Educational Measurement, 29,* 95–110.

Jordan, B. T. (1980). *Jordon Left-Right Reversal Test.* San Rafael, CA: Academic Therapy Publications.

K

Kamin, L. (1974). *The science and politics of IQ.* Potomac, MD: Erlbaum.

Kamin, L. (1981). Some historical facts about IQ testing. In H. J. Eysenck & L. Kamin (Eds.), *The intelligence controversy* (pp. 90–97). New York: Wiley.

Kanfer, F. H., & Grimm, L. G. (1977). Behavior analysis: Selecting target behaviors in the interview. *Behavior Modification, 1,* 7–28.

Kaufman, A. S. (1979). *Intelligence testing with the WISC-R.* New York: Wiley.

Kaufman, A. S., & Kaufman, N. L. (1983). *Kaufman Assessment Battery for Children.* Circle Pines, MN: American Guidance Service.

Kaufman, A. S., & Kaufman, N. L. (1985). *Kaufman Test of Educational Achievement.* Circle Pines, MN: American Guidance Service.

Kavale, K. (1990). Effectiveness of special education. In T. B. Gutkin & C. R. Reynolds (Eds.), *The handbook of school psychology* (2nd ed., pp. 868–898). New York: John Wiley & Sons.

Kavale, K., & Mattison, P. D. (1982). "One jumped off the balance beam": Meta-analysis of perceptual-motor training. *Journal of Learning Disabilities, 26,* 121–134.

Kazdin, A. (1974). Self-monitoring and behavior change. In M. J. Mahoney & C. E. Thoresen (Eds.), *Self-control: Power to the person* (pp. 218–246). Monterey, CA: Brooks-Cole.

Kazdin, A. (1984). *Behavior modification in applied settings* (3rd ed.). Homewood, IL: Dorsey Press.

Kazdin, A. E. (1977). Assessing the clinical or applied importance of behavior change through social validation. *Behavior Modification, 1,* 427–451.

Kazdin, A. E. (1979). Situational specificity: The two-edged sword of behavioral assessment. *Behavioral Assessment, 6,* 57–76.

Kelly, T. L. (1927). *Interpretation of educational measurements.* Yonkers-on-Hudson, NY: World Books.

Kern, L., Childs, K. E., Dunlap, G., Clarke, S., & Falk, G. D. (1994). Using assessment-based curricular intervention to improve the classroom behavior of a student with emotional and behavioral challenges. *Journal of Applied Behavior Analysis, 27,* 7–19.

Kirk, S., McCarthy, J., & Kirk, W. (1968). *Illinois Test of Psycholinguistic Abilities.* Urbana: University of Illinois Press.

Kirk, S. A. (1963). Behavioral diagnosis and remediation of learning disabilities. *Proceedings of the annual meeting of the conference into the problems of the perceptually handicapped child* (Vol. 1). Urbana: University of Illinois Press.

Koppitz, E. M. (1964). *The Bender-Gestalt Test for Young Children.* New York: Grune & Stratton.

Koppitz, E. M. (1975). *The Bender-Gestalt Test for Young Children* (Vol. 2). New York: Grune & Stratton.

Kopriva, J., Lowrey, K., & Martois, J. (1994, April). *Validity issues in performance assessment for ELL and English only elementary students.* Paper presented at the American Educational Research Association annual meeting, New Orleans.

Kramer, J. J. (Ed.). (1993). *Curriculum-based assessment: Examining old problems, evaluating new solutions.* Lincoln, NE: Buros Institute of Mental Measurements.

Kramer, J. J., & Conoley, J. C. (Eds.). (1992). *Eleventh mental measurements yearbook.* Lincoln, NE: Buros Institute of Mental Measurements.

Kramer, J. J., Henning-Stout, M., Ullman, D. L., & Schellenberg, R. L. (1987). The viability of scatter analysis on the WISC-R and SBIS: Examining a vestige. *Journal of Psychoeducational Assessment, 5,* 37–47.

Kratochwill, T. R., & Bergan, J. R. (1990). *Behavioral consultation in applied settings.* New York, NY: Plenum Press.

Kretschmer, R. R., & Kretschmer, L. W. (1978). *Language development and intervention with the hearing impaired.* Baltimore: University Park Press.

L

LaBerge, D., & Samuels, S. J. (1974). Toward a theory of automatic information processing in reading. *Cognitive Psychology, 6,* 293–323.

Lahey, M. (1988). *Language disorders and language development.* New York: Macmillan.

Lambert, N., & Windmiller, M. (1981). *AAMD Adaptive Behavior: School edition.* Monterey, CA: McGraw-Hill.

Lamberts, F. (1979). Describing children's language behavior. In D. A. Sabatino & T. L. Miller (Eds.), *Describing learner characteristics of handicapped children and youth* (pp. 253–291). New York: Grune & Stratton.

Lamp, R. E., & Kron, E. J. (1990). Stability of the Stanford-Binet Fourth Edition and K-ABC for young black and white children from low income families. *Journal of Psychoeducational Assessment, 8,* 139–149.

Langdon, H. W. (1989). Language disorder or difference? Assessing the language skills of Hispanic students. *Exceptional Children, 56,* 160–167.

Larry P. et al. v. Wilson Riles et al. (1979). United States District Court. Northern District of California. Case No. C-71-2270 RFP. Injunction in 1972 & 1974. Opinion in October 1979.

Larry P. v. Riles. 343 F. Supp. 1306 (N.D. Cal. 1972) (preliminary injunction). Aff'd 502 F. 2d 963 (9th cir. 1974); 495 F. Supp. 926 (N.D. Cal. 1979) (decision on merits). Aff'd (9th cir. no. 80–427 Jan. 23, 1984). Order modifying judgment, C-71-2270 RFP, Sept. 25, 1986.

Larsen, S. C., & Hammill, D. D. (1975). The relationship between selected visual skills and school learning. *Journal of Special Education, 9,* 281–291.

Lee, L. (1971). *Northwestern Syntax Screening Test.* Evanston, IL: Northwestern University Press.

Lentz, F. E. (1988a). Effective reading interventions in the regular classroom. In J. L. Graden, J. Zins, & M. J. Curtis (Eds.), *Alternative educational delivery systems: Enhancing instructional options for all students* (pp. 351–370). Washington, DC: The National Association of School Psychologists.

Lentz, F. E. (1988b). Direct observation and measurement of academic skills: A conceptual review. In E. S. Shapiro & T. R. Kratochwill (Eds.), *Behavioral assessment in the schools: Conceptual foundations and practical applications* (pp. 76–120). New York: Guilford Press.

Leonard, L. B., Perozzi, J. A., Prutting, C. A., & Berkley, R. K. (1978). Nonstandardized approaches to the assessment of language behaviors. *American Speech and Hearing Association,* 371–379.

Lewontin, R. C., Rose, S., & Kamin, L. J. (1984). *Not in our genes: Biology, ideology, and human nature.* New York, NY: Pantheon Books.

Lindeman, R. H., & Merenda, P. F. (1979). *Educational measurement.* Glenview, IL: Scott, Foresman.

Linn, R. L. (1993). Educational assessment: Expanded expectations and challenges. *Educational Evaluation and Policy Analysis, 15,* 1–16.

Linn, R. L., Baker, E. L., & Dunbar, S. B. (1991). Complex, performance-based assessment: Expectations and validation criteria. *Educational Researcher 20*(8), 15–21.

Lippmann, W. (1976). The abuse of the tests. In N. Block & G. Dwokin (Eds.), *The IQ controversy.* New York: Pantheon. (Originally published in 1922.)

Little, S. G. (1992). The WISC-III: Everything old is new again. *School Psychology Quarterly, 7,* 148–154.

Livingston, S. A., & Zieky, M. J. (1982). *Passing scores: A manual for setting standards of performance on educational and occupational tests.* Princeton, NJ: Educational Testing Service.

Lovitt, T., Eaton, M., Kirkwood, M., & Pelander, J. (1971). Effects of various reinforcement contingencies on oral reading rate. In Eugene Ramp & Bill Hopkins, (Eds.), *A new direction for education: Behavior analysis* (pp. 54–71). Lawrence, KS: University of Kansas.

Lovitt, T. C., & Fantasia, K. (1980). Two approaches of reading program evaluation: A standardized test and direct assessment. *Learning Disability Quarterly, 3,* 77–87.

M

Macmann, G. M., Barnett, D. W., Lombard, T. J., Belton-Kocher, E., & Sharpe, M. (1989). On the actuarial classification of children: Fundamental studies of classification agreement. *The Journal of Special Education, 23,* 127–149.

MacMillan, D. L., Gresham, F. M., & Bocian, K. (1996). *Curing mental retardation and causing learning disabilities: When Performance IQ is used to estimate aptitude.* Manuscript submitted for publication.

MacMillan, D. L., Gresham, F. M., Siperstein, G., & Bocian, K. (in press). The labyrinth of I.D.E.A.: School decisions on referred students with subaverage general intelligence. *American Journal on Mental Retardation.*

Macmillan, D. L., & Meyers, C. E. (1980). Larry P.: An educational interpretation. *School Psychology Review, 9,* 136–148.

MacMillan, D. L., Siperstein, G., Gresham, F. M., & Bocian, K. (in press). Mild mental retardation: A concept that may have lived out its usefulness—Enter LD, exit MR. *Psychology in Mental Retardation and Developmental Disabilities.*

Markwardt, F. C. (1989). *The Peabody Individual Achievement Test-Revised.* Circle Pines, MN: American Guidance Service.

Marsh, H. (1988): *Self-Description Questionnaire-1.* San Antonio, TX: Psychological Corporation.

Marston, D. B. (1989). A curriculum-based measurement approach to assessing academic performance: What it is and why do it. In M. R. Shinn (Ed.), *Curriculum-based measurement: Assessing special children* (pp. 18–78). New York: Guilford Press.

Marston, D., & Magnusson, D. (1985). Implementing curriculum-based measurement in special and regular education settings. *Exceptional Children, 52,* 266–276.

Marston, D., & Tindal, G. (1995). Performance monitoring. In A. Thomas & J. Grimes (Eds.), *Best practices in school psychology III* (pp. 597–608). Washington, DC: The National Association of School Psychologists.

Martens, B. K., Steele, E. S., Massie, D. R., & Diskin, M. T. (1995). Curriculum bias in standardized tests of reading decoding. *Journal of School Psychology, 33,* 287–296.

Martens, B. K., Witt, J. C., Daly III, E. J., & Vollmer, T. R. (in press). Behavior analysis: Theory and practice in educational settings. In C. R. Reynolds & T. B. Gutkin (Eds.), *The handbook of school psychology* (3rd ed.). New York: John Wiley & Sons.

McCallum, R. S. (1985). [Review of *Peabody Picture Vocabulary Test-Revised*]. In J. V. Mitchell, Jr. (Ed.), *Ninth mental measurements yearbook.* Lincoln, NE: Buros Institute of Mental Measurements.

McCarthy, D. (1972). *McCarthy Scales of Children's Abilities.* New York: Psychological Corporation.

McConnell, J. V. (1989). *Understanding human behavior* (6th ed.). New York: Holt, Rinehart & Winston.

McDaniel, E. L. (1973). *Inferred Self-Concept Scale.* Los Angeles: Western Psychological.

McPherson, K. S. (1985). On intelligence testing and immigration legislation. *American Psychologist, 40,* 242–243.

Meehl, P., & Rosen, A. (1955). Antecedent probability and the efficiency of psychometric signs, patterns, and cutting scores. *Psychological Bulletin, 52,* 194–216.

Mehrens, W. A. (1992). Using performance assessment for accountability purposes. *Educational Measurement: Issues and Practice, 11,* 3–9, 20.

Mehrens, W. A., & Lehmann, E. J. (1978). *Standardized tests in education.* New York: Holt, Rinehart & Winston.

Menyuk, P. (1971). *The acquisition and development of language.* Englewood Cliffs, NJ: Prentice-Hall.

Menyuk, P. (1972). *The development of speech.* Indianapolis: Bobbs-Merrill.

Mercer, J. R. (1970). Sociological perspectives on mild mental retardation (pp. 179–209). In H. Haywood (Ed.), *Social-cultural aspects of mental retardation.* New York: Appleton-Century-Crofts.

Mercer, J. R. (1979). *SOMPA technical manual.* New York: Psychological Corporation.

Mercer, J. R., & Lewis, J. (1978). *The System of Multicultural Pluralistic Assessment.* New York: Psychological Corporation.

Merwin, J. C. (1966). The progress of exploration toward a national assessment of educational progress. *Journal of Educational Measurement, 3,* 5–10.

Messick, S. (1984). Abilities and knowledge in educational achievement testing. In B. S. Plake (Ed.), *Social and technical issues in testing.* Hillsdale, NJ: Lawrence Erlbaum Associates.

Meyers, C. E., Nihira, K., & Zetlin, A. (1979). The measurement of adaptive behavior. In N. R. Willis (Ed.), *Handbook of mental deficiency: Psychological theory and research.* Hillsdale, NJ: Lawrence Erlbaum Associates.

Miller, J. (1981). *Assessing language production in children.* Austin, TX: PRO-ED.

Mills v. Board of Education of District of Columbia, 348 F. Supp. 866 (D.D.C. 1972).

Moran, M. R. (1978). *Assessment of the exceptional learner in the regular classroom.* Denver: Love Publishing Company.

Mowrer, D. E. (1989). [Review of the *Goldman-Fristoe Test of Articulation*]. In J. C. Conoley & J. J. Kramer (Eds.), *Tenth mental measurements yearbook* (pp. 323–325). Lincoln, NE: Buros Institute of Mental Measurements.

Mullis, I. V. S. (1992). Developing the NAEP content-area frameworks and innovative assessment methods in the 1992 assessments of mathematics, reading, and writing. *Journal of Educational Measurement, 29,* 111–131.

Myers, P. I., & Hammill, D. D. (1976). *Methods for learning disorders.* New York: Wiley.

Myers, P. I., & Hammill, D. D. (1982). *Learning disabilities: Basic concepts, assessment practices, and instructional strategies.* Austin, TX: PRO-ED.

N

Nagle, R. J. (1979). The McCarthy Scales of Children's Abilities: Research implications for the assessment of young children. *School Psychology Digest, 8,* 319–326.

National Council of Teachers of Mathematics (1989). *Curriculum and evaluation standards for school mathematics.* Reston, VA: Author.

Nelson, R. O., & Hayes, S. C. (1986). *Conceptual foundations of behavioral assessment.* New York: Guilford Press.

Noell, G. H., & Gresham, F. M. (1993). Functional outcome analysis: Do the benefits of consultation and prereferral intervention justify the costs? *School Psychology Quarterly, 8,* 200–226.

O

Oakland, T. (1979). Research on the Adaptive Behavior Inventory for Children and the estimated learning potential. *School Psychology Digest, 8,* 73–80.

Office of Technology Assessment, U.S. Congress (1992, February). *Testing in American Schools: Asking the right questions (OTA-SET-519).* Washington, DC: U.S. Government Printing Office.

Olson, A. E. (1995). *Evaluation of an alternative approach to teaching and assessing spelling performance.* Unpublished Master's thesis, University of Wisconsin–Madison: Madison, WI.

O'Reilly, C., Northcraft, G. B., & Sabers, D. (1989). The confirmation bias in special education eligibility decisions. *School Psychology Review, 18,* 126–135.

O'Shea, L. J., Munson, S. M., & O'Shea, D. J. (1984). Error correction in oral reading: Evaluating the effectiveness of three procedures. *Education and Treatment of Children, 7,* 203–214.

P

Page, E. B. (1985). Review of the Kaufman-Assessment Battery for Children. In J. V. Mitchell, Jr. (Ed.), *The ninth mental measurements yearbook.* (p. 357) Lincoln, NE: Buros Institute of Mental Measurements.

Paraskevopoulos, J., & Kirk, S. A. (1969). *Development and psychometric characteristics of the Revised Illinois Test of Psycholinguistic Abilities.* Urbana, IL: University of Illinois Press.

PASE (Parents in Action on Special Education) v. Joseph P. Hannon. U.S. District Court, Northern District of Illinois, Eastern Division, No. 74 (3586), July, 1980. Also 506 F. Supp. 831 (N.D. Ill. 1980).

Patterson G. R. (1982). *Toddlers and delinquents: Variations on a theme of anti-social behavior.* Paper presented at the annual meeting of the American Psychological Association, Washington, DC.

Pennsylvania Association of Retarded Citizens v. Commonwealth of Pennsylvania. 343 F. Supp. 279 (E.D. Pa. 1972).

Peterson, D. R. (1968). *The clinical study of social behavior.* New York: Appleton-Century-Crofts.

Pfeiffer, S. I. (1980). The school-based interprofessional team: Recurring problems and some possible solutions. *Journal of School Psychology, 18,* 388–394.

Pfeiffer, S. I. (1981). The problems facing multidisciplinary teams: As perceived by team members. *Psychology in the Schools, 18,* 330–333.

Piers, E. (1984). *Piers-Harris Children's Self-Concept Scale* (revised manual). Los Angeles, CA: Western Psychological Services.

Prescott, G. A., Balow, I. H., Hogan, T. P., & Farr, R. C. (1992). *Metropolitan Achievement Tests.* San Antonio, TX: Psychological Corporation.

President's Committee on Mental Retardation. (1970). *The six-hour retarded child.* Washington, DC: U.S. Government Printing Office.

The Psychological Corporation. (1992). *Wechsler Individual Achievement Test.* San Antonio, TX: The Psychological Corporation.

Psychological Corporation. (1996). *Stanford Achievement Test.* San Antonio, TX: Author.

Public Law 94–142. Education for All Handicapped Children Act of 1975 (1975, November 29).

Q

Quay, H. C. (1983). A dimensional approach to behavior disorders: The Revised Behavior Problem Checklist. *School Psychology Review, 12,* 244–249.

Quay, H. C., & Peterson, D. (1983). *Manual for the Revised Behavior Problem Checklist.* Coral Gables, FL: University of Miami.

R

Rashotte, C. A., & Torgesen, J. K. (1985). Repeated reading and reading fluency in learning disabled children. *Reading Research Quarterly, 20,* 180–188.

Rehabilitation Act of 1973. 20 U.S.C. Section 794.

Reid, D. K., Hresko, W. P., & Hammill, D. D. (1989). *Test of Early Reading Ability-2.* Austin, TX: PRO-ED.

Reschly, D. J., Genshaft, J., & Binder, M. (1987). *The 1986 NASP survey: Comparison of practitioners, NASP leadership, and university faculty on key issues.* Washington, DC: National Association of School Psychologists.

Reschly, D. J., & Gresham, F. M. (1989). Current neuropsychological diagnosis of learning problems: A leap of faith. In C. Reynolds & E. Fletcher-Janzen (Eds.), *Handbook of clinical child neuropsychology* (pp. 503–520). New York: Plenum.

Reschly, D. J., Kicklighter, R., & McKee, P. (1988). Recent placement litigation part III: Analysis of differences in *Larry P., Marshall, and S-1* and implications for future practices. *School Psychology Review, 17,* 39–50.

Reschly, D. J., & Sabers, D. (1979). Analysis of test bias in four groups with the regression definition. *Journal of Educational Measurement, 16,* 1–6.

Reschly, D. J., & Ysseldyke, J. E. (1995). School psychology paradigm shift. In A. Thomas & J. Grimes (Eds.), *Best practices in school psychology III* (pp. 17–32). Washington, DC: The National Association of School Psychologists.

Reynolds, C. R. (1982). The problem of bias in psychological assessment. In C. R. Reynolds & T. B. Gutkin (Eds.), *The handbook of school psychology* (pp. 178–208). New York: Wiley.

Reynolds, C., & Fletcher-Janzen, F. (1989). (Eds.). *Handbook of clinical child neuropsychology.* New York: Plenum.

Reynolds, C. R., & Kamphaus, R. (1992). *The Behavior Assessment System for Children.* Circle Pines, MN: American Guidance Service.

Richmond, B. O., & Kicklighter, R. H. (1980). *Children's Adaptive Behavior Scale.* Atlanta: Humanics.

Robinson, D. Z. (1973). If you're so rich you must be smart. In C. Senna (Ed.), *The fallacy of IQ* (pp. 18–30). New York: The Third Press.

Rogers, B. G. (1992). [Review of the *Peabody Individual Achievement Test-Revised*]. In J. J. Kramer & J. C. Conoley (Eds.), *Eleventh mental measurements yearbook* (pp. 652–654). Lincoln, NE: Buros Institute of Mental Measurements.

Roid, G., & Fitts, W. (1988). *Tennessee Self-Concept Scale* (revised manual). Los Angeles, CA: Western Psychological Services.

Rothlisberg, C. H. & McIntosh, D. E. (1991). Performance of a referred sample on the Stanford-Binet IV and the K-ABC. *Journal of School Psychology, 29,* 367–370.

S

Salvia, J., & Ysseldyke, J. (1978). *Assessment in special and remedial education.* Boston: Houghton Mifflin.

Salvia, J., & Ysseldyke, J. E. (1991). *Assessment.* Boston: Houghton Mifflin Company.

Sattler, J. (1988). *Assessment of Children* (3rd ed.). San Diego: Author.

Science Research Associates. (1987). *SRA Achievement Series.* Monterey, CA: CTB Macmillan/McGraw-Hill.

Semel, E., Wiig, E. H., & Secord, W. A. (1995). *Clinical Evaluation of Language Fundamentals 3.* San Antonio, TX: The Psychological Corporation.

Shapiro, E., & Derr, T. (1987). An examination of overlap between a reading curricula and standardized achievement tests. *Journal of Special Education, 21,* 59–76.

Shapiro, E. S. (1996). *Academic skills problems: Direct assessment and intervention* (2nd ed.). New York: Guilford Press.

Shapiro, E. S., & Eckert, T. L. (1993). Curriculum-based assessment among school psychologists: Knowledge, attitudes, and use. *Journal of School Psychology, 31,* 375–384.

Shapiro, E. S., & Elliott, S. N. (in press). Curriculum-based assessment and other performance-based assessment strategies. In T. B. Gutkin & C. R. Reynolds (Eds.), *The handbook of school psychology* (3rd ed.), New York: Wiley.

Shavelson, R. J., & Baxter, G. P. (1992). What we've learned about assessing hands-on science. *Educational Leadership,* 49(8), 20–25.

Shinn, M. R. (1988). Development of curriculum-based local norms for use in special education decision making. *School Psychology Review, 17,* 61–80.

Shinn, M. R. (Ed.). (1989). *Curriculum-based measurement: Assessing special children.* New York: Guilford Press.

Shinn, M. R., & Marston, D. (1985). Differentiating mildly handicapped, low achieving and regular education students: A curriculum-based approach. *Remedial and Special Education, 6,* 31–45.

Shinn, M. R., Rosenfield, S., & Knutson, N. (1989). Curriculum-based assessment: A comparison of models. *School Psychology Review, 18,* 299–316.

Shouksmith, G. (1970). *Intelligence, creativity and cognitive style.* New York: Wiley.

Sinclair, H. (1970). The transition from sensorimotor behavior to symbolic activity. *Interchange, 1,* 119–126.

Snider, V. E. (1992). Learning styles and learning to read. *Remedial and Special Education, 13,* 6–18.

Skinner, C. H., Turco, T. L., Beatty, K., & Rasavage, C. (1989). Cover, copy, and compare: A method for increasing multiplication fluency in behavior disordered children. *School Psychology Review, 18,* 412–420.

Sommer, R., & Sommer, B. A. (1983). Mystery in Milwaukee: Early intervention, IQ, and psychology. *American Psychologist, 38,* 982–985.

Spady, W. G., & Kit, J. (1991). Beyond traditional outcome-based education. *Educational Leadership, 49*(2), 67–72.

Sparrow, S. S., Balla, D. A., & Cicchetti, D. V. (1984). *Vineland Adaptive Behavior Scales,* Circle Pines, MN: American Guidance Service.

Spearman, C. E. (1927). *The abilities of man.* New York: Macmillan.

Spivack, G., & Seift, M. (1967). *Devereux Elementary School Behavioral Rating Scale.* Devon, PA: The Devereux Foundation.

Staats, A. W., & Butterfield, W. A. (1964). Treatment of nonreading in a culturally deprived juvenile delinquent: An application of reinforcement principles. *Child Development, 36,* 925–942.

Staats, A. W., Minke, K. A., Finley, J. R., Wolf, M. M., & Brooks, L. O. A. (1964). A reinforcer system and experimental procedure for the laboratory study of reading acquisition. *Child Development, 35,* 209–231.

Stanley, J. C. (1976). Test better finder of great math talent than teachers are. *American Psychologist, 31,* 313–314.

Stephens, T. (1978). *Social skills in the classroom.* Columbus, OH: Cedars Press.

Sternberg, R. J. (1979). [Review of "Six authors in search of a character: A play about intelligence tests in the year 2000"]. In R. J. Sternberg & D. K. Detterman (Eds.), *Human intelligence: Perspectives on its theory and measurement* (pp. 257–268). Norwood, NJ: Ablex Publishing.

Sternberg, R. J. (1982). Who's intelligent? *Psychology Today, 16,* 30–36.

Sternberg, R. J. (1984). *Beyond IQ: A triarchic theory of human intelligence.* New York: Cambridge University Press.

Sternberg, R. J., & Davidson, J. E. (1982). The mind of the puzzler. *Psychology Today, 16,* 37–44.

Stiggins, R. J. (1987). Design and development of performance assessments. *Educational Measurement: Issues and Practice, 6*(3), 85.

Stiggins, R. J. (1991). Facing the challenges of a new era of educational assessment. *Applied Measurement in Education, 4,* 263–274.

Stiggins, R. J. (1992). High quality classroom assessment: What does it really mean? *Educational Measurement: Issues and Practice, 8*(2), 35–39.

Stiggins, R. J. (1994). *Student-centered classroom assessment.* New York: Merrill.

Strauss, A. A., & Lehtinen, L. (1947). *Psychopathology and education of the brain-injured child.* New York: Grune & Stratton.

T

Taylor, R. L., Tindal, G., Fuchs, L., & Bryant, B. R. (1993). Assessment in the nineties: A possible glance into the future. *Diagnostique, 18,* 113–122.

Telzrow, C. (1989). Neuropsychological applications of common educational and psychological tests. In C. Reynolds & E. Fletcher-Janzen (Eds.), *Handbook of clinical child neuropsychology* (pp. 227–246). New York: Plenum.

Terman, L. M., & Merrill, M. (1973). *Stanford-Binet Intelligence Scale: 1973 Norms Edition.* Boston: Houghton Mifflin.

Thorndike, R. L., Hagen, E. P., & Sattler, J. M. (1986). *Stanford-Binet Intelligence Scale* (4th ed.). Chicago: Riverside.

Thorndike, R. M. (1990). Would the real factors of the Stanford-Binet Fourth Edition please come forward? *Journal of Psychoeducational Assessment, 8,* 412–435.

Thurlow, M. L. (1994). *National and state perspectives on performance assessment and students with disabilities.* Reston, VA: CEC.

Thurlow, M. L., & Ysseldyke, J. E. (1979). Current assessment and decision-making practices in model programs for learning disabled students. *Learning Disability Quarterly, 2,* 15–24.

Thurstone, L. L. (1938). Primary mental abilities. *Psychometric Monographs* (Whole No. 1).

Tindal, G., & Parker, R. (1989). Development of written recall as a curriculum-based measurement in secondary programs. Shool Psychology Review, 18, 317–343.

Trachtman, G. M. (1972). Pupils, parents, privacy, and the psychologist. *American Psychologist, 17,* 32–45.

Tyler, R. W. (1966). The objectives and plans for a national assessment of educational progress. *Journal of Educational Measurement, 3,* 1–4.

V

Van Hattum, R. J. (Ed.). (1980). *Communication disorders: An introduction.* New York: Macmillan.

Vargas, J. S. (1984). What are your exercises teaching? An analysis of stimulus control in instructional materials. In W. L. Heward, T. E. Heron, D. S. Hill, & B. Trap-Porter (Eds.), *Focus on behavior analysis in education* (pp. 126–141). Columbus, OH: Merrill.

Venesky, R. L. (1976). Prerequisites for learning to read. In J. R. Levin & V. L. Allen (Eds.), *Cognitive learning in children* (pp. 96–122). New York: Academic Press.

W

Wahler, R. G., & Cormier, W. J. (1970). The ecological interview: A first step in outpatient child behavior therapy. *Journal of Behavior Therapy and Experimental Psychiatry, 1,* 279–289.

Walker, H. (1983). *Walker Problem Behavior Identification Checklist.* Los Angeles, CA: Western Psychological Services.

Walker, H., & McConnell, S. (1988). *Walker-McConnell Scale of Social Competence and School Adjustment.* Austin, TX: PRO-ED.

Walker, H., & Severson, H. (1992). *Systematic Screening for Behavior Disorders.* Longmont, CO: Sopris West, Inc.

Wallace, G., & Larsen, S. C. (1978). *Educational assessment of learning problems: Testing for teaching.* Boston: Allyn & Bacon.

Wardrop, J. L. (1989). [Review of the *California Achievement Tests*]. In J. C. Conoley & J. J. Kramer (Eds.), *Tenth mental measurements yearbook* (pp. 128–133). Lincoln, NE: Buros Institute of Mental Measurements.

Wechsler, D. (1991). *Wechsler Intelligence Scale for Children-III.* San Antonio: Psychological Corporation.

Wechsler, E. (1974). *Wechsler Intelligence Scale for Children Revised.* San Antonio: Psychological Corporation.

Weiss, C. E., & Lillywhite, H. S. (1976). *Communication disorders: A handbook for prevention and early intervention.* St Louis: C. V. Mosby.

White, M., & Miller, S. R. (1983). Dyslexia: A term in search of a definition. *Journal of Special Education, 17,* 5–10.

White, O. R. (1974). *Evaluating educational progress* (working paper). Seattle: University of Washington Child Development and Mental Retardation Center, Experimental Education Unit.

White, O. R., & Liberty, K. (1976). Behavioral assessment and precise educational measurement. In N. Haring & R. Schiefelbusch (Eds.), *Teaching special children* (pp. 31–69). New York: McGraw-Hill.

Wiggins, G. (1989). Teaching to the (authentic) test. *Educational Leadership, 46,* 41–47.

Wiggins, G. (1990). Standards, not standardization. Evoking quality student work. *Educational Leadership, 47,* 18–25.

Wiggins, G. P. (1993). *Assessing student performance: Exploring the purpose and limits of testing.* San Francisco: Jossey-Bass.

Wilen, D. K., & Sweeting, C. V. M. (1986). Assessment of Limited English Proficient Hispanic Students. *School Psychology Review, 15,* 59–75.

Wilkinson, G. S. (1993). *Wide Range Achievement Test-3.* Wilmington DE: Wide Range, Inc.

Wise, S. L. (1985). *Determining cutoff scores for the PPST.* Unpublished manuscript. University of Nebraska–Lincoln, Lincoln, NE.

Witt, J. C., & Gresham, F. M. (1985). [Review of the *Wechsler Intelligence Scale for Children-Revised.*]. In J. V. Mitchell, Jr. (Ed.), *Ninth mental measurements yearbook* (pp. 1716–1719). Lincoln, NE: Buros Institute of Mental Measurements.

Wolf, D. P., LeMahieu, P. G., & Eresh, J. (1992). Good measure: Assessment as a tool for educational reform. *Educational Leadership, 49*(8), 8–13.

Wolf, M. M. (1978). Social validity: The case for subjective measurement or how applied behavior analysis is finding its heart. *Journal of Applied Behavior Analysis, 11,* 203–214.

Wolery, M., Bailey, D., & Sugai, G. (1988). *Effective teaching: Principles and procedures of applied behavior analysis with exceptional children.* Boston, MA: Allyn & Bacon.

Woodcock, R. W. (1980). *Woodcock Language Proficiency Battery.* Hingman, MA: Teaching Resources.

Woodcock, R. W. (1981). *Bateria Woodcock de Proficiencia en el Iddioma-Version en Espanol.* Hingman, MA: Teaching Resources.

Woodcock, R. W. (1987). *Woodcock Reading Mastery Tests, Revised.* Circle Pines, MN: American Guidance Service.

Woodcock, R. W. (1991). *Woodcock Language Proficiency Battery.* Allen, TX: DLM Teaching Resources.

Woodcock, R. W., & Johnson, M. B. (1989). *Woodcock-Johnson Psychoeducational Battery-Revised.* Allen, TX: DLM.

Woolfolk, A. (1987). *Educational psychology,* (3rd ed.). Englewood Cliffs, NJ: Prentice-Hall.

Wright, D., & Piersel, W. C. (1987). Group administratered tests for decision making: How useful? Depends on the question. *Journal of School Psychology, 25,* 63–71.

Wyne, M. D., & O'Connor, P. D. (1979). *Exceptional children: A developmental view.* Lexington, MA: D. C. Heath.

Wyne, M. D., & Stuck, G. B. (1979). Time-on-task and reading performance in underachieving children. *Journal of Reading Behavior, 11,* 119–128.

Y

Ysseldyke, J. E. (1973). Diagnostic-prescriptive teaching: The search for aptitude-treatment interactions. In L. Mann & D. Sabatino (Eds.), *The first review of special education* (Vol. 1). Philadelphia: Journal of Special Education Press.

Ysseldyke, J. E. (1977). Aptitude-treatment interaction research with first grade children. *Contemporary Educational Psychology, 2,* 1–9.

Ysseldyke, J. E. (1979). Issues in psychoeducational assessment. In G. Phye & D. J. Reschly (Eds.), *School psychology: Perspectives and issues.* New York: Academic Press.

Ysseldyke, J. E., & Algozzine, B. (1982). *Critical issues in special and remedial education.* Boston: Houghton Mifflin.

Ysseldyke, J. E., Algozzine, B., Richey, L., & Graden, J. (1982). Declaring students eligible for learning disability services: Why bother with the data? *Learning Disabilities Quarterly, 5,* 37–43.

Ysseldyke, J. E., & Christenson, S. L. (1987). *The Instructional Environment Scale.* Austin, TX: PRO-ED.

Ysseldyke, J., & Christenson, S. (1993). *The instructional environment system-II.* Longmont, CO: Sopris West, Inc.

Ysseldyke, J. E., & Mirkin, P. (1982). The use of assessment information to plan instructional interventions: A review of research. In C. Reynolds & T. B. Gutkin (Eds.), *Handbook of school psychology* (pp. 395–409). New York: Wiley.

Ysseldyke, J. E., & Thurlow, M. L. (1984). Assessment practices in special education: Adequacy and appropriateness. *Educational Psychologist, 9,* 123–136.

Index

A

B

C

D

E

F

G

H

K

L

N

O

P

T

U

V